THE AMERICAN CLASS SYSTEM

The American Class System

AN INTRODUCTION TO SOCIAL STRATIFICATION

DANIEL W. ROSSIDES

BOWDOIN COLLEGE

HOUGHTON MIFFLIN COMPANY · BOSTON
Atlanta · Dallas · Geneva, Ill.
Hopewell, N.J. · Palo Alto · London

For Marilyn, as in everything

Quotation on page 159 reprinted from *The Political Economy of the Black Ghetto* by William K. Tabb. By permission of W. W. Norton & Company, Inc. Copyright © 1970 by W. W. Norton & Company, Inc.

Printed in the U.S.A.
Library of Congress Catalog Card Number: 75-31001
ISBN: 0-395-20624-3

Contents

Preface

SOCIAL STRATIFICATION has been studied scientifically and with considerable success on a relatively sustained basis since the 1920s, but it cannot be said that a consensus has emerged about the main issues in the field. Indeed, the prevailing picture is one of controversy, especially if one looks at the state of the field on an international basis. Despite notable achievements, the field of stratification is still inchoate and in flux. This is all the more regrettable since the achievements are considerable and indeed make up one of the best (if not the best) ways to understand the nature of society, especially industrial society. In attempting to pull together the disparate and discordant strands of the stratification tradition, I have tried to present a comprehensive picture of current theoretical and empirical work and at the same time suggest ways in which even greater conceptual mastery can be gained over the phenomena of inequality.

As a text, this study is designed for students with some background in social science and is especially directed at the introductory social stratification course. Though its focus is on the American class system and on the current state of the field of social stratification, it contains considerable amounts of historical-comparative material and could easily be used as the main text in a comparative stratification course. Instructors will also find it useful in courses on minority groups since it has an extended discussion of three representative minorities, black Americans, Mexican Americans, and Jewish Americans, plus a summary of the social class position (and prospects) of racial and ethnic minorities in general. There is also a discussion of age and sexual stratification as distinct from social stratification, a discussion which can be expanded and focused to suit the interests of instructors.

No study can avoid organizing assumptions even when presented in the name of science (as this one is). Accordingly, I have tried to state where I stand as early and as clearly as possible. The book's basic theoretical framework is derived from two aspects of Max Weber's work (as well as the work of others):

One, his insistence on clear analytical models, which in the case of stratification analysis means an insistence that the dimension of class (the economic hierarchy), prestige or status (subjective forms, consumption, and interaction in social groups), and power (political-legal hierarchies) be kept analytically separate;

Two, Weber's unique comparative-historical perspective, which not only provided an empirical foundation to his work but also led him to stress the diversity, relativity, and instability of social phenomena. To focus all these aspects of social phenomena in contemporary stratification language, Weber had both a conflict and functional approach to industrial (capitalist) society, seeing it, on the whole, as inherently unstable because of its rich, complex, and contradictory institutions, but at the same time as subject to deep stabilizing pressures from bureaucratization and state centralization.

In adopting the Weberian orientation, I have not interpreted his multidimensional approach to mean that modern society is a hodgepodge of hierarchies with no coherent or structured system of inequality, or that it can be understood in terms of functional differentiation. And in adopting his anti-Marxian perspective, I have tried to avoid the temptation (which is so strong in American society and sociology) to overemphasize subjective (prestige) factors or to give them priority over economic (class) variables. Weber himself was more than aware of the preeminent role of economic forces and would no doubt have disavowed some of the uses that have been made of his multicausal approach in stratification analysis.

In analyzing the American class system, I have tried to present a balanced and relatively full treatment of the nature and interrelations of all three major stratification dimensions. Not only do areas hitherto neglected, such as law, politics, government, and legislation, receive extensive treatment, but also there is a relatively full treatment of class variables, such as income, wealth, occupation, and education, as well as prestige variables, such as self-perception and attitudes, consumption, and differences in associational life. In tackling the broad and complex materials of social stratification, every effort has been made to introduce ideas in an orderly sequence and to allow students to extend their grasp of these materials in a cumulative manner. Given the lack of consensus about social stratification, I have tried to represent rival positions as accurately and as fairly as possible, hoping in this way to let readers form their own judgments about the complex issues of stratification analysis while at the same time making it as easy as possible for instructors to follow their own bent in designing their courses. As a further aid toward this latter end, and to stimulate and reinforce student interest, there are extensive bibliographic notes, including references to paperback editions and reprints, flowing directly out of the text as well as numerous references to research topics and areas.

The overall study is divided into five parts. Part 1 is a broad introduction to the problems, goals, and achievements in stratification analysis. The empirical analysis of the American class system begins in Part 2 and extends through Parts 3 and 4. In Part 2, America's economic classes are identified, along with the class position of our three representative minorities. The relations between class position, on the one hand, and family life, basic personality structure, physical and mental health, and the education of children, on the other, are explored at length. In Part 3, the prestige dimension (what Americans think of themselves, and how they consume and associate), including the prestige positions of the three representative minorities, is analyzed and related to class. In Part 4, the hierarchies of class and prestige are related to such things as political representation and participation, access to public office, political attitudes, legislation, and the dispensation of justice (the realm of political-legal stratification). The overall social class position of the three representative minorities is rounded out by relating their class-prestige position to political-legal forces. And in Part 5, the study concludes with an interpretation and summary of the overall American class system with special attention to the forces that make it work (despite its failure to reflect American values), to the lessons it holds for understanding industrial and other systems of stratification, and to the nature of its overall system of social power.

With the growth and establishment of liberal democracy, most people (more certainly among the general public in the United States) have come to believe that equality either has been or can be achieved within the near future. As the reader will see, this view is questionable, as are many other beliefs about modern stratification structures and processes. Perhaps the major conclusion of our study is that the United States is a highly unequal society, in many ways running counter to its basic ideals, and that on balance there appears to be no evidence that it is making any progress toward more equality, putting aside for the moment the special issue of racial inequality. Our study also broaches the possibility (cautiously and reluctantly) that the United States is incapable of modifying its structure of inequality — that far from being a dynamic system progressively realizing its ideals, it may well be a nondirectional class society, a permanent halfway house mired in the mud of ascriptive property relations and liberal ideology.

Though books usually have one author, they are never written alone. Authors owe a great debt to scholars, teachers, students, colleagues, spouses (an especially heavy debt in my case), and to reviewers, and I am no exception. I was particularly fortunate in having conscientious reviewers, and I should like to extend my thanks to Edward O. Laumann (University of Chicago), Cora V. Baldock (Baruch College, CUNY), Raymond J. Murphy (University of Rochester), and especially Paul Sites (Kent State University) for valuable criticisms and suggestions, even for those that I lacked the wit to accept.

Daniel W. Rossides

PART 1

Sociology and the study of social stratification

1

An introduction to stratification analysis

INEQUALITY IS A PERVASIVE feature of human society and a subject that has fascinated both social theorists and laymen from time immemorial. Social inequality is the stuff of which the drama of history is made: the power and pageantry of kingship, the struggle for supremacy among feudal barons, the executioner's block, the stench and brutality of a slave galley, the vast chasm between Brahman and untouchable, the mind-deadening routine of an assembly line, the factory owner, and the welfare mother all evoke vivid images of the ways in which stratification has been manifested at different times and places.

American history also evokes dramatic images of inequality, such as the bonded servant, the plantation owner and slave, the robber baron, the immigrant, the Depression, and the Dust Bowl. Americans have also witnessed some unique efforts to institute relations of equality, such as the Bill of Rights, the Homestead Act, the Fourteenth and Fifteenth Amendments, the sit-down strike, collective bargaining, and the war on poverty. In trying to understand these and other manifestations of the ceaseless drama of inequality and equality, sociologists must ask many questions: Who or what process determines who shall work in the fields and who in a factory, office, or laboratory? Who or what process decides who shall stand in an unemployment line or suffer the humiliation of welfare allotments? How is it possible in a democracy that

3

millions have second homes while many live in rat-infested tenements? Why do people tolerate hardship in the face of plenty when they have the franchise? Has rising prosperity made Americans more nearly equal? Have reforms made any headway against the forces of ascription, exploitation, and unequal opportunity?

As a distinct discipline within modern social science, sociology has long studied such questions. Despite decades of creative research and theorizing, however, there is still no integrated body of research and theory to account for the way in which a hierarchy of castes, estates, or classes is produced, maintained, and transmitted from one generation to the next. Given the complexity of this subject, it is understandable that there are many rival theories about the nature and destiny of social inequality, ranging from those that describe industrial society as spearheading a long-term drive toward equality, personal achievement, and consensus to those that interpret it as characterized by privilege, conflict, and repression.

All these questions and controversies will be discussed in some depth in the next three chapters as a preliminary to our search through the empirical record. The main purpose of the chapters that make up Part One is to provide an overview of the study of social stratification, particularly its accomplishments, and to introduce the reader to the many controversies and problems that both afflict and nourish the field. In providing this overview, I have assumed that readers will be better prepared to absorb the large amounts of empirical data contained in subsequent parts if they are first acquainted with the overall structure of problems and ideas that stratification theorists have confronted in their efforts to explain inequality. Part One also contains comparative case studies of the three major types of stratification — caste, estate, and class, illustrated respectively by India, Western feudal society, and the Soviet Union; a discussion of some major attempts to develop a general or unified theory of inequality; and a brief discussion of processes by which structures of stratification undergo systemic change, illustrated by the sharply contrasting ways in which feudalism was supplanted by industrial society in France and Japan.

The major purpose of this chapter is to provide an overview of the main issues and goals of stratification, and a working definition of social stratification (including a brief preliminary description of the American class system). We shall begin by considering a theme basic to Western social thought, the attempt to understand the relationship between human nature and inequality. Because the literature that addresses this theme is exceedingly rich, we can do no more than discuss representative examples of the two major positions: the view that seeks to explain social inequality in terms of factors in human nature (the biopsychological position) and the view that seeks to explain it in terms of social variables (the sociocultural position). It will become apparent that each of these orientations is quite complex, and that particular theories often combine elements of these two general positions.

Inequality and the nature of man
The biopsychological explanation of inequality

The type of stratification theory that is most pervasive and influential in Western society attributes inequality to various alleged differences among individuals *qua* individuals. This explanation can be called *biopsychological* (or *naturalistic* or *ahistorical* or *nonsocial*) in that it argues that deep innate differences exist among human beings and that society derives (or should derive) its structure from the hierarchy of "talent" identifiable among human beings. This position assumes, in other words, that one can equate behavior and human nature: behavior is a function of human nature, and differences in the behavior of individuals result from differences in their natures.

One of the most famous and influential expressions of the biopsychological view is Plato's *Republic,* in which he introduced many of the fundamental elements of social inquiry and supplied Western thought with many of its basic concepts. One of the most enduring of these concepts is his definition of society as a network of cooperation, a complex exchange of goods and services for mutual benefit. In the language of modern sociology, Plato thought of society as a system of interdependent functions.

Plato was not the first to articulate the ancient idea that there is a congruence between human nature and society, but he gave it a revolutionary cast by combining it with the novel assumption that the nature of that congruence could be identified by means of rational analysis. Society, argued Plato, has always been nonrational, or even irrational, based more on blind than on conscious cooperation. Instead of being founded on and governed by reason, society is governed by myth and custom. And because human beings have not understood themselves, they have not understood the nature of society. As a result, they have argued over the worth of their respective roles in the social division of labor, causing widespread inefficiency, instability, and civil war. To bring about the good society, Plato insisted, one must derive social and ethical conclusions from rational analysis. The division of labor that is the essence of society has an analogue in the division of labor in the human personality, or soul. According to Plato, the structure of the personality is hierarchical: reason is at the top, followed by the "spirited" or executive capacity, and then the appetites. This specialization within the human being is matched by specialization *among* human beings. In the aggregate, human beings have different aptitudes: some men and women have the capacity to reason, some are specially equipped to manage, and others are suited for work and work alone. In his famous metallic analogy, Plato described the hierarchy of human talent as composed of three groups of individuals who correspond respectively to gold, silver, and iron-brass.

The structure of society, therefore, corresponds to the division of labor in the human personality. In order to function, it must have a reasoning element (philosopher-king or -kings), administrators (guardians), and workers (presumably farmers, merchants, artisans, and slaves). To establish a rational society, one must see to it that the human beings suited by nature to each of these functions are identified and appropriately educated. To do so, however, would not have been as easy as it might seem, since Plato complicated his prescription by introducing a number of other revolutionary ideas. Gold parents, he argued, can have iron-brass children, and iron-brass parents can have gold or silver children; in other words, the distribution of talent is not determined by family birth, nor is it insured by property or a function of sex. For Plato, society could not be constituted on any of the traditional grounds. Only when the innate hierarchy of individual ability (enhanced by education) matches the intrinsic hierarchy of social functions can one speak of the good — and thus stable, just, and happy — individual and society.

Plato's emphasis on society as a set of functions and insistence that only qualified people should perform these functions led him to a rather full commitment to inequality. However, Plato did not develop a theory of social classes.[1] The basic thrust of his thought was to bring the economic and social division of labor under rational control. Plato was fully aware that society controls human beings, and not the reverse. He knew, in other words, that social classes are formed by the economic division of labor and maintained by family, religious, and political institutions. He was also aware, as were most of his contemporaries, that social classes are transmitted across generations by the institution of the family and that they were the primary source of social conflict, instability, and even civil war. Actually, it was largely because of the evils associated with social classes that Plato sought to shed the assumptions and values associated with them. His effort to transcend the society he knew is implicit in all aspects of his work: the recourse to abstract thought; the ahistorical, utopian nature of the *Republic*; his search for a firm foundation on which to place the social division of labor and its attendant inequalities; and his rejection of established norms and values of kinship, sexual inequality, and property. Perhaps the most direct evidence of Plato's rejection of social class is his requirement that the small ruling elite (made up of the philosopher-king or -kings and the guardians) give up the distractions of family and property.

Plato's interpretation of society as a functional system, staffed by those innately equipped to perform certain social functions, has had a long and varied career in Western social theory. But it is one thing to posit an ideal society free from the exigencies of history and another thing to talk about how people and societies actually behave. As we shall see when we examine some contemporary thinking about inequality, whenever a functional definition of society predominates (for example, those of John of Salisbury and other feudal social theorists, Adam Smith, James Madison, fascist corporate theorists, Joseph Stalin, and some contemporary stratification theorists), the concept of social class — especially its emphasis on illegitimate and exploitative ascriptive

1. A working definition of *social classes* will be supplied shortly; a full definition must be pursued gradually in this and subsequent chapters.

factors — is relegated to a secondary position.[2] And we will also find that the rulers of society invariably prefer to have their dominions depicted as characterized by a harmonious, equitable, and natural division of functions based on human nature and to avoid forms of thought that stress ascription, exploitation, and conflict. In brief, this social philosophy takes the form of what Ossowski has called *nonegalitarian classlessness,* or the belief that social inequality is based on natural factors and not on arbitrary definition or the use of force.[3] In the United States, nonegalitarian classlessness is expressed as the belief that inequality is determined by the innate differences in individuals as revealed by equal opportunity and competition.[4]

Biopsychological inequality: the liberal world view

In the modern world, the biopsychological explanation has developed in a unique way. The emergence of capitalism gave rise to the novel proposition that society and social position should directly reflect the personal natures of individuals as individuals, a social philosophy known as liberalism[5] or bourgeois social theory. Expressed in its fullest earliest form in the social contract theories of Thomas Hobbes (1588–1679) and John Locke (1632–1704), this revolutionary redefinition of human nature (and thus of society) gradually broadened and deepened, and eventually triumphed over the feudal view of man and society. Expressed in terms of stratification theory, liberal thought attacked the hereditary principle and fixed hereditary estates of feudal society, and in their place sought to establish the achievement ethic. Henceforth, it declared, inequality was to be a function of personal ability, especially in economic pursuits.

The new focus on achievement in the West acquired a deep biopsychological cast in the period between 1650 and 1850. During this unusually creative period in social thought, theorists in their efforts to explain behavior and inequality catalogued an enormous variety of biological and psychological

2. For an historical survey of functional stratification thought that notes this similarity between apologists for very different social systems, see Stanislaw Ossowski, *Class Structure in the Social Consciousness,* trans. Sheila Patterson (New York: Free Press, 1963), pp. 172–180.

3. Ossowski, *Class Structure in the Social Consciousness,* chap. 7. A similar idea is found in Pareto's biopsychic theory of "the circulation of elites."

4. Another characteristic of the American biopsychic orientation is the constant emphasis on the need for leadership, as opposed to institutional restructuring.

5. The meaning of the term *liberalism* will unfold gradually, especially over the next few pages. Essentially, it refers to the acceptance of private property, private economic motives and actions, and political and legal equality as central social institutions. Thus, both Democrats and Republicans in the United States are liberals; that is, both accept the validity and superiority of capitalist (liberal) society while disagreeing on how to run it. For a fuller discussion of historical and European developments in liberal social thought, see George H. Sabine's classic commentary, *A History of Political Theory,* 4th ed. (New York: Dryden, 1973), and *The Encyclopedia of the Social Sciences* (New York: MacMillan, 1930–1935) or its successor, *The International Encyclopedia of the Social Sciences* (New York: MacMillan and Free Press, 1968).

forces: pugnacity, reason, hunger, sex, the will to power, self-interest, moral traits, genius, I.Q., and so on. In French thought, the fathers of sociology, Saint-Simon (1760–1825) and Auguste Comte (1798–1857), found the explanation for behavior and inequality directly in human nature. Both theorists divided human beings into brain men, sensory men, and motor men, each category having special functions to perform for society.[6] According to Saint-Simon and Comte, these three biopsychic capacities, while shared by all individuals, are distributed unevenly. Education can develop the dominant capacity in each individual, but it cannot change the category in which nature has placed him.

In English social thought, the biopsychological approach is a prominent feature of the work of Herbert Spencer (1820–1903) and Francis Galton (1822–1911). Spencer never developed a rigid classification of biopsychological types, but his thought — the first to be based on the scientific theory of evolution — was heavily influenced by biological analogies. (The basic capacity, according to Spencer, is the ability to adjust to conditions, a capacity that is not solely a function of thinking.) For Spencer, the individual is a real but unknown quantity in the operation of society. Since it is not possible to identify the capacities of individuals precisely, it is necessary for society to provide competitive situations; thus Spencer's emphasis on the law of contract, the free market, private property, limited government, and open competition. Francis Galton, who worked in the early period of quantitative social science, argued on the basis of statistical data that "genius" (by which he meant ability in general) is biological in nature and is distributed differently among individuals, races, and nations. By examining the families of eminent Englishmen, Galton concluded that ability is clustered in families and is transmitted by biological inheritance, especially from father to male offspring.

The idea that inequality stems from differences among individuals is the dominant theme of American political and social theory. James Madison, for example, argued in the *Federalist* paper number 10 that government is necessary because of conflicts over property, and that differences in amounts and types of property individuals own are due to "diversity in the faculties of men." Since social conflict has this natural basis, it cannot be eliminated without doing violence to nature. "The protection of these faculties is the first object of government," argued Madison, and its proper role is to contain or control the effects of conflict, not to eliminate conflict as such. The main virtue of representative government, Madison concluded, is that it transfers natural economic conflicts and inequalities to a different arena and mitigates their impact on the body politic.

In American sociology, the thought of William Graham Sumner (1840–1910) best exemplifies the biopsychological approach. Like Madison, Sumner emphasized the importance of economic conflict in human behavior. History, he argued, is a struggle between economic interests, though only in the modern

6. Comte used the terms *men of intellect, men of feeling,* and *men of action.*

period has society evolved to a point at which this struggle can be made explicit and thus more "rational." All societies, according to Sumner, are divided into the masses and the classes; the former embody the society's *mores* and resist change, while the latter introduce variation and change. Society cannot change individuals, but it can select and develop those who best serve its interests. There is a natural distribution of human talent, ranging from the few individuals of genius and talent to the defective and delinquent. Modern society, which has evolved from a system based on customary status to one based on rational contract, provides individuals with an opportunity to prove themselves. Merit is inherent in the individual; society merely brings it out by means of education and competition. Thus, concluded Sumner, all schemes to help the weak and less talented are wrongheaded interferences with nature.

Many other examples of the biopsychological explanation of social inequality can be cited, but enough have been provided to serve our purpose. On the surface, this is a plausible view. Whenever we observe human behavior, we observe human beings; it seems an obvious conclusion that the individual who exhibits a certain behavior is its cause. However, the biopsychological explanation has serious flaws. Perhaps the primary argument that social science has developed against this highly seductive position is that the forces alleged to characterize human nature tend to vary widely with time and place. In addition, the effort to identify the innate forces in human nature — variously called instincts, reason, I.Q., drives, needs, and propensities — produced such an abundance of alleged attributes by the beginning of the twentieth century that social science eventually had to reconsider the entire enterprise. Of great importance to this reappraisal was L. L. Bernard's investigation of the concept of *instinct* and his report that 412 authors had in 495 books identified no less than 14,046 separate instincts of 5,759 types![7]

The biopsychological approach constituted the core of the liberal world view from the seventeenth through the nineteenth centuries, and was deeply related to the needs of emerging capitalism. At its inception, the liberal emphasis on equality of opportunity and inequality of native endowment was both a metaphysical attack on feudalism and a legitimation of the emerging liberal society. With the consolidation of liberal society, the same position was used to attack theories of reform and assorted forms of socialist thought.[8] Eventually, however, the biopsychological explanation of social inequality had to be drastically modified, not only on scientific grounds, but also because it no longer suited the needs of a maturing industrial society. A complex industrial society requires a great deal of coordination, and many of its members require long years of preparation for adult roles. It is not surprising, therefore, that the idea that society should simply reflect the natures of individuals was gradually

7. L. L. Bernard, *Instinct: A Study in Social Psychology* (New York: Henry Holt, 1924), chap. 9.

8. Antisocialist arguments are prominent in the thought of such leading sociologists as Georg Simmel, Max Weber, Emile Durkheim, William Graham Sumner, Vilfredo Pareto, Charles Horton Cooley, Franklin Henry Giddings, and Talcott Parsons.

questioned and modified. The shift to a more sociocultural explanation of behavior has been the major trend in liberal intellectual-scientific circles during the past century. This does not mean, however, that the biopsychological tradition is dead. On the contrary, it is dominant among laypeople and still a vital force in social science, as is attested to by the work of Konrad Z. Lorenz, Lionel Tiger, Desmond Morris, Robert Ardrey, Arthur R. Jensen, H. J. Eysenck, and Richard J. Herrnstein. Nevertheless, the cutting-edge of creative social science has come to place primary emphasis on sociocultural variables in explaining behavior. It is to this tradition that we now turn.

Inequality and the nature of society
Rousseau and the sociocultural explanation of inequality

The other dominant theme in Western social theory treats inequality as the outcome of social variables. Rousseau's remarkable essay, the *Discourse on the Origin of Inequality* (1754), is an early modern expression of a mode of thought that has become the cornerstone of creative social science. In brief, Rousseau argued that those who attribute inequality to human nature are mistaken; they are confusing the effects of society on human beings with man's original constitution. Man in his original state, Rousseau suggests, can only be hypothesized about. At best, he is merely a compassionate bundle of emotions motivated by his own welfare and self-preservation, and repelled by others' pain and death. By and large, he is equal to his fellows in his weakness and nakedness. Only in the society of others does he develop language, property, law, and inequality; in this process his original nature is distorted and corrupted by reason and civilization. Above all, the division of labor and the attendant convention of property create mutual dependence and enslave not merely the subordinate groups in society but everyone.

Rousseau's thesis is an outstanding example of the sociocultural view of behavior and inequality. Of special importance is the fact that his analysis contains a conception of the division of labor totally different from Plato's (and from those of most "functional" theorists). While Rousseau defined society as a network of functional specialization, unlike Plato he saw the division of labor as resulting not in mutual profit or peace but only in corruption, injustice, and violence. He was an adherent of the "conflict school of inequality," which regards social factors, and often the basic structure of society, as detrimental to man and incompatible with social harmony and justice.

Sociocultural inequality: Karl Marx and Max Weber

The sociocultural explanation of inequality has many sources, but its most influential contributors have been Karl Marx (1818–1883) and Max Weber (1864–1920). Indeed, the basic conceptual elements both of the contemporary sociocultural explanation of social stratification and of conflict theory are found in their original forms in the theories of these two men. Both Marx and Weber explicitly rejected the Anglo-American liberal view that capitalist society and the inequality that characterizes it stem from the individual. Despite serious disagreements, both theorists maintained that the biopsychological approach was a thorough mistake. The reasons for their rejection of it transcend the undoubted genius of these two men. Gradual economic growth and small-scale enterprise had misled English and American theorists into believing that individualism had caused capitalism. As Germans, Marx and Weber had not grown up in a social environment permeated by the logic of individualistic explanations. The growth of capitalism in Germany was an abrupt, disruptive process spawned largely by military and political considerations. Lacking the long phase of small-scale enterprise characteristic of capitalist growth in other countries, German capitalism took the form of a relatively large-scale factory system from the outset. This abrupt growth, due to corporate formation and state action, made it as impossible for Germans to develop a theory of individualism and *laissez-faire* as it was for them to explain capitalism and its resulting system of social stratification in biopsychological terms.[9]

Though Marx and Weber agreed that behavior is the outcome of sociocultural forces, they disagreed markedly about the nature of these forces. Marx, who was greatly influenced by such classical liberal economists as Adam Smith and David Ricardo, by and large accepted their definition of society as a functional division of economic and social labor.[10] But Marx rejected the notions that an individual's place in the functioning of society rested on his or her innate talents and that the division of labor (as found in any known society) was compatible with social harmony and justice. For Marx the key determinant of human behavior and human consciousness is man's relationship to nature. Marx referred to this relationship as *the forces of production* or *the material conditions of life* (resources, technology, and technical skills). A given level of production, he argued, leads to a distinctive set of social relations or *mode of*

9. In this connection, see Norman Birnbaum, "Conflicting Interpretations of the Rise of Capitalism: Marx and Weber," *British Journal of Sociology* 4 (June 1953): 125–141; also available as Bobbs-Merrill reprint S-26.

10. The substance of Marx's theory of social stratification may be found in *The Communist Manifesto* and, on a more sophisticated level, in *The German Ideology*. Two good anthologies of various aspects of Marx's thought, including social stratification, are T. B. Bottomore and Maximilien Rubel, eds., *Karl Marx: Selected Writings in Sociology and Social Philosophy,* trans. T. B. Bottomore (New York: McGraw-Hill, 1964), paperback edition, originally published in 1956; and Lewis S. Feuer, ed., *Basic Writings on Politics and Philosophy: Karl Marx and Friedrich Engels* (Garden City, N.Y.: Doubleday, 1959), paperback edition.

For a succinct description and analysis of Marx's views on class, see Reinhard Bendix and Seymour M. Lipset, "Marx's Theory of Social Classes" in *Class, Status, and Power: Social Stratification in Comparative Perspective,* 2nd ed., eds. Reinhard Bendix and Seymour M. Lipset (New York: Free Press, 1966), pp. 6–11. For a full-length depiction of contemporary class systems in the United States and other industrial societies from a Marxist viewpoint, see Charles H. Anderson, *The Political Economy of Social Class* (Englewood Cliffs, N.J.: Prentice-Hall, 1974).

production. The core of these social relations is the legal order, especially property forms; forms of the state; and the ideological order, including religion, philosophy, and art. In brief, as Marx put it, "the hand mill will give you a society with the feudal lord, the steam mill a society with the industrial capitalist."

History is essentially the story of man's changing relation to nature. As the forces of production change, they come into conflict with the mode of production (or superstructure), leading to a conflict between classes and eventually to revolution. As the forces of production crystallize into a new modal technology, they give rise to a new set of social relations that corresponds to the new needs it creates, including a new type of human being. For Marx, therefore, society derives its essential structure from the prevailing level of technology, and it is the individual's relation to the means of production, rather than innate abilities or drives, that determines one's class level, personality, and consciousness. Rather than seeing economic and social structures as the result of human talents, drives, or needs, Marx always focused on social variables, particularly technology and the economic system in which it was embedded.

Strictly speaking, the crucial factor in the creation of classes is not technology as such but the ownership of technology, or the means of production. The simple dichotomy between owner and nonowner is the ultimate basis of Marx's conception of social stratification. All other factors, such as income, occupation, education, and political power, are derivative and secondary. Fundamental to Marx's conception of class is the fact that all material value is the result of labor. But because of the power inherent in property, the owners of the means of production receive more than they produce by their own labor. Therefore their interests and those of the nonpropertied producers of labor are inherently antagonistic.

Economic classes (determined on the basis of the ownership and nonownership of land, tools, factories, and the like) are synonymous with social classes, according to Marx, because beliefs and values (consciousness) and overt behavior outside of work correspond to economic behavior, beliefs, and values. Also crucial to Marx's explanation of class formation, as well as his theory of the dynamics of class struggle and social change, is his assumption that one can distinguish between progressive and reactionary technological forces. The basic criterion that Marx used to make this distinction is the concept of *human fulfillment*. Some technological forces (and the social systems that embody them) retard and some promote the progress of human beings toward emancipation from historical necessity. A class is progressive when it represents the emergence of new forms and levels of liberating technology; an example is the middle class between the sixteenth and nineteenth centuries. Inevitably, however, such a class becomes conservative and reactionary — a "ruling class" — because it can make larger and larger profits without distributing the fruits of the machine to the general populace; an example is the "upper middle" class or *grande bourgeoisie* in the nineteenth century. In other words, individuals are subject to a distortion of their nature as long as material scarcity exists.

Technology, Marx argued, is the key to the reduction and eventual elimination of both material and moral scarcity. Once material abundance is achieved, historical systems of inequality (caste, estate, and class), and the corresponding structures of moral scarcity (original sin, noble versus ignoble birth, master-slave, lord-serf, owner-worker, government-citizen, policeman-criminal) will also disappear and a "classless" society of human fulfillment will emerge.

Marx's amplification of economic causation into a unitary theory of inevitable historical progress, while widely influential in Western intellectual culture, and in Western and non-Western politics, failed to make much of a mark on Western social science. Actually, Marx's metaphysical scenario of the emergence of unitary classes and their confrontation and death struggle had a negative effect on social science, an irony he would probably have appreciated: it was and still is used as the main theoretical rationale for denying the existence of social classes.

Marx's identification and analysis of economic causation was perhaps the most important contribution to social science in the nineteenth century. However, the monocausal or deterministic version of economic causation that he proposed had to be considerably modified before it was accepted into stratification theory and sociology. The theorist largely responsible for its modification was Max Weber. While acknowledging the importance of economic causes in the formation of social strata, Weber insisted that noneconomic sociocultural variables are not only influential but often more influential than economic factors in controlling the distribution of material and symbolic benefits. Religious beliefs and values, for example, significantly influence man's relationship to nature, the definition of work, and the worth of material values. And such factors as family beliefs and values, canons of taste or consumption, considerations of race or ethnicity, and philosophical, political, legal, or military beliefs and values can often exert powerful controls over economic forces.

Weber developed his multicausal theory of behavior in a lifelong analysis of the rise and nature of capitalism.[11] While acknowledging the importance of the economic factor, Weber came to the conclusion that the economic breakthrough to capitalism would have been impossible had medieval Europe not possessed a congenial religious and social tradition. With regard to social stratification, Weber concluded that a simple economic determinism was not consonant with the historical record.[12] He insisted, therefore, that the analysis of social inequality required the analytical separation of three major causal variables: class (market factors, property, technology, income, wealth), status (cultural evaluations expressed in group life, involving such matters as family, religion, race, morality, ethics, consumption, breeding, and general style of life),

11. For Weber's summary of the rise of capitalism, see his *General Economic History*, tr. Frank H. Knight (New York: Greenberg, 1927), Collier paperback, 1961, pt. 4.
12. Weber's theory of stratification is outlined in his influential essay "Class, Status, Party" in H. H. Gerth and C. Wright Mills, tr. and ed., *From Max Weber: Essays in Sociology* (New York: Oxford University Press, 1946), chap. 7. The introduction to this volume by Gerth and Mills is invaluable.

and party (access to the state, ability to create and enforce law). In developing this analytical model, Weber raised all the problems that confront contemporary stratification theory, especially those associated with his stress on multiple causation. The multiplicity of causes influencing the formation and composition of social classes and the reciprocal relations between causes, he argued, make it necessary to posit a scheme of causation characterized by mutual action and reaction. Economic wealth, for example, can be used to obtain prestige and political-legal power, and, conversely, one can use prestige (in the form, say, of noble birth or skin color) to secure economic wealth or political-legal benefits. So too, one can use political-legal power (such as military skill or the ability to organize voters) to secure economic benefits or prestige.

Weber's insights into social stratification illuminate further shortcomings of a simple economic explanation of social class. A wealthy individual, such as a junk dealer, may have low prestige, and a person of high prestige, such as a clergyman, may have an inferior class (economic) position. Poorly paid workers and even the unemployed, though their class and prestige position is inferior to other classes, can nonetheless enjoy equal political-legal benefits (the vote, due process of law) on a formal level and to some extent in practice. But there is no need either to pursue these difficulties now or to stress any further the differences between Marx and Weber. It is their similarities that are relevant to our present task of distinguishing the theories that focus on human nature from those that focus on society as the cause of inequality. Marx and Weber agreed that no such phenomenon as human nature can be identified as a cause of behavior; what we call human nature is the result of sociocultural forces, and the deep observable differences among human beings are the *result* of social stratification, not its cause.

A working definition of social stratification

It should be apparent from the foregoing that social theorists are deeply divided over the root causes of inequality. This is not surprising, given the complexity of the problem and the fact that a thorough discussion of inequality touches on every topic that human beings consider important. Despite decades of scientific research, social scientists are still far from unanimous about how and why human beings become unequal. Thus it seems wise to adopt an explicit working definition of social stratification and to provide a brief description of America's social classes in order to illuminate the maze of materials and issues we will encounter later. Toward this end, we must first distinguish between inequality in general and social stratification in particular.

Social differentiation and social stratification

All human societies are differentiated by various forms of specialization, only one of which should be called *social stratification*. The advantages of specialization are obvious and every society is characterized by a division of labor, no matter how rudimentary. Simple societies invariably use sex, age, and kinship to ascribe rights and duties to their members. That these three biological attributes are universally used to assign people to social functions, however, does not mean that sex, age, and kinship actually cause behavior. We have become too aware of the wide variations in behavior within each of the sexes and age groups, and among parents and children, to accept a simple bio-psychological explanation of behavior. The way in which power groups *define* these human attributes is the crucial determinant of how people are assigned to social functions. However, regardless of the historical circumstances of or specific reasons for a structure of power, or of the definitions it provides, the differentiation of social tasks on the basis of age, sex, and kinship leads to certain forms of inequality. Specifically, the old are usually given authority over the young, parents over children, and males over females.

When differentiation results in a more complex division of economic and social labor, some men become subordinate to other men. The social pattern becomes even more complex when the young acquire power over the old, female employees gain authority over males, or a great industrialist becomes subject to the authority of a doctor or a meter maid. For various reasons, those who hold certain positions in the range of tasks (for example, those of priest, landlord, warrior, doctor, factory owner) tend to receive more material and moral benefits than those in lower positions. Given the existence of families and a structure of differential rewards based on *alleged* differences in functional importance, there emerges a distinct form of inequality that we call social strati-fication. *Essentially, social stratification is a hierarchical configuration of families (and in industrial societies in recent decades, unrelated individuals) who have differential access to whatever is of value in the society at a given point and over time, primarily because of social, not biopsychological, variables.*

It is simple to illustrate the difference between inequality resulting from social stratification and inequality resulting from differentiation. While a society may declare all women inferior to men, the processes of social stratification make some women superior not only to many other women but to many men as well: one need only compare the wives of lawyers, business executives, and generals, for example, to lower- and working-class wives and their husbands to see social stratification in operation. To take another example, a servant in a millionaire's home will have two sources of authority over the children of his or her employer — adulthood and functional position — but the children under his or her authority occupy a much higher position in the total hierarchy of values. To use Max Weber's telling term, their *life chances,* measured in terms of material comfort and security, personal fulfillment, occupation, and so on are superior to the servant's or his or her children's.

Still another way to understand the nature of social stratification is to imagine an unstratified hunting and gathering tribe in which all males are fairly equal in hunting ability, and therefore equal socially. Then imagine the ap-pearance of an individual who is exceptionally fleet of foot and keen of vision. Social stratification begins when he becomes the leader of the hunting party and is given authority, prestige, and a larger share of the catch. It is crucial to note that both he and his family will rank above those who are average in ability and who in turn will rank above those who are lame or nearsighted. But such a stratification hierarchy is only a partial system because the superior hunter cannot insure his son's future position as a leader. His wife and children will enjoy more food and prestige during his lifetime, but unless the son inherits his father's physical traits he will sink in the hierarchy upon reaching adulthood. Indeed, if no biologically superior or inferior individuals emerge in our hypothetical society, the stratification hierarchy itself will disappear. A full system of social stratification emerges only when parents can see to it that their children inherit or acquire a social level equal or superior to their own regardless of innate ability.

The key to intergenerational transfer of social level is the development of high occupational positions that can be filled only by those who possess or acquire a given range of *social* assets, such as property, leisure, motivation, education, personality traits, noble birth, military or other skills, and so on (or those who have socially defined, valued, and cultivated biopsychological abilities associated with such occupations as basketball player, opera singer, or mathematician). Thus, *stratification inequality* is the condition in which social positions are ranked in terms of importance, rewarded differentially, acquired by individuals (and thus their families), and transmitted over generations quite independently of biological or psychological attributes. Futhermore, the definition of what is functionally important and the ways specified to achieve given social functions are quite arbitrary and based as much on force as on rationality, moral insight, or social necessity. The fact that modern society allows some individuals to rise above their parents' station (or to drop below it) does not alter the fact of social stratification. There is far less mobility than is popularly believed, and it neither diminishes the distance between tops and bottoms nor interferes much (despite considerable rhetoric to the contrary) with the hereditary transmission of stratification level.

Caste, estate, and class forms of stratification

Once a society abandons direct dependence on nature, social stratification inequality emerges prominently.[13] Economic surplus is easily translated into prestige and power and readily transmitted from one generation to the next. On the other hand, those who elevate themselves above others by the exercise of personal qualities (such as hunting, military, or religious skills) cannot easily transmit their prestige or power to their offspring unless the transfer also has an economic base. In short, economic surplus provides the wherewithal for

13. For an ethnographic study of fourteen aboriginal Polynesian cultures that finds a direct relationship between productivity and degree of social stratification, see Marshall D. Sahlins, *Social Stratification in Polynesia* (Seattle: University of Washington Press, 1958). This general point has been usefully elaborated by Gerhard Lenski; for a fuller discussion of his work, see Chapter 2.

social stratification: if property is esteemed, parents can guarantee that their children will be esteemed by giving them property; if abstinence from economic work is valued, those who can live off property or the work of others will be elevated above those who must work; if education is necessary to attain high occupations, those whose parents can motivate and support them through long years of schooling will have a decided edge over those who cannot.

Though economic variables are crucial to social stratification, they do not function in any mechanical or unitary fashion. As Weber pointed out, moral relationships (status or, in our terms, prestige) emerge to legitimate property relations and often become strong enough to disguise and even counteract economic forces. The diversity of causation and the variety of structures that social stratification assumes make it difficult to impose conceptual order on this form of inequality. Actually, past and present systems of stratification are exceedingly diverse, and while scholars of social stratification have made great strides in historical and comparative study in recent decades, they are far from agreed on how to classify or interpret the various types of social stratification. We will pursue this matter at some length in Chapter 2. However, for our immediate purpose of developing a brief working definition of social class, we only need note that it is generally accepted that social stratification, considered in the abstract, takes three general forms:[14]

1. Caste stratification, in which an agrarian society defines social level and function in terms of a hierarchy of religious worth (or some other strict ascriptive[15] criterion).

2. Estate stratification, in which an agrarian society defines social level and function in terms of a hierarchy of family worth.

3. Class stratification, in which an industrial society defines social level and function in terms of a hierarchy of differential achievement by individuals, especially in economic pursuits.

The analysis of class stratification

Class stratification appears in societies with expanding economies and is a phenomenon peculiar to industrial society. The development and nature of

14. The following definitions are minimal. For case studies of each, see Chapter 2.

15. Following Ralph Linton's classic discussion of ascribed and achieved statuses in his *The Study of Man* (New York: Appleton-Century-Crofts, 1936), chap. 8, the term *ascription* has come to mean the relatively arbitrary and permanent assignment of individuals to social statuses based on factors and processes over which they have almost no control. Thus birth and biological factors such as blood relationship, sex, and age are used quite universally to assign statuses. In addition, birth into a given geographical territory or religious-ethnic or even economic group can also be subject to ascription; thus an individual is assigned a nationality and caste, or class position (and a resulting set of life chances). As opposed to ascription, achievement statuses emerge when power groups establish a contrary tradition stressing values and norms such as individualism, equal opportunity, competition, hard work, voluntarism, choice, and the like. Achievement statuses also "require" institutional practices such as free education, legal universalism, political mobilization, research, the nuclear family, and the like with the ostensible purpose of opening economic and social statuses to individual achievement.

class stratification have varied by country, and one can detect interesting variations in class structure among England, France, Germany, the United States, and Eastern Europe.[16] Essentially, however, an expanding economy requires functional expertise in many sectors of its specialized occupational system, and needs flexibility in its labor, commodity, and credit markets (to use Weber's breakdown of class variables). Because of these needs, expanding economies undermine feudal norms and practices based on static lineage, prestige, and legal criteria. Thus the emergence of class over estate stratification occurred in modern Western Europe.

Much of the widespread confusion over the meaning of class inequality results from a failure to note two things: (1) class stratification emerged primarily in societies with well-developed systems of estate stratification; and (2) class stratification in such countries has undergone two distinct stages: an initial period during which classes crystallized into relatively self-conscious antagonistic strata,[17] and a contemporary stage in which an expanding standard of living, political-legal equality, and state welfare programs have succeeded in muting class hostility.

Though the United States was spared the early stage of class crystallization experienced by most European nations, it would be a mistake to assume that social classes do not exist in the United States. The essence of class stratification is that economic status prevails openly, steadily, and strongly over all other statuses. What Americans are worth on the labor, commodity, and credit markets is the primary determinant not only of their standard of living but also of their worth in the realms of prestige and power. As we shall see, American social classes do not form a strict and clearly defined set of strata. There are multiple dimensions of inequality, which, while under the general sway of economic status, remain distinct and somewhat independent. Thus our overall analytical model is based on the general orientation provided by Max Weber. Our model assumes, first, that the causes of behavior are socio-cultural rather than biopsychological, and it accepts the primacy of economic factors even as it stresses multiple causation. Because of the number of factors affecting social stratification, analysis is made easier if these factors are grouped under three broad headings — class, prestige, and power,[18] each of which has subdimensions. (See Table 1-1.)

In the abstract, the values within the dimension of class range from affluence and economic power and security at the top to destitution and economic powerlessness at the bottom. Some of the variables or subdimensions of class

16. For a sophisticated comparison of the historical development of class stratification in the United States and Europe, see Norman Birnbaum, *The Crisis of Industrial Society* (New York: Oxford University Press, 1969).

17. The terms *social class* and *social stratum* will be used interchangeably throughout this text, though this is not always the case in the literature of stratification.

18. There are semantic, as well as conceptual, difficulties with these terms that will be explained shortly. To avoid confusion, the components of each are often referred to in parentheses to indicate how the term is being used: for example, class (income, occupation, education). Needless to say, readers should avoid reifying these or any other concepts.

Table 1-1 Basic Dimensions of Social Stratification (with the range of values within each dimension and examples of subdimensions[a])

Class						Prestige					Power			
Income	*Wealth*	*Occupation*	*Education*	*Family stability*	*Education of children*	*Occupational prestige*	*Subjective development*	*Consumption*	*Participation in group life*	*Political participation*	*Political attitudes*	*Legislation and gov'tal benefits*	*Distribution of justice*	
Affluence; economic security and power						Integrated personalities; consistent attitudes; psychic fulfillment due to deference, valued associations, and consumption					Power to influence public mechanisms, giving control over social values			
Destitution; worthlessness on economic markets						Unintegrated personalities; inconsistent attitudes; sense of isolation and despair					Political powerlessness; lack of legal recourse or rights			

a. For expository purposes, religious-ethnic and racial rankings are omitted.

are listed in Table 1-1. A fuller list of class-related variables would include not only income, wealth, occupation, education, family stability and values, and the education of children, but also basic personality structure, physical and mental health, and life expectancy. In analyzing this domain, we are interested in the variables that determine life chances in all dimensions. None of these variables has any scientific meaning, however, until we specify a relationship to something else; a given income, for example, has little meaning unless we relate it to the total universe of incomes or to other variables.

The classic definition of class is Max Weber's. "We may speak of a 'class'," says Weber,

> when (1) a number of people have in common a specific causal component of their life chances, in so far as (2) this component is represented exclusively by economic interests in the possession of goods and opportunities for income, and (3) is represented under the conditions of the commodity or

labor markets. [These points refer to "class situation," which we may express more briefly as the typical chance for a supply of goods, external living conditions, and personal life experiences, in so far as this chance is determined by the amount and kind of power, or lack of such, to dispose of goods or skills for the sake of income in a given economic order. The term "class" refers to any group of people that is found in the same class situation].[19]

The variables that compose the dimension of prestige are occupational prestige, certain aspects of personality, associational life, and consumption or style of life. Again, these variables are not intrinsic entities; they must be understood in relation to each other and to variables in other dimensions. At one end of this scale of values are those who tend to have integrated personalities and to enjoy personal fulfillment through valued associations and consumption. At the other end are those who tend to have distorted, underdeveloped personalities and to live lives of isolation and despair.

The dimension of power is made up of rights to political participation and access to public office, political attitudes, legislative benefits, and governmental treatment, including the distribution of justice. In all areas, and perhaps especially in this one, it is necessary to see beyond the rhetoric of formal institutional analysis to the operational reality. As we will see in abundant detail later, the people at the upper end of this scale have far more power to influence the state, and thus the distribution of values in all dimensions, than do those at the bottom, protestations of democracy and equal rights notwithstanding.

Weber's cross-cultural comparisons and his acute eye for historical variations enabled him to see things that most stratification theorists overlooked. He not only insisted that prestige and political-legal factors were important in modifying and even counteracting economic forces, but also stressed the importance of distinguishing between three kinds of economic markets — credit, commodity, and labor. For Weber, class was no simple dichotomy between the propertied and nonpropertied (though he, like Marx, considered this phenomenon central to social stratification), but rather a series of hierarchies that interact to produce the inequality of social stratification. Even the central economic markets of credit, commodities, and labor could be powerfully influenced by prestige and political-legal forces. This suggests the importance of Weber's insistence that the various dimensions and subdimensions of social stratification be kept analytically separate so that their relationships could be disclosed on an empirical rather than verbal basis.

Weber quite rightly stressed the diversity among societies, as well as *within* society, especially the early industrial society. But Weber also sensed the strengthening grip of rationality — the efficient coordination of means and ends — on Western life, and feared that it would usher in an "age of icy

19. Max Weber, "Class, Status, Party" in H. H. Gerth and C. Wright Mills, tr. and ed., *From Max Weber: Essays in Sociology* (New York: Oxford University Press, 1946), p. 181. Reprinted by permission of the Oxford University Press. The sentences in brackets are from other contexts in Weber's *Economy and Society*.

darkness," by which he meant meaningless efficiency and centralization. The main agency of this trend, according to Weber, was bureaucratization. We shall stress both aspects of Weber's work, the need to give due regard to the empirical complexity of society and the need to see the empirical interconnectedness that constitutes a social system. Since Weber's day it has become apparent that industrial society has found ways to stabilize itself. In short, while we will keep the dimensions of class, prestige, and power analytically separate, we will assume that coordinating mechanisms and processes at strategic points connect them empirically to form an identifiable system.

We will differ from Weber, however, in a number of respects. Weber tended to regard education as a prestige phenomenon even when it was used as the basis for occupation, the classic example being his analysis of the Chinese literati, the scholar-civil servants of Imperial China. For our part, we will regard education primarily as a class phenomenon. Since Weber's day diplomas and degrees, whether functionally necessary or not, have become the prime qualification for occupational status at many levels, thus making education an explicit class phenomenon. Education is also the main means by which families pass on their class positions to their children, and therefore an indispensable part of the process of class continuity and consolidation of advantage. And it is quite clear that both students and educators (more, perhaps, in the United States than elsewhere) look upon education as a way to enhance economic status. But education is not totally a class phenomenon, and we will note its implications for prestige and power as well.

Our use of the key but ambiguous term *power* will also vary somewhat from Weber's. In differentiating the major variables of social stratification, Weber used the terms *class, status,* and *party* (rather than *power*), and his discussion of party was quite fragmentary. Implicit in his analysis of stratification and in his work as a whole, however, was the recognition that political institutions have much to do with social stratification. The term *power,* therefore, will refer to any and all political-legal forces that stratify a population in the political realm and that influence stratification elsewhere. However, Weber would also have insisted, and rightly, that all three realms — the economic, the social, and the political — are complexes of power. Furthermore, it must be understood that in a class system the most important form of power as such is economic power; as a matter of fact, it is crucial in all societies. Thus, while we will speak of power as a separate dimension for analytical purposes, the concept of *social* power refers to the combined effects of class, prestige, and power variables.

Whatever terminology is used, however, the basic objectives of stratification analysis are to locate a population along the axes of class, prestige, and power and to understand the causal processes that produce any given distribution of values. Location on any one dimension, while important, cannot be relied on to yield a social class — that is, a class of units characterized by common benefits and behavior across the dimensions of class, prestige, and power. In addition to avoiding a monocausal emphasis on economic status (class), or any other variable, we must also guard against a semantic difficulty that characterizes the use of the concept of class[20]: for one thing, the word *class* is used to refer both to the economic dimension and to the general system of stratification in an industrial society. A closely related complication is the use of the term *class* to denote both economic class and social class. And to make matters worse, the word *class* can refer both to the type of society that provides freedom and opportunities for individuals to transcend their origins (the liberal achievement ethic as opposed to caste and estate systems based on family, sexual, religious, ethnic, or racial ascription) *and* to the ascriptive advantages or disadvantages that attend birth in an economic class. Every effort has been made to keep these diverse meanings clear and distinct in the following pages, and the reader is urged to examine each such usage carefully.

In analyzing the locations of various aggregates on the hierarchies or dimensions of inequality, there are a number of things we want to determine. First, the three major dimensions of stratification represent the basic components of social existence, and we want to know how they are distributed. For example, what percentage of total income or wealth is enjoyed by a given percentage of families? Is access to valued forms of association (prestige groups) distributed unequally, and, if so, on what basis? With regard to the distribution of goods and services, are there noticeable breaks in the income hierarchy? In other words, more broadly, does the distribution of economic values take the form of a vertical continuum with no discernible gaps in the various hierarchies of income, wealth, occupation, and education?

Second, we want to know whether location and behavior in one dimension, or any of its subdimensions, can be related to location and behavior in any other dimension or subdimension. For example, does location at the bottom of the class (economic) dimension also locate one at the bottom of the prestige (moral evaluation) and power (political-legal) dimensions? In asking this general question, our basic objective is to identify social classes or strata (those social units sharing a composite of statuses in each of the three major dimensions from which they derive a common level of benefits and behavior). This effort, of course, raises the question of how overall location is determined. No single factor appears to be a reliable indicator of location on all other dimensions. On the other hand, it is not necessary to know everything about social units before ranking them. Researchers have found many consistent correlations between social factors; for example, education is a good predictor of attitudes about civil rights, lifetime income, consumption styles, and the like. Since no one factor — not even occupation, the central status of modern society — can predict social class, researchers have developed ways of combining factors to do so. (We will discuss these methods more fully in Chapter 3.)

20. And many other terms commonly used in social stratification.

Third, we want to know how units acquire their positions on any or all of the hierarchies. Do they inherit a given rank, achieve it, or inherit a set of advantages and then achieve? To what degree is social class location due to economic, governmental, educational, religious, or other factors? How much mobility is there across the "breaks" in each dimension and what forms does such mobility take?

Fourth, we want to examine all of the foregoing questions in terms of time. Is the distribution of values more or less equal today than at selected points of time in the past? Have the lower classes made any relative gains *vis à vis* the upper classes? Are minorities improving their overall positions in society? Are changes in a minority's position attributable to an absolute improvement in the positions of majority and minority alike or do they represent relative gains — that is, gains against the majority? What changes, if any, have taken place in mobility rates? Has the relative causal power of any dimension changed: for example, is any aspect of the power dimension (such as government) getting relatively stronger *vis à vis* any aspect of class (such as the economy or economic classes)?

Fifth, we want to know how well American ideas and values coincide with the empirical record. Do Americans — either the general population or specific categories such as farmers, business people, labor leaders, or sociologists — have adequate and realistic images of the forces that produce equality and inequality?

Social class in the United States

It is time to give substance to our formal definition of social class (the inequality that results from the operation of class, prestige, and power variables over time); to outline the number, content, and size of America's social classes (see Table 1-2); and to discuss some of the key processes affecting them. To avoid undue complexity in what amounts to a summary of a summary, we will not refer here to minority groups; the location of some representative minority groups and the positions of minorities in the American class system are discussed more fully in later chapters and summarized in Chapter 16.

A social class is made up of families and unrelated individuals who share similar benefits across the three dimensions of class, prestige, and power. (In 1973, the counted American population numbered about 55 million families and 18 million unrelated individuals.) The criterion for distinguishing between social classes is relative level of social benefits; that is, as a given social unit moves from one social class to another, it should experience a noticeable rise or drop in the overall amount and quality of social values available to it. This is not to say that important differences do not exist, say, between the bottom and the top of the working class, or that class boundaries (such as between the working and the lower-middle class) are clearcut. Furthermore, there are no easy equations among the three major dimensions, and changes

Table 1-2 The American Class System in the Twentieth Century: A Composite Estimate[a]

a. This estimate is based on a variety of sources: the federal government, especially the Census Bureau; community, metropolitan, and national studies; and interpretive works. The proportion of the total population represented by each class is given as a percentage range to emphasize that this is an estimate. For expository purposes, racial and ethnic minorities are not included.

CLASS

Class (and percentage of total population)	Income	Property	Occupation	Education	Personal and family life	Education of children
Upper class (1–3%)	Very high income	Great wealth, old wealth	Managers, high professionals, high civil and military officials	Liberal arts education at elite schools	Stable family life	College education by right for both sexes
Upper-middle class (10–15%)	High income	Accumulation of property through savings	Lowest unemployment	Graduate training	Autonomous personality Better physical and mental health	Educational system biased in their favor
Lower-middle class (30–35%)	Modest income	Some savings	Small business people and farmers, lower professionals, semiprofessionals, sales and clerical workers	Some college High school	Longer life expectancy	Greater chance of college than working class children
Working class (40–45%)	Low income	No savings	Skilled labor Unskilled labor	Some high school Grade school	Unstable family life	Educational system biased against them Tendency toward vocational programs
Lower class (20–25%)	Poverty income (destitution)		Highest unemployment Surplus labor	Illiteracy, especially functional illiteracy	Conformist personality Poorer physical and mental health Lower life expectancy	Little interest in education, high dropout rates

Table 1-2 (continued)

Class (and percentage of total population)	PRESTIGE			
	Occupational prestige	Subjective development	Consumption	Participation in group life
Upper class (1–3%)	High occupational prestige	Consistent attitudes; Integrated self-perception	Tasteful consumption; Affluence and comfort	High participation in groups segregated by breeding, religion, ethnicity, race, and function
Lower-middle class (30–35%)			Modest standard of living; Consumption of mass "material" and "symbolic" culture	
Working class (40–45%)	Low occupational prestige	Inconsistent attitudes; Unrealistic self-perception; Greater prevalence of mental illness	Austere consumption	Low participation in group life
Lower class (20–25%)	Stigma of worthlessness on the labor market		Physical suffering; Acute economic anxiety	Social isolation

Table 1-2 (*continued*)

| | POWER | | | |
Class (and percentage of total population)	Participation in political processes	Political attitudes	Legislative and governmental benefits	Distribution of justice
Upper class (1–3%)	High participation	Belief in efficacy of political action	Greater governmental	Legal order biased
Upper-middle class (10–15%)	in voting and other forms of political participation; Monopoly on governmental positions	Support for civil rights and liberal foreign policy	benefits than classes below despite smaller numbers	in support of their interests and rights; Much greater utilization of legal processes than classes below
Lower-middle class (30–35%)		Negative attitude toward governmental intervention in economy and toward welfare programs; Tendency to discount value of political action		
Working class (40–45%)	Tendency not to vote or participate in politics	Except for minorities, opposition to civil rights	Governmental neglect, some repression, some paternalism	Legal order biased against lower classes
Lower class (20–25%)		Support for more nationalist foreign policy and governmental programs that provide economic help and security		Little utilization of legal processes

are taking place at all levels that are difficult to interpret. But, as Table 1-2 indicates, existing research points to five relatively distinct strata in the United States, and to a fairly pronounced integration of the three dimensions, whose center of gravity is the class dimension.

A brief description of these five classes will stand us in good stead when in subsequent chapters we confront the intricacies and nuances of stratification analysis. First, the United States has an upper class (or, as it is called elsewhere, a stable top): a relatively small group of families possessing enormous wealth and great power over the economy, much of it a result of gradual accumulation and inheritance. At this level family lineage is important, and careful attention is paid to such matters as breeding, education, and general style of life. Consumption of both "material" and "symbolic" culture is high and tasteful. Members of this class are active in primary and secondary groups, many of which are carefully guarded against outsiders. The upper class participates fully in political processes and is a major recipient of public benefits. The overall social power of this class will be discussed in due course; in Marxian literature, this class is considered to be the ruling class of contemporary industrial society.

Next is the upper-middle class, composed of successful business people, executives, professionals, and high civil and military officials. Some of its members have considerable wealth and most have high incomes relative to those of the bulk of the population. The economic status of this class is high enough not only to provide an affluent way of life for most but also to allow for savings. In addition to the economic power that stems from the ownership of businesses and professional practices, this group exercises such power through its occupational roles. For many of its members, economic status depends on educational credentials; it is this segment of the upper-middle class that professes, represents, and passes on the scientific ethic, and whose prestige is enhanced thereby. The upper-middle class is also active in voluntary groups, providing a disproportionate percentage of the leadership of the United States' charitable, aesthetic, fraternal, reformist, educational, and political groups, and much of their memberships. It is an especially potent participant in political processes and a major recipient of public benefits.

The lower-middle class, composed of small business people and farmers, lower-level professionals, semiprofessionals, and sales and clerical workers, is in many ways the most heterogeneous economic class. One segment of this class is economically powerful because of its property and because the economic interests of small business and small farming are intertwined with and supported by government. Included in this class are professionals who earn less and have less prestige and influence than the leading segments of their professions; such individuals are often found in small towns, as well as in large cities. The lower-middle class also contains a substantial and apparently growing segment of semiprofessionals — such as nurses, fire fighters, police officers, and teachers — though the largest and fastest-growing segment is sales and clerical workers. Though many members of the lower-middle class are dependent workers subject to the same insecurities and confining routines as most wage workers and seem to have incomes, views, and politics similar to those of substantial portions of the working class, there are sufficient grounds for including them in the middle classes, not the least of which are a more stable family life and a greater ability to see their children through college.

The working class, composed of skilled and unskilled factory, field, and service workers, is the largest class; it too is economically heterogeneous. It is by and large a dependent economic group that enjoys fewer overall economic rewards than the classes above it (though some workers earn higher incomes than some middle class income units). The working class is also less secure economically than many of the classes above it, trade unionism notwithstanding. It is characterized by less education and prestige than the classes above it, and its family life is unstable relative to that of the middle and upper classes. Participation in the associational life of society, including politics, is relatively restricted, and despite its size and its unions the working class tends to have less political power than the classes above it. All in all, there is little evidence that the working class is disappearing or becoming submerged in a great middle class mass; this holds true even for highly paid skilled workers.

The lower class is composed of the chronically unemployed, underemployed, and underpaid, abandoned mothers, and the poor who are sick, disabled, or old. Because it is worth little economically, it has little prestige and political power. The lower class is characterized by unstable family life, and it is too weak and divided to exert itself against the dominant classes above it.

It should be apparent from the foregoing that America does not have a rigid hierarchy of classes. Needless confusions can be avoided, however, if it is clearly understood that sociological knowledge is expressed primarily in terms of statistical modalities. One must take care not to fall prey to old-fashioned generalizations that admit of no exceptions. Statistics is a language equipped to describe the behavior — actually, rates of behavior — of aggregates, not individuals — and it is understood that every individual does not behave in the same way. Aggregates, whether ears of corn, gas molecules, or income classes, can exhibit regular or patterned attributes or behavior, and thus can be generalized about even though particular ears of corn, gas molecules, or income units deviate from the norm.

To understand the class system of industrial society, one must also avoid importing concepts derived from previous systems of inequality. The idea that there are strict boundaries between the levels of society is derived from agrarian society and from certain historical forms of class crystallization and antagonism that emerged during the transformation from estate to class stratification. However, unlike static societies, or societies undergoing social system change, a dynamic, expanding, established industrial society is bound to exhibit a certain fluidity and overlap between its various levels and to have some inconsistency among its types of inequality, especially due to vestiges of the past.

Perhaps the best way to sum up these points is to say that the analyst of social stratification must be wary of confusing abstractions with reality. Above all, one must keep the multidimensional analytical scheme constantly in mind in order to make sense of the empirical complexities of American stratification. But while the United States is far from possessing a neatly articulated set of self-conscious social classes, neither is it a seamless series of functionally differentiated hierarchies. There is little doubt that each of the major hierarchies contains relatively distinct levels, and that the various levels are related across all three major dimensions. Thus, even as we stress the need to employ a model of analysis in which variables are kept analytically separated, we must recognize that these variables are empirically connected. On the basis of the empirical record, the class dimension contains the most important causal variables. In other words, behavior and benefits in the prestige and power dimensions can be predicted by focusing on such class variables as income, wealth, occupation, and education. One of the most important conclusions to emerge from the many empirical studies we will review is the extent to which class (economic institutions) in America has penetrated the dimensions of prestige and power. As we shall see, it is very difficult for prestige or political-legal forces in the United States (and presumably in all established liberal societies) to counteract the influence of the class dimension or for individuals to rise or remain at a given level without a secure economic base.

This point can also be understood differently. While the United States' economic classes are relatively heterogeneous in terms of economic interest, consumption patterns, religion, ethnicity, race, class of origin, and even political outlook, they are distinct in overall economic values and form separate social classes largely because of influences stemming from powerful economic factors. This relative diversification of economic and social classes, incidentally, has a consequence of considerable importance: it prevents the formation of solidary, self-conscious strata. We will have much more to say about this feature of contemporary class society in due course.

From the standpoint of overall social power — we will state this more tentatively and cautiously than is our wont — there appears to be a basic cleavage, though not overt conflict or struggle, between the upper and middle classes (here defined as the upper, upper-middle, and lower-middle classes, which make up approximately 40 percent of the population) and the classes below (the working and lower classes, which compose the remaining 60 percent). The relationship between these two sets of classes appears to reflect the basic power structure of the United States, though we will explore the possibility that the upper and upper-middle classes, either separately or in concert, are the real locus of social power.

Our empirical studies have revealed some other stratification processes that should be presented at the outset, since they contradict much conventional thinking. It appears that overall stratification inequality is not declining in the United States, or in any industrial country; that the rate of upward mobility in the United States is not as large or as different from those of other industrial countries as most people think; that achievement processes are not overcoming ascriptive processes; that equality of opportunity is not being increased; and that while there is little class consciousness in the United States, there is a significant amount of unacknowledged class conflict, exploitation, and waste, all deeply institutionalized and thus not easily recognized or eradicated. In sum, let us keep in mind, as we proceed, the image of a deeply unequal society that is moving up an inclined plane of increasing benefits for most, but exhibiting little if any reduction in its overall degree of stratification inequality, producing inequality by means of a poorly understood mixture of class inheritance and achievement, and possessing legitimating symbols that are at wide variance with the facts.[21]

The special problems of age and sex stratification

In recent years a number of neglected areas of social inequality, notably age and sex, have come into prominence — thanks in good measure to the growing awareness and militancy of the affected parties. No model or depiction of the American structure of social stratification would be complete if it did not treat, at least briefly, the relationship between social stratification and age-related and sexual stratification. Inequalities based on age and sex are not as totally distinct from social stratification as we might have implied earlier.

Age, for example, importantly influences the economic, and thus class, status of individuals. There is a tendency, too, for those who are born poor to be poor when they are old and for those who are born rich to remain so as they age. But unlike social stratification, which allows for individuals and families to move upward or downward or to remain stationary in the scheme of rewards, age is a one-way, irreversible process. By and large, the inequalities of age do not have to correspond to the inequalities of social stratification — the old can be either poor or rich, and so on. Perhaps the most important point about age is that its meaning can vary enormously from one society to another: for example, in different societies a fourteen-year-old male can be either a married adult or a child with many years of school ahead of him; an elder can be revered as a fount of wisdom or put to death as an economic burden; and so on. Since age has an obvious bearing on an individual's worth on economic, prestige, and political markets, stratification analysts must keep an eye on norms and values that define stages in the life cycle (for example, school-leaving or retirement age) and on factors that affect longevity (for example, sanitation, nutrition, and medical care). There is another way in which age exerts a significant influence on social stratification: if large numbers of young or elderly people lack secure economic statuses, this fact will be reflected in all other stratification hierarchies. If large numbers of affluent or impoverished elderly cluster in retirement centers, this phenomenon will have repercussions at all political levels. And, to take a final example, a life

21. As will be explained later, the improved position of black Americans (and other depressed minorities) is primarily a movement out of "caste" and into, not up, the class system.

expectancy of seventy, instead of thirty-five to forty, means that women's lives do not begin and end with bearing and raising children, and allows them to pursue other goals. In sum, it should be apparent that age and social stratification are distinct but related phenomena. However, the analysis of the relation between age and social inequality is in a preliminary stage and much remains to be done.[22]

Analysis of the relationship between sexual and social stratification has only begun, and much hard thinking and research will be necessary before precise linkages can be established.[23] Social stratification theorists have always identified the family as the ranking unit, and by and large this stance is correct. As we indicated earlier, the rationale for this position is that all family members are equals in terms of class (or estate or caste). Thus, to repeat our earlier argument, even when a prejudiced and discriminatory society makes women subordinate to men, the nature of social stratification makes some women (mostly the wives of successful men and women with careers of their own) superior to other women and to many men as well. As long as women are subordinated to men in the family system, and as long as families can be ranked in terms of differences in economic, prestige, and power values, social and sexual stratification will remain two distinct forms of sociocultural inequality.[24]

However, women are no longer as fully subordinated in the family system as they once were. Thanks to forces that have been gestating for generations, many women now fill roles outside the home and marriage. The thrust of industrial society is to individualize behavior, and stratification theorists can no longer assume that the family is the only unit of social stratification. It is not just that one must account for the many individuals whose lives are lived outside of marriage and family life; of perhaps greater significance is the increase in individualism *within* the family, especially at middle class levels. It is significant that the women's liberation movement is primarily a middle class phenomenon. The reason for this is not difficult to discern: middle (especially upper-middle) class parents tend to treat their male and female children alike, even to the extent of providing both with higher education and the motivation to pursue careers. As a consequence, middle class females have experienced a deep contradiction between, on the one hand, an upbringing focused on personal worth and training for productive citizenship, and, on the other, subordination to a husband and children, what some feel is the relatively degrading

22. For a comprehensive introduction to all aspects of the sociology of age, see *Aging and Society,* written under the direction of Matilda White Riley, 3 vols. (New York: Russell Sage Foundation, 1968–1972).

23. For a criticism of stratification theorists for neglecting this relationship and some suggestions on how to proceed to study it (some of which are pursued below), see Joan Acker, "Women and Social Stratification: A Case of Intellectual Sexism," *American Journal of Sociology* 78 (January 1973): 936–945.

24. In defining *social stratification,* we may seem to imply that age-related and sexual stratification are not social. Nevertheless, age and sex are culturally defined and thus overwhelmingly "social" in nature.

role of housewife, and institutionalized inferiorities and inequities in economic, political, legal, and moral statuses.

The changing relation between women and men reflects the growing participation of women in the work force. How it has affected family life at the various class levels cannot be stated with precision. At the upper levels, the "two-person career," in which the wife is "gainfully unemployed" helping her husband, may be diminishing somewhat in frequency as husband and wife each pursue a career (with or without children).[25] At lower levels, large numbers of wives and daughters now work, at least intermittently, to supplement family income. It is quite probable that working wives and daughters help some male breadwinners achieve mobility in their own careers, help their family units to save and thus maintain or raise their class levels, and help to equalize the relations between husband and wife and father and daughter. None of this pertains usefully to the task of linking sexual and social stratification, however, until we know how "class" achievements are affected by sex. If all women's incomes, types of occupation, and prestige were equivalent to those of men with the same backgrounds, sexual inequality would not be relevant to or different from social stratification. But women are an exploited portion of the labor force even after education, type of work, and lifetime experience are taken into account.[26] That women are concentrated in low-paying stereotyped occupations is not the main issue here; so are many men, for that matter. Central to the relation between sex and social stratification is the fact that women are not treated as men's equals once they enter the labor force. They receive less pay for the same work, are not subject to the same standards of evaluation and promotion as men, and are prevented from entering certain occupations. Furthermore, when the male dies or disappears they must assume the extraordinary burden of heading the household (which means that many widows and abandoned mothers and their children sink to and remain at the bottom of the social hierarchy). When we analyze the relation between sex and social stratification we must distinguish between inequalities, just and unjust, to which men and women are both subject and those that pertain only to women (or, for that matter, only to men[27]).

Implicit in the foregoing is the view that if stratification theory is to be comprehensively related to age and sexual inequality, we must think hard about how to rank individuals. Of course, the census bureau already keeps track of unrelated individuals, a group composed increasingly of the aged living in

25. For an analysis of the two-person career, see Hanna Papanek, "Men, Women, and Work: Reflections on the Two-Person Career," *American Journal of Sociology* 78 (January 1973): 852–872.

26. For a valuable analysis, focused especially on lifetime experience, that reveals considerable sexual inequality in economic statuses after other factors are controlled, see Larry E. Suter and Herman P. Miller, "Income Differences Between Men and Career Women," *American Journal of Sociology* 78 (January 1973): 962–974.

27. For example, men are uniquely subject to military service, and inequitably burdened by muscular wage labor and the anxieties and hurts of economic insecurity and failure.

separate households. Census data are also collected on family and individual incomes and on income by age and sex. Of special importance for understanding the relation between women and social stratification is the analysis of the behavior of individuals who are members of families.

The stratification of religious-ethnic and racial groups

The inequality of ethnic and racial groups can be related to social stratification much more easily than can age or sex, for a simple reason. In a society with an ethnic-religious or racially diverse population, a hierarchy based on ethnic-religious or racial status is easily established using the traditional ranking unit, the family.

An upper class must contain all ages and sexes, but it need not include all ethnic, religious, and racial groups. Thus a relatively sharp hierarchy based on ethnicity, religion, or race can easily be established and maintained over generations. Indeed, the clustering of economic and political power around distinctive ethnic, religious, or racial statuses is a commonplace of social stratification, not only in the United States but in all societies that are or have been heterogeneous in these regards. In industrial societies such stratification is an important aspect of the prestige dimension, sometimes coinciding with class and power stratification and sometimes not. In preindustrial societies, religious-ethnic and racial stratification more often coincide with class and power stratification and thus partake of the more explicit and thorough separation of strata characteristic of such societies.

Stratification analysis: a summary

The purpose of this chapter was to provide a broad overview of the general field of social stratification. To do so we have examined and discussed the relative merits of the biopsychological and sociocultural explanations of inequality, finding the latter more persuasive. In developing a working definition of social stratification, we relied heavily on Max Weber, and especially on his insistence that the various areas of inequality — the economic (class), the social (prestige), and the political (power) — be kept analytically separate. We explained that the purpose of stratification analysis is to locate social units on each of these three dimensions (and their subdimensions) over time, and to relate the various hierarchies to each other, also over time. Again following Max Weber, we assumed that though these dimensions vary in importance over the course of history, they tend with time to coalesce and form either castes, estates, or classes — that is, aggregates of social units that share given social benefits across all three dimensions.

We identified five social classes in the United States and indicated that the popular explanation for American inequality is unacceptable: Americans are not made unequal by their biopsychological natures but by social variables, which are for the most part ascriptive in nature. In other words, social class at birth explains success or failure for Americans in the aggregate better than does the idea of talent or the philosophy of nonegalitarian classlessness. Social stratification, as the institutionalized ranking of family units containing both sexes and all ages, was carefully distinguished from sexual and age-related inequality. And, finally, we pointed out that since religious-ethnic and racial aggregates are composed of family units, they can be stratified as aggregates by more powerful religious-ethnic or racial groups.

2

Social stratification and the problem of a general theory

THE GOAL OF EVERY field of science is to develop a unified depiction of its subject matter, and social stratification is no exception. The heart of such a unified or general theory would consist of generalizations applicable to all systems of stratification. Our task in this chapter, therefore, is to review the progress that has been made toward a general theory of stratification and to identify some of the barriers standing in the way of its realization. We will also ask whether it is possible to make generalizations about the innumerable and complex phenomena of stratification, and even suggest that social scientists must limit themselves (at least for the time being) to generalizations about specific past or existing systems of stratification.

We will initially approach the problem of a general theory by presenting case studies of the three major forms of stratification — caste, estate, and class, illustrated respectively by India, feudal Europe, and the Soviet Union. Once we have gained some familiarity with the diverse ways in which stratification manifests itself, we will examine some of the theories that claim to find unity in the historical record. And, finally, we will examine change in stratification systems, using France and Japan as representative examples.

The diversity of stratification: selected case studies

In the following analysis, each of the major types of stratification will be depicted in ideal-typical terms — that is, in terms of how each would work if it adhered to its basic principles — and also in terms of how it actually works.

Following Max Weber's usage, it should be noted that the use of an ideal type is not a value judgment. An ideal type is simply a freely and logically constructed model in which the constitutive principles of the phenomena under examination are identified and formulated purely, even exaggeratedly, so that the empirical world can be brought into relief more easily.

The caste system: India

The most explicit, thoroughgoing, and inflexible structure of social stratification is the caste system. In general, a caste system declares that a differential in some ascriptive condition is supremely important and forms an unalterable and inviolate basis for the unequal distribution of all social benefits. While a number of societies (for example, Ceylon, parts of Africa, Japan, and the United States) have developed approximations of caste stratification, probably the only true example is India.[1]

In approaching any stratification system, one must be wary of accepting traditional explanations and justifications. The written and oral tradition of a people is invariably in the hands of those who benefit most from the status quo. In pronouncements about the nature of their society, dominant strata always put their best feet forward: they stress consensus on values and beliefs and the mutual benefits derived from institutions, and excuse their mistakes, hide their unwarranted privileges, and blame social problems on human nature and other forces beyond human control. Our knowledge of India's stratification system during its classic period is derived primarily from the religious writings of the upper caste; to accept such a description at face value is tantamount to accepting a Fourth of July speech as an accurate depiction of how the American stratification system works.

Disregarding origins and historical irregularities, what appears to have happened on the Indian subcontinent is that the Hindu religion crystallized in such a way as to transcend class and power, and came not only to express economic and political forces but to dominate them. This is not to minimize the importance of economic and political factors. Reading the following description of the underlying religious rationale for caste, it should be kept in mind that India was an agrarian society, the vast bulk of whose population worked in a labor-intensive, low-technology agricultural economy. Given a static village economy, it is not surprising that a complex, sophisticated religion

1. For a wide-ranging historical and comparative analysis of various stratification systems, which sees class forces behind caste divisions including racial slavery in the American South, see Oliver Cromwell Cox, *Caste, Class and Race* (Garden City, N.Y.: Doubleday, 1948). Allison Davis' classic article, "Caste, Economy, and Violence," *American Journal of Sociology* 51, no. 1 (July 1945): 7–15 (also Bobbs Merrill reprint no. 61), calls attention to the failure of the American South to apply the principle of caste to economic institutions, and thus helps to confute any facile claims of equivalence between caste in India and racial domination in the pre- or postplantation American South. In using the concept of caste to draw attention to the similarities between caste in India and racial slavery and segregation in the United States, we will use quotation marks to signify this lack of total equivalence.

such as Hinduism could provide the simple productive system with a religious sanction and eventually envelop it altogether. And the same thing is true of family, governmental, and military relations: together with economic functions, these realms too were eventually absorbed into a hierarchic mosaic of religiously defined castes and subcastes. With behavior in all areas of life subject to a religiously determined division of social labor, the individual castes were self-sufficient in terms of marriage and reproduction, the socialization of the young, eating patterns, kin obligations and mutual help, the settlement of disputes, and the practice of religion *per se*; at the same time they were committed to occupations and caste relations that incorporated them into village-wide, regional, and all-India divisions of social labor.

In all societies always, there is a basic thrust toward consistency of class, prestige, and power (especially at the upper levels), and India was no exception. Modern empirical research has revealed considerable inconsistency — even conflict and mobility — in twentieth-century India,[2] but evidence suggests a high degree of consistency in the classic period among the statuses of each caste and subcaste in each dimension of stratification. The system of caste and subcaste cannot be described exactly. On a very abstract and relatively unrealistic level, Indian society was a hierarchy composed of four *varnas* (broad all-India castes) and the untouchables (the outcaste). This scheme was derived from a religious literary tradition three thousand years old; while it is not accurate empirically — (the reality of Indian stratification is its thousands of subcastes) — it provides a first approximation of the essential spirit of caste.

Formally speaking, therefore, the classic caste system of India was based on the all-pervasive importance of religious status at birth (Hinduism).[3] Both the Hindu religion and the social system it eventually brought under its sway

---

2. Oscar Lewis, *Group Dynamics: A Study of Factions Within Castes in Village Life in Northern India* (Urbana: University of Illinois Press, 1954); Adrian Mayer, *Caste and Kinship in Central India; A Village and Its Region* (Berkeley: University of California Press, 1960); Andre Beteille, *Caste, Class, and Power: Changing Patterns of Stratification in a Tanjore Village* (Berkeley: University of California Press, 1965); James Silverberg, ed., *Social Mobility in the Caste System in India* (The Hague: Mouton, 1968). For a series of interpretive essays on various aspects of modernization in India, see M. N. Srinivas, *Caste in Modern India and Other Essays* (New York: Asia Publishing House, 1962).

3. For an excellent formal description of the extraordinarily complex phenomenon known as the Indian caste system, see Egon E. Bergel, *Social Stratification* (New York: McGraw-Hill, 1962), pp. 35–67. For a theoretical discussion of caste, see Anthony de Reuck and Julie Knight, eds., *Caste and Race: Comparative Approaches* (London: J. and A. Churchill, 1967), especially chaps. 1, 5, and 7; also in paperback. The classic scholarly treatise by J. H. Hutton, *Caste in India: Its Nature, Function, and Origins*, 4th ed. (London: Oxford University Press, 1963) is useful, especially for its details. Probably the best introductions for the beginning reader are Taya Zinkin, *Caste Today* (London: Oxford University Press, 1962), paperback, and Gerald D. Berreman, "Caste in India and the United States," *American Journal of Sociology* 66 (September 1960): 120–127 (also Bobbs-Merrill reprint no. 22); and "Caste in the Modern World" (Morristown, N. J.: General Learning Press, 1973). Though useful to a point, Berreman's attempt to interpret racial inequality in the American South in terms of caste should be resisted.

are vastly different from the religions and societies Westerners are accustomed to. They lacked the theology, explicit organizational structures, functional staff (clergy, civil servants), and degree of legalization and formal political authority that Westerners associate with religion and society. Despite the apparent formlessness of the Indian caste system, however, it effectively controlled Indian society for well over two thousand years. This is all the more remarkable in light of the fact that the castes and subcastes could never be precisely identified, described, ranked, or even numbered. Each of the four main castes — the Brahmans (priests and scholars), the Kshatriyas or Rajputs (princes and warriors), the Vaishyas (merchants), and the Sudras (peasants, artisans, laborers) — contained many subcastes, and the total numbered in the thousands. Below these, the outcastes (untouchables) made up approximately 20 percent of the population.

It is impossible to understand the absolute inequality that prevails under the Indian caste system without understanding the main tenets of Hinduism:

1. *Samsara,* or reincarnation, is life after death — in this world not another.
2. *Dharma,* or correct ritual behavior, specifies the behavior appropriate to one's caste.
3. *Karma,* or causality, is dependent on how well one adheres to correct ritual behavior (dharma) independently of social conditions.

In Hinduism, there is no supreme creator: life, or the soul, has always existed and manifests itself in caste. One can improve one's caste in the next (social) life, and failure to adhere to the dharma of one's caste can cause one to be downgraded either in this social life or the next one, but no one can climb the social hierarchy during any given lifetime.

There is little that is obligatory for all Hindus. All must respect the Brahmans, believe in the sacredness of the cow, and accept the castes into which they are born. The main thrust of Hinduism (and thus of Indian culture) is toward prescribing different modes of behavior and different benefits for each caste. There is no universal standard of right and wrong, and no improvement is possible in this life; all deprivations and hardships are ordained and explained by religion, and the only recourse against worldly suffering and avenue to social mobility is the possibility of a better life in some future reincarnation. Unlike Christianity, which has universal moral rules (the Ten Commandments) and universal ethical ideals (love and brotherhood) and declares all individual souls equal before God, Hinduism sets a radically different course for each caste and subcaste, saying in effect that different castes are worth different amounts in the divine scheme of things.

The enormous power and stability of the Indian caste system resulted from the extension of religion into every aspect of behavior: occupation, marriage, eating and drinking, friendship, and many other pursuits were explicitly regulated by caste status. The radical particularism of religion thus resulted in a social and cultural particularism so deep that it precluded even a minimal degree of equality. The Indian subcaste was a prestige group without parallel in the history of stratification. It constituted the consciousness of its members and controlled their economic and political relationships down to the smallest particular. A Westerner's deeply implanted sense of the public, ingrained universalism, and easy use of abstractions in dealing with himself, with others, and with nature make the cultural diversity (particularism) represented by India's thousands of subcastes almost incomprehensible. Nevertheless, the caste system was not random or unpatterned. Relations between the subcastes were strictly prescribed according to a logic provided by the Hindu concept of ritual purity — a concept blurred obviously by such phenomena as conquest, migration, British imperial control, urbanization, and industrialization.

Given this strict and narrow definition of identity, there is no formal consistency between the hierarchies of class, prestige, and power. Formally, each of the top three castes monopolized the top of one hierarchy and each was formally positioned hierarchically in relation to the others: Brahmans (prestige), Kshatriyas or Rajputs (power), and Vaishyas (class). But beneath the forms of the Indian caste system there is a general consistency of status in the major dimensions of stratification: all three of the top castes, for example, enjoyed high or substantial economic status and were roughly equivalent in their other statuses. Let us investigate these equivalences by briefly examining the Brahman caste. Only a minority of Brahmans followed a priestly calling; while Brahmans could not pursue certain occupations, such as medicine and money-lending, without jeopardizing their caste positions, they were landlords and practiced all the learned professions. As the following description of their overall social position indicates, dominant strata do not ordinarily allow inconsistencies of class, prestige, and power to develop, especially with regard to themselves:

> Nor did the Brahman fail to make the most of his privileged position as interpreter and arbiter of holy writ, at any rate according to the Code of Manu. A Brahman need observe mourning for ten days only, but a Kshatriya for twelve, a Vaishya for fifteen and a Sudra for a month. A Brahman is initiated, and in the process born again, in his eighth year, a Kshatriya in his eleventh, a Vaishya in his twelfth, and a Sudra never. A Sudra may use only the southern gate of a town for carrying forth his dead, and his killing by a Brahman is equivalent merely to the killing of a cat, a mongoose, a blue jay, a frog, a dog, a lizard, an owl, or a crow. To serve a Brahman learned in the vedas is the highest duty of a Sudra, and if he be pure and serve humbly he may in another incarnation attain the highest class. The Brahman is by right the chief of this whole creation; whatever exists in the universe is the wealth of the Brahman, who is entitled to it all by his primogeniture; in virtue of which he is entitled to treasure trove and his property never escheats to the king. He is the deity on earth by divine status and the intelligent one by his innate comprehension. He may without hesitation take the property of a

Sudra for the purpose of sacrifice, for a Sudra has no business with sacrifices. If a Sudra mentions the name and class of the twice-born with contumely an iron nail ten fingers long shall be thrust red hot into his mouth. "If he arrogantly teaches Brahmans their duty, the king shall cause hot oil to be poured into his mouth and into his ears." But no reciprocal punishments are prescribed for cantankerous Brahmans—though they follow mean occupations Brahmans are to be honoured in every way "for each of them is a very great deity." Such are the injunctions of the Code of Manu; the Padma Purana says that immoral Brahmans are to be worshipped, but not Sudras, though subduing passions, for "the cow that eats things not to be eaten is better than the sow of good intent." Vedic rites and prayers are required of the twice-born castes, but they are prohibited to Sudras who may learn only the Puranas and the Tantras. The Code of Manu says that a king shall never execute a Brahman "though convicted of all possible crimes," but may banish him "with all his property secure and his body unhurt. No greater crime is known on earth than slaying a Brahman; and the king, therefore, must not even form in his mind an idea of killing a priest." "A Brahman, be he ignorant or learned, is a great divinity."[4]

Industrialization has caused the dimensions of prestige, class, and power to separate. As Weber wrote:

> When the bases of the acquisition and distribution of goods are relatively stable, stratification by status [prestige] is favored. Every technological repercussion and economic transformation threatens stratification by status and pushes the class situation into the foreground. Epochs and countries in which the naked class situation is of predominant significance are regularly the periods of technical and economic transformations. And every slowing down of the shifting of economic stratification leads, in due course, to the growth of status structures and makes for a resuscitation of the important role of social honor.[5]

Changes in the Indian stratification system, however, have not paralleled (as yet) the sharp displacement of prestige by class that occurred in the Western world. The power of caste and the enormous economic problems India faces have prevented such an occurrence. Nonetheless, caste has been undermined in some important ways (such as when industry or government ignores caste in hiring labor or dispensing services) and strengthened in others (such as when new occupations are monopolized by castes, or political candidates reflect caste voting strength). Of course, even in the classic period there was probably a considerable amount of both rivalry between castes and subcastes and upward and downward mobility (of subcastes, not individuals) due to military conquest, the settlement of new lands, the emergence of new occupations, and British rule. But all this notwithstanding, the classic Indian caste system was a uniquely rigid system of virtually total inequality.

4. From J. H. Hutton, *Caste in India: Its Nature, Functions and Origins,* 4th ed. (London: Oxford University Press, 1946, 1963), pp. 92f., by permission of the Oxford University Press.
5. Max Weber, "Class, Status, Party" in H. H. Gerth and C. Wright Mills, tr. and ed., *From Max Weber: Essays in Sociology* (New York: Oxford University Press, 1946), pp. 193–194, by permission of the Oxford University Press.

The estate system: feudal and feudal-authoritarian society

Inequality by estates[6] is the most commonplace system of stratification among precommercial horticultural and agricultural societies. Two subtypes can be distinguished:

1. Feudalism, or the highly localized and personalized lord-vassal relation based on hereditary linkages to land, in which the lord has explicit governmental, religious, military, and economic power over his dependents.[7]

2. The feudal-authoritarian form, in which a relatively strong central government emerges and is superimposed on the feudal system. Ordinarily, an hereditary absolute monarchy rules bureaucratically through officials recruited from the feudality.[8]

The estate structure of stratification can vary considerably depending on geography, economic variables, patterns of conquest and migration, type of religion, and other factors.[9] Thus societies as dissimilar as ancient Egypt, the Inca and Maya, medieval Europe and Imperial Russia, and China and Japan all belong in the general category of estate stratification. But regardless of variations, even some important ones, one overriding pattern characterizes preindustrial estate society: a small group of families has succeeded in institutionalizing its domination of the vast majority through legitimated economic, political, military, religious, and intellectual power. Regardless of origin or

6. For an extended formal analysis of stratification by estates or orders, see Roland Mousnier, *Social Hierarchies: 1450 to the Present*, trans. Peter Evans, ed. Margaret Clarke (New York: Schocken, 1973), part 2. Mousnier neglects economic variables throughout, and his attempt to interpret "totalitarian" regimes (Jacobin France, Fascist Italy, Nazi Germany, and the Soviet Union) as societies stratified by orders is not altogether successful. Nonetheless, his analysis of preindustrial estate societies is a valuable contribution to stratification theory.

7. For an historical and comparative analysis of, and search for the essential elements of, feudal society, see the valuable essays in Rushton Coulborn, ed., *Feudalism in History* (Princeton: Princeton University Press, 1956).

8. For a broad sociological usage of the term *feudalism* that subsumes both subtypes (and caste society), see Gideon Sjoberg, "Folk and 'Feudal' Societies," *The American Journal of Sociology* 58 (November 1952): 231–239; also available as Bobbs-Merrill reprint no. 270.

For a valuable sociological analysis of an example of the feudal-authoritarian form of estate stratification, see Hsiao-Tung Fei, "Peasantry and Gentry: An Intrepretation of Chinese Social Structure and Its Changes," *The American Journal of Sociology* 52 (July 1946): 1–17; also available as Bobbs-Merrill reprint no. A-63.

9. Arthur L. Stinchcombe has provided a valuable analysis of the various forms and systems of stratification that various types of commercial or capitalistic agricultural enterprise give rise to. See his "Agricultural Enterprise and Rural Class Relations," *American Journal of Sociology* 67 (September 1961): 165–176; reprinted in Reinhard Bendix and Seymour M. Lipset, eds., *Class, Status, and Power*, 2nd ed. (New York: Free Press, 1966), pp. 182–190. Despite the fact that Stinchcombe analyzes precommercial and quasi-commercial systems (the manorial and family tenancy systems), the thrust of his article and the other three types of systems he defines (family freeholding, plantation, and ranching systems of agriculture) are oriented toward market economies and thus toward class stratification.

specific history, a complex agrarian society tends to become "feudalistic" — that is, to develop as a hierarchy of explicitly articulated hereditary estates. (Occasionally some develop in the direction of caste stratification, of which India is the solitary pure type.)

The complex agrarian society develops a considerable economic surplus, thanks to an advanced technology and division of labor. Literacy, restricted to the elite in power, leads to the accumulation of technical knowledge and of a corpus of sacred writings, all easily transmissible under the custody of a privileged profession of priests or scholars. It is characterized by many mighty public works, such as aqueducts, temples, roads, and fortresses, but little accumulation of productive capital; most production is for consumption. Any surplus over subsistence is expended on luxury, "public" buildings glorifying the upper estates and the beliefs and values that benefit them, and warfare. In other words, the surplus produced by the masses is used to reinforce and perpetuate the system that dominates and exploits them.

Like the caste system, the estate system is focused formally on prestige rather than economic status. However, institutionalized inequality in estate society relies much more explicitly and heavily than caste society on power (monarch, magistrate, state religion, tax collector, the military). Though economic variables are important in the origination of such societies, they eventually succumb to such power and prestige variables as military force, law and administration, a mighty religion, styles of consumption, traditions of family honor, intellectual-educational forces, and the like.

The estate system of stratification is similar to the caste system in other ways, too, though a full silhouette requires contrasts with class society. Both caste and estate societies lack a coherent and viable state or system of public authority relative to modern society. When estate stratification is compared only with the Indian caste system, however, one finds in the former a much higher degree of formal definition, especially in the area of law. While the estate system is also governed by ascription, it is family, not religious status at birth, that is the crucial determinant of social position in an established estate system.

Medieval society in the West contains both subtypes of estate stratification. Due to the prime social importance of force during the settlement of barbarian Europe after the fall of Rome, skill at warfare became the most important form of social behavior. The retreat into the countryside and the primitive technology of the time made land the most important economic value. The warrior soon turned his skill at violence into an economic asset through plunder and control of land under a system in which protection was exchanged for food and labor, and eventually succeeded in legalizing and legitimizing his ascendant position through chivalry, *noblesse oblige,* and privilege or superior legal rights.

While the full-fledged estate system has a relatively higher degree of explicit social specialization than the caste system, it is much less specialized, and differently specialized, than modern society. The modern social system specializes the behavior of individuals according to an intricate occupational system, but also demands considerable versatility from individuals. Thus individuals (especially males) are Jacks-of-all-functions in that they must obtain educations, work, attend to the formation and functioning of their families, be responsible for the legality and morality of their actions, seek out salvation, participate in public affairs, and fight in the nation's wars. In the feudal system the upper stratum (nobles) did the fighting, administered the manors, dispensed justice, engaged in "politics," and did the thinking and praying.[10] The serfs were a dependent group who followed the decrees of custom and lord. They raised families, of course, and went to church, and were even pressed into military service on occasion, but by and large the normative tradition confined them to manual work, a dishonorable activity regarded as punishment for sin.

The estate legal system in the West stipulated that legal status was a function of family birth and provided for different rights and duties (privilege) depending on social position. The noble was not subject to arrest or trial in the same manner as were commoners; his fiefs were not inherited in the same way as were other properties; his rank gave the nobleman exclusive access to high religious position; his person was specially protected against his inferiors; he had the right of private vengeance; he enjoyed special rights with regard to consumption and personal adornment; and he was able to substitute military service for the usual burdens of taxation.

The feudal idea of privilege must be seen in the context of a pronounced system of cultural particularism. Feudalism was characterized by few abstractly defined functional institutions, and there was little that was shared by all. Its emphasis, rather, was on the different rights and duties of the different strata. The relation between lord and serf was a highly personal, rigid, and pervasive structure of supersubordination that encompassed all spheres of existence. Of great significance to this system was the privatization of political power; what today is defined as public authority or public office was defined under feudalism as the attribute or possession of private persons.

Despite the static nature of feudal stratification, a certain measure of social mobility was both possible and legitimate. In the Western estate system, for example, marriage between social unequals (strictly forbidden in a caste system) was possible though not common, nonnobles could be knighted in exceptional circumstances (usually military), noble status and high office could be purchased, and the nature of the Christian Church blurred the strict distinction between noblemen and serfs by permitting the latter to become priests. Furthermore, Christianity tended to give all a common religious and moral status, thus lending the moral force of religion to a minimal acknowledgement of equality.

Western feudalism was modified, of course, by the emergence of absolutism or feudal-authoritarian society. Attempts to impose absolute monarchy on feudalism account for a great deal of the histories of England, France, Prussia,

---

10. The upper clergy were eventually drawn only from noble families. Thus the disputes between Church and state, however real, were disputes between two estates that shared fundamental stratum (class, prestige, and power) attributes and interests.

Russia, and other countries. The essential new contribution by the authoritarian estate system was bureaucratic administration in government, a hierarchy of governmental occupations requiring training and the attachment of individuals to a centralized means of administration. While this subtype emerged throughout the world, it developed most fully in the West, where it was eventually transformed into the class system when the "state" passed out of the hands of the monarch and nobility into the hands of the middle class. As Sjoberg points out, however, the emergence of liberal democracy represented less of a break with the past than we imagine. Thus, while the class system of stratification will be treated as a distinct type, important continuities and similarities with the estate system will be noted in due course.[11]

The class system: the Soviet Union

The caste and estate systems stratify their populations along lines that are formally independent of economic statuses. A third type of stratification emerges whenever economic variables emerge to upset prestige and power variables, such as in republican city-states and the various plutocratic societies, and especially when economic variables develop to the point that they receive society's highest moral blessing. It is in this latter situation, of course, that we confront the genuine class system of stratification. Class inequality is an outcome of industrialization, and appears in a variety of forms in all kinds of industrial society, capitalist and communist alike.

The issue of whether or not communist countries — also called socialist, state socialist, state capitalist, classless, and elite versus mass societies — are class societies is not settled, and our own assessment is based on what appears to be the most reliable evidence and analysis.[12] The essentials of class society appear when science and human effort make mastery over nature feasible and turn it into a supreme value. The depiction of man's destiny as inextricably bound up with the mastery of nature is common to liberal and Marxian thought, and both types of societies claim to be classless — that is, merely unequal because of functional differentiation. However, the central aspect of class — significant economic inequality and its transmission through the family — is present in all industrial societies. While there are historical variations in the emergence of industrialization, the overall impact of sustained economic growth is relatively uniform. The state socialist societies may be under more direct political control (though the difference between them and liberal democracies in this respect should not be exaggerated) and may reveal more social mobility and less extreme cleavages between the various strata, but these characteristics

11. See "Continuity With the Past" in Chapter 16.
12. For a judicious examination of the various positions on this issue, which concludes that the key question about socialist society is whether it can maintain its openness in the long run, see Frank Parkin, *Class Inequality and Political Order* (London: MacGibbon and Kee, 1971), chap. 5. For an analysis that finds the similarities between systems of stratification in different industrial societies to far outweigh the differences, see David Lane, *The End of Inequality?: Stratification Under State Socialism* (Baltimore: Penguin, 1971).

are probably due to the rapidity of industrialization and the urgency of eliminating vestiges of the past. In all communist countries high technical and occupational competence is being rewarded handsomely (as it is in capitalist countries), and managerial and professional groups have established themselves and developed considerable autonomy *vis à vis* the party machinery.

Thus either the United States or the Soviet Union (or any industrial society) can serve as an example of class stratification. We will assume, therefore, for the purpose of gaining some comparative perspective, without closing the issue,[13] that regardless of previous cultural tradition or present ideology, any country that successfully industrializes has by definition changed its principle of stratification from caste or estate to class. Industrial countries also reveal marked similarities, again despite ideology and previous cultural tradition, in the relationship between class status (occupation, income, education) and responses to questions of belief and value.[14] Despite obvious differences, the Soviet Union is similar to the United States in a number of fundamental ways: both have a family system that is characteristic of other industrial countries at similar stages of development[15]; both recognize and encourage achievement by *all* citizens in the struggle against nature and in the management of society; there are striking inequalities in economic, prestige, and power statuses in both countries, related (at least ideologically, and to some extent in practice) to functional achievement; in contrast to preindustrial society, and insofar as it can be measured, the two nations have considerable social mobility and similar problems of motivation, rigidity, and privilege; and both have pronounced tendencies toward the transmission of occupational (and, in general, stratum) position by means of the family and education.[16] Furthermore, there is a marked similarity in their legal systems, though the Soviet Union has adopted European rather than Anglo-American legal practices.[17]

Communist thought and policy in the first decade after the Russian Revolution tended toward egalitarianism.[18] But by the early 1930s a systematic policy

13. Disputes about whether or not one can refer to the Soviet Union as a class society will be touched upon later in this chapter, in "The Ideology of Convergence."

14. See the compilation of cross-national data by Alex Inkeles, "Industrial Man: The Relation of Status to Experience, Perception and Value," *American Journal of Sociology* 66, no. 1 (July 1960): 1–31; also available as Bobbs-Merrill reprint no. 131.

15. See H. Kent Geiger, *The Family in Soviet Russia* (Cambridge, Mass.: Harvard University Press, 1968).

16. See Seymour M. Lipset, "Commentary: Social Stratification Research and Soviet Scholarship," in *Social Stratification and Mobility in the U.S.S.R.,* ed. and trans. Murray Yanovitch and Wesley A. Fisher (White Plains, N.Y.: International Arts and Sciences Press, 1973), pp. 355–391.

17. For a classic study, see Harold J. Berman, *Justice in Russia* (Cambridge, Mass.: Harvard, 1950). For two more recent general introductions, see Kazimierz Grzybowski, *Soviet Legal Institutions: Doctrines and Social Functions* (Ann Arbor, Mich.: University of Michigan Press, 1962), and E. L. Johnson, *An Introduction to the Soviet Legal System* (London: Methuen, 1969).

18. For Soviet developments up to 1950, see Alex Inkeles, "Social Stratification and Mobility in the Soviet Union: 1940–1950," *American Sociological Review* 15 (August 1950): 465–479; also available as Bobbs-Merrill reprint no. S-132.

of encouraging social differentiation (by means of such practices as the increasingly precise definition of occupations, the establishment of piecework, large differentials in income between salaried and wage workers, and bonuses) led to the emergence of a definite hierarchy of social classes. Inkeles distinguishes ten such classes, which appear to be ranked in the following order:

1 Ruling elite
2 Superior intelligentsia
3 General intelligentsia
4 Working class aristocracy
5.5 White-collar
5.5 Well-to-do peasants
7 Average workers
8.5 Average peasants
8.5 Disadvantaged workers
10 Forced labor

During and immediately after World War Two, the process of formalizing the class system continued. Especially significant was the widespread adoption of civilian uniforms, the practice of awarding prizes and honors for outstanding achievement, and a tax system that allowed high income groups to keep most of their money and even to pass it on to their children.

Another aspect of the development of the Soviet class system has been apparent since the 1950s. Leadership and brainwork cannot be emphasized in a universalistic achievement-oriented society without risking demoralization and deviance at the bottom levels. The position of the upper range of occupations cannot be shored up without risking the development of castelike obstructions to competition and achievement. And it is dangerous to monopolistic political power to allow a rigid hierarchical system to develop or to permit social groups to become too structured and thus somewhat autonomous. Recognizing all this, the Communist party has deliberately sought to prevent such developments by asserting the fundamental class principle of individual achievement.[19] It has appealed for "popular participation" to curb administrative incompetence and nepotism; abolished many civilian uniforms; upheld the dignity of manual work; modified income structure in favor of lower income groups (though differences in the distribution of economic values are still considerable and equalitarianism is still denounced); and increased opportunities for the lower classes, especially through educational reform.[20] Indeed, many of the internal

19. And, of course, by the systematic undermining of such groupings, in the earlier years of communist rule, through the use of terror, forced labor camps, and the like, and, since the 1950s, through censorship and harassment as well as positive economic and social programs.
20. This depiction of events during the 1950s relies heavily on Robert A. Feldmesser, "Toward the Classless Society?," *Problems of Communism,* vol. 9 (Washington: United States Information Agency, 1960), pp. 31–39; reprinted in Reinhard Bendix and Seymour M. Lipset, eds., *Class, Status, and Power: Social Stratification in Comparative Perspective,* 2nd ed. (New York: Free Press, 1966), pp. 527–533.

political events in the Soviet Union since the 1950s bear striking resemblances to political struggles and reforms in the United States such as the war on poverty, federal aid to education, and the like.

These similarities indicate the problems that are common to the management of urban-industrial social systems. They do not imply that the United States and the Soviet Union are identical, nor that either has created a classless system of individual merit and functional differentiation. The reformist ferment within the Soviet Union (and, as we shall see, in the United States) is best understood as an attempt to maintain the momentum of industrial expansion by means of a differential reward system while preventing the least privileged from dropping behind or other levels from losing pace. As is true of the United States, internal reform in the Soviet Union appears not to have lessened the overall structure of social inequality or to have threatened the ability of the privileged strata to transmit their positions to their children.

The diversity of stratification: the problem of a general theory

The primary purpose of the remainder of this chapter, in addition to providing more information about the astonishingly varied record of human inequality, is to identify the basic difficulties involved in constructing a general or unified theory of stratification. Analyzing a particular system of stratification presents the usual scientific problems of identifying variables and demonstrating relationships between them; but these problems are minuscule compared to the difficulty of establishing generalizations applicable to all systems of stratification. Even the concepts of caste, estate, and class — our most advanced means of ordering the phenomena of stratification — tend to distort the historical richness of systems of inequality if they are not properly qualified. The same is true of the even more abstract distinction between agrarian and industrial systems of inequality, or among, for example, primitive, feudal, and bourgeois systems of inequality. And, of course, none of these is a unitary scheme; at least for the time being, there seems to be an irreducible diversity in the record of social stratification.

The idea of diversity does not sit well with intellectuals, and, of course, does not lend itself easily to the type of legitimation that most dominant strata seem to want and need. In approaching the construction of a general theory of stratification, it is first necessary to escape from the legitimating symbols of class stratification. (If we were living in caste or estate systems, we would have the underlying assumptions of those systems to worry about.) We have already warned against the simple functionalism that confuses differentiation and social stratification, and against the ideology of "nonegalitarian classlessness." We will now also warn against a premature adoption of unitary schemes by discussing two main types, evolutionary Marxism and evolutionary liberalism. We will begin with a brief discussion of evolutionary Marxism and then devote the bulk of our attention to evolutionary liberalism, the complex of ideas that supplies the legitimation for class stratification in the United States and other capitalist societies.

Evolutionary Marxism

The great drama of secular salvation depicted by Marx is one of many monuments to human beings' ceaseless search for a way to escape from history. Marx's theory, and the assorted revisions and extensions undertaken by his disciples, represents a rich branch of social science and social philosophy, and it is not our wish to dismiss it out of hand. We have already acknowledged Marx's insight into economic causation as the most important contribution to nineteenth-century social science. Here we wish simply to raise some general objections to his theory of social evolution and to acknowledge his idea of a classless society as a moral ideal.

Briefly, the major objection to Marx's prediction of human progress through class struggle is that it has not been fulfilled. A dynamic economy is the exception, not the rule, in world history. All non-Western societies, including the great civilizations of China and India, reached a certain point of economic development and then stagnated. Even in the West, Marx's prediction of the future of capitalism has failed to materialize. Industrial society has not been split apart by polarized classes, and the working class has not risen to proclaim the end of private property and thus of social exploitation. What appears to have happened instead is that modern society has been diversified internally into a number of social classes, and has evolved a number of practices for adjusting (and even disguising) the relations between them. To refute Marx's metaphysics, however, is not to accept evolutionary liberalism or "nonegalitarian classlessness." Modern society is a class structure that is not easily related to any of the explanations offered on its behalf.

It is true that Marx foresaw future developments quite accurately in many respects. Modern society is characterized by a high concentration of economic power and a deep interpenetration of economic and political power. It is exploitative and wasteful, and its legitimating symbols contain much ideology (the symbolic justification of an outmoded status quo)[21] and even hypocrisy. And there is also a considerable amount of "false consciousness," or acceptance by the lower classes of upper-class symbols that are not in their true interests. But modern society has not fulfilled Marx's prediction of class polarization and struggle. In all industrial countries, including those where class hostility was once pronounced, the forces of economic expansion and political reform have diversified and diffused the structure of social classes. As a result, class

21. In sociology, *ideology* refers to selective theorizing. It is defined sometimes as compatible with the growth of knowledge and truth (such as by Marx and Durkheim), sometimes as an inescapable feature of man's historical nature (such as by Weber), and sometimes simply as a defense or justification of particular interests. For a review of this branch of sociology, see Robert K. Merton, *Social Theory and Social Structure,* rev. ed. (New York: Free Press, 1968), chap. 14.

society is far more stable and adaptable than Marxists (and others) are wont to believe. Instead of a dynamic system containing the seeds of its own destruction, one must think of capitalism as a society that successfully reproduces itself generation after generation despite and often because of exploitation and misery. We will explore the various agencies by which this is accomplished in due course, but central to any study of social stability are the ascriptive processes inherent in the idea of social class itself.[22]

The image of a classless society (about which Marx said very little) is surprisingly similar to the liberal idea of nonegalitarian classlessness. By positing a society based on the fulfillment of all individuals, it sets a high standard for human hopes and aspirations. But, as Marx himself understood only too well, moral values reflect the realities of economic life. As we examine the realities of class in one industrial society, the United States, we will find ample proof of the power of economic life over society and of the way in which it reflects and disguises itself in appealing moral terms, not the least of which is the belief that a classless society has already been achieved.

Evolutionary liberalism

The main metaphysical legitimation of capitalist society has also taken an evolutionary form — that of evolutionary liberalism.[23] This metaphysical orientation is composed of various elements: the doctrine of progress developed during the French Enlightenment, Utilitarianism, representative government, Social Darwinism, liberal reformism, and related phenomena. Though the evolutionary theory of social development was rejected by social science in the early decades of this century as teleologically biased and inconsonant with the facts, the idea was too firmly planted to be even partially erased from the public consciousness. It lives on in various guises: "nonegalitarian classlessness"; functionalism in sociology; the theory of convergence; faith in progress, especially through economic growth; and the denial that classes exist. In its simplest form, it is a belief that industrial capitalism is uniquely capable of carrying mankind toward a better future for all. Let us examine some of the variations of this position, beginning with the ideology of convergence.

The ideology of convergence

The English sociologist John Goldthorpe argues that some American theorists of stratification have carried the abstract definition of class society too far in stating that a general convergence in stratification is taking place in all industrial

22. For Lenin's theory of imperialism as the means by which capitalism has prolonged its life, see "Class and International Relations" in Chapter 15.
23. For this term, see the valuable critique of American stratification theory by John Pease, William H. Form, and Joan Huber Rytina, "Ideological Currents in American Stratification Literature," *The American Sociologist* 5 (May 1970): 127–137.

societies.[24] The reason cited for this alleged convergence, says Goldthorpe, is the "logic" of industrialization, a logic that standardizes social development through three basic processes:

1. differentiation based on achievement, accompanied by growing equality in all dimensions of stratification

2. consistency, or the integration of class (economic position), status (prestige position), and power (political-legal position)

3. common patterns and increasing rates of social mobility.

Goldthorpe rightly challenges the concept of convergence by demonstrating that these three alleged trends are at variance with a great deal of empirical data. He points out that there is considerable evidence against the belief that there is a growing equalization of income and wealth in industrial societies. He also notes the powerful currents in occupational differentiation that separate industrial populations in terms of culture, power, and general way of life (though he fails to point out that ascriptive differentials based on religion, ethnicity, and race are still powerful and undiminished where they exist in industrial societies). With regard to the third alleged feature of convergence, Goldthorpe says that patterns of mobility, while common in some respects, are also divergent. He concludes by asserting flatly that it is a mistake to call the system of stratification in communist countries a class system, since it is subject to monolithic political control rather than market forces. The latter point aside, Goldthorpe's analysis is a healthy corrective to both monocausal explanations and evolutionary biases in stratification theory. And he is probably correct in citing as one of the factors responsible for the widespread misreading of the data of stratification in industrial society "ethnocentric bias, that failure of the imagination which leads the sociologist to accept his own form of society, or rather some idealized version of this, as the goal toward which all humanity is moving."

Goldthorpe probably goes too far, however, in suggesting that each modern society exhibits a unique form of industrialization, creating a diversity of development over and above the divergence between capitalist and communist development. While correctly questioning belief in a convergence based on growing equality of income and wealth, Goldthorpe has not recognized that a different type of convergence seems to have appeared, one based on sharp and stable inequality in these areas. Similarly, the development of different subcultures, amounts of power, and life styles among the various classes of industrial societies is evidence not against convergence, as Goldthorpe claims, but for a different kind of convergence. Finally, Goldthorpe's flat denial that the Soviet Union and capitalist countries have similar systems of stratification is unacceptable. Both are achievement societies committed to world mastery through the development and application of technology and science. Both na-

24. "Social Stratification in Industrial Society," in *Class, Status, and Power: Social Stratification in Comparative Perspecitve*, 2nd ed., eds. Reinhard Bendix and Seymour M. Lipset (New York: Free Press, 1966), pp. 648–659.

tions have similar family, occupational, and educational systems, and high rates of social mobility in contrast to preindustrial societies. Despite differences in their political systems and ideologies, both rely heavily on law — Goldthorpe is in error when he says that law is absent in the Soviet Union — and on bureaucratic administration to manage, coordinate, and direct their affairs, including their economies. The two countries are even similar in their denials that they have classes and their acceptance of the ideology of convergence (the gradual realization of "nonegalitarian classlessness"). In short, industrial societies do have important structural features in common — features that differ considerably from those alleged by theorists who have not yet escaped from their national ideologies of industrialization.

The evolutionary liberalism of Davis and Moore

In 1945 Kingsley Davis and Wilbert E. Moore wrote an essay on social stratification at the level of general theory; that is, they articulated what they claimed were the universal principles of stratification. Written in the spirit of functionalism and with only an implied evolutionary framework, this work, which is not characteristic of the work of these two eminent sociologists and which has since been modified by their other writings, stimulated a wide and valuable debate among stratification theorists.

In keeping with the basic strategy of sociology, which is to establish generalizations about human behavior, sociologists in the functional tradition argue that phenomena that occur universally must stem from the inherent needs of society itself. Thus, society is defined naturalistically, as having given structural features that can be identified despite empirical or historical variations and changes. Working in this tradition, and leaving aside "variable" or historical issues, Davis and Moore argue that the "main functional necessity explaining the universal presence of stratification is precisely the requirement faced by any society of placing and motivating individuals in the social structure."[25] Assuming that different positions in society require different incentives and rewards, they conclude that "social inequality is an unconsciously evolved device by which societies insure that the most important positions are conscientiously filled by the most qualified persons." The thrust of their argument is that despite both historical variations in the way inequality manifests itself and the failure of given societies to live up to their own values and norms, inequality as such is generic to society, intrinsic to its nature. All societies, say Davis and Moore, simply must define some positions — in general, the leadership of major institutional areas — as more important than others and must structure the distribution of social, cultural, and personality benefits so as to insure an adequate supply of personnel for these positions, which require various talents, arduous training, and heavy responsibility.

25. Kingsley Davis and Wilbert E. Moore, "Some Principles of Social Stratification," *American Sociological Review* 10 (April 1945): 242–249; also available as Bobbs-Merrill reprint no. S-68.

A number of general points should be made about the Davis-Moore position. First, whether palatable or not, their argument is a scientific effort and should not be attacked on the basis of value judgments. Second, they are in no way culpable for having overlooked the dysfunctions of inequality or the imperfections in given empirical systems of inequality; they deliberately separate such questions from their main concern, which is to determine in what way inequality is related to the universal nature of society.[26] Their position is simply that society, however variously organized to emphasize different abilities in individuals, must always — if it is to be a society — make human beings unequal.

A first criticism of this particular statement of the functional position[27] is that it is really a discussion of differentiation, not stratification. Secondly, the critics of the Davis-Moore position, Tumin especially, have sensed the basic emptiness of their generalization. By and large, conflict theorists — those who see society and inequality as a means by which the strong can induce the weak to do more for less — tend to bypass the Davis-Moore analysis. It is one thing to argue that differentiation must take place — that individuals must be motivated and trained to occupy different statuses in the hierarchies of work, or leisure, or warfare, or whatever — and quite another to decide how all this is to be done. Invariably, the placement of individuals has been a result of social stratification, not individual achievement or natural social processes, which is to say that at some point in history families are ranked with regard to general economic, social, and political power and worth, and that this hierarchy of families then becomes the basis for the next generation's hierarchy of families. Equally important, the hierarchy of strata that emerges eventually controls the definition of functional positions and recruitment into them. It is, according to the critics of functionalism, the radical inequality of ascriptive conditions that lies at the heart of stratification analysis, regardless of the type of society. The fact that liberal democracy (or communist dictatorships, for that matter) demands high levels of achievement does not alter the fact that

26. This paragraph recapitulates the general line Davis has taken in replying to criticism on both these counts by Melvin M. Tumin, "Some Principles of Stratification: A Critical Analysis," *American Sociological Review* 18 (August 1953): 387–397. The original Davis-Moore essay, Tumin's article, the reply by Davis, and a comment by Moore are available as Bobbs-Merrill reprint no. S-68.

27. This is a convenient point at which to assert that there are many forms of functionalism and to dispel any impression that functionalism is *ipso facto* wrong or sterile as a school of sociology. Actually, as we will argue in Chapter 3, the functional method is synonymous with science and informs a good deal of our own analysis. Indeed, the functional position with regard to social stratification is a rich and valuable legacy drawing on the work of the classical economists, Karl Marx, Charles Horton Cooley, and Talcott Parsons to name only a few. We have singled out Davis and Moore's essay only because it stimulated a valuable debate within sociology about a topic badly in need of attention. For an excellent summary of this debate, which has taken stratification theory considerably beyond the original Davis-Moore statement, see George A. Huaco, "The Functionalist Theory of Stratification: Two Decades of Controversy," *Inquiry* 9 (1966): reprinted in Melvin M. Tumin, ed., *Readings on Social Stratification* (Englewood Cliffs, N.J.: Prentice-Hall, 1970), pp. 411–428.

birth into the class hierarchy determines, by and large, who will be trained to succeed and who to fail.

As opposed to the abstract analysis of differentiation, therefore, stratification theory must question whether there is any correspondence between social rewards and the performance of social functions, and even whether functional positions can be precisely defined as to value. Indeed, so great is the disparity between the legitimating symbols of society and its actual operation that stratification theory must also take into consideration that the explanation of inequality is itself a product of the overall stratification system.[28]

The Davis-Moore view of inequality has been discussed for two reasons. First, it is a distortion of the essential nature of social stratification, which is the analysis of the institutionalized means by which society gets its work done. These means invariably involve ascriptive privilege, conflict, waste, exploitation, and ideology; in short, they are means by which some profit at the expense of others for no functional purpose. Second, it tends to resemble the dominant lay tradition in the United States, "nonegalitarian classlessness," or the view that while Americans are unequal they deserve their positions because all have an equal chance to show their worth. As our subsequent analysis will show, the United States has extensive ascriptive and exploitative elements that appear to be deeply institutionalized, and may even be "necessary" features of industrial society. The view that America has found a way to distribute rewards on the basis of individual achievement is thereby rendered problematic. We will encounter many obstacles to understanding stratification structures and processes in America, but none will rival the view that the United States is already an equal-opportunity achievement society or can become one given time and judicious reform.

The evolutionary liberalism of Gerhard Lenski

Gerhard Lenski has made a notable contribution to stratification analysis at the level of classification and description.[29] His attempt at a unified or general theory of inequality, however, has not succeeded. Indeed, his alleged synthesis of stratification phenomena is simply unabashed evolutionary liberalism. Lenski bases his theory almost exclusively on the concept of power, providing (in Chapters 3 and 4) a number of penetrating and highly useful comments about its employment, consequences, and general nature. His comments, however, are quite *ad hoc*, and his definition of power eventually becomes a synonym for causation (or all the variables in stratification analysis).

Not surprisingly, Lenski makes no attempt to characterize systems of

28. Ralf Dahrendorf has criticized the functional approach, and all other approaches, only to propose something quite similar to Davis and Moore's argument. Society is always a moral community, he argues, and the very act of imposing norms and sanctions will make individuals unequal; see his *Essays in the Theory of Society* (Stanford, Calif.: Stanford University Press, 1968), pp. 151–178.
29. *Power and Privilege: A Theory of Social Stratification* (New York: McGraw-Hill, 1966).

stratification; to recognize that caste, estate, and class systems are viable historical structures is not compatible with a unitary theory. Lenski constantly refers to the variety of ways in which various forces behave, depending on time and place, and then solves the problem of causation by imposing an evolutionary pattern on his wayward and unstructured historical materials. His analysis of power (or the materials of social stratification) is further vitiated by the introduction of certain constant human (nature) needs and propensities, most of which are suspiciously similar to the behavior characteristic of liberal society.

To fully appreciate Lenski's theory and obtain its many potential benefits, one must focus mainly on his fascinating description and classification of the ways in which inequality has manifested itself throughout history. Basically, says Lenski, the variety of inequality a society exhibits depends upon how the "power" system distributes material surplus, especially food. Focusing his analysis on the basic techniques of subsistence, Lenski develops the typology of societies illustrated in Figure 2-1, each type having a distinguishable degree of inequality.

Lenski's focus is almost exclusively on the five types of societies in the center column, and the peripheral types can be ignored. A brief description of each of these five types of society, with examples, and of the degree of inequality within each follows:

1. Hunting and gathering societies.[30] A societal type characterized by pronounced equality because of deep and thus shared economic scarcity. Any superiority that exists is based on personal skills and abilities, a form of superiority that cannot be transmitted socially to children. The Andaman Islanders exemplify this type of society.

2. Simple horticultural societies.[31] Institutionalized inequality first emerges with horticulture, or farming based on the digging stick, the fundamental tool of a gardening economy. The domestication of plants leads to a more dependable supply of food, which in turn is associated with the emergence of a division of labor; specialized economic occupations and full-time occupations in politics and religion develop. There occur increases in the production of noneconomic items of largely prestige-symbolic importance (temples, masks, and the like) and in noneconomic (leisure) activities such as warfare and ceremonial life. Socially, a distinction develops between a person and his or her social statuses, a distinction related to functional specialization. This distinction is crucial to stratification because it provides a mechanism for passing social positions and their benefits from one generation to the next. The Zuni Indians of the American Southwest and the Arapesh of New Guinea are examples of this type of society.

3. Advanced horticultural societies.[32] A significant increase in inequality accompanies the development of the hoe, which allows for better utilization of the soil than does the digging stick, and of terracing, irrigation, fertilizers, or

30. *Ibid.,* chap. 5.
31. *Ibid.,* chap. 6.
32. *Ibid.,* chap. 7.

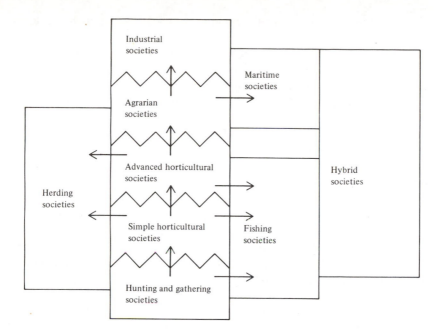

Figure 2-1 Lenski's Societal Typology: Subsistence Techniques as the Basis
of Society

SOURCE: From *Power and Privilege: A Theory of Social Stratification* by Gerhard
Lenski, p. 92. Copyright 1966 by McGraw-Hill, Inc. Used with permission of
McGraw-Hill Book Company.

metallurgy. While this level of technology leads to an increase in economic
specialization, its outstanding feature is a striking increase in inequality as a
result of variability in political power. The elaboration of formal social statuses
is matched by sharp increases in property rights (including rights over human
beings, or slavery) and transferable assets (money, cattle, slaves). From the
standpoint of stratification, this stage of technological and social development
sees the emergence of well-defined hereditary strata. Examples of this type of
society are the Incas, the Aztecs, the Maya, and sub-Sahara tribes characterized
by "African despotism," such as the Dahomey.

4. Agrarian societies.[33] This type of society is characterized by a technology
of agriculture, rather than horticulture. Agriculture appears with the plow, the
harnessing of animal energy, and metallurgy (which makes possible the iron
plow). The significant increase in food production that results from this
technology leads to advances in transport, communication, engineering, and
military technology. The latter is especially significant for stratification because
it lays the foundation for a professional military, which is eventually transformed
into a superior hereditary social group (estate or caste). Social inequality is
markedly increased by the advent of agrarian society, whether it takes the

33. *Ibid.,* chaps. 8 and 9.

form of a city-state, a bureaucratic empire, or feudalism. Though the long-range causes of this increase in inequality are economic, the major focal point and short-range source of inequality is "government." Examples of this type of society are ancient Greece, Rome, China, India, the Byzantine Empire, the Ottoman Empire, and medieval Europe.

5. Industrial societies.[34] The emergence of an industrial technology represents a profound change in the "means of subsistence" available to society. As a consequence, sharp increases take place in production and in specialized economic activity. Lenski claims that the resulting material surplus does not lead, as in the past, to increases in inequality but to a reversal of this historic trend. While economic, prestige, and political inequality is still considerable, it is less marked than in agrarian societies. The top 2 percent of income units, for example, receive at most 15–20 percent of the total income, as opposed to 50 percent in agrarian societies, and the emergence of universal suffrage represents a diffusion and popularization of political power. The main reason for this reversal of the trend toward increased inequality is that industrial society is too complex to be run personally or arbitrarily. The upper groups tend to find it in their interests to involve the lower and intermediate groups in economic and political processes. Examples of this type of society are liberal (capitalist), communist, and "socialist": the United States, France, Canada, Britain, the Soviet Union, and Sweden.

The foregoing is only a rough sketch of Lenski's rich portrayal of human inequality through the ages. Indeed, the materials he presents are so rich that they could easily be interpreted as irreducibly diverse and nondirectional. Actually, Lenski's classification and description of human inequality raise the same questions as a general theory: What primary and secondary causes function in human affairs, and how can they be welded together into a single comprehensive explanatory scheme? What analytical tools and fact-gathering procedures best reveal whatever patterns exist in the record of human behavior, and how does one escape or guard against the biases induced by one's own sociocultural system? Unfortunately, Lenski has not treated the analysis of historical and comparative materials in this way. His classification of a wide variety of societies would have been perfectly acceptable scientific procedure had he limited himself to searching for their similarities. But locating his types in a scheme of evolutionary development begs all the important questions in social science. Above all, Lenski never addresses himself to the basic question of why one agrarian society — Western feudalism — transformed itself into industrial society while the rest "stagnated." What was to Max Weber and most of the classical theorists of sociology a great novelty in need of explanation presents no problem for Lenski, since he assumes that the basic ideas and values of capitalism are normal to human nature. Instead of trying to explain the unique historical phenomenon of liberal society, he unabashedly attributes liberal values and behavior to human nature. To assume that liberal society is natural to man is also to assume that all other societies are distortions or pale

34. *Ibid.,* chaps. 10–12.

reflections of that norm. One can then rest easy with an explanation of the emergence of industrial society consisting of casual references to constitutionalism as the result of "a peculiar combination of historical circumstances," the willingness of elites to delegate authority to markets, the rapidity and magnitude of increases in productivity (which encourages concessions by the elite), birth control, the great expansion of human knowledge, and the new democratic ideology.[35]

Most of these "explanatory" remarks are not intended as an explanation of the rise of capitalism, which never presents itself as a problem to Lenski, but occur as part of Lenski's assertion that industrial society represents a reversal of the historical trend in which increasing surplus is turned into increased inequality. The argument that industrial society is characterized by a decrease in economic and political inequality relative to agrarian society is a major theme in Lenski's work; it also deserves careful scrutiny since it occupies a central place in the American belief system.

Lenski's careful description of the reduction of certain forms of inequality by industrial society is useful and important. Who cannot be impressed with the dramatic way in which the feudal-authoritarian hierarchy based on birth was shattered by the forces of revolution and reform? Who cannot be impressed with the fact that all individuals (of both sexes) have for the first time in human history been defined as moral entities with the legal right to engage in economic pursuits of their own choice, participate equally in political decision-making, and be treated as legal equals by the state? And it is significant, as Lenski emphasizes, that the top economic elite in industrial society claims a smaller portion of the economic pie than the economic elite of agrarian society.

However, there is no particular reason to stress the reduction of inequality as the salient feature of contemporary society and ignore the fact that the same transformation can also be interpreted as the displacement of one unique historical set of social inequalities by another. The unique inequalities of industrial society are steep and stable enough to warrant at least parallel consideration.[36] Lenski, however, minimizes the problem of inequality in industrial society by framing his analysis primarily as a broad comparison with the past, and by stating that the full flowering of industrial society is yet to come, implying further reductions in inequality.[37] He obscures the development of stratification analysis by his highly idiomatic use of the terms *power, privilege, prestige,* and *class* and by his failure to attempt an overall characterization of the system of stratification in industrial society. Instead, he presents a long

35. *Ibid.,* pp. 60, 313–318.
36. One can question the legitimacy of comparing such dissimilar societies, and it can even be asked whether modern society in fact has more equality than previous societies; for a fuller discussion, see Chapter 4.
37. Lenski actually asserts that inequality is declining *within* industrial society, which is, to say the least, highly problematic (Lenski, *Power and Privilege,* pp. 344, 397, 400–402). For the reasons why it is not possible to say that equality is increasing or decreasing in industrial society, see Chapter 4.

series of *ad hoc* statements about industrial societies' political class system; property class system; entrepreneurial class; class of party functionaries; managerial class; military class; professional class; unemployed and slave-labor classes; educational class system; racial, ethnic, and religious class systems; class system based on sex; and class system based on age. These are followed by a miscellany of statements about mobility, class struggle, prestige, stratification, and the like, and throughout, data are drawn first from one society and then from another.

Although Lenski presents many important and valid ideas and arguments, the result of his analysis is to hide the specific historical system of class stratification from our view. He does so by overemphasizing the contrast between the present and the past (which amounts to a teleological bias in favor of contemporary liberal society), implying a trend toward greater equality within liberal society, and obscuring sociology's hard-won advances in analytic concepts (for example, caste, estate, and class systems; class, prestige, and power variables), concepts that are still our most advanced tools for examining and interpreting the phenomena of inequality without ideological bias.

The evolutionary liberalism of Talcott Parsons

One of the most prominent variations on the theme of convergence is the evolutionary theory of America's foremost sociological theorist, Talcott Parsons.[38] Primarily a specialist in general theory, and the United States' leading exponent of the functional perspective, Parsons has devoted considerable attention to social stratification.[39] His depiction of the American system of stratification is derived largely from an abstract contrast with feudal society. He emphasizes the decline of ascriptive forces and the rise of equality, choice, pluralism, and functional inequality based on achievement processes during the past few centuries. His depiction of stratification is also based on a refutation of Marx (he asserts that property is declining in importance); he sees social class, in the traditional sense, as a transitional phenomenon.

In his most recent contribution to stratification analysis, Parsons has stressed the importance of egalitarian forces, especially equality of opportunity, mass education, and civic rights in government and private associations. These forces, Parsons claims, tend to have real effectiveness in controlling and moderating inequality. The "competence gap" produced by achievement and competition is also modified by fiduciary mechanisms located most prominently

38. Parsons' commitment to evolutionary social theory is explicitly articulated in *Societies: Evolutionary and Comparative Perspectives* (Englewood Cliffs, N.J.: Prentice-Hall, 1966) and *The System of Modern Societies* (Englewood Cliffs, N.J.: Prentice-Hall, 1971).

39. "An Analytical Approach to the Theory of Social Stratification," *American Journal of Sociology* 45, no. 6 (May 1940): 841–862; "A Revised Analytical Approach to the Theory of Social Stratification" in *Class, Status and Power: A Reader in Social Stratification,* 1st ed., eds. Reinhard Bendix and Seymour M. Lipset (New York: Free Press, 1953); and "Equality and Inequality in Modern Society, or Social Stratification Revisited," *Sociological Inquiry* 40 (Spring 1970): 13–72.

in law, government, and the professions. Some ascriptive advantage accrues in the family, but Parsons does not see this as a great problem. Actually, he argues that the concept of social class should be divorced from kinship and property and that we should instead think in terms of hierarchical differentiation. A social class should now be thought of as an aggregate of people who "in their own estimation and those of others" occupy achievement positions of approximately equal status. Basically, social classes "represent a more or less successful resultant of mechanisms dealing with integrative problems of the society, notably those having to do with the balance between factors of equality and of inequality."[40]

The trouble with Parsons' stratification theory, of course, is that he is simply stating as fact or operative ideal what society itself claims to be. In short, beneath his elaborate language and conceptualizing lies an acceptance of liberal society as a valid, progressive, and natural structure and process. Everything that science should consider problematic is accepted at face value. As we will see later in more detail, much of what modern society (actually, its power-holders) says about itself is not true, highly dubious, or as yet incapable of being tested. Many favorable judgments about modern society are based on highly abstract and dubious comparisons with the feudal-monarchical past. But the contemporary United States still has many powerful ascriptive forces, including class ascription, and it is not even possible to say that their efficacy has been reduced during the course of American history.[41] In an interesting analysis of Newburyport, Massachusetts — the same city analyzed by Warner and his associates under the title Yankee City — during its initial period of industrial expansion (1850–1880), Stephan Thernstrom concludes that the significant degree of social stratification in American society (as measured by upward social mobility) has not changed much since the nineteenth century.[42]

40. "Equality and Inequality," p. 24.
41. While such comparisons are difficult, there appears to have been no decrease in social class inequality since our colonial period; see Jackson T. Main, "The Class Structure of Revolutionary America," in *Class, Status, and Power: Social Stratification in Comparative Perspective* 2nd ed., eds. Reinhard Bendix and Seymour M. Lipset (New York: Free Press, 1966), pp. 111–121; Jackson T. Main, *The Social Structure of Revolutionary America* (Princeton, N.J.: Princeton University Press, 1965); and Gary B. Nash, ed., *Class and Society in Early America* (Englewood Cliffs, N.J.: Prentice-Hall, 1970). For an analysis of substantial social inequality during the second quarter of the nineteenth century, the so-called era of the common man, see Edward Pessen, *Riches, Class, and Power Before the Civil War* (Lexington, Mass.: D. C. Heath, 1973).
Robert S. and Helen M. Lynd's classic community studies, *Middletown* (New York: Harcourt, Brace, 1929) and *Middletown in Transition* (New York: Harcourt, Brace, 1937), provide valuable material suggesting a growth in inequality by comparing three years in the history of Muncie, Indiana: 1890, 1924, 1935. An extremely valuable historical analysis of social stratification in New Haven and Connecticut that traces the changing bases of what it depicts as an unchanged relative structure of inequality, may be found in August B. Hollingshead and Frederick C. Redlich, *Social Class and Mental Illness* (New York: John Wiley and Sons, 1958), chap. 3.
42. *Poverty and Progress: Social Mobility in a Nineteenth Century City* (Cambridge, Mass.: Harvard University Press, 1964). Arguing that Newburyport is a

Nor is it defensible to equate existing inequalities with social functions as easily and neatly as Parsons (and others) is prone to do. As we will see, much of what passes for equality in America is empty formalism and rhetoric, and the "educational revolution" Parsons makes so much of is actually a facade masking middle class dominance and privilege.[43] And, finally, Parsons' emphasis on the assumed competence and fiduciary nature of law, government, and the professions is an error of misplaced faith, an uncritical continuation of a technocratic strain in liberal thought that dates back to the sociology of Saint-Simon and Comte. And, in a wider context, Parsons' evolutionary liberalism is part and parcel of the pervasive American faith that the United States is simultaneously at the terminal stage of social development and busily engaged in perfecting itself. It is of no little importance that this faith has also found wide expression in stratification theory.[44]

Evolutionary liberalism as ideology

The ideology of evolutionary liberalism is so widespread that it is important to know where it comes from and why it persists. Pease, Form, and Rytina suggest three sources: the dominant ideology of individualism, the association of social and stratificational explanations with Marxism, and sociology's search for scientific status (which predisposed it toward quantitative methods and which, in turn, predisposed stratification analysts toward the concepts of status or prestige rather than class or power).[45] Our own explanation would acknowledge the ideological causes cited above but we would also ask: where do these ideological phenomena themselves come from? The answer, of course, is history, or, more specifically, American society and its class system. To understand how the American class system works, in other words, is to understand the consciousness of the American people and a good deal about the consciousness of American intellectuals. America's ahistorical seventeenth- and

---

relatively good and our best example of a typical American community, Thernstrom challenges the conclusion reached by Warner and the Lynds that upward mobility is becoming more difficult. It has always been difficult, he argues, no more so today than in the past.

43. For a full analysis, see Chapter 6 and "Government and Education: The Public as Partisan" and "Legislation, Government, and Representative Minorities" in Chapter 13.

44. An example in the functionalist school is Suzanne Keller, *Beyond the Ruling Class: Strategic Elites in Modern Society* (New York: Random House, 1963), also in paperback. Keller contributes a useful analysis relating the wide variety of elites in modern society to the four functional needs (goal attainment, adaptation, integration, and pattern maintenance) Parsons claims all societies must satisfy. But her overall discussion is badly marred by an uncritical acceptance of all the main tenets of evolutionary liberalism: thus Keller argues that property, ascription, arbitrary central power, castes, aristocracies, and classes are declining in favor of professionalism, equality of opportunity, merit, pluralism, and greater material security and equality; in short, that strategic elites have emerged signalling the end of class stratification and the advent of inequality based on merit.

45. "Ideological Currents in American Stratification Literature," *American Sociologist* 5 (May 1970): 127–137.

eighteenth-century rationalism, proclivity for biopsychological explanations, optimistic faith in progress, and moral struggle to overcome the disruptive forces of ascription all combine to distort Americans' insight into their system of inequality. The United States' symbolic culture is itself explicable as the product of a virgin and fabulously rich continent; the selective diffusion of European sociocultural elements; low population density; and high rates of social mobility, relative to agrarian societies, induced by an economic growth unprecedented in human history.

In a broader context, the ideology of progress satisfies an important need for the middle class: it legitimates industrial capitalism as a terminal society while allowing for technological and economic growth under private auspices. In other words, by employing the appealing terms of inevitable moral and material progress, the main beneficiaries of economic expansion can indefinitely postpone the solution of social problems and explain away the social system's failures.

The diversity of stratification: the problem of social system change

We have stressed the difficulties that lie in the way of those who would generalize about social stratification — difficulties that stem from the diversity of inequality. In fact, human history exhibits so much diversity that we were forced to ask whether it is even possible to generalize about social stratification. One of the ways in which we raised this question was to stress the difficulty of analyzing social system change. We shall now elaborate on this question by presenting two brief case studies of such change and indicating the apparent lack of pattern in the ways systems of stratification undergo change.

An obsession with historical diversity can defeat the ends of social science, and it is not our wish to overstress the difficulties presented by the historical dimension in human affairs. On the contrary, our overriding purpose is to develop a depiction of the American class system that is valid in its own right and simultaneously as consonant as possible with the requirements of general theory. But no understanding of contemporary social stratification is possible unless one escapes the teleological bias that clings so stubbornly to contemporary social science. The teleological or prescientific world view based on Aristotelian logic was smuggled into modern liberal (and other) thought as the doctrine of progress. Like the acorn that teleologically matures into the oak tree, its naturally intended final outcome, modern industrial society is thought to be naturally evolving toward progressively higher levels of human fulfillment. Indeed, even pioneer sociologists, for all their talk of science and the positive society, were so struck by the uniqueness of modern society that they too depicted it as the highest state of social development. A partial corrective to such bias is the recognition that history is marked by irrationality (meaningless conflict, stagnation, drift, waste, violence and oppression, diverse causal patterns) as much as it is by rationality (a cosmic pattern, natural law, lawful development, the unfolding of the Absolute, conscious self-direction). It cannot fail to be instructive, and an appropriate conclusion for our discussion of the problem of general theory in stratification analysis, to examine two contrasting ways in which systems of social stratification undergo structural change.

Violent social system change: France, the typical pattern

Societies do not ordinarily change from one system of stratification to another without considerable friction and violence. People take the constitutive structure of their society very seriously, and as a rule react violently to perceived threats to its security. Before the class system institutionalized methods for reforming itself, it was extremely difficult for disputants to settle grievances through peaceful negotiation and compromise. What usually occurred was a metaphysical confrontation between groups prepared to resort to violence. Ancient Greece witnessed perhaps the most savage "class" struggles of all time as oligarch and democrat contended for supremacy in one city-state after another. A transition from one system of stratification to another is not very frequent. One should not confuse systemic change with, for example, Church-state disputes, palace revolutions, *coup d'etats*, collective bargaining, election results, the rise of the welfare state, or the existence of labor governments. India and China, for example, have undergone constant internal turmoil but did not experience challenges to their respective systems of stratification until the twentieth century; that is, their systems of stratification remained intact for over two thousand years. Feudal Europe's transition to a class system was also no abrupt event: it lasted approximately from the eleventh to the nineteenth century. This long and torturous transition to a capitalist society was characterized neither by foresight nor by peaceful adjustment.[46]

Until the eleventh century, there were only "merchants of occasion." The first capitalists appear in the eleventh and twelfth centuries but soon retire from commerce to become landed proprietors. A new batch of men emerged with the burst of capitalist activity that occurred in the thirteenth and fourteenth centuries. But here too the initial momentum of enterprise was soon exhausted, and the trading towns succumbed to rigid guild regulations, business monopoly, and moral and religious pressure. Capitalists sought security and the ability not to challenge the feudality but to enter its ranks. Thus few of the same families were found among the new capitalistic elements of the fifteenth and sixteenth centuries. During these centuries the capitalist economy at last came into its own, but again the dynamism of economic expansion was stifled by conservatism (mercantilism). In the latter part of the

46. The following section is based on the classic analysis by Henri Pirenne, "The Stages in the Social History of Capitalism," *American Historical Review* 19, no. 3 (April 1914): 494–515; reprinted in *Class, Status, and Power: Social Stratification in Comparative Perspective*, 2nd ed., eds. Reinhard Bendix and Seymour M. Lipset (New York: Free Press, 1966), pp. 97–107.

eighteenth century, capitalistic behavior was vastly enhanced by industrialization; this new phase of capitalism, says Pirenne, saw a tenfold economic increase over the previous period. Again the prominent capitalist families of the previous period of economic expansion were unengaged by this new burst of economic energy (except in mining, because of its connection with ownership of land). And once again, during the nineteenth century, the spirit of economic conservatism and security reappeared, in the guise of monopoly and high tariffs.

It is noteworthy in this sequence of events that the notion of a creative and revolutionary middle class is a fiction composed of convenient abstraction and ideology. Actually, there were numerous middle classes, each of which tended to stagnate well short of economic revolution, let alone social reconstruction. To a large extent, each of these capitalistic groups accepted feudal values, the most daring wanting change only in order to make their own lives easier or more profitable. Even on the eve of the French Revolution, the French middle class cannot be said to have had anything more than reform in mind.

The process of transition between estate (agrarian) stratification and class (industrial) stratification was not simply a progressive cycle of innovation and conservatism. It was also marked by blind drift and incredible violence, neither of which is anywhere more dramatically evident than in the development of French society. After centuries of slow economic expansion, France in the eighteenth century harbored in its bosom two contradictory principles, the principle of ascription and the principle of achievement.[47] While most of the French accepted the supremacy of the nobility and the noble way of life, a contradictory element had emerged in French society: a sizable bourgeoisie representing the principle of personal achievement in a nonvalued activity (business). Nothing better illustrates the nonrevolutionary nature of the French middle class than its anxiety to shed the stigma of lowly birth and lowly experience (the making of money). To accommodate this anxiety and to afford the nobility ways to compensate for its relative economic decline, French society developed a number of avenues of social mobility that enabled the bourgeoisie to translate its wealth into enhanced social status. The main method of achieving upward mobility was the purchase of hereditary offices and titles. Marriage to impoverished noblemen was an option for those who could afford large dowries. Status could also be enhanced by the purchase of a military commission. Finally, and importantly, one could enhance one's status by adopting the noble way of life (country house, elaborate dress, idleness, conspicuous consumption).

As long as these avenues of mobility remained open, the bourgeoisie wanted nothing more than to escape the stigma of business and join the dominant

47. Much of the following is neatly summarized in Elinor G. Barber, *The Bourgeoisie in Eighteenth Century France* (Princeton: Princeton University Press, 1955). For an excellent general history, see Georges Lefebvre, *The Coming of the French Revolution* (New York: Random House Vintage paperback, 1947), originally published in 1939.

stratum. They cared little for politics, though there was some grumbling about financial matters. The two principles of ascription and achievement were basically antagonistic, however, and the aristocratic reaction that set in during the eighteenth century brought this contradiction to a head. The aristocracy's growing exclusiveness about noble rank, growing legal monopolization of high political, military, and ecclesiastical offices, and refusal to pay taxes blocked upward mobility. This in turn stimulated revolutionary feelings among a middle class that until the eve of the Revolution had rarely questioned the legitimacy of the feudal way of life. The two principles that France had accommodated for centuries at last collided, causing a revolution in 1789 whose consequences left French society unstable for over a century and a half.

France in the eighteenth century is an example of a deeply *anomic*[48] society, a social system with a relatively large middle class but no symbolic or institutional mechanisms to legitimate or ingest such a group. The result was the typical pattern of blind drift and violence: first, the development of social fictions to disguise the problems created by change, followed by a growing self-consciousness on the part of threatened groups, and finally the descent into the abyss of confrontation and civil war. So deep were the wounds inflicted by the Revolution, the Terror, and the Restoration that France still suffered from estate-class conflicts long after it began to experience the problems of industrialization and the conflicts emerging from *within* the class system.

Peaceful social system change: Japan, an exception

In analyzing transitions between types of stratification, it is not even possible to find comfort in the generalization that such transformations are always accompanied by violence; the case of Japan is a major exception to such a generalization.[49] Before 1600 Japan was an estate society, characterized by a hierarchy of warrior, peasant, artisan, and merchant estates. Each estate was theoretically closed and restricted as to permissible occupations, residence, food, and dress. Despite the growth of a merchant class, there was no middle class to threaten the supremacy of the warrior estate. Japan had all the ear-

---

48. *Anomic* is derived from *anomie,* a term we will come across again. Associated strongly with Durkheim's famous analysis of the social nature of suicide, *anomie* now refers to a condition in the group or normative life of a society that causes individuals or groups to deviate. The conditions associated with deviation include the breakdown, absence, or contradictory nature of the statuses that individuals or aggregates are expected to adopt. The deviance that results from anomie can either exist without disturbing the stability of society — indeed, it can contribute to it — or undermine the social system, as in the case of France.

49. The following section is based on Thomas C. Smith, "Japan's Aristocratic Revolution," *Yale Review* 50 (March 1961): 370–383; reprinted in Reinhard Bendix and Seymour M. Lipset, eds., *Class Status, and Power: Social Stratification in Comparative Perspective,* 2nd ed. (New York: Free Press, 1966), pp. 135–140.

marks of a static hierarchical society. But something happened in the period between 1600 and 1868 that allowed a peaceful revolution to sweep away the estate structure and inaugurate a society based on individual (male) achievement (class).

The two-and-one-half centuries of peace (the Tokugawa Period) after 1600 obviously made difficulties for the warrior estate. A few thousand warrior families were set apart by lineage and income, but the bulk of such families ("several hundred thousand") were quite poor. Changes in the warrior estate itself were of great importance to the transformation of the Japanese system of stratification. Unthreatened from below, the warrior estate was transformed internally in directions leading away from feudalism. Basic to this change was the appropriation from most warriors of direct control of land and direct personal responsibility for social functions (such as justice). Instead, the lord restricted his warrior vassals' power over their fiefs, forbade them to administer local justice, relocated them in the towns that grew up around his castle, decreed the taxes they could collect, and eventually collected taxes himself, paying his warrior vassals stipends in money or in kind. Japan could be governed in this nonfeudal manner only by means of extensive bureaucratization. The advent of bureaucratic government was accompanied, significantly, by a decline in the personal bonds between the dominant warrior lords and their subordinate warriors and by the rise of impersonality and functional ability in office.

In 1868 there emerged a central government that swept away the local empires of the dominant warrior families. The new government abolished estate restrictions and gave extensive civic — though not political — rights to all. Especially important was the establishment of free public schools and the principle of qualification for office and occupation. The bulk of the warrior estate, having been separated from the land and having had centuries of experience in office-holding, did not view this phenomenon as a threat to its estate privileges — especially in contrast to, for example, the French nobility. On the contrary, it saw in these reforms new and fresh opportunities for achievement. After 1868 there occurred an explosion of individual energies as the lesser warriors took the lead in developing careers in business, industry, and the professions. Thus a peaceful revolution *within* its warrior aristocracy allowed Japan to transform itself from above and to make the transition to a class system without experiencing the bitter social cleavages that marked such transitions in the West.[50]

50. On contemporary aspects of the Japanese class system, see Joseph H. Kahl, ed., *Comparative Perspectives on Stratification: Mexico, Great Britain, Japan* (Boston: Little, Brown, 1968), paperback, Part 3. For historical analyses of the emergence of modern Japan, see Barrington Moore, Jr., *Social Origins of Dictatorship and Democracy* (Boston: Beacon Press, 1966), chap. 5, also in paperback; and Everett E. Hagen, *On the Theory of Social Change* (Homewood, Ill.: Dorsey Press, 1962), chap. 14.

The diversity of stratification and general theory: a summary

It is apparent from our case studies of the three types of stratification and of the two contrasting ways in which stratification system change took place in Japan and France that the development of a general theory of social stratification will not be easy. The radical diversity of inequality in history, and its varying fortunes, have confounded both evolutionary Marxism and evolutionary liberalism. It is time now to abandon this high level of abstraction in order to discuss the concrete achievements of stratification analysts and some of the research problems they face as they struggle to understand a phenomenon that has long intrigued and baffled theorists.

3

Stratification analysis: basic concepts and problems

IN THE PRECEDING CHAPTERS we have discussed some of the broad theoretical concerns that have occupied stratification theorists. In this chapter we will concern ourselves with the basic concepts, methods, and problems of contemporary stratification analysis, with a special focus on American developments. Despite continuing controversy, theorists of social stratification have made solid progress toward understanding the why and how of inequality. We will begin our analysis of this achievement by surveying the historical background of American developments, then discuss the development of class indices and the ideas basic to the analysis of status consistency and social mobility, and finally identify some of the strengths of sociological analysis proper that stratification analysts can rely on.

The historical background
The monopoly of liberalism

Though most of the pioneer American sociologists paid at least some attention to social stratification, interest in stratification was minimal in American sociology until the 1920s.[1] This relative lack of interest in class theory before

1. For an analysis of the class theories of many of the leading figures in early American sociology, see Charles H. Page, *Class and American Sociology: From Ward to Ross* (New York: Dial Press, 1940); for a critical review and analysis of

the twentieth century reflects the unusual lack of class consciousness in American history. While Americans have always been much concerned with questions of equality and inequality, they have not until recent decades conducted their discussions and disputes in terms of class categories. From the 1920s on — perhaps especially since the 1930s, as a result of the shock of the Great Depression — interest in social stratification has grown, and a veritable flood of material about stratification has developed. Today, even the general public analyzes behavior and social problems in the broad language of class (often in euphemisms and rarely in the language of class antagonism), which would have been inconceivable fifty years ago.

As we have suggested earlier, and as we will see in abundant detail later, not only is the United States a deeply unequal society but its structure of class inequality differs very little from those of other industrial societies. Given this general similarity, why is it that American thought, on the part of laypeople and experts alike, has ignored European developments in class theory? In Europe, and especially on the Continent, stratification theory has tended to acknowledge the reality of social classes and to assume widespread economic, social, and political conflict among them. In the United States, however, theorists have tended to deny the existence of class conflict, and even the reality of social classes. The reasons for this divergence lie in the nature of American social and cultural development. Of special importance is the absence in American history of a feudal or authoritarian past. The American middle class did not have to gird itself against either a deeply entrenched nobility and clergy or an authoritarian state, as did its counterpart in Europe. This allowed liberal theorists in the United States to define American society in the universalistic terms of the French Enlightenment and the optimistic individualism of John Locke. As a consequence, American thought has concentrated on the problem of relating the interests of the individual with those of society, rather than on the conflicting interests of classes.

From the beginnings of the American republic, American experience with conflict and inequality has always involved functionally specific issues dividing functionally specific groups. The major subjects of conflict in American history have been highly specific and issue-oriented: for example, the national bank, tariffs, canals, railroads, silver, the Haymarket riot, the Pullman strike, monopolies, pure food and drug acts, Prohibition, sit-down strikes, collective bargaining, social security, the National Recovery Act, the Taft-Hartley Act, civil rights, and war on poverty. American thought divorced conflict from the idea of a confrontation between classes, and conflict as such was defined in such a way as to emphasize ultimate harmony or mutuality of interest between· individuals and groups. Given the widespread uniformity of economic

---

class theory and research from the 1920s to the 1950s, see Milton M. Gordon, *Social Class in American Sociology* (Durham, N.C.: Duke University Press, 1958). Gordon's search for conceptual clarity in the field of social stratification, which results in an elaboration of the multidimensional approach, constitutes a valuable contribution to stratification analysis in its own right.

conditions and of religious and ethnic background in the early agrarian United States, it is no wonder that inequality and conflict were interpreted in a non-class way. Given the social reality of individualism (small farms and businesses, local markets, local politics, the relative absence of external and internal military threats), it is not hard to understand why the United States accepted the Newtonian-inspired image of a natural economic and social system. And it is also easy to understand why the United States accounted for the increased conflicts and social evils of hectic industrialization by grafting Darwin's doctrine of evolution and natural selection (the survival of the fittest) to the doctrine of *laissez faire*.[2]

During this period, when gross inequality in wealth and power had become commonplaces of private and public discourse, and conflicts between economic groups (class) and between status groups (prestige) and their various mixtures had become troublesome in the extreme, there was no pronounced tendency to view the United States' problems in class terms. There were too many factors preventing the growth of class consciousness: the United States was experiencing real economic expansion and unprecedented rates of upward social mobility; immigration not only enhanced mobility but tended also to make economic classes extremely heterogeneous in religious and ethnic composition; and, of course, the vitality of the American political process allowed for enough reform to channel discontent away from radicalism and to turn injustice and exploitation into political rather than class issues.

All in all, the American experience gave rise to a widespread consensus that social inequality is natural. If it is assumed that the United States is a free society, what could be more natural than to believe that inequality reflects the natural distribution of talent among human beings? And, being natural, inequality and the conflicts that resulted from it posed no threat to society, though it did create problems of adjustment. If these adjustments could not be made by free economic markets, they could be undertaken by the United States' free political markets.

American sociology's development of an interest in social class must be seen as basically continuous with the evolution of the United States' symbolic culture. Every effort should be made to avoid interpreting this symbolic evolution as anticapitalistic or as a harbinger of socialism. Nothing better illustrates the power of American liberalism than the shift from early to late liberalism. Late liberalism is characterized by a greater appreciation of the power of social variables over human behavior, or, in other words, by a shift from a bio-psychological to a moderate sociocultural view.[3] But despite the emphasis on the social roots of behavior in the thought of late liberal theorists like Charles

---

2. See Richard Hofstadter, *Social Darwinism in American Thought,* rev. ed. (Boston: Beacon Press, 1955), paperback, originally published in 1944.

3. For intellectual histories of this relatively important shift, see Morton White, *Social Thought in America: The Revolt Against Formalism* (New York: Viking Press, 1949), and Henry Steele Commager, *The American Mind: An Interpretation of American Thought and Character Since the 1880's* (New Haven: Yale University Press, 1950), also in paperback.

Horton Cooley, W. I. Thomas, John Dewey, and Charles Beard, and in late liberal reform movements like Progressivism, the New Freedom, the Square Deal, the New Deal, the Fair Deal, and the Great Society, late liberalism is continuous with the past. The purpose of reforms, even when they involve extensive changes in the social environment, is not to change society but to make it more consistent with its basic principle — the emancipation of unequal individual talent through equality of opportunity — and thus produce a natural and just society, or system of "nonegalitarian classlessness." To accomplish this, however, it is necessary to know how society promotes or retards personal achievement. Along with the other social sciences, sociology responded to this intellectual challenge, and the development of stratification research and theory represents an important part of its response.

During the twentieth century American sociologists have pursued some of Weber's ideas in developing stratification theory, though on the whole they have extracted only as much from him as suited the distinctive flavor of American sociology and American culture and society. Heeding Weber's admonition to see more than the economic dimension, they identified the three general dimensions of class, prestige, and power. During the formative years of stratification analysis, sociology neglected the power dimension in favor of prestige and then of class. Since World War Two, there has been a shift toward treating economic status as the central focus of stratification. Despite mistakes and errors of emphasis, there emerged from this richly creative period a clear recognition of the major problems of stratification analysis. How does one construct indices in the economic realm (income, wealth, occupation, education) that make for causally meaningful and valid economic classes? How does one establish gradations of prestige and power that are causally meaningful and valid? Above all, how does one relate class, prestige, and power gradations? Or, in other words, how does one turn formal analytical categories into a synthesis that expresses the behavioral reality of social stratification?

The small-town focus

The American tradition of stratification research and theory emerged as a focus on the small town. From the 1920s on, American social scientists developed a complex set of skills for analyzing social stratification and a fairly sophisticated understanding of social class (and "caste") in small-town America. While an important aspect of this tradition was a search for the typical community, almost every kind of community and region was studied. From this massive effort emerged a rich and colorful picture of regional and other variations in inequality: from the well-established and differentiated class structure of the northeast and south to the frontier communities of the middle and far west, from complex industrial communities to homogeneous farm and mining communities, from ethnically and racially homogeneous communities to those richly diversified by ethnicity and race, and from small towns to metropolitan centers and suburbs.[4]

Despite variations in the approaches of the pioneer analysts of class, certain common characteristics may be noted. Virtually all researchers chose communities of manageable size — small enough for the observer (often a team) to get to know it fairly well, and, even more importantly, for the inhabitants to identify each other in terms of stratification categories. The customary point of entry to the sociological reality of social classes was the classes themselves, namely, individuals' subjective evaluations of each other. Thus community members evaluated families on a number of different bases (income, amount and type of wealth, occupation, club memberships, breeding, power, and so on), and the observers presumably allowed the reality of social class to emerge.

The main outlines of this tradition stemmed from the work of the social anthropologist W. Lloyd Warner, who with many collaborators investigated a number of communities, starting in 1930 with Yankee City (Newburyport, Massachusetts). In 1949 Warner and his associates published a manual[5] in which they formalized their method, presenting two different procedures for determining social class: Evaluated Participation, or the subjective determination of social classes by community members themselves; and an Index of Status Characteristics, or an average of weighted scores for occupation, source of income, house type, and dwelling area. The results obtained by using these two procedures were found to correlate quite well in the case of a small town; and presumably the Index of Status Characteristics could be substituted for the more cumbersome interview procedure to allow for the study of larger population complexes whose members do not know each other well enough to judge others' class positions.

The small-town tradition is characterized by many difficulties, notably its basic assumption that studying the small town is tantamount to investigating the nature of the United States.[6] This assumption was probably not justified even at the time such studies were being conducted, and their current relevance to the dynamics and structure of the American system of stratification is even

---

4. For a useful review of representative examples of this tradition between the 1920s and 1950s, see Milton M. Gordon, *Social Class in American Sociology* (Durham, N.C.: Duke University Press, 1958), chaps. 3–5.

5. W. Lloyd Warner et al., *Social Class and America: A Manual of Procedure for the Measurement of Social Status* (Chicago: Science Research Associates, 1949); also available with additional chapters as a Harper paperback.

6. W. Lloyd Warner, the leading researcher associated with small-town studies, states this explicitly in the foreword to *Democracy in Jonesville* (New York: Harper and Row, 1949; also in paperback), and implicitly in the titles of the first four volumes of the Yankee City series (5 vols.; New Haven: Yale University Press, 1941–1959): *The Social Life of a Modern Community* and *The Status System of a Modern Community*, both with Paul S. Lunt; *The Social Systems of American Ethnic Groups*, with Leo Srole; *The Social System of the Modern Factory*, with J. O. Low. The fifth volume is entitled *The Living and the Dead*.

more problematic. Aside from their diverse orientations and conclusions, these studies all focused on something that has since virtually disappeared, small-town America.[7] The great creative period of small-town (or small-city) stratification research lasted from the mid-1920s to the early 1940s; it occurred, in other words, at the same time that the United States was rapidly becoming an urban society dominated by a national economy and governed by a national state.[8] Today even the concept of an autonomous national state is inadequate; one must think in terms of an international economy and politics.[9]

The small-town tradition has other shortcomings which we will mention only briefly here and discuss more fully later. Its emphasis on prestige tends to distract attention from the major determinant of stratification, the economy. And its subjective, or reputational, method and choice of subject matter tended to emphasize stability and homogeneity; to highlight prestige phenomena without tracing them to their historical roots, especially economic developments; and to substitute the judgments of lay individuals for those of social scientists. To put the latter point differently, the small-town tradition tended to allow the man in the street to settle scientific questions.

These local studies were not without value, however. They gave rise to extremely fruitful research methodology and revealed most of the problems basic to stratification analysis. And small-town studies are important for another reason: despite differing methodologies and emphases, they all agree on one fundamental point, that the United States is a deeply stratified society.

The national focus: the development of class indices
The shift from subjective to objective data

The insufficiency of a narrow concentration on small communities was sensed by Warner, who, as we have said, eventually developed a more efficient procedure for analyzing stratification phenomena than the reputational approach he had used earlier. However, credit for the transition, both theoretical and practical, from study of the small town to study of the metropolitan center belongs to August B. Hollingshead. Early in his career, Hollingshead had used the reputational approach to study the impact of social class on education in Morris, Illinois, a small midwestern town of 6,000 inhabitants.[10] Though Hollingshead's procedures were a model of explicitness and simplicity compared

7. Small towns are still plentiful in the United States, but most are caught up in the dynamics of a national economy and state; for a pioneering study along these lines, see Arthur J. Vidich and Joseph Bensman, *Small Town in Mass Society: Class, Power, and Religion in a Rural Community* (Garden City, N.Y.: Doubleday Anchor Books, 1960), originally published by Princeton University Press, 1958.

8. Warner himself has intimated that he is aware of this transformation in Volume 4 of the Yankee City series, in which he notes the development of a "break in the skill hierarchy" and points out that "Yankee City loses control of its factories."

9. Though the relation between international affairs and social stratification is beyond the scope of this study, some of the ideas and problems basic to it are set out in "Class and International Relations" in Chapter 15.

10. *Elmtown's Youth* (New York: John Wiley and Sons, 1949).

to those of Warner, who studied the same town,[11] both essentially relied on the subjective awareness of the townspeople themselves. (Hollingshead's findings were corroborated by Warner's analysis.) Later, Hollingshead became interested in the relations between social class and mental illness, which he studied in New Haven, Connecticut, a metropolitan center of 240,000. (His research will be discussed later.) Unable in such a large city to rely on subjective awareness of social class, Hollingshead developed an "objective" substitute, the Index of Social Position.[12] After intensive interviews with a cross-sectional random sample of 552 households, Hollingshead and his associate Meyers ranked the families. Working independently, they agreed, by and large, on the ranking of the families in a scheme of five classes. They then extracted the three basic criteria they had used to rank the families: (1) place of residence; (2) occupation; and (3) education (which was taken to indicate associational and cultural life). Each of these factors was scaled and weighted, and the resulting range of scores produced five distinct classes (see Table 3-1).

Socioeconomic status

A number of other indices that focus on economic status have been developed in an effort to understand the distribution of values in the class dimension. Perhaps the best-known measure of economic status was developed by the United States Census Bureau; known as SES (socioeconomic status), it is based on occupation, educational attainment, and family income (or, as the case may be, individual income of unrelated individuals).

The bureau's most recent study of SES is based on a 5 percent sample of the population selected to include families and unrelated individuals, inmates of institutions, members of the armed forces, students in college dormitories,

Table 3-1 The Class System of New Haven

Hierarchy of classes	Number of families as percentage of total
I	2.7
II	9.8
III	18.9
IV	48.4
V	20.2

SOURCE: August B. Hollingshead and Frederick C. Redlich, *Social Class and Mental Illness: A Community Study* (New York: John Wiley and Sons, 1958), Appendix 2, p. 395. Used by permission of John Wiley and Sons, Inc.

11. William L. Warner *et al., Democracy in Jonesville* (New York: Harper and Row, 1949), also in paperback.
12. For a full explanation, see August B. Hollingshead and Frederick C. Redlich, *Social Class and Mental Illness: A Community Study* (New York: John Wiley and Sons, 1958), Appendix 2.

and rooming-house residents. Using Census Bureau definitions, scores for socioeconomic status were derived as follows:

1. The occupation, education, and income of the chief income recipient were identified.

2. Scores were then developed for occupation, education, and family income by computing a cumulative percentage for family income and for the education of the chief income recipient as of 1959 (see Tables 3-2 and 3-3). For example, persons with five or more years of college were assigned to the 96th–100th percentiles. An individual's score in a given category was the midpoint of the cumulative percentage interval for that category; thus persons with five or more years of college were given scores of 98. Scores for occupation (based on 1950 data) were developed by averaging the incomes and education of given occupations, and then constructing a cumulative percentage distribution (see Table 3-4).[13]

Table 3-2 SES Scores for Categories of Family Income (or Income of Persons Not in Families)

Category	Score	Category	Score
$25,000 or more	100	$5,000 to 5,499	49
15,000 to 24,999	98	4,500 to 4,999	41
10,000 to 14,999	94	4,000 to 4,499	34
9,500 to 9,999	89	3,500 to 3,999	27
9,000 to 9,499	87	3,000 to 3,499	21
8,500 to 8,999	84	2,500 to 2,999	17
8,000 to 8,499	81	2,000 to 2,499	12
7,500 to 7,999	78	1,500 to 1,999	08
7,000 to 7,499	74	1,000 to 1,499	05
6,500 to 6,999	69	500 to 999	03
6,000 to 6,499	63	Loss, none or less	
5,500 to 5,999	57	than 500	01

SOURCE: U.S. Bureau of the Census, *U.S. Census of Population: 1960*. Subject Reports. Socioeconomic Status, Final Report PC (2)-5c (Washington, D.C.: U.S. Government Printing Office, 1967), Appendix 4.

13. These scores correspond quite closely to subjective appraisals of the worth (prestige) of occupations by the American public-at-large. See "The Hierarchy of Occupational Prestige" in Chapter 8 for these appraisals; also see Peter M. Blau and Otis Dudley Duncan, *The American Occupational Structure* (New York: John Wiley and Sons, 1967), pp. 119–128, for the correlation between socioeconomic status (and occupation category scores) and occupational prestige rankings. For a review of the various testing devices used to study all aspects of occupation, and a review and discussion of findings, see John P. Robinson, *et al.*, *Measures of Occupational Attitudes and Occupational Characteristics* (Ann Arbor, Mich.: Institute for Social Research, 1969).

Table 3-3 SES Scores for Categories of Years of School Completed

Category	Score
College	
5 or more	98
4	93
3	89
2	86
1	83
High school	
4	67
3	49
2	42
1	34
Elementary	
8	23
7	13
5 and 6	08
3 and 4	04
1 and 2	02
None	01

SOURCE: U.S. Bureau of the Census, *U.S. Census of Population: 1960.* Subject Reports. Socioeconomic Status, Final Report PC (2)-5c (Washington, D.C.: U.S. Government Printing Office, 1967), Appendix 3.

Table 3-4 SES Scores for Categories of Major Occupation Groups (Compiled on the Basis of Average of Education and Income)

Category	Score
Professional, technical and kindred workers	90
Managers, officials, and proprietors, except farm	81
Clerical, sales, and kindred workers	71
Craftsmen, foremen, and kindred workers	58
Operatives and kindred workers	45
Service workers, including private household	34
Laborers, except farm and mine	20
Farmers and farm managers	16
Farm laborers and foremen	06

SOURCE: U.S. Bureau of the Census, *U.S. Census of Population: 1960.* Subject Reports. Socioeconomic Status, Final Report PC (2)-5c (Washington, D.C.: U.S. Government Printing Office, 1967), Appendix 2.

3. Once the chief income recipient's scores in each area were determined, a simple average was computed — that is, the three scores were given equal weight — to produce a socioeconomic score indicating socioeconomic status, or SES (see Table 3-5).[14]

These scores are not absolute measures of socioeconomic status. They fail to take into account, for example, nonmoney income received in farming, religious, and social welfare occupations. Furthermore, the methodology used, especially the simple averaging of the three components of SES, tends to locate more people in the middle ranges than in the extremes.

Of even more importance for our purposes is the fact that the SES hierarchy does not serve as a hierarchy of economic or social classes. Like all methodological instruments, it provides only what the instrument defines and collects as data. The hierarchy of SES scores, for example, does not tell us much about those who possess great wealth and control the United States' giant corporations. To take another example, the bottom rung on the SES ladder is only a small portion of the United States' destitute population. And by using family income as a criterion, SES tends to obscure the important difference between families with identical incomes but different numbers of earners. The class position of black Americans is markedly improved, for example, if comparison between whites and blacks are made on the basis of family income.

Table 3-5 Socioeconomic Status (Average of Scores in Occupation, Education, and Income) of the American Population, 1960

Socioeconomic status score	Percentage distribution
90–99	5.4
80–89	7.7
75–79	5.1
70–74	6.0
60–69	13.7
50–59	15.0
40–49	14.1
30–39	11.7
25–29	4.9
20–24	4.3
10–19	7.7
0–9	4.4

SOURCE: U.S. Bureau of the Census, *U.S. Census of Population: 1960*. Subject Reports. Socioeconomic Status, Final Report PC (2)-5c (Washington, D.C.: U.S. Government Printing Office, 1967), Table A.

14. For a full explanation of the method of determining SES, see U.S. Bureau of the Census, *U.S. Census of Population: 1960*. Subject Reports. Socioeconomic Status, Final Report PC (2)-5c (Washington, D.C.: U.S. Government Printing Office, 1967), pp. ix–xix.

The SES hierarchy has its uses, but leaves a crucial question unanswered: what is the meaning of a given rank, or, better still, what does location in a given rank indicate about the behavior of an individual or family? The SES hierarchy's rankings are too narrow to be symbols of behavioral differences. In other words, ranks should be combined if there is no appreciable difference between them in terms of family life, health, interaction patterns, cultural activities, voting, and so on of the families and unrelated individuals in question. Warner and Hollingshead used data and procedures similar to those of the Census Bureau, but employed wider ranges for their economic data in order to relate them to inequalities in the prestige and power dimensions. If SES is to be fully useful in stratification analysis, it must avoid a narrow, formal statistical approach and gear itself to the realities of behavior. The problems this entails is our next topic.

Strategy and pitfalls in the analysis of class

After a hierarchy of objective income, education, and occupation has been developed, how does one identify discontinuities in this hierarchy that can be called economic and social classes? The federal government has developed a widely known index that allegedly identifies a break between poverty (destitution) and nonpoverty. In 1973 a nonfarm family of four with an income of $4,540 or less was considered poor.[15] Of course, extremes can be identified with relative ease: a family of four with an inheritance of $100,000,000 and an annual income in the millions and a family of four with an income of $3,000 may both be called American and may have certain things in common, but will live in far different worlds. The same is true of extremes in occupation and education: the president of a large corporation, a judge, a physicist, and a professor and their families will all live in worlds far removed from those inhabited by a night porter, an elevator operator, or a grape picker.

But after extremes have been identified, what is the next step? How does one dissect the income hierarchy to reveal stratification differences? Is it meaningful to distinguish $0–3000 from $3000–6000? Assuming that we can identify destitution and wealth, at what point is a family (or unrelated individual) of modest means rather than poor, and how is the former distinguished from the well off, and it in turn from the affluent? The only way to answer this question is to determine empirically what happens to families and unrelated individuals in a given range of income, occupation, or education — or, better still, a given range of a mixture of these statuses.

A useful approach to determining the relation between income distribution and standard of living has been made by the United States Department of

15. U.S. Bureau of the Census, *Current Population Reports,* Series P-60, no. 98, "Characteristics of the Low-Income Population: 1973" (Washington, D.C.: U.S. Government Printing Office, 1975), p. 1. It should be noted that there is considerable dispute about the validity of the "official" definition of poverty; few experts argue that it is too inclusive. For a further discussion of poverty, see "Prosperity and Poverty: Opposites or Correlates?" in Chapter 4.

Labor. The department's Bureau of Labor Statistics has developed measures for distinguishing three living standards for two types of income units, an established urban family of four with one earner and a retired couple living in an urban area. These measures are not based on actual expenditures, which the bureau hopes to report on in the future, but on definitions and estimates. With understandable caution, the bureau's three living standards have been labeled lower, intermediate (or moderate), and higher.[16]

As can be seen in Table 3-6, an urban family of four with an income of $8,181 in 1973 had a lower (not poverty-level) standard of living, a family with an income of $12,626 had an intermediate budget, and a family with an income of $18,201 had a higher budget. It should be noted that these are comprehensive budgets that include recreation, socializing, and tax expenses. The corresponding figures for 1973 for a retired couple living in an urban area were approximately $3,763, $5,414, and $8,043. (These are approximations because they do not include taxes.)[17]

Unfortunately, the bureau does not report how many families fall into each budget category, which is something well worth knowing. In a valuable earlier study, the bureau reported that in 1970 16 percent of families of four with a

Table 3-6 Summary of Annual Budgets for a 4-person Family at 3 Levels of Living, Urban United States, Autumn 1973

Component	Lower budget	Intermediate budget	Higher budget
Total budget	$8,181	$12,626	$18,201
Total family consumption	6,580	9,761	13,450
Food	2,440	3,183	4,020
Housing	1,627	2,908	4,386
Transportation	563	1,014	1,315
Clothing	696	995	1,456
Personal care	205	275	390
Medical care	660	664	692
Other family consumption	389	722	1,191
Other items	385	611	1,024
Taxes	1,216	2,254	3,727
Social security and disability	492	647	647
Personal income taxes	724	1,607	3,080

SOURCE: U.S. Department of Labor, Bureau of Labor Statistics, *Monthly Labor Review* 97 (August 1974): 57.

16. The explanation of these measures is available in Bulletin 1570-5, "Three Standards of Living for an Urban Family of Four, Spring 1967" and Bulletin 1570-6, "Three Budgets for a Retired Couple in Urban Areas of the United States, 1967–68," Bureau of Labor Statistics, U.S. Department of Labor. The three budgets are updated annually in the Bureau of Labor Statistics' *Monthly Labor Review.*
17. U.S. Department of Labor, *Monthly Labor Review* 97 (October 1974): 57.

full-time experienced worker and a nonworking wife were below the lower budget, 28 percent between the lower and intermediate, 30 percent between intermediate and higher, and 26 percent above the higher budget (see Table 3-7).

However important, these measures of urban budgets ignore substantial portions of the population[18] and do not tell us directly how families at each income level behave in a wide variety of other areas. But the question these measures seek to answer is central to stratification analysis: what does a given economic status mean for behavior? This is the basic strategy we will employ in later chapters as we report on the research sociologists and others have conducted on a wide variety of topics in social stratification. Though these studies vary somewhat as to date conducted, universe analyzed, reliability, and definition of economic or class status, they are similar enough to tell cumulatively a powerful and fairly complete story about the structure and processes that make up the American class system.

In developing our portrayal, we will be on the alert for gaps in our knowledge, especially gaps that result from systematic bias (whether well-intentioned or inadvertent). As a minor example, we can determine the number of people employed in thousands of occupations, but we do not know how many prostitutes there are. It is not unrealistic to guess that the United States has five hundred thousand prostitutes. This is a sizable number of human beings occupying a distinctive stratification position, and yet we know little about them because the Census Bureau does not recognize prostitution as an occupation. As a matter of fact, the total number of people in illegal occupations (pimps, bookies, pickpockets, confidence men, fences, and so on) is probably high.

Table 3-7 Budget Levels in Relation to Income for Urban Family of Four with One Earner, 1970

Income level	Percentage of families	Number (thousands)
Below lower budget ($6,543 or less)	16	887
Between lower and intermediate budgets ($6,544–$10,064)	28	1,552
Between intermediate and higher budgets ($10,064–$14,571)	30	1,662
Above higher budget ($14,572 or more)	26	1,441
Total families	100	5,542

SOURCE: Bureau of Labor Statistics, "Three Budgets for an Urban Family of Four Persons, 1969–70," Supplement to Bulletin 1570-5, p. 7.

18. For our rough estimate of the distribution of family and unrelated individual income units by standard of living, see Tables 4-1 and 4-2.

In other words, researchers do not always use the total universe of human beings when they formulate their research designs. In addition to illegal occupations, they often overlook unrelated individuals, inmates of mental and penal institutions, uncounted members of society (significant numbers are missed by the census), illegal immigrants (estimated at five-to-ten million) [19] and "immigrant" workers.[20] Perhaps the best-known bias in stratification research is its systematic neglect of the very poor prior to the 1960s.

The failures of stratification research can be partially attributed to powerful American myths about inequality. Part of the reason for the neglect of the poor, for example, is the American belief that the poor would inevitably be eliminated by prosperity. Other examples are easy to cite. Since Hollingshead's study of New Haven, the problem of analyzing the metropolitan center has been tackled; we now have some extremely useful empirical data pointing toward (but not identical with) national patterns.[21] However, unlike Hollingshead's, some of these studies contain judgments at odds with our data. Hodges, for example, has accepted the popular beliefs that income differentials are being reduced and that the welfare state has brought about a reduction of class differentials. In the case of the Coleman-Neugarten study, the mistaken idea (also subscribed to by Warner in his later work) that the United States is becoming a three-class system characterized by an upper class, a lower class, and a great middle-majority, is given a tentative endorsement. Despite the gains represented by these and other empirical studies, and by some broad interpretive studies,[22] we still lack a satisfactory picture of the overall American

19. The impact of illegal immigration is an important, though little researched, aspect of the American class system. Illegal aliens are a subproletariat who do many forms of low-paid, undesirable work, and who benefit from few civic rights or public services.

20. The term *immigrant* is used for many types of noncitizens: those who enter a country intending to stay; those who come intending to work for short periods (and stay for long periods); those who come as part of a short-term imported labor force, and others. For a valuable study of the impact of "immigrants" on the class systems of European countries, see Stephen Castles and Godula Kosack, *Immigrant Workers and Class Structure in Western Europe* (London: Oxford University Press, 1973). No comparable study exists for the United States.

21. Examples of this research are Harold M. Hodges, Jr.'s 1960 study of a three-county area of 2,000,000 people near San Francisco, which wisely does not claim to be a theory of our national class system, "Peninsula People: Social Stratification in a Metropolitan Complex," *Education and Society: A Book of Readings*, eds. W. Warren Kallenbach and Harold M. Hodges, Jr. (Columbus, Ohio: Charles E. Merrill, 1963), pp. 389–420; Richard P. Coleman and Bernice L. Neugarten, *Social Status in the City* (San Francisco: Jossey-Bass, 1971), a Warner-type study of Kansas City, Missouri, during the 1950s that attempts and in our judgment fails to derive a national structure of stratification from the study of a metropolitan population of 800,000; and Edward O. Laumann, *Prestige and Association in an Urban Community* (Indianapolis: Bobbs-Merrill, 1966), a careful study of two suburbs of Boston.

22. For example, C. Wright Mills, *White Collar: The American Middle Classes* (New York: Oxford University Press, 1951), and *The Power Elite* (New York: Oxford University Press, 1956); E. Digby Baltzell, *The Protestant Establishment: Aristocracy and Caste in America* (New York: Random House, 1966), a Vintage paperback, and Suzanne Keller, *Beyond the Ruling Class: Strategic Elites in Modern Society* (New York: Random House, 1963), also in paperback.

system of stratification. And, more to the point, much mythology has to be cleared away before our picture can be brought into focus.

The area of subjectivity — how individuals feel about and appraise themselves and each other — also has its pitfalls. There is little doubt that we need to know how and what individuals think and feel in order to understand the nature of inequality and equality. As we have indicated, the area of subjectivity has not been neglected. Stratification analysis has developed two different ways to obtain data in this area, the reputational and the "subjective" methods. The reputational approach was referred to earlier in our discussion of the small-town approach; it consists of asking individuals what they think of other individuals, and involves the evaluation of others on the basis of family, religion, race, occupation, income, wealth, and similar factors. Far more valuable to the study of metropolitan and national patterns of stratification is the subjective approach, which seeks to determine what people think and feel about themselves and about a variety of issues, such as education, politics, sense of power and ability to control life, work satisfaction, class self-identification, and the like.

Measurement of popular beliefs and values is extremely widespread today. We have become accustomed to this practice largely by our experience with public opinion polls. Perhaps less well-known is the practice of market and advertising research. And stratification researchers have extensively explored and interpreted the area of subjectivity. National studies of occupational prestige ranking are of special importance because of the central position of occupation in the modern system of inequality; we will have more to say about them later.[23]

Here again, as in the use of data derived from the study of overt behavior, caution must be exercised. Subjective data do not represent the natural outcome of human nature, and the simple description of what people feel and think is not an answer to the basic questions about social stratification. Just as the opinions of the public have no special scientific validity with regard to such issues as fluoridation, the safety of nuclear power plants, and policy in Southeast Asia, they have no special scientific validity with regard to the nature of social stratification. It is one of the central insights of stratification theory that the class system precedes perception and judgment; indeed, class factors are constitutive forces, not mere influences. Thus, if the general public says that social classes do not exist, or offers contradictory definitions of class, the issue of whether or not classes exist is not automatically decided. On the contrary, one may well conclude that the class system is so structured that its existence is hidden from the population it affects. However, though what individuals and majorities believe is not necessarily scientific, the data establishing what they believe *are* scientific; that is, if the data are compiled

---

23. See "Occupational Prestige" in Chapter 8. As we noted above, there is a substantial correlation between occupational scores developed from objective data about income and education and the hierarchy of occupational prestige that has emerged from subjective evaluation.

according to the canons of science, they accurately reflect what people actually feel and think.

In orienting ourselves toward stratification analysis, we must be wary of two assumptions that have led analysts astray. On the one hand there are the assumptions that the United States' system of inequality is based on functional differentiation and that the hierarchy of inequality is a continuum of fine gradations or contains a very large middle mass and two small extremes of rich and poor. On the other hand there is the tendency to think in terms of strong correlations between the various dimensions of inequality, leading to well-defined strata. The empirical evidence, however, contradicts both conceptions of the nature of class stratification.

There is little doubt that the approximately 55 million families and 18 million unrelated individuals that made up the counted American population in 1973 cannot be arranged in a hierarchy of well-defined social classes. It is not possible, in other words, to find significant discontinuities in class that correlate precisely and completely with significant breaks in prestige and in power. It is undeniable that families and unrelated individuals with the same incomes may be ranked quite differently in prestige because of color, religion, or style of life, and that members of the same income group may behave quite differently politically or be treated quite differently by those who exercise power.

This does not mean, however, that the concept of social class should be abandoned. On the contrary, there are a number of ways in which stratification analysis can circumvent this problem. One of the most important of these is to employ statistical generalizations, which predict the behavior of aggregates, and avoid old-fashioned generalizations, which predict the behavior of all particulars. The heart of sociological analysis is to identify tendencies or rates of behavior within aggregates. In other words, the statistical approach identifies lawful, predictable, modal behavior, rather than the behavior of each and every particular. Thus, to take a demographic example, the American birth rate in the coming year can be predicted quite accurately, though we cannot predict what contribution every sexual pair will make to it. To render this example in class terms, we can predict the birth rates of specified income groups — and the accuracy of our prediction can be increased if we take into account occupation, education, or religion — but we cannot predict the number of children each sexual pair in such categories will produce. Therefore, despite our present inability to predict the behavior of every family and individual, it is undeniable that aggregates who share a common location on the axis of class are deeply affected in every aspect of their behavior. In other words, we should not be prevented from concentrating on the very real and important consequences that flow from stratificational variables simply because such variables have not yet been incorporated into a unified or general theory of social class. To deny the reality of social class in America because the data have not yet satisfied the requirements of general theory, or because they do not conform to the Marxian definition of class, is to mask the reality of inequality, distort the nature of social problems, and hinder the formulation of public and private policy.

Status consistency as a mode of analysis

The problem of finding significant discontinuities in class that correlate with discontinuities in prestige and power is central to stratification analysis. The lack of correlation — or, more accurately, the inconsistency between positions held in the various dimensions and subdimensions of stratification — has produced a great deal of research, to which we now turn.

Status consistency or crystallization

The essence of the concept of status crystallization (or status consistency) is old, though its specific terms are associated with Gerhard Lenski.[24] All caste and estate societies are marked by a high degree of consistency in the ways in which individuals and families are ranked and those at any given level behave. Since high prestige status leads to high power status, and high prestige-power leads to high class status, and so on, caste and estate systems of stratification develop not only unified strata (consistency in class, prestige, and power) but also relations between strata that are rigid and stable over time. When status inconsistency appears in a caste or estate system (as in the case of the bourgeoisie in prerevolutionary France), one can speak of deviations from the normative sociocultural system.

Class societies also reveal considerable status consistency, though they are also marked by considerable inconsistency, especially among the lower classes. And, of course, status consistency (or class consolidation) leads to class perpetuation, since parents tend to pass on their high or low positions to their children. Broadly speaking, consistency analysis seeks to establish relations within and between each of the major hierarchies:

1. Status Consistency or Crystallization. One employs this concept to describe families and unrelated individuals characterized by comparable or consistent benefits across the various hierarchies of inequalities. Examples are a white Presbyterian doctor, a white Methodist skilled worker, and a white Baptist farm laborer.

2. Status Inconsistency. This concept is used to describe families and unrelated individuals characterized by different or inconsistent levels of benefits in the various dimensions of stratification. Examples are a black Presbyterian doctor, an Italian Roman Catholic building contractor, and a Jewish lawyer.

24. "Status Crystallization: A Non-Vertical Dimension of Social Status," *American Sociological Review* 19 (August 1954): 405–413.

One of the most advantageous features of the concept of status consistency is that it enables an analyst to demonstrate that class position is often perpetuated without superior achievement.[25] Speaking more generally, status consistency reveals a great deal about the fundamental causal process in social stratification. Stated abstractly, this process occurs as follows: those with high incomes, occupations, and education tend also to enjoy high prestige, stable families, more and varied opportunities for interaction, and greater political-legal power; and these factors in turn tend to protect and enhance high economic status. Such families also have the resources, motives, and skills to insure a high social class position for their offspring, especially through the careful management of socialization.

The same causal process is discernible at the bottom of the class hierarchy. The poor have low income, educational, and occupational statuses, and thus tend toward low prestige, unstable families, and isolated social interaction patterns. These factors not only reinforce each other but tend to give rise to a process of class "inheritance"; that is, the offspring of the poor tend to inherit the general class position of their parents.[26]

Some of the more extreme incongruities in stratification status are found among minority groups: middle class blacks suffer serious status inconsistency, for example, as do Jews of high economic or professional achievement. The same thing is probably true of well-to-do Irish, Italian, Japanese, and other minority Americans, including women. Exact comparisons between power and the other dimensions of inequality are difficult to make, but those who live in big cities and have fairly substantial incomes (middle management and skilled workers) are probably not enjoying political power consistent with their class positions.

While such status inconsistencies can be described in formal terms, as we have just done, it is much more difficult to identify the causes and consequences of status inconsistency or consistency in precise empirical terms. Extreme caution should be used in employing this mode of analysis. The need for precise models for analyzing status consistency and inconsistency is obvious, and a simple model for the class dimension[27] has been constructed by the demographer Donald Bogue. Bogue argues that *occupation* is an ambiguous term and that a more accurate prediction of socioeconomic status (or what he calls *socioeconomic achievement status*) can be arrived at by averaging income

25. For a discussion of how this takes place in and through education, see "Class and Educational Shortage, Waste, and Privilege" in Chapter 6.

26. For an analysis of the concept of "intergenerational welfare dependency" that emphasizes how little we know about this process, see Norman C. Weissberg, "Intergenerational Welfare Dependency: A Critical Review," *Social Problems* 18, no. 2 (Fall 1970): 257–274.

27. On the basis of ideas from Max Weber and Marx, Norbert Wiley has developed a more complex analysis of consistency and inconsistency within the class dimension and has related it to political behavior; see his "America's Unique Class Politics: The Interplay of the Labor, Credit and Commodity Markets," *American Sociological Review* 32 (August 1967): 529–541. For a discussion of this essay, see "America's Unique Class Politics" in Chapter 11.

and education.[28] An initial step in the analysis of status consistency can be taken, Bogue believes, by determining average incomes for different amounts of educational attainment standardized by age. Among the major occupational categories, some display consistency between income and education (professional, technical, and kindred workers; clerical and kindred workers; sales workers; craftsmen, foremen, and kindred workers; operatives and kindred workers; service workers, except private household workers), and some reveal significant inconsistency between income and education (managers, officials, and proprietors; private household workers; farmers and farm managers; farm laborers and foremen; laborers, except farm and mine). Within the inconsistent categories, specific occupations are characterized by significantly more income than their education-by-age normally warrants (physicians, bank managers, and lawyers); and some by significantly less (nurses, elementary teachers, library attendants, fishermen and oystermen, hospital attendants, kitchen workers, farm owners and tenants, and farm and food canning laborers). Some of this inconsistency, Bogue argues, is attributable to differences in ability, especially as such differences are reflected in education. But Bogue also argues that some inconsistency is due to differences in economic power; accordingly, he develops a threefold categorization of consistents and inconsistents along the lines of economic power:

1. Economic dominants — those who receive significantly more income than their education normally warrants.
2. Full participants — those who receive the income normal to their level of education.
3. Economic subordinants — those who receive significantly less income than their education normally warrants.

However interesting and potentially useful Bogue's analysis of economic dominants, full participants, and economic subordinants, one cannot predict how those in these positions will actually behave. So far, in this text and elsewhere, the analysis of status consistency has remained too formal and abstract to serve as a good predictor of behavior. All in all, therefore, important information is still needed before we can understand behavior as an outcome of inconsistency within the realm of class (income, occupation, education), within the realms of prestige and power, or as an outcome of inconsistency between one or more major dimensions. Analyzing the consistency of positions in the hierarchies of class, prestige, and power calls into play all the fundamental questions in social theory, questions involving social causation, mobility, pluralism, and integration,[29] as well as the dynamics of personality.[30] In a

28. Donald J. Bogue, *Principles of Demography* (New York: John Wiley and Sons, 1969), chap. 14.
29. H. M. Blalock, Jr., "Status Inconsistency, Social Mobility, Status Integration and Structural Effects," *American Sociological Review* 32 (October 1967): 790–801.
30. James A. Geschwender, "Continuities in Theories of Status Consistency and Cognitive Dissonance," *Social Forces* 46 (December 1967): 160–171; reprinted in

general way, the explanation of behavior by reference to social disjointedness and incoherence is central to the entire tradition of modern social science. Any number of social theorists have explained major social trends and stresses and breaks in the social system in terms of a society's internal conflicts and contradictions. A good example of social breakdown as a result of internal contradictions is the French Revolution, which resulted when the middle class's prestige and power statuses were badly out of line with its class position. Obviously, the idea that there can emerge a class that contradicts the society it is a part of, and is thus revolutionary while other classes are reactionary, is central to the Marxian tradition. In sum, there is little doubt that consistency analysis is a valuable tool, but it has not yet proven itself fully and the dangers inherent in its use must be noted.

The dangers in consistency explanations

The concept of stratification consistency is intriguing and seductive, and suits intellectuals' professional predilections for logic and abstraction. However, serious questions have been raised about its empirical validity as a mode of explanation, and about the ideological biases it might contain. In recent years a great many attempts have been made to apply this concept — that is, to determine whether specific forms of behavior can be related to stratification consistency (or the lack of it). Researchers have sought to explain political attitudes and behavior, including extremist behavior and attitudes toward power, in terms of consistency in stratification variables (income, education, occupation, and ethnicity).[31] In addition, social participation,[32] psychological stress,[33]

Edward O. Laumann, Paul M. Siegal, and Robert W. Hodge, eds., *The Logic of Social Hierarchies* (Chicago: Markham, 1970), pp. 500–511.

31. Gerhard E. Lenski, "Status Crystallization: A Non-Vertical Dimension of Social Status," *American Sociological Review* 19 (August 1954): 405–413; Irwin W. Goffman, "Status Consistency and Preference for Change in Power Distribution," *American Sociological Review* 22 (June 1957): 275–281; James W. Vander Zanden, "The Klan Revival," *The American Journal of Sociology,* 65 (March 1960): 456–462; (also available as Bobbs-Merrill reprint no. S-299); Daniel Bell, ed., *The Radical Right* (Garden City, N.Y.: Doubleday, 1964); Gary B. Rush, "Status Consistency and Right-Wing Extremism," *American Sociological Review* 32 (February 1967): 86–92; Gerhard E. Lenski, "Status Inconsistency and the Vote: A Four Nation Test," *American Sociological Review* 32 (April 1967): 298–301; David R. Segal, "Status Inconsistency, Cross Pressures, and American Political Behavior," *American Sociological Review* 34 (June 1969): 352–359; Larry L. Hunt and Robert G. Cushing, "Status Discrepancy, Interpersonal Attachment and Right Wing Extremism," *Social Science Quarterly* 51 (December 1970): 587–601.

32. Gerhard E. Lenski, "Social Participation and Status Crystallization," *American Sociological Review* 21 (August 1956): 458–464.

33. Elton F. Jackson, "Status Consistency and Symptoms of Stress," *American Sociological Review* 27 (August 1962): 469–480; Elton F. Jackson and Peter J. Burke, "Status and Symptoms of Stress: Additive and Interaction Effects," *American Sociological Review* 30 (August 1965): 556–564.

middle class juvenile delinquency,[34] religious identification,[35] and class consciousness[36] have been related to status discrepancy.

Consistency-inconsistency explanations, however, have been strongly refuted on both empirical and methodological grounds. Other investigators have failed to find a relationship between status discrepancy and political attitudes,[37] voting behavior,[38] and prejudice.[39]

The extensive literature on inconsistency has been cited because it illustrates an important pitfall in sociological thinking in general, and in stratification thinking in particular. Basically, consistency theory seeks to show that predictable effects (dependent variables) result from the combination or interaction of statuses (variables), and that these effects differ from the effects of several independent variables. In addition to the empirical evidence against this view, methodological critiques of this approach have argued that though a causal effect may result from the interaction of variables, it is not possible to distinguish this causal process from the process that results from an additive model.[40]

The question posed by attempts to explain behavior in terms of status consistency can be put more simply: do all the inconsistencies in class, prestige, and power statuses that exist logically (or even statistically) actually affect the behavior of Americans? There is little question that the behavior of Americans is deeply affected by the ambiguities, conflicts, and contradictions in American society. However, individuals and aggregates do not behave in a specified manner simply because their social and stratificational statuses are illogical or

34. Robert H. Bohlke, "Social Mobility, Stratification Inconsistency and Middle Class Delinquency," *Social Problems* 8 (Spring 1961): 351–363; reprinted in Edmund W. Vaz, ed., *Middle Class Juvenile Delinquency* (New York: Harper and Row, 1967), pp. 222–232; available in paperback.

35. N. J. Demerath III, *Social Class in American Protestantism* (Chicago: Rand McNally, 1965).

36. John C. Leggett, *Class, Race, and Labor: Working Class Consciousness in Detroit* (New York: Oxford University Press, 1968).

37. William K. Kenkel, "The Relationship Between Status Consistency and Politico-Economic Attitudes," *American Sociological Review* 21 (June 1956): 365–368; D. Dennis Kelly and William J. Chambliss, "Status Consistency and Political Attitudes," *American Sociological Review* 31 (June 1966): 375–382; D. Stanley Eitzen, "Social Class, Status Inconsistency and Political Attitudes," *Social Science Quarterly* 51 (December 1970): 602–609.

38. Leonard Broom and F. Lancaster Jones, "Status Consistency and Political Preference: The Australian Case," *American Sociological Review* 35 (December 1970): 989–1001.

39. Robert W. Hodge and Donald J. Treiman, "Occupational Mobility and Attitudes Toward Negroes," *American Sociological Review* 31 (February 1966): 93–102; Donald J. Treiman, "Status Discrepancy and Prejudice," *American Journal of Sociology* 71 (May 1966): 651–664.

40. H. M. Blalock, Jr., "Status Inconsistency, Social Mobility, Status Integration and Structural Effects," *American Sociological Review* 32 (October 1967): 790–801; Robert W. Hodge and Paul M. Siegal, "Nonvertical Dimensions of Social Stratification" in *The Logic of Social Hierarchies,* ed. Edward O. Laumann *et al.* (Chicago: Markham, 1970), pp. 512–520.

incongruous. Lurking behind this mode of explanation, it would seem, is the early liberal assumption of the rational individual. Early liberals tended to assume that behavior results from a continuous series of pleasure-pain, profit-loss calculations. Basically, early liberalism explained behavior by reference to the alleged rationality of economic markets and to a primitive psychology of basic hunger and gain drives, and by assuming that the unity of statuses found among the successful classes must be psychologically normal. The consistency explanation in social science is probably best seen as a modern version of this assumption.

Sociocultural systems are often contradictory and ambiguous in the demands they place on individuals, and as a result personalities become contradictory and ambiguous. There is little evidence, in other words, that human beings have any psychological need to think things out or to introduce coherence into their lives. Despite the sophisticated psychological concepts that abound in this area,[41] the simple fact remains that unless people are taught to integrate their values and thoughts they do not do so, and do not recognize or regret the lack of such integration. In short, the consistency explanation is in large part a product of social scientists' attribution of their own predilections to ordinary people (and thus to the empirical nature of society).

Doubts about the usefulness of the consistency mode of explanation do not mean that contradictory or unsatisfactory statuses have no relevance to behavior. A great many auxiliary ideas must be introduced, however, to extract whatever utility this idea possesses. It is interesting that consistency theorists have begun to employ a perceptual variable involving subjective awareness of inconsistency, and a variable involving degree of attachment to groups, or the nature of an individual's interpersonal relations, to aid them in their analysis. In doing so they are drawing on the full inventory of sociological analysis and enlarging considerably on consistency theory as such.

Consistency analysis does raise an interesting question: how does American society cohere, given its enormous number of actual and potential contradictions? An initial step toward an answer to this question is to sharply qualify the notion of the rational individual, and to search instead for the processes associated with actual behavior. What we want to know, in other words, is how Americans actually *experience* their society. When we have determined that, we will see that social systems have many ways to protect themselves against rationality (consistency).

In any case, we will assume throughout our study that there exists a causal process composed of a host of variables: income, wealth, occupation, education, family stability, age and expectation of life, mental and physical health, level

41. A prime example may be found in Leon Festinger, *A Theory of Cognitive Dissonance* (Evanston, Ill.: Row, Peterson, 1957). For a discussion of this and other psychological theories in relation to consistency analysis, see James A. Geschwender, "Continuities in Theories of Status Consistency and Cognitive Dissonance," *Social Forces* 46 (December 1967): 160–171; reprinted in Edward O. Laumann, Paul M. Siegal, and Robert W. Hodge, eds., *The Logic of Social Hierarchies* (Chicago: Markham, 1970), pp. 500–511.

and type of consumption, participation in group life, personality, and the operation of political and legal forces. But despite the fact that we must adopt a model of multiple and reciprocal causation and be on the alert for the special effects of status inconsistencies, our primary assumption will be that a number of key variables — especially income, wealth, occupation, and education — best account for the phenomena of inequality in America, and for levels of consistency and inconsistency as well.

The analysis of social mobility

Inconsistency of positions in the various dimensions of stratification is associated strongly with a class system, or economically expansive society. In other words, uneven mobility up (or down) the various dimensions of stratification, induced by industrialization and other factors, causes inconsistency. For this and other reasons, therefore, sociologists have devoted a great deal of attention to social mobility.

Types of mobility

In stratification analysis, *mobility* refers to movement (or lack of movement) between different social classes or strata. In the past, disproportionate attention has been paid to upward mobility, though, of course, reference to any type of vertical mobility logically implies downward mobility and lack of mobility. While numerous studies of mobility exist, it cannot be said that our knowledge of this phenomenon has advanced significantly. However, a number of assertions can be made with relative confidence. It appears that most upward and downward mobility takes place between adjacent strata; large jumps, such as from the working class to the upper middle class (professional and managerial occupations), are rare. Second, overall rates of upward mobility are not as large as is popularly believed; overall rates in the various industrial countries do not differ very much; and there appear to have been no obvious changes in mobility rates over time.

S. M. Miller has suggested that downward mobility is a better indicator of stratification fluidity than is upward mobility. In his comparative analysis, Miller found considerable amounts of downward mobility across a large number of societies at various stages of development.[42] As he cautioned, however, comparisons and generalizations in this area are difficult because research is not based on standard categories and faulty interpretations are easy to make. Of special significance is the fact that the high rates of downward mobility from nonmanual to manual labor are not necessarily significant. Indeed, the differences between lower white-collar and manual strata may be much less than people think. (This point affects our interpretation of upward mobility as well.) In any case, we have little recent data about downward

42. S. M. Miller, "Comparative Social Mobility: A Trend Report and Bibliography," *Current Sociology* 9, no. 1 (1960): 1–89.

mobility, and exact knowledge in this area is one of the most urgent tasks in stratification research.

The essence of the clumsy term *lack of mobility* is that individuals and families do not move from the stratum into which they are born. A number of distinctions should be kept in mind with reference to this idea. Static stratification positions based on ascription are characteristic, of course, of caste and estate systems (usually referred to as closed systems of mobility), as opposed to class societies (usually referred to as open systems).[43] Thus, one meaning of a zero rate of mobility in industrial society is that ascriptive barriers — such as racism, poverty, religious-ethnic discrimination, and, in a special sense, sexism — prevent people from rising on the social ladder. The degree of rigidity of such barriers is of interest because it is also a measure of equal opportunity mobility. (An important mobility analysis that contains a measure of equal opportunity mobility will be discussed shortly.) A lack of mobility also exists when an absolute increase in benefits is unaccompanied by a relative increase (a distinction that will be discussed more fully shortly).

People can be stationary in a variety of other ways, however. *Horizontal mobility* (accompanied or not by geographic mobility)[44] is a change of occupation *within* a stratum. For example, a sales manager for a corporation becomes an advertising executive; a scientist for the Department of Interior becomes a professor of geology; a milk-truck driver becomes a bus driver; and so on.

Intragenerational, intergenerational, and social-origins mobility

Sociologists have focused on three distinct aspects of social mobility, usually emphasizing vertical mobility. The first is *intragenerational or career mobility. Here the analyst follows individuals' careers to see what paths they follow, the barriers they face, how far they progress, and so on.* The lives of successful people are of perennial interest, and much has been written about and by individuals who have struggled and prevailed against great obstacles. A good deal of fiction has also been written on this theme, most notably Horatio Alger's novels.[45] Alger's 135 novels, written during the latter third of the nineteenth century, were not far from some important truths about social mobility. His heroes were middle class boys, carefully socialized to Protestant bourgeois

43. That *open* and *closed systems of mobility* are misleading terms will become apparent.

44. Geographic mobility is of interest because it alerts us to some interesting consequences of the clustering and dispersion of class elements: thus the high concentration of particular class elements in political capitals, residential neighborhoods, research and development centers, and retirement areas all help to produce stratification-related phenomena of considerable importance.

45. Much of the following is based on R. Richard Wohl, "The Rags to Riches Story: An Episode in Secular Idealism" in *Class Status, and Power: Social Stratification in Comparative Perspective,* 2nd ed., eds. Reinhard Bendix and Seymour M. Lipset (New York: Free Press, 1966), pp. 501–506.

ways, who began the ascent to success only through a lucky break. Despite their mechanical plots, wooden characters, and unabashed vulgarity, these novels were phenomenally successful, perhaps mostly because they offered a detailed, colorful picture of city life in an age when America's rural migration to the city was in full swing. The Horatio Alger theme has undergone modernization during the course of the twentieth century. It is now embodied by slum children who gain success through hard work and virtue and, as such, is a proper target of ridicule for those who are knowledgeable in the ways of social mobility.

The Horatio Alger myth, like all stories about virtuous, talented individuals who rise from humble beginnings, should be scrutinized carefully and even with suspicion. For one thing, such stories are far from typical; for another, the individual's "humble" beginnings are often staged apprenticeships for well-placed sons, such as the son who begins his career by driving a truck in his father's factory and within a few years becomes a vice-president.

Too much attention is usually given to occupational mobility, diverting attention from the numerous other channels of mobility: marriage, political life, carefully planned consumption (on a number of fronts), crime, education, friendship, family connections, and the operation of religious, ethnic, and racial forces. But occupation is undeniably central to mobility in industrial society, and increasingly such mobility (or the lack of it) occurs within the various bureaucracies that now dominate our institutional life.[46]

The growing importance of mobility in organizations is part and parcel of a major transformation in American society, the relative decline of small economic enterprises as channels of mobility and the relative growth of mobility through formal and vocational-professional education.[47] The role played by education in mobility (which is much misunderstood, as we will see later) focuses attention on an individual's family-of-origin, since education takes place during the formative years of an individual's life. Thus we arrive at the second aspect of mobility: *intergenerational mobility, or analysis of the relation between parents' class position and their children's, especially sons'*. (Because studies in this area mostly involve father-to-son mobility, our report focuses on males and neglects females.) The analysis of intergenerational mobility is attractive superficially because it appears to tell us how open or closed a social system is over time. Its study, however, is fraught with diffi-

46. The importance of occupational context, as well as the need to examine other channels and forms of mobility, is emphasized by Harold L. Wilensky, "Measures and Effects of Social Mobility" in *Social Structure and Mobility in Economic Development,* eds. Neil J. Smelser and Seymour M. Lipset (Chicago: Aldine, 1966), chap. 3. Some hints about the variety and nuances of mobility can be culled from Anselm L. Strauss, *The Contexts of Social Mobility* (Chicago: Aldine, 1971). For a pioneering attempt to construct mathematical models to aid in the analysis of organizational mobility, see Harrison C. White, *Chains of Opportunity: System Models of Mobility in Organizations* (Cambridge, Mass.: Harvard University Press, 1970).

47. Small business is still a powerful theme in American life, and large numbers continue to move into and out of the self-employed category. We are talking here, it should be emphasized, of a relative decline.

culties, and it cannot be said that such studies[48] have enlightened us much about the openness or rigidity of the American class system. One need only realize, for example, that the son of a black postman has a better chance of upward mobility than the son of a white Protestant doctor to appreciate the conundrums in this area. Of first importance in tracing father-to-son mobility is the difficulty of matching occupations from one generation to the next. Second, it is hard to identify generations, since "fathers" and "sons" can range over a large agespan.[49] Third, the decision to focus on the father-to-son relation makes for the omission of fathers who had no sons and households run by divorced, unmarried, and widowed women, many of whom raise sons.

Other complications that stand in the way of a more precise prediction of a son's career in terms of his father's class can be mentioned in passing. Sons can skip college, for example, and inherit a business directly; they can enter college after spending a few years traveling or being self-employed; or they can voluntarily live, at least for a while, below their class level of origin, and thus be ignored by some methods of collecting data. And sons can obviously be affected differently by such social events as economic booms or busts, war, governmental science policies, and the like, depending on their location in rural or urban areas, their age, and so on. Despite all this, we know that a father's class position exerts a significant influence on the amount and quality of education received by his son, which is, in turn, a major determinant of the son's future occupation.[50]

The inability to make precise comparisons between generations, and thus to make judgments about the openness or rigidity of a given phase of social development, does not mean that father-to-son studies are not valuable. When they take the form of *social origins mobility, they tell us from what social level the occupants of various occupations have been recruited.* Here the analyst seeks to determine whence the incumbents of various positions have come. Whether school teachers, for example, are drawn primarily from the

48. Perhaps the most successful of these is Natalie Rogoff, *Recent Trends in Occupational Mobility* (New York: Free Press, 1953). For an appreciation and criticism of this work and a general discussion of the methodological complexities in studying this and other forms of mobility, see Otis Dudley Duncan, "Methodological Issues in the Analysis of Social Mobility" in *Social Structure and Mobility in Economic Development,* eds. Neil J. Smelser and Seymour M. Lipset (Chicago: Aldine, 1966), chap. 2.

49. The study of mobility — indeed, all sociological analysis — must account for the age factor much more accurately than has so far been done. It is not overly productive, for example, to compare "fathers" in one generation, ranging in age from 20 to 50, with "fathers" in another generation, who in turn vary enormously in age.

50. For the educational and other mechanisms that mediate between socioeconomic background and occupational and income achievement, see Otis D. Duncan and Peter M. Blau, *The American Occupational Structure* (New York: John Wiley and Sons, 1967); Otis D. Duncan, David L. Featherman, and Beverly Duncan, *Socioeconomic Background and Achievement* (New York: Seminar Press, 1972); and William H. Sewell and Robert M. Hauser, "Causes and Consequences of Higher Education: Models of the Status Attainment Process," *American Journal of Agricultural Economics* 54 (December 1972): 851–861.

lower or upper segments of the middle class will make a big difference in the nature of that occupation. Similarly, if the officer ranks of the military or the senior officials of the State Department are drawn from a narrow class base, occupational performance can be expected to be different than if their class base were broad. Many key occupations have been studied, including business people, teachers, civil servants, legislators, and the military. We will have occasion to refer to such studies later.

Structural versus equal opportunity mobility

In assessing mobility phenomena, care should be taken to distinguish between structural or "forced" mobility and equal opportunity or "circulation" mobility.[51] A great deal of social mobility is due to causal processes that alter economic opportunities. Examples are technological innovation, war, public and private credit policies, depressions, and public tax and land-use policies. One of the most dramatic transformations in American society in the past century has been the radical decline of farming and rise of factory and office occupations. A great deal of father-to-son upward mobility, therefore, should be seen as the "forced" departure from the land of millions of rural people, including blacks. Much of this structural mobility is the result of the growth of white-collar occupations, a process which should be interpreted with great care. A great many white-collar jobs, for example, are difficult to distinguish from working class jobs (the distinction between mental and manual work notwithstanding). Also, most of the mobility into white-collar ranks involves working-class individuals, which lends lower-level white-collar ranks a working class outlook that matches their objective economic functions and income. And, finally, a large percentage of the increase in white-collar occupations is accounted for by women, who for the most part share the class levels of their fathers or husbands and therefore should not automatically be assumed to increase the number of white-collar families.[52]

It is important to keep structural mobility in mind when trying to assess the relative roles played in the mobility process by human nature, talent, equal opportunity, individualism, and equal competition (roughly, equal opportunity or "circulation" mobility). It would seem, basically, that mobility is socially induced, but occurs so fitfully and selectively as to create the misleading impression of stemming from the capricious way in which nature distributes ability and ambition. In their valuable analysis comparing intergenerational mobility rates in Australia, Italy, and the United States, Broom and Jones

51. This distinction is derived from an important paper on mobility, Leonard Broom and F. Lancaster Jones, "Father-to-Son Mobility: Australia in Comparative Perspective," *American Journal of Sociology* 74 (January 1969): 333–342.

52. In this connection, see Richard F. Hamilton's warning against exaggerating the difference between the lower-middle and working classes, "The Marginal Middle Class: A Reconsideration," *American Sociological Review* 31 (April 1966): 192–199. Hamilton has explored the political implications of this insight in an important book, which we will come across again, *Class and Politics in the United States* (New York: John Wiley and Sons, 1972).

conclude that while the United States has the highest rate of overall mobility, Australia has a higher rate of equal opportunity mobility (a larger amount of the American rate being structural in nature).

Absolute versus relative mobility

Of decisive importance in studying social mobility is the distinction between absolute and relative mobility. *By absolute mobility is meant the general upward absolute movement of the class system itself as measured by income (rising standard of living), occupation (more brainwork, less manual labor), and education (more literacy, more years of school completed).* Seen in this way, the entire American population has experienced upward mobility during the last century (see Figure 3-1), a phenomenon that resembles structural mobility (economic expansion). *Relative mobility, on the other hand, is movement by individuals and families (and various other collectivities and groups) up, down, or across the line(s) separating one social class or stratum from another.* Relative mobility also stems from economic expansion, which provides opportunities for some individuals to rise above their class of origin; and, of course, economic contraction can plummet individuals into the classes below. Relative mobility can also stem from noneconomic "equal" opportunity institutions, such as education, and governmental efforts to subsidize training or combat discrimination, but it is very difficult to measure the impact of such institutions and their power must not be exaggerated. There is a strong tendency to assume that equal opportunity leads to relative mobility, as well as to structural mobility (economic expansion). Actually, the reverse is more accurate: economic expansion leads to structural and relative mobility, as well as to efforts to promote equal (and unequal) opportunities.

Keeping the foregoing distinctions in mind, it is easy to understand how it is possible for a family to experience dramatic improvements in its absolute class position over two or more generations but to remain in the same social stratum. Of considerable importance in understanding this process is the knowledge that abundance does not eliminate or even reduce overall scarcity. Industrial society elaborates new forms of scarcity ("needs") to replace old ones, and one should not automatically assume that absolute increases in affluence, or in educational and occupational skills, reduce the relative distance between the various classes.[53] Confusion of absolute and relative mobility is perhaps the major source of errors about class stratification, and every effort should be made to keep this distinction clearly in mind.

A valuable contribution to understanding this distinction has been made by Norbert F. Wiley, who has identified a special variety of absolute movement unaccompanied by class mobility and aptly termed it a *mobility trap*.[54]

53. For a fuller discussion, see Chapter 4.
54. "The Ethnic Mobility Trap and Stratification Theory," *Social Problems* 15 (Fall 1967): 147–159; reprinted in Peter I. Rose, ed., *The Study of Society: An Integrated Anthology,* 2nd ed. (New York: Random House, 1970), pp. 397–408.

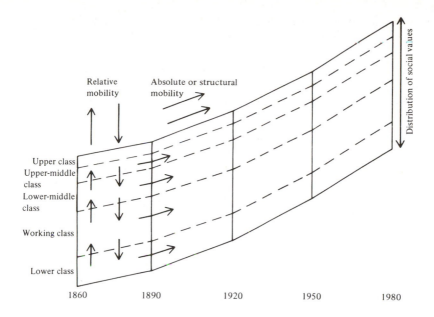

Figure 3-1 A Nonempirical Construct Depicting the Absolute Upward Movement of the American Class Structure and the Absence of Change in the Relative Distribution of Social Values Despite Upward, Downward, and Lack of Mobility

The mobility trap is mobility *within* a stratum. Though Wiley focuses on the ethnic mobility trap, he lists four distinct types:

1. The "age-grade trap," or the tendency of age and sex groups to adopt prestige values that conflict with those of older age groups. Thus, popularity as a sports star or beauty queen in high school may well be a barrier to social mobility for those who cannot break into professional sports or the field of entertainment.

2. The "overspecialization trap," or lower-level highly specialized administrative jobs from which one cannot be promoted.

3. The "localite trap," or the pursuit of local prestige at the expense of national standing. Certain occupations, such as social worker, planner, school superintendent, professor, and clergyman, increasingly allow for mobility only on a nationwide basis.

4. The "minority group trap," or advancement within a minority group in lieu of advancement into majority structures.

Absolute and relative ambition

LaMar Empey has made an important distinction in the area of ambition (or aspirations) that has significant bearing on a number of problems in stratification analysis, including social mobility. In his study of high school seniors in the State of Washington in 1954, Empey found that one must distinguish between absolute and relative occupational aspirations. If one asks the various classes about their aspirations in terms of a single hierarchy of occupations, it is clear that the upper classes aspire to upper occupations more frequently than do the lower classes. But if one examines the strength of aspirations in terms of starting-point, it becomes clear that the lower classes want to move beyond their class positions at birth as much if not more than those in the classes above them. Testing further, Empey also found little difference between preferred and anticipated occupational goals.[55]

The implications of Empey's findings have been followed up by Ralph Turner in his sophisticated study of the social factors affecting ambition. To help us conceptualize mobility in an open class system of stratification, Turner uses the analogies of a race and a ladder. By studying high school seniors selected to represent as accurately as possible the nonethnic twelfth-grade population of Los Angeles, Turner also found strong educational and occupational mobility aspirations among all classes in both an absolute and a relative sense.[56] The implication is clear: one must envisage mobility in the United States as both a race to the top and a climb up a ladder, and must be careful to specify which is being referred to. And, of course, one must carefully distinguish between aspirations and actual mobility.

Mobility and class consistency

As we have noted, there is a tendency in all systems of stratification for families and individuals to receive consistent types of benefits in each of the major dimensions and subdimensions of stratification and for "hereditary" strata to appear. This tendency is more pronounced in caste and estate systems, but one must be careful in those cases, too, not to overestimate the amount of consistency or to assume an identity between the hierarchies of class, prestige, and power. Maintaining a rigorous distinction between class, prestige, and power is even more important in the class system of stratification, since its various dimensions tend not only to interlock and merge but also to oppose and contradict each other in some respects. For example, two Americans with the same incomes may have occupations of widely disparate prestige; or they may have the same incomes and occupations but widely disparate prestige because of race, religion, family lineage, taste, or other factors. Disparities between the various dimensions of inequality are made possible by the unique capacity of the human personality to harbor incongruities and contradictions and by the capacity of society to function not only despite such contradictions and incongruities, but often because of them. The general

55. LaMar T. Empey, "Social Class and Occupational Aspiration: A Comparison of Absolute and Relative Measurement," *American Sociological Review* 21 (December 1956): 703–709.

56. Ralph H. Turner, *The Social Context of Ambition* (San Francisco: Chandler, 1964), chap. 3.

causes of such disparities are the rich complexity of values pursued by modern society — for example, the American population simultaneously pursues the values of success, equality, educational and professional achievement, self-discipline, high consumption levels, salvation, nationalism, internationalism, religion, ethnicity, religious and ethnic superiority, and racism[57] — and the lack of formal coordination of its various institutional sectors. Given well-established but incongruous values and beliefs, it is not surprising that individuals and groups may rise in one dimension without a corresponding rise in the others (for example, the *nouveau riche*, the economically successful Jew); or may descend in one dimension, such as the economy, without a corresponding decline in another dimension, such as the polity (for example, small business people, certain types of farmers). It is important, in other words, to distinguish between mobility in one hierarchy and movement or lack of movement in the several hierarchies that compose the full system of stratification.

Class mobility and rigidity

In thinking about class rigidity and class mobility, care must also be taken to avoid the obvious mistake of assuming that these two processes are mutually contradictory. A substantial rate of social mobility is perfectly compatible with a high degree of class rigidity. What this means in simple terms is that it is possible for individuals and families at the top of a class hierarchy to remain stationary even though other individuals and families are moving up. To understand this process one need only remember that the size of an upper class relative to other classes may remain unchanging in terms of percentage while its absolute numerical size increases greatly. Thus, if 10 percent of the American population is considered to be upper-middle class between 1900 and 1975, the absolute numbers in this class will be much larger in 1975 than in 1900. It is possible, therefore, for most of the families composing the top 10 percent in 1900 to remain at the top because of class perpetuation and simultaneously for considerable social mobility to take place. What this means, in effect, is that the original 10 percent (minus any that have succumbed to downward mobility) is joined by families that have risen with the expansion of the American economy and population.

This point can be stated differently by focusing on the fact that different social classes have different birth rates, the upper classes consistently producing fewer children than the lower. What happens, in other words, is that the upper-middle class produces only enough sons to replace part of itself, and vacancies at the top have to be filled from below (overwhelmingly from the ranks of the lower-middle class). (As daughters in the upper classes become more important sources of recruitment into the upper reaches of our occupational system, they may deprive the lower classes of some mobility.)

57. This is an idiomatic list drawn from perhaps the best classification and analysis of American values, Robin M. Williams, Jr., *American Society: A Sociological Interpretation,* 3rd ed. (New York: Alfred A. Knopf, 1970), chap. 11.

It is necessary to keep this overall compatibility in mind whenever we refer to these two salient features of class stratification: the tendency for benefits at various levels to congeal and reinforce each other, producing class rigidity, and the tendency in an expansive society for various elements to move up and down in the class system.

The dysfunctions of social mobility

We are so accustomed to thinking of upward mobility as a good thing that a brief word of caution about this process is in order. Melvin Tumin has identified some unintended dysfunctional consequences of the tradition of achievement and success.[58] A high rate of social mobility gives rise to insecurity among the newly mobile, which interferes with performance of role responsibilities in their newly won positions. In addition, the general approval and encouragement of social mobility, as well as the reality of success, make role responsibility difficult at *all* levels as *all* think of rising above their present positions. This blurring of status and role responsibilities as a result of high rates and high expectations of mobility, Tumin claims, induces insecurity at the personal level and *anomie* at the social level. Another latent function — or, rather, dysfunction — of social mobility, according to Tumin, is the buying-off of intellectuals and the stifling of social criticism. Surprisingly, Tumin fails to cite the tendency of social mobility to rob lower groups of their leadership through co-optation, a process of enormous consequence for, say, the black American. Perhaps this process is now known well enough and practiced consciously enough to qualify as a manifest function.[59]

The general pattern of American mobility

Because the foregoing ideas about social mobility violate some commonsense understandings and accepted *mores*, it might be useful to summarize them even at the risk of oversimplification. Perhaps the most important thing to keep in mind about stratification in America, and industrial countries in general, is that the class structure as a whole has moved upward. Thus, there have occurred a consistent absolute rise in income, but little relative equalization of income; a consistent upgrading of occupational skills, but little relative equalization of occupational statuses; and a consistent absolute rise in the number of years of school completed, but little relative equalization in education.[60] As a consequence, one must undertake any analysis of mobility with

58. "Some Unapplauded Consequences of Social Mobility in a Mass Society," *Social Forces* 36 (October 1957): 32–37; reprinted in Jack L. Roach *et al.*, eds., *Social Stratification in the United States* (Englewood Cliffs, N.J.: Prentice-Hall, 1969), pp. 575–582.
59. For example, many public policies are designed to pacify the black American by providing employment or welfare. An extended discussion of manifest and latent functions follows shortly.
60. For an empirical analysis of these areas, see Chapter 4.

the image in mind of a class structure that is static insofar as relative differences in income, occupation, and education (and other factors) are concerned, but that is moving up an inclined plane (see Figure 3-1). In employing this model, however, it is important to note that while the American class structure is static in terms of the abstract distribution of its central social values (aggregate income, wealth, occupational status, education), the families composing any given class do not necessarily remain stationary throughout the lifetimes of a particular set of parents or over generations (relative mobility).

The salient features of social mobility can be listed succinctly: (1) mobility rates are composed of structural as well as equal opportunity segments; (2) aggregates of individuals are prepared for mobility, or the lack of it, by the existing class structure (that is, by their class or family-of-origin); and (3) upward mobility does not necessarily mean that families at any given level are displaced. Downward mobility, like upward mobility, should be interpreted in social terms and not merely as the result of personal demerit. For example, an upper class manufacturer of wooden office furniture is ruined by the advent of metal furniture; a semiskilled worker, aged forty-five, is replaced by a machine and never works regularly again.

Perhaps the greatest pitfall in the analysis of class dynamics is the confusion of apparent mobility (absolute upward movement) with real mobility (relative gains). It must be remembered that absolute gains in such class factors as income, occupation, and education do not necessarily represent movement from one class to another. To illustrate the latter point, one can cite a number of hypothetical family histories characterized by absolute gains in class factors unaccompanied by upward mobility. If, for example, the grandson of a blacksmith who earned $500 per year is an automobile worker earning $10,000 per year, one cannot speak of upward social mobility; in fact, this could be a case of downward mobility. If the grandson of an independent farmer with no formal education is a bank teller with a high school education, one again cannot speak of mobility from one class to another. (See Figure 3-2, which contrasts types of mobility.)

The greatest source of confusion about contemporary stratification is incompletely thought-out comparisons between modern and premodern societies. It cannot be overemphasized that the transition from agrarian estate systems to industrial class systems is a movement not toward equality but toward a *new type* of inequality. Economic expansion has made most people wealthier, healthier, more skilled, better educated, and the like than their forebears, but modern populations are just as unequal, relative to their own societies, as people were in the past. The changing composition of human populations due to the impact of absolute or structural mobility and the unchanging degree of inequality are depicted graphically in Figure 3-3.

In analyzing social mobility, therefore, it is essential not to prejudge trends. It is especially important not to assume automatically that overall mobility is producing a society composed primarily of middle class families and individuals, or that such mobility represents progress toward the abolition of

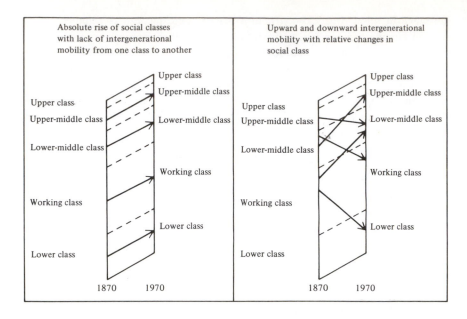

Figure 3-2   Absolute (or Structural) and Relative Intergenerational Mobility

ascriptive barriers to mobility. (This is the ideology of convergence.) To do so is to confuse affluence (absolute mobility) with equality of opportunity and substantive equality. The United States has been and remains a very unequal society, characterized by significant differentials in ascriptive advantage (birth into different classes), and there is as yet no way to tell whether these differences are increasing or decreasing.

Social stratification and sociological analysis

Before ending our discussion of the current state of stratification analysis, let us look briefly at the relation of stratification analysis to some of the key ideas and problems in sociological analysis. We will begin by discussing the central and creative role played in sociology by the functional mentality.

Stratification and functional analysis

During the period of the early development of capitalism, liberal theorists denied the reality of existing social groups, whether in the form of families, established churches, guilds, state monopolies, or estates. In opposition to what they alleged were parasitic, irrational, and artificial bodies based on birth and custom, liberal theorists set out to identify the real and natural individual and society, invariably defining the real and natural in terms of functional (especially economic) performance. The basic outlook of the functional mentality is to think in terms of concrete causes and consequences and to evaluate institutions

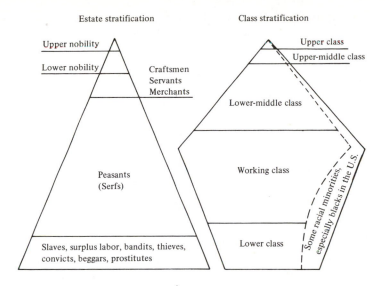

Estate stratification   Class stratification

Upper nobility

Lower nobility

Craftsmen
Servants
Merchants

Upper class
Upper-middle class

Lower-middle class

Peasants
(Serfs)

Working class

Slaves, surplus labor, bandits, thieves,
convicts, beggars, prostitutes

Lower class

Some racial minorities, especially blacks in the U.S.

Figure 3-3   Economic Expansion (Absolute or Structural Mobility), Changing
Population Composition, and Unchanging Degree of Inequality

and social systems in terms of operational success and failure. Its basic stance
is to reject philosophies that allege that society's source is God, tradition,
or logic.

In the Anglo-American world the functional outlook took the form of
laissez-faire theory during the eighteenth and nineteenth centuries, and much
of English and American history of the past century or so may be interpreted
as an attempt to evaluate the laissez-faire theory critically as an economic and
social philosophy. The gist of laissez-faire theory is that society has an inherent
functionality provided that human beings are allowed to pursue their own
interests. Basic to this argument is the assumption that there exists a rational
mechanism called the free market, which will see to it that the activities and
interests of such diverse groups as bankers, manufacturers, farmers, and
workers are meshed and harmonized, and that each gets his or her just deserts.
Differences and conflicts between economic groupings are precisely that:
economic or functionally specific differences that are natural and that will be
settled by the logic of free, competitive economic markets.

The development of a functional perspective in sociology is no accident,
given this general background. As we have indicated, one emphasis of the
functional school is highly detrimental to class theory — namely, the tendency
to define society as a functionally interdependent naturalistic system containing
inherent processes that integrate its various parts. This model of society has
its uses, but class theory is starved if processes that make for dysfunction, such
as instability, exploitation, and conflict, are neglected. (This is the conflict
school of social stratification.) In our analysis of the United States' class

system, we will try to give sufficient attention to both traditions in stratification theory: the one that sees society groping to develop functional structures and processes and the one that sees it as an exploitative system generating conflict and instability.

In conducting our analysis we will rely heavily on the functional or scientific method, which is not the same thing as a functional substantive theory of society and stratification. Sociologists disagree about the meaning of functional analysis, and there are numerous controversies surrounding it. For our part, we have adopted a simple definition: *functional analysis* is the identification of causes and consequences in human behavior, with due regard to conceptual and other methodological problems such as the use of logic, semantic analysis, and the construction of research designs, and to the need for empirical verification of assertions. In this sense, functional analysis is synonymous with science.[61]

Historically, the functional outlook has been used to support a variety of substantive functional theories of society by such theorists as Plato, Aristotle, John of Salisbury, Adam Smith, Karl Marx, Joseph Stalin, and some contemporary functionalists in sociology. Provided it does not commit itself to any single inclusive conception of society, or substantive or normative theory, the functional method — the analysis of how something works or fails to work — need not be biased.[62] To rid itself of bias, however, a functional analysis must establish standards against which judgments of function and dysfunction can be made, and must define the meaning of such slippery terms as *ongoing system, functions, functional units,* and *integration.* One of the main safeguards against ideological bias that has emerged in functional thought is the distinction between manifest and latent functions. This distinction helps to avoid one of the most dangerous pitfalls in stratification analysis, the tendency to take one's own society's definition of itself, and of its stratification system, at face value.

Manifest and latent functions in stratification analysis

The basic problem to which the idea of manifest and latent functions addresses itself is an old one, and it has elicited many different solutions during the course of human history. Human beings have long recognized that human behavior often has unpredictable, arbitrary, and ironic consequences. Things do not turn out as expected or desired; the best-laid plans are thwarted. In other words, fate or luck or providence seems to play a large part in the affairs of mankind. Often the very words used to describe this problem presuppose prescientific explanations. The words *fate, luck, irony* and *providence,* for

61. See Kingsley Davis, "The Myth of Functional Analysis as a Special Method in Sociology and Anthropology," *American Sociological Review* 24 (December 1959): 757–772; also available as Bobbs-Merrill reprint no. S-567.

62. See Robert K. Merton, *Social Theory and Social Structure,* rev. ed. (New York: Free Press, 1968), chap. 3; also in his *On Theoretical Sociology* (New York: Free Press, 1967), chap. 3; available in paperback.

example, are all prescientific solutions to the problem of unpredictability in human affairs.

Perhaps the first scientific approach to this problem was the work of Emile Durkheim, though it had been anticipated by many. Durkheim insisted that social facts must be used to explain social facts, and that to employ this concept of causation properly one must develop the idea of function. It is undeniable that people consciously intend certain functions (or outcomes) of their behavior, such as when they undertake to build a house, fight a war, or unify a nation. Durkheim's originality lies in his conscious identification of the unintended consequences of social facts. In analyzing crime, for example, he pointed out that though crime is dysfunctional to society, it also has functional consequences. For example, crime stimulates revulsion and thus rekindles and reinforces conventional sentiments and beliefs. Further, crime is part-and-parcel of normal behavior in that it stems from the same motives and skills that animate law-abiding citizens, such as creativity, ambition, and the sanctity of individual conscience.

In contemporary sociology the formal definition of this idea and the terms used to describe it — *manifest* and *latent functions* — are the work of Robert K. Merton.[63] Thanks to Merton's work, sociologists are now easily alerted to the insufficiency of analyzing causation and consequences simply in terms of the motivations or manifest intentions of an actor, whose attempt to achieve a stated objective may have unintended consequences — recognized or not — for himself and/or others. And sociologists are now aware that "bad" behavior, such as crime, apathy, and poverty, is the outcome of "good" behavior, such as ambition, achievement, and prosperity. In other words, deviance and social problems stem from the central institutional structures of society.[64]

The concept of manifest and latent functions and dysfunctions is highly germane to the field of stratification analysis. For example, the strong American tradition of equality has the manifest functions of promoting equality of opportunity, restricting racism, granting women the vote, and the like. But the tradition of equality also has an important and less well-known latent function. The most obvious manifest meaning of *equality* is the opposite of inequality. For purposes of understanding class stratification, however, the cultural norm of equality must also be seen as a necessary supplement to cultural norms and values that recognize and accept inequality. Inequality in an achievement society requires a mechanism to spur all of its members to compete for scarce positions and a means of justifying itself ideologically: this is the special latent function of egalitarianism. If equality of opportunity and competition for positions conform to rules and standards of achievement, the

63. *Social Theory and Social Structure*, rev. ed. (New York: Free Press. 1968), chap. 3; also in his *On Theoretical Sociology* (New York: Free Press, 1967), chap. 3; available in paperback.
64. This is the central theme of perhaps the best overall sociological examination of the nature of social problems, Robert K. Merton and Robert A. Nisbet, eds., *Contemporary Social Problems*, 3rd ed. (New York: Harcourt Brace Jovanovich, 1971).

structure of inequality is alleged to reflect the unequal distribution of innate talents and acquired skills in individuals. It is through the ideology of equality, in other words, that the class system of stratification affirms both the indispensability of inequality and the validity of its own structure of inequality. At the same time it spurs all individuals to exert their best efforts within that system. The result is the "classless" society of popular thought, or the "nonegalitarian classlessness" referred to by Ossowski. Those who are satisfied with society see these outcomes as latent functions; those who are discontented with society see them as latent dysfunctions.

There are many other examples of latent functions and dysfunctions in the field of social stratification. Merton himself uses Veblen's insight into the latent prestige functions of some economic activities to illustrate the distinction between manifest and latent functions, and to point out that conspicuous consumption is now often engaged in consciously. A latter-day variation of Veblen's classic insight is the analysis of the world of fashion by Bernard Barber and Lyle S. Lobel.[65] According to Barber and Lobel, women's fashions help to reconcile "the dilemma between equality and difference" by simultaneously stressing uniformity and variation in women's clothing styles. Strain between these two emphases is reduced by the "trickle down" process whereby upper class fashions are eventually copied and made available to the classes below.

The analysis of latent functions is fraught with difficulties, especially if one engages in the exploration of unconscious motives. But it is clear that one cannot understand social structure simply by examining and recording public opinion or the conscious beliefs and values that prompt behavior. Stratification theorists who rely exclusively on such data will, in other words, be blind to certain processes that promote or undermine America's system of social stratification. To restrict stratification analysis to what people think and feel and to examine the data of behavior in terms of the assumptions of progress, equality, and competition for success is to be objective in the ideological sense of the term. It is to study the *results* of social stratification and to use only a selected range of social data to define, and thus legitimate, the existing structure of social power and its class system. Such analysis, in other words, has the latent function of supporting the existing structure of stratification, and such support throws the weight of sociology on the side of those who benefit most from the present order of things and people. It prevents recognition of the possibility that the United States, like all other societies, is an historical rather than a natural society, a society fashioned from a particular configuration of power factors and still subject to the problems of social power.

65. " 'Fashion' in Women's Clothes and the American Social System," *Social Forces* 31 (December 1952): 124–131; also available in Reinhard Bendix and Seymour M. Lipset, eds., *Class, Status, and Power: A Reader in Social Stratification,* 1st ed. (New York: Free Press, 1953), pp. 323–332.

The dangers of universalism

Ironically, one of the pitfalls confronting those who seek knowledge about the American class system is the United States' penchant for rational discourse, its universalistic way of analyzing itself. This tendency characterizes lay as well as scientific thought. An example of this universalistic bias is the American preoccupation with formal equality: the vote, equality before the law, common citizenship and territory (nationalism), equal opportunities, liberty and justice for all, and fair competition. The theme of equality is broadly related to the middle class's tendency to think in terms of a universe of individuals with relatively fixed, equal attributes and to its proclivity for employing universalistic (that is, universally valid) norms to evaluate individual performance: I.Q., achievement tests, grades, industry, sobriety, frugality, punctuality, honesty, self-discipline, rational control, futurism, personal responsibility, and self-reliance.

The symbolic forms that characterize the American world view have roots in the basic institutional pattern of modern society. The logic of a mass-production money economy predisposes all to think of homogeneous units of labor and materials disposable and interchangeable through standardized, abstract currency units; common needs, likes, and dislikes; and common consumption patterns and facilities (public transit, public parks, cars, plumbing, beer, cigarettes, packaged food). Symbolic homogenization is reinforced by the mass media, whose content and advertising both present standardized and idealized versions of human nature, family life, romance and marriage, moral and political issues, and the like. Similar themes are apparent in politics. The logic of liberal democracy — for example, majority rule — leads to campaign platforms designed for universal appeal, and the liberal legal system enjoins judges and lawyers to think and act in terms of a universalistic legal code. The educational system affirms the universal rightness of the middle class way of life, while the Judaic-Christian religious tradition affirms the existence of a universal god and a universal moral code. All in all, the universalistic symbolic world is unique. Unlike the particularism of the caste and estate systems, which declare and expose inequality openly, the universal symbols of class society tend to disguise the nature of inequality and even to hide its existence.

Even the universalism of science can distort the perception of inequality. Though valid when used properly, the tendency to define modern populations by means of statistics is biased against the reality of inequality if a disproportionate emphasis is placed on averages, national or per capita; absolute figures relative to total population; or percentages of total population. We should exercise caution when we are told, for example, that average income or average life expectancy is a certain figure. Caution is also called for when we hear that a given number of people owns stock in America's corporations, that a given percentage of the electorate voted in the last federal election, or that the birth rate, crime rate, or divorce rate per 1,000 is a given figure. A quantitative approach to social analysis is proper and valuable — indeed, indispensable — for without it precise comparisons would be impossible. But we must not allow figures based exclusively on averages to predispose us to assume that a fictional average individual actually exists, or, at best, to think too much in terms of homogeneous fictional types. Furthermore, used to make absolute comparisons with the past, such figures tend to reinforce evolutionary liberalism, or the faith that progress is being made toward equality.

The problem of the comparative method

Comparison is indispensable to science, but valid comparisons are not easy to make. The comparison of two social systems presents special difficulties. For example, it is a truism in American thought that the United States is egalitarian as compared with preindustrial society. As we have suggested, however, even this belief is not unproblematic. The serf whose hardships are accounted for and compensated for by a vital religion is not necessarily worse off than a black American whose expectations are raised but never satisfied. Who can find comfort in comparing an American assembly-line worker, whose work provides no satisfaction or identity, with a medieval craftsman? Such comparisons are very difficult and subject to subtle distortions of all kinds, but it is exactly these sorts of comparisons that are commonly made. In other words, the analysis and evaluation of American society is confused when we derive satisfactions from real or alleged superiorities to other societies, since comparisons are invariably selective. For example, Americans might be prone to compare themselves with others in terms of wealth (plumbing, automobiles, telephones, food), hygiene, punctuality, and zest for work and to neglect other value areas. Of course, social scientists must compare societies if they hope to achieve certain levels of critical detachment and insight. Indeed, without comparison thought is impossible. But comparisons must be made of comparable categories. To compare an idealized version of the United States with a realistic version of other countries fosters not self-appraisal but complacency. To compare categories of ideas or values from one cultural context with superficially similar categories from other cultural contexts is to misdirect mental effort.

Those who practice the comparative method in social science are certainly more aware of these analytical problems than the lay public. But the scientific urge to develop abstractions tends to obscure the cultural uniqueness of every society, even similar societies. In addition to making sure that similar phenomena in different societies are compared, one must also compare societies with reference to their own ideas and values. But even when Americans compare their society with their ideals — a vital tradition in American history — they do not always escape the stereotypes all societies develop to justify the actual, or to fuse it with the ideal. In the United States, fusion of the actual and the ideal takes the primary form of a deep faith in the capacity of existing institutions, either in their present forms or with limited changes, to realize the American Dream. Social science, however, cannot afford the security the lay public derives from such a faith. It must always cultivate a critical stance toward the very phenomena that are considered most normal or natural. In other words, the treatment of *all* behavior as problematic marks the difference between science and ideology.

In our analysis and evaluation of the American class system, therefore, we will use the United States' own values and beliefs as our major reference-point, paying due regard to other forms of comparative data. We will discover what evidence exists to support our claim of a wide discrepancy between what America professes and what it practices. Perhaps we will conclude that the difficulty of achieving American values and beliefs lies not in human nature but in the values and beliefs themselves and the social structure which embodies them. The principle of equal opportunity is violated in the United States not because human nature is deficient but because Americans also believe in and value, for example, family life. As long as parents can pass on their own achievements or failures to their children, American values will conflict with one another. Other values and beliefs that impede achievement and equality of opportunity are not difficult to find. Many Americans, for example, place high values on skin color, religion, and national origin, all of which are irrelevant to achievement but highly relevant to social stratification.

It is time now to end our long introduction to the field of social stratification and to turn to direct analysis of the empirical materials of stratification in the United States. This introduction to social stratification was intended to familiarize the reader with the field's main issues and controversies, and with its goals, concepts, and methods. Such an introduction invariably spends more time talking about science than practicing it. In the next three parts, devoted respectively to class, prestige, and power, we will undertake stratification analysis itself.

PART 2

The American class dimension

4

The hierarchy of economic class values

IN THE CHAPTERS that make up Part Two, we will analyze the various aspects of the hierarchy of class. The distribution of income, wealth, occupations, and education will be the subject of Chapter 4. Given their intimate connection with economic status, family behavior and personal health have been defined as aspects of the overall class dimension and are analyzed in Chapter 5 as integral parts of the class hierarchy. And because education not only contributes to one's worth on economic markets, but also serves to transmit class standing from one generation to the next, we will analyze the relation between class origin and education in Chapter 6.

Income distribution
Absolute and relative income levels

The distribution of income and wealth is roughly uniform in all industrial countries. Despite variations due to historical circumstances, political ideology, and tax, defense, and welfare policies and the like, the oustanding characteristic of the material culture of industrial society — aside from the dramatic increase in the standard of living — is its radically unequal distribution. Of perhaps equal importance is the fact that this sharp inequality in the distribution of goods and services has been remarkably stable over the entire period for which we have reliable data. The inequality of income in the United States, for example, seems to be fixed over time and not to be affected by rising productivity, taxation, or the rise of the welfare state.[1] No understanding of class (economic) stratification is possible, therefore, unless one guards against the popular equation of rising productivity, progressive tax schedules, and the inauguration of the welfare state with a growing equality of material conditions. As we have suggested, one must distinguish clearly between criteria that determine absolute levels of goods and services and criteria designed to establish relative shares of income. It is especially important not to succumb to the popular ideology that equates rising productivity and income with a more egalitarian distribution of life chances. In fact, the evidence suggests quite the opposite: left to itself, a dynamic economy seems invariably to make everyone richer and more unequal. Of course, economies are no longer left to themselves, if they ever were. However, despite the growth of state management of economic and social phenomena, the evidence points to a general uniformity in the distribution of income and wealth over the entire period for which we have records. To appreciate fully the fact that a rise in the absolute standard of living has not significantly affected the *relative share* of national income enjoyed by the various income classes of any given industrial population, one may think of modern structures of stratification as a fleet of ships in a harbor: an incoming tide — rising productivity and a rising standard of living — does not diminish the differences between rowboats, cabin cruisers, cargo vessels, and giant ocean liners. Governmental policies are often interpreted as leading to equalization, but this is true only in a special sense. The net historical effect of all tax and public spending policies has not been to increase material equality but rather to prevent further extremes in income and wealth. In other words, whatever equalization has resulted from such policies has remained within certain boundaries; the data point to a remarkably unequal and stable distribution of income and wealth before and after taxes and before and after government spending.

Nearly all scholars in the field of income-wealth distribution in the United States now agree that there is no trend toward equality. Their agreement is most complete for the post–World War Two period. As we will see, the relative share of goods and services during this period — usually measured by comparing income fifths over time — was startlingly stable, despite unprecedented increases in the gross national product and in real living standards. The disagreement among scholars involves changes that may have taken place between approximately 1910 and 1945. Gabriel Kolko, for example, argues that no significant change in the structure of material inequality in the United

1. For a valuable popularization of this difficult subject, see Herman P. Miller, *Rich Man, Poor Man,* 2nd ed. (New York: Thomas Y. Crowell, 1971). While we will cite other studies in order to raise technical questions and provide up-to-date figures, Miller's book is a good summary of problems and trends in this area. For an excellent collection of readings on various aspects of economic inequality, see Edward C. Budd, ed., *Inequality and Poverty* (New York: W. W. Norton, 1967).

States occurred from 1910 on.[2] Other scholars have argued that a small but significant decrease in the relative share of income received by the top 5 percent and top 20 percent of income units took place in the period preceding World War Two. All in all, the latter position appears more persuasive.[3]

Analyzing the distribution of income is extraordinarily complicated, though some highly refined statistical techniques provide a fairly reliable picture of how income is distributed. The prevailing disputes about income distribution in the pre-1945 period result either from lack of data or from the noncomparability of data over time.

Comparative income distribution

Comparisons between countries are even more difficult, and for similar reasons.[4] By way of introduction to American income distribution, it is useful to note that the United States is no exception to the rather profound income inequality characteristic of industrial countries. The distribution of income from employment (which is less dispersed than total income) is remarkably similar, for example, in Denmark, the United Kingdom, Sweden, Yugoslavia, Poland, the Federal Republic of Germany, Canada, Belgium, the United States, and Austria, though there are variations in particulars.[5] Of special importance is the fact that industrial countries are not characterized by greater equality of income than the underdeveloped nations, except in one important respect: in the underdeveloped countries the top 5 percent receives a greater share of total income. Among the remaining 95 percent, however, income is distributed more equally than in developed nations. Furthermore, it is not widely known that the bottom 20 percent of income units in the rich nations receives a significantly lower percentage of total income than the bottom 20 percent in underdeveloped countries, or that the bottom 60 percent in both types of countries receives approximately the same percentage of total income.[6]

On the basis of income from employment (as opposed, again, to total income, which is more widely dispersed), it appears that New Zealand, Australia, and most communist countries have less income inequality than the Western

2. Gabriel Kolko, *Wealth and Power in America* (New York: Frederick A. Praeger, 1962), also in paperback.

3. For the reasons, see Herman P. Miller, *Income Distribution in the United States: A 1960 Census Monograph* (Washington, D.C.: U.S. Government Printing Office, 1966), chap. 1.

An important criticism of the concepts and data used to support the view that economic equality has increased in the United Kingdom may be found in Richard M. Titmuss, *Income Distribution and Social Change: A Critical Study in British Statistics* (Toronto: University of Toronto Press, 1962).

4. For a technical analysis stressing the difficulty, if not impossibility, of comparing economic inequality in agrarian and industrial societies, see Harold Lydall, *The Structure of Earnings* (London: Oxford University Press, 1968).

5. *Ibid.*, p. 156.

6. Simon Kuznets, *Economic Growth and Structure* (New York: Norton, 1965), p. 289f.

capitalist countries.[7] The use of a broader measure of economic inequality —
one that takes into account welfare programs, income, physicians available,
infant live births, and caloric and protein intake — appears to suggest that
some economic equalization occurs during the initial phases of industrialization.
(It should be noted that the measures used are crude, and that disentangling
absolute growth in material existence from its relative distribution is not easy.)
However, this trend is soon replaced by a stable and still steep economic
inequality that persists despite economic growth, egalitarian political intentions,
and political democracy.[8]

Income distribution in the United States

There is little doubt that the American standard of living (as expressed in
income) has grown spectacularly since World War Two. Between 1947 and
1973 the median income in constant dollars for families climbed from approximately $6,000 to $12,000 and the median income for unrelated individuals
rose from about $1,950 to about $4,130. The doubling of America's standard
of living as expressed in median income does not tell the whole story, however;
during the same period the distribution of income was steeply and stably
unequal.

Like all facts, income data cannot speak for themselves and must be interpreted carefully. Great care must be taken, for example, to identify the
type of income unit in question. It makes a great deal of difference whether
one is referring to families; unrelated individuals; families with two or more
earners; families with experienced workers; large or small families; black, white,
Indian, or Spanish-origin families, and so on. The meaning of one income level
as opposed to another must also be defined. What criteria does one use to
determine cutoff points? Is it meaningful to distinguish between annual incomes
of $10,000 and $11,000 for families of similar size? When grouping income
data, the analyst must ask what a group or class of incomes represents.
Obviously, income data can be grouped in many different ways. We can draw
the profile of income distribution, for example, in terms of consumer units
that can afford to buy a Pinto or Vega as opposed to those that can afford a
Cadillac or Lincoln Continental. Different profiles will emerge if we determine
which income classes visit the dentist regularly, which travel more than a
thousand miles on their holidays, which vote for the Democratic as opposed to
the Republican Party, and so on.

Since our purpose here is to present a comprehensive picture of income
distribution in the United States, we have defined income "classes" in terms of

7. Lydall, *The Structure of Earnings*, pp. 156–162. Differences in the overall
levels of economic inequality of communist and noncommunist countries should not
be exaggerated.

8. For a review of the existing literature and an argument along those lines based
on analysis of a cross-section of sixty Western and Third World countries, see Robert
W. Jackman, "Political Democracy and Social Equality: A Comparative Analysis,"
American Sociological Review 39 (February 1974): pp. 29–45.

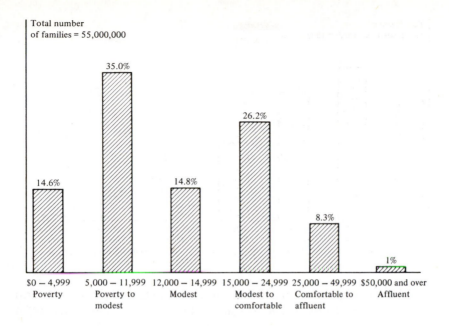

Total number
of families = 55,000,000

35.0%

26.2%

14.6%   14.8%

8.3%

1%

$0 — 4,999   5,000 — 11,999 12,000 — 14,999 15,000 — 24,999 25,000 — 49,999 $50,000 and over
Poverty   Poverty to   Modest   Modest to   Comfortable to   Affluent
              modest   comfortable   affluent

Figure 4-1   Family Income Distribution in the United States by Estimated
Standard of Living, 1973 (as of March 1974)

SOURCE: Estimates made from income data supplied by the U.S. Department of
Commerce, *Current Population Reports,* Series P-60, no. 97, "Money Income in
1973 of Families and Persons in the United States" (Washington, D.C.: U.S. Government Printing Office, 1975), Table 25.

a rough estimate of overall living standards for two types of income units,
families and unrelated individuals. In Figure 4-1 we have grouped 1973
income levels into categories of economic and social well-being and have computed the percentage of families in each income class. Thus, in Figure 4-1,
14.6 percent of approximately 55,000,000 families, or about 8,000,000 American families, live in poverty ($0–4,999); about 8 percent, or about 4,400,000
families, live in the range of comfort to affluence ($25,000–49,999); and 1
percent, or 550,000 families, live in affluence ($50,000 and over).

The income classes presented in Figure 4-1 are only gross indications of
how well people eat, how they are housed, how much they can spend for
entertainment or travel, and the like. The United States Department of Labor's
two measures for distinguishing lower, moderate, and higher living standards[9]
are of no help here because they focus on an urban family of four with one
experienced earner and on an urban retired couple. The data in Figure 4-1, on
the other hand, are derived from small and big families, rural and urban
families, the employed and the unemployed, all ages, all "races," all educational
and occupational groups, and families with one as well as more than one

9. See "Strategy and Pitfalls in the Analysis of Class" in Chapter 3.

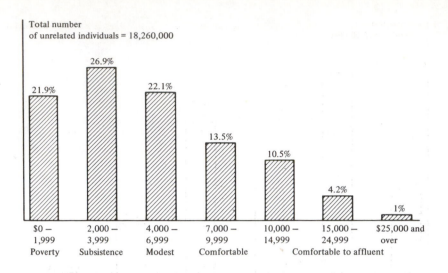

Total number
of unrelated individuals = 18,260,000

21.9%	26.9%	22.1%	13.5%	10.5%	4.2%	1%
$0 – 1,999	2,000 – 3,999	4,000 – 6,999	7,000 – 9,999	10,000 – 14,999	15,000 – 24,999	$25,000 and over
Poverty	Subsistence	Modest	Comfortable		Comfortable to affluent	

Figure 4-2 Income Distribution for Unrelated Individuals in the United States by Estimated Standard of Living, 1973 (as of March 1974)

SOURCE: Estimates made from income data supplied by the U.S. Department of Commerce, *Current Population Reports,* Series P-60, no. 97, "Money Income in 1973 of Families and Persons in the United States" (Washington, D.C.: U.S. Government Printing Office, 1975), Table 25.

earner. Even the simple fact that the cost of living in the United States varies as much as 25 percent from one place to another should make one cautious about deriving hard-and-fast generalizations from the data in Figure 4-1. Nonetheless, the profile of family income distribution reveals considerable inequality.

Figure 4-2 illustrates the income distribution for unrelated individuals. These data too must be interpreted with caution, since they refer to a wide variety of individuals who live alone or in households with nonrelatives: the young, the old, those in their middle years, residents of rural and urban areas and of all regions, and all "races." Nonetheless, the data paint a dramatic picture of inequality. Of the unrelated population of 18,260,000, almost 22 percent or 4,017,200 live in poverty ($0–1,999), while approximately 15 percent or 2,739,000 are in the comfortable-to-affluent range ($10,000 and over).

Our awareness of income inequality in the United States is heightened if we compare per capita personal income in 1973 — that is, the amount each individual would receive if total personal income were divided equally, or $4,921 — with (1) the present income of unrelated individuals (Figure 4-2), and (2) the income of a fictional universal family of four (derived from Figure 4-1). Such a hypothetical society brings our actual society into sharper relief. Of the unrelated individuals in the United States, 48.3 percent have incomes of less than $4,000, and 58.1 percent have incomes of $4,999 or less. (The median income in 1973 for unrelated individuals was $4,134, which means that half earned less and half earned more than this figure.) In our hypothetical society of income equality, a family of four would have an income of $19,684. A comparison of this figure with the actual distribution of family income in Figure 4-1 highlights the inequality of present income distribution. Approximately 65 percent of American families had incomes of less than $15,000 in 1973. (Median family income in that year was $12,000.) Of course, the percentage under $19,684 is much higher, but because the Census Bureau does not provide a breakdown of incomes in the $15,000–24,999 range the exact percentage cannot be computed.

The above data are for one year. What about trends in income distribution? As Table 4-1 shows, income distribution for families and unrelated individuals has been remarkably stable over the entire period for which we have reliable and comparable records. Of family income units, each fifth received an almost unchanging percentage of total income each year from 1947 to 1973, the top 20 percent receiving approximately 40 percent of the total income and the bottom 20 percent receiving approximately 5 percent. The small overall decline in the shares of the top 5 percent and top 20 percent income classes should be noted, but its significance is far from clear. In any case, for interpreting the degree of both income inequality and income trends, it is important to know that the Census Bureau's data are not completely accurate because they fail to consider nonmoney income, realized capital gains, and retained corporate earnings, and suffer from underreporting, especially in the areas of interest, rents, and dividends. On the whole, underreporting and the omission of certain kinds of income tend to cause the Census Bureau to understate the degree of income inequality.[10]

In summary, income in the United States has been rising steadily without becoming more equal. As we will now see, this is true, by and large, of income distribution both before and after taxes and governmental spending.

Income, taxation, and governmental spending

Existing studies indicate that no significant equalization of income occurs as a result of taxation. In its study of the impact of total taxation (federal, state, and local taxes, including both personal and business taxes), the Tax Foundation reports that approximately the same percentage in taxes is taken from all incomes up to $15,000. (In both 1961 and 1965 the tax rates for incomes up to $15,000 ranged between 26 and 31 percent; for incomes over $15,000 the rate was 44 percent). The net result of the total tax burden, therefore, is to leave the relative distribution of income between $0 and $15,000 largely untouched. (In 1961 this range of income accounted for ap-

10. For a discussion, see Howard P. Tuckman, *The Economics of the Rich* (New York: Random House, 1973), pp. 48–53 (paperback).

Table 4-1 Percentage Share of Aggregate Income Received by Each Fifth and Top 5 Percent of Families, 1947 to 1973

| Year | Percent distribution of aggregate income | | | | | |
	Lowest fifth	Second fifth	Middle fifth	Fourth fifth	Highest fifth	Top 5 percent
1973	5.5	11.9	17.5	24.0	41.1	15.5
1972	5.4	11.9	17.5	23.9	41.4	15.9
1971	5.5	12.0	17.6	23.8	41.1	15.7
1970	5.4	12.2	17.6	23.8	40.9	15.6
1969	5.6	12.4	17.7	23.7	40.6	15.6
1968	5.6	12.4	17.7	23.7	40.5	15.6
1967	5.5	12.4	17.9	23.9	40.4	15.2
1966	5.6	12.4	17.8	23.8	40.5	15.6
1965	5.2	12.2	17.8	23.9	40.9	15.5
1964	5.1	12.0	17.7	24.0	41.2	15.9
1963	5.0	12.1	17.7	24.0	41.2	15.8
1962	5.0	12.1	17.6	24.0	41.3	15.7
1961	4.7	11.9	17.5	23.8	42.2	16.6
1960	4.8	12.2	17.8	24.0	41.3	15.9
1959	4.9	12.3	17.9	23.8	41.1	15.9
1958	5.0	12.5	18.0	23.9	40.6	15.4
1957	5.0	12.6	18.1	23.7	40.5	15.8
1956	4.9	12.4	17.9	23.6	41.1	16.4
1955	4.8	12.2	17.7	23.4	41.8	16.8
1954	4.5	12.0	17.6	24.0	41.9	16.4
1953	4.7	12.4	17.8	24.0	41.0	15.8
1952	4.9	12.2	17.1	23.5	42.2	17.7
1951	4.9	12.5	17.6	23.3	41.8	16.9
1950	4.5	11.9	17.4	23.6	42.7	17.3
1949	4.5	11.9	17.3	23.5	42.8	16.9
1948	5.0	12.1	17.2	23.2	42.5	17.1
1947	5.1	11.8	16.7	23.2	43.3	17.5

SOURCE: U.S. Bureau of the Census, *Current Population Reports,* Series P-60, no. 97, "Money Income in 1973 of Families and Persons in the United States" (Washington, D.C.: U.S. Government Printing Office, 1975), Table 22.

proximately 98 percent of all families and approximately 91 percent of total income.) While there is a significant jump in the tax rate for incomes above $15,000, it is far from confiscatory.[11]

11. *Tax Burdens and Benefits of Government Expenditures by Income Class, 1961, and 1965* (New York: Tax Foundation, 1967), tables 3, 7, and B-8. For a similar conclusion about the relative burden of taxation on income in 1958, see *Allocation of the Tax Burden by Income Class* (New York: Tax Foundation, 1960). It should be noted that for technical reasons, the definition of income applied in these studies

Perhaps our most sophisticated study in this area has concluded that in 1966 "the United States tax system was essentially proportional for the vast majority of families and therefore had little effect on the distribution of income." [12] One of the virtues of this study is that it analyzes the data along alternate lines in keeping with economists' differing views on the impact of various taxes. Whatever assumptions one makes, however, it is clear that total taxation has little impact on income distribution and that the very rich pay significantly higher, as opposed to moderately higher, rates only if one assumes that corporations' income and property taxes are not borne by the consumer.

The reason why taxation does not alter income inequality significantly is now fairly well known. Property, sales, and social security taxes are regressive in nature; that is, flat or equal tax rates take a larger percentage of lower than higher incomes and burden large families more than small. In addition, the federal income tax is not, in effect, very progressive. Miller reports, for example, that in 1962 the top 5 percent income class received 20 percent of total income before taxes, and that its share of income received was reduced only to 18 percent after taxes.[13] The reason for this can be seen in Table 4-2, where effective rates of taxation are compared to the formal progressive rates. This table demonstrates that the actual rates of taxes paid are far lower and much more uniform than the formal progressive rates imply.

The reasons for the wide disparity between effective income taxation and the formal progressive schedule allegedly based on ability to pay are also fairly well known. Over the years, legislation (often unpublicized and even secret) has filled the Internal Revenue Code with shelters and "loopholes": capital gains, "fast writeoffs," expense account deductions, exemption from taxation of interest from state and municipal bonds, oil and mineral depletion allowances and the treatment of drilling costs as business expenses rather than capital investment, and contributions to charity either in the form of property (antiques, stocks) or through the use of foundations.[14]

Granted that taxation does not equalize, what about public spending? Does not the expenditure of tax funds, however collected, benefit the lower income classes more than the higher, in effect equalizing income distribution? Criteria for determining who benefits most from public budgets are not without their controversial aspects, and answering this question is not easy. There exists at present only

is income after personal taxes. There are differences, therefore, between the income data in these studies and income data reported elsewhere.

12. Joseph A. Pechman and Benjamin A. Okner, *Who Bears the Tax Burden?* (Washington, D.C.: Brookings Institution, 1974), p. 10. In Pechman's and Okner's opinion, the general pattern of tax burdens has not changed since 1966 (p. viii).

13. Herman P. Miller, *Income Distribution in the United States: A 1960 Census Monograph* (Washington, D.C.: U.S. Government Printing Office, 1966), p. 41.

14. For a brilliant and comprehensive analysis of the federal tax structure, which also cites the special tax treatment accorded the blind, the aged, the married, the homeowner, and the like, see Philip M. Stern, *The Great Treasury Raid* (New York: Random House, 1962) and *The Rape of the Taxpayer* (New York: Random House, 1973).

Table 4-2 Percentage Distribution of Federal Income Tax Returns by Effective Tax Rate Classes, 1969 (by Amended Gross Income Classes, 1969 Levels)

Amended gross income ($000)	Effective tax rate classes													
	0–5	5–10	10–15	15–20	20–25	25–30	30–35	35–40	40–45	45–50	50–55	55–60	60–65	65–70
0– 3	68.0	0.3	1.4	6.0										
3– 5	14.5	2.3	10.9	63.0	5.6									
5– 7	3.9	2.0	22.2	71.6	0.1									
7– 10	0.9	1.0	22.2	70.5	5.3									
10– 15	0.7	0.8	6.3	85.2	6.6	0.4								
15– 20	0.6	1.5	4.8	71.2	19.8	2.2								
20– 50	0.9	1.6	7.0	27.9	45.2	13.5	3.0	0.6	0.2					
50– 100	1.2	0.8	3.3	7.5	12.7	21.6	31.2	16.4	3.9	1.2	0.2			
100– 500	1.9	1.3	1.9	6.1	17.9	15.9	11.5	14.1	14.4	8.7	4.1	1.9	0.3	
500–1,000	2.1	0.7	0.8	0.7	31.9	32.8	6.3	4.3	3.0	2.4	3.1	4.6	6.7	0.4
1,000 & over	2.5	0.4	0.3	0.4	36.6	37.8	4.3	1.7	1.8	2.1	1.2	1.3	6.1	3.4

SOURCE: From an article by former Secretary of the Treasury Joseph W. Barr, "Tax Reform: The Time Is Now," *Saturday Review*, 22 March 1969; data compiled by the Office of Tax Analysis, Office of the Secretary of the Treasury.

the beginning of a scientific study of the impact of public spending.[15] Though their conclusions differ, the authors of existing studies agree, by and large, that governmental expenditures produce a significant equalization of income since the poor tend to benefit more from public spending than the rich. However, all these authors agree that their analyses rest on assumptions that are open to legitimate questions. For example, governmental spending is seen as tending to equalize American society only if one computes per capita benefits from expenditures on defense, health, education, highways, the arts, and so on, an approach obviously based on an image of society as a vast, amorphous collection of equal individuals. But educational expenditures and benefits, for example, are very unequal in actual practice, and their inequality corresponds closely to class inequality. Does it make sense, therefore, to compute educational expenditures (and benefits) on a per capita or per child-in-school basis? Does it make sense to compute the cost of defense spending on a per capita basis? Is the benefit of a missile or a tank equal for an industrialist, a doctor, a carpenter, a farm worker, and an unemployed person, or should the allocation of benefits be weighted to account for the greater benefits derived from defense by those with higher incomes and more property?

When income distribution is related to a type of governmental spending that economists call *transfer payments* — such things as Social Security and railroad retirement payments, public assistance, workmen's compensation, unemployment insurance, veteran's disability compensation and pensions, Medicare, food stamps, and public housing subsidies — one can see a reduction of income inequality.[16] A number of qualifications apply, however, to the impact of transfer payments on income distribution. First, the overall reduction of income inequality is not large, and income distribution remains sharply unequal both before and after transfer payments. Second, the largest transfer payment, Social Security pensions, is really a form of postponed income or investment income, and is not properly thought of in the same terms as other transfer payments. In the early years of Social Security, many retirees received a great deal without contributing much, but workers who are retiring today have made huge contributions and should be thought of as reaping the rewards of an investment. Social Security is thus different, for example, from public assistance, which uses tax revenues to help those in need. In the latter case, income is taken from some and granted irretrievably to others. Given the regressive nature of the Social Security tax and the fact that large numbers of the lower classes either never reach the age of sixty-five or live shorter lives

15. R. A. Musgrave *et al.*, "Distribution of Tax Payments by Income Groups: A Case Study for 1948," *National Tax Journal* 4, no. 1 (March 1951): 1–53; W. Irwin Gillespie, "Effect of Public Expenditures on the Distribution of Income" in *Essays in Fiscal Federalism,* ed. Richard A. Musgrave (Washington, D.C.: Brookings Institution, 1965); and the Tax Foundation, *Tax Burdens and Benefits of Government Expenditures by Income Class, 1961 and 1965* (New York: Tax Foundation, 1967).

16. Benjamin A. Okner, "Individual Taxes and the Distribution of Income" in *The Personal Distribution of Income and Wealth,* ed. James D. Smith (New York: National Bureau of Economic Research, 1975), chap. 3.

than the upper classes, it is not at all clear that the Social Security system has a redistributive effect on income. Finally, it should be noted that transfer payments help the poor in a selective manner: the chief beneficiaries are the aged and female-headed families; poor and near-poor families headed by working males are underhelped and overtaxed.[17]

Public discussions of governmental spending and taxation and such related issues as the public debt and welfare spending are characterized by many flagrant and harmful distortions of meaningful issues. For some reason, Americans in general consider it permissible for private individuals, families, and businesses of all kinds to go into debt — they are even encouraged to do so — but not for governments to do so. Thus private debt is infinitely larger than all public debts combined. Consider too that our control of the public debt relies on ceilings set in absolute figures, whereas a much more meaningful ceiling would be based on the criterion used in private borrowing, what the borrower is worth. Thus the federal debt should more properly be expressed as a percentage of gross national product (GNP), or what the country is worth. Actually, the federal debt, which has risen in absolute terms during the twentieth century, has not really risen at all — it has even declined — if computed in relation to GNP. Again unlike private budgets, not much attention is paid to the distinction between public spending that represents cost and public spending that represents investment. Another significant distortion of the role of governmental spending is division of the federal budget into (1) social welfare and human services and (2) military and administrative overhead components. From 1889 to 1972–1973, the proportion of total government spending devoted to "social welfare" has increased significantly, from 2.4 percent of GNP to 17.6 percent. But if one subtracts social security system expenditures, which are based on a heavily regressive tax, from the definition of "social welfare" spending, the overall figure shrinks considerably, to 10.6 percent. And if one subtracts educational expenditures, which are beneficial mostly to the upper and middle classes, the figure shrinks to 5.3 percent. To put the matter more directly, the most important form of help to the poor, welfare or public aid to the needy, has risen from 0.9 percent of GNP in 1949–1950 to 2.3 percent in 1972–1973.[18]

To relate governmental spending and legislation to the structure of class realistically, one must also remember that most federal (civilian) spending must be channeled through state and local governments. Keeping this in mind makes it easier to understand why federal spending in general (including military expenditures) tends to benefit the middle and upper classes and why much of the money intended for the poor never reaches them. If one (1) thinks of the tax code as a system of expenditures, consider-

17. Harold W. Watts and Jon K. Peck, "On the Comparison of Income Redistribution Plans," in *The Personal Distribution of Income and Wealth,* ed. James D. Smith (New York: National Bureau of Economic Research, 1975), chap. 4.

18. Alfred M. Skolnik and Sophie R. Dales, "Social Welfare Expenditures," *Social Security Bulletin* 37 (January 1974), Table 3, p. 11.

ing each exemption and deduction as a decision for private rather than public spending,[19] (2) remembers that the tax code benefits the rich and moderate rich the most, and (3) remembers that the United States is one of the least severely taxed industrial countries, one can understand the conservative uses to which Keynesian economic theory — the belief that the public welfare is best promoted by government if it in turn promotes private consumption and private economic activity — has been put. None of this is surprising, given the fact that political participants, public policy-making structures, and governmental personnel are drawn almost exclusively from the middle and upper classes. (See Chapter 12.) Ironically, the public does not recognize that the monies actually appropriated to fund public programs fall far short of the well-publicized figures initially requested, and is thus deluded into believing that far more is being undertaken by government than is actually the case. Meanwhile unsatisfied expectations continue to rise.

Prosperity and poverty: opposites or correlates?

It is an article of faith with modern populations that economic growth is the ultimate solution to social problems, in that it will equalize material benefits, eliminate poverty, and promote social harmony and moral growth. Today, however, it requires no great sophistication to recognize that this is a highly questionable assumption. The belief that economic growth will equalize people is not limited to the lay public. Almost every sociologist who addresses the subject of social stratification cites the dramatic growth of real income in the United States. Except for a small minority, however, these sociologists fail to point out that no significant change in the relative share of income or wealth has taken place in the entire period for which we have reliable records. Indeed, it is astonishing how many texts, in both general sociology and social stratification, either blandly equate a rising standard of living with growing equality or use blatantly defective contrasts to prove the same point.[20] With one exception,[21] every textbook in social stratification that interprets trends in the distribution of income is characterized by this confusion and error.[22]

19. For a valuable analysis of the federal income tax code from this perspective, see Paul M. Dodyk, "The Tax Reform Act of 1969 and the Poor," *Columbia Law Review* 71 (May 1971): 758–802.

20. The related notion that industrial countries have more equal incomes than nonindustrial countries is also taken for granted and stated in a more or less unqualified way in the few instances where the subject is raised.

21. Charles H. Anderson, *The Political Economy of Social Class* (Englewood Cliffs, N.J.: Prentice-Hall, 1974).

22. Of the ten textbooks on social stratification I have examined, two do not refer to trends in income or wealth, one refers to them in order to note how little we know about them, and the other six declared that the trend is toward greater equality. Of the seven collections of readings in social stratification I found, only three included a selection on income (by Herman P. Miller, in which the axiom of growing equality of income is questioned). In a quick perusal of forty-seven introductory texts, I found that twenty-five do not treat trends in income or wealth and that twelve of the remaining twenty-two assert that incomes are becoming equal (the

Textbook authors must rely on the specialized work of researchers, and in this case the erroneous identification of a trend toward equality of income is based on a number of influential articles that appeared in the early 1950s.[23] The basic argument of these articles is based on empirical data showing a decline in income inequality from the mid-1930s to the late 1940s. A contrast between a period of deep economic depression and a period of high prosperity, separated by ten–fifteen years, is such a blatantly unsound basis for deriving historic trends that here as elsewhere one is probably witnessing not so much error as acts of faith (evolutionary liberalism).[24]

Lack of interest in income trends is as interesting as errors of interpretation. One suspects that the failure to mention income trends is as much an expression of faith in the beneficence of technological expansion as it is haste to demonstrate a trend toward income equality. In any case, it is one thing to assert that industrialization will among other things promote the growth of equality of opportunity — in other words, that equality is realized when individuals are given a fair chance to find themselves in the structure of inequality ("nonegalitarian classlessness") — and quite another to say that individuals are actually becoming more equal.

The widespread assumption that industrialization and growing prosperity will eliminate poverty is also problematic. Of all the misconceptions about inequality, this one is perhaps the easiest to excuse. At the advent of industrial society, poverty was a fairly clear-cut phenomenon that entailed physical suffering due to the lack of adequate food, clothing, and shelter. So serious and widespread was this type of poverty that being poor came to have one definition: "biological" poverty or physical deprivation. Unfortunately, this is still what people mean when they refer to poverty. It is not surprising that with the spectacular growth of real income and the development of a standard of living that allows average citizens to enjoy amenities previously denied to emperors, belief in the elimination of poverty became widespread. The Keyserling Report of 1962 [25] and Michael Harrington's *The Other America* in 1963,[26] however, proved to Americans that the United States still had a con-

---

more recent the text the more likely that income will be discussed and discussed accurately).

23. Gideon Sjoberg, "Are Social Classes in America Becoming More Rigid?" *American Sociological Review* 16 (December 1951): 775–783; Joseph J. Spengler, "Changes in Income Distribution and Social Stratification: A Note," *American Journal of Sociology* 59 (November 1953): 247–259; William Petersen, "Is America Still the Land of Opportunity? What Recent Studies Show About Social Mobility," *Commentary* 16 (November 1953): 477–486.

24. The other major piece of evidence used to support the growth of income equality is a comparison of the relative shares of income and wealth of the top 1 and 5 percent of income units between 1929 and the 1940s. Not only is this drop far from impressive, but the data are also not easily compared.

25. Conference of Economic Progress, *Poverty and Deprivation in the United States* (Washington, D.C.: Conference on Economic Progress, 1962).

26. (New York: Macmillan), available in paperback.

siderable amount of poverty. Characteristically, a war on poverty was mounted, and the federal government developed criteria to define poverty and to measure its extent. While there is some disagreement about the definition of poverty, and thus about the number of poor, Americans tend to agree on one point: that the number of poor will decrease steadily, since rising prosperity will lift more and more families above the poverty line. Given the wealth pouring out of the American economy and certain governmental efforts, Americans feel that poverty will gradually be eliminated.

But this perspective on poverty has several serious shortcomings. First, and perhaps most important, it fails to address itself to the question of whether America's very unequal distribution of income and wealth is justified on economic, political, social, or moral grounds. It should be remembered that the attack on poverty was undertaken, aside from humanitarian motives, in the name of equality of opportunity, not of actual equality. Second, there is the lack of realism about the possibility of eliminating "biological" poverty.[27] And third, there is the fact that industrial society has produced a new kind of poverty, a "psychological" or subjective poverty that is difficult to measure but no less real than objective or "biological" poverty. For example, a family whose income is precisely the amount used by the federal government to define poverty ($4,540 for a nonfarm family of four in 1973)[28] has a material existence undeniably superior to that of the poor in the past (peasants, slaves, and serfs) and in some ways to that of past aristocrats and monarchs. But such a family does not ordinarily compare itself with serfs or royalty. Its reference group is the contemporary United States, and its level of "felt" poverty (relative deprivation) is determined by comparisons with contemporaries. It is comparison with modest, comfortable, and even affluent income groups, in other words, as well as "biological" poverty (which is, of course, also "felt") that defines poverty for the American underclass.

To state the point differently, the index in terms of which poverty is defined assumes a *fixed* standard of living; thus the figure defining poverty rises each year only because inflation makes necessary a higher income to buy the *same* amount of goods and services. In an economy predicated on a rising standard of living, in which real income normally goes up for most people, poor people are thus legally tied to a very low and unchanging living standard. As a result, a widening gap develops between those who are poor and the rest of the population whose incomes normally rise faster than the cost of living. In monetary terms, the gap between the average income of poverty families and the average income of nonpoor families rose from $7,843 in 1959 to $11,216 in 1972

27. The elimination of objective or "biological" poverty is a far more complex matter than is generally recognized. There are too many groups that profit from poverty, and, perhaps more importantly, foresee the destruction of the American way of life if effective measures to eliminate poverty are adopted.

28. U.S. Bureau of the Census, "Characteristics of the Low-Income Population, 1973," *Current Population Reports,* Series P-60, no. 98 (Washington, D.C.: U.S. Government Printing Office, 1972), p. 1.

(in constant dollars). The gap between poor families and rich families increased by even more.[29]

Comparison with other Americans, in other words, is what defines poverty for the poor. Indeed, if one remembers that the achievement ethic is a constant stimulus to better one's position and a continuous source of dissatisfaction with the present, one can speak of institutionalized discontent at all class levels. Thus the norm of success has its inevitable counterpart in the norm of failure, and the constantly rising level of prosperity produces rising expectations and a subjective sense of poverty. A relative sense of failure and poverty, it should be noted, is a chronic or institutionalized feature of American society, and obviously grips many individuals and families at levels above those conventionally defined as poor.[30] In short, the concept of *institutionalized discontent* and such related ideas as *relative deprivation, reference group,* and *psychological poverty* are central to an understanding of the contemporary class system.

The distribution of wealth
The basic pattern: concentration

It is very revealing that, with one recent exception, hard data about the wealthy are not readily available. Despite the reams of data on the economic behavior and status of Americans that are collected each year, we have almost no direct, accurate, and comprehensive information on wealth distribution or of the economic status of the very rich (and we know very little about many other aspects of the upper class). However, census and income tax data, and such other materials as biographies and histories of old families and successful leaders, allow us to compose a fairly accurate portrait of wealth distribution and its trends. Scholars in this field are generally agreed that the basic pattern of the distribution of wealth is high and relatively steady concentration.[31] Whether analyzed and measured in terms of liquid assets, personal property, real estate, stock ownership, ability to save, or income from property, the distribution of wealth in the United States is characterized by the same pro-

29. Herman P. Miller, "Inequality, Poverty, and Taxes," *Dissent* (Winter 1975): 46f.

30. For example, the presiding judge of the Appellate Division of the New York State Supreme Court resigned in 1975 because continuing on the bench "would work a financial deprivation on his family" (*New York Times,* 29 January 1975, p. 33). His salary was $55,266, an income that located him in approximately the top 1 percent of all income units.

31. General summaries of the distribution of wealth may be found in Gabriel Kolko, *Wealth and Power in America* (New York: Frederick Praeger, 1962), chap. 3; G. William Domhoff, *Who Rules America?* (Englewood Cliffs, N.J.: Prentice-Hall, 1967), chap. 2; Edward C. Budd, ed., *Inequality and Poverty* (New York: W. W. Norton, 1967), pp. 80–90, 114–122, and 128–139; Ferdinand Lundberg, *The Rich and the Super-Rich* (New York: Lyle Stuart, 1968); and Howard P. Tuckman, *The Economics of the Rich* (New York: Random House, 1973), available in paperback.

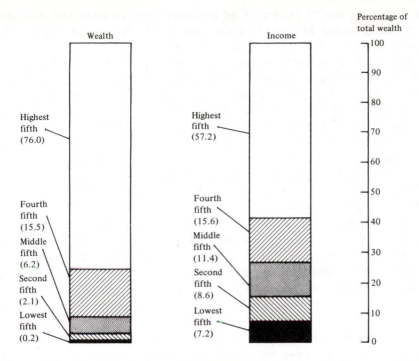

Figure 4-3 The Distribution of Total Wealth: Fifths of Consumer Units Ranked by Wealth and Income, 1962

SOURCE: Executive Office of the President, Office of Management and Budget, *Social Indicators, 1973* (Washington, D.C.: U.S. Government Printing Office, 1973). Chart 5/15.

nounced pattern of concentration.[32] The degree of concentration of total wealth in 1962 is illustrated in Figure 4-3. Total wealth is the sum of assets less debts: homes, automobiles, businesses and professions, liquid assets (funds in checking and savings accounts and United States savings bonds), investment assets (marketable securities, investment real estate, and mortgages), profit-sharing plans, money held in trust, oil royalties, and patents. Ranked in terms

32. Basic data about types of wealth in the United States, its size distribution — that is, amounts owned by income, age, sex, and racial groups —*and trends in wealth distribution may be found in "1953 Survey of Consumer Finances," *Federal Reserve Bulletin* 39 (September 1953): 940–947; Survey Research Center, *1960 Survey of Consumer Finances* (Ann Arbor: University of Michigan, 1961); Robert J. Lampman, *The Share of Top Wealth-Holders in National Wealth, 1922–1956* (Princeton: Princeton University Press, 1962); George Katona and John B. Lansing, "The Wealth of the Wealthy," *Review of Economics and Statistics* 46, no. 1 (February 1964): 1–13; "Survey of Financial Characteristics of Consumers," *Federal Reserve Bulletin* 50 (March 1964): 285–293; Dorothy S. Projector and Gertrude S. Weiss, *Survey of Financial Characteristics of Consumers* (Washington, D.C.: Board of Governors of the Federal Reserve System, 1966); and Robin Barlow *et al., Economic Behavior of the Affluent* (Washington, D.C.: Brookings Institution, 1966).

of wealth, the top 20 percent of all consumer units (families and unrelated individuals) owned 76 percent of the total wealth. Ranked by income, the top 20 percent owned 57.2 percent of the total wealth.

The degree of concentration of wealth also appears to be stable: despite rising levels of output and the fact that millions of people own property and even shares in business, no significant trend toward either the equalization of property or the development of a "people's capitalism" is discernible. Though we still do not collect data on wealth directly, a recent study has penetrated the veil of semidarkness that surrounds stock ownership, the most important form of wealth in industrial society.[33] The data on stock ownership illustrate both the steep inequality of wealth and its relative stability over time. As Tables 4-3 and 4-4 indicate, the small trend toward equalization in effect since 1958 has ended, leaving the distribution of stock ownership highly concentrated. As Table 4-3 shows, in 1971 families and unattached individuals earning over $50,000 annually (1 percent of all income units) owned 51.1 percent of the total market value of stock and received 46.9 percent of total dividend income. At the other extreme, income units earning below $5,000 in 1971, which accounted for 22 percent of all families and unattached individuals, owned 2.4 percent of the total stock and received 2.8 percent of total dividend income.

Trends in the distribution of stockownership are illustrated in Table 4-4. As we already know from our analysis of income, the distribution of income is remarkably stable and concentrated, whether seen in terms of fifths (as in Table 4-1) or of the top 1, 5, 10, or 50 percent of income units. When the distribution of dividend income and stock ownership is analyzed, the top 1 percent of income units ($50,000 and over) has maintained a remarkably stable percentage of both stock value and dividend income. The top 5, 10, and 50 percent of income units accounted for a declining percentage of dividend income and stock values between 1958 and 1969, and have had stable and still high percentages since 1970. In assessing the historical studies in this area, the authors conclude that while a significant decline in the concentration of stock ownership and dividend income took place from the 1920s through the 1960s, the amount of decline has been highly exaggerated. In other words, the present distribution of stock wealth and stock investment income is still highly concentrated. Incidentally, the overall picture of wealth ownership may be distorted in the direction of equality by the tendency of tax laws to encourage the wealthy to invest a greater percentage of their wealth in tax-free municipal bonds and the booming tax-sheltered real estate market — that is, into forms not captured by Blume, Crockett, and Friend's study, which is based on income tax data. And as the authors warn, the reduction of corporate stock concentration does not imply a reduction in concentrated economic power. We will turn to this matter shortly.

33. Marshall E. Blume, Jean Crockett, and Irwin Friend, "Stockownership in the United States: Characteristics and Trends," *Survey of Current Business* (U.S. Department of Commerce) 54, no. 11 (November 1974): 16–40.

Table 4-3 Percentage Distribution of Families,[a] Dividend Income, and Value of Stock by Family Income Level, 1958–1971

Family income[b]	1958	1960	1964	1969	1970	1971
		Number of families				
Under $5,000	48.75	43.9	37.2	26.9	23.9	22.0
$5,000–$9,999	37.9	39.4	38.6	32.7	31.9	31.4
$10,000–$14,999	8.5	10.6	16.0	21.8	23.1	23.5
$15,000–$24,999	3.5	4.6	6.0	15.2	15.9	17.3
$25,000–$49,999	1.1	1.2	1.7	2.3	4.3	4.8
$50,000–$99,999	.2	.25	.4	.7	.7	.8
$100,000 and over	.05	.05	.1	.2	.2	.2
Total	100.0	100.0	100.0	100.0	100.0	100.0
		Aggregate dividend income				
Under $5,000	4.6	5.0	4.0	3.0	2.9	2.8
$5,000–$9,999	10.5	10.7	10.6	9.9	8.6	8.2
$10,000–$14,999	12.9	11.7	11.0	9.4	9.4	9.3
$15,000–$24,999	17.4	18.2	15.1	14.6	14.1	13.8
$25,000–$49,999	20.7	21.8	20.5	20.2	19.7	18.9
$50,000–$99,999	15.5	13.5	17.2	19.8	20.1	20.0
$100,000 and over	18.4	19.1	21.6	23.1	25.2	26.9
Total	100.0	100.0	100.0	100.0	100.0	100.0
		Aggregate market value of stock				
Under $5,000	4.4	4.8	3.9	2.6	2.5	2.4
$5,000–$9,999	10.2	10.3	10.3	8.6	7.4	7.0
$10,000–$14,999	12.6	11.2	10.7	9.0	8.4	8.9
$15,000–$24,999	17.2	17.6	15.0	13.7	13.2	12.8
$25,000–$49,999	20.6	21.9	20.4	19.2	18.8	17.8
$50,000–$99,999	15.8	14.0	17.4	20.7	21.2	20.9
$100,000 and over	19.2	20.2	22.3	26.2	28.5	30.2
Total	100.0	100.0	100.0	100.0	100.0	100.0

[a] Definition of families includes unattached individuals.
[b] Family personal income before income taxes.

SOURCE: Marshall E. Blume, Jean Crockett, and Irwin Friend, "Stockownership in the United States: Characteristics and Trends," *Survey of Current Business* (U.S. Department of Commerce) 54 (November 1974). Table 3, p. 26.

Concentration and the ability to save

Thrift is a virtue basic to liberal society and is undoubtedly practiced by millions of Americans. Realistically speaking, however, the ability to save is restricted to relatively few people, basically those in high income groups.[34] To

34. Analyses of the ability to save may be found in Charles Liniger, "Estimates of Rates of Saving," *Journal of Political Economy* 72 (June 1964): 306–311; U.S.

recognize this is to know a great deal about the basic class structure of American society. The fact that only high income groups can save helps to explain the high concentration of wealth; conversely, the high concentration of wealth helps to explain high income. The ability of high income groups to save creates extra income (dividends, interest, capital gains, stock appreciation), which in turn promotes the unequal ability to save, and so on. If we examine three factors — (1) the sources of income from property, (2) the ways in which such income is protected against taxation, and (3) the ways in which estate and inheritance taxes permit the transmission of wealth from one generation to the next — a set of relationships become apparent that go far toward explaining the highly concentrated and highly stable distribution of America's material culture.[35] That this is a statistically derived feature of American society — that is, the individuals and families who make up the top, the middle, and the bottom groups are not always the same because of upward and downward mobility — and that a correction for age has to be made should not be allowed to obscure the reality of the processes that produce a high and stable inequality of property in the United States.[36]

The concentration of economic power

The pattern outlined above can also be expressed as a high concentration of economic power. Social classes are not merely statistical aggregates; they exist in organized form as corporations, trade and professional associations, farm groups, labor unions, cooperatives, and the like. When wealth is considered in this fashion it becomes clear that the high concentration of wealth and its continuity over time is attributable primarily to the business enterprise, and notably to the large corporation.

When analyzing economic concentration it is probably best to speak of *market power* — the ability of a participant or group of participants to influence price, quantity, and the nature of products in a given market and thus

Bureau of Labor Statistics, *Consumer Expenditures and Income, Total United States, Urban and Rural, 1961,* Bureau of Labor Statistics Report no. 237-93 (February 1965); Dorothy Projector, "Consumer Asset Preferences," *American Economic Review* 55B (May 1965): 227–251.

35. For an analysis of the basic economic, governmental, and educational forces that produce highly concentrated ascriptive wealth, and for some proposed remedies, see Howard P. Tuckman, *The Economics of the Rich* (New York: Random House, 1973), available in paperback. Because of the scarcity of data, Tuckman's definition of wealth is based on high income and ability to save (aided by favoritism in the tax laws and elsewhere).

36. It is interesting to note that the concentration of power over material culture is a more or less standard feature of every industrial society, regardless of past history, type of culture, or the ascendancy of a capitalist (liberal or fascist), socialist, or communist government. The techniques of concentration and control — interlocking directorships; intercorporate stockholding; favorable tax laws; private corporate concentration; nationalized industries with private managerial control; public corporations; governmental ownership and supervision by monopolistic political parties — vary considerably, of course.

Table 4-4 Trends in the Distribution of Stock Ownership by Selected Total Income Percentiles, 1958–1971

	Percentage of total income received by highest				Percentage of dividend income received by highest				Percentage of stock value owned by highest			
	1%	5%	10%	50%	1%	5%	10%	50%	1%	5%	10%	50%
1958	7.5	19.9	29.4	76.7	50.6	72.8	82.6	95.2	51.7	73.7	83.2	95.5
1960	7.2	19.4	29.0	76.8	48.4	69.8	78.3	93.5	50.5	71.3	79.5	94.0
1964	8.0	20.0	30.0	77.6	48.5	69.3	75.9	93.1	49.1	70.5	77.1	93.3
1969	n.a.	n.a.	n.a.	n.a.	45.9	63.9	72.1	91.3	50.4	66.6	74.5	92.5
1970	7.6	19.2	29.2	77.1	46.9	64.8	72.1	91.1	51.5	68.0	75.4	92.4
1971	7.5	19.1	28.9	76.7	46.9	63.8	71.6	90.5	51.1	67.1	75.1	92.0

N.a. Not available.
NOTE.— The percentages 1, 5, 10, and 50 refer to the specified percentage of families with highest total income.

SOURCE: Marshall E. Blume, Jean Crockett, and Irwin Friend, "Stock ownership in the United States: Characteristics and Trends," *Survey of Current Business* (U.S. Department of Commerce) 54 (November 1974), Table 4, p. 27.

to earn profits higher and more dependable than would be possible with competition — rather than economic concentration, bigness, or monopoly.[37]

The size of American corporations is difficult to fathom. In 1965 General Motors, our largest corporation, made more in after-tax profits than any individual state except California and New York collected in tax revenues. As a matter of fact, its profits were larger than the combined revenues of our eighteen smallest states. Bigness alone, however, is not synonymous with market power. Market power is likely to be a function of some combination of the following factors: the firm's size and share of the market relative to other firms; informal cooperative arrangements to control competition, including barring entry to newcomers; and relative size, diversification, and vertical patterns relative to outside markets. Judged in these terms (and despite the Sherman Anti-Trust Act of 1890, the Clayton Act of 1914, and the Celler-Kefauver Act of 1950), the growth of market power has continued unabated. Measured in terms of concentration ratios, share of total assets, profits, sales, or value added, the largest 100, 200, and 500 firms in the United States increased their shares of the total from 1947 through 1967, and there is no reason to expect that when data for recent years are available the trend will be reversed. Oligarchic competition is pronounced in manufacturing, in finance, and with exceptions, in transport and utilities. All in all, Shepherd concludes, at least 35 to 45 percent of all market activity is subject to substantial market power. According to Shepherd, there appears to be no technical necessity, such as efficiency, for the existing amount of oligarchic competition, let alone for an increase.

The causes of market power are complex: it stems from technology, the control of information, the advantage well-established firms wield over new firms (especially if they have learned to "cooperate" smoothly), and governmental policies. For their part, governmental policies are decisive in promoting market power by means, for example, of research support; cash subsidies; controls (safety, tariffs, import quotas, production quotas); rate-setting; tax laws that favor mergers and diversification (conglomerates); defense and other governmental purchasing; utility regulation; the distribution of patents, licenses, and franchises; and antitrust policy and implementation.

The failure to acknowledge oligarchy in the automobile industry is especially interesting. Shepherd estimates that oligarchic competition in the manufacture of automobiles costs the consumer approximately 25 percent of the price of a new car.[38] In class terms, this means that the automobile industry and related busi-

37. For an excellent summary and analysis of theories and data pertaining to market power, see William G. Shepherd, *Market Power and Economic Welfare* (New York: Random House, 1970). For a comprehensive selection of readings on all aspects of market power, see Werner Sichel, ed., *Industrial Organization and Public Policy: Selected Readings* (Boston: Houghton Mifflin, 1967), and Ralph L. Andreano, ed., *Superconcentration, Supercorporation* (Andover, Mass.: Warner Modular Publications, 1973).

38. Helen Leavitt estimates that in 1969 Americans spent $120 billion on automobiles. In other words, one out of every nine dollars in the nation's economy is spent on the automobile. See her *Superhighway — Superhoax* (Garden City, N.Y.:

nesses and interests have the power to redistribute income: money is taken from one set of classes by means of the price system and given to another. Oligarchic competition also contributes to inequality in the distribution of wealth by enhancing the value of stock in oligarchic companies, and adversely affects opportunities for minority ethnic and racial groups to acquire desirable jobs.[39]

Agencies of power are invariably surrounded by myths, and the corporation is no exception. In the nineteenth century there developed the legal fiction that the corporation was a person and that its rights were absolute under the Constitution. Endorsed by the United States Supreme Court between 1865 and the 1930s, this myth facilitated the rise of the large corporation and the oligarchic economy. More recently, other myths have developed to camouflage the power of corporations. One such fiction is that the rise of labor unions has provided workers an effective check on managerial power. There is no evidence of any equalization of either income or wealth since the rise of trade unions in the 1930s.

Another myth is that the power of property has declined in favor of managerial power, and that the corporation, under the guidance of well-educated executives, has become socially responsible. This idea, which is widespread in sociology and throughout the social sciences, is now being reexamined, since it implies that a basic change has taken place in liberal society. Implicitly, and often explicitly, it is held that the prevailing elites have won their positions in open competition and can exercise power objectively because they are not tied to special interests, such as property. Recent studies have cast doubt on the proposition that the power of property has declined and that occupation has supplanted it as the modal control force in the modern economy.[40] Actually, it is best to think of a mutuality of interests and motivations between property-owners and managers. As Zeitlin reports,[41] there is no difference in profit orientation between family-controlled and manager-controlled businesses, and dollar profit and rate of return on equity are major determinants of executive compensation. Indeed, it is probably better to think of the ownership of corporate property as a chain linking many otherwise disparate groups to a capitalist order of society: not only managers (who are

---

Doubleday, 1970), also a Ballantine paperback, for a fascinating account of the power structure behind the national interstate highway system and the political activities of the deeply entrenched automotive establishment.

39. For an analysis of these areas, see William G. Shepherd, *Market Power and Economic Welfare* (New York: Random House, 1970), pp. 208–220 and chap. 15.

40. For a careful analysis of the data that finds a significant degree of family control in big business, see Philip H. Burch, Jr., *The Managerial Revolution Reassessed* (Lexington, Mass.: D. C. Heath, 1972). For a case study of an alliance or "interest group" formed by a number of wealthy families, see James C. Knowles, "The Rockefeller Financial Group" (Andover, Mass.: Warner Modular Publications, module 343, 1973, pp. 1–59). For a review of the literature in this area that finds the alleged divorce of ownership and control highly problematic, see Maurice Zeitlin, "Corporate Ownership and Control: The Large Corporation and the Capitalist Class," *American Journal of Sociology* 79, no. 5 (March 1974): 1073–1119.

41. Zeitlin, "Corporate Ownership and Control": 1094–1095.

important stockowners) but also labor unions, universities, churches, professional associations, and voluntary organizations of all kinds have their funds invested in corporate stocks. We will turn to this important matter again as we examine the American occupational structure.

The American occupational structure

The transformation of occupational structure over the past century or so has been noted and commented on by many social scientists. The analysis of occupational structure, or the nature of society's labor force, has many important functions for social theory and policy. The occupational system puts deep and complex demands on the personality, as well as on the family, education, religion, and politics. In the area of social stratification, its importance is difficult to exaggerate. In an industrial society, work is a powerful and pervasive factor in behavior, and its demands are given precedence over almost all other institutional obligations. The extreme specialization of labor in modern society is of particular interest to sociologists. The great French sociologist Émile Durkheim (1858–1917) was perhaps the first to understand that the diversity of interest and experience that is inherent in occupational specialization is not necessarily a threat to social unity and stability. Indeed, Durkheim argued in *The Division of Labor in Society* (1893) that the occupational norms that control behavior in specific work contexts are a positive force for social integration; this insight is now generally accepted.

The specialization of labor

The fact of extreme specialization cannot be denied. For example, *The Dictionary of Occupational Titles* [42] listed 21,741 separate occupations in 1965. The extensive specialization of industrial society is also attested to by the fact that no single occupation accounts for more than a tiny percentage of the total labor force. For example, of the total American work force in 1970 (76,553,599 workers aged sixteen and over) 0.36 percent dispensed justice (272,401 lawyers and judges); 0.37 percent ministered to Americans' health (280,929 physicians); 0.34 percent handled real estate transactions (262,161 real estate agents and brokers); 0.40 percent managed Americans' banking (309,438 bank managers and financial officers); 0.33 percent delivered mail (252,524 mail carriers); 1.05 percent repaired automobiles (804,772 automobile mechanics); 0.004 percent repaired shoes (31,163 shoe repairmen); 0.53 percent operated precision machines (411,093 precision machine operatives); 0.009 percent collected America's garbage (71,417 garbage collectors); and 0.22 percent gave American males haircuts (167,256 barbers). [43]

42. 3rd ed. (U. S. Department of Labor, 1965), 2 vols.
43. U.S. Bureau of the Census, *Census of Population, 1970: Occupation By Industry,* Final Report PC(2)-7C (Washington, D.C.: U.S. Government Printing Office, 1972), table 8.

The new distribution of occupations

The Census Bureau keeps track of the distribution of occupations in three different ways: (1) it keeps a "detailed occupation classification" of 479 categories; (2) it groups all occupations into twelve major categories; and (3) it makes intermediate groupings based on selected characteristics. To highlight gross historical trends, the twelve major categories are sometimes consolidated into three comprehensive categories:

1. Primary: Agriculture[44]
2. Secondary: Manufacturing, construction, mining
3. Tertiary: Trade, communication, transportation and services (personal and professional)

When a society commences the process of industrialization, the initial occupational trend is from primary to secondary occupations. Eventually, however, a second trend occurs: primary occupations continue to decline, secondary occupations become stabilized, and there is an enormous growth of tertiary occupations. In a few countries, such as the United States, Canada, and Australia, the majority of the labor force is now employed in tertiary occupations. The trend in this direction is clear in all other industrial countries.

Precise historical comparisons of trends in occupational distribution are rendered impossible by the absence or noncomparability of data. However, it would not be inaccurate to postulate that at least three-fourths of the American population was engaged in agriculture at the beginning of the nineteenth century. In Table 4-5, figures from 1900 projected to 1975 reveal the dramatic decline in the relative importance of agriculture and the equally dramatic rise of tertiary occupations.

Another way of characterizing these trends is to note that Americans are increasingly being drawn away from direct contact with nature. Vast and complex layers of culture (machinery, drugs, air conditioners, mathematics, and so on) now mediate almost all of our relationships with natural forces. Implicit in this trend is a reduction in brute physical labor as such and a dramatic rise in physical and mental skills. Americans now manipulate symbols (invoices, checks, reports, blueprints), operate complex machinery (simple and automated lathes, jetliners, computers), and direct other people (bureaucracy) far more commonly than they have direct dealings with nature (clearing and plowing land, lumbering, fishing, making their own furniture and clothes, and so on).

It is of considerable importance that though America is now a society of employees, its basic values and beliefs originated in a period when Americans lived in an agrarian society of small independent farmers serviced by a small segment of independent businesspeople and professionals. This intimate connection between property, work, family, and politics characteristic of small-town rural America has long since been lost. In its place, Americans now

---

44. Fishing, forestry, and mining are sometimes considered primary and sometimes not. In any case, the number involved in these pursuits is very small.

Table 4-5 Distribution of Primary, Secondary, and Tertiary Occupational Groups as Percent of Total Labor Force from 1900 Projected to 1975

	1900	1940	1950	1960	1970	1975
Primary:						
Total	37.6	18.5	12.1	8.1	5.3	4.5
Farmers, farm managers, laborers, foremen	37.6	18.5	12.1	8.1	5.3	4.5
Secondary						
Total	35.8	36.7	40.3	36.3	34.3	33.4
Craftsmen, foremen, and kindred workers	10.5	11.6	14.0	12.8	12.8	12.8
Operatives and kindred workers	12.8	18.1	20.1	18.0	16.9	16.3
Laborers, except farm and mine	12.5	7.0	6.2	5.5	4.6	4.3
Tertiary						
Total	26.6	44.7	47.5	55.6	60.4	62.1
Professional, technical, and kindred workers	4.3	8.0	8.8	11.2	13.3	14.2
Managers, officials, and proprietors, except farm	5.8	8.1	9.0	10.6	10.7	10.7
Clerical and kindred workers	3.0	9.8	12.5	14.7	15.9	16.2
Sales workers	4.5	6.9	7.0	6.6	6.7	6.7
Service workers including private household	9.0	11.9	10.2	12.5	13.8	14.3

SOURCES: D. L. Kaplan and M. C. Casey, "Occupational Trends in the United States, 1900–1950," U.S. Bureau of the Census, Working Paper No. 5; U.S. Bureau of the Census, *U.S. Census of Population: 1960,* Vol. I, "Characteristics of the Population," Table 89; U.S. Department of Labor, *Monthly Labor Review,* March, 1963, "Employment Projections, by Industry and Occupation, 1960–1975," Table 2. Differences in methods and classifications employed and differences due to corrections and the updating of data all tend to change somewhat the meaning of each of these percentages and their relationships. However, the basic ratios and trends are not altered significantly by this qualification.

experience a world in which property and work are divorced and the relations between work, family, and politics have become increasingly tenuous, ambiguous, and complex. In other words — speaking modally, of course — Americans now work not as autonomous individuals whose endeavors and competitions are mediated by impersonal markets (commodity, credit, labor) but as employees of large bureaucratic organizations. The implications of this change are enormous, but, as we shall see, exceedingly difficult to analyze.

The classic (and controversial) analysis along these lines is C. Wright Mills'. The most salient aspect of occupational and stratification trends for Mills is the transformation of American property and occupational structures as a result of the rise of the large business enterprise. For Mills there are two Americas, the early liberal society dominated by the old middle class and the late liberal society dominated by the new middle class. Before its rapid industrialization after the Civil War, America was a society of small-scale economic agents: freeholding farmers; small financial, commercial, and manufacturing units; and professionals who practiced their professions as self-employed entrepreneurs. The early liberal economy was characterized by a congruent and relevant ethic: it was widely held that liberty, equality, competition, and individualism, within the framework of self-balancing economic and political markets, guaranteed social harmony and progress. With industrialization, however, all this changed. The concentration of property and the transformation of the labor force from self-employed, property-owning individuals into employees of large bureaucracies rendered the liberal ethic problematic, if not obsolete. The corporation, the administered economy, and the coordination of economy and state are all outside the scope of conventional liberal ideas. Indeed, Mills says, to understand these developments we must look beyond both the liberal and Marxian frames of reference. What we have witnessed, he claims, is the emergence of a white-collar society (clerks, salespeople, salaried professionals, and managers) and a power elite, an illegitimate establishment composed of a small number of individuals and families who straddle and control the upper reaches of class (the corporate elite), prestige (still hidden and undefined), and power (the federal executive and the military).[45]

The analysis and interpretation of occupational structures and trends is characterized by difficulties of all sorts. For one thing, considerable distortion is introduced by occupational stereotypes. The much referred-to American farmer, for example, does not exist except as a high-level abstraction and misleading myth. There are considerable differences between family farms and industrial farms; between truck farms, wheat farms, and cotton farms; and between all these and cattle ranches, horse farms, and gentlemen's farms. And, equally obviously, there are differences in the occupations of people who work on farms: owners, managers, foremen, laborers, native migrant laborers, illegal foreign laborers ("wetbacks"), legal foreign laborers (*braceros,* quotas from the British West Indies), and tenants and sharecroppers. Similar complexities attend such other occupational abstractions as *working person, business person,* and *professional.* Even the Census Bureau's categories are misleading unless handled with care. For example, its category "professional, technical and kindred workers" includes doctors, lawyers, bellydancers, Shakespearean actors, embalmers, and quarterbacks. The category "sales workers" includes high-income stock and bond salespeople, real estate agents and brokers, newsboys, and sales clerks. Of course, the real difficulty begins when low-level

45. Mills' theory is presented in what should be viewed as two volumes in a single study, *White Collar: The American Middle Classes* (New York: Oxford University Press, 1951) and the *Power Elite* (New York: Oxford University Press, 1956), both also in paperback.

stereotypes such as these are strung together to form generalizations. An important and dangerous example is the now-popular concept of a postindustrial society.

The advent of postindustrial society?

The trend toward white-collar occupations has led a number of commentators to conclude that we are experiencing the advent of a postindustrial society. This outlook is related to a theme we explored earlier, the mistaken belief that there has been a radical divorce between property and management. Given the rise of bureaucracy, some commentators have come to believe that society is no longer centered on an entrepreneurial class of property-owners, but on an educated set of elites, especially business executives and professionals.

The idea of a postindustrial society is also an aspect of the liberal ideology of convergence, the belief that society is leaving behind the period of ascription, property, factory work, and centralized power and entering an era of achievement, administration, "strategic" elites, and a pluralist power structure.[46] One of the more sophisticated versions of this mistaken perspective is that of Ralf Dahrendorf, who believes we are in a postcapitalist era. Dahrendorf stakes much of his argument on the erroneous belief that industry and politics have been separated and mutually insulated and that industrial conflict has been muted and self-contained. Industry, argues Dahrendorf, no longer supplies the model for the organization of the rest of society. Dahrendorf has also fallen prey to other liberal clichés. He claims that occupation is no longer a dominant force in a worker's life or personality, that there has occurred an equalization between strata, especially with regard to living conditions, and that these developments have helped to separate industrial and political conflict. However, Dahrendorf does not stress the idea of convergence, correctly emphasizing that modern society remains hierarchical. His main point is that society is now pluralist, a series of discrete "imperatively coordinated associations." In this new pluralist system, conflict has been localized and wealth and political authority have been separated. Indeed, governmental elites (the heads of governments, legislatures, and the judiciary) form the heart of the new ruling class.[47]

The main thrust of Dahrendorf's analysis is directed at Marx, especially at Marx's belief that industrial society is heading toward open conflict between two highly organized and self-conscious social classes. In pointing out that this has not occurred and that conflict is now managed (presumably) within institutional sectors on an issue-by-issue basis, Dahrendorf is undoubtedly right. And he is no doubt correct in pointing to the enhanced role of political

46. See Chapter 2 for a discussion of the ideology of convergence and evolutionary liberalism, and Chapter 16 for an analysis of the ideology of pluralism.
47. Ralf Dahrendorf, *Class and Class Conflict in Industrial Society* (Stanford, Calif.: Stanford University Press, 1959), especially chaps. 7 and 8.

authority. However, he is wrong to think that class and power, industry-wealth and political authority have been separated. On the contrary, the modern state is still an adjunct of the market economy, and one must at all times think in terms of an imperatively coordinated social system in which the needs of the economy are the needs of the state and society.

One of the latest versions of the postindustrial perspective is Daniel Bell's.[48] Bell hedges his ideas — they are too *ad hoc* to be called a theory — by stipulating that he is talking about changes in the economy (which for some reason he refers to as "the social structure" or as "postindustrial society"). The essence of these changes, Bell claims, is a shift to a knowledge-centered economy, which is in turn creating unique problems for society to solve. The ultimate shape of the new society cannot be predicted because each industrial country (the United States, Germany, the Soviet Union, Japan) will handle its problems in terms of its own traditions and political institutions. Essentially, Bell is arguing that the economic system needs political direction; indeed, that the shift from an economy-centered to a politically centered society has already occurred and is a key aspect of the postindustrial age. Bell rejects both Marxian and functional (sociological) theories, claiming that both err by focusing on the total sociocultural system. It is best, he says, to think in terms of autonomous subsystems pulling in various directions, some known and some still unknown.

Bell's argument is also framed in terms of the decline of industrial workers relative to service workers, which is the equivalent of the growth of theoretical knowledge as the "axial" principle of society. The empirical support for Bell's views is derived from census data on the changing composition of the labor force. In 1947 goods-producing jobs accounted for 51 percent of the total; in 1968, 35.9 percent; and in 1980 such jobs will account for only 31.7 percent of the total. The service-producing totals for the same years are 49, 64.1, 68.4 percent respectively. Accordingly, argues Bell, "if industrial society is defined as a goods-producing society — if manufacture is central in shaping the character of its labor force — then the United States is no longer an industrial society."[49] Bell acknowledges that service work is not always white-collar work, including as it does transport workers and automobile repair men (and, we might add, barbers and beauticians). Also, many blue-collar workers service machines. And Bell also recognizes that much of the increase in the white-collar category is accounted for by minor clerical and sales jobs (a significant portion of which are held by women). But, he argues, the male labor force has also been transformed in the direction of white-collar work. Whereas in 1900 only 15 percent of American men (mostly independent small businessmen) wore white collars, in 1970 almost 42 percent of the male labor force held white-collar jobs. Of these almost 60 percent were managerial, professional, or technical workers, "the heart of the upper middle class." (Blue-

48. *The Coming of Post-Industrial Society* (New York: Basic Books, 1973).
49. *Ibid.*, pp. 132–133.

collar workers were 35 percent of the total labor force in 1900, 40 percent in 1920 and 1950, 36 percent in 1968, and will be only 32.7 percent in 1980).[50]

Bell's reference to managerial, professional, and technical workers as the heart of the American upper-middle class is both correct and misleading. While they include the upper-middle class, a very large percentage of these categories is composed of teachers, nurses, dental assistants, entertainers, and the like. But even if we focus exclusively on the upper-middle class, it is not easy to depict it as a revolutionary force. One has only to list some of its members — doctors, lawyers, engineers, business executives, scientists, college professors — to realize that it is anything but revolutionary.

The rise of white-collar jobs cannot be interpreted, therefore, as a break or qualitative change in the nature of liberal society. As we will see, lower-level white-collar workers are different from blue-collar workers in important respects, but the differences do not represent a break with industrial society: *white-collar workers are different from blue-collar workers because most of the former belong to industrial society at a higher level.* As for upper-level white-collar workers, they are hardly proponents of even a liberalizing, let alone a revolutionary, political ethic. All evidence points to a basic economic and political conservatism among the upper-middle class, a conservatism often characterized by a pragmatic, reformist outlook and behavior.

Bell is mistaken in many of his assumptions. As we have noted, it is far from certain that property is divorced from management, that the property-owner has lost control of his property, or that there is any significant tension between property-owners and managers. Secondly, it cannot be said that the economy is declining *vis à vis* the state, but only that we are now more aware of the role of the state and the shortcomings of the economy. The economy and state have always served each other, and the former has always been the obvious pacesetter and beneficiary. Also, Bell implies that theoretical knowledge (a new intellectual technology) has come into play, but fails to cite any empirical evidence suggesting a consequent or eventual transformation of society. All in all, the new white-collar occupations appear to be firmly embedded in bureaucracies oriented toward private property and a market economy and society.

Bell's prophecy that a postindustrial society is upon us appears to be another variation on the technocratic theme in liberalism, which has its sources in the views of Condorcet, Saint Simon, and Comte. To his credit, Bell avoids the easy optimism of early liberalism. Instead, he stresses the inchoate nature of social change and is willing to predict only that the future will pose unique problems to tax humanity's political and moral capabilities. Despite his caution, however, Bell endorses many liberal myths: he believes that equality of opportunity is a feasible ideal; that meritocracy is possible and is at odds with substantive equality; that prosperity has reduced inequality; and that the power of bureaucracies has been curtailed by committees and the popular de-

50. *Ibid.,* pp. 134–135.

mand for participation. These beliefs supplement his overriding belief that property and management have been divorced and that knowledge (embodied in upper-middle class managers and professionals) has replaced property and economic entrepreneurialism as the "axial" principle of society.

In sum, the best interpretation of the growth of white-collar occupations has been undertaken outside the liberal tradition. Though many questions are still unsettled, it seems best to think of the growth of white-collar occupations as a change *within* industrial (liberal) society. The classic analysis along these lines remains C. Wright Mills'. Leaving aside many of Mills' tendentious conclusions,[51] the basic thrust of his argument is sound. The new service or white-collar or professional occupations represent a change *within* the middle class. Far from transcending class or industrial society, the new occupations are firmly embedded in economic, political, and social structures based on private property, managed markets, upper-level coordination, and bureaucratic administration. That significant portions of the new middle class are propertyless does not dilute their commitment (unconscious as well as conscious) to a property-oriented market society.

The distribution of formal education

Formal education is a jealously guarded prerogative of most dominant strata, and until the nineteenth century only a tiny fraction of any given population could read and write. With the advent of industrialization, whether or not it was accompanied by political democracy, the requirements of occupation and citizenship made literate populations necessary. In the United States, as in other industrializing nations, a dramatic surge in education brought about almost universal literacy in less than a century.

The United States is also characterized by educational attainments that go far beyond basic literacy.[52] As Figure 4-4 shows, only 2 percent of American seventeen-year-olds were graduating from high school in 1870. In 1910, 15 percent of the fourteen–seventeen age group were in high school, and by 1957 this figure had risen to 90 percent. Significantly, by 1957, 62 percent of seventeen-year-olds were earning high school diplomas. The rise in college attendance and achievement is equally dramatic. In 1940 only 15 percent of the college-age group (eighteen–twenty-one-year-olds) was enrolled in America's colleges and universities. In 1954 this figure had risen to 30 percent, and by 1960, it was approximately 37.5 percent. Trow cites an estimate (since proven correct) that in 1970 the percentage would be anywhere from 50 to

51. Most of which are in Mills' sequel to *White Collar, The Power Elite* (New York: Oxford University Press, 1956), where he argues that the new white-collar society, in losing its former legitimacy, has succumbed to a tiny power elite made up of the apex of the corporate world, the federal executive, and the military.
52. For a brilliant summary of educational developments in the United States, and analysis of the controversies attending them, see Martin Trow, "The Second Transformation of American Secondary Education," in *Class Status, and Power: Social Stratification in Comparative Perspective,* 2nd ed., ed. Reinhard Bendix and Seymour M. Lipset (New York: Free Press, 1966), pp. 437–449.

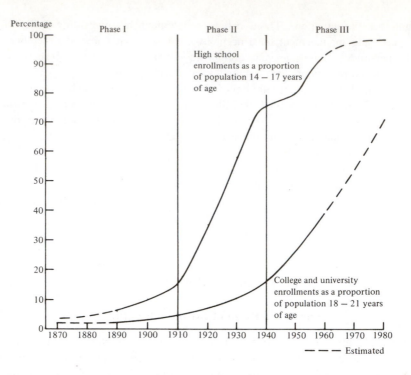

Percentage

Phase I   Phase II   Phase III

High school
enrollments as a proportion
of population 14 – 17 years
of age

College and university
enrollments as a proportion
of population 18 – 21 years
of age

1870 1880 1890 1900 1910 1920 1930 1940 1950 1960 1970 1980

– – – Estimated

Figure 4-4   Development of Mass Secondary and Postsecondary Education in
the United States

SOURCE: Martin Trow, "The Second Transformation of American Secondary Education," *International Journal of Comparative Sociology* II, no. 2 (September 1961): Figure 1, p. 153. Used by permission.

55 percent and that in 1980 it will rise to 70 percent. (It should be noted that the rate of expansion in college enrollments slowed significantly in the early 1970s, making Trow's projection for 1980 rather high.)

Another way to illustrate developments in education is to focus on years of school completed and on high school and college graduates. As Table 4-6 reveals, 63.8 percent of the American population aged twenty-one or over as of March 1974 had at least completed four years of high school. Comparisons of the number of school years completed by different age brackets illustrate the historical dimension of American education. For example, 83.4 percent of twenty-two–twenty-four-year-olds had completed four years of high school or more by March 1974, as opposed to only 61.2 percent of those twenty-five years old and over. For the same two age brackets, those who have completed four or more years of college account for 16.6 percent and 13.3 percent respectively.

Table 4-7 is especially useful because it focuses on diplomas and degrees

Table 4-6 Years of School Completed by Persons 14 Years Old and Over, March 1974 (Numbers in thousands)[a]

Percent distribution	Total population	Elementary				High school				College				
		0 to 4 years	5 years	6 and 7 years	8 years	1 year	2 years	3 years	4 years	1 year	2 years	3 years	4 years	5 years or more
Total, 14 years and over	100.0	3.4	1.3	6.1	11.1	7.0	7.8	5.9	33.8	5.0	5.5	2.3	6.7	4.2
14 and 15 years	100.0	0.4	0.6	26.7	44.9	25.7	1.5	0.2	0.1	—	—	—	—	—
16 and 17 years	100.0	0.4	0.1	1.9	7.2	25.7	39.9	22.4	2.2	0.1	0.1	(Z)	—	—
18 and 19 years	100.0	0.4	(Z)	1.1	2.3	4.1	7.6	20.2	51.6	11.3	1.1	0.2	0.1	(Z)
20 and 21 years	100.0	0.6	0.1	1.2	1.9	3.5	4.3	4.8	43.8	15.9	15.1	7.4	1.2	(Z)
22 to 24 years	100.0	0.6	0.3	1.5	2.1	3.0	4.5	4.2	41.3	8.4	10.2	7.3	13.5	3.1
25 years and over	100.0	4.4	1.6	6.0	10.8	5.0	6.5	4.4	36.1	4.3	5.5	2.0	7.9	5.4
25 to 29 years	100.0	1.2	0.3	1.9	2.9	3.1	4.7	3.9	41.9	7.4	8.3	3.7	13.7	7.0
30 to 34 years	100.0	1.3	0.5	2.4	3.5	3.7	5.9	4.8	43.6	5.8	6.8	2.5	10.5	8.6
35 to 44 years	100.0	2.2	1.0	4.1	5.8	4.9	6.7	4.8	42.3	4.6	5.7	2.1	8.9	6.8
45 to 54 years	100.0	3.4	1.4	5.2	9.5	5.4	7.0	5.2	40.1	4.0	5.2	1.7	6.9	5.0
55 to 64 years	100.0	5.3	1.9	8.1	16.2	6.0	7.8	4.8	32.0	3.2	4.6	1.4	5.2	3.7
65 to 74 years	100.0	9.5	3.5	11.9	22.1	6.8	6.7	2.9	21.2	2.3	3.9	1.2	4.9	3.2
75 years and over	100.0	16.0	5.1	13.1	26.8	4.9	4.7	2.4	15.3	2.0	3.4	1.4	3.5	1.7
21 years and over	100.0	4.0	1.5	5.5	9.9	4.8	6.2	4.4	36.7	4.9	6.1	2.8	8.2	5.1

a. The March 1974 survey includes 1,067,000 members of the Armed Forces and the March 1973 survey includes 979,000 members of the Armed Forces in the United States living off post or with their families on post. All other members of the Armed Forces are excluded.

SOURCE: U. S. Bureau of the Census, *Current Population Reports*, Series P-20, no. 274, "Educational Attainment in the United States: March 1973 and 1974" (Washington, D.C.: U.S. Government Printing Office, 1974), Table 1.

Table 4-7 High School and College Graduates 25 Years Old and Over, 1957 Projected to 1985

Year	High school graduates[a]		College graduates[b]	
	Number (thousands)	*Percent*	*Number (thousands)*	*Percent*
1957 and 1959	41,113	42.3	7,606	7.8
1964 to 1966	50,519	49.0	9,764	9.5
1970	58,492	53.8	11,466	10.5
1975	69,123	58.9	13,627	11.6
1980	83,156	63.8	16,764	12.9
1985	94,977	68.5	19,240	13.9

a. Persons who completed 4 years of high school or beyond.
b. Persons who completed 4 or more years of college.
SOURCE: U.S. Department of Commerce, "Projections of Educational Attainment 1970–1985," *Current Population Reports — Population Estimates,* Series P-25, No. 390, March 29, 1968, Table A.

earned and contains a projection of probable developments in American education through 1985. As Table 4-7 shows, the percentage of the population over twenty-five years of age that has at least completed high school is expected to jump from 49 percent in 1964–1966 to 68.5 percent in 1985, while the percentage completing four or more years of college is expected to rise from 9.5 percent to 13.9 percent in the same period.

All of the foregoing figures are significant and dramatic. (Whether education has kept pace with the needs of the American economy or with the complex issues facing American citizens are questions that need not concern us at this point.) Of course, these figures should not be taken to imply a relative gain in education on the part of any given social class or category of American (black, ethnic, female).[53] Like the rise in income and occupational skill levels, it is best to think of the rise of educational attainment as resembling the rise of boats of unequal sizes on an incoming tide.[54]

The class positions of some representative minorities

The purpose of this chapter is to provide a broad overview of the distribution of economic values in the United States. In painting an abstract statistical portrait of America's economic classes, we are laying a foundation for our

53. Data on education among black and Mexican Americans are presented in the next section.
54. A full portrait of the role of education in the American class system may be found in Chapter 6.

ultimate objective, the analysis of the American class system as a behavioral structure. Whatever the value of treating the American population as a whole, failure to identify the positions of minority groups within that whole would be a serious distortion of our picture of social inequality in America. As the data on the following pages demonstrate, the American population has been deeply scarred by racism, religious and ethnic discrimination, and military subjugation.

A *minority* is any collectivity made an inferior social group by the power of a dominant group(s). It is obvious that minorities exist in the United States because American society, despite its universalistic norms and values, has treated some of its members in a particularistic fashion. In analyzing the positions of minority groups in the American class system, we have also tried to determine whether there has been any relative change in their positions. Interpreting change in this area is not easy. As we will see, even the extension of the achievement ethic to minorities often works to perpetuate the historic legacy of inequality rather than to undo it.

The United States has a number of minorities, some large and some small, some with serious problems and others whose problems seem to be abating. In selecting the minorities on which we will report, we have eliminated most of the immigrant groups from Europe. Both Protestant and Roman Catholic immigrants from Europe (and Canada) have more or less made their peace with the United States (though, as we will see, ethnicity and religion are still important forces in the American stratification system). From among European immigrants, we have selected Jewish Americans for analysis, because they represent not only an important historic example of minority oppression but also an interesting contrast to the other minorities we will study, blacks and Mexican Americans.

The reasons for selecting the two latter groups should be obvious. Both are large, and both have legacies of deeply rooted racist oppression. As such, they can stand for smaller "racial" groups that have borne or still experience the pervasive pain of American racism. Racism in the United States has various flavors, depending on the group in question. For one thing, white Americans have employed a hierarchy of skin color to distinguish among races: the lighter the skin the "better" the race. Secondly, the term *race* — which has no scientific standing as an explanation of behavior, since no causal relation between skin color, hair texture, eyelids, and other physical attributes, on the one hand, and behavior, on the other, has ever been established — is commonly confused with *sociocultural identity*. Thus Jews and Mexicans, though commonly referred to as races, should be thought of as sociocultural or religious-ethnic groups.

Our neglect of the other "races" in the United States is largely a matter of space. It should be noted, however, that though these other "races" — American Indians, Eskimos, Chinese, Japanese, Filipinos, Hawaiians — have been subject to exclusion and deep humiliation, they are not represented in large numbers and their position in the American class system is only now being explored and documented.[55]

Minority groups are differentiated internally by class, skin color, variations in religious outlook, immigrant status (time of arrival, rural or urban location, and the like), and so on. Extreme caution should be exercised, therefore, in generalizing about them. Before we outline some of the salient class features of our representative minority groups, it would be useful to note the sizes of America's various disadvantaged racial and cultural groups (see Table 4-8). It is interesting that exact numbers were not readily available until the 1970 census. Excluding Jewish Americans, approximately 17 percent of the Ameri-

Table 4-8   "Racial" and Cultural Minorities in the United States, 1970

Total American population	203,212,000
Blacks	22,580,000
Latins (Total, 1971)	8,956,000
Mexican	5,023,000
Puerto Rican	1,450,000
Cuban	626,000
Central or South American	501,000
Other Spanish	1,356,000
Jews	5,870,000
American Indians	793,000
Japanese	591,000
Chinese	435,000
Filipinos	343,000
All other "races"	
(Asian Indians, Koreans, Polynesians, Indonesians, Hawaiians, Aleuts, Eskimos, and others not listed separately)	721,000

SOURCE: *Statistical Abstract of the United States, 1973* (Washington, D.C.: U.S. Government Printing Office, 1973), Tables 31, 33, 41, and 63.

55. For a valuable study of the Japanese American in the continental United States, see Harvey H. L. Kitano, *Japanese Americans: The Evolution of a Subculture* (Englewood Cliffs, N.J.: Prentice-Hall, 1969). The violence and deceit practiced against the American Indian is vividly portrayed in Dee Brown, *Bury My Heart at Wounded Knee* (New York: Holt, Rinehart and Winston, 1971). For a valuable introduction to the history of the North American Indian and a comprehensive analysis of contemporary American Indian life (with exceptionally good bibliographic notes), see Murray L. Wax, *Indian Americans: Unity and Diversity* (Englewood Cliffs, N.J.: Prentice-Hall, 1971). The racial situation in Hawaii is described carefully and rather noncommitally by Andrew W. Lind, *Hawaii, The Last of the Magic Isles* (New York: Oxford University Press, 1969).

can population is subject to deep disadvantage, most of it due to racist oppression. Including 5,870,000 Jews among the disadvantaged raises this figure to approximately 20 percent.

In analyzing the class positions of our three representative minority groups, we will continue to emphasize the distinction between absolute and relative data. Absolute data reveal a group's position at any given time or even over time, while relative data denote a group's position relative to that of the dominant group, especially over time.

Black Americans

The Census Bureau began to collect data on black Americans alone only a few years ago; previously it had used the general categories "nonwhite" and "Negro and other races" to lump all nonwhite "racial" groups together.[56] Nevertheless, the overall class position of black Americans can be established clearly enough, and even with relative precision. In terms of absolute class position (income, occupation, education), black Americans' fortunes changed dramatically for the better as a result of migration from southern farms to northern and western cities.[57] Thanks largely to technological displacement from agriculture, a burgeoning industrial economy, and wartime labor shortages, the black American also made class gains relative to whites between the end of the nineteenth and the middle of the twentieth centuries. Most of these gains are attributable to the quickened economic pace and subsequent boom produced by World War Two. Between 1939 and 1954, black median annual income jumped from 37 to 56 percent of white income. While black Americans' movement out of agriculture and into the lower reaches of the urban-industrial labor force did not improve their position very much, it still represented a significant upgrading of occupational status. And gains both absolute and relative were made in education.

The 1950s tell a different story, however. What happened, basically, is that the rate of growth for blacks slowed and in some ways stagnated or worsened.

56. On the whole, wherever data on nonwhites are presented, black Americans (who account for approximately 92 percent of America's nonwhite "races") can be assumed to be below (more unequal than) other minorities.

57. For an excellent short history and analysis of the black American's economic position, see Charles C. Killingsworth, *Jobs and Income for Negroes* (Ann Arbor, Mich.: Institute of Labor and Industrial Relations, 1968). Extremely good collections of readings on the economic status of black Americans are Louis A. Ferman *et al.*, eds., *Negroes and Jobs* (Ann Arbor: University of Michigan Press, 1968). and John F. Kain, ed., *Race and Poverty: The Economics of Discrimination* (Englewood Cliffs, N.J.: Prentice-Hall, 1969). For a sophisticated analysis that treats black oppression as a necessary feature of the overall economic-political system of capitalism (and the ghetto as an internal colony), see William K. Tabb, *The Political Economy of the Black Ghetto* (New York: W. W. Norton, 1970), also in paperback. Along the same lines, see Robert L. Allen, *Black Awakening in Capitalist America* (New York: Doubleday, 1971), paperback. Basic data about the black American are provided by the U.S. Bureau of the Census, *Current Population Reports,* including an annual summary, "The Social and Economic Status of the Black Population in the United States," Series P-23.

The white-black income ratio did not change during this decade, and there occurred a significant relative decline in the income of black males. Small gains in occupational status continued, but were entirely attributable to migration out of agriculture. And there was actually an increase in the black-white unemployment ratio from approximate equality in 1930 and 1940 to 1.6:1.0 in 1947–1949 and 2:1 in the 1950s, a two-to-one ratio that has persisted into the 1970s. *Indeed, the emergence of a relatively constant class relation between blacks and whites is the basic pattern for the post-1950 period.*[58]

Perhaps the most dramatic index of black Americans' class position is their unemployment rate, especially relative to white unemployment. The high rate of black unemployment and the two-to-one ratio of black and white unemployment can be seen in Table 4-9. In addition, Table 4-10 shows that unemployment among blacks is significantly higher regardless of occupation (with

Table 4-9 Unemployment Rates and Ratios by Race: 1960–1973

| Year | Unemployment rate | | Ratio: Negro and other races to white |
	Negro and other races	White	
1960	10.2	4.9	2.1
1961	12.4	6.0	2.1
1962	10.9	4.9	2.2
1963	10.8	5.0	2.2
1964	9.6	4.6	2.1
1965	8.1	4.1	2.0
1966	7.3	3.3	2.2
1967	7.4	3.4	2.2
1968	6.7	3.2	2.1
1969	6.4	3.1	2.1
1970	8.2	4.5	1.8
1971	9.9	5.4	1.8
1972	10.0	5.0	2.0
1973	8.9	4.3	2.1

SOURCE: U.S. Bureau of the Census, *Current Population Reports,* "The Social and Economic Status of the Black Population in the United States, 1973" (Washington, D.C.: U.S. Government Printing Office, 1974), Table 28. Official unemployment rates are far from reliable. For a persuasive technical argument that general rates, as well as rates for blacks and other minorities, are seriously underreported, see John C. Leggett and Claudette Cervinka, "Countdown: Labor Statistics Revisited," *Society* 10 (November/December, 1972): 99–103.

58. The rising expectations of blacks, nourished by their real class gains during the 1940s and by wartime propaganda, were no doubt frustrated by this slowdown, a factor that should be considered by way of explaining black militancy in the 1960s. Incidentally, blacks made some gains in the late 1960s, but these were largely erased in 1970–1975.

Table 4-10 Unemployment Rates by Occupation and Race, 1973

Occupation	Total Negro	White
Total, all civilian workers	9.3	4.3
Experienced labor force	7.8	3.7
White-collar workers	6.7	2.7
Professional and technical workers	4.5	2.0
Managers and administrators, except farm	2.2	1.4
Sales workers	11.5	3.4
Clerical workers	8.2	3.8
Blue-collar workers	8.0	5.0
Craft and kindred workers	5.3	3.6
Operatives, except transport	9.4	5.6
Transport equipment operatives	5.1	3.9
Nonfarm laborers	9.5	8.1
Service workers	8.7	5.0
Private household	6.8	2.9
Other	9.2	5.2
Farm workers	6.0	2.2

SOURCE: U.S. Bureau of the Census, *Current Population Reports,* "The Social and Economic Status of the Black Population in the United States, 1973" (Washington, D.C.: U.S. Government Printing Office, 1974), Table 34.

some narrowing among blue-collar and service workers). The uniformly higher rates at the upper occupational levels suggest that even education is no guarantee that blacks will enjoy the same rates of employment as whites. Among black teenagers, unemployment is chronically of crisis proportions and more than twice the rate for white teenagers (see Table 4-11).

Table 4-11 Unemployment Rates by Race Among 16–19 Year-Olds of Both Sexes: 1963, 1968, and 1973

Race	1963	1968	1973
Negro and Other Races	30.4	25.0	30.2
Negro	NA	NA	31.4
White	15.5	11.0	12.6
Ratio of Negro and Other Races to White	2.0	2.3	2.4
Ratio of Negro to White	NA	NA	2.5

Note: Data for 1968 and 1973 are not strictly comparable with 1963 data because of basic changes in concepts and definitions introduced in January 1967.
NA: Not available.
SOURCE: U.S. Bureau of the Census, *Current Population Reports,* "The Social and Economic Status of the Black Population in the United States, 1973" (Washington, D.C.: U.S. Government Printing Office, 1974), Table 30.

Table.4-12 Median Family Income by Race, 1950 to 1973
(In Current Dollars)

| Year | Race of head | | | Ratio of Negro and other races to white | Ratio of Negro to white |
	Negro and other races	Negro	White		
1950	$1,869	NA	$3,445	0.54	NA
1951	2,032	NA	3,859	0.53	NA
1952	2,338	NA	4,114	0.57	NA
1953	2,461	NA	4,392	0.56	NA
1954	2,410	NA	4,339	0.56	NA
1955	2,549	NA	4,605	0.55	NA
1956	2,628	NA	4,993	0.53	NA
1957	2,764	NA	5,166	0.54	NA
1958	2,711	NA	5,300	0.51	NA
1959	3,161	$3,047	5,893	0.54	0.52
1960	3,233	NA	5,835	0.55	NA
1961	3,191	NA	5,981	0.53	NA
1962	3,330	NA	6,237	0.53	NA
1963	3,465	NA	6,548	0.53	NA
1964	3,839	3,724	6,858	0.56	0.54
1965	3,994	3,886	7,251	0.55	0.54
1966	4,674	4,507	7,792	0.60	0.58
1967[a]	5,094	4,875	8,234	0.62	0.59
1968	5,590	5,360	8,937	0.63	0.60
1969	6,191	5,999	9,794	0.63	0.61
1970	6,516	6,279	10,236	0.64	0.61
1971[b]	6,714	6,440	10,672	0.63	0.60
1972[b]	7,106	6,864	11,549	0.62	0.59
1973[b]					
United States	7,596	7,269	12,595	0.60	0.58
South	6,495	6,434	11,508	0.56	0.56
North and West	8,943	8,378	13,049	0.69	0.64
Northeast	8,027	7,762	13,230	0.61	0.59
North Central	9,076	9,109	13,128	0.69	0.69
West	10,208	8,233	12,661	0.81	0.65

NA: Not available. The ratio of Negro to white median family income first became available from this survey in 1964.

a. Revised, based on processing correction.

b. Based on 1970 census population controls; therefore, not strictly comparable to data for earlier years.

SOURCE: U.S. Bureau of the Census, *Current Population Reports,* "The Social and Economic Status of the Black Population in the United States, 1973" (Washington, D.C.: U.S. Government Printing Office, 1974), Table 6.

Black Americans' absolute income has risen steadily, and they have even made small relative gains *vis à vis* whites. But despite America's greatest period of prosperity and strenuous efforts at reform, there is still a sharp disparity between black and white income. As Table 4-12 shows, black family income as a percentage of white income rose from the low 50s to a high of 61 percent in 1969–1970 (and fell back to 58 in 1973). But even these small gains are attributable mostly to a number of extraneous factors: continued migration out of agriculture, the Vietnam war, and the fact that the greatest black gains were made during a period when black families had multiple earners more often than white families. (The decline in black family income since 1971 is accompanied by a sharp decline in black families with multiple earners). The ratio of black-to-white family income is significantly higher outside the south, as Table 4-13 shows. But the overall stability of ratios on both national and regional bases is also noteworthy.

As we have noted, the class position of black Americans underwent a marked improvement as a result of their exodus from the rural south which lasted from the end of the nineteenth century through World War Two. But, as we have just seen with regard to unemployment and income, the black American's class position has not improved much relative to that of non-blacks since the 1950s. The same pattern is apparent in the black American's occupational status. Comparing contemporary occupational data with data from the past is difficult because the Census Bureau made large-scale changes in its occupational classification scheme in 1970. The data we have for the 1960s, however, are important because they reflect the first large-scale black experience with an urban-industrial environment. Despite some relative gains, the pace of improvement in the 1960s was extremely slow (see Table 4-14).

The occupational status of black Americans in 1973 as a percentage of those employed in various occupational categories can be seen in Table 4-15.

Table 4-13 Negro Family Income as a Percentage of White by Region, 1959, 1966, 1970, 1971, 1972, 1973

Area	1959	1966	1970	1971	1972	1973
United States	51	58	61	60	59	58
North and West	71	71	74	69	68	64
Northeast	69	67	71	67	64	59
North Central	74	74	73	69	70	69
West	67	72	77	71	71	65
South	46	51	57	56	55	56

SOURCE: U.S. Bureau of the Census, *Current Population Reports,* Series P-23, nos. 42, 46, and 48. "The Social and Economic Status of the Black Population, 1971, 1972, 1973" (Washington, D.C.: U.S. Government Printing Office, 1972, 1973, 1974), Tables 19, 7, and 6 respectively.

Table 4-14 Negro and Other Races as a Percentage of All Workers in Selected Occupations, 1960 and 1969 (Annual averages for 1960 and January-November averages for 1969)

	1960	1969
Total, employed	11	11
Professional and technical	4	6
Medical and other health	4	8
Teachers, except college	7	10
Managers, officials, and proprietors	2	3
Clerical	5	8
Sales	3	4
Craftsmen and foremen	5	7
Construction craftsmen	6	8
Machinists, jobsetters, and other metal craftsmen	4	6
Foremen	2	4
Operatives	12	14
Durable goods	10	14
Nondurable goods	9	14
Nonfarm laborers	27	24
Private household workers	46	44
Other service workers	20	19
Protective services	5	8
Waiters, cooks, and bartenders	15	14
Farmers and farm workers	16	11

SOURCE: U.S. Bureau of the Census, *Current Population Reports,* Series P-23, No. 29, "The Social and Economic Status of Negroes in the United States, 1969" (Washington, D.C.: U.S. Government Printing Office, 1970), p. 43.

Though comparisons with the past are difficult, it is safe to say that black Americans have made both absolute and relative gains in occupational status. But they are still heavily underrepresented in top occupations. Whether black Americans can consolidate and extend their small relative gains remains to be seen. It is apparent, however, that black gains in occupational status reflect structural changes in the American economy. The rise in the overall economic status of blacks (and whites) is largely due to the drastic displacement of agriculture from the center of the American economy and the emergence of a manufacturing and white-collar economy. Situated in marginal occupations, in the sense that they are subject to technological change and cutbacks during recessions, black Americans are displaced more often than whites, which goes far toward explaining their higher level of unemployment. However, they also find jobs at higher skill levels; thus their occupational upgrading, however slow. All in all, black Americans have not made any breakthrough into the white collar ranks despite their presence on the urban-

Table 4-15 Occupations of the Employed Population by Race, 1973 (Annual Averages in Thousands)

Occupation	Total	Negro	White	Percent Negro of total
Total employed	84,409	8,061	75,278	9.5
White-collar workers	40,386	2,302	37,545	5.7
Professional and technical	11,777	684	10,876	5.8
Engineers	1,094	15	1,053	1.4
Medical and other health	1,939	124	1,754	6.4
Teachers, except college	2,916	253	2,644	8.7
Other professional and technical	5,828	291	5,426	5.0
Managers and administrators, except farm	8,644	280	8,270	3.2
Salaried workers	6,815	202	6,548	3.0
Self-employed	1,829	78	1,722	4.3
Sales workers	5,415	167	5,207	3.1
Retail trade	3,074	123	2,921	4.0
Other industries	2,342	44	2,286	1.9
Clerical workers	14,548	1,171	13,192	8.0
Stenographers, typists, and secretaries	4,206	269	3,880	6.4
Other clerical workers	10,342	902	9,313	8.7
Blue-collar workers	29,869	3,411	26,147	11.4
Craft and kindred workers	11,288	713	10,479	6.3
Carpenters	1,078	49	1,018	4.5
Construction craft workers, except carpenters	2,357	185	2,152	7.8
Mechanics and repairers	2,903	170	2,702	5.9
Metal craft workers	1,159	65	1,086	5.6
Blue-collar supervisors, n.e.c.	1,460	87	1,364	6.0
All other craft workers	2,333	158	2,157	6.8
Operatives, except transport	10,972	1,410	9,425	12.9
Transport equipment operatives	3,297	467	2,814	14.2
Drivers and delivery workers	2,798	370	2,416	13.2
All other	498	98	398	19.7
Nonfarm laborers	4,312	821	3,429	19.0
Construction	854	178	665	20.8
Manufacturing	1,100	230	859	20.9
Other industries	2,358	413	1,905	17.5
Service workers	11,128	2,130	8,814	19.1
Private household	1,353	509	833	37.6
Service workers, except private household	9,775	1,621	7,981	16.6
Cleaning service workers	2,076	577	1,470	27.8
Food service workers	3,402	401	2,907	11.8
Health service workers	1,596	352	1,225	22.1

Table 4-15 (*cont.*)

Occupation	Total	Negro	White	Percent Negro of total
Personal service workers	1,543	177	1,346	11.5
Protective service workers	1,158	115	1,033	9.9
Farm workers	3,027	219	2,772	7.2
Farmers and farm managers	1,664	51	1,602	3.1
Farm laborers and supervisors	1,363	168	1,170	12.3

SOURCE: U.S. Bureau of the Census, *Current Population Reports,* "The Social and Economic Status of the Black Population in the United States, 1973" (Washington, D.C.: U.S. Government Printing Office, 1974), Table 40.

industrial scene for at least two generations. Thus they are not only heavily overrepresented in blue-collar occupations, but perhaps chronically so. A closer look at white-collar data also reveals that black Americans are concentrated at the lower reaches of the white-collar world, especially with regard to managerial positions, and that they tend to practice their professions in a segregated context.[59] Among blue-collar workers, black Americans are highly underrepresented in elite trade unions and have had very little success in expanding their representation despite considerable efforts since 1968.[60]

In education, black Americans have made significant absolute and relative gains against formidable odds (see Table 4-16). These gains extend to higher education, even though (as Table 4-17 shows) the overall ratio of black and white college graduates remained stationary between 1960 and 1971, black absolute increases being offset by white increases.

However, blacks have made relative gains in the percentage of eighteen–twenty-four-year-olds enrolled in college (see Table 4-18). It is significant that a majority of black college students are now enrolled in predominantly white institutions (see Table 4-19), although a majority of black college students in the south attend predominantly black institutions. It should also be noted that a significant slowdown of black and minority college enrollment occurred in 1973.[61]

It is important to recognize that education does not benefit blacks in the same way it does whites. As we have seen, black unemployment is higher than white regardless of occupation (and, by implication, regardless of education), and black income is lower regardless of occupation. And, as Figure 4-5

59. For data on the underrepresentation of black Americans and other minorities in white-collar occupations, especially in one hundred large corporations based in New York City, see United States Equal Opportunity Commission, *Hearings on Discrimination in White Collar Employment* (Washington, D.C.: U.S. Government Printing Office, 1968).
60. Equal Employment Opportunity Commission report, *New York Times,* 9 February 1971, p. 20.
61. *Chronicle of Higher Education* 7 (11 February 1974): 1.

Table 4-16 Years of School Completed, by Race, 1940 to 1973

	All persons					Negro				
	Percent of persons not high school graduates		Percent of persons with 4 years of high school or more		Median school years completed	Percent of persons not high school graduates		Percent of persons with 4 years of high school or more		Median school years completed
Age and year	Total	Completed less than 5 years of school	Total	College, 4 years or more		Total	Completed less than 5 years of school	Total	College, 4 years or more	
25 Years and over										
1940	75.5	13.7	24.5	4.6	8.6	92.7	42.0	7.3	1.3	5.7
1950	67.5	11.1	34.3	6.2	9.3	88.3	32.9	12.9	2.1	6.8
1960	58.9	8.3	41.1	7.7	10.5	81.8	23.8	20.1	3.1	8.0
1970	44.8	5.3	55.2	11.0	12.2	66.3	15.1	33.7	4.5	9.9
1972	41.8	4.6	58.2	12.0	12.2	63.5	12.8	36.6	5.1	10.3
1973	40.2	4.5	59.8	12.6	12.3	60.8	12.6	39.2	6.0	10.6
25–29 Years										
1940	61.9	5.9	38.1	5.9	10.3	(NA)	27.7	11.6	1.6	7.0
1950	49.5	4.7	52.8	7.7	12.1	80.4	16.8	22.2	2.7	8.6
1960	39.3	2.8	60.7	11.1	12.3	62.3	7.0	37.7	4.8	9.9
1970	24.6	1.1	75.4	16.4	12.6	43.9	2.5	56.2	7.3	12.2
1972	20.2	0.8	79.8	19.0	12.7	36.0	1.3	64.1	8.3	12.3
1973	19.8	1.0	80.2	19.0	12.7	35.8	1.5	64.2	8.1	12.3

NA: Not available.
SOURCE: U.S. Bureau of the Census, *Statistical Abstract of the United States, 1974* (Washington, D.C.: U.S. Government Printing Office, 1975), Table 186.

Table 4-17 Percentage of Population 25–34 Years Old Who Completed 4 Years of College or More, by Race and Sex, 1960, 1966, 1970, and 1971

Year	Negro			White		
	Total	*Male*	*Female*	*Total*	*Male*	*Female*
1960	4.3	3.9	4.6	11.7	15.7	7.8
1966	5.7	5.2	6.1	14.6	18.9	10.4
1970	6.1	5.8	6.4	16.6	20.9	12.3
1971	6.3	6.5	6.2	17.2	21.1	13.4

SOURCE: U.S. Department of Health, Education, and Welfare, *Digest of Educational Statistics: 1970 Edition* (Washington, D.C.: U.S. Government Printing Office, 1970), Table 66.

shows, black median family income is also lower when the education and age of the family head are held constant.

The foregoing data tell a story of class subordination, a phenomenon that will not be easy to overcome. One of the reasons why blacks in the aggregate have not been able to make significant gains is the extent of black poverty. Not only was 31 percent of the black population living in poverty in 1973, as opposed to 8 percent of whites, but a higher percentage of poor blacks were children under eighteen and a higher percentage of black children were

Table 4-18 College Enrollment of Persons 18 to 24 Years Old, by Race and Sex, 1965 and 1971 (in Thousands)

Sex and race	1965			1971		
	Total, 18–24 years old	Enrolled in college		*Total, 18–24 years old*	Enrolled in college	
		Number	*Percent of total*		*Number*	*Percent of total*
Negro	2,041	210	10	2,866	522	18
Male	935	99	11	1,318	262	20
Female	1,106	111	10	1,547	259	17
White	16,505	4,213	26	20,533	5,594	27
Male	7,641	2,593	34	9,653	3,284	34
Female	8,864	1,620	18	10,880	2,310	21

SOURCE: U.S. Department of Health, Education, and Welfare, *Digest of Educational Statistics: 1970 Edition* (Washington, D.C.: U.S. Government Printing Office, 1970), Table 67.

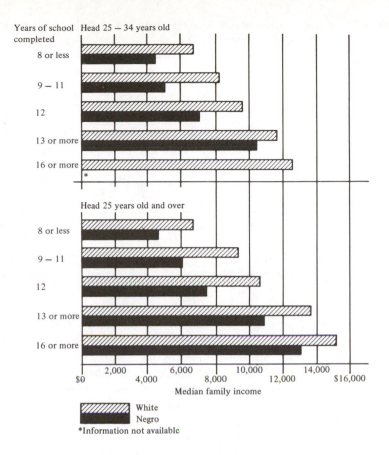

Years of school Head 25 — 34 years old
completed

Head 25 years old and over

2,000   6,000   10,000   14,000
$0   4,000   8,000   12,000 $16,000
Median family income

White
Negro
*Information not available

Figure 4-5 Median Family Income by Education, Age, and Race of Family
Head: 4-Year Average, 1968–1971

* Not available.
SOURCE: Executive Office of the President, Office of Management and Budget,
Social Indicators, 1973 (Washington, D.C.: U.S. Government Printing Office, 1973),
Chart 5/6.

growing up in single-parent families headed by females.[62] Ominously, the
number of female-headed black families with children under eighteen has
continued to grow, and the percentage of female-headed families with children
under eighteen increased significantly between 1960 and 1973.[63]

62. U.S. Bureau of the Census, *Current Population Reports,* Series P-60, No. 98,
"Characteristics of the Low-Income Population: 1973" (Washington, D.C.: U.S.
Government Printing Office, 1975), pp. 1–8.
63. U.S. Bureau of the Census, *Current Population Reports,* "The Social and
Economic Status of the Black Population in the United States, 1973" (Washington,
D.C.: U.S. Government Printing Office, 1974), Table 54.

Table 4-19 Black Undergraduate Students Enrolled in College by Type and Region of Institution, 1970

Subject	Total	North and west	South[a]
Total, enrolled	356,836	161,580	195,256
Enrolled in predominantly minority institutions	158,500	31,181	127,319
Percent of total	44.4	19.3	65.2
Enrolled in other institutions (not predominantly minority)	198,336	130,399	67,937
Percent of total	55.6	80.7	34.8

a. Includes the State of Missouri, not regularly included in Census standard definition of the South.

SOURCE: U.S. Department of Health, Education, and Welfare, *Digest of Educational Statistics: 1970 Edition* (Washington, D.C.: U.S. Government Printing Office, 1970), Table 70.

Blacks' prospects for improving their overall position in American society can also be analyzed in terms of the strengths and weaknesses of the black middle class. The black professional-managerial class has been and continues to be small relative to whites. Within it there is a lopsided emphasis on medicine, law, the ministry, and teaching, at the expense of business administration and the natural sciences. The situation is similar with regard to black businesspeople: they are few in number relative to whites, and their number has been shrinking as desegregation has undermined their protected markets. And within black business there is a significant pattern of specialization in small business. Of the few black-owned businesses, most tend to be eating and drinking establishments, grocery stores, personal services (barber shops, beauty salons), and insurance companies.[64] With regard to the black middle class as a whole, a significant change may have taken place. E. Franklin Frazier's depiction of the black bourgeoisie [65] as a status-conscious, fantasy-filled caricature of the white middle class may no longer be accurate. There is evidence that the black middle class is no longer shunning the black masses but instead becoming a source of black leadership.[66]

No depiction of the black American's class position would be complete without considering whether or not the black ghetto (and, by extension, the *barrio* and other ghettos) is an internal colony.

64. Andrew F. Brimmer, "The Negro in the National Economy," in *Race and Poverty: The Economics of Discrimination,* ed. John F. Kain (Englewood Cliffs, N.J.: Prentice-Hall, 1969), pp. 88–89.
65. E. Franklin Frazier, *Black Bourgeoisie* (New York: Free Press, 1957).
66. For a report on Charles V. Hamilton's preliminary assessment along these lines, based on his careful study of Harlem, see Alex Poinsett, "Class Patterns in Black Politics," *Ebony* 28 (August 1973): 35–42.

The economic relations of the ghetto to white America closely parallel those between third-world nations and the industrially advanced countries. The ghetto also has a relatively low per-capita income and a high birth rate. Its residents are for the most part unskilled. Businesses lack capital and managerial know-how. Local markets are limited. The incidence of credit default is high. Little saving takes place and what is saved is usually not invested locally. Goods and services tend to be "imported" for the most part, only the simplest and the most labor-intensive being produced locally. The ghetto is dependent on one basic export — its unskilled labor power. Aggregate demand for this export does not increase to match the growth of the ghetto labor force, and unemployment is prevalent. As consumer goods are advertised twenty-four hours a day on radio and television, ghetto residents are constantly reminded of the availability of goods and services which they cannot afford to buy. Welfare payments and other governmental transfers are needed to help pay for the ghetto's requirements. Local businesses are owned, in large numbers, by non-residents, many of whom are white. Important jobs in the local public economy (teachers, policemen, and postmen) are held by white outsiders. The black ghetto, then, is in many ways in a position similar to that of the typical underdeveloped nation. Can such relationships be termed colonial? And to what extent is the issue one of race and how much one of class? [67]

By and large, the black American's class position can be summarized as follows:

1. Black Americans' absolute class position (income, occupation, rate of employment) improved as a result of their migration to America's large cities during the first half of this century, and especially during the 1940s, despite their lack of marketable skills.

2. Blacks arrived in the cities at a time when muscle labor was declining as an economic asset.

3. Blacks were ghettoized by poverty and discrimination, as well as by prosperity, which allowed prosperous whites to leave the city. In some ways, the

67. William K. Tabb, *The Political Economy of the Black Ghetto* (New York: W. W. Norton, 1970), pp. 22f., also in paperback. For an analysis of the black American's share of power positions in Chicago's business, educational, and voluntary organizations, as well as elected and appointed political offices, which equates Chicago with Mississippi, see Harold M. Baron, Harriet Stulman, Richard Rothstein and Rennard Davis, "Black Powerlessness in Chicago," *Transaction* 6 (November 1968): 27–33; reprinted in Charles H. Anderson, ed., *Sociological Essays and Research* (Homewood, Ill.: Dorsey Press, 1970), pp. 141–151.

For a discussion of Charles V. Hamilton's concept of "conduit colonialism," the process by means of which state welfare funds are funneled through the black ghetto into the hands of white slumlords, merchants, finance companies and the like, see Alex Poinsett, "Class Patterns in Black Politics," *Ebony* 28 (August 1973): 35–42.

For a broad-gauged historical and theoretical argument for depicting some of America's minorities as colonies, see Robert Blauner, *Racial Oppression in America* (New York: Harper and Row, 1972).

For a disclaimer against the concept of "internal colony" which emphasizes the scarcity of data on which to base conclusions, see Nathan Glazer, "Blacks and Ethnic Groups: The Difference and the Political Difference it Makes," *Social Problems* 18, no. 4 (Spring 1971): 444–461.

black ghetto appears to have a colonial relationship with white industrial society.

4. At present, black Americans are located in marginal businesses and marginal occupations, a situation that is reflected in their high rate of unemployment and stagnant position relative to white income. After the transformation of black Americans from rural labor to unskilled industrial labor, their occupational upgrading slackened. Subsequent gains have been both minimal and very slow.

5. Blacks' educational attainments are noteworthy, and have narrowed the formerly enormous gap between blacks and whites with regard to completion of high school, median number of years completed, and, to a lesser degree, prevalence of college education. However, for black Americans increased education does not pay off directly in terms of income or occupation, and their relative gains in education (leaving aside the matters of type and quality of education and prestige of degree) should not be seen as automatically producing relative gains in economic status.

Black Americans' position on the bottom rungs of the American stratification structure is so deeply institutionalized that there is little likelihood that they will escape from it in the near, or even distant, future. Unlike many other immigrant groups, blacks came to these shores as slaves. In slavery, they were deliberately deprived of their separate cultural identity and denied schooling, and the black family was deeply disrupted first by slavery and subsequently by economic deprivation. For over three hundred years, blacks were kept subservient, now exploited, now patronized, always degraded. Despite the Emancipation Proclamation and the Fourteenth and Fifteenth Amendments, black Americans in the American south remained subject to a *de facto* "caste" system until well after World War Two; their position there today is still characterized as much by the strictures of "caste" as it is by class.

During World War One and again during World War Two, black Americans migrated to America's northern industrial cities, only to find themselves subject not only to caste discrimination (racism) but to class discrimination as well. Given their experience as rural laborers, the first generation of black migrants was unsuited to any but the most elementary occupations. In the nineteenth century, immigrants to this country could support themselves on strong backs and capable hands. But by the time black Americans entered the urban-industrial labor market the economic value of a strong back had all but disappeared. And there were other differences between the black American migrant and America's immigrants. The weak ethnic identity induced by slavery made black Americans less able to cushion themselves against the novel pressures and problems of urban life than various immigrant groups had been able to do. Lacking the strong sense of peoplehood and family tradition that had supported the early generations of Irish, Italian, Jewish, Japanese, Chinese, and other immigrants, and even the elementary motivation and character traits needed to utilize the superior educational opportunities of the north, blacks were at sea in the class environment of the north.[68] But this situation was not responsible alone for producing the high rates of unemployment, crime, mental illness, school failure, and family instability that were to become characteristic of black behavior. Black Americans were also subject to racist discrimination, especially with regard to employment and residence, and these forms of discrimination greatly compounded the problems they faced in adjusting to the achievement ethic. Residential segregation, for example, not only directly affected black employment opportunities and family life, but also made it easy to curtail the political power of black Americans by means of the gerrymander. And blacks were now subject to the full impact of the American Dream in a way that was not possible while they remained in the rural south. The bitter contrast between the harsh reality of life and blacks' aroused expectations goes far to explain the high rates of black deviance. Black deviance, in turn, became part of the vicious circle of caste (racist) discrimination — "the Negro is by nature lazy and oversexed," which led to class discrimination — "the Negro is not qualified" — which in turn reinforced caste discrimination — "the Negro is by nature shiftless and untalented, and can never qualify."[69] This stratification process has produced what appears to be a deeply institutionalized pattern of inequality. In other words, it is a mistake automatically to interpret the improvements that have taken place in blacks' legal status, income, occupations, and education since their migration to the north as anything more than a change in position from bottom "caste" to the bottom levels of class society. Of course, the concurrent rise in absolute social benefits, especially since World War Two is real and has no doubt eased the physical hardships of black Americans. But the relative position of blacks in American society has not changed. When blacks and whites are compared in the aggregate, blacks are still concentrated at the bottom of every index used to measure the benefits of American life. What is even more important is that the reforms of recent years do not appear to have produced much change in blacks' overall position. *In other words, black gains (with some minor exceptions) are offset by corresponding white gains.*

Another way to understand the changed position of blacks in American society is to recognize that, to put the matter quite crudely, a mature urban-industrial society cannot use or profit from an illiterate, unskilled, and unmotivated rural labor force, whether black or white. Without attributing any conscious design to the overall process that has transformed blacks from a rural to an urban labor group, we must acknowledge that the result has not

68. For a valuable analysis contrasting the weak communal sentiments and skills of black Americans with the more developed sense of community among Japanese and Chinese immigrants, and an argument that these differences played an important part in producing the economic differences between black and Oriental Americans, see Ivan H. Light, *Ethnic Enterprise in America: Business and Welfare Among Chinese, Japanese, and Blacks* (Berkeley: University of California Press, 1972).

69. The classic depiction of this social process is Robert K. Merton's, "The Self-Fulfilling Prophecy," *The Antioch Review* 8 (June 1948): 193–210; reprinted in Robert K. Merton, *Social Theory and Social Structure*, rev. ed. (New York: Free Press, 1968), chap. 13.

been the gradual integration of blacks into white society. (We are defining *integration* to mean the random distribution of black Americans throughout the occupational, income, educational, residential, and associational structures of the country, in effect producing a salt-and-pepper society.) The history of blacks since the Civil War, including the reforms of recent years, is best seen as the incorporation of a black (and white) rural labor force into the lower reaches of an urban-industrial system. Given the forces at work in American society, it does not appear likely that black Americans' position will change soon (though, of course, their absolute level of existence will continue to rise). It should be understood, too, that black Americans are not predominantly situated in the lower class, though they make up a disproportionate percentage of this class. The large majority of blacks are members of fairly stable working class families. But the improvement in blacks' class position and internal stratification should not be misinterpreted: black entry into skilled occupations has been very slow; the black middle class (defined in terms of the income of one earner) is still small; and black income and employment rates are distinctly lower than white rates, regardless of education.

Mexican Americans

Mexican Americans have been called a "charter member minority" — having been residents of the American southwest long before it became part of the United States — but for various reasons they have not loomed large in America's awareness until quite recently. Living primarily in the rural sections of five southwestern states (Texas, California, New Mexico, Arizona, and Colorado), Mexican Americans have been isolated from, and restricted from, the mainstream of American society. With their urban migration and the changed political climate of the 1960s, Mexican Americans suddenly became a focus of political, governmental, and scholarly attention.[70]

Thanks to a high birthrate and influxes of immigrants in the 1920s and again in the 1950s and 1960s, Mexican Americans numbered 6.5 million in 1974; thus they are a significant minority on this basis alone.[71] If we do not define women, the poor, and the working class as minorities, Mexican Americans have now surpassed Jewish Americans in number, and have become America's second largest minority.

70. Students of Mexican American life are indebted to the excellent study by Leo Grebler, Joan W. Moore, Ralph C. Guzman, *et al., The Mexican-American People: The Nation's Second Largest Minority* (New York: Free Press, 1970). Empirical, comprehensive, and interdisciplinary, this study will long remain the standard reference work on Mexican Americans. Its basic theme is that Mexican Americans are taking tentative small steps toward ending their long isolation from, and oppression by, American society, a conclusion derived from an empirical study of Mexican Americans' behavior in the contrasting settings of San Antonio and Los Angeles.
71. U.S. Bureau of the Census, *Current Population Reports,* Series P-20, No. 267, "Persons of Spanish Origin in the United States: March 1974" (Washington, D.C.: U.S. Government Printing Office, 1974), Table 1. The total number of Latin people in the United States is approximately 10.8 million: 1.5 million of Puerto Rican origin, 700,000 of Cuban origin, and 2.1 million of other Latin origin.

Table 4-20   Income in 1973 of All Families and of Families With Head of Spanish Origin by Type of Spanish Origin, for the United States, March 1974

Income	Total	Families with head of Spanish origin			
		Total	Mexican	Puerto Rican	Other Spanish[a]
All families (thousands)	55,053	2,365	1,359	382	625
Percent	100.0	100.0	100.0	100.0	100.0
Under $2,000	2.9	4.4	5.0	5.5	2.4
$2,000 to $2,999	3.2	4.8	5.4	5.0	3.2
$3,000 to $3,999	4.1	6.5	5.9	12.9	3.7
$4,000 to $4,999	4.5	7.3	6.9	10.2	6.2
$5,000 to $6,999	9.4	14.9	15.5	18.6	11.2
$7,000 to $7,999	4.9	7.8	8.2	9.2	6.2
$8,000 to $9,999	10.0	12.3	13.8	10.0	10.2
$10,000 to $14,999	25.5	23.7	23.4	16.0	29.2
$15,000 to $24,999	26.2	15.6	13.9	10.8	22.4
$25,000 or more	9.3	2.8	1.9	1.8	5.3
Median income	$12,051	$8,715	$8,434	$6,779	$11,191

a. Comprises families with head of Cuban, Central or South American, and other Spanish origin.

SOURCE: U.S. Bureau of the Census, *Current Population Reports*, Series P-20, No. 267, "Persons of Spanish Origin in the United States: March 1974" (Washington, D.C.: U.S. Government Printing Office, 1974), Table 9.

The history and conditions of Mexican Americans are best understood if they are seen as a conquered people. America's expansion into the southwest during the nineteenth century was accomplished by force of arms, and the population native to this region was treated as a subject people.[72] Quickly outnumbered by American settlers, the Mexican American's economic decline and eventual subordination resulted from the advent of fenced-in, large-scale, highly capitalized ranching, farming, and mining enterprises. Segregated by economic forces, geography, and reliance on their native language, Mexican Americans have occupied a position in the American class system comparable to that of American blacks.

72. See Fred H. Schmidt, *Spanish-Surnamed American Employment in the Southwest* (Washington, D.C.: U.S. Government Printing Office, 1970), pp. 65–68. For a radical and, on the whole, persuasive revision of the standard historical account of America's expansion into the southwest, see Rodolfo Acuña, *Occupied America: The Chicano's Struggle Toward Liberation* (San Francisco: Canfield Press, 1972).

Mexican Americans made a small relative gain in class position between 1950 and 1960, but the main reason for this gain was the migration of a considerable number of Mexican Americans to prosperous California. Mexican American income during this period was lower than Anglo income, even holding education and occupation constant.[73] Relative to other "immigrant" groups, Mexican Americans are the only group not to exhibit a substantial improvement in socioeconomic status from first to second generation prior to 1950.[74] And the sharp difference in socioeconomic status between Mexican Americans and other "immigrant" groups continued through the 1960 census.[75]

As Table 4-20 indicates, the Mexican American's median family income in 1973 ($8,434) is considerably lower than the median family income for the entire population ($12,051). And the percentage of Mexican Americans below the poverty level in 1973 was 23.5 percent, as opposed to 11.1 percent of the entire population (see Table 4-21).

Table 4-21 Low-Income Status in 1973 of All Persons and Persons of Spanish Origin by Type of Spanish Origin, for the United States, March 1974 (Numbers in thousands)

Origin	Total	Below the low-income level	
		Number	Percent
All persons[a]	207,621	22,973	11.1
Persons of Spanish origin	10,795	2,366	21.9
Mexican	6,455	1,516	23.5
Puerto Rican	1,548	528	34.1
Cuban	689	52	7.5
Central or South American	705	95	13.5
Other Spanish	1,398	175	12.5
Persons not of Spanish origin[b]	196,826	20,607	10.5

a. Excludes unrelated individuals under 14 years of age.
b. Includes persons who did not know or did not report on origin.

SOURCE: U.S. Bureau of the Census, *Current Population Reports,* Series P-20, No. 267, "Persons of Spanish Origin in the United States: March 1974" (Washington, D.C.: U.S. Government Printing Office, 1974), Table 10.

73. Grebler *et al., The Mexican-American People,* pp. 19–33.
74. For an analysis, see Donald J. Bogue, *The Population of the United States* (New York: Free Press, 1959), pp. 366–374.
75. U.S. Bureau of the Census, *U.S. Census of Population: 1960: Subject Reports. Socioeconomic Status,* Final Report PC(2)-5C (Washington, D.C.: U.S. Government Printing Office, 1967), Tables 3 and 5. For data on the post-1960 period, derived from U.S. Equal Employment Opportunity Commission surveys that corroborate the 1960 census and indicate no subsequent changes in occupational patterns, see the excellent analysis by Fred H. Schmidt, *Spanish-Surnamed American Employment in the Southwest* (Washington, D.C.: U.S. Government Printing Office, 1970).

The low occupational status of Mexican American males is apparent in Table 4-22. Of their total, Mexican American males have a distinctly low percentage of the upper ranges of the white-collar world, a high percentage of semiskilled and unskilled blue-collar workers, and an unusually high percentage of farm laborers. As Table 4-23 reveals, the disparity in class between Mexican Americans and the general population is apparent in education too.

Analysis of overall trends in the class position of Mexican Americans cannot be made with precision because data collected after 1970 are not strictly comparable with those from an earlier period. It is safe to say, however, that Mexican Americans have occupied a low class position throughout American history and that their present position is still low and relatively unchanged.

Table 4-22 Employed Men 16 Years Old and Over by Major Occupation Group and Type of Spanish Origin, for the United States, March 1974

Occupation	Total men 16 years old and over	Spanish origin			
		Total	Mexican	Puerto Rican	Other Spanish[a]
Total employed (thousands)	51,678	2,236	1,344	271	621
Percent	100.0	100.0	100.0	100.0	100.0
White-collar workers					
Professional and technical	14.1	6.7	5.2	4.5	11.0
Managers and administrators, except farm	14.1	7.3	5.7	9.7	9.8
Sales workers	6.1	3.0	2.7	4.1	3.4
Clerical workers	6.6	7.0	5.0	13.8	8.4
Blue-collar workers					
Craft and kindred workers	20.9	17.6	19.2	10.8	17.4
Operatives, including trans.	17.9	27.0	26.8	31.6	25.3
Laborers, except farm	7.3	11.5	14.2	7.8	7.1
Farm workers					
Farmers and farm managers	3.0	0.4	0.4	–	0.3
Farm laborers and supervisors	1.8	7.4	11.4	1.1	1.5
Service workers	8.2	12.0	9.3	16.7	15.8

– Represents zero.

a. Comprises men 16 years old and over of Cuban, Central or South American, and other Spanish origin.

SOURCE: U.S. Bureau of the Census, *Current Population Reports,* Series P-20, No. 267, "Persons of Spanish Origin in the United States: March 1974" (Washington, D.C.: U.S. Government Printing Office, 1974), Table 6.

Table 4-23 Percent Completed Less Than 5 Years of School and Percent Completed 4 Years of High School or More, for All Persons and Persons of Spanish Origin 25 Years Old and Over by Type of Spanish Origin, for the United States, March 1974

Years of school completed and age	Total	Spanish origin				
		Total	Mexican	Puerto Rican	Cuban	Other Spanish[a]
Percent Completed Less Than 5 Years of School						
Total 25 years and over	4.4	19.4	26.5	17.6	8.9	6.0
25 to 29 years	1.2	9.1	12.6	7.5	B	2.8
30 to 34 years	1.3	9.6	14.6	9.0	B	1.6
35 to 44 years	2.2	16.3	22.3	18.0	3.8	2.8
45 to 54 years	3.4	23.1	32.0	23.0	9.3	6.1
55 to 64 years	5.3	29.8	39.9	B	16.1	11.0
65 years and over	11.9	47.4	63.6	B	B	B
Percent Completed 4 Years of High School or More						
Total 25 years and over	61.2	36.4	29.1	29.6	47.7	55.9
25 to 29 years	81.9	52.5	46.7	39.6	B	73.7
30 to 34 years	77.9	48.2	41.9	40.3	B	64.0
35 to 44 years	70.4	38.3	31.0	29.5	52.0	60.1
45 to 54 years	63.0	30.2	20.6	18.8	49.0	54.0
55 to 64 years	50.0	17.4	9.6	B	30.2	31.2
65 years and over	33.1	13.3	5.2	B	B	B

a. Comprises persons of Central or South American and other Spanish origin.
B. Base less than 75,000.

SOURCE: U.S. Bureau of the Census, *Current Population Reports,* Series P-20, No. 267, "Persons of Spanish Origin in the United States: March 1974" (Washington, D.C.: U.S. Government Printing Office, 1974), Table 5.

Jewish Americans

Unlike black and Mexican Americans, Jewish Americans have always been primarily urban residents, a circumstance that has helped them achieve a much more satisfactory class position than other minority groups. Much has been written about the relationship between religion and worldly success (class), and there is no doubt that their religion, with its emphasis on law, intellect, education, and worldliness, has helped Jewish Americans succeed. And yet it is equally plausible to attribute Jewish Americans' success to their location in an urban environment. The causal relationship between religion and social achievement becomes problematic, for example, if we compare American Protestants and Roman Catholics from Europe and Canada. Since the 1940s Roman Catholics have made great class gains relative to the Protestant majority, and are now equal with Protestants on almost all important class indexes. But the reason for Roman Catholics' gains is not religion; it seems to be that Roman Catholics are more heavily urbanized than Protestants, and have ridden the main groundswell of America's postwar economic expansion.[76]

Whatever the reason for their remarkable class achievement, Jewish Americans' success (attested to by Tables 4-24, 4-25, and 4-26) is directly associated with a high concentration in urban centers.

These comparisons, it should be noted, are between whites. And because the Jewish group is small and the other two are much larger, comparisons of

Table 4-24 Distribution (%) by Reported or Estimated Annual Income of Families of White Respondents to Four Recent Gallup Polls, by Religious Preference[a]

Income	Protestants	Catholics	Jews	No religion	Total
Under $1,000	4.7	2.3	1.6	4.2	4.0
1,000–1,999	9.0	6.4	6.2	5.4	8.2
2,000–2,999	9.0	6.9	7.5	7.2	8.5
3,000–3,999	10.1	6.7	6.2	7.3	9.1
4,000–4,999	11.7	9.6	5.3	13.1	11.0
5,000–6,999	19.7	27.0	15.2	22.7	21.4
7,000–9,999	19.3	25.3	24.4	18.5	20.7
10,000–14,999	11.6	12.3	24.4	12.7	12.3
15,000 and over	5.0	3.4	9.2	8.8	4.8
Total	100.0	100.0	100.0	100.0	100.0
Under $3,000	22.7	15.6	15.3	16.3	20.7
$7,000 and over	35.9	41.0	58.0	40.0	37.8
$10,000 and over	16.6	15.7	33.6	21.5	17.1
Median ($)	5,460	6,338	7,990	6,118	5,856
N	8,660	2,884	435	260	12,209

a. Income was estimated by interviewer if respondent refused to report income. Income is reported or estimated for 1963 or 1964 depending on the date of the poll.

SOURCE: Norval D. Glenn and Ruth Hyland, "Religious Preference and Worldly Success: Some Evidence from National Surveys," *American Sociological Review* 32 (February 1967), Table 6, p. 78. Used by permission.

76. Norval D. Glenn and Ruth Hyland, "Religious Preference and Worldly Success: Some Evidence From National Surveys," *American Sociological Review* 32 (February 1967): 73–85. It will be remembered that black Americans and Mexican Americans also have made absolute and relative gains by moving to the city.

Table 4-25 Distribution (%) by Occupation of Head of Household Reported by White Respondents to Four Recent Gallup Polls, by Religious Preference[a]

Occupation	Protestants	Catholics	Jews	No religion	Total
Professional and semi-professional workers	12.8	13.1	27.6	38.7	14.0
Farmers and farm managers	10.8	2.2	0.3	1.8	8.2
Businessmen and executives	13.5	14.3	31.4	6.3	14.1
Clerical workers	6.6	8.9	9.4	2.7	7.2
Sales workers	6.4	7.6	13.2	5.0	6.9
Skilled workers	22.1	22.3	4.7	15.8	21.5
Operatives and unskilled workers	17.3	18.1	11.7	18.9	17.3
Service workers	4.9	7.3	0.6	4.5	5.3
Laborers	5.5	6.2	1.2	6.3	5.5
Total	100.0	100.0	100.0	100.0	100.0
Nonmanual workers	39.3	43.9	81.6	52.7	42.2
Lower manual workers	27.7	31.6	13.5	29.7	28.1
Duncan's socioeconomic index	36.1	37.8	53.1	46.0	37.4
N	7,150	2,462	341	222	10,175

a. Only those respondents reporting an occupation are included here. The dates of the polls range from December, 1963, to March, 1965. Therefore, the data are essentially for 1964.

SOURCE: Norval D. Glenn and Ruth Hyland, "Religious Preference and Worldly Success: Some Evidence from National Surveys," *American Sociological Review* 32 (February 1967), Table 7, p. 79. Used by permission.

averages are a little misleading.[77] A comparison between Jews and specific denominations of Christianity usefully reveals class differences within Protestantism and demonstrates that other religious groups also have high class standings. The data in Table 4-27, from the 1966 Detroit Area Study, are roughly comparable to national statistics on class differentiation among Protestants.[78] As the data reveal, Congregationalists, Episcopalians, and Presbyterians enjoy high class standings.

There are a number of interesting aspects of the general class position of American Jews. Jews are disproportionately represented in such white-collar

77. Those who profess no religion, a small group, also enjoy a substantial class position.
78. N.J. Demerath III, *Social Class in American Protestantism* (Chicago: Rand McNally, 1965); Charles Y. Glock and Rodney Stark, *Religion and Society in*

Table 4-26 Distribution (%) by Educational Attainment of White Respondents to Four Recent Gallup Polls, Ages 30 and Over, by Religious Preference[a]

Years of school completed	Protestants	Catholics	Jews	No religion	Total
0–7	15.5	14.1	9.5	9.0	14.8
8	22.4	20.4	10.6	23.2	21.5
1–3 high school	16.9	19.6	8.2	13.6	17.2
4 high school	28.4	31.9	35.7	21.5	29.3
1–3 college	8.2	6.2	15.4	9.6	8.0
College graduate	8.7	7.9	20.5	23.2	9.2
Total	100.0	100.0	100.0	100.0	100.0
No more than 8 years of school	37.9	34.5	20.1	31.2	36.3
At least some college	16.9	14.1	35.9	32.8	17.2
Median years of school completed	11.1	11.4	12.6	12.2	11.4
N	7,294	2,274	376	177	10,121

a. Dates of the polls range from December, 1963, to March, 1965. Therefore, the data are essentially for 1964.

SOURCE: Norval D. Glenn and Ruth Hyland, "Religious Preference and Worldly Success: Some Evidence from National Surveys," *American Sociological Review* 32 (February 1967), Table 8, p. 79. Used by permission.

occupations as the professions, management and proprietorships, and sales (but not clerical work). At present a shift appears to be occurring from the category of Manager and Proprietor (basically, small business) to the professions, as the small business sector of the American economy becomes more precarious and as discrimination in higher education and the professions wanes.

Popular stereotypes to the contrary, American Jews are not concentrated in positions of control in the American economy. Jews are poorly represented in banking, finance, and insurance and are virtually absent from manufacturing, especially heavy industry. Jews tend to be concentrated or a significant influence only in clothing manufacturing, entertainment, waste and scrap businesses, and the liquor industry. According to Carey McWilliams, "Generally speaking, the businesses in which Jews are concentrated are those in which a large risk-factor is involved; businesses peripheral to the economy; businesses originally regarded as unimportant; new industries and businesses; and businesses which

Tension (Chicago: Rand McNally, 1965); Rodney Stark and Charles Y. Glock, *American Piety: The Nature of Religious Commitment* (Berkeley, Calif.: University of California Press, 1968).

Table 4-27 Socioeconomic Characteristics of Fifteen Religious Groups, 1966

Religious group	Total N	Socioeconomic characteristics		
		Median family income	*Median occupational status*[a]	*Median school years completed*
Protestant	499	$10,117	45.3	12.0
Congregational	10	17,500	82.7	16.5
Episcopal	34	13,000	59.9	13.0
Presbyterian	75	11,667	60.3	13.5
Nonden. Protest.	10	11,250	39.9	11.8
Methodist	93	10,703	45.0	12.1
Lutheran	110	10,375	42.9	12.0
Protestant, no denomination specified	32	9,727	48.8	11.5
Baptist	104	9,311	28.6	11.4
Church of Christ	16	8,636	23.3	11.5
Other fundamentalist	15	7,938	26.4	11.0
Roman Catholic	427	9,999	43.2	12.0
Eastern Orthodox	13	9,999	55.0	12.6
Jew	29	14,688	65.0	15.7
No preference, Other	38	10,357	55.0	12.1
Not ascertained	7	.....[b]	...[b]	...[b]
Grand total	1,013	$10,177	45.2	12.0

a. The current occupation of the respondent was first coded into the 6-digit detailed occupation-industry code of the U.S. Bureau of the Census and then recoded by computer to the 2-digit code of Duncan's Index of Socioeconomic Status (cf. Duncan, 1961).

b. Not calculated because the base is too small.

SOURCE: Edward O. Laumann, "The Social Structure of Religious and Ethnoreligious Groups in the Metropolitan Community," *American Sociological Review* 34 (April 1969), Table 2, p. 186. Used by permission.

have traditionally carried a certain element of social stigma, such, for example, as the amusement industry and the liquor industry."[79]

McWilliams' classic analysis of the location of American Jews in the American economy was based on a *Fortune* magazine survey conducted in 1936. Since then, numerous other studies have corroborated and updated the *Fortune* findings.[80] The most recent summary of such data and of new findings concerns the position of Jews in management. A large number of studies under-

79. Carey McWilliams, *A Mask for Privilege: Anti-Semitism in America* (Boston: Little, Brown, 1948), pp. 147f.

80. For a review of such studies through the late 1950s, see Benjamin R. Epstein and Arnold Forster, *"Some of my Best Friends . . ."* (New York: Farrar, Straus and Cudahy, 1962), pp. 234–237.

taken in the late 1960s confirmed that Jews are significantly underrepresented at all levels of management throughout the American economy (utilities, commercial banks, insurance companies, transportation, oil companies, electronics companies, brokerage companies, automobile manufacturing). Furthermore, there is evidence of exclusion of Jews from large law firms that service such businesses. This has occurred despite the fact that Jews possess the same qualifications and display the same interest in business careers as non-Jews.[81]

In sum, American Jews have enjoyed considerable class success without accruing comparable economic power. And the way in which class and economic data about Jews cluster within every important index, rather than being distributed randomly, suggests a pattern of segregation rather than open class competition and achievement. As we will see, the segregation of Jewish Americans is not limited to the dimension of class.

The hierarchy of economic classes: a summary

It is clear from the data that economic values in the United States, and all industrial countries, are steeply and stably graded. Not only is the distribution of income, wealth, occupation, and education very unequal, but there is no evidence that inequality has been reduced significantly either in comparison with past societies or since the inception of industrial society.

Black and Mexican Americans have had particularly depressed class positions for most of their histories. Though the majorities of both groups are stable members of the working class, both make up disproportionate shares of the lower class. Though both minorities have enjoyed increases in their absolute level of economic existence, they have made no significant gains relative to majority Americans in the post-1950 period. Our third representative minority, Jewish Americans, enjoys a middle class position and ranks disproportionately high in income, education, and occupation, but because of systematic exclusion has relatively little economic power.

The most important conclusion to emerge from the foregoing analysis of economic values is that private property, economic competition, and economic growth have not brought about, and do not necessarily lead to, economic equality. As we proceed with our empirical definition of social class, we will also see that a dynamic and expanding capitalist economy does not bring about, and is not inherently related to, equality in other areas of class (family life, health, the education of children), and that the same is true of its relation to prestige and political-legal phenomena. The fundamental image that must be kept firmly in mind about liberal democracy, and industrial society in general, is of a deep, stable, and comprehensive system of stratification whose main differences with the past are not the degree, permanence, and extent of its inequality but rather its sources and forms.

81. United States Equal Opportunity Commission, *Hearings on Discrimination in White Collar Employment,* " 'Restricted Membership' at the Managerial Level: Exclusion of Jews from the Executive Suite" (Washington, D.C.: U.S. Government Printing Office, 1968).

5

Class, Family, and Related Behavior

IN THE PRECEDING CHAPTER we have seen a general statistical picture of the distribution of economic benefits and power in the United States currently and over time. We are now ready to examine the causal and behavioral structures that characterize the *overall* distribution of benefits and power in the United States. Our analysis will introduce a large number of subdimensions, each of which will refer to some concrete benefit or type of behavior (life expectancy, divorce, dropping out, and so on). Our subject is the national structure of stratification, and we will pay relatively little attention to local stratification (the small-town focus) for reasons already advanced.

Almost every conceivable form of behavior has been related to class position: methods of rearing children, types and amounts of interaction, sexual behavior and tastes, levels of information, perception, consciousness, marital styles, consumption, beauty contests, language skills, survival of disasters, combat survival, tolerance, voting, justice, sainthood, the sending of Christmas cards, nudism,[1] and so on.

1. The relationships between class and sainthood, class and the sending of Christmas cards, and class and nudism will not be touched on below; for those who are interested in the upper class bias in the selection of saints, see Katherine George and Charles H. George, "Roman Catholic Sainthood and Social Status," in *Class, Status, and Power: Social Stratification in Comparative Perspective,* 2nd ed., ed. Reinhard Bendix and Seymour M. Lipset (New York: Free Press, 1966), pp. 394–401; for those who want some shrewd ideas and insights into the middle (and

In canvassing the available research material, our general strategy will be to increase our understanding of social class (individuals or groups that share a common location across the dimensions of class, prestige, and power) by identifying its constituent parts gradually. The family is an obvious starting point for analyzing the behavioral consequences of class position. For one thing, the class position of a breadwinner is by definition shared with all members of his or her family. Secondly, the family is the conveyor belt by means of which the class system is transmitted from one generation to the next. Thirdly, and the subject of this chapter, the structure of the family and the fortunes of its members are intimately affected both by type of social stratification and by the family's overall stratum position in a given type of stratification.[2]

It needs no reiteration that modern Western society has shaped the family to suit the needs of an industrial economy. The thrust of its transformation has been to strip the family of most of its social functions, leaving it primarily the functions of reproduction and socialization. Kinship loyalties have consequently been reduced, leaving the individual freer to engage in economic and other activities outside the context of the family: thus the emergence of the nuclear family, the autonomous kinship unit composed of parents and immediate children.

There is a considerable difference between the family system revealed by empirical analysis and the ideal image of the nuclear family. For one thing, the empirical family varies considerably depending on location in the class dimension. Basically, social classes are aggregates of families and unrelated individuals who share similar positions in relation to economic markets (class) and similar positions in relation to prestige and power markets. Thus, at different income-occupational-educational class levels one would expect to find differences in family and related behavior. As the following analysis demonstrates, the evidence in favor of this axiom is overwhelming. The American family conforms to no simple model. The middle class nuclear family is by no means as widespread as popular mythology would have it, nor even, for that matter, as widespread as a great deal of sociological research would have it. Much of our research on the family is based on samples biased in the direction of the middle class; for example, the extensive use of college students in family research deeply slants samples away from the lower classes. And the smaller amount of research on lower class families tends to be oriented toward family problems and pathology. In short, the middle class family is considered

---

upper) class basis and the upward mobility aspirations behind the practice of sending Christmas cards, see Sheila K. Johnson, "Sociology of Christmas Cards," in *Sociology Full Circle,* ed. William Feigelman (New York: Praeger, 1972), pp. 158–164; for those who are interested in the middle class basis of nudism, see Fred Ilfeld, Jr. and Roger Lauer, *Social Nudism in America* (New Haven: College and University Press, 1964), pp. 69–73.

2. It should be noted that stratification theorists have traditionally tended to place the family in the prestige dimension, especially when analyzing estate or caste systems of stratification.

normal and other family forms are treated as abnormal and pathological — a perfect example in family research of the liberal ideology of convergence.[3]

Class, family, and related behavior

It is popularly thought that falling in love, acquiring a wife or husband, begetting children, and weathering the tribulations of marital and family life are attributable to body chemistry or drives (romantic love, sexual energy) and/or moral fiber (innate moral traits). There is evidence, however, pointing to the central role of class in such phenomena as sexual values, beliefs, and behavior; choice of marriage partner; marriage and family styles; number of children; styles of raising children; and family stability.

Class and sexual values and practices

All societies distinguish between legitimate and illegitimate sexual activity, and legitimate sex is by and large synonymous with family institutions.[4] Once institutionalized, the answers to such questions as how one acquires a mate, what mates are suitable, which births are legitimate, and what ties of kinship and descent exist, make up the structure of family life.

Two general types of family system — the extended and the nuclear systems — have been identified by sociology. In the extended family, values and beliefs associated with kinship tend to be deep and comprehensive; the family is often a miniature society performing religious, economic, political, and educational functions in addition to the functions of procreating and raising children. In its many variations, this type of family is often found in societies with caste or estate systems of stratification. In contrast, the nuclear family is characteristic of class societies. A nuclear family, which raises children to be individuals (independent, self-sufficient, adaptable), is obviously well suited to the needs of an economy that requires a mobile labor force — an economy, in other words, that is constantly generating new occupations. And with the emergence and institutionalization of the liberal political norms of liberty and equality, it is no wonder that arranged (instrumental) marriages were abandoned as fundamentally incompatible with the idea that all individuals are ends-in-themselves. It is the special function of romantic love to allow individuals to enter marriage as equals and to find their own class level irrespective of their family of origin.

Only in industrial society are love, marriage, reproduction, and child-raising combined into one basic relationship between a male and a female. In the United States, this unique marital relationship is shaped by a fairly distinct definition of the nature and morality of human sexuality. The causes and legitimate forms of sexual behavior are defined by American society as follows

3. For an analysis of this bias in family research, see Veronica Stolte Heiskanen, "The Myth of the Middle-Class Family in American Family Sociology," *The American Sociologist* 6 (February, 1971): 14–18.

4. Premarital sex is legitimate in some societies; see, for example, Margaret Mead, *Coming of Age in Samoa* (New York: Morrow, 1928).

(in general and without regard to such questions as who holds such views, with what degree of intensity, and with what consequences for behavior):

1. Sexual behavior springs from deep biological urges in human beings.

2. In some general way males are presumed to be more sexual than females.

3. Legitimate sexual relations are heterosexual in nature.

4. Sexual intercourse and reproduction are legitimate (normal and good) only within the confines of monogamous marriage based on love.

5. Certain individuals cannot marry each other, for reasons either of age or kinship.

6. Sexual relations are especially bad if one of the partners is a minor or if force is used.

7. Only certain sexual acts, out of the total range of possible sexual acts, are permissible.

8. The portrayal of nakedness and sexual intercourse in written and pictorial form for popular consumption is bad both morally and in terms of consequences.

The explanation of sexual behavior represented by the foregoing code is not synonymous with the scientific explanation of sexual behavior (either in a sociological or a physiological sense). And the code's definition of permissible or legitimate sexual behavior is not, of course, identical with actual behavior. As we will note, behavior differs considerably from this formal code, with variations among classes. Furthermore, the attitudes represented by the code seem to be changing: however, there appears to be little interclass variation in permissive attitudes.

Premarital sex, for example, is a violation of the American sexual code.[5] Sex before marriage is partially sanctioned by the code itself, of course, in that men are presumed to be more sexual than women; it is accepted, therefore, for men in a partially acknowledged way. The double standard, however, seems to be on the decline within the middle class. The increase in premarital sex among college-educated females (starting past the age of twenty) is associated with courtship, affection or love, eventual marriage, and a claim to equality. In any case, holding age constant, "lower class" females engage in premarital intercourse only slightly more than middle class girls (class in this instance is defined by amount of education).[6]

Premarital sexual intercourse among males varies considerably, however, with class. "Lower class" males engage in premarital intercourse more frequently than do middle class males and are much more prone to using prostitutes. Sexual outlets other than coitus also vary highly by class, the "lower class"

---

5. For a summary of research on class and premarital sex, see Robert R. Bell, *Premarital Sex in a Changing Society* (Englewood Cliffs, N.J.: Prentice-Hall, 1966), chap. 5. Bell's summary contains nothing on the premarital behavior of the upper class, about which we have no data.

6. In the research reported by Bell, the term "lower class" refers to all classes below the middle class, but basically to the working class.

male frowning on and hence being less prone to engage in petting and mastur- bation, or to purchase pornography.[7] In an interesting study of premarital sexual relations among members of different classes, Ehrmann found that male college students engaged in sexual intercourse with females from a class lower than themselves (who were not college students) more frequently than with female fellow students who were equal to or higher than they in class. And college males from the lower classes rarely succeeded sexually when their dates were college females from a higher class.[8]

However, "lower class" men (and women, where the reference is applicable) tend to accept middle class definitions of sexual respectability. They distinguish between women one does and does not marry, are more likely to condemn deviations from the legitimate sexual code and less likely to vary their sexual techniques than the middle class, and tend to accept the definitions of sexual and physical attractiveness of the classes above them. The double standard — the belief that men are more sexual and therefore should have more sexual freedom — is also more prevalent among the "lower class." Despite the more matter-of-fact attitude toward sex characteristic of the "lower class," its members tend to derive less satisfaction from sexual relations than do middle class couples. Bell also reports that rates of illegitimacy vary inversely with class, a particularly high rate prevailing among lower class blacks (even in contrast to lower class whites).[9] Abortions have been illegal until recently, and data in this area are unreliable. Nothing definitive can be said, therefore, about how abortion rates vary among classes and how these rates affect our data about illegitimacy. It would not be amiss, however, to assume that the further up the class ladder the more likely women are to abort unwanted pregnancies.

As for attitudes toward sex, changes appear to be taking place in the formal code. In any case, Reiss has found a significant degree of sexual permissiveness in all classes on the level of attitudes.[10] The interplay between attitudes and behavior is difficult to interpret, but there is no doubt that the double standard is waning among middle class females at the levels both of attitudes and behavior. The growing sexual expressiveness of middle class females is due, in part at least, to the increased education required for adult middle class status, which has caused ever larger numbers of middle class youth to attend coeducational colleges. This deviation from the accepted sexual code on the part of the middle class is far more important than any deviation, however extreme, by the "lower class." As the custodian of American morals, the

7. *The Report of the Commission on Obscenity and Pornography* (New York: Random House, 1970), Part 3, I, G, also a Bantam paperback.

8. Winston Ehrmann, *Premarital Dating Behavior* (New York: Holt, Rinehart, and Winston, 1959), pp. 146–149. Class was defined by father's occupation.

9. Illegitimacy has been used as an index of the malintegration of Indian and former slave populations into the dominant culture; see William J. Goode, "Illegitimacy, *Anomie,* and Cultural Penetration," *American Sociological Review* 26 (December 1961): 910–925; reprinted in William J. Goode, ed. *Readings on the Family and Society* (Englewood Cliffs, N.J.: Prentice-Hall, 1964), pp. 38–55.

10. Ira L. Reiss, *The Family System in America* (New York: Holt, Rinehart and Winston, 1970), chap. 10.

middle class is in a better position to legitimate its deviant practices. For example, pornography seems to be primarily a middle class (male) phenomenon, and the recent general relaxation of legal prohibitions on it probably has a class base.

Class and marriage

Over the long term Americans have been marrying at increasingly earlier ages, and a larger percentage of the population is married today than ever before in our history. Age at marriage varies directly with class,[11] however, reflecting the long preparation for adult economic roles required of middle class youngsters. Another class-related aspect of marital behavior is that Americans tend to marry within their own class (as measured by residential propinquity, education, or occupation of breadwinner in family of origin), and to marry within their own religion, ethnic group, and race. The belief that American men marry women from a lower class than their own, and that women do the opposite, has been questioned.[12] Nevertheless, it would appear that the upper class has the fewest unmarried men and the most unmarried women while the lower class has the most unmarried men and the fewest unmarried women.[13]

The hoary belief (found in many sociology textbooks) that marriages between individuals of different class backgrounds tend to be unstable appears to be an old wives' tale. A recent study found no empirical basis for this belief; indeed, it found limited evidence that marriages between low-origin males and high-origin females were remarkably free of divorce.[14]

An interesting analysis of the college sorority has identified a problem unique to middle and upper class parents of daughters.[15] In a male-dominated society, women tend to acquire their primary adult status in marriage; thus middle class females must marry someone of either superior or equal class status if they are to avoid downward mobility. In a caste society marriage is carefully confined within caste boundaries, but in a class society marriage can (theoretically) take place across ethnic and class lines. Thus education is a threat to upper and middle class families in that it mixes the sexes across ethnic and class lines and creates the possibility that a female will marry outside such boundaries. A college campus, however, serves as an opportunity for middle

11. Donald J. Bogue, *Principles of Demography* (New York: John Wiley and Sons, 1969), pp. 638–644.
12. Zick Rubin, "Do American Women Marry Up?" *American Sociological Review* 33 (October 1968): 750–760; reprinted in Edward O. Laumann, Paul M. Siegel, and Robert W. Hodge, eds., *The Logic of Social Hierarchies* (Chicago: Markham, 1970), pp. 633–643.
13. For a brief review of the literature in this general area, see Richard H. Klemer, *Marriage and Family Relationships* (New York: Harper and Row, 1970), pp. 85–94.
14. Norval D. Glenn, Sue Keir Hoppe, and David Weiner, "Social Class Heterogamy and Marital Success: A Study of the Empirical Adequacy of a Textbook Generalization," *Social Problems* 24, no. 4 (April 1974): 539–550.
15. John Finley Scott, "The American College Sorority: Its Role in Class and Ethnic Endogamy," *American Sociological Review* 30 (August 1965): 514–527; also Bobbs-Merrill reprint no. S-623.

class girls to meet middle class or upwardly mobile boys. It provides a means, in other words, to solve what Scott calls the "Brahman problem": the shortage of suitable marriage partners for high status females and the competition they face from those in the classes below them. The college sorority, Scott argues, is an ascriptive mechanism by means of which parents can channel their daughters' attention away from males in the lower classes and into paths that lead to marriages suitable on both ethnic and class grounds. Sororities have probably declined in influence since their early twentieth-century heyday, but their function is undoubtedly being fulfilled in various other ways.

Commentators on American marriage have identified several class-related variations in the basic structure of monogamous marriage:

1. The companion marriage — largely an upper class phenomenon.

2. The partner marriage — largely a middle class phenomenon.

3. The "husband-wife" or "working class" marriage — largely a working and lower class phenomenon with a number of subvariations.

These categories are descriptive in nature, and one must be careful in using them. For example, the middle class male has been found to be dominant *vis-à-vis* their wives in the selection of friends.[16] Males in the lower classes, though believing in and claiming authoritarian marital and family status, exercise less effective authority over their wives and children than men in the classes above them. According to Blood and Wolfe, the dominance of a working class husband is drastically curtailed if his wife works — an increasingly prevalent pattern.[17] By and large, it appears that the higher a man's position in the class system, the greater his dominance of the family (though a working wife curtails her husband's dominance at all class levels).

Satisfaction from marriage is a complex subject because it takes different forms and is affected by many factors. However, studies tend to show that marital satisfaction rises with class (with education and occupation more than with income), and that it is higher if the class positions of husband and wife are similar (class in this case is determined by education and religion).[18]

While all marriages exhibit class characteristics, the middle class marriage has a number of noteworthy features. For one thing, middle class wives are often "gainfully unemployed" — that is, the wife is often an adjunct to the husband's career. In a classic analysis, William H. Whyte has outlined how the

16. Nicholas Babchuk and Alan B. Bates, "The Primary Relations of Middle-Class Couples: A Study in Male Dominance," *American Sociological Review* 28 (June 1963): 377–384; reprinted in William J. Goode, ed., *Readings on the Family and Society* (Englewood Cliffs, N.J.: Prentice-Hall, 1964), pp. 124–131.

17. Robert O. Blood, Jr. and Donald M. Wolfe, *Husbands and Wives: The Dynamics of Married Living* (New York: Free Press, 1960), pp. 40–41, also in paperback.

18. *Ibid.*, pp. 253–257.

wives of business executives are incorporated into their husbands' companies. Wives are often interviewed when their husbands are being hired; they are expected to get along and to accept the husband's long hours and frequent moves; and they are integrated into the company by such means as prizes, company socials, and norms governing breeding, deportment, and consumption, including place of residence. In effect, the wife becomes an "extra employee."[19] Women are also prominent in voluntary activities of all kinds, activities that closely correlate with class background.[20] All this further indicates an absorption of marriage, including the female personality, by class. And it indicates an absorption of prestige phenomena (consumption, deportment, voluntary activities) by class, a matter we will examine in Part 3.

There is evidence that at all class levels the roles of husband and wife are deeply differentiated,[21] in effect making man-woman and husband-wife relationships difficult. What data exist indicate that role segregation is deepest in working and lower class marriages, and suggest less strongly that there is significant role segregation by sex in upper class families. By contrast, middle class families tend toward the partnership type of marriage. This curvilinear relationship has been partially validated empirically by studies analyzing the roles of husbands and wives in making economic decisions.[22]

Another aspect of marriage with relevance for stratification is miscegenation laws, state laws that make it illegal for members of different races to marry. The recent United States Supreme Court decision declaring such laws unconstitutional represented a further blow to "caste" stratification and an affirmation of the class principle that the behavior and movements of individuals cannot be hampered by legal barriers based on ascriptive criteria.

19. William H. Whyte, Jr. "The Wives of Management," *Fortune* 44 (October 1951): 86ff., and "The Corporation and the Wife," *Fortune* 44 (November 1951): 109ff.

20. For an analysis of the voluntary behavior of upper class women, see G. William Domhoff, *The Higher Circles: The Governing Class in America* (New York: Random House, 1970), chap. 2, also in paperback.

21. The sharp difference between the values and beliefs of upper-middle class Canadian men and women is described in John Seeley *et al., Crestwood Heights* (Toronto: University of Toronto Press, 1956), pp. 383–394. For differences between the sexes in upper-middle class American marriages (based on informal conversations), see John F. Cuber and Peggy B. Harroff, *The Significant Americans: A Study of Sexual Behavior Among the Affluent* (New York: Appleton-Century, 1965), also a Pelican paperback. The sharp separation between masculine and feminine roles among the working and lower class has been documented by, among others, Lee Rainwater, *Family Design: Marital Sexuality, Family Size and Contraception* (Chicago: Aldine, 1964), and "Crucible of Identity: The Negro Lower-Class Family," *Daedalus* 95 (Winter 1966): 172–216; and by Mirra Komarovsky, *Blue-Collar Marriage* (New York: Random House, 1962), also in paperback.

22. Mirra Komarovsky, "Class Differences in Family Decision-Making on Expenditures," in *Household Decision-Making,* ed. Nelson N. Foote (New York: New York University Press, 1961); reprinted in Marvin Sussman, ed., *Sourcebook in Marriage and the Family,* 2nd ed. (Boston: Houghton Mifflin, 1963), pp. 261–266.

Class, birthrates, and birth control

Since 1910 the crude birthrate in the United States has declined from 30.1 per thousand to 15.0 in 1973.[23] Birthrates are related inversely to class (especially using age of marriage, which is class-based, and education to define class), and class differentials in birthrates appear even when "race" and religion are held constant. Bogue speculates that there is a long-term trend toward family planning at all levels, and that there may eventually be a direct relationship between class and fertility: that is, all families will be small and planned, but the couples who can better afford children will tend to have the larger families.[24]

Class, family, socialization, and personality

In 1958 Urie Bronfenbrenner published a paper that reconciled the serious contradictions that had appeared in research into class child-raising practices over a period of twenty-five years.[25] Bronfenbrenner showed that working class mothers had been more permissive than middle class mothers in the 1930s, but that after World War Two this relationship was reversed: middle class mothers became progressively more permissive, and currently surpass working class mothers in this regard. The greater leniency of middle class parents toward the expressed needs and desires of their children is accompanied by higher expectations of their children and the consistent use of reasoning and "love-oriented" techniques of discipline, techniques research has shown to be more effective than physical punishment in controlling and orienting children. Greater permissiveness, in other words, has not lessened the greater amount of normative social control exercised by middle class parents.[26]

One way to illustrate the difference in "home atmosphere" between middle

23. *Statistical Abstract of the United States,* 1974, Table 67.

24. Donald J. Bogue, *Principles of Demography* (New York: John Wiley and Sons, 1969), pp. 693–723.

25. "Socialization and Social Class Through Time and Space," in E. E. Maccoby *et al.,* eds., *Readings in Social Psychology,* 3rd ed. (New York: Henry Holt, 1958); reprinted in Reinhard Bendix and Seymour M. Lipset, eds., *Class, Status and Power: Social Stratification in Comparative Perspective,* 2nd ed. (New York: Free Press, 1966), pp. 362–377.

26. In reviewing the literature on the relationship between class and childhood personality ["Social Class and Childhood Personality," *Sociometry* 34 (December 1961): 340–356], William H. Sewell deplored the unscientific nature of much work in this area, finding little support for lavish claims about the relation between class socialization practices and childhood personality. Sewell, however, fails to cite Bronfenbrenner's synthesis of "contradictory" findings on middle and working class rearing practices. Sewell's article has been reprinted in William J. Goode, ed., *Readings on the Family and Society* (Englewood Cliffs, N.J.: Prentice-Hall, 1964), pp. 136–143. On the basis of fuller data, Howard S. Erlanger questions Bronfenbrenner's generalization that the working class uses physical punishment more often than the middle class (but does not deny that differences by class in socialization practices and outcomes may exist); see his "Social Class and Corporal Punishment in Childrearing: A Reassessment," *American Sociological Review* 39 (February 1974): 68–85.

and working class families is to contrast their value orientations. Using a representative national sample of all men employed in civilian occupations (that is compared with samples drawn from Washington, D.C. and Turin, Italy), Kohn establishes the pre-eminent role of class (education and occupation) in developing the strikingly different value orientations of middle class parents (independence) and working class parents (conformity).[27] The single most important factor in this difference, according to Kohn, is that higher occupations (higher in the sense that they allow for greater independence) tend to emphasize self-direction whereas lower occupations tend to emphasize conformity to external authority. Kohn's findings, it should be emphasized, hold true regardless of age of children, sex, religion, race, region, or urban-rural location.[28] But it should be noted that Kohn studied parental values and expectations; he did not determine whether such parental values are actually transmitted to children.

To answer this question, we must turn to other studies. In a 1953 study, Schneider and Lysgaard developed the concept of *deferred gratification pattern,* the tendency to postpone satisfactions and renounce impulses in favor of long-range benefits.[29] Youngsters who exhibit the deferred gratification pattern (or the Protestant-bourgeois ethic) would be less prone than others to physical violence, free sexual expression through intercourse, and free spending; they would be more likely to stay in school than go to work and to remain dependent on parents. In their analysis of a national sample of high school students, Schneider and Lysgaard found a considerable relationship between student acceptance of the deferred gratification pattern and class origin, those further up the class ladder being more likely to accept it than those further down. Of special interest is the Detroit study, undertaken in the early 1950s, which suggests strongly that as the United States transforms itself from an entrepreneurial to a welfare bureaucratic society, a shift is taking place in its general pattern of child training. Evidence was found that those in "entrepreneurial" occupations continue to raise their children according to the deferred gratification pattern, but that families in "bureaucratic" occupations place less stress on strict impulse management. Since the occupational structure is undergoing a shift toward bureaucratic forms of work, the authors conclude that this trend will be increasingly reflected in child training patterns.[30]

Numerous analyses support the idea that middle class families produce distinctly different children than working and lower class families. Bernard C. Rosen, on the basis of two samples (427 mothers and their sons from four

27. Melvin L. Kohn, *Class and Conformity: A Study in Values* (Homewood, Ill.: Dorsey Press, 1969).
28. For a further discussion of Kohn's important study, see "Class, Personality, and World View" in Chapter 8.
29. Louis Schneider and Sverre Lysgaard, "The Deferred Gratification Pattern: A Preliminary Study," *American Sociological Review* 18 (April 1953): 142–149; reprinted in Alan L. Grey, ed., *Class and Personality in Society* (New York: Atherton Press, 1969), pp. 84–98.
30. Daniel R. Miller and Guy E. Swanson, *The Changing American Parent* (New York: John Wiley and Sons, 1958).

northeastern states, a sample deliberately designed to be very heterogeneous; and 367 boys aged nine to eleven in three Connecticut towns), concludes, among other things, that social class is consistently related to scores on a thematic apperception–type test designed to identify achievement motives,[31] classes I–III scoring significantly higher than classes IV–V.[32]

Basil Bernstein has provided an important analysis of personality differentials by studying ways in which children of different classes develop linguistic skills. Bernstein distinguishes between formal (or elaborated) and public (or restricted) languages. Middle class children acquire a language (less vocabulary than sentence organization) that facilitates comprehension of a wide range of symbolic and social relationships. The lower class child, on the other hand, acquires a language with a lower order of conceptualization and causality and a greater emphasis on affective responses to immediate stimuli. Consequently, concludes Bernstein, the middle class youngster, who knows both languages, is able to respond to and master a wider variety of symbolic and social situations than the youngster whose personality is environed, indeed constituted, by a public language.[33]

A follow-up of Bernstein's theory lends support to his supposition that the various classes impart different language codes to their children.[34] Using a sample of 163 black mothers and their four-year-old children drawn from four different class levels, this analysis focused on the communication process between mother and child. Judged in a number of different ways, the communication process was distinctly different in the various classes, the top classes providing their children with a greater range of linguistic skills than the lower. The relevance of this research to learning and education is obvious, and we will touch on it again later when we explore the relationship between class and education. Indeed, we will find class influence on personality reflected in a wide variety of phenomena: marital stability, mental health, I.Q., values and beliefs in general, and political orientation.

31. A test in which subjects are shown cards depicting inexplicit scenes, usually involving people, and asked to invent stories about them. It is assumed by the interpreters that the subjects will project their feelings, interests, and problems into the scenes depicted on the cards, and thus reveal basic aspects of their personality.

32. Bernard C. Rosen, "Family Structure and Achievement Motivation," *American Sociological Review* 26, no. 4 (August 1961): 574–585; reprinted in Jack L. Roach *et al.*, eds., *Social Stratification in the United States* (Englewood Cliffs, N.J.: Prentice-Hall, 1969), pp. 537–552.

33. Basil Bernstein, "Social Class and Linguistic Development: A Theory of Social Learning," in *Education, Economy, and Society,* ed. A. H. Halsey *et al.* (New York: Free Press, 1961), pp. 288–314.

34. Robert D. Hess and Virginia C. Shipman, "Early Experience and the Socialization of Cognitive Modes in Children," *Child Development* 36 (December 1965): 869–886; reprinted in Robert J. Havighurst *et al.*, eds., *Society and Education* (Boston: Allyn and Bacon, 1966), pp. 74–85. For a general discussion, in which Bernstein's thesis is accepted pending further investigation, see Alan C. Kerckhoff, *Socialization and Social Class* (Englewood Cliffs, N.J.: Prentice-Hall, 1972), pp. 48–52.

Class and family values

The strong, all-encompassing family values characteristic of nonindustrial countries tend not to exist in individualistic, achievement-oriented contemporary industrial society. However, one should not conclude that industrial society has evolved a uniform family system, that extended family ties are lacking in the United States, or that family life conforms in practice to American ideals. The extended family as such is a group of related nuclear families living and working together as a single structure in the performance of most social functions. It does not exist in this form in the United States, except in isolated instances. Cooperation among related nuclear families does exist, however. Within the upper class, for example, a "voluntary" sense of kinship among related nuclear families often persists for generations. Among working and lower class families, it is often necessary for parents and young married couples, or aged parents and married couples, to live together. There is also a strong patriarchical preference among working class males and among some Roman Catholic ethnic groups, although this tradition is not effective in practice. The matriarchical family common among poor blacks lacks normative support but has in practice helped blacks to prevail in slavery and postslavery class society. And, to further qualify the notion that the United States is made up of autonomous, isolated nuclear families, research has found that a considerable amount of financial and other help, socializing, and recreational and ceremonial activities take place among related nuclear families.[35]

Our knowledge of the upper class family is limited, but the partial studies that exist all point in the same direction. Some upper class families place value on the longevity of their family line, their accomplishments as a family line, and loyalty and cooperation between the various nuclear families that compose a stem or general family line. Such families (old wealth, old family) must be distinguished from other upper class families that have as much or even more money but lack a family tradition (*nouveau riche, parvenu* families). This distinction is expressed by the terms *upper-upper* and *lower-upper,* used by Warner. Upper-upper class families have been found in one community after another, and the existence of an urban upper-upper class is attested to by *The Social Register.*[36] Such families enjoy financial security because of family trust funds, high income because of their occupations and savings, and high standards of consumption; they exercise close supervision over their children by means of

35. For a review of the evidence, see Marvin B. Sussman and Lee Burchinal, "Kin Family Network: Unheralded Structure in Current Conceptualizations of Family Functioning," *Marriage and Family Living* 24, no. 3 (August 1962): 231–240; reprinted in part in William J. Goode, ed., *Readings on the Family and Society* (Englewood Cliffs, N.J.: Prentice-Hall, 1964), pp. 170–175; and Paul J. Reiss, "Extended Kinship Relationships in American Society," in *Marriage, Family, and Society,* ed. Hyman Rodman (New York: Random House, 1965), pp. 204–210.
36. For a fuller discussion of the upper class, see Chapter 10.

servants, summer homes, private schools, and controlled socializing. The achievement ethic and the requirements and problems of economic change and competition have prevented such families from transforming themselves into an hereditary social elite. That is, they have not been able to effect a normative merger of family with positions of control in the American economy and state.[37]

Middle class and working class families all exhibit significant amounts of interaction between relatives: visits, communication on ceremonial occasions, help with children, stabilization of broken families, and economic aid either bilaterally or between generations. Reasons for extended kin relations in an achievement society and for a possible increase in such relations have been advanced by Reiss: about twenty years have been added to life expectancy during this century, increasing the number of families in which three generations are living simultaneously; the increased length of required education makes more young couples dependent on their parents; the undisputed primacy of the independent nuclear family makes it possible for kin (and related religious-ethnic) ties to exist without posing a threat to achievement-individualist values; and it may be that the nuclear family (the main focus of the individual's emotional life) yields such sparse psychic satisfaction that emotional need tends to enforce extended family relations. And a point made by Sussman and Burchinal should not be overlooked: modern means of transport and communications make it relatively easy for geographically separated nuclear families to maintain kinship relations.

The significance of extended kinship ties for class analysis has to be approached by means of indirect evidence. Extended family relations account for a much larger proportion of the total interaction of working class families than other families. Or, in other words, the classes above the working class have significantly higher rates of participation in friendship groups and in formal voluntary associations.[38] The extended kin pattern in the working class has been documented in a number of studies, and forms the basis for the belief in the existence of a distinct working class subculture.[39]

It has long been believed that class mobility undermines kinship values. In a pioneering analysis, Tavuchis has cast doubt on this belief by demonstrating that class mobility (among Greek Americans) does not erode family values. Tavuchis relates his findings to other studies that indicate that the stresses of the achievement ethic predispose individuals toward increased, not decreased,

37. In practice, there is a considerable amount of family control over the economy and, to a much smaller extent, a family tradition of public service. The fact that the United States is uncongenial soil for hereditary values does not automatically mean, of course, that it does not have a "ruling class"; for a discussion, see "The Middle Class Establishment" in Chapter 16.

38. See Chapter 10.

39. Michael Young and Peter Willmott, *Family and Kinship in East London,* rev. ed. (Baltimore: Penguin Books, 1962); Herbert J. Gans, *The Urban Villagers: Group and Class in the Life of Italian-Americans* (New York: Free Press, 1962); and Peter C. Pineo, "The Extended Family in a Working Class Area of Hamilton, Ontario" in *Canadian Society: Sociological Perspectives,* 3rd ed., ed. Bernard Blishen *et al.* (New York: Macmillan, 1968), pp. 140–150.

reliance on family and other primary interaction. Tavuchis also suggests that class differences between first and second generations are easier to reconcile when they are large and when individual achievement is linked to the prestige of the family of origin.[40]

As Tavuchis and others have said, there is a need for more research in this area. From the perspective of stratification analysis, it would be useful to know how kinship links that transcend class differences reduce class distinctions and class consciousness. We also need to know more about the exact pattern of kinship links across class lines, especially patterns of mutual aid, and about kinship patterns at all class levels, especially among the upper and the lower classes.

An important index of the tendency of class society to erode or prevent the formation of familism is the steady growth of the category Unrelated Individuals (which consists largely of households made up of older citizens with low income): In terms of training and life experience, both aged parents and children have been trained not to be dependent, and both probably value independence from confining family obligations. Other indexes to the class system of family life are the nursing home, the retirement village, senior citizens' housing, and legislation aimed specifically at easing the economic position of the aged living in separate households.[41]

Perhaps the best-known index of the relationship between class and family values is the "separation" between parents and children that is a "necessary" feature of socialization in industrial society, a separation marked by significant estrangement and conflict.[42] In sum, despite the existence of extended kin ties, the modal family structure in class society is still the nuclear family.

Class and family stability

The disruption of family life can take a number of forms: premature death of the breadwinner, desertion, separation, divorce, and even role impairment, or the inability of one or more family members to perform a family role(s). There are many suppositions about the relation between class and family instability, but little systematic research has been undertaken. There is no direct census data on divorce, separation, and desertion, and much of the research in this area is limited to the middle and upper classes. The data that do exist, however, indicate that class level deeply affects the stability of family life.[43]

40. Nicholas Tavuchis, *Family and Mobility Among Greek-Americans* (Athens: National Centre of Social Research, 1972).

41. Most individuals in an achievement society are drastically declassed by retirement and old age, posing problems peculiar to the class system of inequality.

42. For an old but still unsurpassed analysis of the conflict between generations, see Kingsley Davis, "The Sociology of Parent-Youth Conflict," *American Sociological Review* 5 (August 1940): 523–535; reprinted in Rose Coser, ed., *The Family: Its Structure and Functions* (New York: St. Martin's Press, 1966), pp. 455–471. Most youth, it should be noted, are not estranged from their parents.

43. For an influential pioneering interpretation of scattered data drawn from a few community studies that emphasizes the class nature of family stability, as well

Census data on divorce and separation require considerable reworking to make them meaningful for stratification analysis. In his analysis of the 1960 census, Udry found an unmistakable inverse relation between total disruption rates (divorce and separation) and education for both men and women and for both whites and nonwhites, and a clear inverse relation between marital disruption and occupation and income for all males. The data suggest a direct relation between women's occupations and income and marital instability — the higher the occupation and income, the more marital instability; however, such data cannot be interpreted easily, since occupational status and income are, normatively speaking, not primary class attributes of women and because marital instability itself may lead women into certain types of occupations. The data for women, therefore, should not be taken as contradicting the fundamentally inverse relation between class and marital instability.[44]

The general impact of class on marital-family stability is unmistakable. Surprisingly, the high rate of instability of the lower (as distinct from working) class family has not received much research attention. On the basis of his study of desertion in Philadelphia, Kephart has questioned the validity of generalizations that attribute unusually high desertion rates to lower class white and nonwhite males.[45]

In a pioneering case study conducted during the Great Depression, Komarovsky pointed to the impaired authority (especially in instrumental marriages, as opposed to marriages with a religious base) of the unemployed husband relative to his wife.[46] In her more recent case study of blue-collar marriage, Komarovsky has pointed to the severe estrangement between the sexes that is characteristic of the normal functioning of the working class family.[47] Of some interest in this regard is the opinion of Cuber and Harroff, who conducted a study based on informal conversations with upper-middle class middle-aged couples, that "good" marriages are uncommon at any level. The sexes are so

as the tentativeness of the generalizations proposed, see August B. Hollingshead, "Class Differences in Family Stability," *Annals of the American Academy of Political and Social Science* 272 (November 1950): 39–46; also Bobbs-Merrill reprint no. 118.

44. J. Richard Udry, "Marital Instability by Race, Sex, Education, and Occupation Using 1960 Census Data," *American Journal of Sociology* 72, no. 2 (September 1966): 203–209; and "Marital Instability by Race and Income Based on 1960 Census Data," *American Journal of Sociology* 72, no. 6 (May 1967): 673–674. For a later analysis, based on the "1967 Survey by the Office of Economic Opportunity," that confirms the relation between class (income and education) and family instability, see U.S. Bureau of the Census, *Current Population Reports*, Series P-20, No. 223, "Social and Economic Variations in Marriage, Divorce, and Remarriage: 1967" (Washington, D.C.: U.S. Government Printing Office, 1971), Tables D, 4, and 11. Remarriage rates are also higher at the upper end of the income scale.

45. William M. Kephart, "Occupational Level and Marital Disruption," *American Sociological Review* 20 (August 1955): 456–465; reprinted in Jack L. Roach *et al.*, eds., *Social Stratification in the United States* (Englewood Cliffs, N.J.: Prentice-Hall, 1969), pp. 430–442.

46. Mirra Komarovsky, *The Unemployed Man and His Family* (New York: Dryden Press, 1940).

47. Mirra Komarovsky, *Blue-Collar Marriage* (New York: Random House, 1962), also in paperback.

deeply differentiated, they argue, that "good" marriages are difficult almost by definition.[48] However, the data on marital satisfaction we cited earlier reveal a direct relation between marital satisfaction and class.[49]

One of the more interesting attempts at a general explanation of marital failure, with important implications for class society, is Kirkpatrick's concept of *ethical inconsistency*.[50] Kirkpatrick argues that the United States has three general marital models, defined in terms of the wife's role: the wife-mother, partner, and companion types. Each is related to a specific class and each specifies a different set of rights and duties for the wife. But because all three types are well known beyond the confines of their classes of origin (and because of the society's general encouragement of self-interest), women tend to adopt aspects of each that are in their interest, while men select aspects in the interest of the husband. The result is that marriage at all levels is heavily burdened by contradictory role expectations. Men expect their wives to be hardworking drudges who are also responsible, efficient, pleasant to be with, and glamorous, while women expect credit and respect for household work, economic security, a say in family decisions, and certain forms of indulgence because they are women (romance, luxuries, courtesy). Too much should not be made of Kirkpatrick's limited study. But its theme is reminiscent of Merton's explanation of deviance, which helps to place marital instability in a broad social context and to bring it within the orbit of anomie theory.[51] In any case, the United States' universal encouragement of self-interest, together with its multiple class-related marriage models, makes it highly unlikely that many married individuals at any class level will experience the stability and satisfactions of role complementarity in marriage.

The family life of representative minorities

Our three representative minority groups exhibit marked contrasts in family life. Black and Mexican American families are distinctly less stable than Jewish American families, and blacks have more unstable families than Mexican Americans.

The black American family

The black family does not compare favorably with nonwhite families. Research has unveiled a grim picture, whose features are as follows. (The reader should remember that the following statements are statistical generalizations about

48. John F. Cuber and Peggy B. Harroff, *The Significant Americans: A Study of Sexual Behavior Among the Affluent* (New York: Appleton-Century, 1965), also a Pelican paperback.

49. Robert O. Blood, Jr., and Donald M. Wolfe, *Husbands and Wives: The Dynamics of Married Living* (New York: Free Press, 1960), pp. 253–257.

50. Clifford Kirkpatrick, "The Measurement of Ethical Consistency in Marriage," *International Journal of Ethics* 46 (July 1935): 444–460.

51. For Merton's theory of anomie, see "Class, Universal Goals, and Deviant Behavior" in Chapter 14.

1. Significant numbers of black males are marginal in the economy, and thus in their marriages and families. Black males are more passive at home than whites, and share tasks less with their wives.

2. The male is absent more in black homes than in white homes.

3. There is deeper estrangement between the sexes both before and after marriage among blacks than whites.

4. Lower income and more members place greater financial strains on the black family.

5. Rates of family disruption due to desertion, separation, divorce, and death are much higher among blacks than among whites.[52]

All these data are characterized by marked variations by class; black family life is highly various, ranging from matriarchal-extended forms among poor blacks in both rural and urban areas to the nuclear family among working and middle class blacks.[53] A great deal of attention has been given to the pathology of the lower class black family, while the adaptive mechanisms developed by blacks to cope with a hostile social environment have been neglected; the fact remains that two-thirds of black families are far from pathological. Given the sociocultural realities of slavery and segregation, migration and economic marginality, it is not surprising that the black family has experienced severe instability and malfunctioning. By definition, the nuclear family needs support: steady employment for the breadwinner; a congenial neighborhood of stable families; a compatible, supportive school system, and so on. All these supports were denied large portions of the black population as it struggled to overcome the legacy of slavery and segregation.

Despite the pathology of the black family, scholars (both black and white) have assumed that the black family will gradually approximate the white nuclear family as blacks are incorporated into the modern economy. This is the general thesis, for example, of E. Franklin Frazier's classic study *The Negro Family in the United States*.[54] It is also inherent in Daniel P. Moynihan's policy-oriented report on the pathology of the black family, "The Negro Family: The Case for National Action".[55] To test this general thesis, John Scanzoni studied a group of black families in Indianapolis above the lower class, selected to be roughly representative of the two-thirds of black families that are not

52. For a succinct analysis of black family life within the context of stratification theory, see Robert O. Blood, Jr., *The Family* (New York: Free Press, 1972), pp. 80–88.

53. For a wide-ranging theoretical and historical analysis of the black family, see Andrew Billingsley, assisted by Amy Tate Billingsley, *Black Families in White America* (Englewood Cliffs, N.J.: Prentice-Hall, 1968).

54. Rev. and abridged ed. (New York: Dryden Press, 1948), originally published 1939.

55. For this report and the controversy surrounding it, see Lee Rainwater and William L. Yancey, eds., *The Moynihan Report and the Politics of Controversy* (Cambridge, Mass.: M.I.T. Press, 1967).

poor and atypical.[56] Scanzoni found Frazier's thesis to be partially true and partially false. It was accurate in the sense that blacks overwhelmingly accept the nuclear family of two parents and their immediate children as the normal and most desirable family form. And Scanzoni also found that class background is strongly related to black family behavior; more specifically, as blacks find regular employment, they develop the typical nuclear family form and tend to have more stable families. But while Scanzoni found mostly stable families, he was careful not to endorse Frazier's thesis, since other research shows that while both white and black marriages become more stable with a rise in class position (education, occupation, income), black marriages' disruption rates are uniformly far higher than white marriages' at all class levels. (Black and white rates are parallel for occupation, converge slightly with increased education, and diverge more than slightly with increased income).[57] It is clear, according to Udry, that one must number among the burdens that black marriages bear not only class factors but also the legacy of slavery.

Identifying the causes of black family instability is not easy. Black income, for example, is decidedly lower than white, holding education and occupation constant, and this in itself imposes an enormous strain on the black family. Perhaps a full-bodied historical approach is needed. The legacy of oppression may impose such burdens that even blacks who move up the class ladder do so at greater cost to personality and family than whites must pay. In any case, it is clear that black family problems stem from economic and other forms of deprivation, and that while black family life has begun to approximate white family behavior (since both are inhabitants of an industrial society), even the more stable aggregate of nuclear families composed of regularly employed blacks is markedly less stable than its white counterpart.

The Mexican American family

One of the most prevalent stereotypes of Mexican Americans is that their lives are centered around their families. In a sense, this is true, as it is for all economically and politically marginal people. However, the full-blown stereotype tends to stress the richness of Mexican American family life, its stability, the authority of the male, and a preference for extended kin relations; and here one must distinguish between romantic myth and operational reality.[58] For

56. John H. Scanzoni, *The Black Family in Modern Society* (Boston: Allyn and Bacon, 1971).

57. J. Richard Udry, "Marital Instability by Race, Sex, Education, and Occupation Using 1960 Census Data," *American Journal of Sociology* 72, no. 2 (September 1966): 203–209, and "Marital Instability by Race and Income Based on 1960 Census Data," *American Journal of Sociology* 72, no. 6 (May 1967): 673–674; reprinted as one essay in Charles V. Willie, ed., *The Family Life of Black People* (Columbus, Ohio: Charles E. Merrill, 1970), pp. 143–155.

58. The following passage relies on the empirical study of Mexican American families in San Antonio and Los Angeles by Leo Grebler, Joan W. Moore, and Ralph Guzman *et al.*, *The Mexican-American People: The Nation's Second Largest Minority* (New York: Free Press, 1970), chap. 15.

one thing, it is clear that Mexican Americans prefer the separate nuclear family household. For another, many Mexican American families lack both parents (especially the male), which confutes the widespread notion that the Mexican American family is universally stable. Further, there is considerable doubt that the patriarchical family of normative definition is patriarchical in practice. Though the norm of male dominance is maintained, women in practice exercise considerable power. The use of contraceptives is high, especially among women, attesting both to their independence and to their lack of desire for large families. (The acceptance of birth control is higher among higher income groups.) All in all, the Mexican American family in the prosperous and dynamic setting of Los Angeles tends to exhibit typical urban-industrial (class) values. Though data are scanty, the lower class Mexican American family appears to be more traditional in attitudes and more unstable. All in all, the harsh realities of poverty and isolation have had an impact on the Mexican American family, as they have on all poor people.

The Jewish American family

Data on religious groups and family stability are not collected explicitly or fully by the United States Census Bureau, and here again we must piece together data from a variety of sources. In his study of religion in Detroit, Gerhard Lenski found that Jews had a lower divorce rate than Protestants or Roman Catholics.[59] Lenski's finding was confirmed by Sidney Goldstein and Calvin Goldscheider in their comparison of Jewish and non-Jewish marriages in the Providence-Pawtucket urban area. Jewish family life was found to be characterized by lower divorce and separation rates, indicating considerable stability. There was some evidence of increased divorce and separation with an increase in education and over time, but no indication of a significant growth of family instability.[60]

A different form of instability is intermarriage (which is also related to assimilation). Though rates of intermarriage between Jews and non-Jews are rising, they do not indicate a general trend toward the absorption of the Jewish population into the gentile world.[61]

All in all, the Jewish American family is remarkably stable. The reasons for this stability are varied, and include a strong religious emphasis on family life, a long history of persecution that forced Jews to rely on themselves and their families for survival, and middle class status.

59. Gerhard Lenski, *The Religious Factor: A Sociological Study of Religion's Impact on Politics, Economics, and Family Life,* rev. ed. (New York: Doubleday, 1963), pp. 218–219, an Anchor paperback.

60. Sidney Goldstein and Calvin Goldscheider, *Jewish Americans: Three Generations of a Jewish Community* (Englewood Cliffs, N.J.: Prentice-Hall, 1968), chap. 5.

61. Sidney Goldstein, "American Jewry: A Demographic Analysis" in *The Future of the Jewish Community in America,* ed. David Sidorsky (New York: Basic Books, 1973), pp. 81–89.

Class and differentials in health and life expectancy
Class and health

Despite absolute improvements in nutrition, sanitation, medicine, and knowledge over the past century or so, there is still a pronounced relationship between class and health: each class level enjoys better health and uses medical and dental services more than the classes below, and the correlation between class and health is especially pronounced among the poor, particularly the black poor.[62] While the overall medical plight of black Americans is due to their class position, Richardson cites data showing that nonwhites visit physicians less often than whites, even holding family income constant.[63]

Thanks to surveys conducted in the 1950s, we also have a clear picture of the relation between class and medical expenditures and insurance coverage. In 1953 the bottom third of the family income hierarchy was found to have significantly less health insurance than the upper two-thirds.[64] By 1958 the percentage of all families covered by insurance had increased, but the percentage among the poorest third was virtually unchanged.[65] Unsurprisingly, expenditures for health services per family and per individual rise considerably as one goes up the income ladder.[66]

In an interesting analysis that should not go unacknowledged, Kadushin has argued that the traditional relationship between class and health has been modified significantly in the direction of equality.[67] This proposition must be qualified, however, in a number of ways. Kadushin also notes (perhaps too unemphatically, because it runs counter to his main thesis) that disease and poverty continue to be related, even in the United States. Given that we are

62. William C. Richardson, "Poverty, Illness, and the Use of Health Services in the United States," *Hospitals* 43 (July 1969): 34–50; reprinted in E. Gartley Jaco, ed., *Patients, Physicians and Illness: A Sourcebook in Behavioral Science and Health,* 2nd ed. (New York: Free Press, 1972), pp. 240–249.

63. Richardson, "Poverty, Illness, and the Use of Health Services," p. 245. For a comprehensive review of black Americans' health problems, which notes that the absolute improvement in the health and life expectancy of blacks has not been matched by a relative improvement because of their class position, see Ralph H. Hines, "The Health Status of Black Americans: Changing Perspectives" in *Patients, Physicians and Illness: A Sourcebook in Behavioral Science and Health,* 2nd ed., ed. E. Gartley Jaco (New York: Free Press, 1972), pp. 40–50.

64. Odin W. Anderson with Jacob J. Feldman, *Family Medical Costs and Voluntary Health Insurance: A Nationwide Survey* (New York: McGraw-Hill, 1956), chap. 3.

65. Odin W. Anderson, Patricia Collette, and Jacob J. Feldman, *Changes in Family Medical Care Expenditures and Voluntary Health Insurance: A Five-Year Resurvey* (Cambridge, Mass.: Harvard University Press, 1963), chap. 2.

66. Anderson *et al., Changes in Family Medical Care Expenditures,* p. 17. Incidentally, neither the 1953 nor the 1958 survey analyzes health expenditures or insurance by race.

67. Charles Kadushin, "Social Class and the Experience of Ill Health," *Sociological Inquiry* 34 (Winter 1964): 67–80; reprinted in Reinhard Bendix and Seymour M. Lipset, eds., *Class, Status and Power: Social Stratification in Comparative Perspective,* 2nd ed. (New York: Free Press, 1966), pp. 406–412.

now more aware of the extent and persistence of poverty than when Kadushin wrote, progress toward the equalization of health among the classes should not be exaggerated. Kadushin also points out that, relative to the classes above them, the lower classes feel sicker, worry more about sickness, and are less likely to visit doctors, behavioral patterns that are not unimportant when assessing the relation between class and health.

The relationship between specific diseases and class has probably also declined, but here too a correlation between disease and poverty persists. The pattern appears to be that high-contagion diseases that threaten all, such as poliomyelitis, have been contained, but that low-contagion diseases like tuberculosis still persist among nonwhites and the urban poor.[68] (Actually polio is of more danger to the upper classes than to the lower because the latter have developed immunity to it over the generations.) And as we have noted, there is also a marked difference by class in people's ability to secure medical attention and care.[69]

There is a pronounced relation between class and work-related health benefits, disabilities, and loss of work. Office workers tend to be distinctly better provided for in terms of medical insurance and sick leave than plant workers.[70] Furthermore, workers in manufacturing, trucking, warehousing, and especially coal-mining tend to suffer more, and have more severe accidents and lose more days of work per case, than communication, finance, and insurance workers.[71] There is also a marked difference in days of work lost due to disability relative to education and income and a smaller difference relative to broad occupational categories, the upper levels being favored over the lower in both instances. For the general noninstitutionalized civilian population, there is a significant difference between income and education levels on the one hand, and restricted-activity days and bed-confinement days on the other, and a smaller difference between broad occupation categories.[72]

68. *Statistical Bulletin* 55 (New York: Metropolitan Life Insurance, January 1974): 9–11.

69. For a miscellany of useful information in this area, including a good bibliography, see Bonnie and Vern L. Bullough, *Poverty, Ethnic Identity and Health Care* (New York: Appleton-Century-Crofts, 1972), available in paperback. For a radical indictment of medicine as part of a hospital-insurance-supplier-educational-professional establishment organized for profit before health, see Barbara and John Ehrenreich, *The American Health Empire: Power, Profits and Politics* (New York: Random House, 1970), also in paperback. For an argument stressing the need for radical transformation, rather than reform, of existing health care systems, see Anselm L. Strauss, "Medical Ghettos," *Transaction* 4 (May 1967): 7–15; reprinted in E. Gartley Jaco, ed., *Patients, Physicians and Illness: A Sourcebook in Behavioral Science and Health,* 2nd ed. (New York: Free Press, 1972), pp. 381–388.

70. U. S. Bureau of the Census, *Statistical Abstract of the United States: 1974.* (Washington, D.C.: U.S. Government Printing Office, 1974), Table 584.

71. *Statistical Abstract, 1974,* Table 585.

72. *Statistical Bulletin* 53 (New York: Metropolitan Life Insurance, June 1972): 10–12.

Class and life expectancy

All must die, but death is distributed unequally and without any necessary correspondence to biological superiority. In analyzing the relation between death and class, a number of correlations can be identified: mortality rates, for example, are related roughly inversely to occupational level.[73] An interesting example of class bias in the distribution of death is the sinking of the Titanic. Among the first-class female passengers 4 (3 of whom volunteered to remain on board) out of 143 were lost; among second-class female passengers 15 out of 93 were lost; and in third class 81 out of 179 female passengers were lost.[74]

Taking one's own life also seems to be related to class, higher rates of suicide being evident at the top and very bottom of the class ladder (and among the unemployed and retired). A significant rate of suicide is also apparent among the downwardly mobile.[75] Death is also dispensed by means of assorted forms of private and public violence. *Private violence* refers to homicide and can perhaps be defined to include accidental deaths not associated with occupation (that is, deaths due to accident or negligence in the home, while engaged in recreation, and while driving an automobile). There is strong evidence that class is an important factor in one form of private violence: homicide is clearly a working and lower class crime,[76] victimizing males in the Negro and Other category especially severely.[77]

Public violence includes execution and warfare. Class plays a large role in selecting those who are put to death publicly, as was found in North Carolina and Pennsylvania: lower occupations supply a significantly larger number of death row inmates, and of these blacks are executed at a higher rate than

73. Lillian Guralnick, "Mortality by Occupation and Industry Among Men 20 to 64 Years of Age, United States 1950," U.S. Public Health Service, September 1962; "Mortality by Industry and Cause of Death" and "Mortality by Occupation Level and Cause of Death," Vital Statistics Special Reports, 53(4), U.S. Department of Health, Education, and Welfare (September 1963); cited with tables by Donald J. Bogue, *Principles of Demography* (New York: John Wiley and Sons, 1969), pp. 603–605, 617.

74. Walter Lord, *A Night to Remember* (New York: Henry Holt, 1955), cited by A. B. Hollingshead and F. C. Redlich, *Social Class and Mental Illness: A Community Study* (New York: John Wiley and Sons, 1958), p. 6.

75. Elwin H. Powell, "Occupation, Status, and *Anomie:* Toward a Redefinition of Anomie," *American Sociological Review* 23 (April 1958): 131–139, and Warren Breed, "Occupational Mobility and Suicide among White Males," *American Sociological Review* 28 (April 1963): 179–188, both reprinted in Jack L. Roach et al., eds., *Social Stratification in the United States* (Englewood Cliffs, N.J.: Prentice-Hall, 1969), pp. 452–478; Ronald W. Maris, *Social Forces in Urban Suicide* (Homewood, Ill.: Dorsey Press, 1969).

76. Marvin E. Wolfgang, "Criminal Homicide and the Subculture of Violence" in *Studies in Homicide,* ed. Marvin E. Wolfgang (New York: Harper and Row, 1967), pp. 3–12, available in paperback.

77. *Statistical Abstract of the United States, 1974* (Washington, D.C.: U.S. Government Printing Office, 1974), Table 247.

whites convicted of similar crimes.[78] Death in war is also subject to a class difference: soldiers from lower income areas (measured by median income of residential area) suffered a significantly higher casualty rate (dead, missing, captured) in the Korean war.[79] A study from the Vietnam war shows that the sons of the poor and of workers were much more likely to die in combat than young men from the classes above them.[80]

The relationship between class and life expectancy is neither surprising nor difficult to explain. To have money is to have the material conditions necessary to good health. To have money and education is to have both the wherewithal and the knowledge required to maintain or restore health. And sedentary occupations are healthier than jobs that require heavy muscular labor.

Analyses leave little doubt about the relation between life expectancy and class, even though data on life expectancy are sketchy for the distant past, hard to interpret for the present century, and difficult to compare over time or between countries. It seems, however, that until the sixteenth century life expectancy was low for all; that is, there were no significant differences in the life expectancies of different strata. From approximately 1650, life expectancy began to rise, but more for the upper than the lower classes. The class differential in life expectancy reached its peak in the nineteenth century, when the differences between the various classes began to diminish. The narrowing of the life expectancy gap, however, seems to have ended after the first decades of this century, and a chronic gap between the lowest class (Class 5) and the classes above it (Classes 1–4) seems to have emerged. Thus, while class affects mortality rates at all levels, a significant and perhaps chronic difference exists only between the lowest class and all other classes.[81] Not unexpectedly, given their markedly poorer class standing, American blacks have a significantly higher deathrate than whites (45 percent higher overall, and about 100 percent higher for all age groups up to 54 in 1964). Though both whites and blacks

78. Elmer H. Johnson, "Selective Factors in Capital Punishment," *Social Forces* 36 (December 1957): 165–169; Marvin E. Wolfgang, Arlene Kelly, and Hans C. Nolde, "Comparison of the Executed and the Commuted Among Admissions to Death Row," *Journal of Criminal Law, Criminology and Police Science* 53 (September 1962): 301–311.

79. Albert J. Mayer and Thomas Ford Hoult, "Social Stratification and Combat Survival," *Social Forces* 34 (December 1955): 155–159. It is also fairly certain that during the Korean and Vietnam wars the draft called up more youth from the lower than from the upper classes, even allowing for the much higher rate of rejection for reasons of health and mental fitness among youth in the lower classes; with regard to the latter point, see James W. Davis and Kenneth M. Dolbeare, *Little Groups of Neighbors: The Selective Service System* (Chicago: Markham, 1968), also in paperback.

80. M. Zeitlin, K. A. Lutterman, and J. W. Russell, "Death in Vietnam: Class, Poverty, and the Risks of War," *Politics and Society* 3 (Spring 1973): 313–328.

81. Aaron Antonovsky, "Social Class, Life Expectancy and Overall Mortality," *The Milbank Memorial Fund Quarterly* 45 (April 1967): 31–73; reprinted in Celia S. Heller, ed., *Structured Social Inequality: A Reader in Comparative Stratification* (New York: Macmillan, 1969), pp. 257–270.

enjoy low deathrates relative to those of most nonindustrial countries, no significant reduction has taken place in the difference between overall black and white deathrates during the entire period for which we have accurate records (since 1900), and no reduction of the deathrate for young blacks took place between 1954 and 1964.[82] Kitagawa and Hauser, who investigated the socioeconomic basis of mortality in the United States in 1960 and in Chicago between 1930 and 1960, substantiate the general conclusion that there is an inverse relation between socioeconomic status and deathrate and a sharp and stable difference in life expectancy between the lowest socioeconomic group and the groups above them. Kitagawa and Hauser also point out that blacks (and American Indians) have much higher deathrates than whites. However, making allowances for errors, the difference, while large, is not as large as that reported by Bogue; and there has been some reduction, though not much (and almost none between 1940 and 1960).[83]

The various factors contributing to class-based life expectancy rates cannot be cited with precision. We do know, however, that classes differ in amounts of knowledge about nutrition and disease, definitions of illness, and willingness to place oneself in the care of medical personnel.[84] This class differential in knowledge and faith in experts was manifested in sharply different responses to an offer of free polio vaccination, the "lower class" (skilled workers and below, husband and wife both having less than high school educations) lagging badly behind the classes above it in positive responses.[85] Class has also been correlated with frequency of visits to a dentist,[86] obesity in women,[87] and, of special relevance, marked differences in the quality of diet.[88] In combination, these conditions and forms of behavior are undoubtedly influential in the overall process that determines who will die earlier from who will die later.

82. Donald J. Bogue, *Principles of Demography* (New York: John Wiley and Sons, 1969), pp. 594–597.

83. Evelyn M. Kitagawa and Philip M. Hauser, *Differential Mortality in the United States: A Study in Socioeconomic Epidemiology* (Cambridge, Mass.: Harvard University Press, 1973).

84. Gerald Gordon, *Role Theory and Illness: A Sociological Perspective* (New Haven, Conn.: College and University Press, 1966); John Kosa *et al.*, eds., *Poverty and Health: A Sociological Analysis* (Cambridge, Mass.: Harvard University Press, 1969).

85. Lelia Calhoun Deasy, "Socioeconomic Status and Participation in the Poliomyelitis Vaccine Trial," *American Sociological Review* 21 (April 1956): 185–191.

86. U.S. Bureau of the Census, *Statistical Abstract of the United States: 1966* (Washington, D.C.: U.S. Government Printing Office, 1966), Table 82.

87. Robert G. Burnight and Parker G. Marden, "Social Correlates of Weight in an Aging Population," *Milbank Memorial Fund Quarterly* 45 (1967): 75–92.

88. In 1967 Congress authorized the Department of Health, Education, and Welfare to conduct a comprehensive survey of the incidence and location of serious hunger and malnutrition and related health problems. For a summary of existing work in this area and a preliminary summary of the National Nutrition Survey, revealing sizable amounts of malnutrition among low income groups, see U.S. Senate,

Class and mental retardation

We have only recently come to see a link between class and mental retardation (organic impairment). Presumably, the extremely few naturally defective babies are randomly distributed on the class ladder. However, the bulk of all other defective human beings are products of an environment of poverty: the fetus is injured because the mother is in poor health, receives an unskilled abortion, or is not under a doctor's care; or the child is organically impaired by illness, malnutrition, ingestion of lead paint, rat bites, and the like. Of some significance in understanding the class nature of mental retardation is the fact that its incidence in the United States is much higher than in England, Denmark, and Sweden, which have national maternal and child care programs.[89]

Of perhaps greater significance is the growing suspicion that many of the mentally retarded are not organically impaired at all. Hurley has argued that at least 85 percent of those designated mentally retarded are simply poor people who have been damaged by their experience in a society with a strong propensity for using the middle class as the yardstick of normality and for labeling those who deviate from its norms as genetic defectives.[90]

In an interesting analysis, Farber has argued that modern society has restricted access to valuable social positions by progressively raising standards in all fields, thereby creating a surplus population (the mentally retarded, the unemployed, the mentally ill, the disabled, the criminal, the functionally illiterate, and so on) which he estimates at as high as 20–25 percent of the total population. Farber reports that the best estimate of the proportion of mentally retarded in the United States is between 2 and 3 percent (between 4 and 6 million people).[91] Despite the vitality of the biopsychological tradition, which tends to stress a natural distribution of intelligence and ability in general, it appears that our mentally retarded are victims of the American class system. Farber also suggests that modern society needs to create deviant groups in order to maintain itself, a point we will return to later.[92]

The social creation of mental retardation has also been argued by Mercer in her analysis of the relation between mental retardation and education. Mercer suggests that her analysis is applicable to other social systems besides education: the family, the neighborhood, law enforcement, welfare, churches, and public institutions for the retarded.[93] Mercer reports that empirical studies

---

Select Committee on Nutrition and Human Needs, *Hearings* Part 3 "The National Nutrition Survey" (Washington, D.C.: U.S. Government Printing Office, 1969).

89. Rodger L. Hurley, ed., *Poverty and Mental Retardation: A Causal Relationship* (Trenton, N.J.: New Jersey Department of Institutions and Agencies, 1968), especially chap. 2, Ronald Marlowe, "Poverty and Organic Impairment."

90. *Ibid.,* introductory essay.

91. Bernard Farber, *Mental Retardation: Its Social Context and Social Consequences* (Boston: Houghton Mifflin, 1968), especially chap. 1.

92. For a discussion of an explicit analysis along these lines by Kai Erikson, see "Class and *Anomie:* The Uses of Deviance" in Chapter 15.

93. The social creation of incompetents in general is analyzed more fully in Chapter 6, on the relation between class and education.

in California show that Spanish-speaking and black students tend to be assigned to special classes (thus beginning the process of becoming mental retardates) at significantly higher rates than English-speaking white students, *even white students with similar scores on intelligence tests.*[94] And in a full-scale study of Riverside, California, a city of 85,000, Mercer again documented the class-ethnic-racial basis of mental retardation. Of further value in this study is Mercer's argument that there is a sociocultural (middle class) bias in the evaluation of what is considered normal intelligence, and that this bias is deeply institutionalized in the individualistic clinical approach of professional diagnosticians and in the interlocking network of organizations that allegedly uncover and treat mental retardation — especially the public schools, public-welfare-vocational rehabilitation agencies, law enforcement agencies, medical facilities, the Department of Mental Hygiene, and private organizations concerned with mental retardation.[95]

Class and mental illness

It is not clear whether there has been a general increase in the rate of mental illness over the years.[96] What is clear is that there is a direct correlation between class and amounts of mental illness, certain kinds of mental illness, and the type and effectiveness of professional treatment received. And it is also clear that the higher the class, the more sympathetic, positive, and tolerant the attitude toward mental disturbance and the greater the likelihood that deviant behavior will be attributed to mental illness.[97] The relation between social class and mental illness received little attention from social scientists until the pioneering community analysis undertaken by August B. Hollingshead and Frederick C. Redlich during the 1950s.[98] In their highly sophisticated empirical study of greater New Haven, Connecticut (at that time a metropolitan center of approximately 240,000), the authors posed five hypotheses:

1. The prevalence of treated mental illness is related significantly to an individual's position in the class structure.

94. Jane R. Mercer, "Sociological Perspectives on Mild Mental Retardation" in *Socio-Cultural Aspects of Mental Retardation,* ed. H. Carl Haywood (New York: Appleton-Century-Crofts, 1970), pp. 378–391. This publication is an indispensable reference on mental retardation. The concluding summary by H. Carl Haywood is especially valuable.

95. Jane R. Mercer, *Labelling the Mentally Retarded* (Berkeley: University of California Press, 1973).

96. Absolute numbers of the mentally ill may be rising, but per capita figures for purposes of historical comparison are not easily computed. Most of the available figures are based on those treated or confined, rather than those who need treatment. Reports of a rise in mental illness may be based on such figures, or on figures that mainfest improvements in reporting. (Greater public acceptance of mental illness as a social problem, for one thing, is likely to lead to better reporting.)

97. With regard to the latter point, see Judith Rabkin, "Public Attitudes Toward Mental Illness: A Review of the Literature," *Schizophrenia Bulletin* 10 (Fall 1974): 21–22.

98. *Social Class and Mental Illness: A Community Study* (New York: John Wiley and Sons, 1958).

2. The types of diagnosed psychiatric disorders are connected significantly to the class structure.

3. The kind of psychiatric treatment administered by psychiatrists is associated with the patient's position in the class structure.

4. Social and psychodynamic factors in the development of psychiatric disorders are correlative to an individual's position in the class structure.

5. Mobility in the class structure is associated with the development of psychiatric difficulties.

The data supported a clear affirmative answer to each hypothesis.[99] A follow-up study of the same patients ten years later showed that class is significantly related to the long-term outcome of treatment and to the adjustment of former patients in the community: the higher the class, the less likelihood that a patient would receive custodial hospital care and the greater likelihood that his or her adjustment to the community would be successful.[100]

The most ambitious investigation of mental health in American social science, a study of a midtown Manhattan residential area of 175,000 inhabitants, offers important corroborating evidence of an inverse relation between class and mental illness.[101] A number of other aspects of this study are of special interest: the authors suggest strongly that midtown Manhattan is typical of segments of other highly urbanized centers across the United States and that therefore their findings are not germane only to that locality. Secondly, the study attempts (by means of a questionnaire evaluated by psychiatrists) to diagnose the mental health of the entire population (and not to base its analysis on treated patients, as the New Haven study did). Thirdly, the Midtown Manhattan Study distinguished between the SES of the individuals studied and that of their parents, so that the impact of each on mental health could be studied.

While emphasizing that they are in no way implying that sociocultural processes account for all mental illnesses, the authors conclude (1) that SES-of-origin and own-SES are both significantly related directly to mental health, or, conversely, that both are inversely related to mental illness, with an especially high rate at the bottom levels; (2) that social mobility is associated with a higher level of mental health (which is directly at odds with the general belief that the opposite is true); (3) that there are no differences in the frequency of some forms of mental illness (schizophrenia, anxiety-tension, excessive intake) and parental SES but pronounced inverse frequencies between parental SES and intellectual, affective, somatic, characterological, and interpersonal disturbances; and (4) that the lower the SES, the less likely that those suffering from mental illness will receive treatment.[102]

99. Data supporting the last two hypotheses are presented in Jerome K. Myers and Bertram H. Roberts, *Family and Class Dynamics in Mental Illness* (New York: John Wiley and Sons, 1959).

100. Jerome K. Myers and Lee L. Bean, *A Decade Later: A Follow-up of Social Class and Mental Illness* (New York: John Wiley and Sons, 1968).

101. Leo Srole *et al., Mental Health in the Metropolis: The Midtown Manhattan Study* (New York: McGraw-Hill, 1962), chaps. 11–13.

102. Our understanding of the nature of alcoholism and its relation to class is limited. We do know, however, that the diagnosis and treatment of alcoholism vary

Class, family, and related behavior: a summary

Considerable research demonstrates that differences in income, occupation, and education are associated strongly with differences in family values and stability and with differences in personality, health, life expectancy, mental retardation, and mental illness. Those higher in the class dimension (income, wealth, occupation, education) tend to have more stable families and personalities and to lead longer and healthier lives. The basic cleavages in the distribution of benefits are between the middle and upper classes, on the one hand, and the working and lower classes, on the other, though in some instances, especially health and life expectancy, the lower class receives markedly fewer benefits than the classes above it.

Because of their histories of association with the lower classes, black and Mexican Americans tend to receive distinctly lower levels of benefits in the areas of family and personal values than other Americans (except, of course, other poor minorities). For various reasons, Jewish Americans rank high in the distribution of family and personal values.

Our definition of social class at this point can be expressed as follows: *the American population is characterized by a hierarchy of families and unrelated individuals who exhibit differences in behavior throughout the entire range of family and personal values depending on their relation to economic markets.* The next step toward comprehensive definitions of both the class dimension and of social class is to examine the relation between the class status of parents and the education of children.

---

with class position and that this variation favors the upper classes. See Wolfgang Schmidt, Reginald G. Smart, and Marcia K. Moss, *Social Class and the Treatment of Alcoholism* (Toronto: University of Toronto Press, 1968).

6

Class and Differentials in the Educational Careers of Children

ONE OF THE fundamental ingredients in America's social philosophy of "nonegalitarian classlessness" is its faith in the power of education. For Americans, it is axiomatic that there should be no arbitrariness in the relation between social rewards and personal worth. Since the founding of their new Jerusalem, Americans have believed that they at last had found the way to realize nature's hierarchy of talent and to put unequal rewards on a just and natural basis. For Americans, the key to overcoming the artificial barriers of social condition, religion, ethnicity, and race and to revealing the true universe of individuals is equal opportunity and competition in the spheres of economics, politics, and education.

In this trinity of free markets, education holds a special place in American hearts. It is alleged to have great power to improve people and solve problems; nothing is more characteristic of an American faced with a problem than to attribute it to a lack of education. The power of education is thought to be enormous, largely because Americans attribute great power to ideas and knowledge. This faith in ideological causation — in the power of truth over ignorance and evil — along with the difficulty of running a regionally, racially, economically, and ethnically diverse society, has led the United States to assign a heavy burden of functions to education. And given their belief in biopsychological causation, Americans find it easy to equate the absence of formal barriers to education and the existence of free public schools with equality of opportunity.[1] For an American, an opportunity is something one seizes or makes use of; inequality in any field is simply the record of those who did and did not have it in them to profit from opportunities available to all.

The small-town focus of early stratification research (1925–1945) gave us a good portrayal of the mixed-class educational system that prevailed under the sway of this tradition of educational equality.[2] With some modifications, which will be noted, this system was probably characteristic of the United States from the advent of mass public education in the middle of the nineteenth century until close to the middle of the twentieth. Under this system the various classes throughout rural, small-town, and small-city America (probably) attended the same schools at every educational level through high school. Most of America's educational norms date from this period: free tax-supported compulsory education; a curriculum stressing literacy, abstract knowledge, patriotism, and the Protestant-bourgeois virtues; and a testing and grading system that supposedly revealed the hierarchy of talent ordained by nature. The fact that rich and poor often attended the same school, in combination with heavy educational expenditures, rising overall levels of education, and the great normative appeal of education, gave a semblance of reality to the norm of equal educational opportunity. However, Hollingshead's finding that Elmtown's schools were deeply biased in favor of its upper classes is much closer to the reality of American education, then and now.

Awareness of the relation between class and education has grown consistently in the twentieth century. In the early part of the century, progressive educators began to question the wisdom of imposing a uniform education on a student body composed of a mixture of social classes.[3] Though it took massive effort and caused deep controversy (and still does, for that matter), progressive educators managed somewhat to diversify the school to make it more suitable for a diverse student body. Accordingly, students were grouped into classes on the basis of their speed of learning; various types of programs (vocational, commercial, academic) were offered; and special schools (music and art, science, vocational) were made available for special students. The early efforts to adjust education to students' differing values and skills were motivated by a desire to overcome class differences, including ethnic and linguistic differences, and thereby to make equal education a reality. But progressive educators in

1. The lay definition of *equal educational opportunity* is "an equal chance at the starting line," to use former President Nixon's term. This should not be confused, of course, with equal access to education of some sort or with proposals to provide different or more effective educational opportunities for diverse social classes.
2. The classic example is August Hollingshead, *Elmtown's Youth* (New York: John Wiley and Sons, 1949). This pattern, which suited the class system of rural–small-town and small-city America, did not prevail in the "caste" system of the south, which, after it began to provide education for black Americans, had a legally segregated system based on the doctrine of "separate but equal facilities" accepted as constitutional until 1954.
3. For an excellent history of Progressivism in education, see Lawrence A. Cremin, *The Transformation of the School* (New York: Alfred A. Knopf, 1961), also a Vintage paperback.

the 1920s and 1930s, even when they advocated special programs and special schools, did not (and could not) envisage the trend that developed in the decades after World War Two. The booming economy of the post-1945 period accelerated the process of urbanization and suburbanization, in effect segregating residential and political districts by social class throughout the United States. The inner city became blighted and black, and layers of white working, middle, and upper-middle class suburbs grew up around the decaying core city. What makes this overall process important, of course, is that residential areas are also the economic and political units on which America's schools are based. Given the United States' powerful tradition of political decentralization, this class-structured hierarchy of local communities deeply affects its educational system; indeed, it particularizes education by class so deeply that it is probably a mistake to speak of an American *system* of education at all.

Class and expenditure per pupil

The amount of money spent on education in the United States varies enormously from state to state, and from one school district to another within any given state. The basic reason for these differences is that school expenditures are the responsibility of local communities: since there are enormous variations in the wealth of localities, there is enormous variation in the amount of money expended per pupil.[4]

As part of the Civil Rights Act of 1964, Congress created a commission to study the "lack of availability of equal educational opportunities for individuals by reason of race, color, religion, or national origin in public educational institutions at all levels in the United States, its territories and possessions, and the District of Columbia."[5]

The Coleman Report found considerable variation in the nature of schools as measured by such factors as age of building, average number of pupils per classroom, textbooks, library, science and language laboratories, accreditation, specialized academic programs, teacher tenure, principal's salary, extracurricular activities, and the like. With due regard for the dangers inherent in the use

4. For a discussion of whether or not unequal educational opportunity is unconstitutional, see Charles U. Daly, ed., *The Quality of Inequality: Urban and Suburban Public Schools* (Chicago: University of Chicago Center for Policy Study, 1968), and Arthur E. Wise, *Rich Schools, Poor Schools: The Promise of Equal Educational Opportunity* (Chicago: University of Chicago Press, 1968). Chapter 6 of the latter contains a useful summary of the hierarchy of school expenditures, which varies, for example, from $1,168 to $479 per pupil in two adjacent school districts in Illinois.
5. The formal title of the resulting study is *Equality of Educational Opportunity* (Washington, D.C.: U.S. Government Printing Office, 1966); its informal title is the Coleman Report. It should not go unnoticed that educational opportunity was placed in the context of civil rights and that while many of the factors that enter into social stratification were cited, class as such was ignored in the commission's terms of reference. The research team itself, though not ignoring class, consistently uses the euphemism "family background."

of averages and for the marked regional disparities in the United States, it was found that blacks have access to fewer of some of the facilities that seem to be related to academic achievement.[6] All in all, however, the report did not find as much disparity along these lines as many thought existed.[7]

The Coleman Report also found distinct differences in academic achievement between majority (white) students and ethnic-racial groups (Puerto Ricans, Indian Americans, Mexican Americans, and blacks), and by implication between social classes. Variations in academic achievement by class will concern us again shortly, but are of particular interest here in connection with unequal educational expenditures. By holding socioeconomic status constant, the Coleman Report concluded that the quality of a school (library, curriculum, building, teachers' qualifications, and so on) has very little independent effect on the academic performance of students. (Minority students are affected somewhat more by the quality of a school than majority, or white, students.) The Coleman Report (p. 302) did find that students' aspirations and performance are strongly affected by the social composition of a school's student body; but this variable, it should be noted, is a function of class factors.[8]

The Coleman Report (p. 325) summarizes its major finding in these words:

> Taking all these results together, one implication stands out above all: that schools bring little influence to bear on a child's achievement that is independent of his background and general social context; and that this very lack of an independent effect means that the inequalities imposed on children by their home, neighborhood, and peer environment are carried along to become the inequalities with which they confront adult life at the end of school. For equality of educational opportunity through the schools must imply a strong effect of schools that is independent of the child's immediate social environment, and that strong independent effect is not present in American schools.

The approach that emphasizes equalization of expenditures per pupil in order to equalize educational opportunity would appear to be futile. The difficulty of equalizing expenditures per pupil would itself be overwhelming, affecting as it would the deeply entrenched tradition of decentralized political control of schools. In any case, the strategy of focusing on educational expenditure as the key to equal opportunity is rendered suspect by the Coleman Report. One should not be surprised at this finding, since it is consonant with what is known about socialization. People learn from social relationships, not from buildings, libraries, cafeterias, or contact with curricula and teachers remote from and irrelevant to their previous (class) socialization. A well-educated teacher with middle class beliefs and values in a plush school is likely to be ineffectual if the pupils come from lower class families; indeed, such ineffectualness has a

6. *Ibid.,* pp. 8–15.
7. The Coleman Report is a broad abstract study of national and regional data, and caution should be exercised when its findings are cited. Shocking disparities between individual, black urban schools and upper class suburban schools, for example, obviously exist.
8. This is discussed further in "Class and Educational Aspirations."

cumulative effect, making relations between the student and the school increasingly difficult. The same teacher in a run-down, ill-equipped school attended mostly by middle class youngsters would probably be far more effective; the social environment of the school would mesh with and complement the values and beliefs acquired by the students at home. On any objective test the latter students would in all likelihood score higher than the former.

The error of relating equality of educational opportunity with equality of educational expenditure has a practical component: virtually insurmountable political barriers confront those who want to equalize (or make more equitable) educational expenditures.[9] But even if these barriers were overcome and an equal amount of money spent on each child in America, there would still be wide differentials in academic achievement — differentials best accounted for by the class structure.

Class and educational aspirations

The American commitment to education is well known: masses of people attend and service schools, great sums of money are spent on them, and the numbers rise every year.[10] The high value Americans place on education must be qualified carefully, however, if we are to understand its social meaning. For one thing, Americans do not value education as an end in itself. Always, and often explicitly, it is a means to other ends. And of special significance is the fact that Americans value education unequally by class. Discussing the relation between class and personality, we pointed to sharp differences in the values of parents in the higher classes and those of parents in the lower classes. The relevance of these differences to education is apparent. Speaking broadly, families in the higher classes prepare and motivate their children for success in school, while families in the lower classes prepare and motivate their children for average academic performance or even failure. One way to examine this link between family socialization by class and education is to interpret the significant differences in the value placed on education by the various classes. In his pioneering secondary analysis of data from a number of national surveys, Herbert H. Hyman investigated the differential value placed on education by Americans.[11] The data clearly disclosed that American adults and youth (in

9. Even when federal funds are directed at equalization, the realities of political power at the federal and state levels dictate that such monies are funneled through state governments that at best distribute them equally, leaving the relative positions of local school systems unaffected, as our experience with the Title I funds of the Elementary and Secondary Education Act of 1965 indicates.

10. Educational expenditures as a percentage of the gross national product have risen from 3.1 percent in 1929 to 7.7 percent in 1972. U.S. Department of Health, Education, and Welfare, *Digest of Educational Statistics, 1973* (Washington, D.C.: U.S. Government Printing Office, 1974), Table 27.

11. Herbert H. Hyman, "The Value Systems of Different Classes," in *Class, Status, and Power: Social Stratification in Comparative Perspective,* 2nd ed., ed. Reinhard Bendix and Seymour M. Lipset (New York: Free Press, 1966), pp. 488–499; originally published in 1953.

separate surveys) place different values on college education according to class.[12]

Data on educational aspirations are extremely revealing, since education is increasingly the key to high class status (and therefore to upward mobility). In one study, educational aspirations were directly related to class (father's occupational prestige) independently of I.Q.[13] In another, educational aspirations were directly related to class (based on a modified verison of Hollingshead's Index of Social Position, essentially father's occupation and education) independently of ethnicity and race.[14] And class was related to plans to attend college independently of academic achievement.[15]

An important study shows that all classes have higher aspirations (and do better academic work) when a student body is composed of a mixture of classes dominated by middle or upper-middle class students, and, conversely, that all classes set their aspirations lower (and do poorer academic work) when a student body is dominated by lower class students.[16] This analysis of a single school system is corroborated by one of the major findings of the Coleman Report.

It is important to bear in mind here that the studies just cited tend to refer to absolute aspirations — that is, to aspirations framed in terms of a single hierarchy of educational success. Given the phenomenal growth of junior colleges, vocational training, and open admissions, aspirations to certain kinds of education appear to be strong at the lower levels of American society.

Class and academic achievement (I.Q., achievement tests, grades, degrees)

The Coleman Report contains a valuable survey of academic achievement (as measured by ability and achievement tests)[17] among pupils in grades 1, 3, 6, 9, and 12 in public educational institutions throughout the United States. Since

12. The data also reveal direct relationships between class and occupational and income aspirations and between class and belief in the existence of the opportunity to succeed.

13. William H. Sewell, Archie O. Haller, and Murray A. Straus, "Social Status and Educational and Occupational Aspiration," *American Sociological Review* 22 (February 1957): 67–73.

14. Bernard C. Rosen, "Race, Ethnicity and the Achievement Syndrome," *American Sociological Review* 24 (February 1959): 47–60.

15. Natalie Rogoff, "Local Social Structure and Educational Selection," in *Education, Economy, and Society,* ed. A. H. Halsey *et al.* (New York: Free Press, 1961), p. 246, also in paperback. For a fuller discussion of this study and Project Talent, which contains a similar conclusion, see "Class and Educational Shortage, Waste, and Privilege" in this chapter.

16. Alan B. Wilson, "Residential Segregation of Social Classes and Aspirations of High School Boys," *American Sociological Review* 24 (December 1959): 836–845.

17. The Coleman Report assumes that "ability" tests (often called intelligence tests and thought to test inborn ability) and "achievement" tests (tests that determine what one has learned) are both "culture-bound" and that what they measure most reliably is cultural intake by class. The Coleman Report, it should again be noted, tends to use the euphemism "family background" instead of the term *class.*

Congress requested that inequalities in educational opportunity be investigated in terms of race, color, religion, and national origin, the results indicate only approximately the role that class plays in academic achievement. These results, which are summarized in Table 6-1, clearly show a marked relation (except in the case of Oriental Americans) between minority-majority (white) status and academic achievement.

Another national study (of all American cities with fifty thousand or more inhabitants) reached a similar conclusion: children's socioeconomic (SES) origin is directly and strongly related to all forms of academic achievement, including I.Q.[18] The same finding has been documented for "Big City,"[19] "River City,"[20] and Chicago.[21]

Differentials in expenditure per pupil, educational aspirations, and academic achievement are not the only ways in which class influences education. While almost every aspect of education is implicitly embraced by these three categories, it should also be noted that pupil and teacher turnover, emotional health,

Table 6-1 Nationwide Median Test Scores for 1st and 12th Grade Pupils, Fall 1965

	Racial or ethnic group					
Test	*Puerto Ricans*	*Indian Americans*	*Mexican Americans*	*Oriental Americans*	*Negroes*	*Majority (white)*
1st grade						
Nonverbal	45.8	53.0	50.1	56.6	43.4	54.1
Verbal	44.9	47.8	46.5	51.6	45.4	53.2
12th grade						
Nonverbal	43.3	47.1	45.0	51.6	40.9	52.0
Verbal	43.1	43.7	43.8	49.6	40.9	52.1
Reading	42.6	44.3	44.2	48.8	42.2	51.9
Mathematics	43.7	45.9	45.5	51.3	41.8	51.8
General information	41.7	44.7	43.3	49.0	40.6	52.2
Average of the 5 tests	43.1	45.1	44.4	50.1	41.1	52.0

SOURCE: James S. Coleman *et al., Equality of Educational Opportunity* (Washington, D.C.: U.S. Government Printing Office, 1966), p. 20.

18. Robert E. Herriott and Nancy Hoyt St. John, *Social Class and the Urban School* (New York: John Wiley and Sons, 1966).
19. Patricia Cayo Sexton, *Education and Income* (New York: Viking Press, 1961).
20. Robert J. Havighurst *et al., Growing Up in River City* (New York: John Wiley and Sons, 1962).
21. Robert J. Havighurst, *The Public Schools of Chicago: A Survey Report* (Chicago: Board of Education, 1964).

regularity of attendance, regular promotion in grade, school-leaving rates, enrollment in college preparatory programs, participation in clubs, receipt of scholarships, parent participation in school activities, and school board composition are all directly related to class level. Surprisingly enough, even enriched and remedial classes and subsidized milk and food programs benefit middle and upper class youngsters more than those who come from the lower classes.[22]

Of no small importance in assessing the relation between class and education is the class position of the public school teacher. Recruited largely from middle class backgrounds, teachers absorb the ethos of middle class America, including the hunger for professional status, regardless of background.[23] As a result, they develop an image of the ideal student and an ideology of education highly inappropriate to many of the actual students and situations they face.[24] It has even been argued that teachers behave in such a way as to elicit from lower class pupils the low achievement they expect.[25]

The class explanation of success or failure in school is part of the overall sociocultural approach to behavior. Though modern scholarship has tended in this direction, there persists a pronounced tendency to include biopsychic factors in explanations of educational and other behavior.[26] And there is still vitality in the tradition that places the burden of explanation on biopsychic variables, especially on the alleged existence of significant differences in inborn intelligence.[27]

22. For a lucid and comprehensive presentation of data on all these areas from "Big City" (and from other studies), see Patricia Cayo Sexton, *Education and Income* (New York: Viking Press, 1961). For a careful compilation of material linking poverty, poor health, poor nutrition, and poor learning, see Herbert G. Birch and Joan Dye Gussow, *Disadvantaged Children: Health, Nutrition and School Failure* (New York: Harcourt Brace Jovanovich, 1970).
23. Robert E. Doherty, "Attitudes Toward Labor: When Blue Collar Children Become Teachers," *School Review* 71 (Spring 1963): 87–96; reprinted in Robert J. Havighurst *et al.*, eds., *Society and Education: A Book of Readings* (Boston: Allyn and Bacon, 1967).
24. Howard S. Becker, "Social Class Variations in the Teacher-Pupil Relationship," *Journal of Educational Sociology* 25 (April 1952): 451–465; reprinted in Robert R. Bell and Holger R. Stub, eds., *The Sociology of Education: A Sourcebook,* rev. ed. (Homewood, Ill.: Dorsey Press, 1968), pp. 155–166.
25. Ray C. Rist, "Student Social Class and Teacher Expectations: The Self-Fulfilling Prophecy in Ghetto Education," *Harvard Educational Review* 40 (August 1970): 411–451. The reader will remember the claim (see Chapter 5) that most of the ostensibly mentally retarded are neither naturally nor organically impaired but are the creations of middle class institutions (including public education) that deal with individuals in the lower classes.
26. For example, Christopher Jencks *et al.*, *Inequality: A Reassessment of the Effects of Family and Schooling in America* (New York: Basic Books, 1972).
27. The biopsychic explanation owes much to a long scholarly compilation of studies (which allegedly verify the argument that behavior results from the unequal endowment of individuals and races) by Arthur R. Jensen, "How Much Can We Boost I.Q. and Scholastic Achievement?" *Harvard Educational Review* 39 (Winter 1969): 1–123. For a more readable version of the radical genetic explanation of behavior, see Richard Herrnstein, "I.Q.," *Atlantic Monthly* 228 (September 1971): 43–64, expanded into bookform as *I.Q. in the Meritocracy* (Boston: Little, Brown,

Higher education: the capstone of class education

Throughout much of its history (approximately from 1500 to 1850) the nascent class society of the West required little formal training or education in the socialization process. By the mid-nineteenth century the social need for literacy had enforced the inauguration of mass public education, and by the end of the nineteenth century the free high school was becoming a standard feature of American education. Between 1900 and 1940 enrollment in America's high schools rose from about 5 percent to over 90 percent of the relevant age group. But in the post-1945 period the terminal high school systems were asked to expand their college preparatory programs as the United States inaugurated a system of mass higher education. In 1940 only 15 percent of eighteen–twenty-one-year-olds were enrolled in institutions of higher education; by 1970 this figure exceeded 50 percent.[28]

American institutions of higher education developed in a decentralized fashion during the nineteenth century. As a result, a vast variety of what Jencks and Reisman[29] call "special-interest" colleges emerged: colleges for each of the many Protestant denominations; for Roman Catholics and for Jews; for men or women only; for whites or blacks; for farmers, engineers, or teachers; for inhabitants of a given town, city, or state; for adolescents or adults; and for the rich and not-so-rich. While the composition of the governing boards of institutions of higher education was necessarily affected by this diversity, analysts have agreed that by and large such boards exhibit a common trend: a decline in the power of clergymen and a corresponding rise in the power of businesspeople and professionals. Though there are variations among institutions, it is clear that farmers, manual workers, lower white-collar workers, ethnic and "racial" groups, intellectuals, scientists, labor union officials, and artists (as well as women and young adults) are not represented on governing boards in proportion to their numbers or importance.[30]

1973). For a radical indictment of the I.Q. as a weapon of class domination, see Samuel Bowles and Herbert Gintis, "I.Q. in the U.S. Class Structure," *Social Policy* 3, nos. 4 and 5 (1972–1973): pp. 65–96; reprinted, along with other essays (both radical and liberal) emphasizing the sociocultural basis of I.Q., in Alan Gartner, Colin Greer, and Frank Reissman, eds., *The New Assault on Equality: I.Q. and Social Stratification* (New York: Harper and Row, 1974), available in paperback.

28. For these developments, see Martin Trow, "The Second Transformation of American Secondary Education" in *Class, Status and Power: Social Stratification in Comparative Perspective,* 2nd ed., ed. Reinhard Bendix and Seymour M. Lipset (New York: Free Press, 1966), pp. 437–449; also see Chapter 4 above.

29. Christopher Jencks and David Reisman, *The Academic Revolution,* (Garden City, N.Y.: Doubleday, 1968), also in paperback.

30. For a review of previous studies and a corroborating analysis of a sample of private and public universities, see Hubert Park Beck, *Men Who Control Our Universities: The Economic and Social Composition of Governing Boards of Thirty Leading American Universities* (Morningside Heights, N.Y.: King's Crown Press, 1947). For the most comprehensive body of empirical data on the composition and attitudes of governing boards, see Morton A. Rauh, *The Trusteeship of Colleges and Universities* (New York: McGraw-Hill, 1969). Though not intended as a representa-

The 1960s witnessed a considerable amount of unrest on college campuses, accompanied by demands for the democratization of power and reforms that would orient educational institutions toward teaching and the student. A 1971 study of sixty-eight representative universities, which was compared with an earlier (1964) study of the same institutions, found that the turmoil of the 1960s produced very little change in universities' goals or power relationships. Administrations and boards still prevail, faculties have acquired somewhat more power, and students have been granted only a small say in how universities should be run. It is of considerable interest that higher education can no longer claim to be an interconnected, multilevel meritocracy. It is what it has probably always been, a fragmented set of unrelated, noncompetitive clusters. High-quality, high-prestige institutions, especially private ones, continue to emphasize elitist goals (pure research, liberal arts, preservation of the cultural heritage, an intellectual atmosphere of free inquiry). Such goals also further faculty members' professional careers and assign a low priority to teaching, especially at the undergraduate level. Lower-quality, lower-prestige institutions, usually public, appear to have given up trying to compete with the front-ranking universities and have come to be characterized by different goals: vocational programs, applied research, teaching, service to the immediate community, and equality of opportunity.[31]

Institutions of higher education have many concrete ties with the worlds of business, the professions, and politics, and we need to know much more about such relationships.[32] Our lack of knowledge about higher education extends in all directions. We have no precise data about the class composition of post-secondary student bodies, the class composition of students enrolled in different types of programs,[33] or about academic records. Nor do we have any method for evaluating the relation between a student's experience and performance in school and performance outside school. Nevertheless, a fairly accurate portrait of higher education can be pieced together from a variety of sources.

It should surprise no one to learn that higher education is deeply implicated in our class system. It is important at the outset, however, to insist on viewing higher education as a class phenomenon and to resist the notions that colleges are attended exclusively by an elite of personal merit, and that such extraneous factors as race, ethnicity, religion, or class, though perhaps influential at the lower levels of schooling, have somehow been overcome or neutralized by the

---

tive sample of all American colleges and universities, the survey includes 654 selectively chosen institutions in a number of basic categories.

31. Edward Gross and Paul W. Grambsch, *Changes in University Organization, 1964–1971* (New York: McGraw-Hill, 1974).

32. For an anecdotal but enormously insightful analysis, see James Ridgeway, *The Closed Corporation: American Universities in Crisis* (New York: Random House, 1968). We will return to this general subject later when we explore the role of higher education in the national structure of power; see "Government and Higher Education" in Chapter 13.

33. Both types of data have long been collected in Canada as part of census-taking. The U.S. Bureau of the Census has at last begun to collect some elementary data on the class backgrounds of college students; see footnote 34 in this chapter.

time students enter college. As we will see, the student bodies of our colleges and universities not only do not include all the available academic talent, but also are havens of class privilege.

Two patterns of class causation can be identified in our twenty-five hundred or so institutions of higher learning: first, access to higher education is class-based, and, second, choices of institution and program of study are class-based. Access to higher education is deeply rooted in the American class system, as Table 6-2 indicates. The data in Table 6-2 leave little doubt that despite the growth of mass higher education, access to college is still dominated by the middle and upper classes.[34] While the figures in Table 6-2 indicate a gradual increase in the percentage of working class (actually upper-working class) children attending college, one must qualify this finding by noting another pattern. There seems to have developed a distinct class pattern *within* higher education, a pattern that takes two forms. First, institutions of higher education are themselves class-based and class-oriented. The typology of institutions and estimates of class composition of their student bodies in Table 6-3 are highly suggestive. The increase in college attendance among the lower classes should not be misinterpreted. Postsecondary education for the lower classes takes place overwhelmingly at junior colleges, which now account for over 40 percent of postsecondary enrollments.[35]

Table 6-2 Social Class Origins of College Entrants (% of Each Class Attending College)

Social class	1920[a]	1940[b]	1950[c]	1960[c]	1965[c]
Upper and upper-middle	40	70	75	80	85
Lower-middle	8	20	38	50	54
Upper-working	2	5	12	25	30
Lower-working	0	0	2	4	6
Percent of total age group entering college	6	16	22	33	37

a. 1920 — estimated by the authors from scattered data.

b. 1940 — estimated by the authors on the basis of several studies of the occupations of fathers of college students.

c. 1950, 1960, and 1965 — composite figures from several studies of social class and college attendance.

SOURCE: From Robert J. Havighurst and Bernice L. Neugarten, *Society and Education,* 3rd ed. (Boston: Allyn and Bacon, 1967), Table 4-1, p. 98. Copyright © 1967 by Allyn and Bacon, Inc., Boston. Reprinted by permission.

34. The class basis of college attendance is also documented in U.S. Bureau of the Census, *Current Population Reports,* Series P-20, No. 241, "Social and Economic Characteristics of Students: October, 1971" (Washington, D.C.: U.S. Government Printing Office, 1972), Figures 3 and 4.

35. For a careful compilation of evidence showing the pronounced separation by class that exists at this level, see Jerome Karabel, "Community Colleges and Social

Table 6-3 Social Class Composition of Students in Various Types of Post-secondary Institutions (in estimated percentages)

Class status	Cosmo-politan university[a]	Ivy college[b]	Oppor-tunity college[c]	Warnell[d]	State college[e]
Upper and upper-middle	30	75	5	40	20
Lower-middle	45	20	40	50	50
Working	25	5	55	10	30

a. Large state or municipal institutions with low tuition and high standards maintained by large freshman failure rate.

b. Private liberal arts colleges for men and/or women, with high standards and high prestige.

c. Colleges and junior colleges with lower admission standards and low tuition, oriented toward middle class vocational skills.

d. A general name for small city liberal arts colleges, often church-related or -originated, which provide good quality education for middle class youth.

e. State or local institutions with low tuitions, often founded as teacher training centers and oriented toward upwardly mobile farm and lower-middle class youth.

SOURCE: The estimates and typology of institutions in this table are from Robert J. Havighurst and Bernice L. Neugarten, *Society and Education,* 3rd ed. (Boston: Allyn and Bacon, 1967), Table 4-2, p. 107. (The descriptions of college types are from pp. 104–106.) Copyright © 1967 by Allyn and Bacon, Inc., Boston. Reprinted by permission.

The second form of class streaming within higher education is evident in the strong relation between SES and choice of undergraduate major and graduate field of study. According to the National Opinion Research Center's analysis of a national sample of graduating seniors in 1961, law and medicine attract high SES students; education, engineering and other professions relatively lower SES students, and nursing low SES students.[36] It is sometimes thought that class ceases to matter once students enter college and that ability alone determines academic success or failure. In his study of an entering class (1952) at the Urbana campus of the University of Illinois, Eckland found that significant numbers of students with low academic ability graduate while significant numbers of high-ability students drop out. He found further that, among college dropouts, class (regardless of ability) is a factor in determining whether an individual sinks in the class structure. Eckland also found that

Stratification," *Harvard Educational Review* 42 (November 1972): 521–562. The recent trend toward open admissions should also not be misinterpreted. It is clear, for example, that open admissions in New York City is drawing working and lower class students primarily into junior colleges and that the dropout rate for such students is very high (as it is for students at community colleges in general).

36. James A. Davis, *Great Aspirations: The Graduate School Plans of America's College Seniors* (Chicago: Aldine, 1964), and *Undergraduate Career Decisions: Correlates of Occupational Choice* (Chicago: Aldine, 1965).

while class is not related to rates of graduation among high-ability students, among low-ability students likelihood of graduation bears a distinct relationship to class origin.[37]

Education and income: social mobility and immobility

The relation between class and education offers a valuable insight into what is now the central process affecting social mobility. Until recently the main avenues to mobility were directly economic. But the unprecedented levels of technical, symbolic, and character skills required to participate and succeed in a maturing industrial economy have increasingly made formal education the medium through which class status is attained, lost, and perpetuated.

How education contributes to upward and downward mobility is difficult to determine, since much apparent improvement in class position is actually absolute gain within a given class position. Without clear criteria to demarcate the various levels of a class hierarchy over time, it is difficult to say precisely what has occurred with regard to upward, downward, or lack of mobility. In order to understand the overall process (which seems to be marked by a significant amount of class perpetuation), one needs to understand the relation between education and income. As Figure 6-1 reveals, there is a significant correlation between the number of years of school completed and lifetime income. Of special significance is the marked differential between completion of high school or one–three years of college, on the one hand, and graduation from college, on the other.

The process by which families perpetuate themselves at given class levels can be better understood if we remember that parents' class position is a heavy determinant of children's performance in school. Parents at the upper levels of the class system provide their children with the motives and skills that insure academic success. In turn, success in school means high income and occupation, and thus high class position, a process that is then recapitulated in the next generation.[38] At lower class levels, parents provide their children with lower levels of academically relevant interests and skills, and fewer opportunities for personal enrichment, all of which is reflected in a lower level of school performance. In turn, poorer school performance leads to poorer jobs and lower income. Since job markets are increasingly controlled by educational credentials, here again class achievement is tightly circum-

37. Bruce K. Eckland, "Academic Ability, Higher Education, and Occupational Mobility," *American Sociological Review* 30 (October 1965): 735–746; and "Social Class and College Graduation: Some Misconceptions Corrected," *American Journal of Sociology* 70 (July 1964): 36–50.

38. As we will point out, a formal college education provides the credentials but not usually the qualifications to perform in an occupation. It also appears that the high-quality colleges have relatively little impact on the future occupations of their students, since the type of student they recruit more adequately explains future success. See Duane F. Alwin, "College Effects on Educational and Occupational Attainment," *American Sociological Review* 39 (April 1974): 210–223.

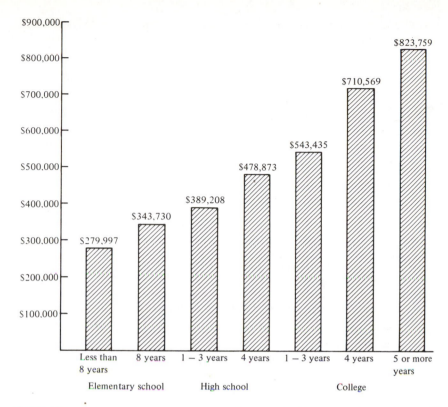

$900,000

$800,000 — $823,759

$700,000 — $710,569

$600,000

$543,435

$500,000 — $478,873

$400,000 — $389,208

$343,730

$300,000 — $279,997

$200,000

$100,000

Less than 8 years	8 years	1 – 3 years	4 years	1 – 3 years	4 years	5 or more years
Elementary school		High school		College		

Figure 6-1 Lifetime Income Based on Arithmetic Means for Men (Ages 18 to Death), by Years of School Completed, 1972

SOURCE: U.S. Bureau of the Census, *Current Population Reports,* Series P-60, no. 92, "Annual Mean Income, Lifetime Income, and Educational Attainment of Men in the United States, for Selected Years, 1956 to 1972" (Washington, D.C.: U.S. Government Printing Office, 1974), Table 6.

scribed by class ascription. Of the many functions of American education, the legitimation of this process of inheritance is surely one of the least understood. Our understanding of this function will be considerably enhanced if we examine it as a "cooling-out" process.

The cooling-out function of education

Social mobility in the United States is thought to be, to use Turner's term, a contest between equals. Unlike the English system of "sponsored" mobility, in which members of the elite identify likely elite prospects in the classes below and consciously recruit them into the higher levels of society, American society regards upper status as a prize to be won by the worthiest individuals. Maintaining loyalty to the social system is a problem all societies face, says Turner.

The most conspicuous control problem is that of ensuring loyalty in the disadvantaged classes toward a system in which their members receive less than a proportional share of society's goods. In a system of contest mobility this is accomplished by a combination of futuristic orientation, the norm of ambition, and a general sense of fellowship with the elite. Each individual is encouraged to think of himself as competing for an elite position so that loyalty to the system and conventional attitudes are cultivated in the process of preparation for this possibility. It is essential that this futuristic orientation be kept alive by delaying a sense of final irreparable failure to reach elite status until attitudes are well established. By thinking of himself in the successful future the elite aspirant forms considerable identification with the elitists, and evidence that they are merely ordinary human beings like himself helps to reinforce this identification as well as to keep alive the conviction that he himself may someday succeed in like manner. To forestall rebellion among the disadvantaged majority, then, a contest system must avoid absolute points of selection for mobility and immobility and must delay clear recognition of the realities of the situation until the individual is too committed to the system to change radically. A futuristic orientation cannot, of course, be inculcated successfully in all members of lower strata, but sufficient internalization of a norm of ambition tends to leave the unambitious as individual deviants and to forestall the latter's formation of a genuine subcultural group able to offer a collective threat to the established system.[39]

American education is structured, Turner continues, in keeping with the cultural ethos of contest mobility. American educational institutions avoid sharp separation (or *tracking*) of students, and the avenues from one program to another are kept open. Education is overtly viewed as a means to get ahead; it is avowedly vocational or practical; a great deal of effort is expended on keeping students in school as long as possible to insure a fair contest; and much attention is paid to skills of "social adjustment," since the upward aspirant has no homogeneous elite on which to model his or her behavior and must not lose contact with the masses.

It should be noted, however, that behind the rhetoric and attempts to provide for equal opportunity and competition, the United States has a well-developed class-based tracking system. Actually, it appears that there is very little difference between the United States and England in continuity of social level from father to son, or in the relative importance of social origin and ability in the son's educational attainment. And while the two nations' educational systems differ greatly, the tracking of students into academic and non-academic streams reflects class origin and ability almost identically. It appears, in other words, that the two countries use different mechanisms to produce the same results.[40]

39. Ralph H. Turner, "Sponsored and Contest Mobility and the School System," *American Sociological Review* 25 (December 1960): 859; reprinted in A. H. Halsey, Jean Floud, and C. Arnold Anderson, eds., *Education, Economy, and Society* (New York: Free Press, 1961), pp. 121–139, also in paperback. Used by permission.

40. For this comparison, see Alan C. Kerckoff, "Stratification Processes and Outcomes in England and the United States," *American Sociological Review* 39 (December 1974): 789–801.

Turner's classic analysis concentrates on the way in which education is used to institutionalize and legitimate upward mobility, or success. It ignores, except by implication, the way in which failure (or relative failure or only moderate success) is institutionalized. Addressing himself to the latter problem, Burton R. Clark has suggested that the junior college performs a "cooling-out" function.[41] The United States, says Clark, must somehow solve the problem created by the contradiction between its encouragement of all to succeed and the ability of the social structure to provide success only for a few — and a deeply graded structure of relative success and failure for the rest. Deliberately structured to diminish the enrollment pressure on colleges and universities, the junior college charges either low or no tuition and provides considerable choice among technical, commercial, and academic programs. But, says Clark, those who enroll in academic programs in the hope of eventually transferring to four-year colleges cannot all succeed, and a need exists to shift potential transfer students into terminal programs. Rather than allow for outright failure, says Clark, the junior college has developed an elaborate but disguised process for easing students into terminal programs and allowing all to save face. Among the features of this process are pre-entrance achievement tests, regular counseling interviews, a mandatory orientation course devoted to "realistic" vocational goals, an elaborate system of supervision in courses, and the routine use of probationary status.

It is important to recognize that standards of academic achievement (in all fields) are norms derived from the behavior in school of middle and upper class students. These norms, despite much popular nonsense to the contrary, have risen consistently over the entire period for which we have records, largely because rising educational levels and aspirations have caused parents to better motivate and prepare their children for school.[42] Departures from established academic norms are then labeled C or F students, low-I.Q., "two years behind in reading," culturally deprived, dropouts, A+ students, brilliant, "college material," and so on. Conformity to such upper and middle class norms is, by definition, harder for working and lower class youngsters, rendering the concept of equal educational opportunity (no matter how defined) highly problematic. What exists, in other words, is an unacknowledged tracking system or, actually, nonsystem, made up of noncompeting clusters heavily related to class. Any

41. "The 'Cooling-Out' Function in Higher Education," *American Journal of Sociology* 65, no. 6 (May 1960): 569–576. The term *cooling-out* is taken from the work of Erving Goffman and refers to the management of disappointment. Goffman illustrates his argument by reference to the confidence game, which often features a means to mollify the victim and thus prevent him from alerting the police. Clark's article is reprinted in A. H. Halsey, Jean Floud, and C. Arnold Anderson, eds., *Education, Economy, and Society* (New York: Free Press, 1961), pp. 513–523, also in paperback.

42. The early 1970s witnessed a decline on one measure of academic ability, the Scholastic Aptitude Test (*Chronicle of Higher Education*, Vol. 10, 3 March 1975, p. 1). Scholars are puzzling over this finding, but the explanation is probably simple: families, schools, and other agencies of socialization have changed their norms somewhat and the S.A.T.s have not.

assumption or argument that the hierarchy of achievement produced by this interplay of class and education coincides with (or approximates) the structure of ability ordained by nature is thoroughly suspect. And, finally, it means that we have no way of knowing how good our best really are.

The nature of education is seen in quite a different light, of course, by laymen and, I suspect, many professional educators and social scientists. I.Q., achievement and aptitude tests, grades, prizes, diplomas, degrees, and the like are all commonly viewed as reflecting native ability and motivation. The wide diversity of types of education (the class-based tracking system) is seen both as a wise provision for tapping and developing differences in native ability and as a moral universe allowing choice and providing a redemptory process for "late bloomers." Scholarships, graduate school grants, and low or no tuition charges at quality colleges (which in reality represent a vast subsidy for middle and upper class students, since it is primarily they who meet admission requirements) are viewed as a contribution to equal educational opportunity.[43] And low or no tuition and low admission standards at good or poor institutions are also seen in this light, despite the fact that such opportunities are often accompanied by deliberately created high failure rates.

American education is through and through a class phenomenon, complete with mechanisms for mollifying average and marginal students. What the United States offers is educational opportunity, not equal opportunity; to fail to recognize this simple distinction, as well as the class nature of American education, is not to understand why and how American society produces shortage, waste, and privilege in the development of its woman- and man-power.[44] But to understand all this fully, one must first examine education as a "great training robbery."

Education: the great training robbery

It is almost universally accepted that the two chief goals of education are to prepare (sift, train, and sort) the young for an ever-more demanding occupational hierarchy and to prepare them for citizenship. The value placed on education and the powers attributed to it are apparent in many ways: education is used to reward demobilized soldiers; it is considered responsible for the success or failure of the nation's science; it is thought of as a bulwark of defense; it is a basis for exempting citizens (college students) from military obligations; it allegedly reduces delinquency, unemployment, underemployment, and unemployability; it is associated with economic progress, and is thus used

43. See Chapter 13 for an analysis of how public higher education redistributes income from the lower classes to the middle and upper classes.

44. The Carnegie Commission on Higher Education, composed of the usual complement of important figures from various upper walks of life, consistently confuses (uses interchanged) *educational opportunity* and *equal educational opportunity;* see its *A Chance to Learn: An Action Agenda for Equal Opportunity in Higher Education* (Hightstown, N.J.: McGraw-Hill, 1970).

by employers who require more and more formal education all the time as a criterion for hiring in almost every line and level of work; and it is alleged to raise the income of the poor, and thus to make them viable citizens.

As education was assigned ever more explicit economic and social functions, Americans came to think of it as a natural or objective process for sorting out and training the talent manifested in each generation. In this sense, education has come to resemble the United States' central institutional system, its economy. But because education has been so deeply imbued with sacred social purposes, it has not been possible for Americans to ask fundamental questions about its actual social role. Of course, Americans have been quite critical of their educational institutions. They have spent and will no doubt continue to spend enormous amounts of time and energy debating their performance. What the empirical record suggests, however, is that America's fundamental premises about education are wrong; that is, a sizable amount of evidence indicates that formal education bears no positive relation to economic behavior. If anything, education is associated with negative economic consequences!

Perhaps the simplest way to look at this evidence is to examine Ivar Berg's indictment of education as a "great training robbery."[45] Summarizing the considerable evidence on the relation between formal education and work performance and satisfaction, as well as a study of his own, Berg found no relation between formal education and work productivity, low absenteeism, low turnover, work satisfaction, or promotion. If anything, he found an inverse relation between amount of formal education and occupational performance. While the studies reported by Berg varied with regard to the type and reliability of their data, the impression gained from reviewing data on blue-collar, white-collar, and engineer-scientist workers is that formal education plays one single role: it determines where one enters the occupational system.[46] What is crucial, in other words, is that employers believe that formal education makes better workers and therefore use it as a criterion for hiring. But once hired, workers with more and less formal education exhibit no significant difference in work performance. The only apparent difference is in income, because workers with more formal education enter the labor force at higher levels and change jobs more often.

45. Ivar Berg, assisted by Sherry Gorelick, *Education and Jobs: The Great Training Robbery* (New York: Praeger, 1970).
46. All this does not necessarily mean that education is not an "investment in human capital." It means that, aside from both the economic value of basic literacy and vocational and professional education, no positive proof has yet been found that formal education is related to job performance. The relevance of formal or academic education to job performance is probably high, however, in occupations that are academic in nature, such as teaching. Thus, a holder of a Ph.D. in sociology can certainly perform better as a professor of sociology than can a seventh-grade dropout. But the Ph.D. holder might have been a better professor (at a younger age) and the seventh-grade dropout might have stayed in school longer had "irrelevant" formal elements been eliminated from their educations.

Berg also found no relation between formal education and success in the military or the civil service. In one highly demanding occupation (air controller) for which the Federal Aviation Administration was forced to train its own employees quickly, no difference in performance was found between high school and college graduates. And, interestingly enough, the demand that teachers have undergraduate and even graduate degrees is associated with high turnover and departure from the profession. Thus Berg and others suggest that formal education is mostly a means of assigning credentials that control the supply of labor, and thus access to jobs and income. Given the close relationship between class and the acquisition of educational credentials, the American system of education is thus, as much as anything else, a way of transmitting class position from one generation to the next.

The suspicion that formal education has little economic significance (in a conventional positive sense) is corroborated by Randall Collins' sophisticated and intensive analysis of this overall question. Reviewing the literature and the data on the increased schooling required for employment in the United States, Collins found that education is better understood as a status-conferring process by means of which dominant groups seek to control occupations by imposing irrelevant cultural requirements than as a reflection of the greater skills needed on the job due to technological change.[47]

But what about class mobility? Do not significant numbers of young people climb the economic ladder after having climbed the ladder of education? Of course, but mobility (or the lack of it) looks quite different if one thinks of it as a function of economic, political, or military need (structural mobility) rather than as a result of education and personal ability (equal opportunity mobility). At great psychic cost, the United States compels all youngsters in the lower classes to compete for a relatively small number of vacancies in the classes above them. The conclusion that should be drawn is that education is among other things a way of controlling the supply of labor, without acknowledging that this is being done, and of incorporating youth — those who fail as well as those who succeed — into American society. And education performs these functions without presenting a challenge to the principle of class (the ideology of nonegalitarian classlessness) or to the incumbents of favored class levels.

Awareness is spreading that formal knowledge is not directly related to job performance, at least judging from the challenges to the use of tests to determine job entry, retention, and promotion being mounted by minority groups. Significantly, the courts have struck down the use of some tests because of their irrelevance to job performance. Since the practice of applying irrelevant formal educational criteria affects most occupations including public occupations (civil servants, teachers), at all class levels, it remains to be seen what progress can be made in lifting the burden of free academic education from the backs of the American people.

47. Randall Collins, "Functional and Conflict Theories of Educational Stratification," *American Sociological Review* 36 (December 1971): 1002–1019.

Education and social integration

In the nineteenth century, Americans believed that education in a common school could provide moral and intellectual cement to bind the nation together. Children would acquire a shared outlook and spirit, it was thought, by growing up together under adult supervision. The common curriculum in the common school was no doubt inspired by, or at least congruent with, the social experience of most Americans in the early nineteenth century. Most Americans shared the experience and values of Protestantism, Newtonian cosmology, farming, and small-town life, which no doubt made it natural for them to think in terms of a common school. Later, the common school was also seen as a corrective to the increased diversity brought about by urbanization and immigration. Even when the school was diversified at the high school level, there persisted the faith (among whom and how strongly is difficult to say) that educational homogenization was gradually taking place and/or that ever higher levels of education were good for society.

A century and a quarter after the advent of mass public education, Americans are probably no more united by common values and beliefs acquired through education than they were before public education. As Norval D. Glenn has shown, the popular belief — prevalent even among social scientists — that cultural differences due to region, race, religion, and social level have declined is not borne out by the facts. Far from being homogenized by education, Americans are quite divided in values and beliefs, perhaps more so now than ever before.[48]

Why Americans persist in thinking of education as a mechanism for promoting social integration through homogeneity cannot be explained with precision. Whatever its source, however, the ideology of homogeneity in education (equality of opportunity, objective-national norms, professional standards, accreditation, national programs) helps to conceal an unfair contest for social position. In fact, beneath the rhetoric of homogeneity and universalism, American society has created wide diversification: it has diversified its high school system so that even students who attend the same school receive different educations; it has created a highly diversified hierarchy of colleges, universities, and junior colleges; it has diversified its entire elementary and high school systems by class, as a result of residential segregation and the tradition of the neighborhood school; and it has taken class diversification one step further to create severe racial isolation in all parts of the nation.[49] But educational diversification disguised by the rhetoric of equality and competition serves important latent functions. The truth of the matter is that the American educational nonsystem

48. Norval D. Glenn, "The Trend in Differences in Attitudes and Behavior by Educational Level," *Sociology of Education* 39 (Summer 1966): 255–275; reprinted in Ronald M. Pavalko, ed., *Sociology of Education: A Book of Readings* (Itasca, Ill.: F. E. Peacock, 1968), pp. 218–238.

49. U. S. Commission on Civil Rights, *Racial Isolation in the Public Schools,* 2 vols. (Washington, D. C.: U. S. Government Printing Office, 1967).

does create social stability, but in a manner extremely incongruous with normative ideology: the class-based tracking system protects those with power and legitimates the failure of those without power.

Class and educational shortage, waste, and privilege

A class system of education is not *ipso facto* bad, either morally or socially. That rich or affluent parents can see to it that their children are better prepared and motivated for academic success than children in the lower classes means nothing by itself. In fact, this process can be considered a positive feature of the American class system: it insures a large supply of trained and motivated people for the increasingly complicated role structure of industrial society. But the ideology of "nonegalitarian classlessness" (personal responsibility, open competition, equality of educational opportunity, "objective" criteria for determining grades, all on the assumption that a natural hierarchy of talent exists) tends to obscure the fact that the American system of education can be faulted, according to American standards, on a number of other counts.

If education is seen as a mechanism for preparing youth for occupational statuses, serious questions about its performance must be raised. For one thing, the United States seems to have far more functional illiterates than is commonly believed.[50] The functionally illiterate include school dropouts and the large number of untrained, unmotivated (actually negatively motivated) individuals, disproportionately young and black, predictably produced by our social system. The inadequacy of citizen development can be seen in yet another light: American educational institutions fail to utilize a great deal of available talent, or, in other words, American society develops more talent than it has yet found ways to harness. There is undoubtedly a large difference between the number of eighteen–twenty-one-years-olds with I.Q.s and other test scores high enough for college work and the number who actually enroll. And data cited earlier show that significant numbers of youngsters in the lower classes with high academic qualifications do not attend college.

The resulting waste is particularly offensive in view of what appears to be a considerable amount of class privilege. Table 6-4, drawn from a national sample of high school students, shows that significant numbers of students plan to (and do) attend college despite academic records inferior to those of students who do not plan on college; these data correlate strongly with class position. Holding class constant, it is apparent that scholastic ability is associated with plans to go to college. But holding scholastic ability constant, it is also apparent that students' class of origin is influential, so much so that more of the low achievers among the well-to-do students (53 percent) plan on college than high achievers among the poor (43 percent).[51]

50. David Harman, "Illiteracy: An Overview," *Harvard Educational Review* 40 (May 1970): 226–243.
51. For data from Milwaukee showing that sizable percentages of students in the lower classes with high I.Q.s do not plan to go to college, while large percentages of students from the upper classes with low I.Q.s do plan to go, see William H. Sewell

Project Talent, the large-scale attempt to identify and analyze the characteristics of American high school students, provides similar data (see Table 6-5), except that the poor achievers among the well-to-do were not found to have a higher probability of attending college than the top achievers among the poor. Table 6-5 illustrates once again that, holding ability constant, the higher one's position in the class hierarchy, the greater one's chance of entering college. It should be noted, however, that Table 6-5's focus on the relation between ability and socioeconomic status is not characteristic of the overall approach of either the follow-up or the original study.[52] While the data collected by this project are a valuable inventory of high school students' academic achievement, interests, and backgrounds, and of the United States' massive waste of talent, the study as a whole tends to take American society for granted, making it appear that students are the independent variable. This unconscious early liberal stance is most readily apparent in the various project writers' characteristic use of the terms "talent," "human resources," "human abilities," "high school students" interchangeably. The identification of American behavior as human behavior tends, of course, to render much of what is observed nonproblematic.

And, to make matters worse, educational privilege, in combination with the class bias of education in general, calls into question the objective validity of high grades and high educational achievement in general. The existing array of

Table 6-4 Percentages of High-School Seniors Planning to Attend College, According to Scholastic Ability (in Quartiles) and Socioeducational Status of the Family, 1955

Scholastic-ability quartile		Family-status quintile						Number of cases
		Top 5	4	3	2	Bottom 1	All quintiles	
Top	4	83	66	53	44	43	61	8,647
	3	70	53	37	29	29	44	8,709
	2	65	41	31	20	21	33	8,696
Bottom	1	53	30	22	16	18	24	8,509
All quartiles		72	47	35	26	24	40	
Number of cases		6,520	6,647	6,465	8,116	6,811		34,561

SOURCE: Reprinted with permission of Macmillan Publishing Co., Inc. from "Local Social Structure and Educational Selection" by Natalie Rogoff in *Education, Economy, and Society*, ed. A. H. Halsey *et al.* (New York: Free Press, 1961), Table 2, p. 246. Copyright © 1961 by The Free Press of Glencoe, Inc.

and J. Michael Armer, "Neighborhood Context and College Plans," *American Sociological Review* 31 (April 1966), Table 6, p. 166.
52. John C. Flanagan *et al.*, *Project Talent: The American High School Student* (Pittsburgh: University of Pittsburgh, 1964).

Table 6-5 Probability of Entering College, By Ability and Socioeconomic Status, for High School Juniors, 1960

Ability quarter		Socioeconomic quarter			
		Low 1	2	3	*High* 4
		Males			
Low	1	.06	.12	.13	.26
	2	.13	.15	.29	.36
	3	.25	.34	.45	.65
High	4	.48	.70	.73	.87
		Females			
Low	1	.07	.07	.05	.20
	2	.08	.09	.20	.33
	3	.18	.23	.36	.55
High	4	.34	.67	.67	.82

SOURCE: John C. Flanagan and William C. Cooley, *Project Talent: One-Year Follow-Up Studies* (Pittsburgh: University of Pittsburgh School of Education, 1966), Tables 5-3 and 5-4, p. 96. Used by permission.

achievement may well be the best, but the best might have been better had class-based waste and privilege not been present. In other words, academic (and professional) norms are based largely on what middle and upper class youngsters actually do. They are not based on raw ability or on open competition. And what middle and upper class youngsters do is predicated on predictable rates of socially induced failure and mediocrity, largely among the lower classes, and on the weeding-out of many highly able youngsters before and during the period of higher education. The norms that are derived from the class-structured system of education continue to rise, but the only standards for evaluating educational performance are norms derived from yesterday's class system. And, of course, one of the latent functions of rising academic and educational standards in general is to guarantee and legitimate the defeat of each generation of youngsters from the lower classes.

While efforts have been made to diversify education in order to supply better-trained people for the various levels of the American occupational structure, the success of such efforts is doubtful. The mythology of a free, private, rational labor market; the deep bias in favor of college-preparatory programs; the vast power labor unions and professional associations exercise over the supply of trained personnel; our tradition of racial discrimination; and our general bias toward according prestige only to professional occupations all serve to make the development of citizens a highly irrational process. Perhaps all these points can be summed up by saying that Americans believe a class society can provide classless education.

Class and education: a summary

As the evidence amply demonstrates, class exerts a heavy influence, even control, over all aspects of education. Class is related strongly and directly to the amount of money spent per pupil; educational aspirations; I.Q., grades, prizes, diplomas, and degrees; rate of attendance and years of school completed; choice of school and program of study; income and occupation; and success in school without superior academic achievement. Academic education does not seem to be related to occupational performance, and it does not produce social integration by developing homogeneous citizens. The main (latent) function of education appears to be control of the flow of woman- and man-power into the economy; or, more exactly, its main function appears to be to insure that the elite occupations are not oversupplied with qualified people. Academic education, in short, is primarily a means of maintaining and transmitting the existing class structure. But since it is not genuinely related to economic performance, academic education is really a prestige phenomenon masquerading as a personal achievement process, thus concealing the fact that entry into the valued levels of American society is primarily due to class birth.

Our definition of social class to this point can be stated thus: the American population is composed of a hierarchy of families and unrelated individuals separated into levels on the basis of worth in various economic markets. Different levels are characterized by significant differences in family values and stability, life expectancy, and mental health, and by pronounced differences in the ability to put children through school successfully, an overall structure and process that tends to produce a static class system over time (as measured by the distribution of the above class values) and a considerable amount of class perpetuation (ascriptively based achievement and nonachievement).

We turn now to an analysis of the relation between inequality in the class dimension and stratification by prestige.

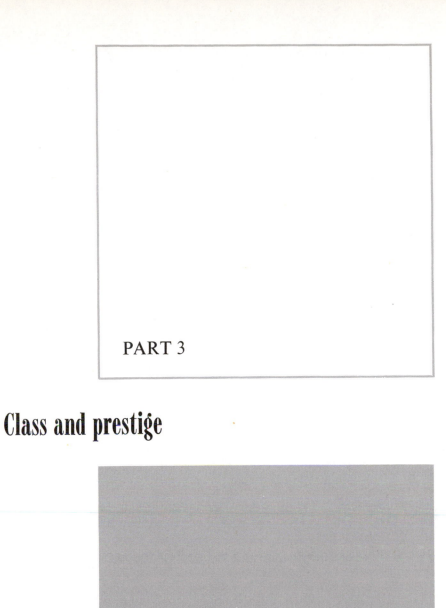

PART 3

Class and prestige

7

The nature of prestige

IN ANALYZING PRESTIGE, we will again deal with some of the phenomena we encountered in the analysis of class. This time, however, we will use a finer analytical framework, and will focus more explicitly on group formation and structure and on the development and distribution of psychic resources and satisfactions. In our analysis of the class dimension, we tended to focus on the abstract distribution of aggregate income, wealth, occupation, education, personal values, and physical and mental health, though we also stressed the importance of organized economic groups and gave some attention to the stability and instability of one important social group, the family. While we will refer to such matters again, we will do so for the purpose of identifying prestige variables and determining their role in the overall American class system.

In the next three chapters, we will consider three aspects of the area of prestige: Americans' views of themselves, in Chapter 8; style of life, or the consumption of "material" and "symbolic" culture, in Chapter 9; and the way in which Americans associate, or the structure of prestige groups, in Chapter 10. This chapter serves as background to the complex and often slippery materials we will encounter when we analyze these three subdimensions of prestige.

The realm of evaluation

The area of prestige has never been adequately analyzed, and in the following discussion we will be treading on less than firm ground. The classic analysis remains Max Weber's. Weber identified status or prestige stratification as a realm separate from, though related to, class stratification. Stratification by status, he argued, is based on the distribution of honor (or prestige) and can take a number of forms:

> The term of "social status" is applied to a typically effective claim to positive or negative privilege with respect to social prestige so far as it rests on one or more of the following bases:
> a. mode of living,
> b. a formal process of education which may consist in empirical or rational training and the acquisition of the corresponding modes of life, or
> c. on the prestige of birth, or of an occupation.[1]

According to Weber, prestige differentials stem from usurpation, but their long-range stability and effectiveness require successful conventionalization and often require added support from the legal order (privilege). Though the bases of prestige can be as varied as birth (into a religious, family, ethnic, or racial status), breeding, property, occupation, education, or some mixture of these, the prestige hierarchy is always opposed to the free play of market (class) forces. Prestige stratification thrives, says Weber, when the distribution of economic power is stable. It reaches its highest development when a prestige group(s) succeeds both in embedding property and occupations in a hierarchy of prestige values, thus making them immune to the play of economic forces, and monopolizing education and other opportunities for subjective development. Impersonal economic forces threaten prestige stratification because they cannot be relied on to honor the special prestige status of persons, property, or occupations. Dynamic economies undermine and transform prestige hierarchies beyond recognition. In short, Weber argued that class and prestige inequality were different though related and that, in a broad sense, classes stemmed from the production of goods and services, while prestige groups were derived from the consumption of ideal and material values.

1. *Max Weber: The Theory of Social and Economic Organization,* tr. A. M. Henderson and Talcott Parsons, ed. with an intro. by Talcott Parsons (New York: Oxford University Press, 1947), p. 428. For Weber's major discussion of prestige, see Max Weber, "Class, Status, Party," *From Max Weber: Essays in Sociology,* tr., ed. and with an intro. by H. H. Gerth and C. Wright Mills (New York: Oxford University Press, 1946), chap. 7.
    The area of prestige is still commonly referred to by the term *status,* following Max Weber's usage. Edward Shils prefers the term *deference* because it connotes an exchange in which some give and some take; see his essay "Deference" in John A. Jackson, ed., *Social Stratification* (Cambridge, England: Cambridge University Press, 1968), pp. 104–132. Shils points — mistakenly I believe — to a general decline of deference (prestige) in the modern period, and mistakenly suggests that social stratification results from deference definitions. His tendency to define social classes in terms of prestige is consistent with the once prevalent American tradition exemplified best by the Warner school of stratification.

Weber directed his analysis of prestige against Marx's argument that class is the universal basis of social stratification. But Weber never meant to replace class with prestige as the universal source of stratification; he was simply against the use of metaphysical generalizations. And he would no doubt have interpreted prestige phenomena *within* class society in economic terms as we have done. In any case, while adhering to Weber's general approach to prestige phenomena, we have grouped the elements of prestige a little differently to relate them better to contemporary American society.

During the formative years of stratification analysis (1925–1945), American theorists tended to emphasize prestige more than class, though in recent years this pattern has changed and may even have been reversed. The reasons sociologists have found the idea of prestige (or status) rankings more congenial than class have been identified by Leonard Reissman: America's tradition of antiaristocracy, frontier psychology, Protestant ethic, antiradical tradition, and unique processes of urbanization and industrialization. The idea of class smacked too much of impersonal forces stronger than the individual to be attractive to Americans. The idea of status or prestige, on the other hand, jibed better with the American mentality, because it implied the democratic right and responsibility of a community to judge an individual.[2]

Today, the economic basis of prestige is commonly acknowledged. But it is still necessary to distinguish between the economic and evaluative realms. Perhaps the best way to understand this distinction is to cite some examples. When an individual buys a house to shelter his or her family, we can associate this event with class by calling it a real estate transaction, relating it to income distribution, using it to determine whether the demand for housing is elastic or nonelastic, and so on. But when an individual buys a house (especially one he or she cannot quite afford) because it or the neighborhood has prestige, or when someone acts to prevent those who can afford the same house from buying it because they are black or *nouveau riche,* the event involves the special moral realm of prestige (style of life, status evaluation, snobbery, deference, exclusiveness, social etiquette, values, consciousness, honor, breeding, taste, racism, and the like).

Other examples of prestige-related behavior come readily to mind. When an employer hires a less qualified individual for a position in preference to a better qualified Jew, Roman Catholic, black, or Protestant, this act also inhabits the realm of moral appraisal (prestige). If we assume that there are ten, twenty, or fifty colleges that provide educations equivalent or even superior to that of, say, Harvard College, the higher cash or occupational value of a Harvard degree is attributable to an unwarranted academic reputation (prestige). Prestige (or status) considerations are paramount when an upper class woman cannot be seen shopping for food or carrying packages, and when a widow cannot work because work is considered demeaning in her "class." Every culture has its own peculiar prestige-related associations and taboos. There is

2. Leonard Reissman, *Class in American Society* (New York: Free Press, 1959), chap. 1.

an interesting story of an African student at a midwestern American university who reported a faculty member as an impostor because he saw the man washing his car, something no faculty member would ever do in the student's country.

The class order, then, is a hierarchy of families and unrelated individuals (embedded in economic groups such as business enterprises, professional and trade associations, public service occupations and associations, and labor unions) ranked on the basis of ability to prevail in various economic markets. In our discussions of income distribution, wealth, occupation, education, family stability, family values, basic personality structure, mental and physical health, and education, we have identified the salient features of the United States' class hierarchy. Our task now is to consider the class dimension as a hierarchy of families and unrelated individuals who not only face economic markets but also behave as moral agents, acting to maintain and enjoy various levels of psychic and social existence.

The relationship between class and prestige is not one-directional, however. In the history of social stratification, free economic markets are scarce; in fact, free markets are analytical fictions created by economists. Whatever their origin, prestige groups exert moral pressure on economic behavior and on the uses to which economic goods and resources are put. In some societies, families withdraw homes, land, and labor from economic markets — by means, for example, of entail and primogeniture or of family trust funds — in effect lodging these "economic" values in a structure of familistic values.[3] In preindustrial societies occupations tend to be assigned on the basis of family or religious status at birth. Even today a prestige order can deeply affect the operation of economic markets by defining a labor force in racial, religious, ethnic, sexual, and/or family terms, often making occupations hereditary. High prestige groups can bias the uses to which a society's economic resources are put by monopolizing the use of some goods and benefits (for example, forbidding lower prestige groups to own land, hunt, or wear fur); by creating and supporting a demand for luxuries; by demanding abstention from work on the Sabbath and/or holidays; or by abstaining from work in favor of conspicuous leisure. The prestige order can also affect consumption-related behavior by, for example, requiring segregated facilities on railroads or segregated barbershops and restaurants. It can also — and this is of considerable importance in the United States — promote the value of residence in one-family houses in the suburbs, a phenomenon that entails a specific pattern of allocating economic resources (land, labor, building materials, automobiles, highways).

The prestige order is composed, therefore, of standards considered to be moral, decent, civilized, and/or in good taste. What is considered honorable or civilized obviously entails an enormous range of behavior, and the beneficiaries (or, to use Max Weber's term, usurpers) of prestige differentials are, by

3. Chekhov's *The Cherry Orchard* is the story of an aristocratic family that keeps its cherry orchard off the real estate market despite the fact that it is facing economic ruin.

definition, those who have social power. Clearly, therefore, no analysis of social stratification can overlook the prestige groups that exercise power over the evaluative or moral realm. But one must also recognize that prestige-based norms, values, and behavior are mostly habitual "agreed-upon" patterns maintained and enforced by routine interaction: they are rarely enforced by overt coercion (though there is, of course, the ever-present use of ridicule and the implicit threat of force). Overt coercion in any significant degree is a sign of the breakdown of a particular prestige system and the advent of a new one. Two examples are the aristocratic reaction to the rise of the middle class in eighteenth-century France and white violence against blacks demanding their civil rights in the American south.

Achieved and ascribed prestige

The distinction between ascribed and achieved prestige is crucial to the understanding of stratification, even in the United States. The decisive difference between achievement and ascriptive prestige is not the difference between equality and inequality; both ascriptive and achievement standards lead to pronounced and lasting hierarchies of inequality. Its nature may instead be defined by asking whether a given prestige status is achievable or not — that is, by asking whether it is accessible to individuals and their families on the basis of training and competition or is assigned to them by criteria deemed important and unalterable.

The major source of achieved prestige in industrial society is occupation. Given its ultimate value-idea that mastery of the world is possible through science and human effort, industrial society accords the major share of prestige to occupations directly related to control of the social and natural environments.[4] Ascriptive barriers to occupational achievement, therefore, not only deny individuals and groups the benefits of class but prevent them from acquiring prestige as well. Achieved prestige can also be found outside of occupation among students, in the realms of taste and consumption, and among members and participants in nonprofit, professional, fraternal, philanthropic, civic, sports, and cultural groups. Achieved rankings in these areas again presume individuals or families to be qualified (or unqualified) for inclusion according to an achievable criterion: for example, achieving an A average or good grooming; being an architect, a manager of a bank, or a college alumnus; being interested in opera or heart research; and the like. When a fixed attribute such as race, religion, ethnicity, family, or sex is used to withhold prestige or to deny membership in prestige-giving organizations or activities, regardless of an individual's performance *vis-à-vis* the relevant achievement standards, one is dealing with an ascribed form of prestige.

Like all other societies, the United States uses age, sex, and family to determine an important range of social statuses. American society far exceeds the elementary use of ascription by also ascribing statuses on the basis of religion,

4. Occupational prestige is discussed at length in Chapter 8.

ethnicity, family lineage, and "race." The United States' denial of equal prestige to newly arrived and unfamiliar religious-ethnic groups is a commonplace ethnocentric phenomenon. Speaking generally, most societies (in-groups) characteristically view other populations (out-groups) as "foreigners," inferiors, threats, immoral, barbarians, and so on.[5]

The areas of ascriptive evaluation in the United States that are fully contradictory of the achievement ethic are sex and race: women, Indians, Chinese, Japanese, dark-skinned groups, and especially blacks have at one time or another all been categorized as permanent outsiders unfit to participate in the full range of available social statuses. Sexual ranking does not figure directly in social stratification, since females who are wives (or daughters) generally receive the class position of their husbands (or fathers). It is germane to the case of many working females, who are subject to deep ascriptive discrimination in pay and employment. However, the tradition of sexual inequality in America has never had the sustained ideological and political-legal base of racist inequality, and while women have not always been treated well they have never suffered the overt systematic degradation visited on nonwhite racial groups, especially blacks.[6]

Moral (or prestige) equality

Stratification analysis does not always give due recognition to America's deep commitment to moral equality. Many of the definitive components of moral equality have been standard features of Western society since the ancient Greeks and Hebrews. Until the modern liberal period, however, moral equality in the West simply meant that all individuals were subject to universalistic moral norms, such as the Ten Commandments, and that all should aspire to certain universalistic ethical goals, such as love and brotherhood. While this tradition helped to prevent the development of a caste system in the West, it was perfectly compatible with an estate system of inequality (feudal Christendom). With the rise of liberal society, this moral tradition blended with the economic and political needs of capitalism to give rise to a more comprehensive definition of moral equality. It is not sufficiently understood that moral equality is an indispensable feature of industrialization. Prestige differentials based on birth invariably subsume and ultimately rigidify economic behavior, and are therefore the deadly enemy of economic expansion. The modern tradition of moral equality should also be understood, in other words, as a means of inviting all to participate in the new economy of capitalism or, in effect, as a moral sanction

5. It should be noted that some societies, especially subregions, tend to denigrate themselves, and that the elites of various societies often hold each other in greater esteem than they do their respective populations.

6. But no comparison of their minority statuses can fail to note the enormous similarity in the ways in which women and blacks have been treated and defined. For a classic analysis, see Helen Mayer Hacker, "Women as a Minority Group," *Social Forces* 30 (October 1951): 60–69; also available as Bobbs-Merrill reprint no. 108.

for dissolving feudal ties and developing an abstract labor force. Though the principle of moral equality emerged differently in countries, it has come to mean, speaking ideally, that all individuals either are or have the right to become persons — that is, self-propelled, responsible actors in and of the society in which they live. As a result, the state and society are defined in such a way as to confirm and promote (at least as an ideal and often in practice) the equal right of all citizens to influence the state and to participate in social life.[7]

The American version of moral equality is unique, given the absence of a feudal tradition.[8] The American state is unrivaled, except by France, in its formal acceptance of the almost absolute reality and rights of individuals. This atomistic-egalitarian definition of political-legal relations is matched by a widespread egalitarianism in social matters. Speaking broadly, Americans expect their leaders to be folksy, and they resent titles, uniforms, and badges denoting supersubordination.[9]

On the whole, prestige forces tend to make populations unequal. Indeed, in the Indian caste system prestige forces were at one time so radically inegalitarian that they ruled out even token notions of equality. In the West, however, an important prestige force stemming from the Judaic-Christian tradition, democratic ideology, and secular humanism emphasizes the equal worth of individuals as moral-spiritual entities. At one level, in the United States, this realm underlies the widespread institutionalization (outside of occupation) of peer relations and "democratic manners"; at another level, it undergirds the egalitarianism that pervades the ideology (but not the practice) of American political-legal institutions. Americans resent attempts to translate occupational superiority into personal superiority. The deep streak of egalitarianism in the United States has been a constant theme in the work of commentators since the time of Tocqueville. A rare empirical example of the vitality of America's democratic folkways is the widespread resentment among American enlisted men during World War Two of the privileges of officers.[10]

The new "free" time (leisure)

Many of the most important forms of prestige behavior take place outside of work. For this reason, a full discussion of the general nature of prestige must be developed in terms of a clear perspective on the nature of noneconomic or "free" time. There is a widespread tendency to think that people today have more "free" time than their forebears, and that modern populations are being

7. The town-hall version of democracy and the various communal experiments in America even imply that all should influence equally.
8. The United States is not without "feudal" elements, however; see "Continuity With the Past" in Chapter 16.
9. For an impressionistic analysis of the strengths of various values, including egalitarianism, in four English-speaking liberal democracies (Australia, Canada, Great Britain, and the United States), see Seymour M. Lipset, *The First New Nation* (New York: Basic Books, 1963), chap. 7.
10. Samuel A. Stouffer *et al., The American Soldier,* 4 vols. (Princeton, N.J.: Princeton University Press, 1949), vol. I, chap. 8, Section I, Part 1.

gradually emancipated from the compulsions of work. It is widely assumed, in other words, that as an economy grows it relaxes its grip on the personality and allows people to develop and elaborate morally valuable prestige pursuits. It is a central tenet of liberal democracy that economic growth leads to an increase in goods and services (discretionary income) and an increase in freedom from work (discretionary time), which in turn lead to an enhanced morality, higher culture, and personal fulfillment. That industrialization has brought about a growth in goods and services and an increase in time spent away from work since industrialization cannot be denied. But as we shall see in examining consumption (of both "material" and "symbolic" culture), it is not at all clear that there have been increases in discretionary income and time, if by *discretion* one means the capacity to choose freely from a meaningful set of alternatives. Data on the consumption of goods and services and the strong connection between economic consumption and social stratification are readily available. But the actual nature of leisure time is not as well understood, and it is imperative that we take a hard look at the popular belief that leisure is increasing and try to determine the kind and amount of "free" (or nonwork) time people actually have.

It is undeniable that industrial society has brought about changes in the amount of "free" time as well as in the way in which time away from work is spent. This is apparent in the contrast between contemporary "free" time and the definition and use of "free" time in preindustrial society. Preindustrial societies are invariably characterized by aristocracies with little interest in economic activities and a penchant for lavish consumption. Industrial society has obviously foreclosed the possibility of the dominant stratum being a leisured, nonworking group of this sort. Indeed, as we will emphasize, to understand contemporary society it is necessary to explore the fact that the powerful middle classes, and probably the upper class as well, are work-oriented.

Exactly what developments have taken place, then, in "free" time? Our contemporary economy has reduced the percentage of the labor force engaged in hard physical labor and produced a dramatic increase in the standard of living, changes that are obviously germane to understanding how people feel and behave off the job. There has also been a well-known decrease in the average work week. But the consequences of these changes have been badly misinterpreted. One analyst of leisure has been led to the erroneous conclusion (shared with many commentators in this area) that affluence and the reduced work week have produced a style of life (consumption, use of time) that reflects a dissolution of classes.[11] Just as we saw little evidence of the growth of a middle class mass in our analyses of income, wealth, occupation, education,

11. Max Kaplan, *Leisure in America: A Social Inquiry* (New York: John Wiley and Sons, 1960), chap. 6. Kaplan's work is primarily a miscellany of conventional information and ideas. For an important article pointing toward a genuine sociology of leisure, see Bennett M. Berger, "The Sociology of Leisure: Some Suggestions," *Industrial Relations* 1 (February 1962): 31–45; reprinted in John Scanzoni, ed., *Readings in Social Problems* (Boston: Allyn and Bacon, 1967), pp. 259–276.

and family and related behavior, we will find little evidence that the classes are converging in the area of prestige. It is important, therefore, that the deeply ingrained belief that economic growth leads inexorably and directly to moral growth (the dissolution of classes, growing participation in and harmony between groups, a rise in the levels of personal fulfillment and social service) must be carefully qualified if we are to understand prestige phenomena. For one thing, it is not at all certain that modern society has made more free time available. In a pioneering analysis, Wilensky has pointed out that the work week lengthened from the Middle Ages through the nineteenth century.[12] Preindustrial societies are characterized by a great deal of what in modern terms we would call unemployment and underemployment, and in this sense burden their populations with enforced idleness. Modern society, in other words, employs its population far more fully and effectively than do preindustrial systems. In an insightful analysis, Linder has argued that it makes more sense to say that time has become increasingly scarce.[13] In addition to a more fully employed work force, one must also consider housewives (whose work week does not necessarily decline as a result of labor-saving devices — they simply become more productive); work and time devoted to personal maintenance; and work and time devoted to using and maintaining high-yield consumption goods.

Thus idleness has declined since the preindustrial period (and is now an attribute of despised categories of people) and "cultural time" (time devoted to cultivation of the mind and spirit) since full industrialization may not be rising as much as we think. Certainly our "cultural time," which accounts for a great deal of our prestige behavior, does not approximate our ideals in this area, most of which are derived from ancient Greece.[14]

Linder argues that people experience the modern shortage of time in many ways: as a sense of being endlessly busy, a hectic tempo, compulsive punctuality, a yearning for simpler times, and a constant need to calculate the highest yield for any unit of time (either at work or during "free" time). This shortage of time stems from a class-based definition of time. In thinking about this and other aspects of "free" time in industrial society, a number of considerations should be kept in mind. First, the reduction of the work week appears to have ended during the post-1945 period; second, "free" time is distributed very unevenly; third, the use of "free" time differs qualitatively by class; and

12. Harold L. Wilensky, "The Uneven Distribution of Leisure: The Impact of Economic Growth on 'Free' Time," *Social Problems* 9 (Summer 1961): 32–56.
13. Staffan Burenstam Linder, *The Harried Leisure Class* (New York: Columbia University Press, 1970), chaps. 1–5, also in paperback.
14. The Greek conception of leisure emphasized self-fulfillment through participation in a social order designed for that purpose. The Greeks viewed work as the chief enemy of self-fulfillment, but looked upon any specialization and lack of balance with horror. Leisure for the Greeks meant a rigorous schooling in moral balance and harmony, schooling provided by participation in a challenging but congruent social order. The ideal behind this conception of the good life was *aretê*, or versatility combined with excellence. Almost every introduction to Greek life stresses this ideal: perhaps the best is H. D. F. Kitto, *The Greeks* (London: Penguin, 1951).

fourth, the basic uses of "free" time (prestige) are deeply embedded in and difficult to distinguish from "unfree" time (economic behavior and values).

More will be said about these various aspects of "free" time in subsequent chapters on prestige. At this point, we need clarify only one of the many misconceptions in this area, the tendency to assume that the work week has declined significantly for all and that it will continue to do so. It is undeniable that the work week itself has declined: during the nineteenth century it was well over sixty hours, in 1909 fifty-one hours, and by 1929 it had declined to forty-four hours. Since 1945, however, the work week has remained at about forty hours, which represents not only no decrease but also not much of a change since 1929. Averages (which include part-time work) are misleading and so are comparisons with the past, when more people worked in agriculture. Also, the legal work week should not be confused with the actual work week, since many workers put in overtime (much of it compulsory) and approximately 5 percent of the employed labor force holds two or more jobs. Though data in this area tend to be crude, one general conclusion seems justified: the reduction in the work week has ceased during the post-1945 period.[15]

Wilensky has also argued against the popular notion of increasing leisure, claiming that the decline in the work week during the last century or so is vastly misunderstood. Basically, he argues, upper occupational groups work very long hours, and much of the apparent new leisure is actually involuntary under- or unemployment among the lower classes. The more favored occupations and classes, concludes Wilensky, "have what they have always had — the right to choose work as well as leisure."[16]

Wilensky's general theme is borne out by retirement studies showing that the upper classes tend to retire later than the lower classes, but that they also anticipate and plan more for retirement and experience less of a loss in self-esteem and, of course, income than the lower classes.[17]

It should be noted that one of the functions of leisure in the preindustrial West was to enable elites to resist the baser demands of society and to work for its improvement. It was always assumed that only society could provide awareness and fulfillment and only society could deny it — thus the need for institutionalized ways to escape society and reflect on its shortcomings. However varied the manifestations of this ideal before the rise and consolidation of industrial society, it always allowed some group to live "above" society — in other words, to examine it, to criticize it, and to experience tension between the demands of philosophy, beauty, religion, family, love, morality, politics, or warfare, on the one hand, and the demands of society on the other. Of considerable importance is the possibility that industrial society has put an end to this tradition by linking the psychic satisfaction of both elites and nonelites

15. Linder, *The Harried Leisure Class,* pp. 135–137.
16. Harold L. Wilensky, "The Uneven Distribution of Leisure: The Impact of Economic Growth on 'Free' Time," *Social Problems* 9 (Summer 1961): 56.
17. Frances M. Carp, ed., *Retirement* (New York: Behavioral Publications, 1972), pp. 176f.; 251f.

to the needs of a mass-production, mass-consumption economy. While such a question cannot be answered easily or conclusively, there are some data pointing in this direction. As we will see in subsequent chapters, consumption patterns are linked to class; higher per capita income has not led to a reduction of prestige differentials in consumption; the growth of free time has not led the working class into middle class pursuits or values; and self-fulfillment and participation in aesthetics and thought-life tend to conform to the structure and needs of industry and class. Indeed, so pervasive is the linkage between economy and society (or, in our terms, between class and the prestige realm of subjectivity, "material" and "symbolic" consumption, and group life) that one must at least seriously consider Marcuse's claim that industrial society has so thoroughly structured man's psychic energies that for the first time in Western history there exists no significant power group that can see past the structural defects of society.[18]

The primacy of class

The distinction between class evaluation and prestige evaluation is an analytic convention, not always easy to substantiate empirically. To complicate matters, the distinction between class and prestige belies an underlying unity. Nevertheless, even when prestige phenomena can be explained in economic terms, they often take on lives of their own and become causes in their own right. As a rule, however, the two spheres are not often distinct entities. In the long run the "social order" and the class hierarchy are brought into harmony — but prestige always appears as a separate realm. Sheer property is never accepted as an absolute credential for social honor or admittance to valued forms of social interaction. In consequence, there is always a tension between these two spheres of inequality, though it is often concealed by the dominance of one over the other. In this there appears to be no set pattern: sometimes class dominates prestige (the class system associated with industrial society), but more often prestige has subsumed the class order (the caste and estate systems of stratification associated with agrarian society).

The power of prestige *vis-à-vis* class (or power) in industrial society must not be exaggerated. Weber reminds us that the market is no respecter of persons. Once unleashed, economic forces can upset even the most deeply rooted prestige structures, such as when colonial powers promote extraction, commerce, and industry and thereby undermine the authority of tribal elders and the family; or when considerations of efficiency hasten the absorption of blacks into the labor force and weaken commitment to racially segregated waiting rooms and toilets; or when businesspeople endow universities, receive honorary degrees, and eventually come to dominate their governing boards.

The rise of capitalism represents a major transformation in the relationship between prestige and class (and power). The basic thrust of liberalism in the

18. Herbert Marcuse, *One-Dimensional Man* (Boston: Beacon Press, 1964), available in paperback.

past five hundred years has been to free land, labor, and prices — and values and beliefs in general — from their subordination to moral, religious, and ascriptive-feudal standards. For this reason one must not exaggerate the autonomy of prestige within liberal society.[19]

Analyzing American prestige stratification in the following chapters, we will assume that prestige phenomena can tell us a great deal about the nature of class, and vice-versa; indeed, we must always assume that there are deep relationships between the realms of class, prestige, and power. These relationships are often distorted by historical forces (such as slavery, immigration, and technological speed-up), but beneath the diversity and even disjointedness of these three hierarchies, the underlying power of economic institutions can always be discerned.

While prestige phenomena cannot withstand the logic and pressures of class for long, this does not mean that economic forces are rational-efficient and prestige forces are emotional-inefficient. Liberal social theory tends strongly to suggest that the health of society is a function of the operation of free economic markets and that foreign bodies in the social organism are lodged in the dimensions of power and prestige. The idea of free economic markets is, however, a fiction; the American economy, though freer and more efficient than preindustrial economies, cannot operate without considerable assistance from prestige and political-legal forces. Roughly, the prestige order is a major source of motivation for economic activity, while power (the state) obviously supports the economy by performing such functions as the protection of property, the issuance of patents and franchises, the adjudication of economic disputes, the granting of subsidies, and the creation of favorable tax climates.[20]

Two striking examples will illustrate the primacy of class over prestige: the commercialization of blood-giving in the United States and the Miss America beauty pageant. In a profound and disturbing analysis, Richard Titmuss has probed the deeper social meaning of the ways in which various societies (especially the United States, Great Britain, the Soviet Union, and Japan) supply patients with blood. Titmuss destroys the myth that most blood in the United

---

19. On the other hand, it is of some significance that Christianity provided much of the moral lubrication needed to bring about the free interaction of entire populations, a freedom indispensable to a dynamic economy. Thus Christians (unlike Hindus, for example) regarded themselves as well as non-Christians as human beings capable of having social relations; in this connection see, for example, St. Paul's *Epistle to the Romans*. In recent American history, Christianity has played a similar role in bringing blacks into American life. Though framed in terms of morality and civil rights, the drive for black equality (often spearheaded by black churches) can also be seen as an effort to incorporate a despised rural labor force ("caste") into America's abstract, mobile, industrial force (class).

20. In stressing the primacy of class and the general compatibility of class, prestige, and power, one must not overlook the cases of serious incompatibility between these dimensions. It need hardly be said that American society is far from having overcome the racism spawned by the plantation economy of the south or the religious-ethnic diversity and discrimination spawned by mass immigration. The other serious shortcoming in rounding out American society is the persistence of many elements from our preindustrial political system, a matter we will explore more fully when we analyze the dimension of power.

States comes from volunteers. Actually, less than 10 percent of it is derived from voluntary donations, or gifts from individuals to unknown strangers.

Titmuss finds that

> despite all the statistical inadequacies in the data presented, the trend appears to be markedly in the direction of increasing commercialization of blood and donor relationships. Concomitantly, we find that proportionately more blood is being supplied by the poor, the unskilled, the unemployed, Negroes and other low income groups, and with the rise of plasmapheresis, a new class is emerging of an exploited human population of high blood yielders. Redistribution in terms of "the gift of blood and blood products" from the poor to the rich appears to be one of the dominant effects of the American blood banking systems.[21]

Titmuss' overall conclusion (pp. 245f.) about the dominance of class in this area of "voluntary" behavior is also worth quoting. Using the all-volunteer and far more socially representative British system of blood-giving as a reference point, Titmuss concludes that the American

> commercialization of blood and donor relationships represses the expression of altruism, erodes the sense of community, lowers scientific standards, limits both personal and professional freedoms, sanctions the making of profits in hospitals and clinical laboratories, legalizes hostility between doctor and patient, subjects critical areas of medicine to the laws of the marketplace, places immense social costs on those least able to bear them — the poor, the sick and the inept — [and] increases the danger of unethical behavior in various sectors of medical science and practice. . . .
>
> Moreover, on four testable nonethical criteria the commercialized blood market is bad. In terms of economic efficiency it is highly wasteful of blood; shortages, chronic and acute, characterize the demand and supply position and make illusory the concept of equilibrium. It is administratively inefficient and results in more bureaucratization and much greater administrative, accounting and computer overheads. In terms of price per unit of blood to the patient it is a system which is five to fifteen times more costly than the voluntary system in Britain. And, finally, in terms of quality commercial markets are much more likely to distribute contaminated blood; the risks for the patient of disease and death are substantially greater. Freedom from disability is inseparable from altruism.

Our second example of the pervasive and often disguised power of class is the Miss America beauty pageant. At first glance, a beauty contest appears to be a nonclass, even nonsocial, event. Since nature alone bestows beauty, the female offspring of all classes presumably have equal chances of becoming Miss America. A closer look at the Miss America contest, however, reveals that more than (culturally defined) physical beauty is required. To win, a contestant must display a range of skills that are distinctly class-related: musical, dancing, and writing ability; poise; cultivated speech; and grooming. In addition, it appears that contestants from the lower classes are informally screened out long before the finals, as are those who express controversial

21. Richard M. Titmuss, *The Gift Relationship: From Human Blood to Social Policy* (New York: Random House, 1971), p. 119. Copyright 1971 by Pantheon Books, Inc., a Division of Random House, Inc.

opinions on public issues. And the prize, a college scholarship, tends to attract contestants who are already attending college.[22] Of course, the class nature of such contests is probably better recognized than is generally admitted. When Miss America of 1973 was asked why she sought the title, she responded with refreshing candor: "I entered it to make money. And I am going to make a lot more money than I first expected — $200,000 before my year is up."[23]

The foregoing is an introduction to a vast and hazily defined area in stratification analysis. As we explore the evaluations in the United States of things, people, and behavior and analyze the relation of these judgments to class (and power), it is worth repeating that the giving and taking of prestige, like income distribution, life expectancy, or family values, are simply data, which one tries to present as accurately as possible and to interpret in terms of causes and consequences. Causes are often interpreted in terms of value consequences, but science does not and cannot evaluate. The scientist can make personal judgments on specific issues, and can analyze society's values and indicate the value consequences that will result from the adoption of given policies, but cannot act as if values can be substantiated by science. However, the human beings who make up society are constantly evaluating the world around them, and are not bound by the conventions of science. Society and social actors are metaphysical in nature — that is, they do not distinguish between ideas, facts, and values. Indeed, it is impossible to think of society at all except in terms of metaphysically expressed meanings attached to nature and human nature, meanings that make up and energize the relations between individuals and between human beings and nature. It is to these meanings, in a special sense, that we are now turning. As we do so, the reader should remember that though the evaluations made by the public-at-large are not necessarily scientific, their nature can be ascertained and explained with a high degree of scientific precision.

In the next three chapters, we will explore a large and diverse body of data. In exploring this highly complex material, our basic orientation will be to view the dimension of prestige in terms of the logic of a class system of stratification, being careful, however, not to assume that economic institutions are always at odds with ascription or that prestige phenomena are always easy to relate to class.

22. For most of the above, see Mort Weisinger, "The Miss America Contest — Why Some Beauties Can't Win," *Parade Magazine,* 2 September 1973, pp. 6–9.
23. *New York Times,* 2 November 1973, p. 43.

8

Class and how Americans regard themselves

IN THIS CHAPTER, we will examine how Americans regard themselves and explore some of their basic attitudes about the world they live in. This aspect of stratification analysis has a rich history and has yielded important data not only about inequality, but also about the congruities and incongruities between economic life (class) and the world of subjectivity (prestige). Perhaps the most important form of prestige inequality is that attributed to occupational status, a subjective hierarchy that correlates highly with income and education (though there are some exceptions).

Occupational prestige
The hierarchy of occupational prestige

The first scientifically reliable (though deficient) national study of the prestige of occupations was conducted by the National Opinion Research Center (NORC) in 1947.[1] Americans were asked to rate ninety occupations as "excellent," "good," "average," "somewhat below average," "poor," or "don't

1. C. C. North and P. K. Hatt, "Jobs and Occupations: A Popular Evaluation," *Opinion News* 9 (1 September 1947): 3–13. An important analysis of this study, along with a number of essays discussing the study of occupations in stratification analysis, may be found in Albert J. Reiss, Jr. *et al., Occupations and Social Status* (New York: Free Press, 1961).

know where to place." Their answers, though they contained few surprises, composed a valuable profile of occupational prestige in the United States. Highest prestige was consistently accorded to occupations characterized by highly specialized training and high responsibility for the public welfare.[2] The occupations of United States Supreme Court justice, physician, state governor, member of the federal cabinet, diplomat in the United States Foreign Service, mayor of a large city, college professor, and scientist headed the list, and were followed by other professions. Then came skilled and unskilled workers, with garbage collector, street sweeper, and shoe shiner at the bottom of the list.

In 1963 the NORC conducted another study of occupational prestige, reproducing its original study as closely as possible in order to see what changes, if any, had occurred in the intervening period. The results revealed a remarkable overall stability in Americans' views of occupations.[3] Though there was some shifting of ranks, the hierarchy of occupational prestige scores in 1963 (see Table 8-1) remained essentially the same as in the earlier study.

Of perhaps greater importance than the stability of occupational prestige is the striking consensus Americans display about the relative worth of occupations. The fact that a sample representing the American population was in substantial agreement on how to rate occupations is of enormous significance *primarily because it means that those in low-rated occupations voted that their own occupations deserved low prestige*. This finding dramatically illustrates why social inequality is rarely a matter of physical coercion, resting instead on "moral coercion," or, put more politely, socialization. The significance of the American social achievement in this regard is enhanced if one remembers that work is the central source of identity in modern society and that the United States also has a deep commitment to egalitarian values. Perhaps nothing in the annals of functional role specialization equals the way in which Americans combine a commitment to moral and political-legal equality with a consensus on the radically unequal worth of occupations.

2. A follow-up attempt by Richard L. Simpson and Ida Harper Simpson, "Correlates and Estimation of Occupational Prestige," *American Journal of Sociology* 66, no. 2 (September 1960): 135–140, to test the NORC scale found that respondents rated occupations on the basis of "training-education-skill and responsibility" and that their judgments corresponded to the NORC findings. The Simpsons conclude their analysis by suggesting that their findings support the Davis-Moore functionalist explanation of stratification. In a general way this is no doubt true, but even their mild certification is bound to mislead to the extent that it fails to explain behavior as the result of power, creates the image of a natural society, or serves to legitimate the widespread discrepancies between the United States' achievement values and beliefs and its practices.

3. For this study and for additional materials showing stability in the distribution of occupational prestige between 1925 and 1963, see R. W. Hodge, P. M. Siegel, and P. H. Rossi, "Occupational Prestige in the United States, 1925–1963," *American Journal of Sociology* 70, no. 3 (November 1964): 286–302; reprinted in a somewhat longer version in Reinhard Bendix and Seymour M. Lipset, eds., *Class, Status, and Power: Social Stratification in Comparative Perspective*, 2nd ed. (New York: Free Press, 1966), pp. 322–334.

Commentators have pointed out that the hierarchy of occupational prestige is ambiguous, since different respondents may be using different criteria to judge occupations; they may, for example, be according prestige in light of what they believe to be society's evaluation of an occupation; emphasizing income or security or work satisfaction, and so on.[4] For the purpose at hand, however, it is important to remember that the analysis of occupational prestige is not designed to test the sociological or analytical sophistication of the general public but to find out how they in fact feel about occupations. As Gusfield points out, one ought not to assume on the basis of the NORC studies a national consensus on narrow normative or evaluative criteria regarding the intrinsic worth of occupations, but it is still important to recognize (largely because income, education, responsibility, and the like correlate so highly) that these studies reveal a startling unanimity on class stratification, if not on occupational prestige. As Gusfield also points out, this unanimity may reflect individuals' adjustment to the reality of power. Thus when sociologists interpret the NORC findings, they may be approving or condemning the structure of social power as well as analyzing it.

A comparative analysis of occupational prestige has further confirmed the idea that industrial societies have similar class systems, and at the same time shed some light on the possible autonomy of occupational prestige *vis-à-vis* other factors.[5] The authors agree that a gross overall similarity in occupational prestige characterizes industrialized societies. But they also point out similarities between developing and industrial countries in the evaluation of occupations and that there are some differences among industrial countries. The authors' major tentative conclusion is that occupational prestige is not simply a reflection of the level of industrialization; the development of an occupational prestige structure may be a contributing precondition to industrialization.

It is important to note that the hierarchy of occupational prestige is compartmentalized from other areas of social life, and that Americans resist attempts to translate occupational prestige into a more generalized claim to status. The classic German practice of referring to a woman by her husband's occupational title would seem ludicrous in the United States. The relatively sharp separation of occupational prestige from other social areas can be seen

4. Joseph R. Gusfield and Michael Schwartz, "The Meanings of Occupational Prestige: Reconsiderations of the NORC Scale," *American Sociological Review* 28 (April 1963): 265–271.

5. For a summary and analysis of research into occupational prestige in twenty-four countries, see R. W. Hodge, D. J. Treiman, and P. H. Rossi, "A Comparative Study of Occupational Prestige" in *Class, Study, and Power: Social Stratification in Comparative Perspective,* 2nd ed., ed. Reinhard Bendix and Seymour M. Lipset (New York: Free Press, 1966), pp. 309–321. For the similarity (and differences) between the values placed on occupations in the United States and Canada, see the first national study of Canada's occupational prestige system, Peter C. Pineo and John Porter, "Occupational Prestige in Canada," *Canadian Review of Sociology and Anthropology* 4, no. 1 (February 1967): 24–40; reprinted in James E. Curtis and William G. Scott, eds., *Social Stratification: Canada* (Scarborough, Ontario: Prentice-Hall of Canada, 1973), pp. 55–68.

Table 8-1 Occupational Prestige Ratings, NORC, 1963

Occupation	Score	Occupation	Score
U.S. Supreme Court justice	94	Priest	86
Physician	93	Banker	85
Nuclear physicist	92	Biologist	85
Scientist	92	Sociologist	83
Government scientist	91	Instructor in public schools	82
State governor	91	Captain in the regular army	82
Cabinet member in the federal government	90	Accountant for a large business	81
College professor	90	Public schoolteacher	81
U.S. Representative in Congress	90	Building contractor	80
Chemist	89	Owner of a factory that employs about 100 people	80
Diplomat in the U.S. Foreign Service	89	Artist who paints pictures that are exhibited in galleries	78
Lawyer	89	Author of novels	78
Architect	88	Economist	78
County judge	88	Musician in a symphony orchestra	78
Dentist	88		
Mayor of a large city	87	Official of an international labor union	77
Member of the board of directors of a large corporation	87	County agricultural agent	76
Minister	87	Electrician	76
Psychologist	87	Railroad engineer	76
Airline pilot	86	Owner-operator of a printing shop	75
Civil engineer	86	Trained machinist	75
Head of a department in a state government	86	Farm owner and operator	74
		Undertaker	74

SOURCE: R. W. Hodge, P. M. Siegel, and P. H. Rossi, "Occupational Prestige in the United States, 1925–1963," *American Journal of Sociology* 70 (November 1964), Table 1, pp. 290–292. Published by The University of Chicago Press. © 1964 by The University of Chicago.

from another perspective: a boss cannot easily pull economic rank (though possibly expecting deference) if he or she happens to meet an employee in a noneconomic setting. Similarly, while Americans accord high prestige to elected officials, they expect candidates for public office to display a common touch. And in a more general vein, as we will see shortly, American workers do not mind being called members of the working class but resist the term *lower class* because of its connotation of moral inferiority.

Nothing in American (or any class) society matches the importance of occupation for influencing the images people have of themselves and each other. Changing their position in the occupational structure is vital, for example, to enhancing the image and power of minority groups. But for minority and

Table 8-1 *(cont.)*

Occupation	Score	Occupation	Score
Welfare worker for a city government	74	Truck driver	59
Newspaper columnist	73	Fisherman who owns his own boat	58
Policeman	72	Clerk in a store	56
Reporter on a daily newspaper	71	Milk route man	56
Bookkeeper	70	Streetcar motorman	56
Radio announcer	70	Lumberjack	55
Insurance agent	69	Restaurant cook	55
Tenant farmer — one who owns livestock and machinery and manages the farm	69	Singer in a nightclub	54
		Filling station attendant	51
Carpenter	68	Coal miner	50
Local official of a labor union	67	Dock worker	50
Manager of a small store in a city	67	Night watchman	50
		Railroad section hand	50
Mail carrier	66	Restaurant waiter	49
Railroad conductor	66	Taxi driver	49
Traveling salesman for a wholesale concern	66	Bartender	48
		Farmhand	48
Plumber	65	Janitor	48
Automobile repairman	64	Clothes presser in a laundry	45
Barber	63	Soda fountain clerk	44
Machine operator in a factory	63	Sharecropper — one who owns no livestock or equipment and does not manage farm	42
Owner-operator of a lunch stand	63	Garbage collector	39
Playground director	63	Street sweeper	36
Corporal in the regular army	62	Shoe shiner	34
Garage mechanic	62		

majority groups alike, there is a problem that transcends discrimination and prejudice: the problem posed by an economy that not only cannot provide jobs for all, but also contains a great many jobs with negative prestige.

Occupational structure and the lack of prestige

Despite the separateness of occupational prestige and other areas, the division of economic labor in modern society creates serious prestige problems for many workers and, of course, nonworkers. Despite the fact that the values associated with work are central to the American identity, business and political leaders, along with academic, business, and governmental economists — individuals with fairly secure upper-middle class occupations — have defined an unemployment rate of 4 percent as full employment (4 percent of the 1973 labor force of 91 million is 3.64 million unemployed). In addition, there are many occupations (out of a total of approximately twenty-five thousand job titles in the United States) that afford little if any prestige and often burden their occupants with negative prestige. Thus, while there is a hierarchy of occupational prestige, it must be visualized as characterized by sharp breaks: an upper range of high-prestige occupations that coincide, by and large, with high position in all other hierarchies; a middle range of heterogeneous occupations difficult to define easily; a lower middle range of occupations with little or no prestige; a still lower group of negatively evaluated jobs, and beneath them the underemployed and unemployed. Those who occupy these lower occupations, or are chronically out of work or only partially employed, also occupy the lower rungs of other stratification ladders.

The importance of the occupational prestige dimension for unifying and legitimizing the hierarchies of class, prestige, and power is difficult to exaggerate. Those at the top receive the moral blessing of society by virtue of their occupations, which helps to legitimate their activities, benefits, and leadership in other areas; those at the bottom are morally evaluated in a negative way, which tends to legitimate both their economic failure and their overall position at the bottom of society.

The difficulties involving occupational prestige that many experience in industrial society elicit a variety of responses and solutions. Occupations that provide little prestige are invariably associated with close supervision, confining routines, punching a time-clock, and wearing a uniform (though some upper-level occupations, such as admirals and archbishops, also involve uniforms). Perhaps the ultimate prestige difficulty is to be without work. Because the problem of job prestige shades off into other problems, such as work satisfaction, pay, and personal identity, the following remarks have been framed in general terms. There are, first of all, the well-known disastrous consequences to personality and family life of unemployment.[6] There is the tendency to invent ego-inflating occupational titles (such as "sanitary engineer" for janitor) and to provide name plates and other prestige-associated items in the work situation. Workers set informal production quotas to prevent their identities from merging with the incentive-oriented, impersonalized factory system. The "protection of the inept" appears to be widespread as society struggles to find places for average people and noneconomic values.[7] Featherbedding occurs as workers violate achievement norms rather than face the humiliation of unemployment. Low-level and dissatisfied workers retire early when given the choice, and mass-production automobile workers, responding overwhelmingly to early retirement plans, expressed great enjoyment of the freedom of retirement.[8] And the demand for high wages is probably largely understandable

6. The classic pioneering empirical study in this area is Mirra Komarovsky, *The Unemployed Man and His Family* (New York: Octagon Books, 1971; originally published in 1940).

7. See William J. Goode, "The Protection of the Inept," *American Sociological Review* 32 (February 1967): 5–19.

8. Richard Barfield and James N. Morgan, *Early Retirement: The Decision and the Experience* (Ann Arbor, Mich.: Institute for Social Research, 1970), pp. 1–7.

as a compensation for psychologically unrewarding occupations and, in some cases, an overt substitute for social mobility.[9] Some workers, of course, make their peace with the division of labor and "enjoy" their work: for example, an information clerk in a department store retires after thirty-five years and says he loved every minute of it. Many workers with good jobs have a prestige problem because their work is difficult to describe and understand, and is therefore not readily converted into prestige; examples are data processors and systems analysts. And some jobs present particularly onerous prestige problems. The janitor,[10] the cabdriver,[11] and the servant[12] all have clients (and a public) who accord them low prestige on a daily face-to-face basis.

Stratification within classes and occupations

Social classes tend to be roughly uniform in prestige, income, occupation, and power. But a social class can also contain economic statuses that differ in significant ways. For example, within the upper-middle class doctors and professors enjoy comparable prestige but have very different incomes. The same thing is true of ministers, psychologists, and airline pilots.

A similar form of hierarchy is the hierarchy within a given occupation. Thus, some doctors earn more and are accorded more prestige than other doctors, and a similar pattern is apparent in many other occupations. With a few exceptions, stratification within occupations is not well documented.[13] We do know, in a general way, that the world of the corporate executive is permeated with prestige gradations and distinctions. The executive washroom is a well-known example and symbol of the numerous occupationally based benefits that have prestige significance; size and location of office, type of desk, furnishings, and the like make for deep prestige differentiation among members of the same occupation.

The world of government (the legislature, the judiciary, and the executive, including the civil service and the military) also contains obvious hierarchies within occupations. For example, a member of the United States Senate has far more prestige than a senator in the Maine legislature. A judge is only an

9. Ely Chinoy, *Automobile Workers and the American Dream* (Boston: Beacon Press, 1965), chap. 10, paperback, originally published in 1955.

10. Ray Gold, "Janitors versus Tenants: A Status-Income Dilemma," *American Journal of Sociology* 57, no. 5 (March 1952): 486–493.

11. Fred Davis, "The Cabdriver and His Fare: Facets of a Fleeting Relationship," *American Journal of Sociology* 65, no. 2 (September 1959): 158–165.

12. Vilheim Aubert, "The Housemaid — An Occupational Role in Crisis," *Acta Sociologica* 1, no. 3 (1956); David Chaplin, "Domestic Service and the Negro" in *Blue-Collar World: Studies of the American Worker,* ed. Arthur B. Shostak and William Gomberg (Englewood Cliffs, N.J.: Prentice-Hall, 1964), pp. 535–544.

13. An interesting and unexplored avenue to information in this area is analysis of the proliferating Halls of Fame in such areas as sports, aviation, agriculture, the franchise industry, and the like, and among songwriters, actors, cowboys, ethnic groups, and the like, and of the wide variety of achievement awards in such fields as moviemaking, the recording industry, the theater, writing, sports, industry, government, and so on.

abstraction until we know whether he or she works at the municipal, state, or federal level.

The growth of professionalism has undoubtedly led to greater internal stratification in business, government, and other occupations, including the world of sports. Perhaps the best way to conceptualize stratification within occupations is to note two characteristics of occupations: (1) occupations (especially organized occupations) try to maintain and promote the overall social class level of their members, and (2) occupations tend to be stratified internally. Perhaps the best-known example of stratification within an occupation involves lawyers. We know that lawyers enjoy high national prestige when ranked in the abstract. They also have high incomes and exercise great power. In fact, one of the interesting features of the legal profession is its close alliance with the modern corporation as well as with the exercise of political power. No other profession enjoys such enviable access to high stratification benefits in both the class and power dimensions. Straddling the upper reaches of all three dimensions of stratification, lawyers are a strategic link in the structure of social power. However, despite their high abstract class position, lawyers are not a narrowly homogeneous group. Jerome Carlin's empirical study[14] of a substantial number of the lawyers in New York City (who are probably representative of lawyers in most urban areas of the nation) reveals a distinct hierarchy *within* the legal profession. According to Carlin's evidence, the bar of New York City is "a highly stratified professional community" based on a hierarchy of law firms (or business enterprises). The large firms tend to have more respectable clients and to deal more with the upper levels of the court and governmental systems. Their members come from the established classes and the more prestigious colleges and law schools, and tend to be Protestant. The cleavage between the elite firms and those below them tends to maintain itself over time, suggesting an organized pattern of recruitment and retention. Mobility between the various levels is rare and tends to favor those with elite backgrounds. Contact between the levels is also rare, and their separation is formalized by the existence of two separate bar associations. Violations of professional norms occur mostly at the lower levels of this hierarchy. And, finally, the overall organization of the profession results in a decided pattern of distribution of legal services according to social class. The upper classes are well served by the elite firms, the poor are not served at all, and the rest are served by the nonelite firms.[15]

The world of classical music is another example of a self-contained, highly stratified occupational community.[16] Within the world of music, there are

14. *Lawyers' Ethics: A Survey of the New York City Bar* (New York: Russell Sage Foundation, 1966).

15. The latter point is also made by Leon Mayhew and Albert J. Reiss, Jr., "The Social Organization of Legal Contacts," *American Sociological Review* 34 (June 1969): 309–318; reprinted in Donald Black and Maureen Mileski, eds., *The Social Organization of Law* (New York: Seminar Press, 1973), chap. 11.

16. For an analysis of this world, see the poorly titled essay by Joseph Bensman, "Classical Music and the Status Game," *Transaction* 4 (September 1967): 54–59;

distinctions between conductors, soloists, opera stars, and professional orchestra musicians. And further distinctions are made among orchestra musicians, depending on such factors as the type of instrument played and the size and history of the musical group to which one belongs. As Bensman points out, this is a "status community" based on occupation (something that is characteristic of many occupations). The typical male musician devotes himself to music even in his spare time. His friends and often his wife come from the musical world (and his children may well continue in like fashion), and he tends to be oblivious to events in the worlds of, say, law or business. The major focal point of his existence is music and its rewards, including the fine prestige gradations bestowed by other musicians and by specialized status-conferring audiences. In other words, the occupation of musicians, like so many others, operates in relative isolation from other occupations.

The distribution of occupational prestige appears to conform to a number of well-known cultural and social themes and trends. Within an occupation, prestige tends to be highest among those who work for national and international enterprises (corporations, governments), size tending to reflect importance and competence. A similar set of standards operates in other occupations: colleges, universities, and professional schools, for example, are ranked according to national (and international) standards, and professors' prestige in the academic world as well as among the general public is a function of the prestige of the school they work for. Occupations also derive prestige from the clients they serve. Federal politicians and civil servants work for "the people," while local politicians work for the town, city, or state. Research doctors work for humanity, while medical practitioners work for individual patients; doctors with rich patients have more prestige than doctors with poor patients. Professors with well-to-do students gain prestige, while professors at plebian schools lose prestige. Prostitutes with upper-middle class clients enjoy more prestige than streetwalkers. And lawyers associated with corporate or public power enjoy more prestige than those whose activities are confined to divorce and criminal cases.

These well-structured hierarchies of prestige within occupations may forestall a number of prestige problems. (We have no direct evidence on this question.) To the extent that people are oriented toward prestige within occupations, for example, the social system is spared the task of judging the absolute or relative worth of the various occupations. Secondly, the focus on prestige *within* occupations probably leads to absorption with the economic issues pertinent to specific occupations, which may in turn reduce concern about differences in the economic worth of occupations. And, finally, preoccupation with prestige (and economic) status within occupations may make it possible for a social system to avoid having to make precise correlations between standings in the realms of class and prestige (and power). Though this is all mostly conjecture,

reprinted in Irving Louis Horowitz and Mary Symons Strong, eds., *Sociological Realities* (New York: Harper and Row, 1971), pp. 240–245.

it is probably no exaggeration to say that "status communities" based on occupation can reveal a great deal about how modern society remains stable and integrated. And they can probably tell us a lot about the unethical conduct, incompetence, and outright exploitation that are such significant and chronic features of our economic system.

The existence of stratification within various economic statuses raises an important problem for class analysis. Since many economic enterprises and occupations are internally stratified, one cannot automatically assign all members of a given economic status to the same class. This is of special importance when analyzing the middle classes. In other words, individual farmers, business-people, lawyers, doctors, professors, and so on do not have uniform economic statuses; by and large, it appears that some are upper, some upper-middle, and some lower-middle class.

Class self-identification

If Americans are asked what class they belong to, or whether they are upper, middle, or lower class, their overwhelming response is to select the middle class. In his pioneering study based on 1945 data, Richard Centers gave white Americans the choice of these three classes and the working class. As a result of the extra option, he elicited a different response than did previous surveys: 40 percent of his respondents identified with the middle class and slightly more than half identified with the working class.[17]

Drawing on a 1964 NORC study, Robert W. Hodge and Donald J. Treiman[18] found that 16.6 percent of the American population identified with the upper-middle class, 44 percent with the middle class, and 34.3 percent with the working class. Thus, between 1945 and 1964 there occurred a significant decline in the number of Americans who considered themselves working class. Hodge and Treiman also found only modest correlations between class identification and education, family income, and occupation of the main earner, and no cumulative clustering of these three class variables into objective hierarchies. They also found that ownership of various forms of capital had no substantial or direct effect on class identification. Actually, the widespread ownership of capital probably helps to reduce the impact of SES or class variables based on education, family income, and occupation. In addition, neither race nor union membership affected class identification. However, the authors found type of status contacts (relatives, neighbors, friends) to be as important in class identification as SES.

Hodge and Treiman depict a class system characterized by great diversity

17. Richard Centers, *The Psychology of Social Classes* (Princeton, N.J.: Princeton University Press, 1949), Table 18, p. 77.

18. "Class Identification in the United States," *American Journal of Sociology* 73 (March 1968): 535–547; reprinted in Joseph Lopreato and Lionel S. Lewis, eds., *Social Stratification: A Reader* (New York: Harper and Row, 1974), pp. 182–192.

and inconsistency in its objective variables (education, family income, occupation, capital ownership, union membership) and a wide dispersal of status contacts among the various classes. Overall, this image coincides more closely with Max Weber's view of social stratification than Karl Marx's. However, the absence of coherent, well-structured social classes in national samples should not be taken to deny the validity of class analysis. At any given point, the American population represents the push and pull and overlap of many historical forces. Social mobility, for example, diversifies social contacts across class lines, but both mobility in general and those who experience it are related strongly to class factors. Also, the use of family income as a factor is always distorting, since it lumps together single and multiple-earner families. Actually, many factors serve to diversify class statuses. The rise of mass education, a boom-and-bust economy, war, technological speed-up, prolonged prosperity, changes in life expectancy, and the like all tend to diversify the education, incomes, occupations, and property ownership of Americans. Even such a simple matter as inadequately accounting for the many millions of uncounted Americans distorts depictions of the class structure. In short, class self-identification does not contradict the power of class. It is the dynamic diversity and disjointedness of class variables that make it difficult for Americans to locate themselves according to objective and coherent class variables.[19]

Prejudice and discrimination

The belief that some people are unalterably different from and inferior to others is a widespread feature of both the internal and external histories of societies. Essentially, such views are promoted by dominant power groups to support their economic exploitation and political control of their own or subject peoples. This relationship is somewhat obscured in the United States, where the dominant ethos proclaims the moral equality of all human beings and the upper classes tend to voice more tolerant views than the lower classes. Attitude studies, however, should probably be discounted somewhat: the upper groups have greater verbal facility and are conscious of the bad publicity that attends expressed prejudices; in other words, their more tolerant views may contain a certain measure of hypocrisy and rationalization. And perhaps more importantly, attitudes are not the same as behavior. Upper, intermediate, and even lower (nonminority) groups can voice egalitarian views while practicing and benefitting from discrimination. *Formally expressed opinions, in other words, do not necessarily represent people's actual behavior in other contexts.* Therefore, while attitudes are important indices of stratification, they should not be confused or equated with actual behavior. Lofty thoughts and noble

19. For an analysis of class self-identification in Canada that finds considerable similarity to the United States (as portrayed in the study by Hodge and Treiman), see Peter C. Pineo and John C. Goyder, "Social Class Identification of National Sub-Groups" in *Social Stratification: Canada,* ed. James E. Curtis and William G. Scott (Scarborough, Ontario: Prentice-Hall of Canada, 1973), pp. 187–196.

emotions expressed in the abstract are often ineffective when they conflict with contradictory thoughts and values in concrete situations.[20] And lofty thoughts and sentiments often serve to camouflage power relations and important social processes.[21] In the following analyses of attitudes toward black, Jewish, and Mexican Americans, we will see two patterns: the expression of prejudice is related to class, and the growing tolerance and acceptance of these minorities does not mean that they are entering an era of achievement and equality of opportunity.

Changing attitudes toward blacks

Considerations of prestige are central to the resistance encountered by black Americans (and other "racial" groups) in their struggle to enter the mainstream of American society. Prestige elements are difficult to separate from black demands for improved class positions (jobs, housing, medical care, education) and improved power positions (the vote, equality before the law and law enforcement agencies). The improvements black Americans have experienced in the class and power dimensions have undoubtedly helped to improve their general prestige (what they think of themselves, what whites think of them, and their freedom of movement in prestige areas). Thus, the dispersal of blacks outside of menial occupations, their enhanced voting power, Supreme Court decisions outlawing educational segregation and miscegenation laws, the integration of the armed forces, and the passage of civil rights laws upholding equal access to public facilities all serve to enhance the prestige status of black Americans. (How much they do so is another matter.) Similarly, recognition of achievements by blacks in American history and in the realms of science and art has also enhanced their prestige and contributed to the development of black pride and confidence.

Whites' beliefs and feelings about blacks have been polled with some regularity and consistency since 1939, and the overall trend (through the late 1960s) is toward a more favorable view of the capabilities and rights of blacks. This trend, as well as the need to exercise caution in interpreting it, is described in Mildred Schwartz's secondary analysis of an assortment of public opinion polls undertaken between 1939 and 1965.[22] By comparing answers to

20. For example, individuals who sincerely believe in human equality may, because they also believe in protecting or enhancing their own property, resist low-income housing in their community.

21. For example, the civil rights movement is as much a class process (a way of transforming rural labor into an urban-industrial labor force) as it is a political-legal-moral movement.

22. *Trends in White Attitudes Toward Negroes* (Chicago: National Opinion Research Center, 1967). The data in this book are derived from ten surveys by the National Opinion Research Center, one by Roper, and five by Gallup. Emory S. Bogardus, who administered his Ethnic-Racial Distance Scale in 1926, 1946, 1956, and 1966, concluded cautiously (since his sample was not representative of the American population and since sizable amounts of ethnic-racial distance still exist)

similar questions on education, intelligence, housing, jobs, transportation, public services, and future prospects for desegregation, Schwartz discovered a number of trends in attitudes over the quarter-century. White Americans, for example, expressed a clear acceptance of the idea that blacks have the same intelligence as whites; of the black Americans' formal right to equality of opportunity in education, employment, and housing; and of the need to desegregate schools and transportation. But also noteworthy were the smaller majority favoring school integration and the avowal by a large majority of whites that they would not send their children to a school attended mostly by blacks or remain in a neighborhood into which a large number of blacks were moving.

The overall trend in white attitudes, it must be repeated, indicates nothing more than a change in attitudes, which cannot necessarily be equated with other forms of behavior. Nevertheless, while they may still be capable of behaving in a racist manner in specific situations, American whites are less and less willing to justify their actions in racist terms.

Whatever its sources, the general shift in white attitudes toward black Americans represents a significant change in the latter's prestige. But this general shift is counterbalanced by white resistance in the realm of everyday behavior. White Americans, in general, seldom deal with black Americans. The reality of life for most blacks is the ghetto (or rural isolation), and there is considerable resistance on the part of whites who have dealings with the ghetto to acknowledge black complaints or demands. An important study of fifteen major American cities, conducted to supplement the 1968 report of the National Advisory Commission on Civil Disorders (Kerner Commission), reveals deep resistance to the grievances and demands of black Americans on the part of those whites who actually deal with the black masses. While there were considerable differences among the six occupational groups surveyed (police, merchants, and employers tending to deny that there was inequality for blacks, while educators, social workers, and political workers tended to stress the existence of inequality), the overall attitude toward the plight of the black American was one of "optimistic denial":

> The men and women who are the faces of central local community institutions are not fanatical racists, nor are they particularly prejudiced persons. Some are apparently quite concerned over the problems of the ghetto and desire more signs of improvement in the position of Negroes in their cities. But, the main tenor of the interviews with the six occupational groups is one of optimistic denial: there are problems; progress has been made; Negroes want too much and want it to happen too fast; and besides they are fairly close to as much equality as they deserve right now.[23]

that there has been some improvement in ethnic-racial attitudes over the forty-year period. See his *A Forty-Year Racial Distance Study* (Los Angeles: University of Southern California, n.d.)

23. Peter H. Rossi *et al.*, "Between White and Black — The Faces of American Institutions in the Ghetto" in *Supplemental Studies for the National Advisory Commission on Civil Disorders* (New York: Frederick A. Praeger, 1968), p. 76.

Changing attitudes toward Jews

In 1964 the Survey Research Center of the University of California at Berkeley, in cooperation with the National Opinion Research Center of the University of Chicago, conducted the first extensive analysis of anti-Semitism in the United States, using a representative national sample.[24] One of its important findings is that one-third of the American population holds anti-Semitic prejudices in some form or another. Comparisons with other studies suggest, however, that there has been a moderate decline in Americans' negative evaluation of Jews in business and of their social and personal characteristics, and a more pronounced decline in political anti-Semitism. The data also reveal a substantial decline in discriminatory attitudes toward Jews in hiring, in the choice of neighbors, and in voting for a (hypothetical) Jewish candidate for president.

Data on discriminatory attitudes toward intermarriage, social club membership, and Christmas carols in public schools were difficult to interpret, since they involve legitimate concerns about preserving Christian values and identity as well as anti-Semitic prejudices. A substantial number of Americans accept the idea of their child marrying a Jew and are opposed to social club discrimination, but far fewer support abolition of Christmas carols in public schools. All in all, it appears that discriminatory attitudes toward Jews have declined more than have anti-Semitic beliefs.

The 1964 survey on anti-Semitism in the United States contains data on variables associated with both anti-Jewish and anti-Negro attitudes. In both cases, there is an inverse relation with socioeconomic status: the higher one goes in the class hierarchy, the lower the expressed prejudice toward Jews and Negroes. The strongest correlation is with education: the more educated tend to be less prejudiced in their beliefs and less discriminatory in their attitudes, with one exception — the feeling that Jews should be excluded from social clubs is strongest among the best educated.

Selznick and Steinberg are careful to point out that attitudes are not synonymous with behavior, and their analysis includes questions designed to reveal what people are likely to do in concrete situations. The authors also point out that the decline in anti-Semitic beliefs and discriminatory attitudes may be superficial, and that a national emergency combined with the relatively low level of attachment to democratic values they claim exists in the United States could pose a danger to Jews. And they emphasize that a high level of anti-Jewish sentiment exists at all levels of education with regard to social club membership.

Selznick and Steinberg are not as cautious as they might be, however, in analyzing the relation between attitudes and behavior. The authors tend to place a great deal of emphasis on the primacy of attitudes over behavior, tending to equate discriminatory attitudes (which they also refer to as

---

24. For an extended analysis of this data, see Gertrude J. Selznick and Stephen Steinberg, *The Tenacity of Prejudice: Anti-Semitism in Contemporary America* (New York: Harper and Row, 1969).

"behavioral orientations") with actual behavior and stating in two or three places without supplying any supporting data that an actual decline in discrimination against Jews has taken place in the post–World War Two period. All sociocultural systems tend to place much heavier emphasis on the importance of symbols than on actual behavior — the heretic is always seen as a bigger menace than the sinner — and the United States is no exception. Indeed, it may be that the United States emphasizes ideological purity more than most societies. The strong American belief in education as a cure for social problems is one aspect of this stress on ideological causation, not to mention the American mania for inducing symbolic conformity and weeding out alleged forms of un-Americanism. Selznick and Steinberg also stress education as the key variable in antiminority prejudice and discriminatory attitudes (with the exception of social club membership), and leave the impression that further improvement in education holds the best hope for a decline in antiminority attitudes and behavior. Interestingly enough, however, it is the better-educated and more tolerant classes that have systematically excluded Jews from the major power positions of the American economy and that have a stake in the perpetuation of economic anti-Semitism. The authors are not unaware of the economic consequences of anti-Semitism:

> The social discrimination of the educated shows that an aura of social undesirability still stigmatizes Jews. This has important consequences for the position of Jews in the social and economic order, and ultimately for the persistence of anti-Semitism. Excluded from the stable center of the economic order, many Jews end up in marginal industries and marginal economic roles often characterized by marginal business practices. A recent study of the legal profession in New York City showed that Jewish lawyers are still largely excluded from coveted positions in the profession.[25]

But this is the authors' only reference to the economic and class function of anti-Semitism. As we have seen,[26] Jews are indeed excluded from the main power centers of the American economy, and there is no reason to believe that Carey McWilliams' classic analysis[27] of the relation between anti-Semitism and the protection of economic power is any less valid today, on the whole, than it was a quarter-century ago.[28]

Selznick and Steinberg display a cautious optimism about the more positive attitude toward Jews they found, but say little about the actual position of Jews in the behavioral system, as opposed to the symbolic system, of American society. In other words, their analysis treats attitudes and not behavior (except

25. Selznick and Steinberg, *The Tenacity of Prejudice*, p. 187.
26. In "Jewish Americans" in Chapter 4.
27. "Does Social Discrimination Really Matter?" *Commentary* 10 (November 1947): 408–415.
28. In his *The Protestant Establishment* (New York: Random House, 1964), also in paperback, E. Digby Baltzell devotes a great deal of attention to anti-Semitism, tending to see it as a deplorable prestige phenomenon. Aside from a few casual remarks, he too ignores the deep implications of anti-Semitism for the protection of economic power.

insofar as attitudes are a form of behavior), and as such tends to display the misplaced American emphasis on the importance of ideology.

Changing attitudes toward Mexican Americans

There has been no reliable national study of Americans' attitudes toward Mexican Americans. The Bogardus Racial Distance study conducted in 1926, 1946, 1956, and 1966 is based on an unrepresentative sample composed of college students. Given this limitation, the major finding of this longitudinal study is that Americans are becoming more tolerant toward most racial and ethnic groups. But while Mexican Americans' absolute position has improved, their relative standing has not (in 1966 they ranked twenty-third out of the thirty racial and ethnic groups studied).[29] The Bogardus Scale tells us little about class variations, but since it is based on the attitudes of college students we can infer that it pertains to the middle and upper classes.

The growth of tolerance noted by the Bogardus Scale and other studies should not be taken as a sign of inevitable moral progress. The decline of prejudice in the past half-century or so has taken place during a period of unprecedented economic growth — a period, in other words, when dominant groups could afford moral generosity. A slowdown of economic growth, either in the short or the long run, could well bring about a resurgence of prejudice.

The burden of moral equality

The modern belief in the moral (including political-legal) equality of human beings is not an unmixed blessing, and it should not be assumed that this tradition rejects all forms of social inequality. It is unquestionable that the concept of moral equality is deeply incompatible with caste and estate forms of stratification. But it is inadequate to say that moral equality is not necessarily in conflict with class stratification; it actually meshes with and reinforces the class hierarchy. One need only remember that the liberal tradition of moral equality is often posited on the assumption that individuals as individuals are responsible actors to appreciate the way in which this tradition harmonizes with the liberal explanation of social stratification, "nonegalitarian classlessness." Given equality of opportunity, according to this explanation, all social inequality is natural and just since it reflects the innate capabilities of the individual.

One of the best illustrations of the irony contained in the American tradition of moral equality is apparent in the pattern of white attitudes toward blacks. Remember that a comparison of public opinion polls from 1939 on found a dramatic decrease (roughly from 60 percent to 20 percent) in the percentage of white Americans who believe that whites are racially (morally and intellectually) superior to blacks. But when asked in the late 1960s the

29. Emory S. Bogardus, *A Forty-Year Racial Distance Study* (Los Angeles: University of California Press, n.d.), Chart II, p. 29.

cause of the depressed social position of Negroes, a majority of whites answered "Negroes themselves." In other words, acceptance of the black American as an equal entails acceptance of the liberal belief that human beings are free to determine their own destinies and therefore responsible for their own lives.[30] Americans, in other words, have little understanding of behavior as a function of institutions, and the fact that white Americans are discarding racist beliefs does not mean that they have adopted a sociocultural explanation of inequality. What they have done in discarding racist views, it appears, is to explain black behavior in the same way that they explain white behavior, as emanating from forces in individuals themselves.

The ability of the class system to protect itself is enhanced, therefore, by the widespread prestige phenomenon called moral equality. Obviously, the tradition of moral equality is also helpful to minorities in combating inequality; indeed, it is a continuing source of tension in American society, perhaps most when a minority invokes it to demand reparations for past treatment. Our purpose here, however, is to stress the latent consequences of this tradition: to point out that insofar as it rests on the assumption that individuals are free to determine their own destinies, the tradition of moral equality is a burden to those who seek redress for inequities through the reform or restructuring of society.

When the tradition of moral equality is manifested in public policy as equal treatment and equal opportunity, the results are just as mixed. Obviously, it is a gain for minority groups no longer to be discriminated against, but to be treated uniformly does not have the positive consequences our tradition of equality implies. When blacks, Mexican Americans, Puerto Ricans, or Indians in the aggregate are allowed to compete in school and for jobs, fellowships, and so on, the outcome is predictable: they will lose because their social experience has shaped them for failure. Special efforts to offer realistic opportunities to minorities are another matter. But even here no change in the relative position of minorities in the aggregate (as opposed to individuals) should be expected to follow automatically.

The culture hero as an index to prestige
The culture hero in America

Culture heroes personify some of the core values and beliefs of a society, and therefore illustrate the processes that elevate some individuals above others. In the United States, the culture hero [31] par excellence is the individual who

30. For the development of this point by means of a comparison of these two sets of data, see the poorly titled article by Howard Schuman, "Sociological Racism," *Transaction* 7 (December 1969): 44–48. The data on whites' explanations of the black American's depressed condition were gathered by Angus Campbell and Howard Schuman, "Racial Attitudes in Fifteen American Cities" in *Supplemental Studies for the National Advisory Commission on Civil Disorders* (New York: Frederick A. Praeger, 1968) and a national Gallup poll conducted in 1968.

31. Orrin E. Klapp is one of the few sociologists to devote himself to the study of heroes; see his *Heroes, Villains and Fools* (Englewood Cliffs, N.J.: Prentice-Hall, 1963) and *Symbolic Leaders* (Chicago: Aldine, 1965).

is his or her own person and who overcomes adversity by drawing on his or her own resources.[32] American culture heroes are easy to name: George Washington is an obvious choice, as are some of our other presidents, most notably, Thomas Jefferson, Abraham Lincoln, Theodore Roosevelt, and Franklin Roosevelt. Of all our culture heroes perhaps none has achieved the stature of Lincoln, a man who personified all the most vigorous American values: humble origins, hard work amid adversity, intellectual striving, moral strength, and a common touch. Probably the only figure to rival Lincoln as a culture hero is Dwight Eisenhower; in terms of popularity in one's lifetime, no American in our history has enjoyed more popular esteem than this general-turned-politician.

The United States, like most nations, has a rich complement of heroic figures, real and mythical, who serve as models or reference "groups" for its population. As Dixon Wector[33] has pointed out, Americans love character more than brains; earthy secular personalities more than saints; lowbrow more than highbrow types; and men of simple, decent, and honorable traits who are forgiven bad means if the cause is noble. It is noteworthy that our major heroes are Anglo-Saxon and Protestant; that women have rarely been chosen as heroic models; that artists, doctors, and lawyers are bypassed; and that invariably the soldier, the explorer, and especially the wartime leader has been cast as a hero.[34]

Our understanding of the relation between heroes and social stratification has been furthered by Theodore P. Greene's use of magazine biographies to gauge changes in America's images of its heroes.[35] Greene distinguishes three periods in American history, each characterized by a distinctive type of popular hero, as judged by magazine biographies. Between 1787 and 1820 America worshipped "The Idols of Order"; in Greene's terms, the "hero emerges as a Patriot, a Gentleman, and a Scholar in magazines of gentlemen, by gentlemen, and for gentlemen." Between 1894 and 1913 America worshipped "The Idols of Power and of Justice"; according to Greene, the "hero has become the Master of His Environment and gains national stature in new magazines of the people, by business entrepreneurs, for profit." During the latter part of this period the "hero dons some social garments to protect his individualistic frame in magazines at the peak of their power." And finally, from 1914 to 1918

32. Whether or not there has been a shift from this inner-directed type to an other-directed type has been the subject of some discussion in sociology. For the original use of these terms, see David Reisman *et al., The Lonely Crowd* (New Haven: Yale University Press, 1950), also an Anchor paperback.

33. *The Hero in America* (New York: Charles Scribner and Sons, 1941), chap. 18.

34. Religious-ethnic and racial groups have their own heroes (Malcolm X and Martin Luther King, for example, among blacks). It would be interesting to know more about the heroes who serve as models for minority groups, and to know whether there is variation in hero worship by class among both majority and minority groups.

35. *America's Heroes: The Changing Models of Success in American Magazines* (New York: Oxford University Press, 1970).

(and presumably since), America worshipped "The Idols of Organization"; as Greene says, the "hero becomes a Manager of Massive Organizations portrayed in magazines for the masses."

The celebrity

Twentieth-century communications technology has produced a new type of culture hero, the celebrity. What is the significance of celebrities and what images of life are portrayed through them by the mass media? Does their advent represent a significant change in the models held up for Americans to emulate? In the absence of rigorous empirical research, one can only speculate about these and other questions. Does the cult of the celebrity provide vicarious meaning and satisfaction to millions of otherwise drab lives? As C. Wright Mills has suggested, the phenomenon of the celebrity may serve as a distraction from other problems and is probably influential in diverting attention from the shortcomings of society.[36] Exactly how "mass culture" works to distract the masses and distort their image of the world cannot as yet be said scientifically. But questions are easily raised. What is the significance of the theme of violence and aggression in American mass media (the cowboy, the gangster, the private detective, the football star and team)? Does violence, for example, help the audience to discharge in fantasy its resentment of bosses, or competitors, or economic forces? Do the mass media portray a world of clean-cut morality and easy solutions, thus disguising the role of power groups and compounding the ambiguities and conflicts in the workaday world? What is the significance of the hero who uses unsavory or illegal means to achieve his ends? What is the significance of the antihero? Does the United States lack a literature of the rogue, the underground hero who fights the system (as opposed to the roguish private eyes and spies who fight domestic rogues or foreign systems)?

It is possible that the rise of the celebrity signifies a shift from a world of achievement to a world of ascription. Celebrity status is difficult to achieve — after all, an unusual voice, face, figure, height, or agility is inborn. And the cult of the celebrity tends to associate success with luck and inborn traits rather than with hard methodical work. The rags-to-riches theme is prevalent in the world of the celebrity, like the hero, but the celebrity's success is often attributed to good fortune rather than intelligence, frugality, or work. Nonetheless, the phenomenon of the celebrity may serve to keep the American Dream alive among the disadvantaged and oppressed: black youth may derive vicarious satisfaction from seeing Joe Louis, Jackie Robinson, Wilt Chamberlain, or James Brown make it big. There are many analogues for other minorities and for whites as well.

The celebrity may also signify a shift from a production-oriented society to

36. For these points and for a valuable general discussion of prestige, see C. Wright Mills, *The Power Elite* (New York: Oxford University Press, 1956), chap. 4; also in paperback.

one in which consumption must be stimulated and managed. Celebrities are often connoisseurs of consumption, and are used extensively in advertising to encourage and guide others in their consumption. In so doing, celebrities lend their prestige to the world of business and help to develop and legitimate the ethic of consumption. And one must not forget that the various spheres of entertainment in which celebrities perform are big businesses in their own right.[37] Celebrities also involve themselves in politics and in the sphere of voluntary action. They support various political parties, run for office, and are occasionally elected.[38] And celebrities lend the magic of their names and presences to many forms of moral uplift (boys' clubs, neighborhood programs, ghetto youth activities).[39] And, finally, the celebrity signifies the professionalization and commercialization of sports and entertainment, processes related to basic developments in other areas of modern society. Indeed, the realms of sports and entertainment may reveal more clearly than other areas the emergence of a spectator society, a basic cleavage between elite and mass, and the failure of the early liberal ideal of the versatile individual in a participatory society.

The relationship between public and celebrity is a national phenomenon, a true nationwide prestige currency. But, as C. Wright Mills reminds us, prestige relationships based on worship, admiration, and envy of celebrities are difficult to institutionalize, and thus provide no easy way for the economic, political, and "social" elites to legitimate themselves. The celebrity's fame is too personal and ephemeral to serve as a basis for the long-range legitimation of positions acquired by other means. For that reason, says Mills, the cult of the celebrity is primarily a distraction and only an indirect way of enhancing and sanctioning high class and high political power.

Class, personality, and world view

Sociologically speaking, personality is coextensive with culture and society, and is thus discussed indirectly on every page of this text. For example, we have referred to personality, either implicitly or explicitly, in discussing the relation between class and sexual behavior, marriage, birthrates, socialization

37. The shift from the "Ideals of Production" to the "Idols of Consumption" is the main theme of Leo Lowenthal's "Biographies in Popular Magazines," *Radio Research: 1942–1943*, ed. Paul Lazarsfeld and Frank Stanton (N.Y.: Duell, Sloan, and Pearce, 1944), reprinted in Leo Lowenthal, *Literature, Popular Culture and Society* (Englewood Cliffs, N.J.: Prentice-Hall, 1961), chap. 4. Lowenthal also stresses the roles of ascription, easy identification with leaders, lucky breaks, and distraction from social problems in recounting how popular magazines shifted during the 1920s from biographies of important political, economic, and professional achievers to biographies of achievers in entertainment.

38. Elected officials sometimes find it politically advantageous to associate with entertainment celebrities and often strive to gain celebrity status by means of mass media exposure.

39. Occasional celebrities condemn rather than help legitimize the society in which they succeeded; examples are Paul Robeson, Muhammed Ali (Cassius Clay), and Jane Fonda. And, of course, celebrities are not of one mind in the choice of political parties.

practices, linguistic differences, self-directed versus conformist personalities, the deferred gratification pattern, education, racial and religious-ethnic attitudes, occupational prestige, class self-identification, celebrities, and hero worship. Our present purpose is to inquire into how class structure affects the basic disposition (world view, perception, ideology, values, beliefs, sense of power, sense of responsibility, and the like) of the American people. Personality is a vast subject, of course, which pursued fully would encompass the disciplines of psychology and psychiatry and the full range of social and humanistic sciences. It raises questions about alleged racial and sexual determinants of character, identity problems, the relative power of the mass media and other socializing agencies, and similar issues. Though relevant to those issues, our analysis does not focus on them directly. In addition, we will say little about what Americans share by way of basic personality and will limit the present discussion still further by ignoring political attitudes until later.[40] Accordingly, our focus will be on class differences in self-perception and world view, and on class differences in consciousness of class.

From Crèvecoeur and Tocqueville to the present, both foreign and native observers have stressed the distinctiveness of the American character, usually by pursuing broad ahistorical contrasts between the United States and other countries. There is, of course, nothing wrong with an abstract approach of this sort, provided it does not divert attention from differences *within* the American population. Otherwise this approach parallels the interpretation of American behavior in terms of absolute figures, national averages, or per capita data (in such areas as income, life expectancy, birthrates, and crime) and the concomitant neglect of data pointing to class variations. Of course, there are many stereotypes of regional peculiarities in personality: the dour, shrewd Yankee; the slow-moving, gracious Southerner; the open, friendly, backslapping Westerner; and so on. There are also rural-urban stereotypes, such as the country hick and the city slicker. And, of course, there are ethnic and racial personality stereotypes like the clannish Jew, the hard-drinking Irishman, and the shiftless Negro. The validity of such stereotypes is obviously minimal, though they undoubtedly provide clues to prestige stratification.

The most influential and best-known analysis of class and personality is in the work of Karl Marx. Marx had a profound influence on social science by treating not only conventional behavior but also thoughts and emotions (personality) as reflections of class position. Marx, as we have said, held that the key to the nature of classes is the modal technology of the period, and that ownership and nonownership of the means of production is the basic factor in the composition of social classes. However, classes can also be identified by their thoughts and values, according to Marx. Each class, he argued, has a distinctive subjective existence that emanates from its relation to the means of production. Marx's sociology of knowledge — the relation between social experience on the one hand, and values and ideas, subjective existence, and

40. In Chapter 12.

personality on the other — was capped by his concept of ideology. According to Marx, when a class is riding the crest of a new mode of technology, its thoughts and values are rational, valid, and progressive. In time, however, technological change renders these ideas and values obsolete, thereby turning them into ideology, or the symbolic defense of an outmoded social system.

While enormously influential, Marx's ideas about the relation between class and personality are not easy to verify empirically. For one thing, the means of production are now enormously complex, and their ownership is somewhat diffused and enormously varied in nature. For another, the relation between class and property ownership is not at all clear. It is especially difficult to establish a relation between the ownership of productive property and our occupational system. (The distinction between owners and workers is too gross a concept for today's world.) Marx's singleminded focus on the labor market and relative neglect of credit and commodity markets also create analytic distortion.[41] Despite all these difficulties, however, the fundamental thrust of Marx's thought was sound: classes emerge from economic institutions and can be identified by their distinctive world views.

A recent cross-national study by Melvin L. Kohn [42] reveals a profound cleavage in the basic perception of self and reality between higher and lower classes, as distinguished by occupation. Analyzing data from Turin, Italy; Washington, D.C.; and a national sample of the United States representing all men in civilian occupations, Kohn concludes that the intrinsic nature of work is the most important determinant of a worker's values. A self-directed personality and the feeling that one lives in a "benign" society are associated with jobs that are not closely supervised; entail complex work involving data or people, rather than things; and are intricately organized. Workers whose jobs are closely supervised, simply organized, and involve things are likely to be conformists and to feel that they live in an "indifferent or threatening" society.

The variable of occupational self-direction was found to be more important in determining world view than family structure, race, religion, national background, income, or subjective class identification. Other variables of occupation, such as bureaucratic or entrepreneurial settings; governmental, profit-making, or nonprofit employers; degree of time pressure; job satisfaction; ownership of the means of production; and job rights and protections (union contracts, seniority, grievance procedures, tenure, civil service, and such) were also less consequential. The self-directed personality, says Kohn — though related to education, which is itself closely related to occupation — is basically a function of occupational self-direction:

> The conformity of people at lower class levels is in large measure a carry-over from the limitations of their occupational experiences. Men of higher

41. For a fuller development of these distinctions, see "America's Unique Class Politics" in Chapter 11.
42. Melvin L. Kohn, *Class and Conformity: A Study in Values* (Homewood, Ill.: Dorsey Press, 1969), p. 190.

class position, who have the opportunity to be self-directed in their work, want to be self-directed off the job too, and come to think self-direction possible. Men of lower class position, who do not have the opportunity for self-direction in work, come to regard it as a matter of necessity to conform to authority, both on and off the job. The job does mold the man — it can either enlarge his horizons or narrow them. The conformity of the lower social classes is only partly a result of their lack of education; it results also from the restrictive conditions of their jobs.[43]

Kohn's study suggests more than the power of occupation over "personality": his argument also supports the belief that occupation is central to class:

Social class is consistently related to fathers' values for children: The higher their class position, the more highly they value self-direction and the less highly they value conformity to externally imposed standards. This is true regardless of the age and sex of the children — even though age and sex are related to fathers' values. Moreover, the relationship is much the same in all segments of the society — regardless of race, religion, national background, region of the country, and the size of community; in families large and small; for oldest children and for children of every other birthrank. In short, despite the heterogeneity of American society, the relationship of social class to fathers' values is remarkably pervasive and consistent.

The implications are impressive. In this exceptionally diverse society — deeply marked by racial and religious division, highly varied in economy, geography, and even degree of urbanization — social class stands out as more important for men's values than does any other line of social demarcation, unaffected by all the rest of them, and apparently more important than all of them together.[44]

In his empirical study comparing skilled blue-collar workers, lower-level white-collar workers, and managers in Providence, Rhode Island, Mackenzie also found emphasis on conformity in the socialization practices of skilled workers in contrast to the stress on independence among managers.[45]

There is evidence from other sources that class tends to override other allegiances. For example, it is known that Protestants, Roman Catholics, and Jews, as well as whites and nonwhites, who are members of the same class, share similar values and beliefs and develop similar personalities. Indeed,

43. *Ibid.*, p. 190. Used by permission.
44. *Ibid.*, pp. 71f. Used by permission. Inkeles' classic study of the relation between class and world view should also be cited. Using a wide variety of cross-national data, Inkeles showed that classes (occupation, income, education, prestige) tend to develop standard responses to a wide range of questions independently of the nature or strength of the traditional culture. Alex Inkeles, "Industrial Man: The Relation of Status to Experience, Perception and Value," *American Journal of Sociology,* 66, no. 1 (July 1960): 1–31; also available as Bobbs-Merrill reprint no. 131.
45. Gavin Mackenzie, *The Aristocracy of Labor: The Position of Skilled Craftsmen in the American Class Structure* (London and New York: Cambridge University Press, 1973), pp. 51–57. Mackenzie's study, which also focuses on occupation as the crucial source of class behavior, is one of the few empirical studies in the United States devoted to exploring the contention that class boundaries are disappearing. We will refer to it again.

the cultural assimilation of immigrants and acculturation across religious-ethnic-racial lines by class is fairly complete.[46]

Another national survey has given us a more detailed picture of the distribution of values in the American population. In 1968 the National Opinion Research Center administered the Value Survey to a national sample of Americans over twenty-one. Developed by Milton Rokeach, the Value Survey consists of two lists of eighteen terminal and instrumental values, arranged alphabetically. Respondents were asked to rank each list "in order of importance to YOU, as guiding principles in YOUR life." One of the clear findings of the 1968 survey was that values vary considerably by class (income, education), especially between the bottom and top levels.[47]

It should be remembered that different classes have different educational, occupational, and success aspirations. And these differences must be interpreted in both absolute and relative terms; that is, while the lower classes have lower aspirations *vis-à-vis* the top than the upper classes, aspirations to rise above one's class of origin are largely uniform in all classes.[48]

Class and class consciousness

Americans are not very conscious of class and do not consciously frame their lives in class terms. Invariably, they interpret differential striving and differential success in individual terms (as functional competition between individuals of different innate ability). Americans are, of course, aware of the existence of inequality, even radical inequality, but do not characteristically think of it in class terms — that is, they do not explain inequality in terms of economic and social variables. Class consciousness, in other words, is awareness that one's social level derives from an economic and social environment one shares with those in similar circumstances and has little to do with natural forces, human or otherwise. In other words, class consciousness is awareness that basic forms of inequality are historical in nature — that is, changeable, with those at the top of society usually interested in preventing change and those at the bottom (who are class-conscious) wanting a restructuring of economic and social power.

Americans are aware, of course, that some people are rich and others are not rich, some are advantaged and others disadvantaged, some have easy jobs while others have difficult jobs, and that some individuals inherit considerable sums of money while others inherit little or nothing. By and large, though, Americans believe that people's positions are the result of work, brains, drive,

46. The evidence for this assertion is presented by Milton M. Gordon, *Assimilation in American Life: The Role of Race, Religion, and National Origins* (New York: Oxford University Press, 1964), chap. 7; available in paperback. For a fuller discussion of cultural and social assimilation in relation to social stratification, see Chapter 10 in this text.

47. Milton Rokeach, *The Nature of Human Values* (New York: Free Press, 1973), pp. 59–66.

48. For a fuller discussion of absolute and relative aspirations and differences in educational aspirations, see the relevant sections in Chapters 3 and 6.

or even luck or connections; only rarely do they see the distribution of benefits as the reflection of a class system. What consciousness of class does exist is found mostly among the upper classes. Probably the closest approximation of class thinking among Americans is the view that the lower classes face barriers to achievement because of inadequate opportunity.

Americans are also conscious of inequities in their society, but regard them as correctable defects of a fundamentally sound society — sound because it works the way people say it works and because it is flexible and reformable. Invariably, reform is directed at making functional competition between individuals more equal. Despite persistent criticism and occasional denunciations of middle class society, very few have questioned the ability of middle class society to reform itself and become what it is supposed to be: a system based on equality of opportunity leading to "nonegalitarian classlessness."

The theoretical relevance of all this is that a society deeply stratified by economic ascription and economic forces does not have to exhibit class consciousness. Historically, Americans have displayed some "class consciousness," though on the whole protest and reform movements have been issue-oriented rather than class-oriented. However, there are many suppositions about class consciousness, but few studies. The widely accepted notion that the lower-middle class is conscious of its differences with the working class and thus prone to "status panic" has been questioned.[49] Class consciousness and militance have been related to economic insecurity,[50] and, in general, occupations characterized by extreme instability of income or employment (miners, lumbermen, fishermen, stevedores, one-crop farmers) tend to be leftist politically. On the whole, however, advanced industrial societies mute class consciousness, though they still generate forms of insecurity and uprootedness that make those affected conscious of class.[51] Actually, those strongest in class consciousness are the upper classes. Speaking generally, the main reasons for the unusual lack of class consciousness in the United States are:

1. economic expansion, specialization, and mobility, and the corresponding diversification of job experience and economic interests within class contexts

2. diversity within occupational and class levels because of ethnicity, religion, sex, age, and race

3. the pronounced tendency in American culture to formulate goals and to explain success and failure in individualistic (biopsychological) terms.[52]

49. Richard F. Hamilton, "The Marginal Middle Class: A Reconsideration," *American Sociological Review* 31 (April 1966): 192–199.

50. John C. Leggett, "Economic Insecurity and Working-Class Consciousness," *American Sociological Review* 29 (April 1964): 226–234.

51. John C. Leggett, "Uprootedness and Working-Class Consciousness," *American Journal of Sociology* 68 (May 1963): 682–692. Leggett's various explorations in the field of blue-collar consciousness are summarized in his *Class, Race, and Labor: Working-Class Consciousness in Detroit* (New York: Oxford University Press, 1968).

52. For a full discussion of the class, prestige, and power variables that account for the relative lack of class consciousness in the United States, see Chapter 15. For a discussion of the lack of class consciousness that argues against the relevance

Commentators have long referred to distinctive forms of consciousness (personality and life style) among classes, the working and lower classes allegedly having outlooks and ways of life peculiar to themselves and distinctly different from those of the upper classes.[53] Analyzing the mentality of a social class is, however, exceedingly difficult, given the absence of consensus on many fundamental questions. And such analysis can also be contaminated by bias, especially if a middle class analyst looks at the working class or the poor in terms of his or her own values.[54] The absence of consensus on fundamental questions in the United States and other countries has important implications for stratification analysis, and we will return to this subject later.[55]

Class and subjectivity: a summary

In this chapter, we have examined the relation between class and one aspect of prestige, people's attitudes about themselves and each other. The inner world of human beings is not always easy to characterize or interpret. It seems clear, however, that class position is the controlling variable in explaining how people think about themselves and the world they live in. Two extremely important subjective phenomena, occupational prestige and basic personality (self-direction versus conformism), are directly related to class. We found, however, that class self-identification and class consciousness are not sharply delineated or directly related to class. Nevertheless, it is justifiable to explain our findings in class terms: the class dimension and related areas are so complex and inconsistent as to have diffused and blurred subjective awareness of class.

In their attitudes toward our representative minority groups, majority Americans have become more tolerant. But majority Americans are also saddling minorities with the burden of moral equality, the liberal belief that human beings — high or low, rich or poor, strong or weak — are responsible for their own success or failure.

of class analysis in the name of what is in effect evolutionary liberalism, see Harold L. Wilensky, "Class, Class Consciousness, and American Workers" in *Labor in Changing America,* ed. William Haber (New York: Basic Books, 1966), chap. 2.

53. Richard Hoggart, *The Uses of Literacy* (New York: Oxford University Press, 1957); Donald Clark Hodges, "Cynicism in the Labor Movement," *American Journal of Economics and Sociology* (January 1962).

54. For a warning against such biases, see S. M. Miller and Frank Reissman, "The Working-Class Subculture: A New View," *Social Problems* 9 (Summer 1961): 86–97; reprinted in Arthur B. Shostak and William Gomberg, eds., *Blue-Collar World: Studies of the American Worker* (Englewood Cliffs, N.J., 1964), pp. 24–36. For Miller and Reissman's attempt to define the poor more adequately, see their *Social Class and Social Policy* (New York: Basic Books, 1968), Part 2.

55. In "Political Attitudes" in Chapter 12.

9

Class and style of life: the consumption of culture

THE CONSUMPTION OF culture plays an important role in stratifying populations. Economic classes invariably spend their money differently, which tends to result in varying types and levels of prestige. In this chapter, therefore, we are interested in understanding another of the ways in which "economic income" is turned into "psychic income." While we will distinguish between material and symbolic culture in the following section, this distinction is adopted for expository purposes only. All human activities, including consumption, are infused with symbols or meanings of the most varied sort. The purchase of clothing or a dwelling is no mere material or objective act; it has important symbolic-value overtones — overtones relevant in the present context to prestige stratification.

Technically, *culture* is a synonym for all the varied values characteristic of a particular society (tools, food, ideas, emotions, desired forms of interaction, and so on). As such, it tends to infuse — indeed, to constitute — human behavior. This study as a whole focuses on how the American class system distributes culture; or, more precisely, on how various cultural forces combine with other cultural forces to produce a system of stratification. In pursuing this objective, we have already analyzed the distribution of such cultural phenomena as income, wealth, mental and physical health, life expectancy, family stability, and formal education. And in Chapters 7–10 on prestige stratification, we are analyzing and accounting for the distribution of psychic satisfaction and development. In this chapter, our primary focus will be on the prestige implications of "material" consumption as such.[1]

Analysis of the noneconomic or honorific aspects of economic behavior was pioneered by Thorstein Veblen (1857–1929),[2] whose penetrating insights into the ways in which honor is acquired through material accumulation and consumption are the source of much of our present-day understanding of prestige behavior (though, as we will see, his ideas have to be updated somewhat). It was Veblen who focused attention on the fact that men and women above the level of subsistence engage in what he called *pecuniary emulation*. In the past, according to Veblen, men and women created invidious distinctions by accumulating more property than they could use, because to do so gave them prestige and thus made them morally worthier than their neighbors. Modern society makes pecuniary emulation difficult, however: property must be conspicuous if it is to enhance prestige, and much of modern property is inconspicuous because of residential segregation, or because it takes the form of factories, office buildings, and the like, or has no tangible form other than pieces of paper.

Veblen also pointed to conspicuous leisure — careful avoidance of work and cultivation of noneconomic activities and skills — as a way in which high economic position is advertised. Acquiring prestige in this way is difficult in industrial society because of its high valuation of work and utilitarian activity. A final means Veblen identified of translating economic or class position into prestige is conspicuous consumption. It is this phenomenon that has particular relevance to prestige stratification in industrial society, especially if one defines it in combination with pecuniary emulation and conspicuous leisure as the display of all manner of economic assets on a scale and with a flair that has known prestige meaning.

Honorific possessions, consumption, and activities

The concept of conspicuous consumption is probably best introduced by noting Veblen's synonym for it, conspicuous waste. Perhaps the most dramatic example of this form of prestige is provided by Ruth Benedict's portrayal of the value system of the Kwakiutl Indians.[3] Native to the northwest coast of North America, the Kwakiutl enjoyed an economy of abundance (at least relative to other folk societies). The sea provided ample food for slight labor, which allowed for their absorption in self-glorification at the expense of rivals. The specific form their ego rivalry took was the potlatch, a social convention based

1. "Symbolic" consumption — or the intake of intellectual, literary, and artistic symbols and values through books, mass media, and education — is not easy to distinguish from "material consumption." Symbolic consumption is discussed separately later in this chapter.

2. Much of the following is indebted to Veblen's classic, *The Theory of the Leisure Class* (New York: New American Library, 1953; originally published in 1899).

3. *Patterns of Culture* (Boston: Houghton Mifflin, 1959; originally published in 1934), chap. 6.

on the distribution and/or destruction of property. Noneconomic, nonmaterial property such as names, titles, myths, songs, privileges, and pieces of copper were combined with other forms of property such as fish oil, blankets, and canoes to serve as the means of personal rivalry. The object of the potlatch was to enhance personal prestige by shaming a rival, either by giving him property he could not return with the required heavy interest or by destroying one's property in amounts he could not match.

Veblen tended to designate much invidious economic behavior as conspicuous waste. He employed the term *waste* neutrally to signify economic behavior with no immediate or obvious economic utility. Broadly speaking, conspicuous waste has a wide variety of motives and takes many different forms. Something is done or used because it is expensive either of material or of time; because it is aesthetically novel, moral, or true; or because it combines certain of these features. The individual engaged in conspicuous waste can be either aware or unaware of what he or she is doing. Quite often, the compulsions of class position make conspicuous consumption (waste) a necessary aspect of one's standard of living, or thought of differently, part of the minimum level of decency in dress, housing, equipment, and services required to maintain class standing.

Veblen provided an enormous catalogue of prestige pursuits whose consequences, intended or not, were to create invidious distinctions between economic classes: acquired wealth; inherited wealth; abstention from productive labor (by a man, by his wife, and sometimes by both, often accompanied by the employment of slaves, servants, or mechanical devices); the cultivation of nonutilitarian pursuits and skills such as (in Veblen's words) quasi-scholarly, quasi-artistic accomplishments like languages, correct spelling and syntax, domestic music; the latest proprieties of dress, furniture, and equipage; games, sports, and fancy-bred animals; and manners and breeding, polite usage, decorum, and formal and ceremonial observances in general.[4]

Nonutilitarian behavior in industrial society

While Veblen's work contains many insights into the manifest and latent functions of consumption, his analysis is not a complete guide to present-day consumption. Veblen was primarily concerned with identifying vestiges of feudal and barbarian prestige in an emerging industrial civilization. To analyze the prestige patterns developed by a maturing industrial class system, therefore, requires an updating and refocusing of Veblen's ideas. His insights into preindustrial forms of prestige (property accumulation, leisure as avoidance of work, waste, canons of taste that emphasize expense over utility, and the cultivation of a wide assortment of nonutilitarian values and skills) are still pertinent, since consumption is still linked strongly to class, but must be supplemented.

Probably the most important single fact about the American system of

4. Veblen, *The Theory of the Leisure Class*, p. 47.

stratification is that the upper classes are gainfully employed. This appears to be true even of the very rich, though there are no exact studies of how members of this class are employed by sex and age. Members of the upper class of industrial society are undoubtedly different from other classes in their ability to choose not to work and to choose their work from a wide variety of options (though in this respect they are probably similar to the upper-middle class). Nevertheless, the upper class of industrial society appears to be neither a leisure nor a *rentier* class, and it certainly does not specialize in religious, governmental, and military occupations. All available indications are that the upper class is actively engaged in a wide variety of (economic) occupations, chief among which, undoubtedly, is the management and supervision of property interests. The significance of all this is that it is work, not property, that legitimates consumption in industrial society, a phenomenon that makes it difficult to uphold cultivated idleness as a prime social value.[5] In the United States, free time is the mark of the half-citizen: the young, the old, the retired, women, the infirm and disabled, and the unemployed. One enjoys leisure in a positively valued sense only after one's work is done: after five o'clock, after fifty weeks, or after age sixty-five. Given the heavy emphasis on work and on such related values as thrift, economic growth, and technical efficiency, it is also difficult both to uphold waste as a positive value and to place supreme or even high value on nonutilitarian activities such as art, music, classical learning, religion, and exotic hobbies. Activities of this sort exist and even flourish, but by and large run counter to the main thrust of American culture.[6]

The United States never developed deep ascriptive limitations on consumption. The black American, of course, was forced to consume in segregated stores and to use segregated facilities, a tradition that represents the most serious contradiction of pure class consumption in American history. And women have been segregated with regard to certain forms of consumption; examples are the need to have an escort in order to use certain facilities, and moral strictures against smoking and drinking. By and large, however, such ascriptive forces have been overcome by the power of class. The central point about consumption in the United States is that it is legitimate for all to be interested — indeed, very interested — in material consumption. One of the major changes in twentieth-century life is the growing respectability of consumption and the apparent decline of Protestant-bourgeois asceticism. The major reason for this development, of course, is the emergence of a mass-production economy and the consequent economic need to make consumption a major public virtue. In the process, consumption has become a semiofficial

5. Though the rich undoubtedly enjoy their property and its income as much as they do their income from work, it cannot be said that the ownership of property as such has ever established itself in the normative culture of America in the same way that work has.
6. Nonetheless, prestige skills and values in these areas are acquired only after considerable nonutilitarian effort, and Veblen's central concept of waste behavior is still relevant in this respect.

way of establishing prestige and, from a broader standpoint, of establishing and maintaining class position.

The ways in which consumption is promoted are also of considerable importance. Our mass media, for example, do much to support and inculcate consumption values, in terms of both program content and advertising. The mass media cater both to class and prestige mobility aspirations and undoubtedly contribute heavily to creating them in the first place.[7] Even in treating public and personal problems, the mass media invariably rely on the basic values and norms of class society for their framework and solutions. Perhaps the most important factor in analyzing the role of the mass media in consumption and the evaluative realm in general is the fact that they are big businesses in their own right, embedded at the apex of the class hierarchy.

Consumption prestige is also promoted by the power dimension. Tax laws favoring the upper classes permit a wide range of luxury consumption. By declaring holidays, the power dimension specifies the values to be celebrated and preserved; and the legal fiction that the birthdays of some of our national heroes take place on Mondays is partly due to the fact that three-day weekends are good for tourist and recreational businesses and thus of more prestige value to those with the money to travel on such mini-vacations.[8] The state also regulates the work week and vacations; subsidizes postal rates for magazines, newspapers, and books, publications which help to promote many other prestige activities; and grants tax deductions for expense accounts (more stringent in recent years but still a large source of differential prestige through club membership, dining, entertainment, and travel).

The federal government has also begun to subsidize the arts, humanities, and public television, following the lead of municipal and state governments. (There is no better example of the blurred distinction between the private and public realms than the disclosure in 1971 that the chief officer of the public television network received $65,000 in salary and its star reporter $85,000.) The power dimension also supports professional sports in a number of ways: by not holding them strictly accountable to the Constitution and antitrust laws; by granting money to build sports facilities or by backing their bond issues with public credit; and by building the highways that make it possible

7. The phenomenal success of *Playboy* magazine, for example, can no doubt be explained in part by the fact that it provides a guide to upper-middle class consumption patterns for upwardly mobile males. In keeping with this orientation are its articles for college-educated readers and nonsensual packaged treatment of sex.

8. Travel, both in general and in terms of specific categories (visits to friends and relations, business trips and conventions, outdoor recreation, sightseeing and entertainment, weekend travel, and vacation travel) is distinctly class-related. (The relation between class and visits to friends and relatives is not pronounced.) For the way in which higher income, occupation, and education are related to more travel, see U. S. Bureau of the Census, Census of Transportation, 1972, *National Travel Survey: Travel During 1972*, TC72-N3 (Washington, D.C.: U. S. Government Printing Office, 1973), Figures 4 and 5, Tables 7–12.

to locate such facilities in the suburbs (thus marking them accessible to some income groups and not to others). The government also subsidizes differential recreation through its system of national parks, which are used mostly by the middle and upper classes, and it has even paid for public works which have resulted in lakes and recreation areas becoming the preserves of private residential communities.

The blurring of the private (prestige) and public (power) spheres of behavior has occurred on another front as well. Public regulation of the airways lends an aura of legitimacy to private enterprises in radio and television, though the public's control over program content and advertising is minimal. Public regulations on land use, building materials, house and plot size, and the like (zoning) are often tantamount to class and racial segregation; and, of course, public highways make it possible for certain income and racial groups to enjoy the prestige of nonurban living.

In studying the oftentimes bewildering array of consumption behaviors and analyzing the relation of prestige consumption to class, there is a general pattern that helps to structure understanding: some consumption behaviors are based on differences while others, especially in industrial society, result in broad and significant similarities.

Differential consumption: industrial potlatching

Despite the existence of a great many ideas about the relation between class and consumption, little research has been undertaken in this area. To organize what is known about the distribution of consumption prestige, we will examine in turn five areas of consumption: residence, dress, commodities, the consumption of time and "symbolic" culture, and the donation of money and time.[9]

Residence

The importance of residence for identifying and certifying class position needs little emphasis. The significance of residence is apparent in the vividness of such stratification-related images as "the wrong side of the tracks," the Gold Coast, a slum, Nob Hill, the East Side, and so on. Type of house and dwelling area are so important to class position that one school of stratification analysis has used both to construct an index of class position.[10] Prestige stems from one's residence in a number of ways: for example, from its size, architectural style, location, size of plot, and exterior decoration and maintenance. Ob-

9. Even death does not end the search for prestige. One need only think of the tombs of the Pharoahs, the state funerals of the mighty, segregated cemeteries, and the class-oriented appeals of undertakers and cemeteries to appreciate the varied ways in which the lower classes are denied even the democracy of death. For a marvelously insightful analysis and critique of funeral practices in America and the economic groups behind them, see Jessica Mitford, *The American Way of Death* (New York: Simon and Schuster, 1963), also a Fawcett paperback.

10. See W. Lloyd Warner *et al., Social Class in America* (New York: Harper and Row, 1960, available in paperback. first published in 1949), pp. 39–42.

viously, one's residence, especially a single-family house, is an important way to display income and/or wealth. But it is also a way to advertise lineage and good taste. Thus, the Early American style in the northeast suggests continuity of descent as well as good taste; its counterparts are Greek Revival in the south; Spanish in the southwest and California; and Victorian in the midwest. Actually, a house affords many ways of displaying values (furnishings,[11] a separate dining room, a private bedroom for each child, a music room). Geographical location (high ground, distance from commerce and industry), size of plot, and landscaping are all important to the prestige (as well as economic) value of a house. In other words, one's address is often a quick and easy way to know who one is.

The pronounced residential segregation by class found and emphasized by small-town studies is matched by a similar pattern of segregation in large cities.[12] A considerable amount of material on residential segregation in urban areas is available in various general works.[13] An important aspect of residential segregation has been the process of suburbanization, which has given rise to the thesis of the *embourgeoisement* of the working class. Here as elsewhere, there is little evidence of the growth of a middle class mass.[14]

A rise in class position usually calls for a change of residence. In fact, it is one of the functions of differential consumption in general to help to establish

11. Furnishings were considered so important to class standing by one sociologist that he developed what came to be known as the Chapin Scale, which grades living-room furnishings to determine the class to which a family belongs; F. Stuart Chapin, *Contemporary American Institutions: A Sociological Analysis* (New York: Harper and Brothers, 1935), chap. 19. Needless to say, this index has its limitations. Edward O. Laumann and James S. House, "Living Room Styles and Social Attributes: The Patterning of Material Artifacts in a Modern Urban Community" in *The Logic of Social Hierarchies,* ed. Edward O. Laumann, Paul M. Siegel, and Robert W. Hodge, (Chicago: Markham, 1970) explore the living room as a way of predicting social attributes, attitudes, and behavior, especially among old and new upper-income families.

12. See Otis Dudley Duncan and Beverly Duncan, "Residential Distribution and Occupational Stratification," *American Journal of Sociology* 40, no. 5 (March 1955): 493–503, for Chicago, and Eugene S. Uyeki, "Residential Distribution and Stratification, 1950–1960," *American Journal of Sociology* 69, no. 5 (March 1964): 491–498, for Cleveland. For a comprehensive initial step toward analyzing national data and historical patterns of residential segregation by class and race, see Leo F. Schnore, *Class and Race in Cities and Suburbs* (Chicago: Markham, 1972).

13. For valuable material on residential segregation in the metropolis, see E. Digby Baltzell, *Philadelphia Gentlemen: The Making of a National Upper Class* (New York: Free Press, 1958), chap. 9, reissued as *An American Business Aristocracy* (New York: Collier Books, 1962); Sidney Goldstein and Kurt B. Mayer, *The People of Rhode Island, 1960* (Providence, R.I.: Planning Division, Rhode Island Development Council, 1963), which provides an Index of Social Rank (occupation, income, and education) for Rhode Island and Providence derived from census tracts; Richard P. Coleman and Bernice L. Neugarten, *Social Status in the City* (San Francisco: Jossey-Bass, 1971), pp. 30–38, a brief analysis of residential segregation in Kansas City; and Richard F. Hamilton, *Class and Politics in the United States* (New York: John Wiley and Sons, 1972), pp. 159–187, an analysis of residential segregation and its associated characteristics in Milwaukee.

14. For a pioneering study, see Bennett M. Berger, *Working-Class Suburbs; a Study of Auto Workers in Suburbia* (Berkeley: University of California Press, 1960).

people who have moved up (or down) in the class hierarchy. Residence is also an index of low prestige (and power) and low class position. Many black Americans, for example, are badly housed because they are poor, subject to racist evaluations, and unable to protect themselves politically. Of all the minority groups in American history, only black Americans have been unable to overcome residential segregation and diversify themselves by place of residence.[15] Even when black Americans rise in class, they have great difficulty acquiring the type of residence their new economic position calls for. Using census data on city blocks to construct an Index of Residential Segregation for 207 cities across the United States, the Taeubers concluded:

> In the urban United States, there is a very high degree of segregation of the residences of whites and Negroes. This is true for cities in all regions of the country and for all types of cities — large and small, industrial and commercial, metropolitan and suburban. It is true whether there are hundreds of thousands of Negro residents, or only a few thousand. Residential segregation prevails regardless of the relative economic status of the white and Negro residents. It occurs regardless of the character of local laws and policies and regardless of the extent of other forms of segregation or discrimination.[16]

Residential segregation by race does not come about by accident, due to the play of impersonal market forces, or as a result of widely held attitudes. The people and organizations that create and perpetuate residential racial segregation are identifiable: real estate brokers, real estate firms, real estate boards, banking and other lending agencies, and local residential communities themselves, including property and tenant organizations and local governments. Helper has articulated the ideology of racial segregation held by real estate people (in Chicago): "white people do not want Negroes as neighbors, property values decline when Negroes enter an area, racial residential integration is not likely for a long time to come if at all, there are harmful consequences for the people of a white community when Negroes enter, and it is morally wrong or violates some principle or value of the real estate business or of the country to sell or rent to Negroes in a white area."[17]

The argument that blacks depress property vaules when they move into a neighborhood is perhaps the most widely advanced reason for excluding them. In his study of San Francisco, Oakland, and Philadelphia, and his review of research on Chicago, Kansas City, Detroit, and Portland, Oregon, Luigi Laurenti concludes that this is not only not so, but that the evidence (collected

15. Karl E. Taeuber and Alma F. Taeuber, "The Negro as an Immigrant Group: Recent Trends in Racial Segregation in Chicago," *American Journal of Sociology* 69, no. 4 (January 1964): 374–382.

16. Karl E. Taeuber and Alma F. Taeuber, *Negroes in Cities: Residential Segregation and Neighborhood Change* (Chicago: Aldine, 1965), pp. 35f. For an excellent collection of articles on various aspects of racial and class segregation in housing, see Amos H. Hawley and Vincent P. Rock, eds., *Segregation in Residential Areas: Papers on Racial and Socioeconomic Factors in Choice of Housing* (Washington, D.C.: National Academy of Sciences, 1973).

17. Rose Helper, *Racial Policies and Practices of Real Estate Brokers* (Minneapolis: University of Minnesota Press, 1969), p. 144.

during periods of generally rising property values) shows a tendency for property values to rise in neighborhoods experiencing "racial" change.[18]

Residential segregation does not affect black Americans alone. Many other minorities are segregated residentially (though none with such thoroughness and seeming permanence). American Indians on reservations and in urban enclaves; Chinese Americans restricted to Chinatowns and widely excluded from suburban housing developments; white ethnic groups; and Mexican Americans in *barrios* and in rural isolation[19] have all been hemmed in by geographical boundaries.[20] And, of course, geographical boundaries mean social boundaries. The effects of residential segregation, in addition to the loss of comfort and convenience, are to deny some members of minority groups the prestige their class position calls for and to make it difficult for the rest to change their class position (for example, by restricting educational and employment opportunities).

Though we have emphasized the roles of private forces in producing residential segregation, the power of the state is used to the same effect. Though discrimination in most housing sales and rentals is now illegal, an extremely important form of legal protection for property is the widespread use of zoning, a device that serves to segregate minority groups and the poor in general and to make housing scarce for both groups and for others further up the social ladder. In addition, government credit, mortgage, tax, transportation, and general housing policies all work to perpetuate the class-prestige hierarchy of housing (also see the section on housing in Chapter 13).[21]

To move from the palatial residences of the rich to the comfortable homes and apartments of the upper-middle class to the modest homes of the lower-middle and working classes and on to the squalid dwellings of the lower class is to take a quick trip through the American class system. Residence does not signify social class in a mechanical fashion, of course. There is evidence

18. Luigi Laurenti, *Property Values and Race: Studies in Seven Cities* (Berkeley and Los Angeles: University of California Press, 1960).

19. For an analysis of the high residential segregation of Mexican Americans (and blacks) in thirty-five southwestern cities, see Leo Grebler, Joan W. Moore, Ralph C. Guzman *et al., The Mexican-American People: The Nation's Second Largest Minority* (New York: Free Press, 1970), chap. 12.

20. Ironically, the federal government's flagrantly unconstitutional confinement of Japanese Americans in concentration camps during World War Two had the effect of reducing their residential concentration. Upon their release, Japanese Americans had to find new places to live and work, and it can even be said that their consequent exposure to wider challenges and opportunities contributed to their social mobility.

21. The pattern of residential segregation by class has far-reaching political implications, which we will have occasion to discuss later; see "Class-Prestige and the Federal System" and "Class-Prestige and Political Representation" in Chapter 12. For an important step toward conceptualizing the metropolitan area in terms of social stratification and developing measures of governmental inequality in the municipalities that make up the metropolis, see Richard Child Hill, "Separate and Unequal: Governmental Inequality in the Metropolis," *American Political Science Review* 68 (December 1974): 1557–1568. The data, Hill concludes, strongly suggest that inequality in family income, and racial discrimination, lead to residential segregation and governmental inequality — that is, inequality of fiscal resources for producing public goods and services.

that working class people are not overly conscious of residence as a mark of class, and people are not always as mobile as they might be due to ethnic and other ties to their old neighborhoods. A further complication is the shortage of housing: many who might have moved have not done so because of the almost chronic undersupply of housing in the United States. One interesting pattern in American housing is the significant number of second homes. In 1970 there were 2,890,000 second homes,[22] and it is reasonable to assume that the number has grown steadily since then.

Dress

In addition to providing warmth and helping to promote and uphold the sense of modesty, clothing is an important advertisement of class status. The terms *white-collar* and *blue-collar,* for example, signify distinct stratification worlds. Many occupations entail special costumes, the function of which is to identify those who wield authority and to provide for the mutual recognition necessary to efficient work, communication, and exchange of services. Judges, soldiers, doctors, scientists, members of the clergy, police officers, conductors, and chorus girls, for example, all advertise their occupations by their dress and simultaneously establish prestige differentials with their clients and the public-at-large.

A discerning observer can usually identify a man's class by looking at his clothing, even when he is not wearing a conventional occupational uniform. This may be even truer of his wife, since women are strongly encouraged to advertise class status through dress. (And women are used in other ways to manifest status; in some countries, for example, the number of a man's wives is a measure of his ability to support extraneous personnel.) All in all, the norms of dress, or fashion, are widely used to identify those with good taste, money, and exemptions from labor.

Another aspect of the world of fashion should also be noted. According to Barber and Lobel, women's clothes in contemporary society manifest two contrasting principles: first, all are invited to be fashionable along lines that are decreed for all by the fashion industry; second, differences in dress are also allowed for by variations in, for example, cut, type of fabric, and tailoring. Such differences tend to be associated with class levels. These contrary emphases on difference and sameness would tend to cause strain were it not for the "trickle-down" process, whereby upper class fashions are eventually copied and made available to the classes below. The overall effect is to allow some women to stress their class position or to aspire upward, and other women to feel equal to the women in higher class positions.[23]

22. U.S. Bureau of the Census, *Statistical Abstract, 1974* (Washington, D.C.: U.S. Government Printing Office, 1974), Table 1201.

23. Bernard Barber and Lyle S. Lobel, " 'Fashion' in Women's Clothes and the American Social System," *Social Forces* 31 (December 1952): 124–131; reprinted in Reinhard Bendix and Seymour M. Lipset, eds., *Class, Status and Power: A Reader in Social Stratification,* 1st ed. (New York: Free Press, 1953), pp. 323–332.

Commodities

There are many types of goods associated with class that lend prestige to their owners. At the advent of the automobile age, only the wealthy could afford to own cars. Mass production caused car ownership to spread, but until recently the type of car one owned was still an indicator of one's class. Now that the same car is owned by members of many different income groups, mere ownership is no longer an easy guide to class. Ownership of two or more cars, however, still indicates the class to which the owner belongs (as Table 9-1 indicates), as does ownership of extremely expensive or exotic cars.

Many other types of commodities are still strongly associated with class, as Table 9-1 also indicates. Though ownership of some commodities, such as black-and-white television sets, loses its strong association with class over time, possession of most major appliances, such as color television sets and dishwashers, is still a class phenomenon.

The ways in which the various classes spend their money is of obvious interest to the student of stratification. One argument has it that blue-collar families are similar to middle-class families in the percentage of their budgets spent on various consumption categories. There is also some evidence that blue-collar families tend to buy brand-name products and overpriced items, perhaps reflecting insecurity about consumption and a desire to avoid stores where they feel uncomfortable.[24] In any case, the underclass, especially black Americans living in ghettoes, have little choice in this regard. They are forced to buy in inefficient, overpriced small retail shops; and, while some items and services are cheaper, low-income groups by and large tend to get less for their money, especially in food and housing.[25]

The consumption of time and "symbolic" culture

The expenditure of "free" time can be thought of as a form of consumption, and there are evident differences in the ways in which the various classes spend their time away from work.[26] A great many studies have shown that blue-collar

24. James M. Patterson, "Marketing and the Working Class Family," in *Blue-Collar World: Studies of the American Worker,* ed. Arthur B. Shostak and William Gomberg (Englewood Cliffs, N.J.: Prentice-Hall, 1964), pp. 76–80.

25. David Caplovitz, *The Poor Pay More: Consumer Practices of Low Income Families* (New York: Free Press, 1963); Phyllis Groom, "Prices in Poor Neighborhoods," *Monthly Labor Review* 89 (October 1966): 1085–1090.

26. For a general review of the American scene, including some historical background and a useful bibliography, see William R. Catton, Jr., "Leisure and Social Stratification," in *Issues in Social Inequality,* ed. Gerald W. Thielbar and Saul D. Feldman (Boston: Little, Brown, 1972), pp. 520–538. For an interpretive study that identifies various levels of "culture" in America and their relations to class, see Herbert J. Gans, *Popular Culture and High Culture: An Analysis and Evaluation of Taste* (New York: Basic Books, 1974); Gans' basic argument appeared earlier in essay form as "Popular Culture in America: Social Problem in a Mass Society Or Social Asset in a Pluralist Society?" in *Social Problems: A Modern Approach,* ed. Howard S. Becker (New York: John Wiley and Sons, 1966), reprinted in part as "Social Class and Popular Culture" in *The Impact of Social Class: A Book of Readings,* ed. Paul Blumberg (New York: Thomas Y. Crowell, 1972), pp. 452–467.

Table 9-1 Households Owning Cars and Appliances, 1960, 1970–71, Percent Distribution by Income Level, 1970–71

Item	Cars One or more	Cars Two or more	Television Black and white	Television Color	Washing machine	Clothes dryer	Refrigerator	Freezer	Dishwasher	Air conditioner[a]
1960, all households	75.0	16.4	86.7		74.5	17.4	86.1	NA	4.9	12.8
1970, all households	79.6	29.3	77.4	37.8	69.9	40.8	83.3		17.3	20.5[b]
Annual income[c]										
Under $3,000	42.5	4.5	77.3	13.1	50.0	11.8	75.5		3.0	4.3[b]
$3,000–$3,999	64.1	9.7	78.9	23.0	60.7	19.6	77.7		3.8	12.9[b]
$4,000–$4,999	75.7	17.9	78.1	25.2	62.8	26.1	80.0		5.6	14.7[b]
$5,000–$5,999	83.2	17.8	78.9	27.6	62.9	29.0	78.1		6.4	18.9[b]
$6,000–$7,499	88.9	25.3	76.4	38.9	70.5	37.3	83.0		10.2	21.6[b]
$7,500–$9,999	91.6	34.7	75.6	45.5	76.3	49.7	85.5		15.0	28.5[b]
$10,000–$14,999	95.9	48.4	76.9	53.3	82.9	62.9	90.0		29.3	33.7[b]
$15,000–$24,999	96.6	62.2	78.4	61.8	86.2	73.1	91.5		49.8	44.9[b]
$25,000 and over	95.3	66.6	79.2	73.4	88.1	81.8	92.0		71.0	
1971, all households	79.5[d]	30.2[d]	77.6	43.3	71.3	44.5	83.3	32.2	18.8	31.8
Annual income[c]										
Under $3,000	40.6[d]	5.3[d]	77.0	16.1	51.6	13.9	76.5	21.0	1.9	13.5
$3,000–$4,999	68.0[d]	12.6[d]	79.7	26.5	62.0	24.0	80.4	25.3	4.4	21.1
$5,000–$7,499	84.2[d]	23.2[d]	75.3	39.7	68.3	38.2	80.8	30.1	9.5	25.6
$7,500–$9,999	91.3[d]	32.2[d]	74.5	50.3	77.2	51.6	84.4	33.7	15.5	32.8
$10,000–$14,999	94.9[d]	45.6[d]	77.7	58.4	83.4	64.5	88.2	38.9	29.1	43.5
$15,000–$24,999	96.5[d]	58.4[d]	81.8	68.3	86.6	75.2	90.4	43.3	50.7	52.2
$25,000 and over	93.0[d]	66.6[d]	82.1	79.5	89.7	83.9	94.0	56.3	74.8	69.3

NA Not available. a. Includes both room and central systems. b. 1967 data. Based on January 1967 sample survey. c. Total money income (before taxes) of primary family or primary individual in 12 months immediately preceding interview. d. 1972 data. Based on July 1972 sample survey.

SOURCE: U.S. Bureau of the Census, *Statistical Abstract, 1974* (Washington, D.C.: U.S. Government Printing Office, 1974), Table 646. Based on January 1960 and July 1970 and July 1972 sample surveys, except as noted. Ownership is not a direct measure of availability; many renter households live in units where major appliances are provided by the property owner.

workers differ from middle class individuals in that they read less; attend fewer movies, concerts, lectures, and theaters; travel less; display less interest in artistic and musical pursuits; and participate far less in formal associations. Working class individuals spend more time than their middle class counterparts working around the house, watching television, working on their automobiles, taking automobile rides, playing cards, fishing, informally interacting with relatives and friends, and tavern-visiting.[27] There is also little doubt that significant differences in the use of "free" time characterize the poor and the middle class.[28]

Differences in the use of time can also be represented as differences in modes of consuming "symbolic" culture. The term *symbolic culture* is a roomy construct into which we can deposit whatever evidence we have about differential participation in the moral, aesthetic, and intellectual life of society. Remember that symbolic culture is an analytic fiction that should not be taken for a concrete entity. Participation in symbolic culture can take a number of different forms. We have already analyzed the most important form of symbolic consumption in modern society, formal schooling. No conclusion in the realm of education is more important for understanding contemporary inequality and differentials in subjective development and enjoyment than the fact that formal schooling and professional training are largely middle class monopolies. An important variation on this theme is that rising levels of education have led neither to greater homogeneity nor to a greater consensus of values and outlooks. Actually, effective participation in American society is severely limited for many people by functional illiteracy. Judged by role requirements, which

27. For a comprehensive and extremely useful review of earlier research in this area, see Milton M. Gordon and Charles H. Anderson, "The Blue-Collar Worker at Leisure," in *Blue-Collar World: Studies of the American Worker*, ed. Arthur B. Shostak and William Gomberg (Englewood Cliffs, N.J.: Prentice-Hall, 1964), pp. 407–416; also useful in rejecting the thesis that the working class is adopting middle class leisure pursuits are from the same volume, Gerald Handel and Lee Rainwater, "Persistence and Change in Working-Class Life Style" (pp. 36–41); and Richard F. Hamilton, "The Behavior and Values of Skilled Workers" (pp. 42–57). Also see Bennett M. Berger, *Working-Class Suburb: A Study of Auto Workers in Suburbia* (Berkeley: University of California Press, 1960), chap. 5, and Gavin Mackenzie, *The Aristocracy of Labor: The Position of Skilled Craftsmen in the American Class Structure* (London and New York: Cambridge University Press, 1973), chaps. 4 and 7. A denial of British working class assimilation into a middle class style of life may be found in John H. Goldthorpe, David Lockwood, Frank Bechhofer, and Jennifer Platt, *The Affluent Worker in the Class Structure* (London and New York: Cambridge University Press, 1969), chap. 4.

28. Bradley S. Greenberg and Brenda Dervin, with the assistance of Joseph R. Dominick and John Bowes, *Use of the Mass Media by the Urban Poor* (New York: Praeger, 1970). In addition to research reports on differences in the use of the mass media by the poor and the middle class, this book contains a valuable summary and annotated bibliography of all that was known about the "communication behaviors" of the poor, both white and black, at that time.

Useful information about the consumption of leisure time by the lower classes is provided by Harold M. Hodges, Jr., "Peninsula People: Social Stratification in a Metropolitan Complex" in *Education and Society: A Book of Readings*, ed. W. Warren Kallenbach and Harold M. Hodges, Jr. (Columbus, Ohio: Charles E. Merrill, 1963), pp. 389–420.

are probably becoming more demanding, it is likely that as the United States produces increasing numbers of college graduates, it also produces increasing numbers of functional illiterates.

Participation in "symbolic" culture can also take the form of participation in voluntary groups, especially those devoted to religion, reform, and politics. We discuss this form of participation further in Chapter 10, but here again there is little doubt that the stimulation and prestige afforded by associational activity correspond to a general pattern of middle and upper class dominance.

Participation in "symbolic" culture can also be analyzed in terms of differential class consumption (and production) in the aesthetic and intellectual-moral sphere;[29] this issue is the subject of this section. The main American pattern in this area is clear: Americans consume aesthetic, intellectual, and moral values in class-structured ways.[30] The corollary to this pattern is the significant fact that the production of "symbolic" culture is also geared to class audiences. And perhaps of even greater significance is the fact that "symbolic" culture is now in an advanced industrial stage of production and consumption. In other words, organizations engaged in creating and distributing aesthetic, intellectual, and moral values are managed in much the same way as is the economy; they are characterized by narrow upper class "ownership" and control, professional staffs who manage day-to-day operations, and benefits bestowed according to class.[31]

Our knowledge of the relation between class and "symbolic" culture has been advanced by Edward Arian's analysis of the Philadelphia (Symphony) Orchestra.[32] Suggesting that the forces at work in Philadelphia are found throughout the United States, Arian argues that the Philadelphia Orchestra Association is dominated through its board of directors by upper class (old-rich) families, and that they and the upper classes are its chief beneficiaries. To combat mounting costs, the board has instituted a rigidly bureaucratic, efficiency-minded mode of operations; this innovation has enabled the board

29. Two Marxist scholars who have achieved fame exploring the general relation between society (class) and aesthetic life are Georg Lukacs, especially his *The Historical Novel* (London: Merlin Press, 1962) and *Studies in European Realism* (New York: Grosset and Dunlap, 1964), available in paperback, and Arnold Hauser, *The Social History of Art*, 4 vols. (London: Routledge and Kegan Paul, 1962, available in paperback, originally published in 1951). For contemporary examples of Marxist literary criticism, see *College English* for November 1972. For a valuable historical analysis of the class basis of various forms of art, see Vytautas Kavolis, *Artistic Expression: A Sociological Analysis* (Ithaca, N.Y.: Cornell University Press, 1968).

30. For a report on the views and behavior of Americans with regard to a broad range of cultural questions and activities that finds a moderately strong difference between nonmanual and manual occupations and little evidence of a "middle mass," see Norval D. Glenn and Jon P. Alston, "Cultural Differences Among Occupational Categories," *American Sociological Review* 33 (June 1968): 365–382.

31. For a general analysis (and approval) of this trend, see Alvin Toffler, *The Culture Consumers* (New York: St. Martin's Press, 1964). Toffler reviews the evidence on the prevalence of upper class participation in higher culture on pp. 30–37.

32. Edward Arian, *Bach, Beethoven, and Bureaucracy: The Case of the Philadelphia Orchestra* (University, Ala.: University of Alabama Press, 1971).

to retain control, since the orchestra's budget can still be financed by private wealth. One of the interesting by-products of this process is that the orchestra does not play before a wide spectrum of community audiences and performs little modern or experimental music.

Middle and upper class dominance in the general area of aesthetic-intellectual-moral values makes for differences in the amount and type of enjoyment available to the various classes. Furthermore, control of prestigious forms of cultural activity by the upper classes strengthens and supports the general system of stratification by class. To the extent that high culture is thought to bear a special relationship to the integrity of society, the upper and middle classes are seen as its patrons and preservers. To the extent that the aesthetic-intellectual-moral realm has a bearing on social problems and issues, it is the upper classes that control its operations and compose its audiences, thereby deeply influencing the way in which issues and problems are formulated and solved. And, finally, it is the upper and middle classes whose sensibilities are stimulated and wits sharpened by offerings in the worlds of music, theater, painting, dance, sculpture, and quality publications, outcomes that are valuable in their own right and that have applications in the areas of class and power.

The relation between voluntary organizations in the field of "symbolic" culture and government (power) is of growing importance and deserves much greater study. In addition to its growing influence on higher education, the federal government now supports an extensive television network (the Corporation for Public Broadcasting and Public Broadcasting System) and has made large sums of money available to the arts and humanities (through the National Arts Endowment and the National Humanities Endowment). Framed in the image of the independent regulatory commissions, these public bodies resemble their predecessors: ostensibly nonpartisan, objective and aloof from politics in practice, they dispense public monies and public prestige in a manner that coincides with the basic structure of class and political power.

An interesting review of some empirical findings on the mass media suggests that because the logic of economic life, and especially its technology, impels the mass media to try to attract mass audiences, very little of their content is specialized according to class.[33] While blue-collar and white-collar families clearly tend to have different tastes and preferences in broadcast programs and print media (the former preferring more entertainment and less information), the interesting thing, according to Bogart, is that the differences are so small. What the mass media represent, Bogart suggests, is a powerful instrument for inducing working class conformity to a middle class society.[34]

Pressure to conform is one thing; actual homogeneity of outlook and values

33. The growth of publicly supported television has produced significant diversification of television programming. As is true of the other subsidized arts, public educational television represents subsidized stimulation for the middle and upper classes.

34. Leo Bogart, "The Mass Media and the Blue-Collar Worker" in *Blue-Collar World: Studies of the American Worker,* ed. Arthur B. Shostak and William Gomberg (Englewood Cliffs, N.J.: Prentice-Hall, 1964), pp. 416–428.

is another. Despite the mass media, there are significant differences between the symbolic interests and skills of white- and blue-collar Americans. This is not surprising given differences in the amount and type of reading (books, magazines, newspapers), formal education, socialization, travel, community participation, and occupational experience engaged in by the two groups.[35]

The donation of money and time

One of the ways to convert money into prestige is to give it away. Donating money enhances one's reputation among those who benefit from such generosity and among those who are impressed that one can afford to give money away. It also helps to make people forget how one earned one's money. (The classic case is the Rockefeller family, which has succeeded in living down the image of John D. Rockefeller as a robber baron.) Thus individuals give money to hospitals, settlement houses, adoption agencies, colleges, museums, symphony orchestras, and the like, and in return often gain fame and social immortality through the buildings, scholarships, or endowed chairs that memorialize their names.

Another way to gain prestige is to give time to community service. Despite constant complaints that they are overly busy, upper and middle class men often serve on committees or boards associated with the full range of voluntary organizations.[36] Their high class status and skills are useful to voluntary organizations (even if they merely lend their names) and, in turn, the moral prestige of such groups rubs off on volunteers. The wives of such men are also deeply involved in community work, the donation of time in their case also signifying freedom from the need to work. Such women are so secure economically that they can afford to give their time away. They too lend their prestige (actually, the prestige of their families and/or husbands), time, skills, and money to such enterprises, and in return they and their families gain

35. Also important to the analysis of "symbolic" culture are the political-ideological views (which we will discuss in Chapter 12) associated with the United States' various classes and economic groups. See R. Joseph Monsen, Jr. and Mark W. Cannon, *The Makers of Public Policy: American Power Groups and Their Ideologies* (New York: McGraw-Hill, 1965), available in paperback; Martin Trow, "Small Businessmen, Political Tolerance, and Support for McCarthy," *American Journal of Sociology* 64 (November 1958): 270–281; Norbert Wiley, "America's Unique Class Politics: The Interplay of Labor, Credit and Commodity Markets," *American Sociological Review* 32 (August 1967): 529–541; Lloyd A. Free and Hadley Cantril, *The Political Beliefs of Americans* (New Brunswick, N.J.: Rutgers University Press, 1967); Alfred Hero's summary of three decades of public opinion polls in John P. Robinson *et al., Measures of Political Attitudes* (Ann Arbor, Mich.: Survey Research Center, Institute for Social Research, 1968), pp. 38–50; Michael Mann, "The Social Cohesion of Liberal Democracy," *American Sociological Review* 35 (June 1970): 423–439; and Joan Huber and William H. Form, *Income and Ideology: An Analysis of the American Political Formula* (New York: Free Press, 1973).

36. Participation in voluntary organizations is in general a middle and upper class phenomenon; see "Primary Prestige Groups" and "Secondary Prestige Groups" in Chapter 10.

prestige by being associated with projects and organizations dedicated to moral and civic betterment.

The linkage between the upper classes and voluntary organizations probably involves far more than prestige. In a study of the board of trustees of a nonprofit hospital, it was found that economically dominant individuals maintained a steady representation on the board and were influential in controlling the hospital's not inconsiderable economic resources.[37]

Interestingly enough, membership on the boards that control voluntary associations appears to be remarkably homogeneous.[38] Arian's analysis of the Philadelphia Orchestra, cited above, found its board to be not only upper class but predominantly *Social Register* upper class. Further, the board rejected a consulting firm's suggestion that it diversify its membership, arguing that to do so would jeopardize its standards.[39]

We obviously need to know much more about this area of behavior. One can assume that charitable and social service agencies are hampered in their purposes by the exclusion from membership of the people they serve. And, obviously, the absence and exclusion of many professions, ordinary workers, lower-level businesspeople, the semiprofessions, and minorities from the governing boards of voluntary associations also hamper their operation and represents a serious loss of prestige and power for such groups.[40]

An important means of acquiring prestige through the sacrifice of economic assets is public service. Upper class individuals contribute their time to public commissions of all kinds and accept public positions at considerable sacrifice of income. Ambassadors are perhaps the best examples of the latter, but there are many high-income businesspeople and professionals who accept government positions or run for public office at some (temporary) economic sacrifice. Obviously, the prestige of such individuals is enhanced, and so is that of upper occupational and income-wealth groups in general. Above all, this process helps to create and maintain the impression that middle and upper class interests and values are identical with the public interest, an impression fostered by the entire range of voluntary behavior.

37. Robert G. Holloway, Jay W. Artis, and Walter E. Freeman, "The Participation Patterns of 'Economic Influentials' and Their Control of a Hospital Board of Trustees," *Journal of Health and Human Behavior* 4 (Summer 1963): 88–99; reprinted in E. Gartley Jaco, ed., *Patients, Physicians and Illness: A Sourcebook in Behavioral Science and Health,* 2nd ed. (New York: Free Press, 1972), pp. 313–324.

38. The basic analogue is corporate ownership and control. The reader should also remember the homogeneity found to characterize the boards of institutions of higher education, especially private ones.

39. Arian argues that the board's policies actually restrict the orchestra's services to an elite clientele, prevent it from keeping abreast of musical trends, and create severe alienation among rank-and-file performing artists.

40. Also significant is the fact that membership in symphony orchestras tends to be tightly controlled and nepotistic. As in many skilled craft unions, openings are reserved for members' children and friends, thus making it difficult for newcomers, such as members of racial and ethnic minorities, to enter this relatively prestigious occupation.

Common consumption
The logic of mass production

An outstanding and unique feature of consumption in the United States is that large portions of the American population consume the same items and services. The inherent tendency of an industrial economy is to create a national (and international) market for products and services and to transform all citizens into equivalent consumers. A mass-production economy is obviously at odds with norms and values that seek to restrict or differentiate consumption according to social position. Unlike industrial social systems, agrarian societies often develop *sumptuary laws,* or laws that lend the power of the "state" to moral and religious norms governing consumption. Such laws establish differential consumption by, for example, stipulating that only aristocrats can wear fur or silk. In caste, multireligious, or multiethnic societies, there develop strong normative traditions that define appropriate forms of consumption for each level or segment of society, especially in the areas of food, drink, and clothing. But the United States, like other industrial societies, has successfully established the primacy of class position with regard to consumption. One's income, and thus one's relation to the commodity market, is the main legitimate restriction on consumption.[41]

Common consumption does not, it should be noted, mean equivalent expenditures. The various classes obviously spend different amounts in their overall consumption. What is of interest here is that sharp differences in consumption, and resulting sharp differences in prestige, do not exist in the United States in an easily recognizable way. The major reason for this is that the majority of the population consumes a wide range of similar products, often brand-name goods with national prestige: food (staples as well as nonstaples); beverages (milk, soft drinks, beer); household products (soap, polishes, waxes, detergents); household appliances (refrigerators, vacuum cleaners, television); clothing (quality ready-made clothing of all sorts, such as suits, dresses, shoes, underwear); and such other items as cigarettes, entertainment products, and sporting goods. The crucial point is that vast portions of the public consume these goods in common regardless of income. In addition, sizable segments of various classes can afford to consume in common even such expensive goods as automobiles, washing machines, air conditioners, and color television sets.

The meaning of common consumption, and other common behavior, is not self-evident. As Handel and Rainwater have emphasized, there is only a superficial similarity between the working and middle classes even when they seem to be saying or doing identical things. For example, both classes have positive attitudes toward education and home ownership, but the meanings they attach to these values are quite different. The working class views education quite instrumentally, while the middle class also sees it as a process of refinement, a foundation for later learning, a means to enjoy life more, and a way

41. There are, of course, laws prohibiting certain kinds of consumption (such as consumption of drugs), but these laws are applicable to all.

to learn how to get along with people. Similarly, the working class sees home ownership as a way to escape from the landlord while the middle class tends to see it as a "validation of status." In addition, the working class tends to purchase durable goods in common with the middle class, but not such services as meals in restaurants, vacations, home and automobile repairs, clothing, and education.[42]

In his empirical test of the thesis of the *embourgeoisement* of the working class, Gavin Mackenzie also found that the various classes (in Providence, Rhode Island) do not attach the same meanings to similar consumption. It is clear, for example, that skilled blue-collar workers attach a different meaning to home ownership than do white-collar workers, especially managers. Mackenzie's conclusion is the same as Handel's and Rainwater's finding about stable working class families: basically, skilled workers see home ownership as a way to escape accountability to landlords, an urge analogous to their desire to escape their bosses. For their part, members of the lower- and especially the upper-middle classes, though they also stress privacy and freedom, cite the economic advantages and prestige of owning a home.[43]

Public accommodations and facilities

Another category of common consumption is "public" accommodations and facilities, both those that are privately owned — such as restaurants, housing, hotels, movie theaters, and stadiums — and those that are usually run by government — national, state, and local parks, transit systems, highways, beaches, swimming pools, recreation centers, golf courses, hospitals, colleges, libraries, theaters, stadiums, and museums. The United States has a long history of regarding such services and facilities as less than totally public; their use, for example, was deeply affected by racial segregation in the American south.[44] This situation was changed by law during the 1960s. The Civil Rights Act of 1964 forbade discrimination on the basis of race, religion, or national origin in such "public" facilities as private hotels, motels, restaurants, lunch counters, movie houses, gasoline stations, theaters, stadiums, barbershops and taverns located in hotels, restaurants located in department stores, and facilities that receive federal funds (hospitals, schools for the deaf and blind, colleges and universities). A fundamental feature of this act is that it voids on constitutional grounds state laws requiring segregation in private facilities not engaged in interstate commerce, but cannot forbid private discrimination in them.[45] The Housing Act of 1965 also asserted the public nature of most privately owned

42. Gerald Handel and Lee Rainwater, "Persistence and Change in Working-Class Life Style," in *Blue-Collar World: Studies of the American Worker,* ed. Arthur B. Shostak and William Gomberg (Englewood Cliffs, N.J.: Prentice-Hall, 1964), pp. 36–41.
43. Gavin Mackenzie, *The Aristocracy of Labor: The Position of Skilled Craftsmen in the American Class Structure* (London and New York: Cambridge University Press, 1973), pp. 74–77.
44. At one time, Oklahoma even had segregated telephone booths.
45. Many states outside the south have their own laws prohibiting discrimination.

housing and forbade discrimination in the sale or rental of most of the nation's housing stock.

On the whole, there is now full formal access to most such facilities and accommodations. Speaking broadly, use and nonuse is now based on class rather than "caste" for all Americans. In practice, however, there are glaring exceptions to pure class consumption, the most important of which is housing. It appears that, in relative terms, no significant progress has been made in providing black Americans with more, better, or integrated housing. Though systematic data are lacking, the same is probably true of hospital use and a host of public services such as police and fire protection, garbage removal, and the like. And, of course, the ghettoization of black Americans and other minorities means that effective access to many free or low-cost public facilities is severely reduced.[46]

The amount and type of use made of "public" accommodations and facilities is also related to class, but no exact picture can be drawn due to lack of research. Many "public" accommodations (hotels, restaurants, lunch counters, housing) are geared to income, and often psychologically deter people who could otherwise afford them. Many rich and many poor people do not use low-cost public facilities such as subways, buslines, and golf courses, or use them less than do the middle-rich and near-poor. The poor probably do not use public facilities such as highways, libraries, and museums much, speaking both in absolute terms and in relation to higher income groups. And while hospitals are ostensibly open to all, their use depends on money. They are thus segregated internally by class — the poor who use hospitals are identified as charity cases — and little common consumption can be said to take place in this area.

Both the rich and the poor, therefore, are exceptions to the pattern of common consumption of public accommodations and facilities. But while the rich consume privately and out of the public eye (though aided extensively by the power dimension which, for example, protects their privacy, property, and income through favorable and discriminatory zoning and taxation), the poor face important prestige disabilities because they consume minimally and are objects of private and public charity. The prestige implications of poverty in the midst of plenty are difficult to gauge. Earlier in our history, the poor were subject to private charity, which allowed the upper classes to acquire prestige by displaying their concern and generosity. During the twentieth century responsibility for solving the problems of the poor has shifted from private markets and private organizations to government. In any case, the poor continue to suffer from low prestige because of low consumption, but in new ways, and perhaps more severely, now that they are acknowledged to be wards of the state.

In sum, the impact of "public" accommodations and "public" facilities on the

46. Minority groups have in recent years asked for access to the public airwaves (radio and television channels). While this demand has not been met as often or as fully as minority groups would like, it has served to raise the question of how such public facilities denigrate or neglect minorities.

American class system cannot be gauged with precision. It is clear that such accommodations and facilities could not exist under caste or estate systems of stratification. It is also clear that in a society oriented toward private life, many undoubtedly take governmental services for granted, others resent them as unearned gifts to the poor, still others do not use them, and many lack access because rights are not enforced or because equal services are not provided. On the whole, it cannot be said that the common consumption of class society is as egalitarian as a cursory comparison with caste and estate systems might suggest, nor that any significant reduction of inequality can be said to result from it. The formal right to use "public" accommodations and facilities does, however, create the illusion that an important form of common (and thus equal) consumption is taking place. And, like the illusion of equality of opportunity to consume education, this illusion serves to legitimate and stabilize the American class system.

The role of consumption in class stratification

All the evidence about consumption indicates that rising absolute income (and a shorter work week) has not led to the homogenization of the American population into one great middle class (or mass) bounded at the top by the very rich and at the bottom by the very poor. The American working class, including highly skilled workers and their families, has not translated its rising income (class) level into middle class levels of prestige. Even if the idea of cultural consumption is broadened to subsume any use of time or money, or to refer to the intake of intellectual, aesthetic, and civic values in general, no middle class homogenization of the American population is discernible.

Consumption patterns undoubtedly play a role in reducing social stress and producing social stability. How this process works cannot be specified in detail, though general tendencies can be identified with a certain measure of confidence. Large amounts of common consumption (and the illusion of still more) are undeniable. But similar behavior can have very different meanings for different participants, and this seems to be the case for much of what passes as common consumption. Patterns of common consumption do have a moral effect, however: they tend to create and uphold belief in moral (prestige) equality. It is not unimportant in this respect that various income groups, Protestants, Roman Catholics, Jews, Republicans, Democrats, whites, blacks, and other "racial" groups all use or are free to use the "same" soap, drink the "same" water, eat the "same" food, and wear the "same" clothes.

Perhaps more important to social integration than common consumption is differential consumption. To understand the American class system fully, it is essential to recognize that, by and large, the culture of capitalism has successfully established the legitimacy of differential styles of class consumption and resulting styles of differential prestige. Americans at all levels accept the principle of a hierarchy of consumption, which is in keeping with their acceptance of the differential worth of occupations and the legitimacy of a hierarchy of income and wealth. Those who consume well or even lavishly deserve to do so, it is thought, because of their economic accomplishments.[47] As long as differential consumption does not lead to rigid categories of prestige affecting the moral or political-legal worth of individuals, there is little public resentment of differential income classes and differential prestige through consumption.[48] In other words, American society has successfully compartmentalized the forces of liberty and success (inequality) and the forces of equality. Nothing signifies the stability of American society so completely as the fact that its economic groups invariably make demands on each other based on a desire to maintain their present share of the national product. In other words, they do not draw on the tradition of equality to question the principle of class inequality. Normally, Americans discuss the problems created by class within the context of a class system of society. For example, they draw on the tradition of equality to identify lack of equal opportunity in the general system, not to question whether the system is capable of providing it. Similarly, Americans accept differential consumption because it is believed that consumption is related to what individuals earn and thus to what they are worth. But they also expect the economy to provide for continuous increases in consumption, and strains occur whenever the economy falters. Therefore, the health of the system depends on continuous economic expansion and on the relative balance of differential and common consumption — and (as we will now see) on special processes at work within each of these areas.

Consumption and absolute and relative prestige levels

In an interesting essay, Fallers has suggested that the "trickle-down" effect identified by Barber and Loebel in the world of fashions characterizes the entire range of consumption, and that in addition to reconciling the contrary emphases on difference and equality, the trickle-down effect has consequences for society-at-large insofar as it reconciles the emphasis on success and the fact that most must fail.[49] Basically, the trickle-down effect helps to create the illusion of success, and thus to motivate people to continue striving against unfavorable odds. A wide range of products is trickled down — that is, gradually made available to the masses for common consumption.

This form of trickling down is somewhat different from that of the world of women's fashions, and Fallers discusses it in terms of how individuals experience a rising hierarchy of consumption. Of central importance is the fact that many individuals have come to regard an absolute rise in the standard

47. The recent interest in preserving the environment, controlling pollution, and conserving energy may arouse some public resentment of certain forms of consumption. The effect on differential (and common) consumption remains to be seen.

48. This does not mean that Americans do not complain about inequities and inadequacies in living standards and public services.

49. Lloyd A. Fallers, "A Note on the 'Trickle Effect'," *Public Opinion Quarterly* 18 (Fall 1954): 314–321; reprinted in Reinhard Bendix and Seymour M. Lipset, eds., *Class, Status and Power: Social Stratification in Comparative Perspective,* 2nd ed. (New York: Free Press, 1966), pp. 402–405.

of living as normal. As all incomes rise, an absolute rise in consumption does not lead to a relative change for most people. Thus, while their relative consumption position may not change, there is a realistic payoff for most people (and thus for society) as the economy expands: relative to their own past experience, they are consuming at a higher level, and there is no threat to prestige in the fact that others are consuming more. As a consequence, their motivation to work and strive continues unabated even though they are not achieving success in relative terms. Some individuals experience unchanged levels of consumption during an upward shift in real income, and are aware or unaware of a relative loss depending on their consumption level and social location (for example, small town or big city). Others drop in the consumption hierarchy, but the blow is softened by the facts that total consumption is rising and that their slippage in consumption is more moderate than their decline in the prestige hierarchy. And, of course, other individuals can realize relative gains in their prestige status by consuming more, differently, or both.

Figure 9-1, adopted with changes from Fallers, illustrates these processes. (It is an abstract construct and does not refer to actual proportions of income or prestige). As the American economy expands between 1947 and 1970, creating a new level (V) in the hierarchy of total consumption:

D will experience a decline from 1 to 2 in prestige but may not know it.
C will experience a decline from 2 to 4 in prestige but only a one-level decrease in total consumption.
B's prestige will be stationary at 3 but he will experience a rise in total consumption.
A will experience an extreme rise in prestige and in total consumption, rising from I to V and from 4 to 1.

This fundamental process of motivating people to continue working and striving in order to modify or overcome consumption gradations in prestige obviously depends on the continued expansion of the economy. Failure to develop more (and, probably, new) goods and services would lead to serious strain in the relations between classes. Much of the tension created by the black movement in the 1960s may be attributable to the fact that some black advances were made at the expense of the white working class — at the same time that the Vietnam war and inflation hampered the steady growth in real income expected by the American public and required by the American system of society. Decreases in investment in public services also contribute, no doubt, to the feeling that the standard of living is not rising. And, finally, unknown amounts of the gross national product (as well as many undesirable economic by-products) do not constitute real improvements or are difficult to perceive as such: airport noise, the cost of commuting by automobile, tobacco consumption and the medical technology and facilities needed to combat the cancer caused by tobacco; deterioration of products because of pollution; police officers; and, of course, the growth of what is now a large and important segment of our economy, military production and space exploration.

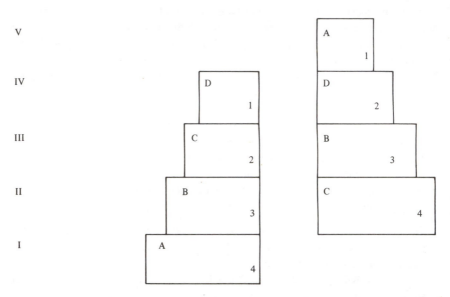

Figure 9-1 columns:

Hierarchy of total consumption, roughly gross national product divided into class levels

Hierarchy of prestige-symbolic consumption, a point in time, say 1947 with a family income median of $5,000

Hierarchy of prestige-symbolic consumption, another point in time, say 1970 with a family income median of $10,000

Figure 9-1 Absolute and Relative Prestige Levels: Consumption Possibilities in an Expanding Economy

SOURCE: Adapted with changes from Lloyd A. Fallers, "A Note on the 'Trickle Effect,'" *Public Opinion Quarterly* 18 (Fall 1954): 318. Used by permission.

Counterfeit and compensatory consumption

C. Wright Mills has suggested that white-collar people in lower-middle class occupations engage in a "status cycle" to alleviate "status panic."[50] The secretary who skips lunches to save money for a wardrobe and a two-week vacation in a plush resort is one example. Many other means of enjoying prestige above one's class level are available to Americans because of the anonymity of modern life: after-hour clothing, a splurge on theater tickets, a new hairdo, inexpensive travel tours, and the like. Again, as is true of so much consumption behavior, we have little data and can only speculate on the extent to which Americans rely on a "status cycle" to alleviate prestige anxieties.

Another way of counterfeiting prestige is to live beyond one's income, either by endangering one's economic position (by, for example, failing to save for retirement, or to own life or medical insurance) or through credit. Of course,

50. C. Wright Mills, *White Collar: The American Middle Classes* (New York: Oxford University Press, 1953), chap. 11, also in paperback.

not everyone who uses a credit card or borrows is living beyond his or her means. Installment credit and mortgages, however, do allow an unknown number of Americans to live on future earnings, a practice that often entails serious psychic and family costs. The role of the state in making credit and mortgage money available (and allowing the interest paid as an income tax deduction) is an indispensable aspect of our prestige system. Expense-account living, also subsidized by the state, is another form of counterfeit consumption; how many engage in it cannot be said with certainty. The role of the state in enforcing one-sided contracts and credit terms also allows for a form of high-cost "compensatory consumption" among the poor. The function of this type of consumption is to provide consumer goods to high-risk customers and thus promote self-respect among the poor.[51] As we have suggested, the integrative function performed by consumption at this level — maintaining loyalty to the system among the poor — is performed by various forms of consumption (common, differential, counterfeit) at various class levels.

A related form of "status cycle" is the practice of spending holidays in ethnically and racially segregated or otherwise "safe" places. There has long existed a domestic circuit of safe places for black Americans to visit, and increasing prosperity has given rise to a black travel bureau business that caters to the domestic and overseas travel needs of the black middle class. The problems related to vacations and leisure encountered by other minorities, and the practices that have developed to overcome them, must still be researched. It is well known, though, that there are hotels, resorts, clubs, and country clubs that cater to various ethnic groups.

We also need to know more about compensatory consumption among various classes. It has long been thought that blacks dissipate their earnings on immediate gratifications and thus fail to save. Not only is this not true, but blacks seem to save at higher rates than whites, holding class constant.[52] Of some interest is the finding in 1963 that *Ebony* had far fewer advertisements for automobiles, furniture, and home improvements and appliances than a similar magazine for whites (*Life*), which partially contradicts the stereotype that blacks overspend on luxuries.[53]

Consumption extremes

Commentators on American society have tended to stress the decline of ostentatious display by the rich, in terms both of the long-term historical transition from feudal society and of developments within industrial society during the twentieth century. (The White House, says Talcott Parsons, is not the Palace of Versailles.) This overall perspective on consumption is sound

51. David Caplovitz, *The Poor Pay More: Consumer Practices of Low Income Families* (New York: Free Press, 1963), chap. 2.

52. Julian A. Simon and Rita James Simon, "Class, Status, and Savings of Negroes," *American Sociologist* 3 (August 1968): 218–219.

53. David Berkman, "Advertising in *Ebony* and *Life*: Negro Aspirations vs. Reality," *Journalism Quarterly* 40, no. 1 (Winter 1963): 53–64.

enough, though some of the conclusions drawn from it are not.[54] Comparisons between modern society and feudal systems, as we have pointed out, are monumentally difficult to make and a source of endless confusion and distortion. For example, most of the French aristocracy during the heyday of Versailles led lives of relatively deep impoverishment and were incapable of flaunting luxurious consumption. It is also true that there has been a decline of splendor in private residences — in the use of gold plumbing, large servant staffs, and the like — simultaneous with the decline of "High Society." The reasons generally adduced for this decline are the income tax (a much-exaggerated cause), the competition for and cost of servant labor, the growth of a democratic spirit, and the decline of a leisure class of nonworking very rich.

There is little doubt that some of the very rich lead quiet, inconspicuous lives, a style of life that is itself a source of prestige vis-à-vis the new rich. Also important is the fact that new wealth is often amassed by highly disciplined, hardworking businesspeople and professionals who find it hard to engage in wasteful, frivolous forms of expenditure. But all this should not obscure the fact that consumption at the upper end of the class system is very high and very luxurious and has enormously important (and unique) consequences for the American class system. The argument that ostentatious display has declined is not only based largely on gross and misleading comparisons but is also an unwitting apology for the low-profile old rich and the new rich of upper-middle class managers and professionals. Dunhill's 1972 Christmas catalogue, for example, lists a $10,500 cigar humidor, a $1,950 pen, and a $835 pipe; the price of the cigar humidor corresponds almost exactly to that year's income for an average American family. Dunhill's chief complaint is the difficulty not of selling such items but of finding craftsmen to make them. Dunhill's merchandising director is even quoted as saying, "When times are good, they're really good for Dunhill. When times are bad, they're quite good for Dunhill." [55]

Of central significance in understanding consumption extremes is the phenomenon of relative deprivation. Industrial populations are now highly urbanized and subject to high levels of stimulation — for example, through the mass media — which among other things make known to them higher and often unattainable levels of consumption. And it is no longer possible to comfort people with the promise of a better life in the next world, or to persuade them that their poverty is due to original sin. The fact remains that an upper class man or woman may routinely spend on clothing an amount that millions of Americans must live on for an entire year. In short, large numbers at the upper levels enjoy multiple dwellings, expensive hobbies, and private boats and planes while significant numbers go hungry, lack plumbing, and suffer from lack of medical care.

54. Actually, the American presidency is embellished by impressive facilities, ceremonies, and protocols.
55. *New York Times,* 25 November 1972, p. 27.

Class and consumption: a summary

The use of property and money has prestige implications, and a wide variety of prestige differences has appeared in industrial society. The hierarchy of class is accompanied by a hierarchy of differential consumption that leads to sharp and enduring differences in prestige. Unlike agrarian societies, however, industrial society is characterized by a sphere of common consumption and promotes expectations of increased consumption at all levels. Given an expanding economy, and thus rising consumption, Americans accept prestige differences in consumption despite the fact that such differences are at odds with their moral egalitarianism. There is little evidence of the development of a great middle mass of consumers. In sum, the area of consumption prestige reflects the nature of an expanding capitalist economy and its steeply and stably graded class system.

10

Class and the structure of prestige groups

IT IS ONE THING to enjoy deference and make prestige claims on others in the realm of universally accepted values, and quite another to expect prestige benefits on grounds external to a social consensus. As we have seen, Americans acquire and grant prestige on the basis of occupation with great unanimity because occupation is central to the American consensus on the value of economic achievement. Americans also accord prestige to certain types of culture heroes with a fairly high degree of unanimity. In addition, majority Americans are now much more likely to accept (on the level of attitudes) the equal worth of ethnic, religious, and "racial" minorities than they were in the relatively recent past. Despite its importance, however, it is a mistake to think that society functions on the basis of consensus, or homogeneity of beliefs and values.

As we saw in Chapter 9, the United States has both common and differential ways of according prestige and psychic satisfactions. We did not, however, stress the point that differential prestige often contributes to stability and integration and, like other forms of social differentiation, should not automatically be defined as socially divisive or disruptive. As we will see in studying the structure of prestige groups, prestige and psychic satisfactions derived from group membership are also distributed differentially, a circumstance that lubricates (as well as disturbs) class relations.

The importance of group membership for personality development and maintenance cannot be exaggerated. In analyzing prestige forms of associational life, we will investigate some of the important forces that produce and perpetuate the American personality — or, rather, the many American personalities — and reflect as well as create America's values and beliefs. Since group structures are the fundamental causal processes behind human behavior, we will also be peeling away some of the veils that obscure the American structure of social power. In analyzing prestige groups, we will maintain our society-wide focus, making few references to prestige structures in local communities (despite the fact that small-town America is still a stronghold of mutually accepted prestige claims). As the nation has urbanized and suburbanized, there has been a pronounced trend toward the segregation of class and prestige groups by residence and political community, and the small-town hierarchy of prestige groups is not an accurate model of contemporary national prestige behavior.

Our analysis will employ some familiar sociological distinctions. We will refer, first of all, to *achievement prestige groups*, which base membership on achievement criteria, and *ascriptive prestige groups*, membership in which is restricted according to religion, ethnicity, family lineage, and/or "race." Secondly, we will distinguish between *primary prestige groups* based on intimate interaction, such as a family or a club, and *secondary prestige groups* based on impersonal interaction, such as charitable or professional associations. And, finally, we will note that, while the United States does not have nationwide prestige groups that make broad, diffused claims to deference from subordinate groups (such as an aristocracy requires from serfs and southern whites have demanded from blacks), prestige claims are part of its working consensus (and thus part of one group's claim on another). At the same time, a wide range of prestige benefits are displayed and enjoyed by groups in relative isolation from each other. In combination with the fact that many secondary organizations have heterogeneous memberships, the segregation of associational life goes a long way toward explaining the lack of class consciousness and class hostility in the United States.

Many of the terms traditionally used to differentiate prestige from class behavior are ambiguous and misleading. The distinction between private and public is not overly useful, since class behavior, for example, can stem from occupations that cut across the economic, social, and political spheres. Much the same problem characterizes the prestige realm: for example, private clubs are prestige groups, but so are publically supported museums, schools and universities, and charity organizations. A preferable approach is to think of the area of prestige as social space particularly amenable to individual choice; indeed, it is often referred to as the *voluntary sector*. Provided it is used with care, this term is probably the most descriptive and accurate that we have.

Voluntary behavior can be both primary and secondary in nature: its focus can be intimate, as is true of love, family, friendship, and some clubs, or it can be reformist, humanitarian, or charitable, like the League of Women

Voters, political parties, the Red Cross, and the Salvation Army. We speak of this realm in terms of the rights of free speech, free association, and petition. But despite such traditional phrases and the appearance of behavior in this area as natural and spontaneous, it would be a mistake to think of prestige as the domain of human nature and of freely chosen behavior. Choices in the realm of prestige are still social choices tied closely to class (and power), and the alternatives that are considered normal effectively rule out many other feasible courses of action.

There are two perspectives that can guide us through the maze of American prestige phenomena as they express themselves in prestige groups. First, voluntary behavior exerts an influence beyond itself to counteract or modify the inequalities and inequities of class and power. A vital tradition of moral egalitarianism, derived largely from Christianity and secular humanism, and especially from the liberal democratic tradition, permeates the voluntary sector and supports its autonomy from the rigid frameworks and compulsions of work and law. It is in this realm that Americans relax and rest, undertake new activities, pursue old interests and values, criticize themselves and their institutions, and launch movements of reform and regeneration. The voluntary realm has seen a significant historical increase in the number of people eligible to participate in important institutional sectors and to consume hitherto restricted goods and symbols. And it is in the voluntary realm that commentators from Tocqueville on have found the essential explanation of America's freedom, equality, and democracy: a pluralistic, decentralized group structure responsive to both personal and public need.

The other perspective that will guide us through the sector of prestige or voluntary groups is equally important, if not more so. As we will see, all the available evidence points to a steeply graded, sharply segregated, and highly stable stratification of benefits derived from memberships in prestige groups. Not only are such benefits distributed unevenly, but there is also a far-reaching interpenetration of class and prestige (and power) structures. The prestige realm, for example, is subject to the same inexorable growth of rational organization (bureaucracy) as the realms of class and power. The United States has an incredible number of formally organized, private associations.[1] Beneath this multiform associational life there is a basic trend toward bigness and concentration. Churches; universities and colleges; fraternal and charitable groups; research institutes; foundations; the mass media and entertainment businesses (radio, movies, television, recording, sports); businesses devoted to hobbies and recreation; publishers of magazines, newspapers, and books; and the world of "high" culture (symphony orchestras, ballet groups, museums) are all characterized by large-scale organization and increased concentration.

1. *Encyclopedia of Associations,* 8th ed. (Detroit: Gale Research Company, 1973). Volume 1, "National Organizations of the United States," lists "more than 17,000 trade associations, professional societies, labor unions, fraternal and patriotic organizations, and other types of groups consisting of voluntary members."

A shift from preindustrial to industrial modes of operation is clearly discernible in the fields of entertainment, religion, "high" culture, philanthropy, education, medicine, and the professions in general. In other words, services formerly provided on the basis of individual need are beginning to be offered in large-scale standardized ways to families, neighborhoods, cities, states, regions, the nation, and even other countries. In other words, private organizations in these areas are in step with the major trend evident in our economy and government.

Prestige processes
Prestige diversity and struggle

American history is filled with rivalries between prestige-seeking groups: whites have oppressed nonwhites; the well-bred have struggled to maintain ascendancy over their social inferiors; native-born American whites have looked down on immigrants and native nonwhites alike; people of property and/or education have expected deference from the poor; unlettered rural people have railed against the city; and so on. The winners of these various struggles are not always easy to determine. It is, however, of no little importance to the development of American prestige patterns that the United States has never had to dislodge a powerful set of feudal families from the upper levels of its economic, religious, educational, and political life. But while it was spared this problem, the United States has witnessed many attempts to translate old wealth and lengthy pedigrees into a prestige (and even power) factor.

Analysts of social stratification in the United States have found deep prestige divisions based on "family lineage" in every community they have studied. This is not to say that Americans assert the superiority of particular family bloodlines (except when families are differentiated according to "race"). Americans believe in biopsychic differences between individuals, which is quite different from the feudal principle of a hierarchy of hereditary families. Where families come to believe themselves superior (or inferior), their prestige claims (or shame) are based on achievable factors such as income, wealth, expensive residence, breeding and good taste, philanthropy, leisure pursuits, or some mixture of these.[2] The American social system encourages and accords achievement prestige in a wide variety of areas: business, science, education, the arts, charity, reform movements, and in such areas of taste as dress,

2. For a history of prestige phenomena in the United States, such as democratic politics, books of etiquette, blue books and *The Social Register,* clubs, the society page, the American search for feudal splendor, and prestige sports, see Dixon Wecter, *The Saga of American Society: A Record of Social Aspiration, 1607–1937* (New York: Charles Scribner's Sons, 1937). Other accounts of the American plutocracy's concern with establishing "society" are Cleveland Amory, *The Last Resorts* (New York: Harper and Brothers, 1948), and *Who Killed Society?* (New York: Harper and Brothers, 1960); and Lucy Kavaler, *The Private World of High Society* (New York: David McKay, 1960).

speech, home furnishings, music, and art. By and large, therefore, when prestige distinctions seem at odds with class, they are really at odds with *newly acquired* class position; thus the distinction between the old rich and the new rich.

The identification of prestige differentials as the basis of social stratification is best exemplified by the Warner school. Their own research and that of others led Warner and his associates to identify six class levels in the more established regions of the country (New England and the deep south) and five levels in the middle and far west.[3] At the top of the six-level system in New England [4] is a tiny upper-upper class composed of rich families possessing old wealth. The men of this class are occupied gainfully as large-scale merchants, financiers, or elite professionals, but the family wealth, ideally speaking, dates from the era when fortunes were made at sea. Almost by definition, a class of families with old wealth is lacking in the less established sections of the country.

The lower-upper class, also very small, is composed of wealthy families with new money — money made in such new industries as shoe manufacturing, textiles, and corporate finance. While they may chafe at the thought that they, the doers, have less prestige than the old-family class whose wealth is essentially hereditary, they work assiduously to acquire the prestige credentials needed for admittance to the upper reaches of the class ladder.[5]

Below the very rich is the upper-middle class composed of professionals and owners of stores and businesses. Members of this class aspire to join upper class prestige groups, Warner claims, but seldom succeed. They are active in civic life, to a large extent furthering the interests of the two tiny upper classes while screening them from public view. Together the three top classes account for approximately 13 percent of the population.

At the top of what Warner calls the common man level is the lower-middle class of clerks and other white-collar workers, small tradesmen, and a few skilled workers. Members of this class have little property, though they are frequently home owners. Included among them are the successful members of such ethnic groups as Italians, Irish, and French Canadians. This group makes up about 28 percent of the population.

The upper-lower class makes up 34 percent of the population and is composed of "poor but honest workers." Below the common man level is the lower-lower class made up of those alleged to be shiftless, improvident, and sexually promiscuous. Research, says Warner, reveals that they are simply poor and lack ambition.

3. W. Lloyd Warner, Marchia Meeker, and Kenneth Eells, *Social Class in America: The Evaluation of Status* (New York: Harper and Row, 1960), pp. 11–24; originally published in 1949 without chaps. 16 and 17, which have been substituted for the original appendix.

4. The six-level system in the deep south is accompanied by a "caste" line separating whites and blacks.

5. An excellent fictional portrayal of these two classes, undoubtedly set in Newburyport, Massachusetts (Yankee City), is John P. Marquand's *Point of No Return* (Boston: Little, Brown, 1949).

The essence of Warner's scheme is to assert the independent force of prestige differences based on old wealth, tasteful consumption, superior breeding, and public service. Critics have pointed out, however, that while these hierarchical prestige differences exist, they are not only lodged in economic status (as Warner is not unaware) but must be seen in historical context: prestige phenomena are not the essence of social class but manifestations of economic positions consolidated over generations.

The main general thrust toward prestige hegemony in the United States has been made by the bearers of white Anglo-Saxon Protestant (WASP) values. Speaking broadly, this thrust has been successful in two different ways:

1. The achievement values established and developed by the original English colonists became the core American culture and served as the criteria on which the American class system is based. These achievement values permeate the worlds of farming, business, and the professions, and include standards of taste, personal deportment, and public service. Thus WASPs and non-WASPs are stratified by the various values of the liberal ethos.

2. The ascriptive values of the original settlers — familistic pretensions, sexism, anti-Catholicism, anti-Semitism, and racism — elaborated in various ways by various classes of WASPs, have, along with the values of others, also left their imprint on American society.

We will discuss each of these two points in the next two sections, first analyzing the upper class as a prestige group and then analyzing ascriptive segregation in associational life.

The upper class as a prestige group

It is an extremely important feature of the American class system that no prestige group has ever been able to establish itself on a nationwide basis. For such a thing to happen one group would need to combine prestige assets with either class or power assets, or both, to form a dominant stratum. On a regional basis, the plantation aristocracy of the old south can be considered such a stratum. And one can interpret the prestige aspirations of the "Four Hundred" at the end of the nineteenth century as an abortive attempt to become a national prestige group. But while that attempt to establish a high society failed, the American upper class — composed essentially of families of old wealth, as described by Warner — has developed a unique and powerful prestige position. Though it lacks public acceptance, the upper class' prestige pursuits and achievements are in keeping with its high class and power position and serve many important functions.

The identification of this class through its prestige practices is primarily the work of E. Digby Baltzell. In his study of the upper class in Philadelphia [6] and

6. E. Digby Baltzell, *Philadelphia Gentlemen: The Making of a National Upper Class* (New York: Free Press, 1958), available in paperback, also issued as a Collier paperback under the title *An American Business Aristocracy.*

subsequent historical study of the upper class on a national scale,[7] Baltzell has traced the parallel fortunes of an emerging national political economy and a national upper class, defined as possessing a common cultural tradition, a sense of solidarity resulting from regular interaction, and a consciousness of itself as a distinct social class.

Though his account of the upper class is badly marred by the assumption that the United States has (and has always had) open class and power dimensions that allow individuals of ability to rise in the economic and political-legal systems, and though he fails to understand that prestige exclusiveness buttresses class and power interests and privileges, Baltzell nevertheless draws a fascinating and insightful picture of what he calls America's "caste-ridden" prestige dimension. Primarily as a response to large-scale immigration but also, Baltzell suggests, as patrician protective devices against populism, progressivism, urban blight, and trust-busting, the WASP upper class began in the 1880s to develop a series of exclusive prestige groups and practices: [8]

1. The trend toward exclusive summer resort communities was ratified when President Eliot of Harvard built a summer cottage at Northeast Harbor, Maine, in 1881.

2. The trend toward exclusive country clubs was initiated by the founding of The Country Club at Brookline, Massachusetts, in 1882.

3. The patrician search for family roots and the craze for genealogy gave rise to the founding of the Sons of the Revolution in 1883, followed by the Colonial Dames in 1890, the Daughters of the American Revolution in 1890, and the Society of Mayflower Descendants in 1894.

4. That important institution for socialization, the exclusive country day school and boarding school, experienced its most rapid growth in the last two decades of the nineteenth century. Andover and Exeter, established in the eighteenth century, and St. Paul's, established before the Civil War, experienced their greatest growth in these decades. They were joined by Groton in 1884, Taft in 1890, Hotchkiss in 1892, Choate in 1896, and approximately seventy other similar schools. Among the exclusive suburban day schools established at the same time are Browne and Nichols (1883) in Cambridge, Massachusetts, and Haverford (1884) and Chestnut Hill (1895) in Philadelphia.

5. The development of exclusive suburban residential areas, initiated by the opening of Tuxedo Park, New York, in 1886, ushered in a flight from the city on the part of the upper class.

6. Graduates of the exclusive lower schools attended high-prestige universities (Yale, Princeton, and Harvard) of, in those decades, somewhat indifferent quality. We must add that there is now a circuit of high (and medium) quality liberal arts colleges and universities, primarily in the north-

7. E. Digby Baltzell, *The Protestant Establishment: Aristocracy and Caste in America* (New York: Random House, 1964), also in paperback.
8. *Ibid.*, chap. 5.

eastern United States, to complete the educational careers of upper class men and women.

7. *The Social Register,* first published in 1887 in New York City, soon added listings for many of America's major cities. This widely imitated register, sold by a profit-making publisher, adheres to no established rules for rejection or ejection. It simply lists details about old wealthy families who stay out of trouble and receive no adverse publicity.[9] *The Social Register* probably contributes considerably to facilitating social events and intercity mobility on the part of the upper class.

8. The metropolitan men's club emerged as a potent adjunct to corporate power during the latter part of the nineteenth century. Baltzell, who makes much of the anti-Semitism and anti-Catholicism of all upper class prestige activities, points out that Jews were excluded from clubs (and some Jewish members expelled) at this time. He fails to note, though, that this was probably necessary because Jews were also being systematically excluded from the upper reaches of the business world.

The development of these prestige groups and practices, says Baltzell, helped to unify the upper class both locally and throughout the metropolitan United States, and in time produced a national upper class. The unity of this upper class results from common socialization; intermarriage; frequent interaction in clubs and resorts, and at parties; and trusteeships of such prestige organizations as schools, clubs, resort associations, and the like. The possibility that the upper class is or could become a dominant stratum does not concern Baltzell, who believes that every society needs a "representative establishment," or an elite that is also an aristocracy — that is, an establishment that represents talent in the spheres of class and power, and expresses a society's highest values in the prestige realm. Assuming that class and power are open elite systems, Baltzell's main concern is that the upper class practices ethnic-religious and racial exclusion and therefore violates in the prestige dimension the moral universalism that should accompany the open merit system of the class and power dimensions. Baltzell is hopeful, given leadership by elite elements of the upper class, that these practices will be abandoned, the upper class will again become a representative establishment, and the United States will cease being a "caste-ridden, open class" system.

Baltzell's evolutionary liberalism pervades his work, and is particularly evident in his failure to see deep connections between the castelike nature of upper class prestige patterns and the protection of class and power interests and privileges. This is not the case with two theorists who have benefited from Baltzell's analysis of upper class prestige practices and have incorporated it

9. Baltzell's analysis of *The Social Register* and comparison of it with *Who's Who in America* may be found in his *Philadelphia Gentlemen* (also titled *An American Business Aristocracy*), chap. 2, and in essay form in " 'Who's Who in America' and 'The Social Register': Elite and Upper Class Indexes in Metropolitan America" in *Class, Status, and Power: Social Stratification in Comparative Perspective,* 2nd ed., ed. Reinhard Bendix and Seymour M. Lipset (New York: Free Press, 1966), pp. 266–275.

into their radical analyses of the American class system. C. Wright Mills treats the foregoing prestige practices as devices to unify the elites who control the apexes of the economic, political, and military orders. As such, these prestige practices are integral features of the United States' power elite, the tiny group of men and families Mills believes to control the nation's basic decisions.[10]

G. William Domhoff, pursuing the approach established by Mills and others, developed a set of social indicators to more positively identify members of the upper class (and has thereby helped to update Baltzell's prestige analysis). According to Domhoff, a male can be considered to belong to the upper class:

1. if he is listed in an edition of *The Social Register* or one of its counterparts.

2. if he, his father, brothers, or father-in-law attended an exclusive prep school.

3. if he, his father, brothers, or father-in-law belongs to an exclusive club.

4. if his sister, wife, mother, or mother-in-law attended an exclusive school or belongs to an exclusive club.

5. if his or his wife's father was a millionaire entrepreneur or $100,000-a-year corporation executive or corporation lawyer *and* if he or she attended any of several private schools or belongs to certain clubs.[11]

Domhoff also offers an interesting analysis of the socialization of upper class women and their leadership of voluntary and reform groups — groups that help to stabilize society and enhance the prestige of the upper class.[12] In addition, he analyzes upper class control of prestigious research and public-interest organizations and their impact on foreign and domestic policymaking.[13]

Mills' view that the United States is dominated by a power elite (and Domhoff's view that we are dominated by a ruling class) will concern us again later. The evidence, however, makes one thing certain: the various elites at the apex of a centralized economy and state have developed prestige groups that provide them with a common psychology and a means to coordinate and protect their interests, values, and privileges. In sum, while the American upper class has not been able to elicit national consensus on its prestige superiority, it has managed in practice to establish formidable prestige barriers between itself and the general public. These barriers support a set of benefits that are enjoyed in their own right, are aped by and thus help to divide and co-opt the classes below them, and above all, protect the economic and political power of this class from being diluted by the free play of economic and political forces. Whether or not the upper class is the dominant stratum in America, these prestige values and practices are essential to the formation and maintenance of its extraordinary wealth and power.

10. This is the theme of Mills' discussion of prestige in *The Power Elite* (New York: Oxford University Press, 1956), chap. 3.

11. G. William Domhoff, *The Higher Circles: The Governing Class in America* (New York: Random House, 1970), chap. 1, also in paperback.

12. *Ibid.*, chap. 2.

13. *Ibid.*, chaps. 5 and 6.

Associational segregation by race, religion, and ethnicity

Associational segregation by race, religion, and national origin is one of the most significant aspects of American prestige group life. The associational segregation of blacks as an aftermath of slavery needs no introduction. However, the pervasive segregation of America's immigrant groups (both "racial" and ethnic-religious groups) requires a word of explanation.

Native-born Americans expressed two responses when confronted with large-scale immigration during and after the latter half of the nineteenth century. The dominant theory of assimilation ("Anglo-conformity") was that immigrants should give up their native cultures and adopt the English-American way of life. The melting pot theory was that native-born Americans and immigrants should merge biologically and socioculturally to forge a new American identity.[14] As Milton M. Gordon has shown, neither of these theories, nor the theory of cultural pluralism advocated by some minority groups, has prevailed. The United States did succeed in assimilating most immigrant groups culturally (language, diet, dress, manner, and general economic and political beliefs and values). On the whole, ethnic groups have tended to abandon their native languages (Spanish-speaking groups are an important exception), and their commitments to familistic values and to their countries of origin have no doubt become diluted. Above all, most foreign-born and second-generation white ethnic groups have entered the American occupational and educational system and have enjoyed rates of upward social mobility that compared favorably, as of 1962, with those of native-born whites.[15]

But if one considers types of assimilation other than cultural assimilation, and compares racial as well as ethnic-religious groups (see Table 10-1), the story is somewhat different. With regard to primary group behavior (structural and marital assimilation), there has been little assimilation (see Table 10-2). The United States is not a unitary melting pot, argues Gordon, or even a "triple melting pot" (Protestant, Roman Catholic, and Jewish), but a multiple melting pot divided on religious, ethnic, and racial grounds. (Gordon argues that intellectuals also form an associational system.) With regard to associational life,

14. These views are analyzed in Milton M. Gordon's excellent theoretical study, *Assimilation in American Life: The Role of Race, Religion, and National Origin* (New York: Oxford University Press, 1964), chaps. 4 and 5, also in paperback.
15. Peter M. Blau and Otis Dudley Duncan, *The American Occupational Structure* (New York: John Wiley and Sons, 1967), pp. 227–238. Assimilation varies among types of immigrant groups. Donald J. Bogue, *The Population of the United States* (New York: Free Press, 1959), in his analysis of assimilation using 1950 census data, reports that most immigrant groups (including immigrants from Japan, China, and the Philippines) show more or less substantial improvement in socioeconomic status between first and second generations. The striking exception is Mexican Americans (pp. 366–374). The continued sharp difference in socioeconomic status between Mexican Americans and other immigrant groups in 1960 may be seen in U.S. Bureau of the Census, *U.S. Census of Population: 1960. Subject Reports. Socioeconomic Status*, Final Report PC(2)-5c (Washington: D.C.: U.S. Government Printing Office, 1967), Tables 3 and 5.

Table 10-1 Gordon's Typology of Assimilation Variables

Subprocess or condition	Type or stage of assimilation	Special term
Change of cultural patterns to those of host society	Cultural or behavioral assimilation	Acculturation
Large-scale entrance into cliques, clubs, and institutions of host society, on primary group level	Structural assimilation	None
Large-scale intermarriage	Marital assimilation	Amalgamation[a]
Development of sense of peoplehood based exclusively on host society	Identificational assimilation	None
Absence of prejudice	Attitude receptional assimilation	None
Absence of discrimination	Behavior receptional assimilation	None
Absence of value and power conflict	Civic assimilation	None

a. My use of the term here is not predicated on the diversity in race of the two population groups which are intermarrying and interbreeding. With increasing understanding of the meaning of "race" and its thoroughly relative and arbitrary nature as a scientific term, this criterion becomes progressively less important. We may speak of the "amalgamation" or intermixture of the two "gene pools" which the two populations represent, regardless of how similar or divergent these two gene pools may be.

SOURCE: From *Assimilation in American Life: The Role of Race, Religion, and National Origins* by Milton M. Gordon (New York: Oxford University Press, 1964), Table 5, p. 71. Copyright © 1964 by Oxford University Press, Inc. Reprinted by permission.

therefore, the implications are clear: the United States exhibits *structural pluralism*, or multiple associational systems along primary religious, ethnic, and racial lines.

At first, prestige differentiation and discrimination in the United States, along with the facts of economic and political life, created clusters of "ethnic communities": separate churches, social clubs, philanthropic organizations, residential areas, and schools; ethnic cultural activities; foreign-language newspapers; and specialized forms of economic life were salient characteristics of first-generation ethnic groups. But the virtual institutional self-sufficiency of ethnic communities gradually disintegrated. In response to the impact of public education and economic mobility, ethnic groups severed ties with the past (illustrated by the decline of foreign-language newspapers), and began to exhibit class differentials among themselves. Thus, to the extent that Irish Americans are rich, middle rich, and poor, and high, middle, and low on the occupational and educational ladders (class differences), they are less likely than before to

Table 10-2 Gordon's Paradigm of Assimilation Applied to Selected Groups in the United States — Basic Goal Referent: Adaptation to Core Society and Culture

Group	Cultural[a] Assimilation	Structural Assimilation	Marital Assimilation	Identificational[c] Assimilation	Attitude Receptional Assimilation	Behavior Receptional Assimilation	Civic Assimilation
Negroes	Variation by class[b]	No	No	No	No	No	Yes
Jews	Substantially yes	No	Substantially no	No	No	Partly	Mostly
Catholics (excluding Negro and Spanish-speaking)	Substantially yes	Partly (variation by area)	Partly	No	Partly	Mostly	Partly[d]
Puerto Ricans	Mostly no	No	No	No	No	No	Partly

a. Some reciprocal cultural influences have, of course, taken place. American language, diet, recreational patterns, art forms, and economic techniques have been modestly influenced by the cultures of non-Anglo-Saxon resident groups since the first contacts with the American Indians, and the American culture is definitely the richer for these influences. However, the reciprocal influences have not been great. See George R. Stewart, *American Ways of Life*, New York, Doubleday and Co., 1954, and our [Gordon's] further discussion on this subject. Furthermore, the minority ethnic groups have not given up all their pre-immigration cultural patterns. Particularly, they have preserved their non-Protestant religions. I have thus used the phrase "Substantially yes" to indicate this degree of adaptation.

b. Although few, if any, African cultural survivals are to be found among American Negroes, lower-class Negro life with its derivations from slavery, post-Civil War discrimination, both rural and urban poverty, and enforced isolation from the middle-class white world, is still at a considerable distance from the American cultural norm. Middle and upper-class Negroes, on the other hand, are acculturated to American core culture.

c. Identification in a modern complex society may contain several "layers." My point is not that Negroes, Jews, and Catholics in the United States do not think of themselves as Americans. They do. It is that they also have an "inner layer" sense of peoplehood which is Negro, Jewish, or Catholic, as the case may be, and not "white Protestant" or "white, Anglo-Saxon Protestant," which is the corresponding inner layer of ethnic identity of the core society.

d. Value and power conflict of Catholics with a large portion of the rest of the American population over such issues as birth control, divorce, therapeutic abortion, and church-state relationships constitute the reason for the entry of "partly" here.

SOURCE: From *Assimilation in American Life: The Role of Race, Religion, and National Origins* by Milton M. Gordon (New York: Oxford University Press, 1964), Table 6, pp. 76–77. Copyright © 1964 by Oxford University Press, Inc. Reprinted by permission.

live together, intermarry, and belong to the same clubs or other voluntary organizations.

The structural melting-down of ethnic groups is prevented, at least in part, by the power of religion. Ethnic and religious discrimination has no doubt also played a part: ethnic groups have not always been able to translate their class positions into prestige or power. In any case, there is still a strong tendency for ethnic groups to maintain separate primary and secondary organizations. There is also a continuing tendency, resulting both from habit and from the effects of discrimination, for ethnic groups to occupy specialized niches in the American economy. And the political realities of gerrymandering and residential concentration tend to give ethnic groups almost official roles in the political life of many localities. But while this state of affairs gives ethnic groups an important means to protect their interests at the local political level, the ethnic basis of local politics, when and where it exists, tends to reinforce the segregation of such groups and to dilute their numerical representation — though not necessarily their political power — at the national level.

We shall now analyze what we know about prestige groups in a more systematic manner and relate it to class. We will discuss primary and secondary prestige behavior separately, and, in keeping with a salient feature of the American class system, subdivide each along religious-ethnic and "racial" lines.

Primary prestige groups
Class and primary behavior

Primary relations (groups) are forms of interaction that usually occur face-to-face, have diffused emotional-moral content, and involve the entire personality in an enduring web of obligations and rights. Friendship, love, marriage, family, neighborhood interaction, as well as dining and certain other forms of socializing, all belong in this category. The fact that primary relations seem normal and spontaneous should not mislead us about their social nature or their relation to the prevailing system of stratification. Class society, no less than estate and caste societies, is characterized by class-related prestige groups that control the basic forms of primary interaction.[16] We know in a general way that class factors play an important role in determining marriage and eating partners, as well as place of residence and membership in clubs.

Though many stratification analysts have long been intrigued by the role of clubs in stratification inequality, no systematic study has been undertaken. Of all the classic empirical studies, perhaps the most systematic, and certainly the most informative, is August B. Hollingshead's *Elmtown's Youth*. Hollingshead found distinctive types of clubs and club affiliations for each of Elmtown's five classes.[17] For their part, E. Digby Baltzell and G. William Domhoff have

16. The classic analyses of social stratification in small-town America contain a wealth of information about the class basis of primary behavior.
17. August B. Hollingshead, *Elmtown's Youth: The Impact of Social Classes on Adolescents* (New York: John Wiley and Sons, 1949), chap. 5.

examined upper class clubs.[18] Though a good deal is known about clubs, much has to be conjectured. It would not be amiss, however, to assume that the exclusive urban men's clubs offer basic psychic benefits in their own right and are important adjuncts of the business world as well. The simplest and most direct clue to the latter relation is that it appears to be common practice for businesses to pay the club dues of their executives. High-prestige clubs of all types often have annual fees and dues that amount to thousands of dollars, and as such obviously represent an exclusiveness based on price (class). There is also an obvious and fairly specific class factor (old wealth) in the membership of exclusive men's clubs: Duquesne (Pittsburgh), Detroit (Detroit), Union, Knickerbocker, Brook, Racquet and Tennis, Century, Union League, Metropolitan, and University (New York), and so on. There are also elite women's clubs such as Colony (New York), Friday (Chicago), Chilton (Boston), and Acorn (Philadelphia). Patriotic-historical-genealogical societies are by definition limited to members of old families (often possessing old wealth).

Class content is also obvious in the membership of country clubs and resorts, some of which are restricted to old wealth, some to wealth, and others of which cater to the middle classes at large. Service clubs such as the Kiwanis and Rotary are anchored in the world of business and the professions, while fraternal orders and lodges and veterans' groups, such as the Elks, Shriners, and American Legion, appear to be largely lower-middle and working class in composition. An interesting new form of primary interaction (in a commercial setting) is the singles club and bar, and the singles weekend at resorts. Though little researched, it is highly likely that this is a primarily middle class activity. In sum, primary relations have a pronounced class basis: fundamentally, only class peers engage in primary or intimate forms of interaction.

One must add that there also exists a relatively sharp qualitative discontinuity by class in the *kind* of primary relations Americans enter into. Working class Americans tend to have fewer friends, entertain less, and belong less to clubs and other organizations devoted to entertainment and companionship than the classes above.[19] And working class marriages and family life provide fewer

18. E. Digby Baltzell, *The Protestant Establishment: Aristocracy and Caste in America* (New York: Random House, 1964), chap. 16, also in paperback; G. William Domhoff, *Who Rules America?* (Englewood Cliffs, N.J.: Prentice-Hall, 1967), chap. 1, available in paperback; and *The Higher Circles: The Governing Class in America* (New York: Random House, 1970), chaps. 1 and 4, also in paperback.

19. For a review of the literature in this area within the context of role theory, see the excellent article by Alan F. Blum, "Social Structure, Social Class and Participation in Primary Relationships," in *Blue-Collar World: Studies of the American Worker,* ed. Arthur B. Shostak and William Gomberg (Englewood Cliffs, N.J.: Prentice-Hall, 1964), pp. 195–207, also in paperback.

For a valuable start toward understanding primary associational structures in our urban-suburban life, see Edward O. Laumann, *Prestige and Association in an Urban Community: An Analysis of an Urban Stratification System* (Indianapolis: Bobbs-Merrill, 1966). Laumann, who used both old and new empirical techniques to study Cambridge and Belmont in the Boston metropolitan area, found a considerable relation between occupation and intimate (primary) relationships, especially friendship, and a more pronounced relation at the top and bottom levels.

and lower-quality satisfactions than characterize those of the classes above. And below the working class is an underclass that experiences deep social isolation, since members of this class do not engage much in either primary or secondary behavior.

As we have suggested, families in similar class positions are not necessarily eligible for primary group relations. The age and source of a family's wealth are important differentiating factors. Primary relations are also affected by forms of consumption: since consumption skills and interests can vary within a given class, individuals and families having similar class positions may enjoy different levels and types of primary interaction. The best-known distinction is between the old rich and the new rich, but such distinctions are applicable at all class levels. However, while style of life (consumption) can be independent of class, it invariably succumbs to class; in other words, given time, an economic position can and does acquire the prestige credentials needed for inclusion in primary prestige groups. It was inevitable, in other words, that Mrs. Astor (old real estate wealth) would call on Mrs. Vanderbilt (new railroad wealth). And, of course, primary relations between families and individuals with similar class positions are strongly differentiated by religion, ethnicity, and "race" — but this issue is best discussed separately.

Class and religious-ethnic primary behavior

Each of the major religious groups — Protestants, Roman Catholics, and Jews — is characterized by unique forms of primary interaction, which are further differentiated by ethnicity. Thus residence, friendship, marriage, forms and functions of family life, socializing at home and in clubs, and worship all tend to take place within the boundaries of religious-ethnic identification. But each of these three religious-ethnic groups is also differentiated internally by class-structured forms of primary relations. Milton Gordon has suggested the term *ethclass* to refer to this behavioral reality:

> The ethnic group is the locus of a sense of *historical identification*, while the ethclass is the locus of a sense of *participational* identification. With a person of the same social class but of a different ethnic group, one shares behavioral similarities but not a sense of peoplehood. With those of the same ethnic group but of a different social class, one shares the sense of peoplehood but not behavior similarities. The only group which meets both of these criteria are people of the same ethnic group *and* the same social class.[20]

Accordingly, there is an upper, middle, and (broadly speaking) lower class type of club and pattern of friendship, marriage, and "church" orientation within each of the broad categories of Protestant, Roman Catholic, and Jew.

20. Milton M. Gordon, *Assimilation in American Life: The Role of Race, Religion, and National Origin* (New York: Oxford University Press, 1964), p. 53; also in paperback.

There is ample documentation of religious-ethnic segregation by class (eth-class) at the primary group level. The classic analyses of social stratification in small-town America do not all offer comparable materials on the primary behavior of ethnic-religious groups, since many of the communities studied were relatively homogeneous. Two studies that stress ethnic-religious segregation in primary (as well as secondary) behavior are Anderson's study of Burlington, Vermont,[21] and, of course, the study of Newburyport, Massachusetts, by Warner and his associates.[22]

Both segregation by ethnicity-religion and the differentiation of segregated groups by class characterize our two representative religious-ethnic groups, Jewish and Mexican Americans. Jewish Americans appear to have continuing strong primary relations largely among themselves. The legendary Jewish family is a source of rich interaction and strength. While the rate of intermarriage with non-Jews has risen, it appears not to threaten the Jewish family. Overwhelmingly, Jews tend to marry Jews and to have Jewish relatives. And Jews tend strongly to have Jewish friends.[23] The involvement of Jews in strong communal forms of religious observance, however, appears to have declined. Jews also have their own social clubs, resorts, and fraternal organizations, largely as a result of explicit and systematic ascriptive discrimination. Remember that non-Jews still believe in excluding Jews from clubs, and that the best educated are the strongest believers. Speaking generally, segregated Jewish primary prestige groups are attributable to the strength and vitality of Judaism; the legacy of persecution and discrimination in employment, residence, and elsewhere; and the attainment of middle class status.

The impact of class on Jewish primary behavior is twofold. Their success in entering the middle and upper-middle class levels has prevented Jewish family life (and other forms of primary behavior) from being undermined by poverty and occupational marginality. In addition, Jewish primary behavior is affected by the class differentiation that does exist. Upper-level Jews tend to have slightly higher rates of divorce and separation, and there are clubs and resorts that cater to the various classes of Jews.

The social world of the Mexican American is far more varied than it was even a few decades ago, and generalizations about it must be made cautiously.[24] The isolation of the Mexican American in the countryside of the American

21. Elin L. Anderson, *We Americans: A Study of Cleavage in an American City* (Cambridge, Mass.: Harvard University Press, 1937).
22. W. Lloyd Warner and Leo Srole, *The Social Systems of American Ethnic Groups* (New Haven: Yale University Press, 1945). This text, Volume 3 of the Yankee City series, is (despite its title) restricted to Newburyport, a city of 17,000.
23. For Jewish friendship patterns, see Gerhard Lenski, *The Religious Factor: A Sociological Study of Religion's Impact on Politics, Economics, and Family Life,* rev. ed. (Garden City, N.Y.: Doubleday, 1963), p. 37.
24. For the following, see Leo Grebler, Joan W. Moore, Ralph G. Guzman *et al.,* *The Mexican-American People: The Nation's Second Largest Minority* (New York: Free Press, 1970), chaps. 16, 17, and 18.

southwest has ended: Mexican Americans have abandoned their castelike positions in rural areas and are now largely members of the urban working and lower classes.

As we noted earlier, the Mexican American family is not as stable as is widely believed. Familism is strong as an ideal, but the harsh realities of poverty have left their mark. And yet the family is still a focal point of Mexican American life, since other forms of primary behavior are lacking. As we will see, Mexican Americans have been unable to develop supportive networks of voluntary groups and have received very little help from government.

In a wide range of primary and secondary relationships, including friends, schoolmates, parish members, and associates at work, there has been a shift away from exclusive association with Mexican Americans both by generation and class.[25] And intermarriage rates are higher than expected, a greater propensity to leave the ethnic fold in this important area of primary behavior characterizing higher class levels.[26]

Class and "racial" primary behavior

It seems best to treat class and "racial" forms of primary behavior separately. Despite the strength of religious-ethnic values and beliefs among whites, there is still enough social and moral elbow-room for members of various religious-ethnic groups to mix (or even to "pass") to make it necessary to distinguish this form of segregation from racial segregation. In the aggregate, American whites and blacks (and Indians, Orientals, and other groups whose skin color is not white) simply do not mix on a primary, or even a secondary, basis.[27] Thus residence, intermarriage, friendship, and socializing at home, in clubs, or at church (even within a given religion) are all sharply bounded by lines based on color and impervious to equality in class.[28] Primary relations among our representative "racial" group, black Americans, do not compare favorably with the primary relations of the rest of the population, primarily because of the historic disorganization of the black family. As we have pointed out, the economically marginal black male has historically played a passive role in his family; he is often entirely estranged. There also appears to be a sharper estrangement between the sexes among blacks, though this is not uncommon in American, and especially in working class, life. The relation between parents and children in economically marginal or depressed black families differs markedly from that of stable families. The absence of adult role models makes for a different form of socialization and means that black children at this

25. *Ibid.*, chap. 17.
26. *Ibid.*, chap. 18.
27. Even death does not unite the "races" — cemeteries have traditionally been segregated, though the practice is now being modified by legislation and court decisions.
28. Upper class blacks and other "races" tend to mix more with whites than their counterparts lower on the class ladder.

level are highly subject to peer control, often in the form of street gangs. And because of their historically depressed economic position, blacks have been unable to develop kinship networks or communal groups to help them face their problems or to provide capital for economic needs and endeavors.[29]

Black American primary relations are also differentiated internally by class. As is true of whites, upper-level blacks enjoy more stable family lives (though not as stable as those of whites at similar class levels), belong to more clubs, and participate in a greater variety of social events than lower-level blacks.[30]

Secondary prestige groups
Class and power and secondary (voluntary) behavior

Secondary interaction involves only a portion of an individual's personality and tends to be functionally specific and emotionally neutral: seeing a doctor, getting on a bus, going to school, working in an office or factory, going to church, voting, being on trial, serving on a committee, joining an interest group, going to the park or a ball game or a restaurant or a movie, and joining a trade union or professional association are all examples of secondary interaction.

Two national studies have clearly established that membership in voluntary organizations correlates with every index of class (income, occupation, education) and that there is a correlation between class and the types of associations Americans belong to.[31] There is not only a relation between class and voluntary participation, but also a sharp difference between the middle and upper classes on the one hand, and the working and lower classes on the other. Indeed, the working and lower classes engage in so little voluntary secondary behavior that one must conclude that qualitatively different life experiences divide these two segments of American society. Not only is the United States not a nation of joiners — excluding trade unions and churches, it is doubtful that even half of the adult American population belongs to a secondary organization — but the evidence clearly indicates that the American social system tends to restrict and routinize the experience of its working and lower classes.[32]

29. For an analysis of the weak primary group development of blacks relative to economic development contrasted with the strong development of economically relevant primary behavior among Japanese and Chinese immigrants, see Ivan H. Light, *Ethnic Enterprise in America: Business and Welfare Among Chinese, Japanese, and Blacks* (Berkeley: University of California Press, 1972).
30. The primary relations of upper-level blacks depicted in E. Franklin Frazier, *Black Bourgeoisie* (New York: Free Press, 1957), chap. 9 can be contrasted fruitfully with the primary relations among lower-level blacks depicted in Elliot Liebow, *Tally's Corner: A Study of Negro Streetcorner Men* (Boston: Little, Brown, 1967).
31. See the valuable secondary analysis by Murray Hausknecht, *The Joiners* (Totowa, N.J.: Bedminster, 1962).
32. There is also evidence that, in addition to relying on family and friends for most of its interaction experience, the working class does not travel as widely as the classes above it, and that its participation in the thought-life of the nation is qualitatively lower than the classes above it. The amount and quality of moral, intellectual, and artistic enrichment is even lower among the lower class.

Participation in secondary prestige groups is a well-known way in which the upper classes exert influence over important activities (outside of class and power) and an important source of moral, intellectual, and aesthetic prestige. It is also a way in which upwardly mobile families establish their claims to full inclusion in a higher social stratum. Of some interest in this connection is Aileen Ross' classic analysis of philanthropic activity in Montreal, in which she found a well-institutionalized relation between business roles and roles in philanthropic fund-raising. Large business firms routinely use fund drives to test the abilities of young executives; and they are quite aware that their participation in such drives is a means to acquire a favorable public image.[33] The ties betweeen the upper levels of the business and professional worlds and institutions of higher education are well documented. We also have considerable documentation of the upper and upper-middle class base of foundations, prestigious research institutes, hospitals, cultural groups, and voluntary organizations in general.

While secondary organizations are primarily middle and upper class groups, the class composition of particular organizations varies. Though data are scarce and often impressionistic, it is clear, for example, that cultural groups like museum or symphony orchestra boards have different class memberships than parent-teachers associations, and that various shades of upper and middle class membership characterize the Rotary, the Kiwanis, the Elks, the Masons, the Young Men's Christian Association, the Democratic and Republican parties, the Red Cross, the American Cancer Society, the American Bar Association, the American Sociological Association, and so on. There is also wide variation by class in type of church and church membership; this matter is best discussed separately, since it touches on differences based on religion and ethnicity.

Any sharp distinction between the dimensions of prestige and power must be fallacious, since the traditional distinction between the private and public sectors has been badly blurred by the dynamics of mature industrialization. Actually, the separation of these spheres was never as complete as we sometimes imagine. For example, the property and income of religious, charitable, and educational organizations have traditionally (and in the case of religion, constitutionally) been exempt from taxation. This practice indicates a broad consensus on the value of such activities, and the exemption from taxation of our churches, foundations, and institutions of higher education is contingent on their political neutrality.

One of the more portentous aspects of the relation between government and the private sector of voluntary organizations is the growth of government by grant and contract.[34] In recent decades, the federal government and lesser

33. Aileen D. Ross, "Philanthropic Activity and the Business Career," *Social Forces* 32 (March 1954): 274–285.
34. The significance of this development was noted by Alan Pifer, president of the Carnegie Corporation, in two essays, "The Nongovernmental Organization at Bay" (New York: Carnegie Corporation *Annual Report,* 1966), and "The Quasi-

governments have sought to achieve a host of purposes by contracting with established private groups such as the National Urban League or the Young Men's Christian Association or financing new organizations to render intellectual and scientific services at home and abroad. ("Not-for-profit corporations" provide advisory and technical services to the military, the Atomic Energy Commission, the Department of State, the Central Intelligence Agency, and so on.) This trend has made many traditional voluntary organizations dependent on government for financing, creating a new type of quasi-voluntary group. As Alan Pifer points out, the trend toward government by contract and grant has important implications for the autonomy of private bodies and poses problems of accountability.[35]

In addition, the federal government has begun large-scale funding of medical, scientific, and educational undertakings, often funneling public monies through "nonpolitical" conduits like the National Science Foundation. In the case of education, institutions of higher education (including private and religious schools) have received direct governmental grants for construction, special programs, research, and (with the Higher Education Act of 1972) normal operation.

The trend toward public institutions of higher education also represents a way in which power is explicitly engaged in serving class values in the realm of prestige.[36] This process also characterizes the many areas in which power endorses the right of private or "public" organizations to certify individuals for high-level occupations and to enforce regulations controlling the behavior of their members (for example, the American Medical Association, the National Association of Securities Dealers, the American Bar Association).

Still another way to examine the interrelatedness of our class-prestige-power systems is to trace the pattern of overlapping personnel and policies in the areas of research, reform, and public policy formation. Presidential and congressional commissions are composed of high-level representatives of various segments of the economy and the professions; and private foundations, associations, and institutes (such as the Committtee on Economic Development, the Rockefeller and Ford Foundations, the Brookings Institution, the Council on Foreign Relations, and the Twentieth Century Fund) cultivate images of public disinterestedness and develop highly influential policy proposals in the realms of business, education, population, foreign policy, medicine, the arts, race relations, and the like.

It is interesting to note the way in which women have been induced to perform class roles in voluntary groups. Women are prominent in voluntary

---

Nongovernmental Organization" (New York: Carnegie Corporation *Annual Report,* 1967).

35. Pifer does not mention that consulting firms that make policy recommendations to government are in a unique position to further the interests of their other clients.

36. For a discussion of the way in which public institutions of higher education subsidize the middle and upper classes, see Chapter 13.

activities of all kinds, activities that correlate closely with class background.[37]

A final noteworthy aspect of the relation between class, power, and prestige is the invasion (redefinition?) of privacy (prestige) by agencies of both class and power: credit organizations probe into the economic and moral worth of individuals; private and public agencies use electronic eavesdropping devices (legally and illegally) to gain information about individuals and organizations; and agencies of the government infiltrate and co-opt private organizations (examples are the co-optation of the leadership of the National Student Association and several intellectual journals by the Central Intelligence Agency in the 1960s, and the infiltration of numerous political organizations by the Federal Bureau of Investigation in the 1970s). In sum, it is clear that the entire realm of secondary prestige groups (along with consumption and primary group behavior) represents an adjunct to economic and political power. It is through various secondary prestige activities that a vital moral and intellectual cement is applied to the overall structure of American inequality. And secondary prestige groups are as narrowly based, unresponsive, and backward in their procedures and policies as corporate and governmental bureaucracies.[38] The function, largely latent, of secondary prestige groups can perhaps be stated more simply: by deflecting attention away from the class (and power) basis of America's social problems, such groups help to preserve the status quo.

Class and religious-ethnic secondary behavior

A great deal of secondary behavior is marked by religious-ethnic segregation, some forced and some self-imposed. By and large, religion and ethnicity are ascriptive forces; children inherit the religion and ethnic identity of their parents, as well as a wide range of interactional experience: worship, the discussion of moral and public issues within a sacred context, and opportunities to participate in charity drives, parochial school education, church-based or related youth groups, men's and women's auxiliaries, hospitals, nursing and retirement homes, credit unions, and intellectual-reform groups.

The concept of ethclass also encompasses this form of group behavior, since religious-ethnic secondary behavior is also differentiated by class. A classic analysis pointing to the dual nature of voluntary behavior is Hollingshead's study of the Junior League in New Haven. Hollingshead found a major trend toward "the development of parallel class structures within the limits of race, ethnic origin, and religion" citing:

> the fact that there are seven different Junior Leagues in the white segment of the community for appropriate affiliated upper class young women. The

37. For a pioneering analysis of the voluntary behavior of upper class women, see G. William Domhoff, *The Higher Circles: The Governing Class in America* (New York: Random House, 1970), chap. 2; also in paperback.
38. For an able defense of private foundations as providing more flexibility, variety, and innovative daring than government, see the report of The Commission on Foundations and Private Philanthropy, Chairman Peter G. Peterson, *Foundations, Private Giving, and Public Policy* (Chicago: University of Chicago Press, 1970).

top ranking organization is the New Haven Junior League which draws its membership from "Old Yankee" Protestant families whose daughters have been educated in private schools. The Catholic Charity League is next in rank and age — its membership is drawn from Irish-American families. In addition to this organization there are Italian and Polish Junior Leagues within the Catholic division of the society. The Swedish and Danish Junior Leagues are for properly connected young women in these ethnic groups, but they are Protestants. Then too, the upper class Jewish families have their Junior League. The Negroes have a Junior League for their top-drawer young women. This principle of parallel structures for a given class level, by religious, ethnic and racial groups, proliferates throughout the community.[39]

The three worlds of Protestantism, Roman Catholicism, and Judaism are a stable feature of associational behavior in the United States. But churches are not immune to the dynamics of class stratification. Each of the three major religions in the United States is heavily differentiated by class. Among Protestants, the upper classes tend to prefer Episcopalian, Congregational, Presbyterian, and Unitarian forms of worship, while the lower classes tend to be Methodist and Baptist.[40] Roman Catholicism has been associated with the working class for much of American history, though less so in recent decades. Internally, Roman Catholicism is less clearly divided by class lines than Protestantism, though there are de facto class lines based on residence. More characteristic of Roman Catholicism is the "national parish," or differentiation by ethnic group: Irish, French Canadian, Italian, Spanish-speaking, and so on. However, there is some evidence that the "national parish" is slowly declining in prevalence.

There is a definite relation between class and branches of Judaism. The Conservative branch of Judaism, which broke with Orthodox Judaism at the beginning of this century, has been interpreted as a response to middle class experience. Reform Judaism, a legacy from Germany, is quite similar to liberal Protestantism and is associated with middle class Jews.

The associational behavior patterns of our two religious-ethnic minority groups are markedly different. Both have derived strength and support from organized religion. Jewish religious organizations, though they have declined in relative importance in recent decades, have performed valuable adaptive functions for immigrant Jews confronting an alien environment. The Roman Catholic Church, which has played a vital role in helping a variety of ethnic groups to adapt to American life, has not performed that function for Mexican Americans. Short of resources and clergy, lacking an English-speaking clergy, and dispersed over vast rural areas, the Roman Catholic Church in the southwest is markedly dissimilar to the English-speaking, Irish-led, and politically skilled Church in other parts of the country.[41]

The same contrast is apparent in other areas of secondary voluntary life. Due

39. August B. Hollingshead, "Trends in Social Stratification: A Case Study," *American Sociological Review* 17 (December 1952): 679–686. Used by permission.
40. Churches in the south have traditionally practiced open segregation by race as well.
41. Grebler *et al., The Mexican-American People,* chap. 19.

to their urban concentration and rise in class position, Jewish Americans have had the human and material resources to develop a large and vital network of groups to support Jewish and community values: charity and service groups of all kinds, groups supporting Zionism, civil rights groups like B'nai B'rith, and the like. In addition, Jews have been active in political life and in the trade union movement. Given the lower and working class status and rural isolation of Mexican Americans, it is not surprising that they have developed few voluntary groups. In this respect, they are worse off than black Americans, who, for various reasons (including help from whites), have had a more viable network of voluntary organizations to help them cope with a hostile environment.

Sentiments of ethnic solidarity are still strong among Mexican Americans. Their political participation is low, though not abnormally so given their aggregate class position, and they favor the Democratic party by an overwhelming percentage. Mexican Americans also overwhelmingly reject a political coalition with black Americans.[42] This attitude, together with Mexican American prejudice against blacks,[43] forestalls cooperation between the two, though they are members of essentially the same classes. Whether the Chicano movement that rose in the 1960s, and which represents a more militant Mexican American stance against economic and political domination by Anglos, can build bridges to the black community remains to be seen.

The historic power of religious-ethnic institutions in the United States is clear. Less clear is how closely Americans still adhere to patterns associated with their religious-ethnic groups of birth.[44] Much of the data is tangential, and much of it is old and focused on small communities. An important recent study comparing three generations of Jewish Americans in Providence, Rhode Island, indicates that the present generation is less likely than its forebears to belong to Jewish organizations and more likely to belong to non-Jewish organizations (especially among college-educated Jews living in the suburbs).[45]

Class and racial secondary behavior

Despite some weakening of the rigid barriers between the white and nonwhite "races," it is still best to discuss racial segregation in secondary groups separately from religious-ethnic segregation. Black Americans do not as a rule belong to white secondary organizations, largely because of class factors — membership in secondary organizations is a middle and upper class phenomenon, and few blacks enjoy such class status (due, it must always be remem-

42. *Ibid.*, chaps. 22 and 23.
43. *Ibid.*, pp. 392–394.
44. We know that Protestants tend to participate more in voluntary groups than do Roman Catholics, even holding class constant, and that there appears to be no difference in rates of secondary behavior between foreign-born and native-born Americans; see Hausknecht, *The Joiners*, pp. 51–56.
45. Sidney Goldstein and Calvin Goldscheider, *Jewish Americans: Three Generations in a Jewish Community* (Englewood Cliffs, N.J.: Prentice-Hall, 1968), chap. 10.

bered, to centuries of oppression). Racist exclusion has also prevailed in many areas, forcing black Americans to found their own organizations.[46] Furthermore, blacks have probably believed that their interests would be submerged and their power dissipated if they joined white organizations. Thus, parallel to white secondary organizations there exist all-black clubs, charities, veterans groups, labor unions, and associations of manufacturers, lawyers, doctors, psychiatrists, ministers, bridge players, cowboys, businesspeople, executives, and the like. Of great importance in the history of black Americans is the all-black religious organization. The racially segregated church is as much a part of the history of blacks and whites as the segregated school or waiting room. So too, the all-black college has played a considerable role in the ability of blacks to survive, though all indications point to its relative decline in the near future.

The best-known black organizations are those dedicated to civil rights and politics: the National Association for the Advancement of Colored People (founded in 1909 as an interracial group but now predominantly black), the Southern Christian Leadership Conference, the Student Nonviolent Coordinating Committee, the Congress of Racial Equality (founded in 1942 as an interracial group but soon thereafter predominantly black), and the Black Panthers. Also well-known is the National Urban League (1910) which works mostly to advance the cause of blacks in the economy and in the field of housing.

The secondary behavior of black Americans is not too well researched, though the class basis of black business and occupational groups is obvious. Class is also associated with residential distinctions among blacks,[47] and there are black upper class "society" organizations and events and magazines devoted to reporting black class achievements. The major such magazine, *Ebony,* bears a marked resemblance to *Life* (now defunct) in both format and acceptance of broad middle class values. In short, the concept of ethclass encompasses both primary and secondary behavior among blacks.

Studies of black participation rates in voluntary organizations do not distinguish, as we have done, between primary and secondary groups. Nevertheless, it is interesting that analysts have found blacks to have generally higher rates of overall participation than whites, holding socioeconomic status and age constant. Earlier studies tended to explain the higher rate of black participation by referring to it as a "compensatory" process. Blacks, it was argued, were seeking a refuge from, and a source of satisfaction and prestige apart from, the racist white world.[48] Recent studies have added another dimension to this explanation: the higher rates of black social participation are due, at least in

46. For the exclusion of black Americans from policy-making posts in voluntary organizations (including universities) in Chicago, see Harold M. Baron with Harriet Stulman, Richard Rothstein, and Rennard Davis, "Black Powerlessness in Chicago," *Transaction* 6 (November 1968): 27–33; reprinted in Charles H. Anderson, ed., *Sociological Essays and Research* (Homewood, Ill.: Dorsey Press, 1970), pp. 141–151.

47. Karl E. Taeuber and Alma F. Taeuber, *Negroes in Cities: Residential Segregation and Neighborhood Change* (Chicago: Aldine, 1965), pp. 180–184.

48. Nicholas Babchuk and Ralph V. Thompson, "The Voluntary Association of Negroes," *American Sociological Review* 27 (October 1962): 647–655.

part, to "ethnic" consciousness and community pressure. Blacks have become more conscious of themselves and of the need to organize, which exerts pressure on individuals to become socially active.[49] Of some interest here is the fact that black activism has led to increased contact with the white world. However, we have little data on the success of racially mixed organizations or on trends in this area.

Our most comprehensive and empirically reliable survey of interaction between blacks and whites, based on a stratified sample of 248 cities throughout the United States and conducted during the early 1950s,[50] indicates that secondary interaction was racially segregated in a wide variety of areas, secondary segregation in one or more of the following characterizing particular cities: the Masons, the American Legion, the Young Men's Christian Association, the Chamber of Commerce, barber shops, hotels, and restaurants. Of great significance is the finding that there is no single pattern of segregation in nonsouthern cities. It is not fear of intimacy, the public character of a particular form of interaction, a question of economic threat or gain, the importance of given facilities or services, or a question of their relevance for power. The only explanation for racial segregation in nonsouthern cities (aside from America's pervasive morality of racism) is historical accident: particular individuals, businesses, and groups established segregated interaction in particular areas and the practice simply became custom. The authors suggest that such segregation can be eradicated much more easily than can the all-inclusive, castelike forms of segregation that characterize southern cities.

The relation between class (and power) and prestige groups: a summary

The United States has an enormously varied array of both primary and secondary prestige groups. There is a distinct class basis to both types of prestige behavior, and a distinct segregation of prestige behavior by ethnicity, religion, and "race." The major function of prestige behavior appears to be to maintain existing class and ethnic-religious-"racial" (and political-legal) inequalities.

The major patterns in prestige group activity (which can be defined broadly to include forms of consumption, education, and use of leisure in general) appear to be:

49. Marvin E. Olsen, "Social and Political Participation of Blacks," *American Sociological Review* 35 (August 1970): 682–697; J. Allen Williams, Jr., Nicholas Babchuk, and David R. Johnson, "Voluntary Associations and Minority Status: A Comparative Analysis of Anglo, Black, and Mexican Americans," *American Sociological Review* 38 (October 1973): 637–646. The latter study found that Mexican Americans' participation in voluntary organizations was equal to that of Anglos, holding socioeconomic status constant.

50. Robin M. Williams, Jr., in collaboration with John P. Dean and Edward A. Suchman with contributions by others, *Strangers Next Door: Ethnic Relations in American Communities* (Englewood Cliffs, N.J.: Prentice-Hall, 1964), chap. 6. While this study focuses on black-white relations, it has valuable material on other minority-majority relations as well.

1. Strong integration and reciprocal support between class, prestige, and power for the upper, upper-middle, and lower-middle classes, and a general pattern of less prestige and support from prestige activities in the working and lower classes.

2. A general pattern of ethnic-religious-"racial" segregation in prestige groups, and a distinct differential within each religious-ethnic and "racial" group by class (ethclass). Each of our three representative minority groups has a distinctly different record of prestige group behavior. Given their strong religious-ethnic identification and urban middle class status, Jewish Americans have developed strong, supportive prestige groups; they differ from the majority middle class, however, in that their political orientation is strongly toward the Democratic party. Black Americans have had poor family primary relations but their voluntary organizations have been surprisingly active and somewhat effective, even though blacks lack a large middle class from which to draw funds and personnel. Mexican Americans have also had poor primary relations (though not as poor as those of blacks). The much-vaunted familism of Mexican Americans is only a partially operative idea — as we have said, there is evidence that the Mexican American family has suffered considerably from poverty. Furthermore, Mexican Americans were unable to develop a network of supportive voluntary organizations due to their poverty and rural isolation. This pattern has changed somewhat since the 1960s, when Mexican Americans began to shed the apathy induced by poverty and oppression and to take steps toward determining their own future.

The wide diversity in types of prestige that is such a salient feature of prestige in a class society, as opposed to the tightly meshed and all-encompassing ascriptive prestige systems of caste and estate societies, has important consequences for the functioning of American society. On the one hand, it leads to struggle and conflict, since those with low ascribed prestige, such as blacks and other racial minorities, can combat their prestige "superiors" with prestige values the latter accept, like accomplishments in science or warfare, the Bill of Rights, and Christian brotherhood.

But prestige diversity can also prevent struggle, since individuals and families have access to a wide variety of traditional and new opportunities to acquire prestige. In this sense, prestige phenomena can be likened to the American economy: both undergo continuous expansion and diversification, thereby avoiding to a considerable extent the *subzero* type of competition in which one person's or group's gain is another's loss.

Despite their functional importance, the autonomy and power of prestige processes and structures should not be exaggerated. The evidence points overwhelmingly to the power of class and power over prestige. Class and power forces determine the boundaries and cleavages in prestige differentiation, and more often than not prestige phenomena are blatantly economic or political-legal in nature. Direct links between class and prestige are abundantly evident, as are the links between power and prestige. For one thing, many prestige activities — including music, art, sports, books, magazines, and consumption in general — are now dominated by profit-making organizations. For another, the staffs of profit and nonprofit organizations in the realm of prestige have similar qualifications, which also makes them interchangeable with personnel in the realms of class and power. It is also well known that many voluntary organizations, such as museums, hospitals, symphony orchestras, universities, and charities, rely heavily on business and professional people and their spouses for policymaking and financial support. An additional link between class and prestige is the investment of the endowment funds of churches, universities, foundations, and other voluntary organizations in the major corporations of our economy. Studies of university and hospital boards reveal that the upper classes exercise strong control over the budgets of voluntary-prestige groups, and thus over the allocation of community resources.

The dependence of prestige groups on the power dimension is also pronounced. Government supports prestige groups in many ways, and thereby endorses private solutions to public problems: it charters private education and allocates tax money to an enormous range of class-oriented educational services. It subsidizes cultural activities and research, and its tax laws exempt a wide range of charitable, religious, and educational groups. Government also has enormous impact, often inadvertent, on the prestige realm through postal rates, highway and recreational programs, mortgage policies, and the celebration of holidays.

As we have said, the consolidation of the existing class system appears to be the major function of the prestige dimension. Perhaps this point can be stated differently. The possibility that class, prestige, and power differentials will lead to social friction is ever-present in a formally egalitarian society, and the specific prestige processes that serve to minimize this danger are of more than passing interest.

Thus it is not unimportant that primary prestige groups exist in relative isolation from each other (or are insulated from each other). By and large, each class level develops distinctive primary prestige groups, and the various classes do not participate in each other's primary forms of interaction. Just as important is the fact that membership in secondary prestige groups, while formally open to all according to achievement criteria, tends to be relatively homogeneous by class. And where membership is heterogeneous, prestige problems are minimized by the segmentalization of interaction; that is, people do not interact as members of a class but as individuals with a common specialized interest, such as birdwatching, stamp collecting, retarded children, and the like. There is also specialized prestige interaction on both primary and secondary levels by religion-ethnicity and "race," though here too each religious-ethnic and "racial" aggregate is differentiated by class. (That is, there is a class hierarchy among Irish Roman Catholics, Mexican Americans, Roman Catholics, Protestants, Jews, blacks, and so on.)

Because of these processes, there is no need for class society to develop a society-wide consensus about all prestige values. The isolation and insulation of primary prestige groups makes it possible for people who would not dream of eating together, let alone intermarrying, to regard themselves as moral, political, and legal equals. Class society avoids, in other words, the general supersubordination by an upper prestige stratum (aristocrat) of a lower prestige stratum (serf). When Americans of different prestige interact, it is invariably in a functionally specific situation (such as at work, in a voluntary group, in a court of law, as a patient).

Thus the American prestige system avoids the spread of one form of prestige into other areas (diffused, categorical-ascriptive prestige) and inhibits the development of behavior that expresses and continuously reinforces the general superiority of one collection of families over another, a prestige system characteristic of caste and estate societies. The operation of these prestige processes allows the United States to avoid tension between its universalistic moral (and political-legal) system and the requirements of a class structure of stratification. And these isolating and insulating prestige processes help to moderate the deep tension between, on the one hand, the tradition of moral equality and achievement and, on the other, the United States' ascriptive values in ethnicity, religion, and especially race relations.

The reader is again warned, therefore, to be wary of the powerful American tradition in stratification theory that focuses on prestige differentiation as the determinant of social stratification and neglects the obvious dominance of economic and political variables. Indeed, Americans in general tend to equate subjective expressions with psychological causation, and are thus partial to psychological or individualistic explanations of all social phenomena. But without the individualizing force of industrial expansion, individualism (either subjective or otherwise) would not be possible. The reader is cautioned to think of prestige phenomena as primarily expressions of and protection for deep-rooted economic forces.

PART 4

The relation between class-prestige and political-legal power

11

The dimension
of power

POWER IS ONE of the most ambiguous terms in social science. Using it in stratification analysis, care should be taken, first of all, to distinguish between *social* power (the combined effects of class, prestige, and power) and *political-legal* power alone. The conceptualization of political-legal power is the least developed aspect of stratification theory, though a rough definition is easy to provide. Following Max Weber's usage, *political-legal power* refers to only one form of social power, the state, or the political-legal forces that promote or reduce social inequality.[1] Max Weber's classic article on social stratification, "Class, Status, Party," contains only a fragmentary discussion of party, or the realm of power. Just as class and prestige do not ordinarily separate or come into conflict in an agrarian (estate or caste) society, Weber tells us, no autonomous political realm emerges unless a movement away from "community" and toward "societalization" takes place. Only when a certain level of rationality is reached does the state emerge. That is, only when conflicting potential courses of action dictate conscious choices and the evaluation of consequences does there appear a specialized, full-time staff to make and enforce the norms called law in the name of social adjustment, integration, and other ideals.

1. For Weber's discussion of law and politics in relation to social stratification, see his "Class, Status, Party" in *From Max Weber: Essays in Sociology,* ed. and tr. H. H. Gerth and C. Wright Mills (New York: Oxford University Press, 1946), chap. 7, Sections 1, 10.

All societies, and particularly the more complex, develop some form of politics to handle conflicts, exact norms, and legitimate the general structure of super-subordination. Political institutions, Weber says, can reflect either class or status (prestige) groups, or a mixture of both. The purpose of political action is to influence or control a specific category of norms, law. Law is said to exist, according to Weber, when a staff can obtain conformity to norms (or punish those who violate them) by either physical or psychic means. When such a staff and such a body of norms are accompanied by accepted procedures for controlling the staff and for legislating law, one can speak of the state (power). Politics, in other words, means access to and influence over the state — that is, the tax collector, the courts, the police, the military, and so on. *Stratified politics* means that the various levels of society have differential access to and differential control over the state.

Our major purpose in this and the following three chapters is to analyze the stratification of politics in America, or, in other words, to find out how the hierarchy of class (and prestige) is related to the hierarchy of power (politics, government, and law). Our strategy will be to relate class (the hierarchy of individuals and families defined in terms of economic market assets and liabilities) and prestige (the hierarchy of individuals and families defined in terms of psychic and interactional or, roughly, moral assets and liabilities) on the one hand, to the structure of power (the hierarchy of individuals and families defined in terms of political-legal assets and liabilities) on the other. For convenience, *class* and *prestige* can be treated as a single entity (*class-prestige*), or referred to (with caution) as *socioeconomic class* or as *socioeconomic status* (SES). To portray a full-fledged social class, in other words, one must examine political-legal power in combination with economic and prestige power. *Formally defined, a social class (or social stratum) is the composite of assets and liabilities that characterizes aggregates of individuals and families (and other groups and collectivities) in the economic realm, the social (or prestige) realm, and in the realm of politics, government, and law.*

In broadening our concept of social class, we will also be accomplishing another purpose: as we discover how class-prestige affects power and vice-versa, we will also be laying bare the overall structure of *social* power. In stratification analysis, the overall structure of social power is synonymous with the hierarchy of social classes.

The formal materials of political-legal power stratification

Much of our thinking about politics (and society) is formal in nature — that is, concerned with appearance, words, and ideals, rather than substance and operational reality. Indeed, so prevalent is formal thinking in American life that it seems best to begin by articulating the conventional or formal view of politics, so that we can devote ourselves fully to examining its validity. To put the matter bluntly, whenever the word *formal* is encountered, the reader should be on notice that the reality of the phenomenon being discussed will be challenged.

The formal separation of state and society

During the seventeenth and eighteenth centuries, and even into the nineteenth, the leading liberal societies (England, France, and the United States), each in its own time and way, struggled to separate the state from society. Liberal theorists assisted this process by asserting individual rights that the state could not violate and by claiming that citizens deserved equal access to and equal treatment by the state. The process of distinguishing the state from society reached its climax in the characteristic liberal separation of law (the state) from morality (freedom of speech, association, worship, and so on), a separation that seeks to limit the discretionary power of the state by specifying in precise legal norms what it is authorized to do and what it cannot do.

The attempt to separate state and society and to define their relations in legal terms is the essence of liberal democracy. As we will see, there is a considerable amount of formality in this formulation: common access to politics and equal treatment by government are far from being operational realities. And *laissez-faire* theory, one of the main devices with which liberal theorists have tried to separate state and society, is also an empty formality. As we will see in abundant detail, it is far more realistic to think in terms of the *intertwining* of state and society — an intertwining that represents a coordination, if not a merger, of the hierarchies of class, prestige, and power. In contradiction to the alleged existence of common rights and equality before the law and the alleged separation of state and society, therefore, we will speak of a corporate state or a political economy. This does not mean, of course, that the formalities of American life have no force or reality; it simply means that they should not be allowed to monopolize our thinking.

The logic of a class system of political-legal power

The interplay between power and the forces of class and prestige has had varied and complex manifestations in American history. The sanctity of the person, which is such a prominent feature of the liberal tradition, led early to the abolition of imprisonment for debt and the development of the law of bankruptcy. Today the law of bankruptcy, which even includes a specific prohibition denying the right of an individual to sell himself into slavery, gives the individual political-legal protection against disastrous economic (class) reversals. The abolition by Thomas Jefferson, as governor of Virginia, of *primogeniture* — the legal requirement that the first-born, usually the first-born male, must inherit the entire family estate — and *entail* — legal prohibition of the owner's right to sell his or her property either in part or as a whole — are other examples of the class logic of power. When primogeniture and entail are in effect, economic and familistic values have blended and been lent added force and legitimacy by the state. Thus the abolition of primogeniture and entail signified the egalitarianism of the United States and its need to free economic assets from familistic and legal controls.

Until well into the nineteenth century, American political institutions were explicitly tied to economic status through the imposition of property qualifications for voting or for holding public office.[2] The official sale of exemptions from military service during the Civil War is a well-known example of the connection between class and power. And until the Fourteenth and Fifteenth Amendments (1868 and 1870), the power dimension was formally tied to class (and prestige) forces in other ways, though practices differed in the north[3] and in the south.[4]

In other countries, political institutions have been subordinated to a variety of prestige statuses, such as religion[5] and family.[6] Quite obviously, any attempt to establish a particular religion or to make it an essential part of the definition of citizenship represents a merger of prestige and power. Perhaps no aspect of the emergence of the liberal state was more difficult than disentangling religious status from citizenship. Though the struggle to sever Church and state was a dominant theme in English and French history from the sixteenth through the nineteenth centuries, the United States was largely spared comparable strife. The practice of selling political and military offices (which figures prominently in the histories of England and France) and the English university constituency (an electoral practice in which university degree-holders could vote twice, once in their residential area and again in a nation-wide constituency of degree-holders) are further examples of direct connections between class-prestige and power.

The formal tension between class-prestige and power

It is not difficult, on a formal level at least, to illustrate the tension between class and prestige on the one hand, and power on the other, and to demonstrate

2. Chilton Williams, *American Suffrage: From Property to Democracy, 1760–1860* (Princeton, N.J.: Princeton University Press, 1960); Margaret Chute, *The First Liberty: A History of the Right to Vote in America, 1619–1850* (New York: E. P. Dutton, 1969). White male suffrage was achieved unevenly after the American Revolution. General elimination of the property qualification and extension of the vote to white adult males was not completed until the 1850s.

3. In extending suffrage, most northern states specifically exempted blacks. Before the Civil War only five northern states (accounting for 6 percent of the blacks in the north) extended the right to vote to black males (Chute, *The First Liberty*, p. 313).

4. The black American's formal right to vote was virtually meaningless in the south, however, until the 1960s. Another ascribed status, which is not directly germane to stratification analysis but which also qualified the full autonomy of political-legal institutions from ascription, was denial of the vote to women until 1919.

5. In England until the early nineteenth century, Roman Catholics and Jews could not hold office or vote.

6. In contemporary Spain, for example, only the male head of the family is permitted to vote in local elections.

the relative autonomy of the power dimension. Political and legal privileges based on ascriptive criteria are incongruent with both the achievement ethic and industrialization, and have been gradually undermined. Today, formally speaking, all American citizens have extensive political and legal rights, and American political-legal institutions are autonomous from class and prestige forces.[7] And, formally, the egalitarian norms of "one person, one vote" and territorial representation are at odds with inequalities based on income or wealth and with inequalities based on prestige, whether derived from occupation, education, sex, family lineage, religion, ethnicity, race, or taste. The corollaries of this norm, majority rule and compromise, mean that in order to win majorities, political parties cannot appeal to narrow class and/or prestige interests, but must evolve programs that cut across class and prestige rankings (provided that constituencies are relatively heterogeneous in composition). And a party that obtains political power must continue to placate and serve interests transcending any single social class if it hopes to remain in power. Given these pressures, groups striving for political power have created and are forced to maintain the concepts of a *public* and of an ideal realm lying above the passions and particularities of the moment.

The tension between class-prestige and power can also be illustrated on another level. The existence of a system of public taxation means that certain functions are accepted as public responsibilities and that all class and prestige groups must make material contributions to the common good. In other words, such phenomena as the progressive income tax, estate and inheritance taxes, and eminent domain promote the presumption that class and prestige forces cannot expect to be left alone when they conflict with public need or the public interest.

There is further formal evidence of the autonomy of political institutions *vis-à-vis* the forces of class and prestige. A merit-based career civil service is at odds with the idea that one is equipped to serve the many simply by virtue of high class or prestige qualifications. Conflict-of-interest norms (such as the requirement that cabinet members and even the president sell stocks or put them in trust funds) also presuppose the differing functions of political status and class or prestige status.[8] And, finally, one can point to the norm of equal justice under law, dispensed by an independent judiciary, as a way in which legal institutions resist the tendency of the class and prestige dimensions to

7. The United States Supreme Court has clearly separated religion and the state in a number of decisions; recent Court decisions requiring legal counsel and other legal rights for the poor and the "despised" (lower class criminal defendants) are evidence of the continued vitality of political-legal rights against the forces of class and prestige. The Supreme Court decision voiding state laws that prohibit marriage between members of different "races" (miscegenation) is also evidence of continued pressure to undermine "caste" forms of prestige inequality. And legislation and governmental pressure to extend the rights of women signify the autonomous role of power *vis-à-vis* ascriptive sexual inequality in the areas of both prestige and class.

8. Conflict-of-interest norms are relatively undeveloped (almost to the point of scandal) for legislators and, excluding the federal judiciary, for judges as well.

make justice subject to privilege. Justice, in other words, is tax-supported and public in nature and, at least ostensibly, the same for all.[9]

Our analysis has to this point stressed the *logic* of a class system of power and the *formal* tension between class-prestige and power. As we explore the actual relation between class-prestige and power, however, we will uncover a very different picture. Every effort must be made to resist the logic of liberal democracy, or, in other words, to avoid taking the rhetoric (formalities) of liberal democracy at face value. Unfortunately, the confusion of rhetoric with empirical reality is widespread, even in sociology. In general, it takes the form of a belief in the efficacy of political-legal institutions to solve social problems and realize social ideals. In effect, it results in a belief in progress, an assertion that liberal democracy is an ultimate social system capable of improving itself without changing (evolutionary liberalism).

The actual operation and autonomy of the political-legal realm are, of course, subject to empirical research. Speaking factually, there is little question that political-legal institutions are under heavy pressure to conform to class and prestige values. As we will see, for example, both the frequency and nature of voting and other forms of political participation are heavily influenced by such factors as economic status and religious and ethnic persuasion. And in many ways the small but powerful upper classes use the political and legal system to further their own interests. Nevertheless the use of political-legal institutions to realize, buttress, and legitimate class and prestige interests considerably modifies their expression and impact.

Late liberal (mature industrial) society: some basic trends
The process of bureaucratization

No understanding of the nature of present-day society is possible unless one recognizes that rationality is now embodied in bureaucratic structures as much as it is in individuals. The classic formal definition of bureaucracy is Max Weber's:

> . . . precision, speed, unambiguity, knowledge of the files, continuity, discretion, unity, strict subordination, reduction of friction and of material and personal costs — these are raised to the optimum point in strictly bureaucratic administration, and especially in its monocratic forms. As compared with all collegiate, honorific, and avocational forms of administration, trained bureaucracy is superior on all these counts.[10]

The actual performance of bureaucracies varies widely from this formal definition, and one must always be wary of confusing empirical behavior in

9. United States Supreme Court decisions guaranteeing due process to paupers illustrate both of these aspects of justice.
10. Max Weber, "Bureaucracy," in *From Max Weber: Essays in Sociology,* tr. and ed. H. H. Gerth and C. Wright Mills (New York: Oxford University Press, 1946), p. 214. Used by permission. This essay has been widely reprinted.

this area with ideal definitions. Nonetheless, bureaucratization in one form or another has come to characterize all spheres of life. Its development can be measured in terms of the increase in white-collar workers and the concentration of resources and power in manufacturing, finance, farming, mining, transportation, entertainment, religion, education, law, medicine, other professions, and, of course, politics and government.

The bureaucratization of politics

Though the tendency to associate bureaucratization only with governmental administration is unfortunate, there is little doubt that the power and effectiveness of public bureaucracies have grown steadily. The growth of government in general is related to social complexity and its attendant frictions and conflicts. And in a related way, the relative growth in power of governmental bureaucracies *vis-à-vis* legislatures is largely due to the political stalemates generated by mature industrialization. Given the highly decentralized structure of American political life (federalism, states' rights) and the complex issues and interests that arise routinely in an advanced industrial system, it is difficult for political parties to forge detailed, coherent programs of action. As a result, the United States' two national parties are loose coalitions of diverse interest groups and classes held together by vague rhetoric and improvised policies. Thus legislatures are not controlled by disciplined parties with coherent mandates; instead, they tend to reflect rather accurately the enormous variety of articulate social interests and thus tend toward stalemate, inaction, or inappropriate action. For this reason, legislatures have declined *vis-à-vis* governmental bureaucracies and elected executives. In other words, interest groups that want concessions from the state tend to place less stress on influencing the traditional political arena (the political party, the politician, the legislature) than on dealing directly with governmental bureaucracies.

One of the significant effects of the professionalization of political life is the relative decline of the political entrepreneur, or political boss. The decline of the political entrepreneur, like that of the economic entrepreneur, should not be interpreted as a radical break with the past. In his classic discussion of the power dimension,[11] Max Weber referred to the boss as a central figure at the advent of representative government — that is, during the initial stage of politics based on mass suffrage. The traditional political boss had no personal economic base and enjoyed little prestige. His strength was derived from his ability to mobilize and control voters, and thus candidates and legislators — or, in effect, his ability to dispense public jobs, and to pass legislation and obtain state concessions for clients. The rise of a merit-based civil service, municipal reform, and the welfare state combined to undermine his power (and, of course, that of political machines and the masses in general).[12]

11. "Politics as a Vocation" in *From Max Weber: Essays in Sociology,* tr. and ed. H. H. Gerth and C. Wright Mills (New York: Oxford University Press, 1946), chap. 6.
12. It was already clear to Max Weber that civil service reform meant a curtail-

This development is in full harmony with the process of rationalization that has transformed other sectors of contemporary society. Those who want to use the state to secure or protect their economic or other interests no longer need to make deals with party bosses. The rise of the regulatory state after the 1890s and increases in explicit legislative lobbying and official and semi-official contacts with political figures and governmental administrators represent a deep intertwining of economic and political institutions. Recourse to boss politics has been left to those who remain outside the corporate economy: small businesses, and blacks and other minorities. Just as boss politics was an outcome of early industrial society, so are the rise of a merit-based civil service, the welfare state, and an administered, expert, "nonpolitical" politics and government in keeping with the rise of a bureaucratic socioeconomic system.

Bureaucratization in politics has also given rise to professional party managers and staffs, professional image-makers, and professional intellectuals. Perhaps the most significant such change in American political life is the growth of the institutionalized presidency.[13] The presidency is the United States' central national office, primary instrument for bringing the problems of the overall social system into focus, and main source of national political leadership. But problems have tended increasingly to be forwarded to Washington for solution, and the presidency has acquired a many-layered bureaucracy as presidents have hired experts and staffs to advise and assist them.

The welfare state as a middle class phenomenon

Perhaps no expression in the lexicon of modern politics is as ambiguous and misleading as the term *welfare state*. This term is sometimes used in the abstract to refer to the interventionist state that developed in the United States after 1890. The growth of the welfare state was significantly advanced in the 1930s when the United States Supreme Court abandoned its tenacious sixty-year-old opposition to governmental intervention in economic matters and allowed the federal government to take measures against the worst depression in the nation's history. The term *welfare state,* however, is rendered ambiguous by its use in a narrower and derogatory sense to mean state action to serve the needs of workers (the legal recognition of trade unions, unemployment insurance, social security, minimum wage, and the improvement of working conditions), and of the working and dependent poor (broken families with dependent children, the aged, the blind, and the disabled and sick).

---

ment of the power of the masses in favor of the educated (and thus the propertied); see his essay "Bureaucracy," chap. 8, Section 14. For background on civil service reform in the United States, see Paul Van Riper, *History of the United States Civil Service* (New York: Harper and Row, 1958).

13. For a valuable discussion of the new presidency and policymaking in the post–World War Two period, see John C. Donovan, *The Policy Makers* (New York: Western, 1970), especially chaps. 2 and 4; also available in paperback.

The nineteenth-century liberal denunciation of state activity, in the name of self-reliance, individual responsibility, and competition, has reverberated to stigmatize efforts to do for workers and the poor what has been done on a much larger scale for other segments of American society. Antigovernmental rhetoric, which stems primarily from small business but also suits the interests of big business and professional groups, should not be allowed to obscure the fundamental reality of American political history: the state has been used actively and extensively by the upper and middle classes to serve their many and varied interests. Actually, the main impetus to an enlarged sphere of activity on the part of government has come from business and upper occupational groups of various kinds: bankers, farmers, transportation businesses, large and small manufacturers, retailers, doctors, and so on. Only during the Great Depression did workers and the needy come to be acknowledged as legitimate recipients of state support (largely because there existed a depressed and badly hurt middle class). It is important to recognize that, by and large, the lower classes have had things done to them and for them (paternalism). Unlike the classes above them, the poor and even the working class (labor unions notwithstanding) neither set the pace nor prevail in American politics.

There is little doubt that *in practice* Americans do not believe in the theory of laissez-faire; and if one judges beliefs by behavior, they have never believed in it. American economic and other interest groups have never hesitated to use political means, including organized violence, to obtain their ends. American history is filled with examples of state action on behalf of interest groups: bank charters, laws protecting slavery, subsidies for canals, land grants for railroads, policies on Indians, territorial annexation, land grants for education, tariffs, gunboat diplomacy, cheap credit, aid to farmers, subsidies for industry, the use of troops to break strikes, antitrust legislation, collective bargaining legislation, the protection of consumers, and so on. And, judging from contemporary public opinion polls, the majority of the American people believes the government should be more active with regard to practical bread-and-butter issues.[14] American politics and American government must be considered in the context of a complex, dynamic industrial economy. Beneath the formalities of political life, it is clear that the main functions of political-legal institutions are to reduce economic and other conflicts, to stabilize or restore economic relations,

14. We will have more to say about this matter later. For a brilliant analysis of the way in which the political wishes of the majority of the American people are thwarted by the upper-middle class, see Richard F. Hamilton, *Class and Politics in the United States* (New York: John Wiley and Sons, 1972). Hamilton's general argument, based on surveys of political attitudes and voting preferences (primarily the 1964 presidential election), is that there is no significant political distinction between nonmanual and manual workers, the former identifying and voting with the latter. While Hamilton's argument is a valuable corrective to views that exaggerate the difference between the lower-middle and the working class or that foresee the absorption of the working class into the middle class, there are sufficient grounds for distinguishing a lower-middle from a working class.

and to enhance and promote opportunities within an expanding industrial society.

Our understanding of government in the United States is enhanced by viewing it from still another vantage-point. It is popularly thought that the federal government has grown bigger and stronger during the twentieth century, and in absolute terms the activities of the federal government have undoubtedly grown, whether measured in terms of expenditures, revenues, number of employees, or functions. But measured in more meaningful terms — such as relative to the growth of the American economy, the labor force, or state and local governments — a very different picture emerges. Using a constant dollar and excepting the special military and international obligations of the federal government and such unusual domestic crises as the Great Depression, there has been an amazing stability in federal domestic expenditures, tax revenues, and numbers of civilian employees, and a steady and sizable decline in the national debt.[15] Finally, it is not always appreciated that federal programs and funds in the area of social welfare are largely administered by local governments, which goes a long way toward explaining why the purposes of federal legislation are so often thwarted.

Exaggeration of the benefits bestowed by government on the poor and on workers and the use of the derogatory term *welfare state* to characterize such assistance probably serves a number of functions. For one thing, it permits middle and upper class Americans to think of the enormous range of money benefits they receive from government in nonwelfare terms, and thus to legitimate state activity on their behalf.[16] Similarly, it helps them to legitimate the enormous range of benefits they receive from governmental regulation (and, often, nonregulation) of such activities as transportation, communications, banking, brokering, and the manufacture of food and drugs; antitrust action, or inaction; tax policies; fair trade laws; price supports; professional certification practices; zoning laws; school policies; and the distribution of franchises and licenses. We can conjecture that these benefits prevent the upper classes from seeing that the problems of workers and the needy are often attributable to governmental policies that aid the middle and upper classes. For example, lavish governmental aid for research leads to technological displacement; urban renewal and highway grants deprive the poor of homes and isolate them from jobs and public services. And such benefits are sufficiently indirect to allow many to avoid recognizing that the natural economy and society

---

15. Good overall reviews of these areas are provided by Frederick C. Mosher and Orville F. Poland, *The Costs of American Governments: Facts, Trends and Myths* (New York: Dodd, Mead, 1964), and Ira Sharkansky, *The Politics of Taxing and Spending* (New York: Bobbs-Merrill, 1969).

16. Cash benefits to middle and upper class Americans are rarely called subsidies, let alone "public assistance." They are invariably defined as ways to make the economy, science, or society work more effectively for the common good. Most middle and upper class benefits are obscured by being linked to tax policy, disaster aid, defense needs, public safety, or public convenience, and by the fact that they take the form of "public interest" franchises, licenses, contracts, and regulations.

posited by laissez-faire liberalism is a myth, and that modern society not only needs political supports, but has received them throughout American history.

The welfare state as an upper and/or upper-middle class phenomenon

To see that the middle class is the main beneficiary of the welfare state is by no means sufficient. It may well be that the real force behind and main beneficiary of liberal political reform since the late nineteenth century is the upper and/or upper-middle class, rather than the middle class (or lower classes). This is a difficult question, and caution should be exercised in confronting it. The middle class imagery of early capitalism (small-town America) is still a vital intellectual tradition[17] with wide support among the lay public, especially small farmers, small businesspeople, and independent professionals. But even though one can be fairly certain that the middle class as a whole dominates American society, there is some justification for thinking in terms of upper and upper-middle class (as opposed to power elite) dominance.[18] Historians have come to question the traditional view that the Progressive era represents a struggle to tame the power of big corporations and corrupt politicians. For one thing, the Progressives accomplished very little by way of concrete reform, rhetoric notwithstanding. And, for another, the upper class (large business interests) was far more active in promoting political reforms that complemented its interests in the developing nationwide and even worldwide economy than people realize.[19]

17. For a characterization of American intellectuals and reformers since the turn of the century as applying small-town imagery to the problems of a national economy and state, see Jean B. Quandt, *From the Small Town to the Great Community: The Social Thought of Progressive Intellectuals* (New Brunswick, N.J.: Rutgers University Press, 1970).

18. C. Wright Mills is one of the few sociologists to treat the reality of the corporate, centralizing economy as the framework for sociological analysis. Actually, he assumed the dominance of the upper and upper-middle class and sought to identify an even smaller group — the power elite — as the central locus of power. For an early indictment of sociology as a middle class ideology that obscures the causes of problems and promotes the status quo, see his "The Professional Ideology of Social Pathologists," *American Journal of Sociology* 49, no. 2 (September 1943): 165–180; for a view of sociology as an upper-middle class apology for a corporate economy and a centralizing state, see Alvin W. Gouldner, "The Sociologist as Partisan: Sociology and the Welfare State," *American Sociologist* 3 (May 1968): 103–116; both essays are reprinted, along with other articles indicting sociology as a liberal ideology, in L. T. Reynolds and J. M. Reynolds, eds., *The Sociology of Sociology* (New York: David McKay, 1970), pp. 129–151, 218–255.

19. For an analysis of municipal reform during the Progressive era as a curtailment of the power of both the masses and the middle class by an upper class of businesspeople, professionals, and old families (in our terms, the upper and upper-middle class), see Samuel P. Hays, "The Politics of Reform in Municipal Government in the Progressive Era," *Pacific Northwest Quarterly* 55 (October 1964); reprinted in B. A. Brownell and W. E. Stickle, eds., *Bosses and Reformers* (Boston: Houghton Mifflin, 1973), pp. 137–161. For an analysis of national politics during the same period as the consolidation of "political capitalism," see Gabriel Kolko,

America's unique class politics

Before addressing the intricacies of political behavior, we need a more explicit framework for understanding the class basis of politics. Specifically, we must look beyond the fairly well-established idea that economic interests are the basis of most political behavior. We need to see economic interests in class terms, which is, ironically enough, difficult to do if we rely exclusively on Marx's conception of politics and government. Marx's conception of class focuses on just one form of class action: the labor market, or the struggle between the buyers and sellers of labor. While this class relationship (which became prominent during the nineteenth century) is of great importance, it is but one of a number of forms of class action.

For Weber, a class is any group sharing a "class situation," a "typical chance for a supply of goods, external living conditions, and personal life experiences, in so far as this chance is determined by the amount and kind of power, or lack of such, to dispose of goods or skills for the sake of income in a given economic order." For Weber, as for Marx, the basic polar determinants of class situation are "property" and "lack of property" — but between these poles a great many class situations must be distinguished. Class situations, says Weber, lead to class protest or struggle only when it is widely recognized that the distribution of life chances is due to a given distribution of property or to the structure of a concrete economic order. Such recognition depends on the general nature of society but especially on "communalization," a process that takes place, according to Weber, when there is interaction between members of *different* classes (and not, as Marx said, when there is interaction between members of the *same* class). The history of class struggle, Weber suggests, is roughly a sequence of the three basic forms of class action and rivalry: the credit market, the commodity market, and the labor market.

The "transparency" of class interest is obscured by general sociocultural conditions, and a number of unusual political consequences flow from the vagaries of class experience. Direct competition between buyers and sellers of labor, for example, is usually bitter while the "unearned" income of the *rentier,* shareholder, and banker go unchallenged. Politically, this situation can lead to varieties of "patriarchical socialism," such as Tory socialism and upper class reformism, or to attempts by threatened prestige groups, such as clergy-

---

The Triumph of Conservatism: A Reinterpretation of American History, 1900–1916 (New York: Free Press, 1963), also a Quadrangle paperback. For an analysis of American foreign policy during the post–Civil War period as a search for a world order favorable to liberal capitalism, see William A. Williams, *The Tragedy of American Diplomacy,* rev. ed. (New York: World, 1962). For the view that the contemporary upper-middle class is the main power-holder in the United States, and consistently thwarts the political aspirations of the majority, see Richard F. Hamilton, *Class and Politics in the United States* (New York: John Wiley and Sons, 1972).

men and intellectuals, to form alliances with the proletariat against the "bour-geosie."[20]

Thus, a full understanding of American political life in class terms is impossible if one relies on Marx's exclusive emphasis on the struggle over the price of labor. Even Weber's suggestion that an evolution has taken place in the modal type of class action is somewhat misleading. But, as Norbert Wiley points out, Weber's theory of class does contain the conceptual elements needed for framing American political behavior in class terms. The United States should be thought of, Wiley says, as characteristically a rich mixture of all three basic forms of class situations, a mixture that gives it a unique class politics. The three basic market relationships are:

1. the labor market (occupational versus property-owning groups)
2. the credit or money market (debtors versus creditors)
3. the commodity market (buyers versus sellers; tenants versus landlords).

One can distinguish, says Wiley, groups that have consistent, inconsistent, and highly inconsistent class interests in their total market or class relationships:

> There are two consistent sets of class attributes, the propertied and non-propertied. The propertied set is that of employer-creditor-seller; the non-propertied that of employee-debtor-buyer. All other sets entail a mixture of the propertied and the nonpropertied, or nonmembership in one or more markets, or membership on both the propertied and nonpropertied sides in one or more markets, or some combination of these. It will be assumed that all sets, other than the two consistent ones, are likely to involve a conflict of economic interest for the person, and it is in this sense that we refer to them as inconsistent. The extent of inconsistency reflects the degree to which the three axes of class conflict divide a population at different points and to that extent a society will have a built-in source of cross-pressures.[21]

American political behavior is obscured for those who fail to recognize that class action takes many forms, and that it is far more likely for the various class relationships to remain separate and mutually antagonistic than for them to coalesce into two camps as Marx predicted. The division of labor in a complex society makes for a rich mixture of class relationships, mixtures that are often inconsistent and unbalanced and whose political consequences are also inconsistent and unbalanced. Those who point to the empirical diversity of American politics to deny the existence of class are mistaking symptom for cause. And those who deny the existence of class because the United States has not crystallized into two warring classes have been influenced more by Marx than by stratification theory and research.

20. Max Weber, "Class, Status, Party" in *From Max Weber: Essays in Sociology,* tr. and ed. H. H. Gerth and C. Wright Mills (New York: Oxford University Press, 1946), chap. 7, sections 2–4; the above quotation is from p. 181.
21. Norbert Wiley, "America's Unique Class Politics: The Interplay of the Labor, Credit and Commodity Markets," *American Sociological Review* 32 (August 1967): 532. Used by permission.

An examination, provided by Wiley, of class-related political behavior in American history is instructive. The most radical political group in American history has been the farmers, whose economic class interests focus on the prices they pay for money (credit), equipment and services (such as railroad transport) on the one hand, and the prices of the products they sell (basically, food), on the other. When the allegedly rational markets in these areas did not perform as expected, American farmers turned to politics to protect and enhance their class interests — interests they defined as cheap money and manufactured goods and high price supports for farm products. In their political and economic struggles, farmers could not readily identify with labor, another class underdog, whose class interests lay in the high price of labor, the high price of manufactured commodities, and the low price of food.

Class analysis is also revealing when applied to other economic groups. Small businesspeople are both buyers and sellers of products; they are often in debt and are small-scale buyers of labor. Thus they are of a classic mixed type who find it difficult to identify with either big business or labor. As an economic group whose class interests are highly inconsistent, small businesspeople are also radical politically, though on the right wing. Others who suffer from high inconsistency in their class positions are workers with property or side income, retired people on small incomes, and white-collar workers. The difficulties experienced by individuals with high (class) inconsistency stem from ambivalence, or, in other words, from the inability to identify a coherent class enemy. Those who are subject to such cross-pressures see the world as capricious and arbitrary and feel psychological pressure to escape into a world of simple certainties. And when class inconsistency is associated with prestige inconsistency, the political situation becomes even more highly charged. All in all, Wiley concludes, the United States has not experienced generalized class warfare because of its rich and inconsistent class structure. Throughout our history, in other words, there has been a different subordinate class in each subdimension of class conflict, and the various subordinate classes have been too diverse to unite; in other words, they have never had a common enemy to rise against.

Class-prestige and power: a summary

We have warned against the uncritical acceptance of a formal definition of political behavior. Over the centuries, a heady mixture of liberal rhetoric has created the impression that invoking the ideas of equal rights and equal treatment by government is the same thing as actually realizing these ideals. In reality, politics and government have a class base. While class forces in the United States are exceedingly complex and lead to a unique form of class politics, there is little doubt that the upper levels of the class structure have more direct access to, exert more influence over, and receive more benefits from the state than their fellow citizens in the classes below.

In the following chapters, we will study this process in a more detailed way. Chapter 12 examines political participation, including voting, lobbying, political careers, political attitudes, and political extremism. In Chapter 13, we will try to determine who benefits most from legislation and governmental action in such areas as taxation, social security, housing, education, and public economic policies. And Chapter 14 investigates the American legal system to see how the distribution of justice is related to the hierarchies of class and prestige.

12

Class-prestige and political participation

IN THIS CHAPTER we will inquire into the relation between the many forms of political participation and class-prestige standing. Thought of in broad historical terms, we want to find out if the growth of representative government marks an increase in the power of the general populace. To put the matter bluntly, has formal political equality resulted in any appreciable measure of actual political equality?

Class-prestige and the federal system

Because the federal government is responsible for issues of war and peace, constitutional questions concerning personal liberty and economic regulation, and personal and corporate income taxation, its activities are better publicized than those of the thousands of "local" governments that are the day-to-day reality of the ordinary citizen's relation with government. However, under America's federal system, state and local governments are extremely powerful. Indeed, so powerful is "local" government that it has successfully made the transition from the agrarian conditions that spawned it to the urban-industrial age.

The history of American political development in this sphere can be related in terms of the growth of that momentous counterweight to central government, the suburb.[1] Contrary to widespread belief, American political development has been characterized by an enormous growth of "local" government, at the state, small-town, and especially suburban levels. Preoccupation with the growth of the federal government causes many to forget that most federal domestic programs (including highways, education, welfare, pollution control, housing, urban development, and most antipoverty programs) must be channeled through "local" government. That the intergovernmental transfer of funds is intricate and extremely confusing compounds misunderstanding of the relation between the federal government and "local" government, and of the relation between the federal government and the rest of society.[2]

The pattern of governmental levels and jurisdictions in the United States can be analyzed quite fruitfully in terms of social stratification. One basic and increasingly prevalent pattern is the segregation of class-prestige groups by political jurisdiction.[3] This is perhaps the most ominous political development of the twentieth century, amounting as it does to a decline in political jurisdictions with mixed constituencies. Much of the vigor of liberal democracy — perhaps, indeed its very existence as a form of government — is attributable to the fact that it has forced those who would exercise political power to persuade a majority of a mixed group of articulate interests (either groups or voters) to support them. The need to search for common interests stimulates and develops the political creativity of candidates and parties. And, once elected, officials and parties are more likely to be independent and broad in their outlooks when their mandates are from mixed rather than homogeneous constituencies. During the founding and early years of the American republic, it was believed that the House of Representatives would be the radical popular body, and that the Senate and the president would act as conservative checks on the people. Quite the opposite has happened, of course, an outcome that is not unrelated to the distinction between mixed and homogeneous constituencies. The pattern of class-related political constituencies implicit in the growth of homogeneous suburban and urban areas poses enormous problems for the United States, since it implies that legislators and governments will eventually come to reflect the class-prestige structure and no longer perform the normal political function of solving the problems created by the forces of class and prestige. The

1. A story well told by Robert C. Wood, *Suburbia: Its People and Their Politics* (Boston: Houghton Mifflin, 1958).

2. For the difficulties of analyzing public spending and for informed comparisons of public spending by governmental level, see Frederick C. Mosher and Orville F. Poland, *The Costs of American Government: Facts, Trends, Myths* (New York: Dodd, Mead, 1964), and Ira Sharkansky, *The Politics of Taxing and Spending* (New York: Bobbs-Merrill, 1969).

3. For a valuable analysis and a pioneering attempt to develop empirical measures of governmental inequality among the municipalities that make up metropolitan areas, see Richard Child Hill, "Separate and Unequal: Governmental Inequality in the Metropolis," *American Political Science Review* 68 (December 1974): 1557–1568. Hill's data point to inequality of family income and racial discrimination as the causes of residential segregation and governmental inequality, and thus of the unequal fiscal resources for providing public goods and services.

problem of political jurisdictions segregated by class and prestige is compounded by a further problem, the lags and imbalances that characterize the American system of political representation.

Class-prestige and political representation

The American population has been badly represented in state and national legislatures, in terms of both numbers and social composition (socioeconomic differences), during the entire period for which we have reliable records.[4] Until the 1960s, this malrepresentation was steadily worsening, to the point that it is not amiss to characterize it as a "rotten borough" system. Numerically smaller portions of the population enjoyed significantly more political power than larger portions, and rural–small-town populations (often synonymous with the smaller portions) were more heavily represented in legislatures than urban populations.

Aside from the dynamics of industrialization and urbanization, two basic processes created these imbalances: (1) legislatures that had the power and often the constitutional obligation to reapportion did not do so (or did not reapportion strictly on the basis of numbers); and (2) legislatures that made wide use of the practice of gerrymandering. The first of these causes of representational imbalance was struck down by the United States Supreme Court in a series of decisions between 1962 and 1964. After having declined jurisdiction in this area, the Supreme Court changed its mind and in a landmark decision[5] gave individuals the right to sue to protect their voting rights, thus making voting rights a constitutional rather than a political issue. The Court did not define the kind of representation required by the Constitution in this decision, but in a later case it held that "the fundamental principle of representative government in this country is one of equal representation for equal numbers of people, without regard to race, sex, economic status, or place of residence within a state."[6] As a result of this and other cases, the basic doctrine of "one person, one vote" was upheld for primaries, and for elections to the House of Representatives and to both houses of state legislatures.

But while the Supreme Court has clearly spelled out the doctrine of equal representation, it will be some time before population imbalances disappear. Resistance to the Court's decision was widespread, especially while there was hope of a constitutional amendment overturning the Court's decision. But even full application of the principle of "one-person, one-vote" will not correct imbalance in the American system of representation as long as legislators

4. Howard D. Hamilton, ed., *Legislative Apportionment: Key to Power* (New York: Harper and Row, 1964), Part 1. This book contains a great many original materials on apportionment, including excerpts from Supreme Court decisions. For a good history and analysis of the problem and politics of representation, see Royce Hanson, *The Political Thicket: Reapportionment and Constitutional Democracy* (Englewood Cliffs, N.J.: Prentice-Hall, 1966).
5. *Baker v. Carr,* 363 U.S. 186 (1962).
6. *Reynolds v. Sims,* 377 U.S. 533 (1964).

are free to gerrymander — that is, to concentrate voters for the opposing party (usually identified in terms of class-prestige factors) in selected constituencies where votes will be wasted in overwhelming victories, and to allot supporters so as to achieve narrow victories in as many constituencies as possible. Since congressional districts (which are reapportioned on the basis of census figures) are drawn by state legislatures, the national House of Representatives is also gerrymandered, and thus represents neither quantitatively nor qualitatively the nature of the American population. The significance of the gerrymander for the student of social stratification is that it allows obsolete or declining class and prestige groups (racists, farmers, small town businesspeople and professionals) to entrench themselves politically. By defining equal representation "as equal representation for equal numbers of people without regard for race, sex, economic status or residence within a state," the Supreme Court presumably has grounds for acting against the gerrymander when the issue comes before it.[7]

Malapportionment is frequently blamed for poor legislation and for the failure of legislative bodies to keep up with social, especially urban, problems. While the equal representation of adult persons is morally important in order to legitimate public policies, one should not expect that equal representation will necessarily lead to better or different public policies. In response to a study claiming that political party competition at the state level is not an important influence on the enactment of social welfare policies, which depend rather on socioeconomic development,[8] a number of studies have sought to analyze the causal power of various political variables. Of special interest here is the finding that at the state level fairer apportionment is unlikely to produce major changes in public policy on employment, education, housing, and the like.[9] Evidence from these and other studies seems strongly to suggest that not only methods of representation, but also political institutions in general (power) are not significantly influential in their own right. (Remember that the studies just cited were conducted at the state level.)[10]

Much of the political history of recent decades can be written in terms of

7. In 1973, however, the Supreme Court modified the "one-person, one-vote" rule for special governmental units, such as water districts, in favor of the principle of property.

8. Richard E. Dawson and James A. Robinson, "Inter-Party Competition, Economic Variables, and Welfare Policies in the American States," *Journal of Politics* 25 (May 1963): 265–289.

9. Thomas R. Dye, "Malapportionment and Public Policy in the States," *Journal of Politics* 27 (August 1965): 586–601, and Richard I. Hofferbert, "The Relation Between Public Policy and Some Structural and Environmental Variables in the American States," *American Political Science Review* 60 (March 1966): 73–82; both essays are reprinted in Donald P. Sprengel, ed., *Comparative State Politics: A Reader* (Columbus, Ohio: Charles E. Merrill, 1971), pp. 413–443.

10. For an analysis of a cross-section of sixty Western and Third World countries, which concludes that political intentions and political democracy do not produce economic equality, see Robert W. Jackman, "Political Democracy and Social Equality: A Comparative Analysis," *American Sociological Review* 39 (February 1974), pp. 29–45.

the dominance of a numerically weak but powerful alliance of elements from the upper classes with rural–small-town interests (the Republican party), an alliance that receives powerful support from racist elements in the south (southern Democrats) and elsewhere (those threatened by black or other minority group gains). Arrayed against this overall coalition is a numerically superior but not always successful coalition composed of intellectuals, trade unions, ethnic and racial groups, and the poor (the liberal wing of the Democratic party). It is one of the great anomalies of American history that American businesspeople and professionals — the historic representatives of reason, liberty, equality, progress, and science — should become the political bedfellows of Southern racists, and that big business and highly trained professionals should share so much with small businesspeople. The decay of large American cities and much of the failure to invest in public services of all kinds can be attributed to this interplay of class, prestige, and power forces. It is of special interest that the process of suburbanization, which has done so much to segregate the United States' political jurisdictions by class and prestige, has become an important component of this broad alignment of political forces. High-income suburbs, which pay heavy local taxes to support high-quality schools and other public services for their own families, are reluctant to pay taxes to support similar public services in the big cities and in working class suburbs. The fact that high income groups often earn their livings in these cities does not prevent them from taking advantage of their political power.[11] In any case, the *ad hoc* growth of local governments (towns, cities, suburbs) characterized by a tangle of overlapping jurisdictions, duplication of services, and unresponsiveness to public complaint and need signifies the power over political life exercised by the hierarchies of class and prestige.

Class-prestige and political careers
Elected and appointed officials

There is considerable evidence that individuals elected to public office at the federal level come largely from the middle and upper classes: professionals, proprietors and officials, and farmers tend to account for the overwhelming majority of those elected to the presidency, vice-presidency, the Senate, and the House of Representatives. The upper levels of prestige hierarchies based on race, ethnic origin, and religion are also overrepresented among elected federal officials.[12] Those elected to state legislatures are considerably higher in class

11. The suburbs are very diverse and have grown so much (while big cities have stagnated or even declined in size) that they are now underrepresented in state and national legislatures.
12. For a review of American data, see Donald R. Mathews, *The Social Background of Political Decision-Makers* (New York: Random House, 1954), pp. 20–30, available in paperback; for data on the class origins of United States senators, see Donald R. Mathews, *U.S. Senators and Their World* (Chapel Hill: University of North Carolina Press, 1960), pp. 17–46. The high position of farmers is explained by the fact that the individuals studied were born around 1900, a period when farmers enjoyed a higher class-prestige position than they do now.

position (as measured by income, education, and occupation) than their constituents.[13] And delegates to both the Democratic and Republican presidential conventions in 1964 had incomes far in excess of the average American's,[14] while the leaders of both parties in Nassau County, New York, were from high — and similar — class levels.[15] It should be noted that the Democratic party broadened the base from which delegates to its 1972 national convention were selected to provide for more representation of lower-income groups and women and other minority groups, but its crushing defeat in the 1972 presidential election led to a severe curtailment of these reforms at the miniconvention of 1974.

The influence of socioeconomic status is also apparent among high federal civilian and military officials. In an analysis of intellectuals who served the Roosevelt administration during the Great Depression, it was found that most of them came from the middle and upper classes, especially the upper-middle class. A study of the occupations of fathers of high federal civilian and military personnel found that the offspring of business executives, owners of large businesses, and professionals were heavily overrepresented, especially in the military.[16] A study of high civil servants in California revealed an over-representation of the middle and upper-middle class at the state level, which is almost identical with Warner's findings at the federal level.[17]

In his study of military leaders, Janowitz found that while they have become more representative of the general population over the years, they are still drawn largely from white Protestant professional and business backgrounds.[18] Janowitz's argument that the military profession has shifted from a career model and an organizational structure based on heroism (in our terms,

13. Harmon Zeigler and Michael A. Baer, "The Recruitment of Lobbyists and Legislators," *Midwest Journal of Political Science* 12, no. 4 (November 1968): 493–513; reprinted in Donald P. Sprengel, ed., *Comparative State Politics: A Reader* (Columbus, Ohio: Charles E. Merrill, 1971), pp. 187–206.

14. Lee Webb, "A Welfare State for the Rich," *Ramparts,* 26 October 1968; reprinted in Glen Gaviglio and David E. Raye, eds., *Society As It Is: A Reader* (New York: MacMillan, 1971), pp. 240–245.

15. Dennis S. Ippolito, "Political Perspectives of Suburban Party Leaders," *Social Science Quarterly* 49 (March 1969): 800–815; reprinted in John Kramer, ed., *North American Suburbs: Politics, Diversity and Change* (Berkeley, Calif: Glendessary, 1972), pp. 237–255.

16. For evidence concerning the social origins of New Deal intellectuals, see Thomas A. Krueger and William Glidden, "The New Deal Intellectual Elite: A Collective Portrait" in Frederic C. Jaher, ed., *The Rich, the Well Born, and the Powerful: Elites and Upper Classes in History* (Urbana: University of Illinois Press, 1973), pp. 338–374. For the social origins of high federal and military personnel, see W. Lloyd Warner *et al., The American Federal Executive: A Study of Social and Personal Characteristics of the Civilian and Military Leaders of the United States Federal Government* (New Haven: Yale University Press, 1963), chap. 2. available in paperback. The finding that there is a significant amount of occupational "inheritance" among members of the military is also of interest.

17. Bruce M. Hackett, *Higher Civil Servants in California: A Social and Political Portrait* (Berkeley: University of California Press, 1967), chap. 2.

18. Morris Janowitz, *The Professional Soldier: A Social and Political Portrait* (New York: Free Press, 1960), chap. 5, also in paperback.

entrepreneurialism) to managerialism (in our terms, bureaucratic administration) is of considerable interest, since it parallels trends in other occupations. It is also important to note that schoolteachers, a large and influential group of public employees, appear to come from the upper third of the socioeconomic scale (and not primarily from lower-middle class backgrounds, as is popularly thought).[19]

Interchangeable careers

It is clear from the foregoing evidence that there is a pronounced trend for the male children of men in high class-prestige positions to move horizontally into high elected and appointed offices. There are many well-known examples of upper class individuals and families who engage in public service careers either full- or part-time. Such people, who enjoy secure, often old, wealth; respected family names and connections; and high-quality prestigious educations, serve both the Republican and Democratic parties. Some are national figures well-known to the public, such as the Cabots, Lodges, Roosevelts, Averell Harriman, Adlai Stevenson, and the Kennedys; others, such as William Bullitt, Francis Biddle, Robert McNamara, C. Douglas Dillon, Robert Lovett, McGeorge Bundy serve in appointed, less publicized positions. There are a number of interesting observations to be made about this general practice. Many political leaders on the federal level, both elected and appointed, do not rise through the ranks of state and local politics and thus must learn their jobs after acquiring them. The practice of ignoring experience and proven worth is perhaps most conspicuous in appointments to ambassadorships (some of which are actually sold), but it is common practice to appoint amateurs at the apex of the federal government. One of the more damaging results of the practice of filling the approximately two thousand high administrative positions at the federal level on a patronage basis is that it has helped to prevent the development of a strong civil service tradition at the upper levels of the federal bureaucracy. One can even conjecture that the prevalence of amateurs at the upper levels of the federal government makes it easier for their predecessors in office, who are now pursuing business and professional careers, to outmaneuver them. And, of course, this practice helps to insure the general control of public policy by the upper classes.

Unfortunately, we have few systematic studies of career interchangeability. What exactly are the trends in the relation between careers in the upper echelons of industry, finance, commerce, law, medicine, university teaching, research, natural science, and the upper reaches of government? Though we do not have sufficient data to answer this question conclusively, there is sizable

19. For data to this effect from Wisconsin, see Ronald M. Pavalko, "Recruitment to Teaching: Patterns of Selection and Retention" in *Sociological Perspectives on Occupations,* ed. Ronald M. Pavalko (Itasca, Ill.: F. E. Peacock, 1972), pp. 239–249; reprinted from *Sociology of Education* 43 (Summer 1970): 340–353.

if unsystematic evidence of considerable traffic among, on the one hand, banks, law firms, universities, and businesses (especially large corporations) engaged in agriculture, transportation, mining, communication, military manufacturing, and the like and on the other, the various departments (civilian and military) and regulatory commissions of the federal government.[20] Career interchangeability is limited, however, by professional ethics, conflict-of-interest laws, and technical occupational requirements.

An important quantitative analysis has helped to clarify the degree of concentration at the apex of American society.[21] The authors of this study analyzed tendencies toward convergence and autonomy in twelve sectors: industry, transportation-utilities-communications, banking, insurance, education, law, civic and cultural associations, foundations, government, the military, personal health, and political finance. Focusing on positions of authority in groups controlling at least 50 percent of the resources in each sector, the authors found a considerable concentration of power: 4,100 individuals controlled 50 percent of the nation's resources through their control of the 5,400 positions at the apex of these institutional sectors. The authors also found a considerable overlap in positions, and a recruitment pattern that flowed from industry to the other sectors. But the authors also note the existence of separate recruitment channels for government, law, and the military, and wisely refrain from applying their mixed findings to all the issues that arise in analyzing social power.

That elected and appointed officials are drawn from the upper levels of the class-prestige structure and that there is considerable interchange between the upper echelons of the "private" and "public" sectors means nothing in itself. As is common in social science, these facts lend themselves to varied interpretations. For some, they raise the specter that the state is a "committee of the ruling class" — that it is subservient to the interests of the rich and economically powerful. Some believe in the existence of a "power elite" (C. Wright Mills), others in a WASP establishment, others in an imperialistic authoritarian system disguised by a smokescreen of liberal rhetoric (Marcuse), and still others in a "military-industrial complex" threatening to our traditional values

20. The interchangeability of careers leads to conflicts of interest; thus there are extensive tie-ins between congressmen and professional (especially law) firms and businesses of all kinds. As yet there are no strict code of ethics or conflict-of-interest laws to regulate the behavior of congressmen, though in 1973 the federal judiciary adopted a code to govern its behavior. (Adherence is voluntary for the Supreme Court.)

Though not strictly their careers, note should be made of the middle and upper class individuals who serve on presidential or congressional commissions and advisory groups or as special appointees to the United Nations and other bodies. This general type of activity is now so widespread and routine that it should be considered "public office"; and some individuals serve in these capacities so often that such service should be considered part of their careers.

21. Thomas R. Dye, Eugene R. DeClercq, and John W. Pickering, "Concentration, Specialization, and Interlocking Among Institutional Elites," *Social Science Quarterly* 54 (June 1973): 8–28.

(Eisenhower). At a slightly lower level of disgust and alarm, the same facts suggest to some the image of a "middle class" society impervious to reform. Generally speaking, those who are morally discontented with society or who adopt a conflict model of social stratification tend to interpret such facts in one of the foregoing ways.[22]

But the same facts can be interpreted positively. It can be argued, for example, that the United States needs even more and better coordination between its various (social) power structures. Whatever coordination now exists can only help American society to identify problems more quickly and reach solutions more intelligently. It can be argued, further, that it is desirable for those in the command-posts of society to come from common backgrounds and share a common value-belief system; otherwise communication between them would be difficult. And, some might ask, what better way is there to enhance the social imaginations of specialists than for businesspeople and professionals to spend time in Washington gaining experience in public affairs? It can also be argued — and freqently is, given the American tendency to explain behavior in biopsychological, social-Darwinist terms — that individuals with talent and drive can always succeed, and that those at the apex of all our occupational ladders deserve their prominence. In short, career interchangeability can be interpreted as signifying the existence not of a ruling class, but of legitimate intelligent government by the most talented. By and large, those who are satisfied with society, and especially those who see society as a functional process of "natural" equilibrium, would probably interpret evidence of elite interchangeability in this way.

Political parties and interest groups

While agrarian societies obviously have internal conflicts, they are on the whole characterized by widespread communalization — that is, by virtually universal acceptance of specific ways of believing and acting. In stratification terms, agrarian societies tend to congeal into static hierarchies of estates or castes. Industrial society, on the other hand, is characterized by a complex and changing social division of labor, and the motivation to perform its myriad activities took the form of "individualism" in the development of Western industrial states. An intricate division of labor means that disputes and conflicts are almost routine occurrences. As a result, modern society has developed specialized groups — especially the state — to keep order and resolve conflict. This trend away from communalization toward "societalization" (or associational or class society) is everywhere accompanied by the growth of political parties and interest groups.

Political parties' financial and voting support, as well as their staff recruitment (both professional and volunteer), are deeply related to class and prestige. And the major interest groups in contemporary society are also related to the

22. This is, of course, simply a modal tendency; it was not characteristic of Eisenhower, for example.

hierarchies of class and prestige and tend to develop ideologies in keeping with their location in the class system.[28] Politically relevant interest groups include learned societies, civic betterment associations, reform movements, groups concerned with particular problems (such as taxation, foreign affairs, or veterans' affairs), professional associations, and, of course, the entire range of pressure groups. Most pressure groups emanate from the American economy, but they also include governmental units themselves, associations of civil service employees, and even associations of elected officials.

Despite the highly visible organizations that represent workers, racial and ethnic minorities, and even welfare recipients, interest groups with direct relevance for political life are overwhelmingly middle and upper class in character. Whether measured in terms of rates of participation by members, the credentials of staff members, mode of operation, or consequences for society, pressure groups basically reflect the interests and power of the middle and upper classes (as do almost all voluntary groups).

Americans have traditionally been uneasy about concentrated power, whether public or private. The early liberal tradition tended to derogate collective action of any kind, and the existence of large private power blocs has been sensed as a threat to individualism throughout American history. This orientation has changed in recent years, and Americans (as we shall see) have come to accept large private groups as permanent, respectable, and even constituent features of social life. Helping to minimize uneasiness about the political and social impact of private interest groups are various laws, regulations, and ethical codes that seek to limit the influence of those with too much money or too few scruples, or both.

Thus various laws (especially the Corrupt Practices Act of 1925, the Hatch Act of 1940, and the Taft-Hartley Act of 1947) have been passed to prevent the financing (and thus control) of political parties by private wealth and private groups. These acts forbid corporations and labor unions to contribute to political parties, and limits have been set on the amounts that individuals can contribute to political parties and the amounts that can be spent on political campaigns. Lobbyists are required by the Federal Regulation of Lobbying Act of 1946 to register and to list their employers, salaries, and activities, and there are conflict-of-interest codes for political appointees and civil servants. The net

23. For an extremely useful analysis of interest group ideology, see R. Joseph Monsen, Jr. and Mark W. Cannon, *The Makers of Public Policy: American Power Groups and Their Ideologies* (New York: McGraw-Hill, 1965). L. Harmon Zeigler and G. Wayne Peak, *Interest Groups in American Society,* 2nd ed. (Englewood Cliffs, N.J.: Prentice-Hall, 1972) provide a summary analysis of American interest groups that is a worthy successor to the late V. O. Key, Jr.'s classic *Politics, Parties, and Pressure Groups,* 5th ed. (New York: Thomas Y. Crowell, 1964). In their study of Muskegon, Michigan, *Income and Ideology: An Analysis of the American Political Formula* (New York: Free Press, 1973), Joan Huber and William H. Form found that the upper classes (as measured by income) were more favorably disposed toward American ideology — equal opportunity, the belief that government and politics work as they should, pluralism, individualism — than the lower classes.

effect of all these efforts to curtail the power of wealth and private interest groups cannot be said to be very great. By and large, such laws have been circumvented or simply ignored, serving more to disguise than to curtail the power of money in American political life.

In 1972 an apparently enforceable federal law was passed limiting campaign spending and requiring scrupulous public acknowledgement of all political contributions of $100 or more. Its impact on political life, however, remains to be seen. The Watergate scandal of 1972 intensified efforts to control political contributions and to further the attempt begun in 1972 to finance political parties from tax funds and to control campaign expenditures. In 1974 the Federal Elections Campaign Act was passed, strengthening the effort to control the power of private wealth in public elections. Contributions by individuals and groups have been limited, matching tax funds are available for campaigns for presidential nominations, tax funds will pay for presidential elections, strict limits have been placed on presidential and congressional campaign spending and enforcement machinery has been created.

The entrenched complexities of the American class-prestige system have had a number of political consequences. One is the general decline of legislatures: for various reasons, political power in general has flowed to the executive branch.[24] The weakness of legislatures has been recognized by interest groups, which continue to pressure legislators, parties, and public opinion,[25] but now also deal directly and on a large scale with governmental bureaucracies. The result is a massive intertwining of interest groups and government, or, more exactly, of particular interest groups and particular governmental agencies, bureaus, and commissions.[26] One of the interesting and not necessarily beneficial consequences of direct interest group involvement in government is that

24. For an interesting interpretation along these lines, see Theodore J. Lowi, *The End of Liberalism: Ideology, Policy and the Crisis of Public Authority* (New York: W. W. Norton, 1969), also in paperback. Lowi charges that laws passed by an interest group-oriented Congress have become increasingly vague, and thus tend to delegate ever larger discretionary powers to the executive branch.

25. Actually, legislators do not have to be pressured to abandon independence and objectivity. Legislators are elected because they agree with the views of this or that constellation of pressure or interest groups. Pressure on legislators should thus be regarded as a means of reinforcing prior commitments.

26. For an overall picture, see V. O. Key, Jr., *Politics, Parties, and Pressure Groups*, 5th ed. (New York: Thomas Y. Crowell, 1964). For a theoretical discussion of the impact of an interest group society on political life, see Bruce M. Hackett, "Public Administration and Governmental Trends in American Society," *Higher Civil Servants in California* (Berkeley: University of California Press, 1967), chap. 4. For an overall history and analysis of the federal regulatory commissions, see Louis M. Kohlmeier, Jr., *Watchdog Agencies and the Public Interest: The Regulators* (New York: Harper and Row, 1969). More detailed analyses may be found in S. Krislov and L. D. Musolf, eds., *The Politics of Regulation: A Reader* (Boston: Houghton Mifflin, 1964); William L. Carey, *Politics and the Regulatory Agencies* (New York: McGraw-Hill, 1967); and the following reports from Ralph Nader's Institute for Responsive Law: Edward F. Cox *et al., The Federal Trade Commission* (New York: Richard W. Barton, 1969); Robert Fellmeth, *The Interstate Commerce Commission* (New York: Grossman, 1970); John C. Esposito and Larry J. Silverman, *Vanishing Air* (New York: Grossman, 1970); and James S. Turner, *The Chemical Feast* (New York: Grossman, 1970).

it has probably strengthened the trend toward objective, expert, and nonpolitical government. As we have pointed out, the professionalization of our class-prestige system has a parallel in the professionalization of our political institutions. Though it is difficult to be certain, the trend toward nonpolitical boards, commissions, and authorities, and the direct cooperation of interest groups and governmental bodies of all kinds appears to be a significant corollary of the modernization of our class system. However, both the neutrality and the accountability of these bodies are highly questionable. Furthermore, the legal status of many such bodies is hazy, and the scope and volume of their economic activities are very great.[27] Of considerable interest are the "nonpolitical" councils, committees, institutes, corporations, advisory boards, and foundations (such as the Council on Foreign Relations, the Rand Corporation, the Committee for Economic Development, the Twentieth Century Fund, and the Brookings Institution), which are characterized by a narrow class composition, direct ties to specific business and professional interests, and great influence over domestic and foreign policies.[28]

Voting and other forms of political participation

Though there are many forms of political involvement by individuals, all have one thing in common: the upper classes tend to monopolize political participation and to receive more from government than do the lower classes.

Voting participation

The act of voting *per se* is clearly related to class position (and, as we will see, to such prestige factors as race, religion, and ethnicity). Those at the upper levels of the class system vote at far higher rates than do those lowest in the class hierarchy. Measured in terms of education, it is clear that those with four or more years of college vote at significantly higher rates even than high-school graduates (see Figure 12-1). The same pattern holds true for major occupational groups, as shown in Table 12-1. White-collar workers of all kinds vote at significantly higher rates than do blue-collar, service, and farm workers. Not surprisingly, income differences are also related to differences in voting partici-

27. The Controller of New York State reports (*New York Times,* 27 December 1972, p. 23) that thirty-four public authorities in that state have "never been legally defined" and that they "have been operating on a scale so massive that, in some instances, they overshadow the fiscal operations of the state itself." A sense of the scale of their operations can be gleaned from the fact that in 1972 the long-term debt of these authorities was $8.9 billion, more than two-and-a-half times the $3.4 billion debt of the state of New York.

For a careful and comprehensive study that concludes that nonpartisan elections at the municipal level favor the upper classes, see Willis D. Hawley, *Nonpartisan Elections and the Case for Party Politics* (New York: John Wiley and Sons, 1973).

28. G. William Domhoff has studied the latter phenomenon closely as part of his argument that the United States is ruled by a small upper class; see his *The Higher Circles: The Governing Class in America* (New York: Vintage, 1971), especially chaps. 5 and 6, available in paperback.

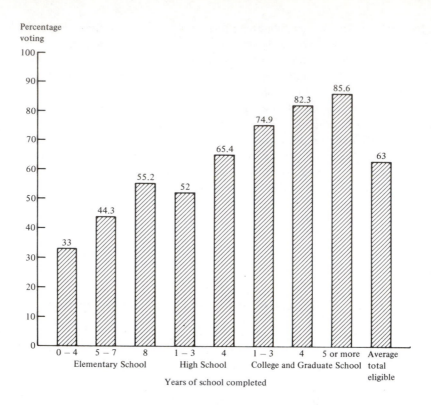

Figure 12-1 Voting Participation By Years of School Completed, 1972

SOURCE: U.S. Bureau of the Census, *Current Population Reports,* Series P-20, no. 253, "Voting and Registration in the Election of November, 1972" (Washington, D.C.: U.S. Government Printing Office, 1973), Table 7, p. 49.

pation. As Figure 12-2 indicates, there is a substantial difference between the 45 percent rate of those with incomes under $3,000 per year and the 79 percent rate of those with incomes of $15,000 or more.

Historically American citizens, especially the poor and minority groups, have faced numerous barriers to voting, including requirements that one register, satisfy literacy and residence qualifications, and pay a poll tax. Though the courts have struck down most of these qualifications, the need to register still seems to curtail voting participation.[29] Kimball has suggested that the registration requirement and various other qualifications were introduced in the late nineteenth century by WASP groups concerned about mass immigration (and with the move to disenfranchise blacks in the south, and efforts to curtail electoral corruption). However, electoral apathy among the lower classes is by

29. For an analysis that focuses on the barriers Americans must overcome before they can vote, see Penn Kimball, *The Disconnected* (New York: Columbia University Press, 1972).

Table 12-1   Reported Voter Participation By Major Occupation Group, 1972

White-collar workers	76.4
Professional, technical, & kindred workers	82.3
Managers and administrators, except farm	76.4
Sales workers	73.1
Clerical and kindred workers	72.7
Blue-collar workers	54.2
Craftsmen and kindred workers	61.0
Operatives, except transport	49.2
Transport equipment operatives	53.2
Laborers, except farm	48.6
Service workers	58.6
Private household workers	51.0
Service workers, except private household	59.7
Farm workers	63.6
Farmers and farm managers	77.8
Farm laborers and farm foremen	42.3

SOURCE: U.S. Bureau of the Census, *Current Population Reports,* Series P-20, no. 253, "Voting and Registration in the Election of November, 1972" (Washington, D.C.: U.S. Government Printing Office, 1973), Table 9, p. 58.

no means attributable solely to the need to register. Electoral apathy must be considered an outcome of class experience: those low on the class structure tend not to lead lives that emphasize active self-direction, and nonvoting is consistent with such experience.

To focus on the upper end of the class hierarchy, the upper classes enjoy a socioeconomic experience that prepares them for and predisposes them toward political involvement. Typically, members of the upper classes (especially the upper and upper-middle classes) have had considerable formal education and are therefore familiar with certain relevant information and with the concepts and skills needed to organize such information. They work in occupations that are, on the whole, more mental than manual. They participate in voluntary-interest groups that focus and reinforce their class-prestige interests, and their participation in voluntary groups in general gives them experience in the verbal and written analysis of public issues. They absorb "higher" levels of stimuli through reading, viewing, listening, and traveling. They are more secure in their finances and in their personalities. And they are quick to perceive political threats to their interests, and to counter them with both symbolic and overt political action. In other words, the typical member of the upper classes (again, especially of the upper and upper-middle classes) is, in contrast to a typical member of the working and lower classes, much more of a self-propelled, conscious decision-maker across a broad range of activities. Thus higher rates of voting participation reflect and reinforce higher rates of involvement in the upper reaches of the hierarchies of class and prestige. And,

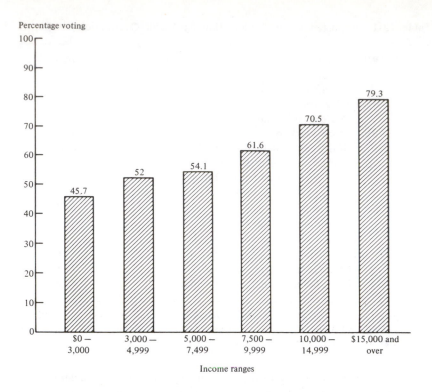

Percentage voting

Figure 12-2 Voting Participation By Income, 1972

SOURCE: U.S. Bureau of the Census, *Current Population Reports,* Series P-20, no. 253, "Voting and Registration in the Election of November, 1972" (Washington, D.C.: U.S. Government Printing Office, 1973), Table 11, p. 96.

as we will see, the upper classes are also more active in other forms of political participation.

The attempt to increase the involvement of the poor in public life, which is one of the purposes of the Community Action Program created by the Economic Opportunity Act of 1964, has not been notably successful. This act, which encouraged the widest possible participation by the poor in federally funded local antipoverty organizations, was not well received by the broad public. In 1967 Congress restricted the membership of the poor on CAP boards, allocating one-third of such membership to the poor and one-third each to local governments and voluntary organizations, and allowing local governments to decide on the form the CAP agencies would take. However, public and congressional reluctance to allow federally funded voluntary agencies to be run by the poor was ill-founded: the mobilization of the poor never took place. Though some community action programs experimented with ways to combat poverty, most (even before Congress' changes) had become social service agencies or devices to dispense benefits to those not being served by local government — that is, the poor, and especially the black poor.[30] Actually, the CAP agencies, which were originally created to allow the poor to bring about the changes needed to transform their lives, were deflected by, and ultimately transformed into adjuncts of, the local middle and upper class power structure.[31]

Political participation in general

Political participation takes a number of forms other than voting: campaigning, contacting governmental officials, contributing money, attending rallies, and the like. In all studies of general political participation, one theme recurs: though there are variations, the political democracies that have been studied exhibit a very low rate of citizen involvement:

> In the United States, only 4 or 5 percent (of the adult population) are active in a party, campaign, and attend meetings. About 10 percent make monetary contributions, about 13 percent contact public officials, and about 15 percent display a button or a sticker. Around 25 to 30 percent try to proselytize others to vote a certain way, and from 40 to 70 percent perceive political messages and vote in any given election.[32]

The most thorough study of American political participation not only supports the generalization that low involvement appears to be characteristic of liberal democracy, but also strongly confirms the class basis of political participation found in numerous other studies.[33] In a national survey conducted in 1967 as part of a cross-national study of political participation (itself part of a larger study, the Cross-National Program on Political and Social Change), Verba and Nie identify six types of political participants and their social characteristics (see Table 12-2). Their conclusion is quite explicit: upper socioeconomic status levels (based on averages of income, occupation, and education scores) dominate all forms of political participation. In a follow-up study to determine the effect of other factors, Verba and Nie found that organizational affiliation increases the participation gap between the classes, since upper levels also dominate participation in voluntary organizations. The participation gap is also increased both by affiliation with a political party

30. Ralph M. Kramer, *Participation of the Poor: Comparative Community Case Studies in the War on Poverty* (Englewood Cliffs, N.J.: Prentice-Hall, 1969).

31. For an analysis of participation in the Los Angeles community action agency, which argues that the poor are co-opted by CAPs, see Dale Rogers Marshall, *The Politics of Participation in Poverty* (Berkeley: University of California Press, 1971). For an analysis of data from a sample of twenty American cities, which shows how the Community Action Program was absorbed into the local power structure, see Stephen M. Rose, *The Betrayal of the Poor: The Transformation of Community Action* (Cambridge, Mass.: Schenkman, 1972).

32. Lester W. Milbrath, *Political Participation: How and Why Do People Get Involved in Politics?* (Chicago: Rand McNally, 1965), p. 19.

33. Sidney Verba and Norman H. Nie, *Participation in America: Political Democracy and Social Equality* (New York: Harper and Row, 1972).

Table 12-2 The Participation Input: A Summary

Type of participant	Pattern of activity	Theoretical dimensions of activity pattern	Leading orientations	Main social characteristics
The inactives (22%)	No activity		Totally uninvolved, no interest, skill, sense of competence, or concern with conflict.	Lower socioeconomic levels and blacks are overrepresented, as are older and younger citizens (but not middle-aged ones) and women.
The voting specialists (21%)	They vote regularly, but do nothing else.	Broad collective outcomes, counterparticipants, and low initiative.	Strong partisan identity but otherwise relatively uninvolved and with low skills and competence.	Lower socioeconomic levels are overrepresented. Older citizens are overrepresented, as are those in big cities. Underrepresented in rural areas.
The parochial participants (4%)	They contact officials on particularized problems and are otherwise inactive.	Particularized outcomes, no conflict, and high initiative.	Some political skill (information) but otherwise no political involvement.	Lower socioeconomic groups are overrepresented, but blacks are underrepresented. Catholic rather than Protestant. Big cities rather than small towns.

The communalists (20%)	They contact officials on broad social issues and engage in cooperative activity. Vote fairly regularly, but avoid election campaigns.	Collective outcomes (but may be narrower than those of elections), high initiative, and relatively no conflict.	High sense of community contribution, involvement in politics, skill and competence. Nonpartisan and avoid conflict.	Upper socioeconomic levels very overrepresented, blacks underrepresented. Protestant rather than Catholic. Overrepresented in rural areas and small towns; underrepresented in big cities.
The campaigners (15%)	Heavily active in campaigns and vote regularly.	Broad collective outcomes, moderate to high initiative, and relatively conflictual.	Politically involved, relatively skilled and competent, partisan and involved in conflict, but little sense of community contribution.	Overrepresentation of upper-status groups. Blacks and particularly Catholics overrepresented. Big-city and suburbs rather than small towns and rural areas.
The complete activists (11%)	Active in all ways.	All characteristics of all acts.	Involved in politics in all ways, highly skilled and competent.	Heavy over-representation of upper-status groups. Old and young underrepresented.
(7% of sample unclassified)				

SOURCE: Table 7-1 "The Participation Input: A Summary" in *Participation in America: Political Democracy and Social Equality* by Sidney Verba and Norman H. Nie (Harper and Row, 1972).

and by political beliefs associated with participation, since the latter reflect the conservative policy preferences of upper-level Republicans.

Comparing their survey with the historical record of American electoral behavior compiled by the Survey Research Center at the University of Michigan, Verba and Nie conclude that the political participation of Americans has been stable for at least two decades. The only factor that reduces the power of socioeconomic status is black group consciousness.[34] Black political participation is low, but not as low as their socioeconomic status would suggest. However, aside from black (and perhaps other minority) consciousness, nothing indicates the imminence of a decrease in the gap between the classes; if anything, it may increase. Political participation is highest in smaller well-defined communities, but the trend is toward unbounded urban and suburban areas where participation is more difficult and lower. This trend may produce an even more class-bound and elitist structure of political participation than now exists.[35]

Verba and Nie also found that the overall policy preferences of both Democratic and Republican activists are much more conservative than those of the population-at-large, and that the conservatism of Democrats is due to SES and that of Republicans to SES and conservative beliefs. Verba and Nie conclude:

> Thus the relationship of social status to participation as well as the relationship of political ideology to participation push in the same direction: the creation of a participant population different from the population as a whole. Our data show that participants are less aware of serious welfare problems than the population as a whole, less concerned about the income gap between rich and poor, less interested in government support for welfare programs, and less concerned with equal opportunities for black Americans.[36]

Verba and Nie leave little doubt that political participation has an impact on policy outcomes: simply put, those who participate most receive the most from government. Since the highest participators are the upper classes, it is they who receive the most. However, activists in the lower classes do not receive much more than the nonactive members of the lower classes, largely because lower-level activists, though vocal and visible, are few in number.[37]

Voting preference

The relation between class and voting preference has become a staple subject of political analysis. Like voting participation in general, voting preference correlates with the hierarchy of class-prestige (though there is little class

---

34. Andrew M. Greeley has suggested that ethnicity and religion are as influential in determining political participation as class; see his "Political Participation Among Ethnic Groups in the United States: A Preliminary Reconnaissance," *American Journal of Sociology* 80 (July 1974): 170–204.
35. Verba and Nie, *Participation in America*, Part 2.
36. *Ibid.*, p. 298.
37. *Ibid.*, Part 2.

consciousness in this regard in the United States). High and middle class-prestige individuals (professionals, managers, proprietors and other white-collar workers, college graduates, and individuals with high incomes) largely support the Republican party, while members of the working class and those with low prestige status regardless of class (manual workers, laborers, blacks, Roman Catholics, Jews) have tended to support the Democratic party, a division that corresponds roughly to the difference between laissez-faire and interventionist views on the economic responsibilities of government.[38]

In analyzing voting preference, it is necessary to separate class factors from ethnicity, religion, and race and to adjust for age, sex, and region. A useful perspective on the relations between class and voting preference in the United States is achieved by comparing it with other countries. In his analysis of voting in four liberal democracies, Robert Alford found distinctly more class-based voting in Great Britain and Australia than in the United States and Canada (see Table 12-3).[39]

The absence of a pronounced relation between class and voting preference in the United States does not mean that class forces are not at the root of American politics. Given the power of class over behavior in general and over other aspects of political life, it would be highly surprising if class and

Table 12-3 Class Voting Within Strata Defined by Two Class Characteristics, Four Anglo-American Countries, Surveys Between 1952–1962 (Means)

Country	Education and occupation	Income and occupation	Subjective social class and occupation	Trade union membership and occupation
Great Britain	57	52	53	51
Australia	43	46	47	46
United States	26	31	35	22
Canada	10	11	12	16

SOURCE: Reprinted with permission of Macmillan Publishing Co., from Robert R. Alford, "Class Voting in the Anglo-American Political Systems" in *Party Systems and Voter Alignments: Cross-National Perspectives,* ed. Seymour M. Lipset and Stein Rokkan (New York: The Free Press, 1967), Table 5, p. 84. Copyright © 1967 by The Free Press, a division of The Macmillan Company.

38. As we will see, on issues concerning civil rights, toleration of dissent and minorities, and foreign policy, the reverse is true: the lower classes are less tolerant and less interested in aiding foreign countries (though there are obvious exceptions by issue).

39. Robert R. Alford, *Party and Society: The Anglo-American Democracies* (Chicago: Rand McNally, 1963); Alford updates his data in his essay, "Class Voting in the Anglo-American Political Systems" in *Party Systems and Voter Alignments: Cross-National Perspectives,* ed. Seymour M. Lipset and Stein Rokkan (New York: Free Press, 1967), chap. 1.

voting preference were not also explicable in class terms. Table 12-3's comparison of the four Anglo-American democracies is useful but also misleading. Despite their common British origin, the four countries are quite dissimilar. Only one, for example, has a class system that grew out of estate or feudal stratification.

Of course, the amount of class voting in the United States appears low even aside from comparisons with Great Britain and Australia. Analysts have noted the strength of ethnicity and religion in voting preference [40] and political participation in general.[41] Others have argued that ideological commitment is a variable in voting.[42] Regionalism has also figured largely in American political analysis; and, finally, it has been generally assumed that affluence would transform the worker into a middle class voter, as well as a middle class consumer.

None of these arguments, however, should be allowed to obscure the direct and indirect class components of such phenomena. "Racial" divisions stem from plantation capitalism; ethnic and religious diversity stem from immigration promoted by industry in order to acquire cheap labor. All in all, the American economy has grown so fast, and become so large and so diversified, that it is not surprising that its various elements do not fit readily into static homogeneous class categories. But one need only recall Wiley's argument about the unique class basis of American politics to see that American political behavior is not as unrelated to class as it appears. Americans, in other words, are subject to cross-pressures and inconsistencies *within* the class dimension unparalleled in other societies. There are also the effects of economic mobility: many white-collar persons who do not vote for the Republican party are not violating the class behavior expected of them, since many white-collar workers are really working class both by origin and by function. And when a blue-collar voter fails to vote for the Democratic party, it may be that his wife works and that their combined income has led to property and rental income; or his wife and daughter may be working in white-collar jobs, thus introducing diversity and cross-pressures into an otherwise blue-collar family. At both the apex and the bottom of the various class hierarchies (commodity, credit, and labor) cross-pressures make it difficult for those in similar economic circumstances to develop a common consciousness (something that is much more difficult to achieve at the bottom). And, of course, differences *within* the class dimension are magnified by ethnic, religious, and "racial" differences.

Each of the arguments that seem to run counter to a class explanation of political preferences deserves some consideration. There is little doubt that regionalism has been an important feature of American politics, but its role

40. Alford, *Party and Society,* chap. 8.

41. Andrew M. Greeley, "Political Participation Among Ethnic Groups in the United States: A Preliminary Reconnaissance," *American Journal of Sociology* 80 (July 1974): 170–204.

42. Gertrude Jaeger Selznick and Stephen Steinberg, "Social Class, Ideology, and Voting Preference: An Analysis of the 1964 Presidential Election," in *Structured Social Inequality: A Reader in Comparative Social Stratification,* ed. and intro. by Celia S. Heller (New York: Macmillan, 1969), pp. 216–226.

in American politics appears to be declining.[43] Actually, there is no reason why sectional political behavior cannot be incorporated into class theory — people do not vote in given ways because of geography *per se*. Historically, southerners voted as they did because of the social structure of the south. The south was dominated by a single party because at one time it had a unitary economy based on capitalistic agriculture (a mixture of plantation, tenant, and freeholding farming) in economic and political rivalry with the industry, commerce, and freeholding agriculture of the rest of the nation.[44] The decline of sectionalism in the south stems from industrialization, an economic development that is producing there a class politics more akin to that of the rest of the country. The new forms of sectionalism that have appeared in the American west and southwest are also forms of class politics — that is, such differences as exist stem from the class-prestige factors unique to that area. For example, the political conservatism of the state of Arizona is in part due to the simple fact that it is a favorite place of retirement for the affluent old.

When citing religion as a political force, it is important to remember that religion is associated with class position and that the political behavior associated with it is perhaps more understandable in terms of class than of religion as such. The historic association of Roman Catholics with the Democratic party, for example, is consistent with stratification analysis, as is the temporary defection of Roman Catholics from the Democrats in the 1950s. As a working class and low-prestige (in occupational and religious-ethnic terms) group, Roman Catholics voted for the most egalitarian party, the Democrats. Given some improvement in their class position by the 1950s, and the alleged international menace of communism, Roman Catholics gave significant support to McCarthy and Eisenhower (right and liberal Republicans) in an effort to improve their prestige (Americanism) and to fight "Godless" Russia. In addition, as Roman Catholics — especially those from European and Canadian backgrounds — have circulated throughout the class structure in recent decades, their political preferences have diversified and their historic association with the Democratic party appears to be ending.

The belief that prosperity will transform workers into middle class voters, a basic tenet of the liberal concept of evolutionary convergence, is not borne out by the evidence. It is clear that neither affluence nor new blue-collar occupations and work settings have lured workers into middle class political outlooks, at least not in Great Britain.[45]

Ideological commitment has also been identified as a variable in voting. Where voters have strong and consistent ideological commitments, their voting

43. V. O. Key, *Politics, Parties, and Pressure Groups,* 5th ed. (New York: Thomas Y. Crowell, 1964), pp. 245–248.

44. The failure to represent urban populations more accurately and the regularity with which southern legislators are re-elected, which gives them seniority and thus control of the all-important congressional committees, provides political support for the perpetuation of sectionalism.

45. John H. Goldthorpe, David Lockwood, Frank Bechhofer, and Jennifer Platt, *The Affluent Worker: Political Attitudes and Behavior* (Cambridge, England: Cambridge University Press, 1968).

bears little relation to class, or bread-and-butter, interests. That individuals can have political attitudes at variance with the ideology of their class is not surprising. Given the almost monopolistic power of liberalism in the United States, significant numbers of Americans have ideologies out of keeping with their bread-and-butter interests. (These attitudes do not, however, prevent them from often voting for their bread-and-butter interests.)

All in all, the class interests of the mass of the American people appear to be distorted and deflected from political expression by a number of factors from the past, including the pervasive ideology of individualism that stems from early capitalist experience. Fundamentally, it appears that the upper and upper-middle classes dominate American politics and provide little political choice for the remainder of the American people. William Gamson has proposed an alternative to the pluralist model of political participation. Though pluralist theory tends to emphasize the openness of the American political system and its responsiveness to public need and changing times, Gamson argues that a model he calls *stable unrepresentation* may be more accurate. He hypothesizes that

> the American political system normally functions to (1) keep unrepresented groups from developing solidarity and politically organizing, and (2) discourage their effective entry into the competitive establishment if and as they become organized. The competitive establishment is boundary-maintaining and the boundary-maintaining process involves various kinds of social control.[46]

In terms of social stratification, stable unrepresentation appears to be deeply embedded in the political dynamics of social class.

Political attitudes

Political attitudes are also linked to location in the class hierarchy (especially occupation) and in the prestige hierarchy (especially religion, ethnicity, and "race"). Generally, the upper classes are more knowledgeable about public affairs, more liberal with regard to civil rights and foreign policy issues, and more tolerant of all forms of dissent than the lower classes. On the other hand, those at the top of the class-prestige ladder are significantly more conservative on economic policy — that is, they have negative attitudes toward federal spending, deficit financing, the federal debt, "socialized" medicine, and welfare legislation in general. The lower classes are the reverse: more conservative with regard to civil rights (with obvious exceptions) and more liberal on economic policy and governmental programs.[47] The American population also divides along class lines when asked about the efficacy of per-

46. William Gamson, "Stable Unrepresentation in American Society," *American Behavioral Scientist* 12 (November–December 1968): 19f.

47. For a valuable summary by Alfred Hero of three decades of public opinion surveys in these general areas, see John P. Robinson *et al.*, *Measures of Political Attitudes* (Ann Arbor, Mich.: Survey Research Center, Institute for Social Research, 1968), pp. 38–50.

sonal political effort. The upper classes, which participate in politics more than the lower classes, also believe more than the lower classes that political effort is efficacious.

When the opinions of the American public are measured on a "liberalism/conservatism" scale, they appear schizoid: on broad ideological issues Americans veer strongly toward conservatism, but on specific bread-and-butter issues they are markedly liberal.[48] If one examines class differences in the consistency with which political attitudes are held, as have Free and Cantril, a significant cleavage appears: the upper classes are far more consistent in their attitudes than the lower, and manual workers — especially whites — are almost "schizophrenic." Upper class individuals tend to be consistently conservative (except for Jews, who are consistently liberal); the only other consistent group is black Americans, who, subject to a uniform environment of disadvantage and oppression, have no trouble agreeing on the political orientation (liberal) most favorable to their interests.

On broad ideological questions concerning the proper role of government and the nature of the American socioeconomic system, there exists broad agreement among the classes (as measured by education and income). There is somewhat less agreement on these ideological issues when individuals subjectively define their own class. On bread-and-butter issues — or, to use Free and Cantril's term, the *operational spectrum* — there is also considerable agreement among the American people, though here the lower classes believe significantly more than the upper classes, whether classes are ranked objectively or subjectively, that government should do more to promote economic well-being.

We have noted a striking difference in personal self-confidence and independence, and in participation in aesthetic and thought life, between the upper and lower classes.[49] If these differences between the classes are considered in combination with differences in political attitudes, some profoundly important questions are raised about the nature and prospects of liberal democracy. In an extremely valuable summary and analysis of a wide range of American and English public opinion surveys on sociopolitical questions, Michael Mann has questioned the dominant belief among social scientists (and Marxists) that society functions because it rests on consensus. (Marxists attribute much of this consensus to false consciousness.) A review of a large number of empirical analyses, says Mann, yields four general findings about contemporary society:

1. value consensus does not exist to any significant extent;
2. there is a greater degree of consensus among the middle class than among the working class;
3. the working class is more likely to support deviant values if those

48. Lloyd A. Free and Hadley Cantril, *The Political Beliefs of Americans* (New Brunswick, N.J.: Rutgers University Press, 1967), especially chaps. 2 and 3.
49. See "Class, Personality, and World View" in Chapter 8 and "The Consumption of Time and 'Symbolic' Culture" in Chapter 9.

values relate either to concrete everyday life or to vague populist concepts than if they relate to an abstract political philosophy;

4. working class individuals also exhibit less internal *consistency* in their values than middle class people.[50]

Society works, Mann claims, not because people agree on values or even on fundamentals, but because most behavior is controlled by specific role systems: individuals come to accept the drudgeries and disappointments of life and tolerate vast contradictions in their roles and in their beliefs. The working class is compliant not because of value-consensus but because it lacks consensus about its deviant values. And it cannot develop a coherent radical sociopolitical philosophy, because its socialization to the dominant symbols of society fragments its mental and emotional world and gives it beliefs and values that are of little aid in interpreting the reality it faces.[51] This is an important insight into the workings of American society, and also helps to explain why Americans are not class-conscious. From this standpoint, it appears that one of the reasons the United States functions is that it provides for the mass of its population a discontinuous experience or *anomic* social world that generates its own stability by promoting attitudinal confusion. As we will see, the United States also purchases some of its stability at the price of high rates of nonpolitical deviance.[52]

Political extremism
Political extremism as a social phenomenon

An outgrowth of Durkheim's classic study of suicide, the sociological explanation of deviance (as opposed to the biopsychological explanation) has been applied to almost every form of nonconformist behavior. The central insight of this tradition is that deviant behavior stems in a rather direct way from the normal institutions of society.[53]

The various forms of extremism and radicalism that characterize American political history are almost all nourished by liberal values and beliefs, or, broadly, by the tradition of individualism. It is interesting to note that the main branches of the American right and non-Marxist left both invoke the traditional American definitions of the individual and society to validate their appeals for change. In short, common to both is a belief in the self-sufficiency of the individual. Both the right and the left believe that people can live in harmony with themselves, with others, and with nature if they are left alone. A corollary to this belief is their common assault on the sources of authority:

50. Michael Mann, "The Social Cohesion of Liberal Democracy," *American Sociological Review* 35 (June 1970): 423–439. Used by permission.

51. Mann cites studies that point to the role of the school in transmitting dominant values and a benevolent view of political authority. This is accomplished largely by ignoring the role of conflict and serious issues affecting the lower classes.

52. See "Class and *Anomie*: The Uses of Deviance" in Chapter 15.

53. For the best treatment of social problems and deviance from this perspective, see Robert K. Merton and Robert A. Nisbet, eds., *Contemporary Social Problems,* 3rd ed. (New York: Harcourt Brace Jovanovich, 1971).

government, the establishment, the power structure, the power elite, the system, the Supreme Court, bureaucracy, the intellectual, the military-industrial complex, and the like.

The class-prestige basis of political extremism

In analyzing American radicalism, much has been made of a phenomenon known as *status politics,* the attempt by prestige groups to protect or enhance their prestige and other interests through political action. Economic change is a threat to prestige groups dependent on old economic structures, and such groups tend to fight to protect their way of life. The French aristocracy during the eighteenth century is a prime example. Threatened by the rise of the middle class, the French aristocracy acted politically to close avenues of mobility previously accessible to middle class money, especially the purchase of titles, offices, and commissions.

"Class" politics, on the other hand, seems to emerge most decisively when economic groups are threatened by adverse economic conditions, especially a depression. Lipset has tended to identify the extremism of status politics with prosperity and that of class politics with depression.[54] This perspective is sound enough if it serves to caution us against the belief that economic expansion is a solution to all social problems. But the distinction between status and class politics should not obscure the pre-eminent role of economic structure in American politics: the rapid bureaucratization and concentration of the American economy; its deep and complex economic-class rivalries; and the rise of stronger, more explicitly directive governments. According to Daniel Bell, it is the groups that have been suddenly "dispossessed" or abruptly involved in the onrush of modern society that exhibit political extremism: the old middle class (the small-town lawyer, independent doctor, small farmer, small manufacturer, real estate agent, small contractor, gas station owner, retail merchant); the unskilled worker; the former farmhand (especially the black American, abruptly thrust into an alien urban environment); the upwardly mobile millionaire or successful immigrant; the isolated worker (lumberjack, stevedore); and the school dropout.

Others have developed similar explanations of political extremism by applying the concept of *status inconsistency,* or the felt contradiction within a given status or between a range of statuses.[55] For example, violence against blacks in the American south has been explained as a function of "caste"-class inconsistency. In the post–Civil War period, southern whites erected an absolute barrier to black mobility in the areas of prestige and power, but so deep was their respect for private property and economic freedom that they could

54. Though I have changed terminology and emphases, I am indebted throughout this section to the essays in Daniel Bell, ed., *The Radical Right* (Garden City, N.Y.: Doubleday Anchor Books, 1964), especially those by Daniel Bell, Richard Hofstadter, and Seymour M. Lipset.

55. For a previous discussion of consistency explanations and their dangers, see Chapter 3.

not bring themselves legally to prohibit blacks from owning property or selling their labor. This inconsistency in the southern "caste" system made it possible for some blacks to rise in the class hierarchy, which in turn occasioned violence on the part of those who were threatened by black class mobility.[56]

In a seminal application of the concept of status consistency to American history, Richard Hofstadter has interpreted the age of reform in the latter part of the nineteenth century as a struggle against a rising plutocracy by a declining old middle class.[57] And Joseph R. Gusfield has interpreted the Prohibition movement as a rear-guard action by a declining rural-Protestant middle class.[58] A pioneering analysis of voting behavior in the 1940 presidential election argued that voters under inconsistent pressures ("cross-pressures") tended to delay their electoral decisions, to be nonvoters, and, on the whole, to be less partisan than other voters. The net result of social inconsistency, according to this study, is to introduce flexibility into the social system, to provide bridges between disparate groups, and to moderate and stabilize political life.[59]

In another application of this mode of analysis, Kornhauser has pointed to the extremist behavior of unattached intellectuals and those in other occupational categories characterized by isolation.[60] There are many such examples of the application of consistency theory to politics. Theorists have explained the rise of Nazism in Germany as a response to the threat posed by rampant inflation to the class position of the German bourgeoisie. Tory democracy can be interpreted as the effort of a landed aristocracy to use its prestige and power assets to make up for its economic shortcomings. And E. Digby Baltzell, who believes society needs an establishment (consistency at the top of the class, prestige, and power hierarchies), found a serious contradiction between the United States' "open-class" elite systems (class and power) and its "caste-ridden" prestige system, a contradiction so serious as to threaten the legitimacy of American institutions.[61] And, finally, members of the working and middle classes who are subject to cross-pressures or status inconsistencies — evoking feelings of ambiguity, indecision, powerlessness, and anxiety — appear to be especially prone to extremism.[62] The manifestations of such extremism can include vigilantism, labor-management violence, riots, electoral support of radical

56. Allison Davis, "Caste, Economy, and Violence," *American Journal of Sociology* 51, no. 1 (July 1945): 7–15; also available as Bobbs Merrill reprint no. S-61.

57. Richard Hofstadter, *The Age of Reform* (New York: Random House, 1955), chap. 4, also in paperback.

58. Joseph R. Gusfield, *Symbolic Crusade: Status Politics and the American Temperance Movement* (Urbana: University of Illinois Press, 1963), also in paperback.

59. Paul F. Lazarsfeld, Bernard R. Berelson, and Hazel Gaudet, *The People's Choice* (New York: Columbia University Press, 1949).

60. William Kornhauser, *The Politics of Mass Society* (New York: Free Press, 1959).

61. E. Digby Baltzell, *The Protestant Establishment: Aristocracy and Caste in America* (New York: Random House, 1964), also in paperback.

62. For a classic social psychological analysis, see Eric Fromm, *Escape From Freedom* (New York: Holt Rinehart, and Winston, 1941), available in Avon paperback.

right- and left-wing parties, and even apathy.[63] (It should be noted that the upper classes often nourish left authoritarianism and the working class often nourishes right authoritarianism.) It is not surprising, of course, that people caught in social situations that isolate them and endanger their personal and economic security behave "neurotically."[64] In sum, extreme cross-pressures in class or prestige position or in a mixture of the two appear to lie at the heart of political extremism, whether of the left or of the right.

In a summary of studies analyzing opposition (often successful) to fluoridation, Kornhauser has demonstrated that those with little education, low occupational status, and low income; members of the old middle class, such as small farmers and small businesspeople; and/or people with little responsibility for or attachment to the community account for most such opposition, which often violates accepted norms of political behavior. Interestingly, the same classes vehemently opposed integration and civil service reform in police and fire departments, suggesting again that much right-wing radicalism reflects changes in the class system. In short, the classes bypassed by the large-scale bureaucratization and professionalization of our economy and government (or, in Arnold Rogow's apt phrase, the "discontinued classes") tend to become political extremists.[65]

The increased activity on the left during the 1930s — socialist and communist movements — largely involved intellectuals and was, on the whole, weak. Lower class and working class Americans did not respond to the crisis of the Great Depression with demands for revolutionary or even drastic social changes. They were largely content to respond to the leadership of middle class reformers and their New Deal programs, as well as to the demagogic appeals of Huey

63. Seymour M. Lipset has compiled and summarized much of the data on political extremism as part of his cross-national studies in political sociology; see his *Political Man: The Social Bases of Politics* (Garden City, N.Y.: Doubleday, 1959, 1960), his more recent collection of essays, *Revolution and Counterrevolution: Change and Persistence in Social Structures* (New York: Basic Books, 1968), and his and Earl Raab's fascinating history of right-wing extremism in America, *The Politics of Unreason* (New York: Harper and Row, 1970). Also see James W. Vander Zanden, "The Klan Revival," *American Journal of Sociology* 65, no. 5 (March 1960): 456–462; also available as Bobbs-Merrill reprint no. S-29a. And see John E. Horton and Wayne E. Thompson, "Powerlessness and Political Negativism: A Study of Defeated Local Referendums," *American Journal of Sociology* 67, no. 5 (March 1962): 485–493.

64. For a broad historical-theoretical exploration of the social conditions that promote "true anxiety" (rational problem-solving) and "neurotic anxiety" (emotional attachment to redemptory leaders or causes), see Franz Neumann, "Anxiety and Politics," in his *The Democratic and Authoritarian State: Essays in Political and Legal Theory* (New York: Free Press, 1967), chap. 11.

65. William Kornhauser, "Power and Participation in the Local Community," *Health Education Monographs No. 6* (Oakland, Calif.: Society of Public Health Educators, 1959); reprinted in Roland L. Warren, ed., *Perspectives on the American Community* (Chicago: Rand McNally, 1966), pp. 489–498. For the best attempt to explore the implications of such findings for social theory, see William Kornhauser, *The Politics of Mass Society* (New York: Free Press, 1959). Also see the partial disclaimer of the automatic equation of mass society and extremism by Joseph R. Gusfield, "Mass Society and Extremist Politics," *American Sociological Review* 27 (February 1962): 19–30; also available as Bobbs-Merrill reprint no. S-588.

Long and Father Coughlin. During the 1960s a decided left extremism arose — the New Left — but again its relation to the class system is difficult to establish.[66] Centered in the universities and in black communities, its manifestations were a civil rights movement directed against the southern "caste" system, and thus not extremist from the standpoint of American liberalism; a small black militant movement, composed of a number of small groups, which saw no hope for blacks (or whites) in American society as presently constituted; and a student movement of diverse groups opposed to educational inadequacies, the capitalist system, and the Vietnam war.[67]

Though violence appeared to increase during the 1960s, the United States has always been a relatively violence-prone society. Interestingly, however, the United States has a relatively low rate of organized political violence.[68] Isolated sporadic acts of political violence, such as assassination, rioting, and bombings, can be thought of as substitutes for rebellion and class struggle. So broad is the consensus on the legitimacy of American political-legal institutions,[69] and on the belief that good and evil reside in the individual, that it is difficult for disaffected Americans to take collective action of a revolutionary nature.

The political participation of representative minorities

Black, Mexican, and Jewish Americans are all strong supporters of the Democratic party. On the whole, 90 percent of the voters in these minority groups tend to support liberal programs and the liberal wing of the Democratic party. Black and Mexican Americans have long been at the bottom levels of the class, prestige, and power hierarchies, and support for a reform party (in the absence of a radical party) is understandable as an effort to improve their positions. Jewish Americans, however, are middle class, and while their heavy commitment to the Democratic party is not necessarily surprising, it represents a deviation from the normal middle class political pattern. However, as members of a religious minority in insecure economic positions, Jews too have a stake in economic reform and in public measures to insure civil rights.

Black and Mexican American rates of political participation are lower than

66. Richard Flacks has suggested that college radicals (as distinct from black, Third World, and white working class youth) came largely from upper-middle class professional backgrounds, especially those of an intellectual cast, and from unstable middle class homes; see his *Youth and Social Change* (Chicago: Markham, 1971), chap. 3.

67. For a good selection of extracts and articles representing the range and focus of the contemporary left, see Priscilla Long, ed., *The New Left: A Collection of Essays* (Boston: Porter Sargent, 1969), and Robert Perrucci and Marc Pilisuk, eds., *The Triple Revolution: Social Problems in Depth* (Boston: Little, Brown, 1968).

68. Hugh Davis Graham and Ted Robert Gurr, eds., *Violence in America: Historical and Comparative Perspectives,* a report to the National Commission on the Causes and Prevention of Violence, 2 vols. (Washington: D.C.: U. S. Government Printing Office, 1969), *passim* and Conclusion.

69. For a comprehensive review of data on the ideology of Americans, which finds substantial consensus on the core principles of the Lockean liberal (political) tradition, see Donald J. Devine, *The Political Culture of the United States: The Influence of Member Values on Regime Maintenance* (Boston: Little, Brown, 1972).

that of the upper classes and even lower than the national rate. But blacks' participation rate is higher than their class standing would suggest, a phenomenon that evidently stems from black consciousness. Jewish Americans have a high rate of political participation, but it appears to be almost completely a class phenomenon rather than a result of ethnic or religious factors. Efforts to protect and enhance black voting rights in the south have been significantly successful. Thanks largely to a series of Civil Rights Acts, especially the Voting Rights Act of 1965, and to the rise in absolute class level among southern blacks, the black voting rate in the south climbed from 44 percent in 1964 to 51.6 percent in 1968. But it is also noteworthy that the overall national voting rate for blacks did not increase; in fact, there was a decline from 58.5 percent to 57.6 percent, as compared to white rates of 70.7 and 69.1, for the years 1964 and 1968.[70] The stabilization of the black voting rate at a low level is even more apparent in the presidential election of 1972. Blacks in the south voted at a rate of 49.5 percent, compared to 59.5 percent for whites; nationally, blacks voted at a rate of 52.1 percent, compared to 64.5 percent for whites.[71]

The relevance for social stratification of the foregoing data on black voting behavior should not be overlooked. While the "caste" forces that prevent black Americans from voting are crumbling, blacks are still subject to the force of class. The decline of "caste" thus has the effect of revealing the class position of blacks in a purer form. Overwhelmingly "lower class" by virtue of income, occupation, and even education, the black American is merely recapitulating the classic pattern of white voting behavior: the lower classes vote less, and markedly so, than the upper classes.

Mexican Americans also have a low rate of voting and political participation. Their unusually low voting rates are attributable to such barriers as the requirement to register, often in unaccessible places; literacy tests, conducted in English; poll taxes; a low rate of naturalization; gerrymandering; and the cooptation of Mexican American leaders by Anglo groups. However, when Mexican Americans in San Antonio are compared with their ethnic counterparts in Los Angeles, it is apparent that Mexican American political behavior begins to approach that of other Americans in the freer and more inviting political atmosphere of Los Angeles: their rate of participation is higher, and upper level Mexican Americans participate more than those in lower levels.

On the whole, Mexican Americans are quite ambivalent about politics, tend to have little confidence in government, and overwhelmingly reject any alliance with black Americans.[72] Viewed nationally, the Mexican American voting

70. U.S. Bureau of the Census, *Current Population Reports,* Series P-20, No. 143, "Voter Participation in the National Election: November, 1964" (Washington, D.C.: U.S. Government Printing Office, 1965), Tables 1 and 2; *Current Population Reports,* Series P-20, No. 192, "Voting and Registration in the Election of November, 1968" (Washington, D.C.: U.S. Government Printing Office, 1969), Tables 1 and 2.
71. U.S. Bureau of the Census, *Current Population Reports,* Series P-20, No. 253, "Voting and Registration in the Election of November, 1972" (Washington, D.C.: U.S. Government Office, 1973), Tables 1 and 4.
72. For general background on the political behavior of Mexican Americans, see

rate is unusually low: in the 1972 presidential election only 37.5 percent of Mexican Americans voted.[73]

It goes without saying that most American minorities are not represented in political positions in proportion to their numbers, especially if one focuses on upper-echelon decision-making positions. Women are obviously vastly under-represented, and, though exact studies are lacking, the same is probably true of other minorities. Black Americans are employed in federal civil service occupations at higher rates than whites, and they have made significant gains in winning elective office in recent years, especially at the local level. However, black Americans are still far from holding a proportionate share of important public positions, at either the elected or the appointed level.[74] The same is true for Mexican Americans and, to a degree, for Jewish Americans.

Class-prestige and political participation: a summary

It is widely believed that the emergence of representative government marks a significant advance in equality, but the realities of political participation require this view to be heavily qualified. It is probably more accurate to say that elections and other forms of political participation are means to translate economic and prestige power into political power. It is clear from the evidence, in other words, that class and prestige control all forms of political participation and that the middle and upper classes dominate political life.

Black and Mexican Americans are at last able to exercise the franchise, though both still manifest low rates of voting and other forms of political participation. This phenomenon is attributable to their class standing: by and large, black and Mexican American participation is comparable to that of other groups in a similar class position, though blacks have somewhat higher rates of political and other forms of voluntary behavior than their class warrants. Jewish Americans are traditionally active in politics, due to their concentration in urban areas and gradual acquisition of middle class status. All three minority groups strongly support the Democratic party.

Leo Grebler, Joan W. Moore, Ralph C. Guzman *et al., The Mexican-American People: The Nation's Second Largest Minority* (New York: Free Press, 1970), chap. 23.

73. U.S. Bureau of the Census, *Current Population Reports,* Series P-20, No. 253, "Voting and Registration in the Election of November, 1972" (Washington, D.C.: U.S. Government Printing Office, 1973), Table 2.

74. For an important analysis at the local level, see Harold M. Baron with Harriet Stulman, Richard Rothstein, and Rennard Davis, "Black Powerlessness in Chicago," *Transaction* 6 (November 1968): 27–33; reprinted in Charles H. Anderson, ed., *Sociological Essays and Research* (Homewood, Ill.: Dorsey Press, 1970), pp. 141–151. For an excellent analysis of the problems black Americans face in acquiring political power, see Harry M. Scoble, "Negro Politics in Los Angeles: The Quest for Power," Institute for Government and Public Affairs, University of California at Los Angeles (1967); abridged and reprinted in Peter Orleans with Sonya Orleans, eds., *Social Structure and Social Process* (Boston: Allyn and Bacon, 1969), pp. 639–650. The federal government, it should be noted, still tends to follow racist hiring practices in southern states, though some changes are discernible.

13

The class-prestige nature of legislation and government

THE HISTORY OF legislation and government in the United States is a vast and complex subject, and ours can be only a preliminary, exploratory analysis. To guide us through the maze of data in this area, we will view the behavior of American legislatures and governments during the past century as an aspect of the process of rounding out and updating liberal society. We will note again that government is far less independent of society (class-prestige) than many think. And we will be wary of a pervasive public theme that is attractive and beneficial in some ways but dangerous and detrimental in others, the hope that society can be run objectively. The liberal world view has always harbored a strong technocratic component, which the United States manifests in many different ways. It is almost axiomatic for Americans that political candidates and even voters should be above politics, that good government is nonpartisan, and that education and knowledge are advantageous in public affairs. The independent voter, the civic-minded citizen, the nonpartisan election, the political neutrality of schools and universities, the use of the tax code to keep politically and socially relevant private groups nonpolitical, and heavy reliance on administration are further manifestations of the technocratic spirit. It is readily apparent that, whatever else this tradition is, it is also a force for protecting the status quo, promoting elitism and narrow professionalism, and disguising the very real partisan consequences that "objectivity" and "neutrality" in social science and other professions have for political and social life.

The class-prestige nature of legislation

There are many classic examples of class-prestige legislation. Every school-child knows that the repeal of the Corn Laws signified the rise of industry in the English economy. In the United States during the nineteenth century, industry and labor erected high tariff walls to protect manufacturing, and farmers tried to pull them down. Banking legislation and governmental credit and monetary policy also reflect the struggle between debtor groups, such as farmers, and creditors, such as bankers. It was governmental policy (the Homestead Act) that encouraged freeholding (capitalist) farming, as well as the private exploitation of minerals, timber, and waterways. And the United States Supreme Court supported property interests in case after case between 1865 and the 1930s.[1]

Before exploring in depth some representative areas of legislation and governmental activity, it will be advantageous to examine some of the stereotypes that prevent accurate perception of political facts and keep observers from seeing the structure of power and the real and often ironic consequences of political-legal action. Let us take a simple example first. It is well known that public authorities evict tenants whose incomes have risen above the maximum level of eligibility for public housing. Initially, one is likely to assume that this is a means of protecting the class interests of the poor. However, such an assumption overlooks the fact that public housing legislation was explicitly formulated to insure that public housing would not compete with private housing. In other words, the eviction requirement is intended to protect the private housing market by guaranteeing that the nonpoor buy their housing from private owners! The net result is that the moral, economic, and political power of the state is used to make housing a private-profit field. Indeed, one of the latent functions of the provision of public housing is to divert attention from the failure of our economic institutions adequately to house our population, and from the possibility that this is a condition chronic to American-style capitalism.[2]

The latent consequences of legislation are obscured because political action is invariably framed in the rhetoric of public interest and moral rectitude. Among the most dramatic examples is our policy of military conscription. The administration of this system was in the best tradition of grassroots democracy:

---

1. For a good review of the Supreme Court during this period, see Arthur Selwyn Miller, *The Supreme Court and American Capitalism* (New York: Free Press, 1968). Caution should be exercised, however, in accepting Miller's suggestion that capitalism was somehow so chastened and modified by the Great Depression and the New Deal that it ceased to exist.
2. Public housing projects (our "penthouse prisons") also have the well-known effects of segregating the residences of white and black Americans and keeping the poor of both races out of the neighborhoods of the nonpoor.

it relied on thousands of local draft boards, "little groups of neighbors" who allegedly represented their communities and were able to render fair judgments on who should serve. During the Vietnam war, however, there emerged a manpower surplus — that is, only a small percentage of the relevant age group was needed to fight a war that, while a major military effort, was something less than a national struggle. Thus one of the main functions of the Selective Service System was to defer men from military service. Subject to scrutiny for the first time, the Selective Service System was shown to be a hodgepodge of varying and contradictory policies, administered by unrepresentative draft boards drawn from the upper socioeconomic levels and deeply discriminatory against the lower classes even when the high rejection rates associated with poverty are taken into account. In other words, the power dimension, in the guise of "little groups of neighbors," brought about the differential distribution of a burdensome civic duty and a differential death rate in war along the lines of class.[3]

As we examine the intricacies of public policy in the realms of taxation, Social Security, housing, education, and economics, the foregoing examples should serve as a warning that things are not always what they seem.

Taxation

Despite a strong verbal tradition affirming "ability to pay" as the underlying principle of taxation, and despite an equally strong commitment to reward work and achievement — and, by implication, not to reward idleness or inherited wealth — the American tax structure at all levels seriously violates these honored American values and beliefs.

The first noteworthy feature of income taxation is that it brings about relatively little change in income distribution; furthermore, there is not much difference in wealth before and after estate and inheritance taxes.[4] The reasons for this phenomenon are now fairly well known:

1. The federal income tax structure, while ostensibly progressive, is not very progressive in effect. The net effect of "tax loopholes" is to produce effective rates of taxation far different from the formal rates. The minimal progressive impact of federal income taxation is reduced, moreover, by regressive federal Social Security taxes and state and local property and sales taxes.[5] The higher rates of taxes paid by the very rich and very poor affect less than 10 percent of total national income. It is noteworthy that a full-scale study reveals that the

---

3. James W. Davis, Jr., and Kenneth M. Dolbeare, *Little Groups of Neighbors: the Selective Service System* (Chicago: Markham, 1968), also in paperback. M. Zeitlin, K. A. Lutterman, and J. W. Russell, "Death in Vietnam: Class, Poverty, and the Risks of War," *Politics and Society* 3 (Spring 1973): 313–328.

4. For a previous analysis, see Chapter 4.

5. In addition, United States Savings Bonds, which have no built-in protection against inflation, tend to discriminate (depending on the relative amounts purchased by the various income groups) against members of lower income groups, who cannot ordinarily protect themselves or profit from inflation.

progressive income tax has little negative effect on work incentives, popular mythology notwithstanding.[6]

2. The federal tax structure tends to reward nonwork. The capital gains tax, which is a low rate of taxation on profits received from the sale of property; rapid initial real estate depreciation, which means that the depreciation of property is assumed for tax purposes to occur at a rapid rate while the property is new; tax-free municipal and state bonds; and oil and mineral depletion and investment allowances all tend to protect income resulting from the investment of money. In light of the fact that individuals on straight salaries or wages are taxed at full rates, it would seem that the federal tax code discriminates against those who work for a living. This is especially true when salaried workers are compared with those who can take advantage of two tax loopholes, such as the oil depletion allowance and capital gains, or rapid depreciation and capital gains. It is interesting that the federal tax code rewards work leading to technological discoveries or inventions by defining income from such property as capital gains, while creative work in the arts is not accorded comparable tax status. Though the justice of this situation may be questioned, it is at least a prejudice consistent with the United States' class values.

3. The United States has ineffective death and inheritance taxes, judged in terms of the much-vaunted American ideal of providing each generation equal opportunity within a framework of equal competition. Again the key word is *effective*, for the impression is widespread that it is pointless to work hard to build an estate since the government will confiscate it when one dies. On the contrary, the American system of taxation promotes a considerable level of familism, since it permits the bulk of one generation's wealth to be passed on to the next.[7]

4. The United States gives strong support to *rentiers* and consumers of leisure. The rentier, or individual who lives off property, profits from the benefits described in (2) above, along with hardworking businesspeople and professionals. The expense account is a device with which the state (Internal Revenue Code) differentiates the American population on the basis of prestige (consumption). While tax regulations on expense account deductions have been tightened, this practice still supports high-consumption groups, mainly businesspeople and professionals, at public expense.

The Tax Act of 1969 contains features that support our contention that state action does little to change the relative positions of class-prestige groups. For

6. Robin Barlow, Harvey E. Brazer, and James N. Morgan, *Economic Behavior of the Affluent* (Washington, D.C.: Brookings Institution, 1966).
7. A married couple can leave $120,000 tax-exempt to their children when they die. Before they die, they can give lump sums of $60,000 in tax-free gifts to their children and $3,000 per year to each child. In addition, various types of trust funds can be created to transfer tax-exempt income to children both before and after the deaths of parents.

one thing, this act — which began as a tax reform movement and ended as a tax cut during the highest inflation since 1945 — provided for proportional cuts throughout the income hierarchy and for all tax-favored groups. Of some interest is the fact that the poor benefited from this tax cut by being removed from the federal tax rolls. While obviously advantageous for the poor, this act of benevolence can also be interpreted as undermining incentive to full citizenship and tending further to make the poor wards of the state.

In sum, it is fairly clear from an analysis of taxation that a power dimension based on universal suffrage, which ignores income and wealth by giving each individual one vote, does not lead to a redistribution of income and wealth despite the fact that lower income-wealth groups (the lower-middle class and below) form a numerical majority. The immunity of concentrated income and wealth to majority rule also characterizes the other liberal democracies. The irrelevance of liberal democratic institutions in this realm is highlighted by noting the similarity in concentrated income and economic power between the liberal democracies and the communist dictatorships. Nowhere are the conflict and contradiction between the ideal of equal opportunity and the class system so vividly apparent as in taxation: the American tax code not only reflects the power and privilege of the class-prestige structure, but also facilitates and legitimates their accumulation over time. Or perhaps the contradiction should be expressed differently: is it reasonable to motivate people to work hard and save on an individual basis and then expect to tax their income and savings to promote social values?

Social Security

The historic Social Security Bill of 1935 was denounced by many, especially the representatives of business, as a "giveaway" and socialistic measure that would promote sloth and social decay. But the actual Social Security Act, including amendments appended to it since 1935, is quite different than the ideological debates would suggest. Basically, it is a contributory insurance system to assist the retired and a public assistance program for those who cannot help themselves. Its components are as follows:

1. Old Age, Survivors' and Disability Insurance (OASDI), a system of benefits financed by a tax paid by workers and employers. Benefits go to retired individuals, disabled workers, and the widows and orphans of employees.
2. Old Age Assistance (OAA) and Aid to Families with Dependent Children (AFDC), a system of welfare benefits paid to the needy aged and to families with dependent children. This is a noncontributory program paid for largely through general federal revenues and administered by the states.
3. Health insurance for the elderly (Medicare), financed by employees' and employers' compulsory contributions.

The social insurance portion of this legislation, enacted quite haphazardly during the Great Depression,[8] has a number of features that need to be much better understood. It is financed by a flat tax rate (5.85 percent in 1975) on a portion of individual income ($14,100 in 1975), with no allowances for dependents or for deductions. All in all, it is a highly regressive tax. The funds collected under this system are then paid out to retirees in terms of the amounts they have paid in, rather than on the basis of need. Actually, lowest-income retirees receive proportionately more than higher-income retirees, but the minimum pensions are extremely small; it cannot be said that income is significantly redistributed, or that this feature alters the regressive nature of the social insurance system.

Furthermore, the amounts collected represent very large sums, amounting in effect to a major tax (second only to the personal income tax) and a considerable burden on most white-collar and almost all working class incomes. Also, many jobs held by the lower classes were not covered between roughly 1936 and the late 1960s and early 1970s, and the retirement age of sixty-five discriminates against the lower classes, whose life expectancy only began to reach that level in the 1970s. (Black males will probably not reach an average life expectancy of sixty-five until the late 1970s or early 1980s.) The lower classes benefit most from the provisions for widows and for disability, since they die earlier and are disabled more frequently, but child support through college favors middle class families. Incidentally, the original Social Security tax was based on extremely conservative actuarial estimates, and from the beginning the monies collected have been put in trust funds earning minimum interest. They cannot be used as instruments of governmental fiscal and monetary policy or to provide capital for housing and other public needs.

Payments to the needy from general tax revenues are designed to alleviate hardship, and are ostensibly distributed according to need. But welfare programs are administered by the states, and there is wide variation in levels of payment, criteria used to establish need, and methods of administration. This portion of the Social Security system is still considered a "handout," an attitude that, along with a mode of administering payments that humiliates and stigmatizes recipients, tends to create a pariah group of public dependents. Not only does the administration of this program tend to invade the rights and privacy of the poor, but its latent function is to support and legitimize the social system that creates this form of poverty.[9]

8. Theodore J. Lowi, in his *The End of Liberalism: Ideology, Policy and the Crisis of Public Authority* (New York: W. W. Norton, 1969), uses Social Security legislation to illustrate the vagueness of legislation passed by the United States Congress. Though conservatively financed for its first thirty-five years, the Social Security system began to experience difficulties in the early 1970s because it had been amended in a number of expensive ways without taking demographic and economic trends into account.

9. For Piven and Cloward's argument that the two central functions of welfare are to quell civil disorder and to enforce work norms among the marginal labor force, see "Regulating the Poor" in Chapter 15.

Housing

The history of housing legislation in the United States is a pre-eminent illustration of class politics.[10] Various stages of public concern about and action on housing can be distinguished, from the beginning of the century to the present. But all such legislation and action has failed to provide housing for the poor: every piece of legislation and every form of implementation has been heavily biased in favor of those Friedman calls "the submerged and potential middle class" and against the poor. What Friedman does not stress, because of his focus on the poor, is that housing is in chronically short supply for many who are not poor.[11]

Though the federal government has a wide variety of housing programs, it has never developed a coherent housing policy. The many piecemeal programs, however, manifest a rather distinct pattern, the *filtering strategy* — concentration on quality construction and subsidies, by far the largest of which is income tax deductions for homeowners, for the middle and upper-middle income brackets, beneficial to the poor only in that older homes eventually become available to them.[12]

The housing shortage can also be interpreted as resulting from a disparity between the price of housing and the American income structure, a partial explanation for which is that housing is a complex durable commodity that has not yet been incorporated into the industrial process. But a full explanation must acknowledge the formidable class-prestige-power forces that stand between Americans and adequate housing. Monopolistic craft unions; outmoded building codes; snob zoning; local tax policies; planning practices; the compliance of real estate boards with snob and racial practices; and the transportation, credit, tax, and housing policies of the federal government all function to mesh the availability, type, and location of housing with the income-wealth and prestige structure of the United States. In sum, there is little doubt that the power dimension at the federal, state, and local levels is deeply implicated in the processes that keep housing scarce and segregated along class-prestige lines.

Government and education: the public as partisan
Elementary and high school education

Given both a "rotten borough" and gerrymandered system of political representation at the state and federal levels and our tradition of political decentralization, it is easy to understand why the distribution of educational resources in local American political districts conforms to class lines. The Serrano-Priest decision

10. For a brilliant summary and analysis of housing legislation and action in American history, with valuable insights into the politics of class, see Lawrence M. Friedman, *Government and Slum Housing* (Chicago: Rand McNally, 1968).
11. As Friedman points out, housing for the elderly has received substantial support, partly because the middle class nuclear family is not geared to accommodate aged parents.
12. Henry J. Aaron, *Shelter and Subsidies: Who Benefits from Federal Housing Policies* (Washington, D.C.: Brookings Institution, 1972).

(1971), in which the California Supreme Court ruled unequal expenditures on education unconstitutional, stimulated an effort to make school expenditures more equal.[13] But even equal expenditures will do little to equalize educational opportunity, since the school itself has negligible impact on differentials in academic achievement.[14]

The impact of class on education is deep and pervasive, even from the standpoint of our political-legal and moral tradition of public education. Elected or appointed school board members and appointed educational civil servants (superintendents, principals, teachers) are overwhelmingly middle and upper-middle class.[15] While school board policies vary (the higher the class, the more liberal the school policy is likely to be), and while an ordinary citizen's outlook may broaden when he or she becomes an elected educational official or professional educator, the fact remains that the basic distribution of educational benefits is controlled by class rather than nonclass forces. Indeed, the independent role education is thought to play *vis-à-vis* class is largely fictitious. Schools may have become complex and bureaucratic, and teachers and administrators may have become more professional, but these changes are quite consistent with a major structural feature of contemporary stratification, the shift from an entrepreneurial to a salaried middle class.

The influence of the power dimension (public election of school boards; free, tax-supported schools; public academic standards; certification standards for school teachers and principals) *vis-à-vis* the class-prestige structure seems to be minimal. In other words, when the state expends its energies and resources to educate the young, it reflects and reinforces the class principle of individual achievement. One of the latent consequences of instituting the principle of individual achievement, moreover, is to give support to the existing class structure; in other words, individual achievement diversifies social classes and prevents the formation of class consciousness. Furthermore, to define educational achievement in this way is to insure middle class dominance, thus perpetuating class advantage and disadvantage. Whatever one's opinion, it should be clear that education is deeply dependent on society and that glib, habitual reference to the need for more education in order to solve the United States' social problems is, wittingly or unwittingly, a way of preserving the status quo.

Of some relevance to the question of whether or not power exerts an independent effect on education is the finding that students who attend parochial (Roman Catholic in New England) schools are not much different from students who attend public schools.[16] The similarity is not explained by the

13. The United States Supreme Court ruled in 1973 that unequal educational expenditures are not unconstitutional.
14. See Chapter 6, especially the first three sections.
15. The Supreme Court has ruled that elections to school boards must be based on the principle of "one person, one vote." But such elections do not ordinarily raise the problem of representation; where they do, school boards will probably become appointed bodies.
16. Peter H. Rossi and Alice S. Rossi, "Some Effects of Parochial School Educa-

public standards to which parochial schools must adhere; what is common to both is the power of American culture over education and religion.

Historically, Congress and the federal government have exerted considerable influence on education, largely through deliberate neglect.[17] Though fought for in the name of equal opportunity, the flow of federal money to the schools, which began in 1958, has not changed the class character of American education. All that can be said is that federal aid may have provided better education for all, but without changing relative differences. Of special significance is the fact that a number of national programs, both governmental and nongovernmental (the National Science Foundation, the College Entrance Examination Board, the National Merit Scholarship Corporation, and the National Defense Education Act), have had a differential impact on high schools, and that such differences correlate with the socioeconomic status of the schools. In a study completed in 1963 of 240 Illinois high schools, it was found that the wealthier suburban and urban high schools participated more fully in the most important of these programs. (Only the National Merit Scholarship program, which requires just a few hours of testing time and does not require reorganization of curriculum or teacher training, was utilized equally.) In other words, while these programs strengthened American education, they did so mostly by strengthening the academic programs of wealthier schools containing the highest percentages of college-bound students.[18]

Another example of differential advantage through "equal opportunity" is the failure of the Elementary and Secondary Education Act of 1965 to equalize educational opportunity. Title I of the act was specifically intended to aid education in poor areas. Preliminary assessments at the end of 1969 revealed that state and local governments were allocating the money equally, in effect, benefiting the nonpoor as much or more than the poor. Thus, while everyone benefits, relative differences are maintained.[19]

tion in America," *Harvard Educational Review* 27, no. 3 (Summer 1957), 168–199; reprinted in Robert R. Bell and Holger R. Stub, eds., *The Sociology of Education: A Sourcebook*, rev. ed. (Homewood, Ill.: Dorsey Press, 1968), pp. 53–77.

17. Notwithstanding the establishment of state colleges of agriculture and mechanical arts by means of federal land grants (Morrill Acts). This encouragement of practical university training obviously helped to modernize American society by bringing about industrial agriculture as well as industrial manufacturing, and such colleges did assist the "industrial classes" they were intended to serve. Federal grants also helped to foster racial segregation, since the annual grants (first enacted in 1890) were withheld unless separate A and M colleges for blacks were established.

18. Roald F. Campbell and Robert A. Bunnell, "Differential Impact of National Programs on Secondary Schools," in *Society and Education: A Book of Readings*, ed. Robert J. Havighurst, Bernice L. Neugarten, and Jacqueline M. Falk (Boston: Allyn and Bacon, 1967), pp. 180–185.

19. For an excellent analysis of the failure to implement this act, which emphasizes that the federal and state governments are subject to deep and controlling pressures from local government, see Jerome T. Murphy, "Title I of ESEA: The Politics of Implementing Federal Educational Reform," *Harvard Educational Review* 41 (February 1971): 35–63.

Government and higher education

Public policy in the realm of higher education also reflects and reinforces the American class system. As we have seen, higher education conforms to the basic pattern of class-structured education.[20] Enjoying much greater freedom from direct public supervision than elementary and high schools, both public and private colleges and universities have greater formal capacity to overcome ascriptive class forces. By and large, however, it cannot be said that institutions of higher education counteract the class system or are even aware that they are part of a class system of education. None of this is surprising, given (1) colleges' and universities' ideals of detachment from society (objective scholarship, political neutrality, and cloistered campuses); (2) their actual deep dependence on and involvement in society (control of their governing boards by business-people, professionals, churches, and state legislatures, the involvement of universities and professors in governmental research and consulting, and the dispensation of knowledge in terms of unconsciously held cultural postulates); (3) the fact that presidents, deans, and faculty enjoy upper and upper-middle class status; (4) and the fact that faculty and administrators are almost without exception innocent of any systematic training in education and of backgrounds in up-to-date social science.

Basically, neither the infusion of public money into higher education nor the establishment and expansion of public institutions of higher education have equalized educational opportunity. For example, the free education made available to all veterans of World War Two and subsequent wars represents an unparalleled educational opportunity for Americans — but making education available to all is not to make it equal. For one thing, not all veterans have availed themselves of their educational rights. While precise data do not exist, it is safe to assume that a larger percentage of the well-to-do than of the poor did so. Secondly, one can assume that rich and poor attend different colleges and schools and pursue different academic programs. And thirdly, the rich are thus enabled to invest the money they would otherwise have spent on education. The net result of the United States' generous support of education for veterans, therefore, was probably to widen the gap between rich and poor (as well as to help many individuals from the lower classes to succeed via education).[21]

The federal low-cost insured loan program for college students (a provision of the Higher Education Act of 1965) is a more recent example of the differential impact of allegedly nonpartisan equal opportunity programs. Designed to lower economic barriers to higher education, this program provides

20. See "Higher Education: The Capstone of Class Education" in Chapter 6.
21. Veterans of the Vietnam war are being treated less well than their predecessors for a number of reasons, not the least of which is the pronounced class bias in the system of drafting men to fight in Vietnam: relative to veterans of previous wars, Vietnam veterans include proportionately far more of the poor and minorities, and thus have less appeal for Congress and other public officials than former veterans.

low-cost loans to college students from families with adjusted family incomes of $15,000 or less. Since an adjusted family income allows for a reduction of at least 10 percent for deductions and a reduction for exemptions, the true qualifying annual income is roughly $20,000; it can be higher if a family has capital gains, pension deductions, and tax-free interest. When these income limits were instituted in 1965, they actually included over 90 percent of American families, though rising incomes and the lack of a provision for inflation has probably caused the percentage to drop.[22] That this program theoretically covers the poor and the general working class is of very little practical consequence. The children of the various classes acquire the motivation and skills necessary for college at different rates, attend college at unequal rates, choose different types of colleges, take different programs, earn different academic records, and complete different amounts of higher education. Thus a formally equal opportunity is far from constituting equality of opportunity or equality of competition in practice. Nor do such programs even necessarily promote a higher level of ability among college populations. It is well known, for example, that there is class bias in the distribution of financial aid by institutions of higher education.[23] Students who can profit from higher education are turned down while students of equal ability who can afford to pay are given public aid, all in the name of equal opportunity (not to mention the unaccomplished well-to-do who feed at the public trough).

Colleges and universities are demonstrably subject to business, religious, and local political control, and one finds higher education explicitly implicated in serving social ends other than detached scholarship and the preservation and transmission of high culture. It is clear that this is the case with regard to public colleges and universities, which were established quite openly to serve students' practical interests and mobility aspirations and to supply skilled woman- and manpower to the economy. That private liberal arts colleges, whether of high or low equality, do the same is less readily appreciated because of the clouds of rhetoric that surround their operations. One need only recognize the deep pre- and early-industrial professional bias of most high-quality liberal arts colleges, which prepare students for medicine, law, natural science, and university teaching, to appreciate the way in which class is disguised by the argument that they are developing the whole person while others, by implication, engage in vulgar practical pursuits. Similar claims are made in the name of liberal arts, general education, the Renaissance man, excellence, and the life of reason.

Our awareness of the class nature of public higher education is based on more

22. Interestingly enough, Section 428, Subsection H of the Higher Education Act of 1965 specifically prohibits state and other loan agencies from denying low-interest loans to students because of lack of need (provided their adjusted family incomes are $15,000 or less)!

23. George A. Schlekat, "Do Financial Aid Programs Have a Conscience?" *College Board Review* 69 (Fall 1968): 15–20.

than insight and hypothesis. Thanks to a study of the California system of public higher education,[24] we are now on firm ground when talking about the educational role played by the power dimension. As is well known, California has an extensive system of post–high school public education, financed by public funds and characterized by low tuition and entrance and retention on academic merit. In their analysis of this system and its relation to class, Hansen and Weistrod conclude that public higher education in California is a system for redistributing income from lower to higher income groups. The authors add that California's reinforcement and aggravation of existing inequality by means of substantial subsidies to middle and upper class students through "public" higher education is probably even more characteristic of the other forty-nine states.[25] Given what we know about public education at all levels, these findings are not surprising.[26] It is difficult not to conclude that the power dimension (local, state, and federal governments and political institutions), as it focuses on education, is an integral and dependent aspect of the American system of stratification. This would be obvious, of course, were it not for the haze of rhetoric that surrounds education. In performing its role in the American system of class, the power structure does more than certify the existing class system; it actually widens differential advantages while labeling its efforts "equality of opportunity," thus creating the impression that it is a neutral promoter of classlessness.

The economic policies of the national government

Each branch of government (legislature, executive, judiciary) has a basic posture with regard to economic issues. Thus it is not easy to characterize the posture of the federal government toward economic affairs, or to measure its independence or difference from the class-prestige forces it is acting upon. Some tentative answers can be hazarded, however, in three general areas: antitrust policy; regulatory policies toward various economic enterprises; and fiscal-monetary full-employment policies.

24. W. Lee Hansen and Burton A. Weistrod, *Benefits, Costs, and Finance of Public Higher Education* (Chicago: Markham, 1969). Hansen and Weistrod's study is also available as "The Distribution of Costs and Direct Benefits of Public Higher Education: The Case of California," *Journal of Human Resources* 4 (Spring 1969): 176–191; and as Bobbs-Merrill reprint no. 133.

25. The authors demonstrate that this is the case for Wisconsin, a state famous for its system of public higher education; see W. Lee Hansen and Burton A. Weistrod, *A New Approach to Higher Education Finance* (Madison, Wis.: Institute for Research on Poverty, University of Wisconsin, 1970). For a study of public higher education in Florida, which corroborates the above findings, see Douglas M. Windham, *Education, Equality, and Income Redistribution: A Study of Public Higher Education* (Lexington, Mass.: D. C. Heath, 1970).

26. It should be noted that public institutions were slated to enroll 68 percent of all students in four-year degree programs in 1971 and that their share of the total is steadily mounting; U.S. Department of Health, Education, and Welfare, *Projections of Educational Statistics to 1978–1979* (Washington, D.C.: U.S. Government Printing Office, 1970), Table 7, p. 24.

Antitrust policy

The United States has a long history of concern about monopolistic economic power, much of it framed in terms of a theoretical ideal of free market competition. Free markets have probably never existed, except in the minds of theorists and in some areas such as labor and agriculture; since reliable records date back only to the last decades of the nineteenth century, it is difficult to cite hard evidence one way or the other. Why this utopian image of economic competition persists is unclear: it may relieve anxiety about failure for some; it may serve others as a rationalization for easy success; and it may be a convenient facade behind which powerful groups can hide. In any case, the American public and the federal government have accepted bigness — or, perhaps more precisely, they tend to assume that the trend toward bigness is compatible with competition, efficiency, and individualism. As Richard Hofstadter points out, the United States had an antitrust movement without antitrust prosecutions between 1890 and 1940, and since has had no antitrust movement (Hofstadter cites a survey indicating public acceptance of bigness) but enough antitrust prosecutions to constitute a real restraint on the growth of market power.[27]

Americans see no contradiction in valuing both competition and bigness, perhaps because they believe that each promotes efficiency. One thing is certain, however: in the United States competition is honored more in ideology than in actual behavior, especially if behavior is measured against the classic ideal of competition, or competition between a large number of equals.

The role of the power dimension in promoting concentrated market power or oligarchic competition is apparent. The federal government is not, on the whole, a trust-busting agency. Its regulatory policies; granting of patents, franchises, and licenses to engage in various businesses, including the production of atomic energy; and import and production quotas clearly promote bigness and noncompetition.

The government's policies with regard to its own purchases of goods and services also contribute heavily to economic concentration, and thus to the redistribution of income and wealth through oligarchic control of markets. The Defense Department, the Atomic Energy Commission, and the National Aeronautics and Space Administration clearly prefer to purchase goods and services (the latter consisting largely of research and development) from a small number of large contractors.

Regulatory policy

Beginning in the late nineteenth century, Congress began to pass legislation to regulate certain forms of economic activity in the public interest. The impact of such governmental regulation of the economy is directly related to class: the

27. Richard Hofstadter, *The Paranoid Style in American Politics* (New York: Alfred A. Knopf, 1965), chap. 6.

regulation of working conditions benefits the working class, a minimum wage aids the working poor, and so on. However, the main beneficiary of governmental economic regulations has not been the lower classes. By and large, the net result of direct governmental regulation of important segments of the American economy is what Kolko has called "consolidation of political capitalism." Supported by big business, the various regulations have tended to rationalize and stabilize economic markets for those already in them, thus completing politically the consolidation of markets begun on the economic level.

Congress specifically exempted many forms of business from antitrust laws, while various government departments and the independent regulatory commissions helped to further the trend toward noncompetition through administrative actions: uniform rates for entire industries, inflexible rates within and between industries, and the curtailment of entry into economic areas through exclusive public franchise and regulations.[28] The nature of federal regulation is such that the regulated actually determine the tone and policies of the regulators. The interests served are those of the respective economic enterprises, rather than those of consumers or the general public. Perhaps the most flagrant example is the government's imposition until 1973 — at the insistence of the oil industry — of import quotas on cheaper foreign oil, which cost consumers billions of dollars each year.

Thus the government pursues contradictory policies, the Justice Department trying to foster competition while various other governmental bodies seek to restrict competition in the interests of the various segments of the economy. Not only does the federal government have no coherent economic policy, but the impression is created that the public interest is being looked after. Public acceptance of bigness (and complacency?) is no doubt due largely to the false impression that the federal government is either preventing or controlling bigness.

Fiscal-monetary full-employment policies

The federal government has always exerted influence on the economy through its tax, expenditure, and monetary policies, but the routine way in which it now employs fiscal and monetary policies to influence the American economy is of fairly recent origin, a response to the crisis of the Great Depression. Governmental economic intervention acquired a developed Keynesian flavor in 1946, when it was wedded to a policy of full employment. If the avoidance of depression is a criterion, governmental economic policies have worked: on the whole, the period since 1945 has been characterized by prosperity and economic stability (recessions rather than depressions), a record unprecedented in American history. Whether or not more precise controls can be developed to stabilize

28. For a good history and analysis of public regulation within this framework, see Louis M. Kohlmeier, Jr., *Watchdog Agencies and the Public Interest: The Regulators* (New York: Harper and Row, 1969).

and direct the economy without explicit economic planning is uncertain. Whether American society should adopt a full commitment to economic planning is not a question that social science can answer easily; it can be said, however, that while the trend is toward increased control, the United States is far from having a planned economy. Indeed, the issue of whether American-style capitalism could achieve full employment was sidestepped by the Employment Act of 1946 when it stipulated that governmental policies were to be implemented within a framework of free enterprise.[29]

Even in the absence of precise criteria, one can draw certain conclusions about the overall consequences of our fiscal-monetary full-employment policies. Despite overall stability and prosperity, the American economy is characterized by a fairly large amount of idle equipment and labor. For another thing, the usefulness of Keynesian economics is yet to be determined. There are indications that even if the government again resorts to wage-price controls, as it did in 1971, economic stability (full employment without inflation) may not be achievable. In 1972 some economists even suggested that *full employment* should mean an unemployment rate of 5 percent rather than 4 percent; in 1973, such a policy would mean 4.55 million unemployed instead of 3.64 million in a labor force of 91 million.[30]

And governmental economic policies can be judged from still another perspective. An enormous backlog of needs seems to have developed in the so-called public sector: hospitals, sewers and sewage treatment plants, garbage disposal facilities, schools, housing, park and recreational facilities, and mass transportation. Federal tax and credit policies and direct governmental expenditures can be characterized as *reactionary Keynesianism* — the use of public economic policy to stimulate private consumption and economic activity in the early liberal faith that "free" private markets rationalize an economy and promote the general well-being. The net result has been to starve public programs and encourage, in Galbraith's words, "private luxury and public squalor."

Finally, despite a highly unsatisfactory employment record, little progress has been made in rationalizing our labor market (such as through job training programs). Ironically, unemployment and underemployment caused by recession, bankruptcies, technological displacement, foreign competition and the like eventually create an underclass of welfare recipients who are denounced as shiftless and made dependent wards of the state. Thus it is apparent that federal economic policies do not run counter to the general structure of economic power and that federal tax, spending, and monetary policies simply reflect and reinforce the American class-prestige hierarchy.

29. It should be noted that the term *full employment* appears neither in the title nor in the body of the act.
30. In discussing unemployment, it is important to keep in mind that actual rates of unemployment (and underemployment) are significantly higher than official figures.

Legislation, government, and representative minorities

The relation between the state and those at the bottom levels of society is never satisfactory, either for the rulers or the ruled. However, the classic relation between top dog and underdog has been complicated and obscured somewhat in the United States by the ideology of liberal democracy. In other words, talk about helping the poor and minorities creates an unreal impression that much is being done to help the lower classes.

One of the difficulties in helping minorities is the tradition of equality itself, a phenomenon we have already referred to as the burden of moral equality.[31] Under the liberal legal system and the American constitution, laws are supposed to be general — that is, they must apply to all (legal universalism).[32] The state cannot enact exceptional or particular laws. This tradition makes it politically, legally, and morally difficult to single out minorities for special treatment. To legislate in the abstract often means that the special needs of minorities are ignored; to legislate directly for their benefit is sometimes unconstitutional and always politically explosive. In practice, of course, Congress and the federal government (as well as state and local governments) enact and administer laws to help particular groups constantly. All that need be done is to frame a general law or regulation in such a way as to apply only to a limited interest or group.

Politically, the United States has changed a great deal since the pre-1930 period when property values enjoyed constitutional supremacy and in effect took precedence over all other values. Since the New Deal, there has occurred a sharp separation of property rights from civil rights and a continuous extension of the latter by means of legislative, judicial, and executive action. And legislatures have modified the power of property by enacting legislation to further other values as well, and ostensibly to help workers, the poor, and minorities. Rhetoric about the poor and other disadvantaged groups has a long history in American politics.[33] During the mid-1960s, a new and in some ways unprecedented approach to the problem of poverty was instituted. Under the general rubric of the War on Poverty and with the help of a number of important Supreme Court decisions, a wide range of opportunities and protections were legislated for lower class Americans. (Though the terminology of class was probably employed more during the 1960s than ever before in our history, lower class Americans are still characteristically referred to as "the poor," "the culturally deprived," or "the disadvantaged.")

Such attacks on class inequality should not be misinterpreted, however. To a significant extent, they represent a disgorging of elements incompatible with

31. See "The Burden of Moral Equality" in Chapter 8.
32. Indian Americans are legally entitled to exceptional treatment, however, because of treaty rights.
33. For a history of the United States' gradual awakening to the problems of poverty between 1830 and 1925, see Robert H. Bremner, *From the Depths: The Discovery of Poverty in the United States* (New York: New York University Press, 1956).

a mature industrial system. However admirable the motivations of our reformers (and there is no question about the high moral intentions of those who have supported the civil rights and antipoverty movements), one must also understand that an advanced technological society has little use for large numbers of unskilled workers with rural backgrounds. Attacks on "caste" and class inequality are thus also efforts to incorporate racial minorities and those left behind by technological advance into mature industrial society, or, in other words, ways of rounding out the liberal universe.

Government and black Americans

The liberal universe is obviously deeply at odds with American traditions that categorize human beings in ascriptive terms (race, sex, religion, ethnicity, and age). It is undeniable that the tradition of class (liberalism) has made inroads into the "caste" structure of the United States.[34] And there is little doubt that its primary victim, the black American, has at least begun a transition from ascriptive inequality to achievement inequality. The explicit use of power to deny blacks the vote or to segregate them socially is now illegal[35] and in growing disuse. The basic landmarks in the abolition of "caste" boundaries are well known: armed forces integration, fair employment laws, school desegregation, and civil rights acts, especially those relating to voting and the use of public accommodations and facilities. Implementation of these decisions has, however, lagged badly. Regardless of party, all national administrations in the post–World War Two period have failed to carry out their clear statutory and constitutional obligation to eradicate "caste" inequality.[36] The inaccuracy of the popular belief that the federal government is an equalizing force is readily apparent if one examines the historic role of the federal goverment in fostering "caste" stratification in the United States. Of course, it was state governments, reflecting the values and wishes of white power groups, that institutionalized racial segregation as a way of life in the American south. State electoral laws systematically disenfranchised black Americans, and state and local laws decreed and enforced segregation in social life.[37] But Congress and the federal govern-

34. We are focusing here, of course, on processes characteristic of industrial capitalism. To the extent that liberalism and Marxism share an interest in actively mastering the natural and social environments, similar processes are taking place in communist countries.

35. Constitutionally speaking, it has been illegal at least since the Fourteenth and Fifteenth Amendments. However, segregation in the south had the sanction of state and local law until the 1960s.

36. It should be noted that the Johnson administration of 1963–1968 achieved significant breakthroughs in establishing the formal rights of minorities in the areas of voting, housing, and use of public accommodations. To some extent this success is attributable to the Goldwater debacle of 1964, which resulted in a crushing defeat for the conservative coalition that had dominated Congress in the post–World War Two period.

37. Among the prime stereotypes that distort our perception of power is the belief that "local" government is more democratic, more personal, and more responsive than national government.

ment looked the other way; indeed, the federal government actually fostered segregation in the armed forces and in federally assisted housing.[38] Meanwhile, the United States Supreme Court accepted and legitimized racial segregation in one decision after the other, not merely before the Civil War but also between 1865 and the 1930s. (The Court issued no major attack on segregation until *Brown vs. Board of Education* in 1954.)

The class bias that characterizes even the most high-minded legislation, insuring that the upper classes gain more from political life than the lower classes, is readily apparent if one examines the impact of legislation on blacks. To use an example we have already discussed, the military conscription laws and practices in effect during the Vietnam war discriminated against those who were not in college — that is, against blacks, and the poor and working class in general. Social Security taxes and minimum ages of eligibility burden blacks unequally because they start work earlier than whites, receive incomes mostly from wages (the only taxable income) and mostly below the taxable maximum, and have larger families (thus being burdened more by the Social Security tax's lack of exemptions). Also, blacks tend to live less long than the classes above them, and thus do not collect Social Security for as long or not at all.

The federal and state trickle-down policy in housing tends to provide housing for blacks only when it is overage; subsidized housing tends to segregate blacks (often far from jobs); and urban renewal is often tantamount to black removal. Governmental policies to stimulate the economy through subsidies, tax depreciation, and low interest rates are another version of the trickle-down philosophy, which can be expressed as, "what's good for the upper classes is bound eventually to be good for the lower classes." However, such policies never seem to have much impact on black unemployment. Furthermore, governmental policies that tolerate inflation burden the poor hardest, as do policies to fight inflation, which invariably amount to socially created increases in unemployment. And the substitute for meaningful employment, the welfare system, has provided only an inadequate level of goods and service and a heavy dose of social stigma.

Fair employment laws have never contained provisions for enforcement, and their ability to create a wider range of opportunities for blacks has thus been minimal. In the 1970s, however, as an aftermath (along with sexual equality laws) of the strong civil rights laws of the mid-1960s, the government and the courts have begun to strike down discriminatory hiring, retention, promotion, and pay practices. The impact of these initiatives has been small, but it represents a significant departure from the hypocrisy of the past.

And, finally, to explore one area in a little more depth, governmental efforts

38. Even the Civil War should not be thought of merely as an attack by the north on the institution of slavery or an effort to preserve the union. The most fruitful interpretation is probably that the Civil War was essentially a military measure to insure the political integrity of an expanding continental economy. In this regard, see Barrington Moore, Jr., *Social Origins of Dictatorship and Democracy: Lord and Peasant in the Making of the Modern World* (Boston: Beacon Press, 1966), chap. 3, also in paperback.

to desegregate schools have had very mixed results. Essentially, the causes of unequal education for blacks are increasingly located beyond the jurisdiction of explicit public policy and in the realm of private life (class position). The pattern of segregation by residence (class) is quite pronounced and becoming more so each day. Black children are just as effectively segregated in public schools, despite equality before the law and equality of opportunity, as they were in the segregated schools of the southern "caste" system. And it is unlikely that the pervasive pattern of class segregation will be modified by the power dimension at the federal, state, or local levels. Not surprisingly, there is evidence that while *de jure* segregation (the overt use of power to segregate schools) has declined in the south, *de facto* educational segregation (based on class forces that segregate the races by income, occupation, and residence) has become well entrenched.[39]

The demands of ethnic and racial minorities for community control of schools during the late 1960s was an important development in the emergence of minority, and especially black, consciousness. Whether such control will help the United States' minorities to preserve their identities or make relative gains *vis-à-vis* majority Americans remains to be seen. It is interesting that education is the only sector of the class dimension in which black Americans seem to have made gains relative to whites during the post-1950 period.[40] But since education seems not to be related to economic advancement for blacks in the way it is for whites, black Americans are probably expending a disproportionate amount of effort in this area. It is clear, for example, that a given amount of schooling benefits blacks much less than whites: it affords significantly less income and is no protection against the greater unemployment rates prevalent among blacks, even for college graduates. It is also significant that relative gains in education by blacks have been confined mostly to the level of high school. Ironically, the worth of a high school diploma began to decline in 1945 (about the same time that blacks began to achieve in this area) with the advent of mass higher education. And, to compound the irony, blacks are now exerting themselves against great odds at the level of undergraduate education just as the B.A. degree is undergoing a relative decline in value and postgraduate degrees have begun to be the educational credential for acquiring positions in the upper classes.

Government and Mexican Americans

Much of what has been said about black Americans' relations to legislation and government also holds true for Mexican Americans. Therefore, after briefly noting these similarities, we will turn our attention to novel features in the Mexican American's relation to public law and authority.

39. "Resegregation: A Problem in the Urban South," *New York Times,* 28 September 1970, p. 1.
40. Relative gains *within* the class system should not be confused with progress in overcoming "caste" barriers blocking blacks' entry *into* the class system.

Mexican Americans, like all others at the lower levels of society, are not affected equitably by laws passed and adminstered by those who dominate the political process. Laws passed for the benefit of typical Americans (such as the Social Security Act) affect those who are below typical levels differently, and usually unequally. National economic policies designed to either stimulate or restrain the economy affect Mexican Americans adversely since they, like all working and lower class people, bear the brunt of economic stagnation and inflation.

Furthermore, Mexican Americans have borne (and still bear) a series of hardships, ranging from minor embarrassment to physical brutality, peculiar to their unique status in American society.[41] As an aggregate, Mexican Americans' legal status as citizens has been continuously challenged and/or ignored by the federal government (Border Patrol), local law enforcement agencies, and even welfare departments. American citizens of Mexican descent are indiscriminately lumped together with Mexicans who have entered the United States illegally, and are constantly required to prove their legal status. During the 1930s, welfare departments throughout the country even helped to "repatriate" thousands of American citizens of Mexican origin who were on welfare, making no attempt to distinguish between citizen and noncitizen.

Governmental agencies tend to have poor relations with working and lower class people because of the incompatibility of their impersonality and rationality and the greater personalism and ignorance of the lower classes. This relation is aggravated in the case of Mexican Americans because of a language barrier and because government in general, never having helped them, indeed having mistreated them, is viewed with suspicion, hostility, and withdrawal.

Mexican Americans have a great deal of trouble with government, partly because laws are passed that ignore them, partly because laws are not enforced, and partly because laws designed to protect American citizens are broken or ignored in their case. To take an important example, some Mexican Americans earn their living grazing sheep; when laws are passed establishing national parks and regulating the use of park land, recreation and aesthetic pleasure for the upper classes are purchased at their expense. State employment bureaus typically think of themselves as agents of employers, and even break laws regulating minimum wages. And local law enforcement agencies, from vigilante groups to the Texas Rangers to the Los Angeles Police Department, have long histories of unconstitutional behavior toward Mexican Americans, including violence and brutality. The relation between law enforcement agencies and minorities will be touched upon again in Chapter 14; it is sufficient here to indicate that law enforcement officials have a long history of siding in economic matters with property-owners against Mexican American workers, even when it means breaking or ignoring the law.

---

41. For much of the following, see Leo Grebler, Joan W. Moore, Ralph C. Guzman, *et al., The Mexican-American People: The Nation's Second Largest Minority* (New York: Free Press, 1970), chap. 21.

The United States Commission on Civil Rights has acknowledged the United States' drastically unequal and discriminatory educational policies toward Mexican American children. Mexican American children go to schools that are ethnically unbalanced, and do less well in their studies and drop out more than majority students. Schools not only do not welcome or reinforce the language and culture of Mexican Americans; Spanish is actively suppressed, and little effort is made to recognize the language barrier in dealing with children or parents. Indeed, the Mexican American community is ignored by the schools when involving parents in education, setting up advisory boards, and hiring consultants. And Mexican Americans are deeply discriminated against in the financing of schools: much less is spent on Mexican American children than majority children, Mexican American communities bear a heavier tax burden for education, and Mexican Americans are not represented on school boards in proportion to their numbers, even in predominantly Mexican American communities.[42]

The Mexican American has been virtually ignored by the federal government (except the Border Patrol).[43] During the unrest of the 1960s, Mexican Americans came to the attention of Congress and the executive branch for the first time. (So ignorant was Congress that an early report on "Mexican American Affairs" was sent to the Foreign Affairs Committee.) The Mexican American's difficulty gaining attention and help from government is illustrated by the antipoverty efforts of the 1960s. Under the Community Action Program, federal money was granted directly to Mexican American organizations — that is, to groups aware of the special needs of a distinct linguistic-ethnic group. For the first time, Mexican Americans had the opportunity to act on their own behalf and to develop the skills to help themselves and to deal with government. For the first time, they had become a constituency for federal legislators and administrators, which is an important prerequisite to acquiring political power and thus governmental attention and help. However, under the Nixon administration between 1968 and 1973, categorical grants and the entire antipoverty program were attacked; and a concerted effort was mounted to return authority and funds to state and local governments. Categorical grants not only allow for the special needs of particular groups to be met and citizen

42. U.S. Civil Rights Commission, *Mexican American Educational Series,* "Report I. Ethnic Isolation of Mexican Americans in the Public Schools of the Southwest" (April 1971); "Report II. The Unfinished Education: Outcomes for Minorities in Five Southwestern States" (October 1971); "Report III. The Excluded Student: Educational Practices Affecting Mexican Americans in the Southwest" (May 1972); "Report IV. Mexican American Education in Texas — A Function of Wealth" (August 1972). All are available from the U.S. Government Printing Office, Washington, D.C.
43. For the following account of relations between Mexican Americans and the federal establishment, see Jerry Rankin, "Mexican Americans and National Policy-Making: An Aborted Relationship" in *Chicanos and Native Americans: The Territorial Minorities,* ed. Rudolph O. de la Garza, Z. Anthony Kruszewski, and Tomas A. Arciniega (Englewood Cliffs, N.J.: Prentice-Hall, 1973), pp. 145–152, available in paperback.

initiative to be fostered; perhaps more importantly, they curtail the power of local governments and, in the case of the Community Action Agencies, bypass it altogether. In the name of returning government to the people, in other words, the Nixon administration's New Federalism and revenue-sharing program were bolstering the power of the state and local governments that have ignored and mistreated Mexican Americans (and other minorities and poor people) throughout their history.

Government and Jewish Americans

The Jewish American has not been subject to the same neglect and lawless mistreatment as have black and Mexican Americans. Predominantly urban before they came to the United States and urban dwellers ever since, Jewish Americans had the motivation and skills to engage in the fairly open political systems that characterized large American cities during the nineteenth century. Riding the wave of economic expansion and able to protect and help themselves politically at the local level, especially through public education, Jewish Americans' relation with government has been far happier than that experienced by other minority groups.

Jewish Americans have also strongly supported civil rights and welfare legislation of all kinds, in effect accounting for much of the pre-1960 leadership of liberal causes in all fields. Jewish Americans have traditionally worked for and donated money to minority causes and organizations, especially those benefiting black Americans.

Since the emergence of black militancy in the 1960s, however, the relation between Jews and blacks has become somewhat strained. For one thing, Jewish Americans became preoccupied with the safety of the state of Israel. Their success in influencing American policy toward Israel has been enormous, especially compared to blacks' lack of success in influencing American policy toward racist regimes in Africa. A second reason for strained relations between Jews and blacks is their differing class interests. In New York City,[44] for example, Jewish businesses hire blacks for low-paying jobs. Though New York City's economy is replete with low-wage industries, and though Jews do not enjoy great economic power, the Jewish businessperson looms large in the black experience as an economic exploiter of black workers.

Jews and blacks also have class differences over education. The black demand for greater control over predominantly black schools constitutes a threat to Jewish school administrators and teachers. Similarly, attempts to increase the number of blacks and other minorities admitted to professional schools are seen as a threat by Jews, who believe (not without cause) that the

---

44. For an enormous fund of information on Jews, blacks, and other minorities in New York City, see Nathan Glazer and Daniel Patrick Moynihan, *Beyond the Melting Pot: The Negroes, Puerto Ricans, Jews, Italians, and Irish of New York City,* 2nd ed. (Cambridge, Mass.: M.I.T. Press, 1970), also in paperback.

extension of professional training for poor minorities will be at their expense. And finally, as urban dwellers, Jews and blacks often jostle up against each other, are class rivals for political favors and housing, and have different views on the problem of crime. Such differences are exacerbated by racist sentiments on the part of Jews and anti-Semitic sentiments on the part of blacks.

In sum, minority groups are divided by ethnic, linguistic, and "racial" differences, and find it hard to cooperate. When they are also divided by class differences, cooperation for mutual advantage becomes exceedingly difficult.[45]

The class-prestige nature of legislation and government: a summary

In Federalist paper number 10, James Madison argued that individuals are unequal by nature, that natural inequality leads to economic inequality, that economic inequality leads to conflict, and that the proper province of government is to mediate and regulate (not change or eliminate) economic differences and disputes. Our own view is that explaining inequality by invoking human nature is a dubious enterprise. Nonetheless, American society is not only based on this view — actually, this view stems from the nature of American society — but has institutionalized Madison's political prescription for coping with inequality. Our analysis of federal legislation and its administration indicates that Madison's view, however dubious from the standpoint of science, accurately describes the performance of American political institutions. Government acts to soften and update inequality, not to curtail it and certainly not to eradicate it. In a sense, of course, government can only reflect the society that spawned it. But the American power dimension is charged with high moral purpose, often expressed in dynamic language. We are constantly led to believe, in other words, that government can and does change things; thus it is important to note that it does not and probably cannot.

In assessing the relation between class-prestige forces and legislation, therefore, we must be careful not to overestimate the independence or power of the power dimension. This subject is exceedingly complex, and generalizations must be made with extreme caution. One conclusion, however, seems to have at least a tentative validity: during the course of American history, political institutions appear to have done little to change the positions of the various groups on the hierarchies of class and prestige. Basic changes and displacements have come about largely as results of economic expansion and inadvertent governmental action. (For example, the government helped to open up the west by subsidizing canals and railroads and by granting homesteads.) In point

45. For an interesting essay on the difficulties and possibilities of cooperation between black and Mexican Americans (and Jews), see Stephen J. Herzog, "Political Coalitions Among Ethnic Groups in the Southwest" in *Chicanos and Native Americans: The Territorial Minorities,* ed. Rudolph O. de la Graza, Z. Anthony Kruszewski, and Tomas A. Arciniega (Englewood Cliffs, N.J.: Prentice-Hall, 1973), pp. 131–138.

of fact, our political institutions either register changes in class or prestige or operate to forestall change. (For example, the economic decline of farmers has been arrested by their political strength.) Thus it is especially important to exercise caution with regard to the role of the federal government *vis-à-vis* class and prestige forces.

In examining federal legislation in the areas of taxation, Social Security, housing, education, and economic policy, the conclusions are inescapable that government changes very little and that politics, legislation, and government are the handmaidens of the class-prestige hierarchy. Though ours is a preliminary, exploratory assessment of a relation not yet fully researched, let alone synthesized, it is unlikely that future research will overturn what must be considered a fairly firm conclusion. Actually, an examination of other areas can only support the conclusion that the power dimension is an auxiliary of the American class and prestige hierarchies. Highway legislation, urban renewal, support for the humanities and arts, funds for pre- and postdoctoral faculty research in science, funds for medicine and mental health, disaster aid,[46] small business loans, the enforcement of safety regulations, antipollution standards, labor legislation, and minimum wage laws are all heavily slanted in favor of the upper classes. And nothing at the local and state levels runs counter to this pattern; if anything, the class-prestige nature of government is even more pronounced and apparent at these lower levels.

46. Both public and private agencies give help to disaster victims in amounts in keeping with the latter's class-prestige standings.

14

The class-prestige nature of law

IN ANALYZING THE relation between class-prestige on the one hand, and legislation and government on the other, we examined a great deal of law — statutory and administrative law pertaining to such matters as taxation, Social Security, housing, education, and civil rights, and laws that manage and regulate myriad economic activities. In this chapter we will focus directly on law as such, and on the relation between those who enforce and those who are affected by the law.

In exploring the relation between law and the hierarchies of class and prestige, our main concern is to see whether the law affects the American population uniformly. More specifically, we want to determine whether obedience and disobedience to the law have anything to do with social class. In enforcing the law and administering justice, does the state — represented by police officers, prosecutors, juries, defense attorneys, judges, court officials and professional auxiliaries, and prison officials — treat individuals equally or in keeping with their positions in the class and prestige hierarchies? In other words, are the agencies of power that specialize in maintaining the law impartial in their treatment of the American people? Or, in short, is there equality before the law?

The law has always been an instrument for upholding the established order, and the modern legal system is no exception. Despite its universalism, liberal law is deeply slanted in favor of political authority, middle and upper class morality, and established economic interests and rights. We will begin our analysis of the relation between law and class society by examining the middle and upper class basis of deviance.

Middle class values and deviance
Class, universal goals, and deviant behavior

Sociologists have long recognized that a great deal, if not most, of deviant (abnormal) behavior is caused by the normal demands society places on its members. Conforming or trying to conform to social norms is, in other words, probably the prime cause of nonconformity. Perhaps the most ironic characteristic of American society is the way in which its rationalistic culture produces nonrational and irrational behavior. The American achievement ethic monopolizes the definition of identity (economic success) and stipulates the means to achieve it (the Protestant-bourgeois virtues).[1] When this moral universalism is promulgated within a deeply structured class system, which by definition cannot allow all to be successful, there are generated social pressures for individuals to acquire success illegitimately (innovation, basically crime) or to compensate for the lack of success (ritualism and retreatism). Merton's depiction of the five ways in which people can respond to cultural goals and the institutional means for achieving them is illustrated in Table 14-1.

Society's response to deviant behavior (categories II–V) is to pass laws, often

Table 14-1   The Five Modes of Adjustment to Cultural Goals and Institutionalized Means[a]

		Cultural goals	Institutionalized means
I	Conformity	+	+
II	Innovation	+	−
III	Ritualism	−	+
IV	Retreatism	−	−
V	Rebellion	±	±

a. Symbol equivalents are: (+) signifies acceptance, (−) signifies elimination, and (±) signifies rejection and substitution of new goals and standards.

SOURCE: Robert K. Merton, "Social Structure and *Anomie*," *American Sociological Review* 3 (October 1938): 676. Used by permission.

1. This is a reference, of course, to Robert K. Merton's classic analysis, "Social Structure and *Anomie*," *American Sociological Review* 3 (October 1938): 672–682; this essay has been widely reprinted, and is also available as Bobbs-Merrill reprint no. S-194. John P. Hewitt's *Social Stratification and Deviant Behavior* (New York: Random House, 1970) falls short of its ambitious title largely because it is sociopsychological in orientation. (The individual's self-esteem in interaction with society is its main theme.) For some reason, this essay contains no reference to Merton's article.

of a type that make the deviance criminal. Innovation and rebellion are heavily criminalized, and if one thinks of some forms of vagrancy, gambling, and drugtaking as retreatism, it too has been criminalized. (Ritualism is heavily stigmatized and ridiculed morally by means of such epithets as *parasite, hack, bureaucrat, pencil-pusher,* and the like.) In sum, the lawless American is no aberration of human nature but an outcome of identifiable social variables.

Middle class morality and the creation of crime

As we have suggested, middle class morality and its legalization is a prime source of crime. To understand this process, one must view crime as a socially defined act, rather than as an intrinsic thing-in-itself. Illustrations of the socio-cultural context of crime are easy to cite. In ancient Athens Socrates' free thinking was judged criminal; in the United States freedom of thought is a constitutional right. A prime example of the creation of crime through the legalization of a moral position is Prohibition. A rural-religious middle class movement, whose morality differed from that of the urban middle class, the lower classes, and even the upper class, succeeded in outlawing the use of alcoholic beverages, and during the 1920s the United States experienced a great deal of crime as Americans in large numbers circumvented Prohibition.

Middle class morality — heavily influenced by biopsychic explanations, agrarian values, nationalism, and religion — has at one time or another come to view a large assortment of behavior as immoral, and consequently made it illegal. Middle class sexual morality, for example, has in combination with other forces made abortion, birth control, and various sexual values and practices (homosexuality, pornography, prostitution) criminal offenses. Middle class morality's emphasis on work and productivity has also given rise to vagrancy laws, which define certain forms of idleness and poverty as criminal offenses. The liberal emphasis on self-control and belief in a rational, predictable universe has led to laws that treat gambling, alcoholism, and drug use as criminal offenses.

The need to lengthen the period of youth and to keep the statuses of young people abstract, so that they can be kept abreast of new knowledge and prepared for new and more demanding occupations, has enhanced the potential for deviant behavior among the male young in industrial society. Anthony M. Platt has charged that upper-middle class reformers (mostly women) invented the concept of *juvenile delinquency* and the judicial process that regulates it largely to protect their own values. According to Platt, many forms of youthful behavior have been labeled delinquent that are innocent enough and unindictable when engaged in by adults. Furthermore, this reform movement helped to consolidate the paternalistic and dependent legal status from which youth still suffer.[2]

Thus it is difficult to escape the conclusion that crime is largely a product of society and its power groups, a view attested to by the history of criminal law.

2. Anthony M. Platt, *The Child Savers: The Invention of Delinquency* (Chicago: University of Chicago Press, 1969).

The English law of theft, for example, was considerably changed by the famous Carrier's Case (1473), in which a court declared that a carrier of goods had committed a crime when, instead of carrying bales of goods committed to his care to their destination, he took them to another place, opened them, and took the contents. English law provided no precedent for declaring this act a crime, because the man had possession of the property he was accused of stealing. Nonetheless, it was declared criminal, thus creating such a precedent. This act of legal creativity was impelled by the fact that the case involved the transport of cloth and wool, the products of England's most important industry.[3]

The English law of vagrancy also illustrates the way in which power groups translate their values and interests into law. In 1349 the first vagrancy statute made it a crime for any citizen to give charity to the unemployed and for an unemployed person to refuse to work for anyone who requested his labor. Quite clearly, this law was passed on behalf of landowners who were losing their supply of cheap labor to competition from a growing commercial and manufacturing town economy; in short, it was intended as a substitute for serfdom. When no longer needed, the law became dormant, only to be revived after 1500 in an effort to control the growing crime problem. The association of idleness (lack of employment) with crime persisted into modern times in both Great Britain and the United States.[4]

The image of society as an arena of free behavior bounded by a static framework of impartial legal rules is a serious error. The law is always biased in favor of power groups, and all behavior is bounded, molded, and defined by law. A society that encourages self-interest, defines identity in terms of middle class ideals, stigmatizes old ways of doing things, and constantly creates new opportunities to get ahead, often at the expense of others — in short, a dynamic industrial-urban society that separates the individual from control by the family, neighborhood, church, or work group — must rely increasingly on explicit legal norms and specialized structures (police, courts, prisons, regulatory commissions, schools) to ensure social control. And this reliance on law results in overcriminalization, which enhances the power of law-related professions and organizations, both public and private, and creates vested interests in legal solutions to social problems.

Class-prestige, crime, and the law

Sociologically, it is impossible to classify legal norms as criminal or civil, constitutional or legislative, public or private, and so on, just as it is unfeasible to distinguish precisely between deviant and conformist behavior or legal and criminal behavior. There is, in other words, no way to define crime precisely,

3. Jerome Hall, "Theft, Law and Society: The Carrier's Case," in *Crime and the Legal Process,* ed. William J. Chambliss (New York: McGraw-Hill, 1968), pp. 32–51.
4. William J. Chambliss, "A Sociological Analysis of the Law of Vagrancy," *Social Problems* 12 (Summer 1964): 67–77; reprinted in William J. Chambliss, ed., *Crime and the Legal Process* (New York: McGraw-Hill, 1968), pp. 51–63.

though working definitions are easy enough to provide. Sociologically speaking, a crime is any violation of a legal norm punishable by the state. But such a definition raises numerous problems. Why are some violations of law not punished? Why is it that some violations of law are punished but not considered crimes by the lawbreaker, his peers, or the general public? Why are various types of crime and of lawbreakers dealt with quite differently by law enforcement agencies? As we will see, the answers to these questions require an understanding of social class.

Class and the definition of crime

The misdefinition of crime has been attributed by Edwin H. Sutherland in his classic study, *White Collar Crime,* to

> the bias involved in the administration of criminal justice under laws which apply exclusively to business and the professions and which therefore involve only the upper socioeconomic class. Persons who violate laws regarding restraint of trade, advertising, pure food and drugs are not arrested by uniformed policemen, are often not tried in criminal courts, and are not committed to prisons; their illegal behavior generally receives the attention of administrative commissions and of courts operating under civil or equity jurisdiction. For this reason such violations of law are not included in the criminal statistics nor are individual cases brought to the attention of the scholars who write the theories of criminal behavior.[5]

Sutherland called this form of illegal behavior "white-collar crime," and defined it approximately "as a crime committed by a person of respectability and high social status in the course of his occupation."[6] He focused his discussion of overlooked crime on corporate business, saying little about the professions. Though the concept of white-collar crime initially evoked considerable controversy, it has achieved widespread general acceptance among criminologists and related professions.[7] Sutherland's conclusions (paraphrased below) about the nature of big business criminality — which is only one aspect of white-collar crime — are quite interesting:

5. Edwin H. Sutherland, *White Collar Crime* (New York: Holt, Rinehart and Winston, 1949), p. 8, also in paperback. Sutherland also refers to a bias of lesser importance, the ability of those in the upper socioeconomic classes to escape arrest and conviction because of their wealth, prestige, and political connections.

6. *Ibid.,* p. 9.

7. There are obvious difficulties inherent in the term *white-collar crime* if one restricts its use to crimes by those of high social status, and primarily to the crimes of big businesspeople. The term *white-collar crime* should also be used (or refined or dropped) to account for the crimes of professionals and semiprofessionals, such as doctors, lawyers, advertising people, police officers, and inspectors; skilled workers in watch repair, television repair, automobile repair, and plumbing; and assorted small and intermediate businesspeople, such as slumlords, manufacturers of misrepresented or misgraded products, butchers who shortweight, fuel companies and gas stations that shortcount, and sales personnel who pilfer ("inventory shrinkage"). From the standpoint of class analysis, it is probably best to think of a hierarchy of types of crime associated with basic class attributes (income, property, education, occupation).

1. Criminality among corporations is persistent; repeaters are as common here as in ordinary crime.

2. Illegal behavior at this level is much more extensive than is indicated by complaints and prosecutions.

3. Businessmen who violate the law do not lose status among their associates, since a violation of the legal code is not a violation of the business code.[8]

4. Crime by businessmen is organized crime, entered into deliberately and in skillful cooperation with others. Criminal businessmen are also like other criminals (for example, the professional thief) in that they are contemptuous of law, government, and government personnel. Such businessmen, however, do not look upon themselves as criminals (here they differ from the professional thief), nor are they looked upon as such by the general public. Businessmen accept the designation "law violator" but on the whole their policy is to profess adherence to law publicly and to make defections from it in secret. While the professional thief must hide his identity, the white collar criminal must hide the fact of crime. Secrecy is possible under the umbrella provided by lawyers, deceptive corporate structures and practices (especially against a divided, weak public) and public relations experts.[9]

Sutherland's insights can help us to answer the questions we raised earlier, which can now be rephrased as follows: why are there such variations in the views on crime of members of the same society? Or, in other words, why was it possible for Sutherland to make a genuinely creative contribution to criminology by pointing out that members of the upper classes who break the law should be called criminals?

Ordinary or lower class crime is more visible and more easily translated into personal terms than white-collar crime. It involves personal loss and violence, which makes it memorable and emotionally evocative. But ordinary crime does not cost as much as white-collar crime; in fact, the money costs of white-collar crime are infinitely higher. And the differential in moral costs is just as large: white-collar crime invariably involves a violation of trust, and if prestige is bestowed on crime by middle class individuals (and eventually on lawbreaking in general), the bases of social respectability and authority could be undermined.

One of the unfortunate by-products of the fact that crime is prevalent at all levels of society is reinforcement of the notion that human nature — allegedly the only factor common to all levels — is the cause of crime. It takes considerable effort to think of economic and social pressures (an *anomic* social structure) as the general cause of crime. And it requires similar effort to pinpoint the specific causes, functions, and dysfunctions of crime at each level and in each sector of society. Fortunately, a good deal of such work has been done. The growth of competition and the practice of competitive bidding in the heavy electrical machinery industry has been identified as an incentive to price-fixing.[10] The decay of a craft tradition has been cited as leading craftsmen to defraud

8. There is an interesting parallel here with youth gangs.
9. *White Collar Crime*, chap. 13.
10. Richard Austin Smith, "The Incredible Electrical Conspiracy," *Fortune* 63 (April, May 1961): 132ff., 161ff.; reprinted in Donald R. Cressey and David A.

the public.[11] And others have pointed out the relation between crime and ambiguity in an occupational role.[12] The hazards and high overhead of retailing in poverty areas have been cited as a cause of the widespread fraud practiced against the consumer; conversely, such cheating can be interpreted as socially valuable, since it enables businesspeople to sell to the poor and the unreliable, and thus provides our underclass with "compensatory consumption."[13] Illegal gambling among the working class may also be thought of as a form of compensatory participation in the success ethic and as a way of venting socially destructive impulses in a harmless form.[14]

Conceivably, the illegal behavior of people in positions of prestige and authority could be defined as crime, and their reputations and positions could become tarnished. The reasons why this has not happened should be clear. While Sutherland's demand that lawbreaking by the high and mighty be called crime has been heeded by criminologists and some related professions, society-at-large has ignored his commonsense judgment. The illegal behavior of people in high social positions is still not seen as identical to the illegal behavior of those in inferior social positions. Robert K. Merton has outlined the nature of this moral hypocrisy in his essay "The Self-Fulfilling Prophecy,"[15] and one of his illustrations is particularly apt: a Jew who studies hard is labeled a grind and a grade-grubber, but a non-Jew who exhibits the same behavior is regarded as intelligent, studious, and ambitious. Similarly, when doctors control the supply of people who go into medicine, they are a professional association; when manual workers do the same thing, they are engaged in a restrictive labor practice. When wealthy, politically influential, and respectable people receive public money, it takes the forms of price supports, grants, tax benefits, or low-cost interest rates; when the lowly and despised receive public money it is called welfare, a handout, or something for nothing. The relevance of this point to the definition of criminal behavior is clear. Behavior has no meaning

---

Ward, eds., *Delinquency, Crime, and Social Process* (New York: Harper and Row, 1969), pp. 884–912.

11. Fred L. Strodtbeck and Marvin B. Sussman, "Of Time, the City, and the 'One-Year Guaranty': The Relations Between Watch Owners and Repairers," *American Journal of Sociology* 61, no. 6 (May 1956): 602–609.

12. Earl R. Quinney, "Occupational Structure and Criminal Behavior: Prescription Violation by Retail Pharmacists," *Social Problems* 11 (Fall 1963): 179–185; reprinted in Marshall B. Clinard and Richard Quinney, eds., *Criminal Behavior Systems: A Typology* (New York: Holt, Rinehart and Winston, 1967), pp. 169–176. It is interesting to note that deviance in the legal profession has been associated with the lower levels of that profession, which are subject to the heaviest social pressures; see Jerome E. Carlin, *Lawyers' Ethics: A Survey of the New York City Bar* (New York: Russell Sage Foundation, 1966).

13. David Caplovitz, *The Poor Pay More: Consumer Practices of Low-Income Families* (New York: Free Press, 1963), chap. 2.

14. Irving Kenneth Zola, "Observations of Gambling in a Lower-Class Setting," *Social Problems* 10 (Spring 1963): 353–361; reprinted in Robert D. Herman, ed., *Gambling* (New York: Harper and Row, 1967), available in paperback.

15. *The Antioch Review* 8 (June 1948): 193–210; reprinted in Robert K. Merton, *Social Theory and Social Structure*, rev. ed. (New York: Free Press, 1968), chap. 13.

until society defines it. It is clear that our class-prestige structure, while not strong enough to prevent the passage of laws detrimental to the interests of the upper classes, has managed to keep the lawbreaking of the upper classes from being associated with that of the lower classes. Crime, in other words, has been successfully defined as something the lower classes do. There is no more dramatic example of the pervasive and powerful influence of the American class system.

The association of crime with the lower classes is most striking in the case of blacks. Everyone knows that blacks have a high crime rate, which undoubtedly serves to reinforce a racist explanation of behavior. But if, instead of comparing the crime rates of blacks and whites (two meaningless causal variables), one compares the crime rates of various classes, the members of any given class seem to commit crime at similar rates regardless of skin color.[16]

The double standard is no doubt partly attributable to the fact that the various classes commit different types of crime. Compared to middle class youth, for example, youngsters from the lower classes seem to engage more in gainful crime and to be more violent and destructive.[17] Similarly, working and lower class adult criminals commit different types of crime and use different techniques than their middle class counterparts. But neither these differences nor differences in the rates of crime and arrest at various class levels are sufficient to explain why we do not equate lawbreaking behavior with criminal behavior at all levels of society. They do not explain why we tend to define the teenage middle class lawbreaker as a "problem child" and the teenage lower class lawbreaker as a delinquent. The only satisfactory explanation is the power of class over our perception of reality, a power to which the universality and majesty of both reason and law are subject.[18]

Class and type of law enforcement

There is a vast difference between the ways in which the law is enforced against the white-collar criminal and against the ordinary criminal.[19] One need only compare the treatment of antitrust violators with the way in which law is

16. Edward Green, "Race, Social Status, and Criminal Arrest," *American Sociological Review* 35 (June 1970): 476–490. The author also specifically challenges the view that higher black crime rates are due to racist discrimination on the part of the general public or the police.

17. Roland J. Chilton, "Middle Class Delinquency and Specific Offense Analysis," in *Middle Class Juvenile Delinquency,* ed. Edmund W. Vaz (New York: Harper and Row, 1967), pp. 91–101.

18. It has been suggested by an experiment that unskilled workers who have criminal records are punished further by loss of employment opportunities, and that unskilled workers who have been *acquitted* of criminal charges are also discriminated against by prospective employers. By contrast, doctors who have been either convicted or acquitted of malpractice suffer almost no ill effects in their subsequent careers; see Richard D. Schwartz and Jerome H. Skolnick, "Two Studies of Legal Stigma," in *The Other Side: Perspectives on Deviance,* ed. Howard S. Becker (New York: Free Press, 1964), pp. 103–117.

19. It should be noted that many white-collar criminals, such as small retailers,

enforced in a black ghetto to appreciate this point. White-collar criminals have fewer dealings with the police than ordinary criminals; are arrested less often; and, if arrested, are rarely subject to pretrial detention.

Another such variation is the selective manner in which laws are enforced, which seems to be related to class. A classic example is urban renewal legislation, all the provisions of which are eagerly obeyed save the requirement that dispossessed families be relocated. Strenuous efforts are made to combat ordinary crime, but the development and enforcement of laws to protect the consumer and to stimulate competition are less than enthusiastic. It is well known that better police protection and public services are usually available in middle and upper class neighborhoods than in working and lower class areas. But the strong are protected in other ways too. Embezzlement laws, which protect the powerful against the weak, were quickly and easily passed when this form of theft first made its appearance. And the Securities and Exchange Commission is, despite its many failings, perhaps the most effective fiduciary structure among the various regulatory commissions. Also striking is the lack of enthusiasm with which the constitutional rights of black Americans are enforced against lawbreaking southern officials and safety laws are enforced against industries and business.[20]

Until recently, public programs of consumer protection were largely ineffective.[21] Consumer problems obviously vary with class level: the lower classes are affected more by the price of food than by the prices of swimming pools or single-family residences. Similarly, the lower classes are affected less by laws designed to protect the environment or establish national parks than the classes above them. Even the routine operation of our courts tends to be biased against the lower classes. For example, members of the lower classes are systematically cheated by an assortment of white-collar criminals and subjected to deceptive advertising, defective goods, tricky contracts, and shoddy services. Not only do they have little chance of legal redress, but the law is actually used against them to enforce tricky contracts, garnishee wages, and collect debts.[22]

---

small service businesses, and landlords, are subject to conventional treatment by law enforcement officials.

20. Public protection measures in such areas as civil rights, fair employment, consumer protection, and factory safety are framed in terms of much-publicized goals, but invariably lack the provisions for enforcement necessary to make them effective. Thus goals are not met and the authority of law and government is diluted.

21. For an outstanding analysis of the consumer problems of the poor, which refers to the way in which law is used to exploit poor consumers, see David Caplovitz, *The Poor Pay More: Consumer Practices of Low-Income Families* (New York: Free Press, 1963). Two other useful references on consumer problems, whose indifference to class is in itself interesting, are Grant S. McClellan, ed., *The Consuming Public* (New York: H. W. Wilson, 1968), and Warren G. Magnuson and Jean Carper, *The Dark Side of the Marketplace: The Plight of the American Consumer* (Englewood Cliffs, N.J.: Prentice-Hall, 1968).

22. Small claims courts, which are now used as collection agencies, were origi-

Class, legal services, and the administration of justice

The Anglo-American legal system reflects the core values of society-at-large. The liberal presumption of the inherent validity of individual action is paralleled by the legal assumption that an individual is innocent until the state proves otherwise. The liberal dichotomy between the individual and society is echoed throughout the judicial process, most dramatically in the standard phrase "The People v. the Defendant." That court proceedings are competitive is obviously related to the liberal belief that competition is good for society. Under the Anglo-Saxon adversary system, it is assumed that justice (like better mousetraps and cheaper pig iron) will result if lawyers engage in combat under the eye of a referee, the judge. Another parallel is that justice must be purchased in much the same way as are food and clothing; thus lawyers must be hired and court expenses and fees paid for before justice is done.[23] The reliability of the accused is also gauged by money (the bail system),[24] and punishment is quite often monetary (the payment of a fine). And the law still assumes, despite modifications, that individuals cause their own behavior. The law is also still centered on the pleasure-pain principle of early liberal psychology in which it is assumed that clear-cut rewards (probation, parole, trustee positions, TV and exercise privileges) and punishments (imprisonment, execution, withdrawal of privileges, solitary confinement) serve as effective incentives and deterrents.

It is not surprising that the parallel between our judicial system and liberal society extends to the relation between law and the class system as well. Indeed, the emphasis on money produces a deep class bias throughout the judicial system. Legal services are performed primarily on behalf of the middle and upper classes, and especially of their most wealthy and powerful elements.[25] Many types of contract favor the rich and powerful, the myth of voluntary equal bargaining notwithstanding.[26] Those with money do not, as we have said, suffer pretrial detention, and if convicted are often given the option of sacri-

---

nally established to allow ordinary individuals to adjudicate small disputes with a minimum of fuss and expense.

23. Of course, the salaries of police officers, prosecutors, judges, court officials and, where clients are indigent, defense lawyers and court fees are paid out of public funds. In spite of this, the judicial process has a pronounced market flavor — the most important cases are handled by private law firms organized as profit-making businesses. And, as we will see, the provision of free justice for the poor has cheapened rather than guaranteed it.

24. The Federal Bail Reform Act of 1966 has modified this situation to some extent in federal courts.

25. Jerome E. Carlin, *Lawyers' Ethics: A Study of the New York City Bar* (New York: Russell Sage Foundation, 1966). Leon Mayhew and Albert J. Reiss, Jr., "The Social Organization of Legal Contacts," *American Sociological Review* 34 (June 1969): 309–318; reprinted in Donald Black and Maureen Mileski, eds., *The Social Organization of Law* (New York: Seminar Press, 1973), chap. 11.

26. Friedrich Kessler, "Contracts and Power in America," in *The Social Organization of Law,* ed. Donald Black and Maureen Mileski (New York: Seminar Press, 1973), chap. 10; reprinted from *Columbia Law Review* 43 (1943): 629–642.

ficing money rather than freedom. The jury system is shunned by defendants from the lower classes, suggesting that they regard a trial by their peers — whether jurors are actually their peers is another matter — as less just than a negotiated conviction. We know very little about the class composition of juries, but prodding by the United States Supreme Court has prompted efforts to curtail the use of flagrantly unrepresentative juries.[27] However, even juries chosen at random and representing a cross-section of the class structure do not guarantee that deliberations will be conducted by equals. One of the rare studies of a jury system that has relevance for class analysis found that jurors of higher occupational status were selected more as foremen, participated more in discussion, had more influence, derived more satisfaction, and were perceived as more qualified for jury duty than jurors from lower occupations.[28]

In general, acquittals, favorable sentences, and commutations of sentence are contingent on the skill of one's lawyer, which is in turn contingent on money. Mere representation by a lawyer does not insure equal justice. One study has shown that among those convicted of murder, especially blacks, defendants with court-appointed counsel were less likely to have their executions commuted. Among blacks, those with private counsel were more likely to have their executions commuted. And sentencing itself varies in regard to identical offenses: drunkenness is a classic instance where social position is a strong determinant of differential sentencing.[29] Where upper and lower class juveniles commit identical offenses, differential treatment and sentencing also appear. And restitution for a wrongful death is explicitly based on the decedent's class position; damages are computed on the basis of his or her projected lifetime income. But type of crime in general is so geared to class that is difficult to establish class bias in sentencing. Data showing that the indigent plead guilty more, are convicted more often, receive probation less often, and so on, while suggestive, do not automatically add up to class bias; the various classes commit different crimes, are involved in crime at different rates, and present a different problem for sentencing and rehabilitation.

27. An otherwise useful full-scale study of the jury system by Harry Kalven, Jr. and Hans Zeisel, *The American Jury* (Boston: Little, Brown, 1966), makes no reference to the relation between class and trial by jury.

28. Fred L. Strodtbeck, Rita M. James, and Charles Hawkins, "Social Status in Jury Deliberations," *American Sociological Review* 22 (December 1957): 713–719; reprinted in W. Richard Scott, ed., *Social Processes and Social Structures: An Introduction to Sociology* (New York: Holt, Rinehart and Winston, 1970), pp. 258–266. The article also notes that court-martialed enlisted men have not taken advantage of a new provision in the military code allowing them to request that fellow enlisted men serve on their court-martial panels — they have preferred to leave their fates to officers.

29. For differences in commutation of execution sentences, see Marvin E. Wolfgang, Arlene Kelly, and Hans C. Nolde, "Comparisons of the Executed and the Commuted Among Admissions to Death Row" in *Crime and Justice in Society,* Richard Quinney, ed. (Boston: Little, Brown, 1969). For different sentencing among those convicted of drunkenness, see Jacqueline P. Wiseman, *Stations of the Lost: The Treatment of Skid Row Alcoholics* (Englewood Cliffs, N.J.: Prentice-Hall 1970), pp. 90–94.

The Supreme Court's guarantee of due process to all, especially its controversial Gideon, Escobedo, and Miranda decisions, has done little to change the class character of justice.[30] Formally, due process means among other things that accused individuals are entitled to free lawyers, trials, and appeals if they are too poor to pay their own expenses, and to the right to remain silent and have a lawyer present at all stages of their dealings with the state. This new interpretation of due process, and the Court's determination to invalidate confessions and other evidence obtained illegally, has been hailed by some as rebalancing the relation between the individual and the state and condemned by others as contributing to the breakdown of law and order. But the real significance of these rulings seems to be to affirm the validity of our traditional adversary system of justice and reassert the traditional liberal view that the individual and the government are enemies. The general power of class over justice is not curtailed; an economic floor has simply been placed under the class system of justice to prevent the poor from being bypassed altogether. There is no doubt that these rulings will curtail shoddy and illegal behavior on the part of some law enforcement officials. But the administration of criminal justice differs markedly from the images conjured by these rulings and by those who applaud or condemn them. Despite these rulings, most crime in the United States will continue to go undetected and unpunished, rates of arrests will not change, rates of confession will continue at previous levels, and the overwhelming majority of defendants (mostly individuals from the lower classes) will continue to plead guilty. (And when they accept trial, they will continue to shun jury trials.) In other words, the reality of criminal justice is not the adversary system (or competition between legal entrepreneurs), abstract rights, or solemn pronouncements. The key to understanding criminal justice is the expression "the administration of justice." There exists a vast system of "bargain justice" in which judges, prosecutors, and private and public defense attorneys negotiate punishment to avoid trials.[31] As Donald J. Newman argues, the idea of bargaining is at odds with a legal process based on facts and rules of evidence, favors the experienced criminal over the first offender, and promotes a general disrespect for law. This assembly-line system of justice is a jerry-built construct created by judges, court officials, probation officers, court psychiatrists, prosecutors, and defense lawyers.[32] As Abraham S. Blum-

30. The definition of due process has evolved slowly through a considerable number of Supreme Court decisions. The basic elements of due process are specified in three famous decisions: *Gideon v. Wainwright,* 372 U.S. 335 (1963); *Escobedo v. Illinois,* 378 U.S. 478 (1964); and *Miranda v. Arizona* 384 U.S. 436 (1966).

31. Donald J. Newman, "Pleading Guilty for Considerations: A Study of Bargain Justice," *Journal of Criminal Law, Criminology and Police Science* 46 (March–April 1956): 780–790; reprinted in William J. Chambliss, ed., *Crime and the Legal Process* (New York: McGraw-Hill, 1969), pp. 209–220.

32. Abraham S. Blumberg, "The Practice of Law as Confidence Game: Organizational Cooptation of a Profession," *Law and Society Review* 1 (June 1967): 15–39; reprinted in William J. Chambliss, ed., *Crime and the Legal Process* (New York: McGraw-Hill, 1969), pp. 220–237.

berg points out, the Supreme Court's rulings upholding the rights of the accused have had the ironic result of enriching the resources of this existing organizational and professional arrangement by providing for a more efficient way of eliciting guilty pleas from defendants.

The administration of justice in the realm of civil law is also heavily weighted against the lower classes. In general, members of the lower classes rarely use the machinery of the law on their own behalf, though they have many legal problems (and legal rights). Our legal institutions assume middle class status: to benefit from the law in practice, one must be educated, informed about one's rights, comfortable in a world of specialization and impersonality, able to take initiative, and, of course, affluent. Members of the lower classes are thus by definition beyond the scope of law as an operational right.[33]

But the law by no means ignores the lower classes, and its impact is not limited to differential treatment by the police and courts in criminal cases. It would not be inaccurate to say that the power dimension supplies one set of legal procedures and even of laws for the lower classes and another set of procedures and laws for the upper classes. Three distinct types of differential treatment of the upper and lower classes in substantive and procedural law have been identified: favored parties, dual law (*de jure* denial of equal protection), and *de facto* denial of equal protection.[34] The law favors landlords over tenants and lenders over borrowers; of course, the favored parties in such cases tend to enjoy higher class status than their adversaries. Dual law for the lower and upper classes characterizes the realms of family law and welfare law.[35] When they concern the lower classes, divorce, property settlements, and support relations are handled as public matters to insure the smallest cost to the public; when they concern the upper classes, such cases are treated as civil matters pertaining to private individuals. Law and legal philosophy also differ with regard to government benefits for the lower classes (public assistance, unemployment insurance, public housing) and the upper classes (licenses, loans, subsidies, contracts). *De facto* bias means that equal application of law

33. Such new developments in law, as federally funded legal aid, especially as provided by the neighborhood or storefront law firm, are designed to overcome some of these class barriers.

34. Jerome E. Carlin, Jan Howard, and Sheldon L. Messinger, *Civil Justice and the Poor: Issues for Sociological Research* (New York: Russell Sage Foundation, 1967). Though the authors use the terms *rich* and *poor* throughout, it is clear that they are referring broadly to the upper and lower classes. Their volume is a brilliant summary of what we know and suspect about the class nature of American justice; it contains a valuable bibliography on the relation between class and law, with special reference to the "poor" (lower classes). Students of social stratification who are interested in this subject will find a collection of articles edited by Jacobus tenBroek and the editors of the California Law Review, *The Law of the Poor* (San Francisco: Chandler, 1966), especially valuable; available in paperback.

35. Jacobus tenBroek, *Family Law and the Poor* (Westport, Conn.: Greenwood, 1971), and "The Two Nations: Differential Values in Welfare Law and Administration" in *Orthopsychiatry and the Law*, ed. M. Levitt and B. Rubenstein (Detroit: Wayne State University Press, 1968); reprinted in Jerome H. Skolnick and Elliott Currie, eds., *Crisis in American Institutions*, (Boston: Little, Brown, 1970), pp. 350–361.

works to the detriment of the lower classes. Impartially applied restrictive abortion and divorce laws actually favor the upper classes; acceptance of common law market precepts ("let the buyer beware") works to the disadvantage of the lower classes in economic transactions. The draft law burdens the lower classes inequitably, since they are less likely to have exempt occupations or to be college students. In general, Carlin, Howard, and Messinger observe, "the law itself serves to define and maintain the position of the poor."[36]

Implicit in these substantive differences between the law of the upper classes and the law of the lower classes are sharp differences in legal procedure. The assembly-line system of justice routinizes, standardizes, and processes a vast percentage of all legal cases involving the lower classes. There is a pronounced tendency to employ criminal proceedings in welfare and family cases involving the lower classes. And the lower classes are treated as wards of the state on the presumption that they are incompetent and that the interests of the state are in harmony with their interests.

The courts that deal with the lower classes tend to dispense with procedural safeguards: they do not give notice; fail to observe rules of evidence; are characterized by a lack of genuine adversariness; and tend to delegate decisions to such nonlegal personnel as probation officers, psychiatrists, and social workers, which results in confusion and diffusion of responsibility. Carlin, Howard, and Messinger also note that the courts for the lower classes are characterized by grossly inadequate resources and least adequately trained and experienced judges and other personnel.

Of course, the net result of this system of mass-production justice is to help create the type of individual the law presumes. The law of the lower classes, in other words, is a self-fulfilling prophecy to the extent that it assumes that people in the lower classes are untrustworthy and incompetent and treats them as such. It is not surprising that, under a regime that deprives them of the opportunity to act as persons, the lower classes see the state and the law as remote and alien phenomena, are suspicious and cynical of its justice, and seem childish and confused. Their experience with the law is consistent with their dealings with authority at home, in schools, at the doctor's or dentist's office, in church, at work, at the unemployment or welfare bureau, and at the employment agency.

The intentions of the state are not in question. That the state "individualizes" justice for juvenile delinquents and the lower classes in an effort to treat all fairly can be taken for granted.[37] But the treatment of some (the upper classes) according to what they do and have and of others (the lower classes) according to who they are is a flagrant violation of the legal theory of the liberal state and contributes heavily to the serious identity problem of the lower classes. According to Carlin, Howard, and Messinger, the ultimate denial

36. Carlin *et al., Civil Justice and the Poor,* p. 21.
37. In fact, however, true individualized justice is restricted to the nonpoor, who can hire good lawyers to particularize and devote attention to their unique legal problems.

of identity by the legal system is that the lower classes are not allowed to mean what they say. Thus, if there is only one possible legal identity — broadly speaking, middle class in nature — those who cannot achieve it must do without a legal identity. (This status rounds out their nonidentity in other areas.) Or, perhaps, to pursue a suggestion by Garfinkel, the successful degradation of the deviant requires the treatment we now give defendants from the lower classes.[38] Whatever the reason for their present treatment, the American legal system would be far different were there equal treatment under law for the upper and lower classes.

Law and representative minorities
Black Americans and the law

The mistreatment of black people by law enforcement agencies is widely recognized, as is the high black crime rate. Though blacks make up about 11 percent of the American population, they account for about 30 percent of all arrests. Blacks are victimized by crime more than whites, even holding income constant, and there is a tendency for offenders to victimize members of their own race.[39] Blacks are also punished more severely than whites accused of similar crimes, and are more likely to be executed. Blacks are often treated illegally by the police, and there is open and explicit police surveillance of black neighborhoods. And blacks are underrepresented throughout the apparatus of law enforcement. What is not known, however, is how much of the mistreatment of blacks by law enforcement agencies is due to race and how much to other factors.

In the south, where blacks have systematically been treated differently by the law, it was generally expected that they would be so treated. Given racist state and local governments, it is not surprising that law enforcement in the south was openly racist in character. But on a national scale, it is not at all clear whether race is any longer a significant factor in the mistreatment of black people. One of the most important findings about black criminal behavior is Green's report, cited above, that black and white crime rates are identical once class is held constant. Though we have no data, it would not be implausible to argue that class is a far more important factor than race in criminal behavior by blacks and in their relation to law enforcement agencies in general. *Basically, law enforcement agencies deal illegally with, and display excessive*

38. Harold Garfinkel, "Conditions of Successful Degradation Ceremonies," *American Journal of Sociology* 61, no. 5 (March 1956): 420–424.

39. Philip H. Ennis, *Criminal Victimization in the United States: A Report of a National Study* (Washington, D.C.: U.S. Government Printing Office, 1967), pp. 32–36. This is a National Opinion Research Center study designed to develop a means of determining the amount of crime more accurate than the Uniform Crime Rate. (Survey data indicate far more crime than the UCR accounts for.) The greater victimization by crime of the lower classes and of Negroes and other races revealed by this survey is also demonstrated in the *Statistical Abstract of the United States, 1972* (Washington, D.C.: United States Government Printing Office, 1972), Table 227.

zeal and force against, all members of the lower classes, whether white, black, yellow, red, Anglo, Mexican American, Protestant, Jewish, or Roman Catholic. In short, the main purpose of law enforcement agencies, like all branches of government, is to defend the existing order of things.

Upper income groups consistently express higher evaluations of the police than do lower income groups (though support in general is high). However, blacks are negative toward the police regardless of income.[40] Generally speaking, blacks dislike the police and suspect them of singling out blacks for mistreatment. Thus one of the (largely latent) ways in which the police defend the existing order of things is to displace the lower classes' resentments toward themselves and away from the class system. In other words, to the extent that blacks interpret their relation to the police and the law in racial terms, they are overlooking the class system, which is the prime source of American behavior.

Mexican Americans and the law

Until recently, the position of Mexican Americans in the southwest has been castelike and somewhat analogous to that of blacks in the south. Mexican Americans' relation to law enforcement agencies, as to government in general, has been thoroughly unsatisfactory.[41] As recently as 1970, the United States Commission on Civil Rights found considerable discrimination against Mexican Americans on the part of law enforcement agencies. The police use excessive zeal and force against American citizens of Mexican descent, are disrespectful of their persons and their rights, and interfere illegally with Mexican American organizations. Adequate remedies against such abuse do not exist and the police retaliate against complainants. Furthermore, Mexican Americans are vastly underrepresented on juries, subject to bail when Anglos are not, inadequately represented by counsel, and greatly underrepresented in law enforcement agencies in general.[42]

The commission's report concentrates on the special treatment of Mexican Americans, in one instance specifically disallowing class factors. There is little question that Mexican Americans are not treated equally or well by law enforcement agencies throughout the southwest. Our own view is that this should be viewed as a stratification phenomenon, a legacy partly of "caste" status and partly of class. Of course, law enforcement officials find it relatively easy to treat distinctive groups such as blacks and Mexican Americans differently. But it is crucial to keep in mind that all types of groupings in the lower

40. Philip H. Ennis, *Criminal Victimization in the United States* (Washington, D.C.: U.S. Government Printing Office, 1967). pp. 52–56.
41. For a good review, see Leo Grebler, Joan W. Moore, Ralph C. Guzman *et al., The Mexican-American People: The Nation's Second Largest Minority* (New York: Free Press, 1970), chap. 21.
42. U.S. Commission on Civil Rights, *Mexican Americans and the Administration of Justice in the Southwest* (Washington, D.C.: U.S. Government Printing Office, 1970).

classes are mistreated by law enforcement officials. The fact that mistreatment takes on a racial or ethnic flavor helps to divide groups with common grievances and interests. In other words, one of the latent functions of the mistreatment of blacks and Mexican Americans by law enforcement agencies is to foster racial and ethnic defensiveness among those mistreated. To the extent that it does so, the affected parties are unlikely to recognize the class factor common to their shared mistreatment.

Jewish Americans and the law

Given their predominantly middle class status, Jewish Americans do not commit crimes at noticeable rates and are not mistreated by law enforcement agencies. Jews are, of course, interested in the enforcement of civil rights and antidiscrimination laws. In recent years they have resisted attempts to establish quotas or to give preference to other minorities in admission to colleges, professional schools, and occupations. And Jews in urban areas have probably been increasingly subjected to crime in recent years, and for this and other reasons have manifested a small trend toward political conservatism.

On issues involving law enforcement, Jewish Americans are probably associated with the status quo: they are property-owners, active in civic and political life, and probably well represented in law enforcement as lawyers and court officials. Whatever the case — we have no exact data — Jewish Americans are probably regarded by blacks (and urban Mexican Americans) as opposing rather than sharing their interests. In cities like New York, Jews are highly visible in the economy, in education and other professions, and in politics and law enforcement; while the extent of their power is problematic, it is easy for those struggling to escape the bottom of the social hierarchy to exaggerate that power. Once again, minority groups with shared interests are divided, this time because they belong to different classes.

New departures in law: reform without change

The law is not a static structure. Thanks to an active legislative process and to judicial interpretation, it is extended and reformed on a continuous basis. To speak of reform without change is not to minimize the impact of legal reform (or pending reform) in the United States; it is only to emphasize that such reforms represent neither change in nor departure from the fundamental principles of class stratification. What legal reform amounts to, in other words, is the modernization of class society.

The redefinition of deviance and crime

The legal code of the United States is being purged of a number of laws defining various kinds of behavior as criminal. In recent years a number of state legislatures have liberalized their abortion laws, in effect making the termination of pregnancy a private matter between a woman and her doctor;

and in 1973 the Supreme Court ruled most antiabortion laws unconstitutional. The incentives for abortion reform have been many and varied: concern over population growth, women's rights, the performance of an enormous number of unsafe abortions every year under criminal auspices, and the fact that the chief victims of antiabortion laws are the lower classes.

Laws against the sale of birth control devices have also crumbled, and public programs have augmented the efforts of private groups to extend the benefits of birth control to the general public. Here too, the lower classes are the chief beneficiaries of a reform for which solid middle class support was necessary.

Homosexuality and other sexual behavior that violates common standards of sexual morality is under review, and efforts are being made to redefine such behavior as a personal matter (or, as the case may be, as a medical or psychiatric problem). Some headway has been made toward defining alcoholism as a medical problem, and there is support for decriminalizing drug addiction.

The Supreme Court has extended the protection of the First Amendment to much of what was once defined as criminal pornography, and a presidential advisory commission has recommended that, by and large, pornography enter the realm of free moral choice for adults and cease to be subject to the criminal code.[43] The more conservative decisions on pornography handed down by the Burger Court in 1973 will undoubtedly modify this trend, though whether it can be reversed remains to be seen. It is of some interest that the chief users of pornography are middle class males, and the successful liberalization of the law in this area is undoubtedly due to middle class support.

Gambling has traditionally been designated a crime in the United States, though some changes in this position can be discerned. The fact that it enjoys widespread public support and is a lucrative source of revenue has prompted some states to legalize certain forms of gambling. Regardless of its disposition by the law, gambling will probably continue for some time to serve as recreation for the successful and as a substitute for success for the lower classes. Whereas these functions were once performed illegally by private business-people, they are now increasingly being performed by public agencies (lotteries and betting parlors). In addition, challenges have been made to the state's right to enforce vagrancy laws. And while not strictly criminal matters, no-fault divorce and no-fault automobile insurance will help to destigmatize certain behavior, especially by removing it from the jurisdiction of courts.

Consumer protection

Consumers are a diverse lot of people, and thus difficult to organize. But because of determined leadership, some notorious scandals, and growing public (especially middle class) apprehension about the quality and safety of a large

43. *The Report of the Commission on Obscenity and Pornography* (New York: Random House, 1970), Part 2; also a Bantam paperback.

number of products, a consumer movement strong enough to achieve significant legal reform emerged in the 1960s.

Safety and quality in automobiles, color television sets, appliances, boats, and other heavy durable goods are obviously more germane to certain classes than to others. In fact, all such issues, from the protection of children from lead poisoning to the effort to protect the natural environment, are related to class. The ways in which government regulates and stimulates industries — by distributing franchises, establishing depreciation rates, setting import and production quotas, and the like — and the way in which it treats oligarchic competition affect the distribution of income (and thus class) because they affect the prices consumers pay for products and services. Standardized packaging, the development of a pricing system based on unit cost, and truth-in-lending will probably be more beneficial to the working class and the poor than to the classes above them.

Programs to aid the poor and minority groups in overcoming consumption disabilities and to make their legal rights effective have had moderate success. The Economic Opportunity Act of 1964, for example, led to the provision of free legal services for the poor. Such help is not limited to the provision of defense in criminal matters; much more importantly, it allows the poor to initiate judicial proceedings to protect their interests and their rights.[44] Of some significance here is the growing use of legal class action (action on behalf of all individuals affected by the practice in question, not of a social class). At present, class actions are much easier to initiate in the federal courts than at the state level. While *class action* is a legal term, some such litigation may be undertaken on behalf of a social class; an example is legal action to protect the interests of all welfare recipients or all dispossessed and unrelocated families. The ability of the poor and working poor to fight back legally may bring about fresh appraisals of a number of social practices that now affect them adversely. The Uniform Commercial Code makes it harder to enforce "tricky contracts," and the use of the garnishee as a way of enforcing consumer payment is now subject to a prior hearing and may be on the decline; indeed, it has already been banned in a number of states.

The Civil Rights Acts of 1964 and 1965 also touched on the area of consumption by making it illegal to discriminate in public accommodations. But

44. Federal funding allows lawyers to be much more independent and to pursue more types of cases on behalf of the poor than the older Legal Aid system. Under the old system, lawyers were dependent for support on local businesspeople, professionals, and, of course, other lawyers; thus the Legal Aid system was a captive of the very people who were causing trouble for the poor. Local and state governments, having themselves been pressured by federally funded legal aid programs to adhere to their own laws, have applied pressure to curtail such programs. In 1974, a Nixon administration proposal to reorganize this service as a "nonpolitical" legal corporation was enacted into law. The effect of such a move cannot be predicted with absolute certainty, but if the history of our "nonpolitical" regulatory agencies is any guide, we can assume that the trend toward equal justice has crested.

legislation outlawing "caste" and ethnic-religious discrimination have minimal effect on the poor as such. It should not go unnoticed that such legislation helps to legitimate the class system by incorporating into our legal understanding and sense of justice the assumption that the law protects only the equal right of poor and rich to consume according to class standing.

The rights of citizens

In the past few decades significant changes have taken place in the definition of the individual's rights, especially in relation to the state. We have already mentioned the provision of free legal services for the poor as a result of the Economic Opportunity Act of 1964. These services have been used in civil actions and in a wide variety of criminal proceedings. Of some importance in enhancing the value of free legal services are the Supreme Court decisions affirming the constitutional right of accused persons, including paupers, to due process. The Supreme Court has also ruled that welfare residency requirements are an infringement of the right to travel and that recipients have a right to formal hearings (due process) before their benefits (property) can be abridged. The Supreme Court is also being petitioned to hear cases involving burdensome court fees for divorce, such fees allegedly precluding equal treatment under the law for the poor. The large and thorny issue of housing, especially zoning and the use of public referendums to curtail low-income housing, is also before the Court, as is the problem of unequal public services.

Reform without change

However substantial and important American legal reform has been, its extent should not be exaggerated. The reform of the law should be seen as one aspect of the modernization of the American class system, and not as the growth of equal justice or as an attack on the basic structure of our class and prestige hierarchies. The law will continue to be a main support of the status quo, but in new ways. While the poor will enjoy more legal rights, they will continue to participate in a legal system structured to assume the validity of property rights and authority relations. Though new property rights (such as the right to welfare benefits) may be acknowledged, they will simply join the existing body of property rights and become subject to the assumption that unequal property is socially desirable and thus socially legitimate. Similarly, welfare recipients' right to due process before their benefits are curtailed also serves to enhance the validity of welfare as an effective and legitimate way to handle the problems of unemployment, racial discrimination, broken homes, illegitimacy, and the like. Welfare recipients will be treated on a national basis: local residency requirements have already been abolished, a national minimum income may someday be established, and national standards for welfare may be adopted. But the real meaning of such changes will be to legitimate class inequality and to incorporate the economically worthless into a nationwide structure of legalized and moralized destitution. Indeed, ironically, it may be that the United States Constitution, middle class efficiency, and Christian compassion are being used to transform welfare recipients into noncitizens.

The growth of publicly supported legal services will no doubt allow the poor to exercise their legal rights more effectively. But here again, the improvement of legal status may serve to distract attention from the hard political decisions necessary if there are to be solutions to the major problems of the poor: inadequate employment, housing, medical care, schooling, and general life experience. Nor should the value of these new legal services be exaggerated. The inadequacy of the newly created legal services and the exaggerated significance attributed to the new legal rights of American citizens (largely the poor) are most dramatically apparent in the case of the new rights of defendants in criminal cases. Remember that the Supreme Court has ruled that all defendants are entitled to full exercise of their constitutional rights: the right not to incriminate oneself, the right to legal counsel, and the right to a full measure of adjudication. This new definition of *due process* seems to sever these legal rights from economic (class) status by making them free if the defendant cannot afford to pay for them. Just as political status was divorced from economic status in the nineteenth century when property qualifications for voting were abolished, the power dimension appears to be freeing itself from economic status when it provides free legal services for the poor. Certainly the impact of these newly established rights would appear to be considerable, judging by the vigorous approval and outraged condemnation they elicited from various quarters. The general controversy over whether or not these rulings leave the public adequately protected against crime appears to be largely irrelevant. Ideally speaking, the Gideon, Escobedo, and Miranda rulings are the glory of liberal civilization. But, practically speaking, they change very little about the United States' basic legal institutions or their relation to the American class structure. Crime will persist at high and perhaps growing rates because of the *anomie* inherent in liberal society. *Law and order* will continue to mean the expenditure of large sums to enforce the law against ordinary criminals while less attention and money are devoted to curtailing far more serious white-collar crime. And, perhaps worst of all, controversy over these rulings and calls for law and order will divert attention from the main question: why is there crime in the first place?

The law's distinctness, alleged separation from society, formality and prestige, and recent reforms do not prevent it from embodying many other features of liberal society. The basic stance of the American penal code is still to assume that potential and actual criminals respond to rewards and punishments much as businesspeople and workers allegedly respond to pleasure-pain stimuli and cost-profit calculations. It assumes that competitive judicial proceedings will produce justice just as competition in economic markets allegedly produces true prices and better products. And it is taken for granted that justice will be available to all because it can be bought much as one buys food, clothing, and housing.

Nevertheless, the bail system will continue to victimize the poor. Police officers, lawyers, judges, jurors, and jailers will continue to employ class-based stereotypes in dealing with clients, defendants, and different types of crimes. Police protection will continue to be inadequate where it is most needed, and middle class efficiency in law enforcement will continue to make the relation between the law and the poor (and some minority groups) tenuous and a source of alienation. Juries will no doubt be chosen more carefully in the future, but the poor will continue to shun trial by jury; thus the chief beneficiaries of jury trials will be white-collar defendants. And our prisons will continue to turn out hardened criminals.

Opposition to legal reforms on the part of vested interests in the legal profession, some police departments, small businesspeople, landlords, and many citizens and politicians may be overcome in the years ahead. But the struggle over legal reform is largely a competition between the rearguard action of an old middle class and the modernizing pressures of the new middle class. The chief beneficiaries of legal reform will not be the poor but the middle and upper-middle classes. Politicians will have more patronage to dispense, civil servants will have more money to spend, police forces will become professionalized, lawyers will enjoy more secure employment, more judges will be needed, and more and better-trained and better-paid court officials and auxiliary professionals will assist them. And the middle and upper classes will complacently conclude that equality under the law is viable in practice.

Class-prestige, law, and justice: a summary

The class-prestige basis of law is clear. The various classes commit different types of crime at different rates; crime is defined differently depending on the class of the lawbreaker; law enforcement agencies treat lawbreakers from the various classes differently; legal services are more readily available to the upper classes than the lower classes; and legal reform rarely affects the essential inequality before the law characteristic of class society. By and large, the working and lower classes enjoy substantially fewer legal rights, inferior legal services, and less justice than the classes above them. It is not clear that black and Mexican Americans, who are mistreated by the law, are abused more than other groups in the working and lower classes.

PART 5

The American class system: an interpretation and summary

15

The American class system: how and why the system works

THE UNITED STATES falls short of its ideals by a considerable margin, and public opinion surveys indicate that the American people know this. Why then has the United States' failure in this regard not led to more popular disaffection? Why, for example, does the deep populist streak in American life not collide more violently with the inegalitarian (achievement-oriented and ascriptive) demands of our economic, familial, social, and political institutions? Why is the legitimacy of American institutions not subject to more widespread questioning, considering the deep and persistent ascriptive inequality that has characterized our history? Why does the irregular performance of the American economy not elicit deeper questioning of the economic system? The failure of the market economy to control pollution is only the latest chapter in a long record of failures to overcome poverty, produce full employment, achieve economic stability and harmony, integrate minority groups, and in general promote achievement and competition. Blatant disparities of wealth and power seem not to stir popular unrest, even though it is widely believed that the American reward system falls far short of matching traditional American norms of achievement. And why is there no concerted attack on the liberal *system* of society when Americans express widespread disbelief in the reality of its central legitimating ideal, equal opportunity?

Some argue that the United States' unsolved problems caught up with the nation in the 1960s, when a number of factors combined to produce considerable internal stress and strain. For one thing, the United States began to feel the effects of a problem unprecedented in its history and in that of any society, the problem of prolonged prosperity. In an important way, the nation's problems are illuminated by being seen in the context of prosperity. In some, prosperity arouses expectations that rise faster than they can be satisfied, and in others it accentuates the sense of relative deprivation, felt differently by different classes. The rising educational and professional requirements brought about by prosperity prolong the period of preadulthood and aggravate the tensions of youth. Prosperity multiplies the number of middle and upper class (and working class) women who receive college educations and then come to feel deprived of their rights and their full humanity in a male-oriented society. It is prosperity that produces geographical and vertical mobility, thus making some rootless and others anxiety-ridden *nouveau riche*. Prosperity based on large-scale economic rationalization undermines small-town and rural life and produces a national and even international economy beyond understanding and control. It is prosperity that divorces economic and political power by locating corporate structures in metropolitan areas and political power in the suburbs and small towns. And it is prosperity that best explains the emergence of militant black consciousness during the 1960s.

The stress of the 1960s also resulted from a long and costly war that lacked national support. The Vietnam war was a source of tension in its own right as the nation debated its wisdom and morality; furthermore, it aggravated old tensions by consuming resources needed to fight poverty, ease the plight of the racially oppressed, and maintain public services. But while its sources were new, it cannot be said that the turmoil in the United States during the 1960s was either threatening or significantly more pronounced than in the past. Comparisons are difficult, but the United States has always had little "rebellions" (as well as one large one), social dropouts (including thousands of utopian communities), and fundamentalist right-wing movements of various kinds. A socialist movement peaked around the beginning of the century, a flurry of Marxism and communism occurred during the 1930s, and so on.

The changes that took place during the 1960s did not revolutionize American society. Black Americans, of course, will no longer be subject to "caste" forces, but as an aggregate they are still at the bottom of American society and their chances of improving their position relative to white Americans are problematic. Nor was American society changed by the War on Poverty. Actually, the antipoverty program failed, and the deeper significance of its failure is that the United States' moral, political, and legal forces seem to be ineffectual against what appears to be a deeply graded and intractable class structure. As for the other themes of the 1960s, they have been either muffled or neutralized: the end of the Vietnam war and the elimination of the draft effectively dissipated student unrest, which had often expressed itself as an indictment of American society. As for women's liberation, no effective assault on American society as a whole can be expected from a highly differentiated female population. As benefits and opportunities comparable to those of their male counterparts are gradually extended to middle class females, they may be expected to behave in a manner that will protect the advantages and privileges of their children, male or female, *vis-à-vis* the children, male or female, of the lower classes. In any case, the 1960s aroused no widespread class consciousness or class struggle. Many disparate types of discontent surfaced, and though some thought that middle class students might be able to weld a coalition of workers, the lower class, and blacks into a generalized structure of opposition to American society, it never materialized.

Among the most interesting things about the American class system, in addition to the absence of class consciousness and class struggle, is its basic stability. Of course, no one should be dogmatic about the basic structure and direction of even simple societies, let alone the United States. Theorists see the United States quite differently: C. Wright Mills sees it as a power elite–mass society, others say that a new American Revolution has taken place,[1] Daniel Bell celebrates the end of ideology and the coming of postindustrial society, and others announce the emergence of a meritocracy of strategic elites.[2] Some see a major modification of industrial society in the direction of Pentagon capitalism,[3] while John K. Galbraith claims that trained intelligence has replaced capital as the key controlling scarcity in capitalist society,[4] and Talcott Parsons foresees the full evolution of American society and the Western system of industrial states within a hundred years or so.[5]

Our study has found little evidence to support any of these assertions and enough evidence to refute some of them. What we have found is that the United States is a highly stable society, that changes in it are more apparent than real, but that nonsystemic changes (basically, economic expansion and political reform) are probably the most important explanation for the nation's stability! From the standpoint of stratification theory, the American population is still defined in economic terms and is as deeply graded in terms of economic success and failure as it has ever been. Achievement and mobility have neither increased nor decreased (to the degree that these complex matters can be analyzed); there is still considerable ascriptive advantage; and American society is still fundamentally organized around private property and private (especially economic) power groups.

Given this general context, what specific processes and structures make America function? This chapter is offered as an exploratory analysis, and is

1. Joseph Bensman and Arthur J. Vidich, *The New American Society* (Chicago; Quadrangle, 1971).

2. Suzanne Keller, *Beyond the Ruling Class: Strategic Elites in Modern Society* (New York: Random House, 1963), also in paperback.

3. Seymour Melman, *Pentagon Capitalism: The Political Economy of War* (New York: McGraw-Hill, 1970), available in paperback.

4. John Kenneth Galbraith, *The New Industrial State* (Boston: Houghton Mifflin, 1967), also in paperback.

5. Talcott Parsons, *Societies: Evolutionary and Comparative Perspectives* (Englewood Cliffs, N.J.: Prentice Hall, 1966), and *The System of Modern Societies* (Englewood Cliffs, N.J.: Prentice-Hall, 1971).

not intended as a complete inventory or a systematic theory.[6] Of first importance in understanding the United States' stability (as well as its tensions, dysfunctions, and inequities) is its economic system.

Economic processes and class stability
Economic expansion and complexity

However difficult it is to interpret the social implications of economic growth, there is no denying that much of the loyalty of the American population to the American way of life is due to promises kept: commitment and adherence to the American way of life has paid off in both psychic and material benefits for broad segments of the American people. Whether there is a better way to run an economy is not likely to become an issue as long as the economy by and large produces the satisfactions it promises. Real economic growth produces an expectation of growth and a belief and faith in progress, and thus makes it easier for people to endure the hardships and disappointments of the moment. A future-oriented psychology is deeply rooted in the needs of capital formation (savings, thrift); socialization processes that stress deferred gratification; and in the middle class sense of order, predictability, and control. All in all, the futurism inherent in an expansive economy is a potent solvent for pessimism and frustration. The impact of American economic values and norms on the American personality has been deep and lasting in other ways as well. The American economy has always provided choice, which goes hand-in-hand with the ethic of individualism and personal responsibility for success and failure. American values have emphasized personal fulfillment from economic endeavor and the nation provided the means of fulfillment for many: cheap, fertile land; a growing and diversifying business and occupational system; many and diverse forms of educational opportunity; and a congenial moral and political climate.

Perhaps the best way to summarize the relation between economic process and class stability is to examine the problem of identity. American society creates many identity problems that can be related to class position. Those who succeed in forging normal identities tend to come from stable homes and to have parents who themselves have secure and consistent identities. Those who do not achieve normal identities tend to come from the lower classes. On a more abstract level, American society is actually structured to prevent the development of stable and easily acquired identities. Each generation is almost immediately a part of the abstract labor force: for Americans, childhood and youth are a period of preparation for undetermined jobs, many of which did not exist at the time of their occupants' birth. And the occupational skill requirements of traditional jobs are upgraded constantly, making long, increas-

6. While I have stipulated the forces that stabilize the American class system somewhat differently, I am indebted to the suggestions of Robin M. Williams, Jr., *American Society*, 3rd ed. (New York: Alfred A. Knopf, 1970), pp. 154–164, originally published in 1951.

ing, and often irrelevant schooling necessary for job entry. And if occupation, the primary social status, is not routinely defined and accessible, it is no wonder that other statuses are vague and that coherent identities are difficult to achieve.

In addition, economic pressures toward social and geographic mobility make it difficult either to identify with a particular place or to develop lasting friendships, group memberships and community attachments — relationships that promote (indeed, constitute) stable, well-defined personalities.[7] As people move from job to job, their attachments to job and community of residence become increasingly superficial. Many individuals may also suffer from insecurity, for they must learn new skills of socializing and consumption as they move up or down the social ladder. Identity is also affected by the nature of work: upper-echelon occupations tend to create more independent and satisfied personalities, while the lower levels produce more withdrawn and conformist personalities. These identity problems lead to behavioral problems of various kinds, but they do not lead to criticism of the social system. Given the almost monopolistic sway of liberalism, Americans tend to interpret identity and behavioral problems as personal failures. Thus their resentments and disappointments tend to be displaced from society and the class system and onto the individual.[8]

Economy and class: a specification

The specific economic processes that promote stability and forestall class struggle can be enumerated without lengthy explanation, since they recapitulate analyses made earlier:

1. Economic growth means a high and growing level of material satisfaction, a phenomenon that has played and continues to play an important role in sustaining the morale of the American population and in lubricating class relations. Readers will recall the highly developed system of differential and common consumption in which Americans participate.[9] This payoff in goods and services is undoubtedly influential in disciplining workers to accept hateful work routines and in persuading others to undergo the arduous training for upper-level occupations. While sizable segments of the lower classes do not believe that real equality of opportunity exists or that achievement lies at the heart of differential rewards, there is nonetheless widespread *personal* acceptance of the possibility of getting ahead, especially if one has what it takes. This faith in the possibility of success is based on the realities as well as the illusions of American experience. It is due partly to rising living standards (without relative social mobility), partly to families' view of themselves as achieving mobility over more than one generation ("I want my kids to have

7. For a fascinating and insightful analysis of the United States from this perspective, see Orrin E. Klapp, *Collective Search for Identity* (New York: Holt, Rinehart, and Winston, 1969), available in paperback.

8. For a further discussion, see "Class and *Anomie:* The Uses of Deviance" later in this chapter.

9. See Chapter 9.

what I didn't have"), and partly to actual vertical mobility, some of it quite spectacular and well publicized. Of considerable importance is the fact that a large proportion of economic growth is distributed within classes — that is, it is not necessary for a family or individual to change class in order to enjoy a rise in standard of living.

2. The American economy has not only continued to generate high levels of opportunity, but has done so largely by diversifying and upgrading its occupational structure. Diversification and upgrading help to stabilize the American class system in a number of ways. For one thing, these processes make possible a variety of ways in which Americans can find work satisfaction, which is of special importance at the middle and upper levels of the occupational structure. The vast increase in the number and types of upper and middle level occupations has made it possible for large numbers of Americans to rise in economic status without having to challenge incumbents at higher class levels. The growth of the professions and semiprofessions is a fundamental aspect of the stabilizing process. Seen in another way, occupational upgrading and diversification are aspects of the deep functional specificity that serves to insulate and cushion relations between superiors and inferiors, professionals and clients, exploiters and exploited.

3. Professionalization is distinct in a number of ways from occupational diversification in general. We are so accustomed to thinking of scientific, business, and professional leadership in terms of innovation and progress that we sometimes forget that these forces also act to preserve the status quo. Our elite structures obviously affirm the old if it is tested and true, pioneer new ways of doing things, and create new knowledge. But they also preserve the old because it is old, and venture into the unknown only within special limits. Thus, whether they are restricting the supply of skilled woman- and manpower or pioneering new ways to spread information, suppressing patents or developing cures for disease, blocking public programs in the interests of private advantage or pioneering new services, our elites should also be thought of as problem-solvers who make a particular social system (one that creates problems peculiar to itself) function.

The many distinguished achievements of our scientific and other professions should not blind us to the fact that professions reflect the society of which they are a part. After all, professionals belong to families, and they and their families enjoy high income, high prestige, and great political-legal power. The educational system is deeply biased in favor of their children. They are well organized to control the flow of labor into their respective fields; they insist on the exclusive right to judge the competence and ethics of their members; and they protect themselves in general against outsiders by maintaining a fiduciary relation to their clients and to society-in-general. To recognize all this is to see the professions in terms of Durkheim's great insight into the stabilizing, integrating nature of the modern division of labor.

No discussion of the professions can fail to note the deep intertwining of professional and economic — especially corporate — interests that has occurred during the twentieth century. Present-day doctors cannot be understood except in relation to giant hospital bureaucracies, developers and manufacturers of complex medical technology, medical supply industries, drug developers and manufacturers, insurance companies, and institutions of higher education, especially those with research hospitals and schools. Lawyers are increasingly employed by corporate and governmental bureaucracies and perform political functions. Professors work increasingly in large universities, often act as consultants to business or government, and write textbooks subject to the vagaries of a complex commercial market. As salaried employees of corporate or public structures, engineers often lend the expertise and prestige of their profession to the furtherance of economic interests. (Transportation engineers and other experts, for example, have furthered the fortunes of the intertwined economic interests that live off the automobile.)

4. The growth of the American economy has also diversified class interests and affiliations. This aspect of the American class system has already been developed fully and needs no further elaboration. In a manner unprecedented in any previous system of social stratification, the United States has developed a rich variety of class relations through its labor, credit, and commodity markets. These class relations overlap and make it difficult for generic class interests to emerge and congeal. It is noteworthy that while new complexities are being added to American class relationships, old forms are not necessarily discarded or eliminated. The most important consequence of class relations of this complexity is to prevent metaphysical confrontations between self-conscious antagonistic strata while promoting a pragmatic, strange-bedfellow mentality.

5. The stability of the American class system also depends on both economic security and insecurity. Though the American labor force and the various economic interests are far from feeling secure, a certain measure of security has emerged in the form of pensions, Social Security, medical and life insurance benefits, seniority and tenure systems, and, of course, trade unionism. We have stressed the importance of collective bargaining as a co-opting process that contributes to the stability of the American class system. The advent and establishment of collective bargaining mean that a large and potentially powerful segment of society has endorsed the validity of capitalism and of its relative position in the capitalist system. Now we enjoy the stabilizing effects of economic grumbling, contractual disputes, and strikes (against companies and even governments, but not against society).

It is highly likely that most members of the American lower-middle and working classes lead marginal economic existences. They do not and cannot save, their pensions do not provide security, and for many there is the constant threat of unemployment. And insecurity is a way of life for many small businesspeople and farmers as well. Given the tradition of Protestant-bourgeois responsibility, economic insecurity undoubtedly induces ritualistic conformity and/or self-blame for economic misfortune. Only as long as the perception of personal economic interest and need is embedded in the liberal mythology of individualism, and as long as there are no large-scale economic breakdowns, will economically dependent classes keep their noses to the social grindstone.

6. Perhaps the most interesting way in which the American economy stabilizes itself, and in turn contributes to the stability of American society, is by being far less achievement-oriented than legend would have it. One of the hoariest clichés characterizing American society (and sociology) is that we live in a dynamic world of competition and achievement in sharp contrast to lesser societies based on the stagnating forces of tradition and ascription. While this is in a sense true, it is also undeniable that we are much less achievement-conscious and competitive than we claim. In a brilliant summary accompanied by an interesting hypothesis, William J. Goode has outlined the various qualifications on our alleged commitment to competition and achievement.[10] Goode notes that the privileged at all levels "try systematically to prevent the talent of the less privileged from being recognized or developed," and points out that "both the able and inept may move into high position." He also notes that every study of workers, higher-level management, and the professions has found institutionalized protection of values other than sheer merit. There is evidence of skill and productivity, to be sure, but allowances are also made for the least able, and for sickness, alcoholism, loyalty, marital and family obligations, friendship, and recreation. And business of all types, including farming, is characterized more by efforts to reduce competition (risk and uncertainty) than by efforts to promote it. Goode concludes by hypothesizing that the much vaunted productivity of modern society is due less to the development of opportunities and rewards for the more able than to the capacity of modern society (thanks to such social inventions as bureaucracy and the factory system) to utilize the inept more efficiently! In any case, the widespread "protection of the inept" is more than a violation of norms and an elaborate social hypocrisy. An achievement-competitive society in any literal sense is an impossibility, a Hobbesian jungle. Americans obviously evade and violate the norms of merit to realize illegitimate values, for example, when they practice nepotism or protect obsolete or vested economic interests from competition. But, as Goode points out, the widespread protection of the inept means that Americans have a large number of legitimate values that for various reasons they insist on realizing directly in their economic institutions. The implications for class stability are obvious.

7. The stability of class society is also due to social mobility, a many-sided process that diversifies social classes and prevents them from becoming solidified and mutually antagonistic. Mobility also allows for the cooptation of potential leaders in the lower classes and undoubtedly plays a role in mollifying and stifling criticism at all levels. Substitutes for mobility are also a stabilizing force. Norbert Wiley's concept of a *mobility trap* is a clue to the nature of this process. Remember that Wiley identified four types of mobility *within* a stratum that prevent mobility *between* strata: the age-grade trap, the overspe-

10. "The Protection of the Inept," *American Sociological Review* 32 (February 1967): 5–19.

cialization trap, the localite trap, and the minority group trap.[11] If we expand the concept of a mobility trap to refer to any process that misleads an individual, family, group, or observer into thinking that an advance in class position is taking place, a substantial list of such traps can be compiled:

a. Gains in real income and/or occupational skill level and/or education over those of one's father are often mistaken for class mobility.

b. Gains in real income and/or occupational skill level and/or education during one's lifetime are also often mistaken for class mobility.

c. Consumption, including such new forms of public consumption as highways, sports stadiums, and recreational facilities, can also be thought of as a mobility trap. (This is a corollary, of course, to rising real income.)

d. Gains in legal or political status that represent a shift from "caste" to class can be mistaken for class mobility. Thus advances made by blacks, Mexican Americans, and other minorities in legal, political, and civil rights, which represent entrance *into* the class system rather than movement *up* the class system, can become substitutes for economic (class) reform.

e. Gains in income through public subsidy, which cannot be transformed into solid class standing, are also mobility traps. In this sense, the welfare system is a giant dependency-creating mobility trap.

f. Much of public education is a mobility trap, in that for many it serves simply to update their skills and income, and in effect allows them to remain in the same class as their parents.

These processes are, of course, both facilitated and disguised by appropriate symbols: the mythology that explains success or failure in personal terms or in terms of luck ("the big break"), that provides convenient rationalizations ("you can't change human nature"), that substitutes illusion for the substance of democracy (Fourth of July rhetoric, democratic manners, folksy politicians), that invests the present in a future that never comes (faith in progress, "tomorrow will be better"), or that exaggerates upward mobility rates (the Horatio Alger tradition).

Prestige processes and class stability
Heterogeneity within strata

The general thrust of the American economy has drawn large numbers of Americans of various economic, religious, and ethnic backgrounds upward (and downward) into strata other than those they were born and raised in. As a result, the various class levels of American society — the stable top, the upper-middle class, the lower-middle class, the working class and the lower class — are heterogeneous in composition, though not all to the same extent or with the same consequences. Thus, in addition to the heterogeneous class (economic) interests that characterize the members of each of these levels, there exists a heterogeneity of religion, ethnicity, race, and previous class condition.

For example, the stable top is diversified by class since it includes holders

11. See "Absolute versus Relative Mobility" in Chapter 3.

of wealth in competitive industries and a variety of competitive elite occupations. And the stable top is further diversified by the entrance of Roman Catholic and Jewish families. However, diversification has probably not proceeded very far among the stable top. The smallness of that class and the fact that membership in it requires extensive socialization (elite education, manners, forms of consumption, and so on) insures a general homogeneity of behavior and outlook, including consciousness of class. At this level, then, it is homogeneity that produces stability as the WASP upper stratum absorbs new elements into its way of life. Actually, the chief function of the small number of Roman Catholics and Jews at this level is probably not to provide religious-ethnic diversity but to serve as token proof that the United States is an open society.

The heterogeneity of American strata increases as one descends the class ladder, leading to a general conclusion that while relative homogeneity produces stability at the top, it is relative heterogeneity that helps to stabilize the classes below it. It is difficult for a distinct consciousness of kind to develop or for concerted class action to take place when each economic class includes a variety of occupations and economic interests. How much more difficult it is when economic classes also contain Protestants, Roman Catholics of various nationalities, and Jews; whites, blacks, yellows, browns, and reds; and old-family achievers as well as new arrivals still bound by ties of blood, friendship, and locality to people and places belonging to higher or lower strata. It is impossible to account for the absence of a revolutionary working class in the United States or of the weakness of the American trade union movement, for example, unless this process of stratum differentiation is taken into account.

Insulating processes

One of the outstanding features of the American system of social stratification is that the various strata do not interact as strata, as is more common to estate and caste systems. Actually, contact between strata is quite limited outside of carefully defined and functionally specific economic relations. By and large, each of the strata is insulated from the others by residential, associational, and political "segregation." In a real sense, the various strata lead full social lives without coming into contact with each other except in class-structured ways. Primary relations, which are heavily structured by class, absorb large amounts of time, and members of all class levels undoubtedly fall back on their primary groups to cushion themselves against the pressures and hurts of secondary, especially economic, relations. Outside their primary relations class members tend to associate with class equals and when they do not, they invariably interact in formally organized or functionally specific situations: work, shopping, education, voluntary groups, professional help. Relations between members of different classes are also smoothed and stabilized by the fact that work, education, professional needs, and voluntary activities are often under the control of members of one's own religion, ethnic group, or "race." The bitter conflicts over school integration through busing and mixed-class housing projects illustrate what happens when different classes come into contact outside class-structured channels.

This process of *institutional closure* varies from class to class and from one region of the country to another. But the existence of class-based subsocieties is quite real, and goes a long way toward explaining why social classes in the United States are not more conscious of or antagonistic toward one another. Marx thought that class consciousness would arise if members of the same class interacted (such as in a factory). Weber had the surer insight — class consciousness is more likely to arise when interaction *between* classes produces a sense of exploitation and oppression.

Stratum insulation occurs at all levels, but is most obviously manifested at the top and at the bottom. Upper class families live in carefully isolated residential areas, are educated, worship, and engage in leisure activities with class peers. Breadwinners in the upper and upper-middle class often have no direct experience of how the other classes live. Even when they leave their residential areas, they often see little of the world they live in. For example, commuters from upper or upper-middle class suburbs or towns see little of how other classes live on their way to or from, or even during, work.

An interesting variation on the process of insulation is created by class segregation combined with religious, ethnic, and/or racial segregation. Ghettoization is only one variant on this pattern, and the well-known separation of black and Mexican Americans from the rest of society need not be gone into again. But a word should be said about segregation at other class levels and of other minority groups. In a real sense, Jewish Americans and European-origin Roman Catholics are also segregated, though not as thoroughly as Mexican and, especially, black Americans. Our perception of this pattern is blurred, as is that of the affected minorities, because we associate a rise in the class (economic) system with freedom and independence.

The crucial point is that Jews and Italian, Irish, Polish, and French Canadian Roman Catholics are not distributed at random throughout our social system. If the distribution of the American Jewish population, for example, were plotted across all the dimensions and subdimensions of stratification, a definite pattern would emerge. While much better off than black and Mexican Americans, American Jews are nonetheless segregated, though at a higher level and less consistently. But because they can live full lives associating largely with other Jews (or, for Roman Catholics, even with Roman Catholics of the same ethnic background), they do not readily perceive the extent to which they are subject to (or have chosen) religious-ethnic segregation.

The overall pattern of insulating the various strata from each other contains some important stabilizing features. But it also contains some serious barriers to successful social adjustment. Much of the existing structure of class separation is due to the process of suburbanization. This process, which is especially characteristic of the post-1945 period, is deeply rooted in the United States' powerful tradition of local government and aided by its deep commitment to rural values (fresh air, open grassy spaces, single-family homes). Postwar affluence has made it possible for the upper-middle and lower-middle classes and even the working class to ape the exclusiveness of the upper class. Given our technology (such as the automobile) and decentralized political institutions, this process of residential and political segregation by class is one of the most ominous trends in our time. The way in which it distorts our political rationality and capacity for social adjustment has already been touched upon, and needs no further emphasis. Let us note, however, that one of its main effects is to prevent various elites from gaining firsthand knowledge and experience of the society they live in. In any case, our present purpose is to examine why the American class system works, not why it does not work well or better. Prominent on a full list of reasons for the absence of class consciousness and struggle in the United States is strata insulation.

The uses of ideology

Laymen and intellectuals alike portray the American personality and society as uniquely activistic and mobile, universalistic and rational, highly secular and pragmatic, deeply committed to individualism and equality, and achievement-oriented and competitive. All this is quite true if one is referring to modal tendencies and making broad contrasts between the United States and preindustrial social systems. To refer to the United States as an achievement society is not accurate, however, if one means that all or even a majority of Americans live their lives according to the achievement ethic, or even believe in it in any coherent way. There is little question that the mastery of the world through human effort and science is the distinctive theme of American culture. But one should not assume that this theme throbs in the hearts of all Americans. On the contrary, the vast majority of Americans — women, black and Mexican Americans, the poor in general, the working class, and much of the lower-middle class — do not live their lives according to the core values of the achievement ethic.

Nonetheless, these beliefs and values enjoy widespread verbal support among intellectuals and laymen, and their persistence indicates that symbolic culture may well play a considerable role in stabilizing the American class system. Many of the nation's cherished beliefs and values are based on a confusion between value and fact, many have been only partially or not at all realized and still others are frankly contradicted by their opposites. Significant numbers of Americans neither share such values and beliefs nor believe that they can be realized. Nevertheless, America's symbols still play a role in legitimating things as they are and preventing other ideologies from arising.

The United States places great emphasis on the power of ideas and ideals, an ideological bias that prompts Americans to think in terms of an eternal and heroic contest between pure ideals (such as representative government) and base practices (such as lobbying), or between good values (freedom) and bad values (racism). And there are those who think that the United States is subject to great stress and strain because of the tension between its ideals and its social practices. The truth of the matter, though, is that ideas are efficacious only if they are rooted in power — that is, rooted in behavior-causing structures and processes. Actually, our symbols do not engage in heroic encounters nearly as much as we like to think. To a great extent, our symbols, like our behaviors, are carefully compartmentalized and insulated from each other both within and between social classes. We will take up each of these themes in turn and suggest, in the relative absence of research, how America's values and beliefs are distributed differentially through the class system, providing it with both lubrication and legitimation (and, of course, with a certain measure of tension and conflict).

The symbols by means of which Americans perceive and evaluate themselves are themselves derivatives of deviant behavior, the middle class struggle to overcome a hostile feudal-religious world. They represent a long struggle to justify productive work against idleness and frivolous consumption, and mobility and individual freedom against the forces of ascriptive custom. Subject to a novel and complex set of market relations, the middle class developed a unique symbolic world to explain and control its new experience. New sources of power (animals, wind, water, coal, oil, electricity), low population density, and other forces combined to undermine gradually an economy based on muscle power (serfdom). In combination with the Greco-Roman and the Judaic-Christian tradition, these dynamic economic forces brought into being the ideas of *the individual, humanity, equality, private property*, and *progress*. Changes in the locus of economic activity, occupation, knowledge, and skill brought into being other ideas and phenomena: an abstract labor force, mobility, competition, and personal ambition. One can identify in this the social functions performed by the powerful modern tradition of equality of opportunity: it justifies inequality by invoking class achievement, but also nourishes equality by providing identification from the bottom to the top of society and vice versa, and by nourishing our tradition of "democratic manners" and our myths of the common man and of individuals arising from or falling to humble circumstances.

Embedded deep in middle class experience are the unpredictability of economic and social outcomes and wide variations in personal fortune and life history. The resulting insecurity has had many symbolic consequences (faith in the magic of evolution or the market, and assorted rationalizations for government support), but one of the most interesting is the widespread acceptance of luck as an explanation of success and failure. The "big break," the "main chance," and the accidental discovery or meeting are persistent themes in the Horatio Alger story, and appear to enjoy widespread popular acceptance as explanations of success and failure.

Also deeply embedded in American culture is the semiacknowledged primacy of economic values. For the middle class especially, individualism takes precedence over family and other loyalties; occupation is blended with marriage, but rarely to the detriment of the former; economic values supersede passion (delayed marriages, birth control); and jobs take precedence over friendship and neighborhood attachments. Indeed, occupation and economic values exercise remarkable authority over behavior, considering America's other values. Individuals are subjected to demanding job regimens, interact as economic segments, and are subject to the influence of economic values in all aspects of their personal lives. The American population has been socialized to accept the existing valuation of occupations, which means that most of them accept the notion that their own job — an important aspect of identity — is worth less than those held by others. Almost as significant is the fact that the claims economic groups make against each other rarely challenge the economic or the social system: such demands are invariably made in the name of a fair share of productivity (which means relative to the demanders' existing share, taking productivity and inflation into account). In other words, beneath the rhetoric of a universal belief and value system (equality, individualism, equal justice under law, equal competition, the public interest, and so on) lies a symbolic hierarchy that tends to support the existing class system and its favored incumbents. The philosophy of laissez-faire, for example, obviously favors the most powerful. The values of achievement and competition (and individualism in general) are obviously biased in favor of the upper classes. And, in the same way, the ideal of equal opportunity disguises what in practice is an unfair contest between the upper and lower classes.

American symbols can also be thought of as providing ammunition for the discontented and oppressed, and for the reformer and revolutionary as well. But they can also be interpreted as a closed system that treats the present as the best and the different as heresy. However, the strength of this symbolic system lies not in its negativism but in the positive way in which it promulgates a value system based on freedom, equality, individualism, progress, and happiness. What prevents such values from causing serious discontent and social unrest is that they are qualified by a master assumption: each of these values, it is assumed, either has been or can be realized within the framework of American society. By and large, all efforts at social analysis and criticism are undertaken in terms of this assumption. The American symbolic system extends far beyond such abstractions as liberty, equality, and achievement. It consists of many particular statements appropriate to particular life problems and contexts. Its inconsistencies are disguised and its absolutes subtly qualified, allowing cakes to be both eaten and had. And while all classes have a minimum core culture in common, the themes of symbolic culture are elaborated and qualified by class level.

Having said all this, we must acknowledge that there has been little research on the exact role played by symbols in our class system. (Some of the existing research will be reported in the next section.) It is not presumptuous, however, to suggest that the United States' symbolic culture is a conserving force and not least because it contains elements that invite people to transcend and critically evaluate the problems of society. In short, postmonarchical liberalism is essentially conservative.

Ideology and social class

While there has been considerable research on the relation between class and beliefs, attitudes, and personality, very little has focused on the main question raised by that research: why have the extreme differences between the beliefs, attitudes, and personalities of different classes not led to more social conflict? In an interesting analysis, Robert E. Lane has suggested that lower-middle and working class men are afraid of equality and that their symbolic world tends to justify the naturalness of society as it is. Lane plumbed the psychology of fifteen such men in intensive interviews and found extensive rationalization of the status quo. By and large, these men accepted the idea that there is enough (though not necessarily equal) opportunity for all, so that all must assume responsibility for their position in life. The significance of the classes above them was minimized in a number of ways: (1) by stating that equality should characterize only people in their own category; (2) by stating that there is no moral difference between people with unequal jobs and incomes; (3) by expressing resigned contentment; and (4) by attributing greater happiness, power, or even income to the working class than to the classes above.

A basic theme of the interviews was the belief that people deserve their status. Explanations of their own humble status, however, often consisted of blaming others (failure to continue education due to lack of family pressure, the family's need for money), youthful irresponsibility, or a fortuitous event (the Depression). In any case, the men believed that the upper classes deserve their status because of both talent and education. Education, says Lane, is often invoked to explain differentials because it does minimal psychic damage (failure to go to college is the fault of an irresponsible youth, not a grown man) and because it is related in the popular mind with economic skills, time spent in preparation, and responsibility, all of which should be rewarded. Likewise, those lower in class level (basically, the lower class) deserve what they get because they don't care and lack ability. In general, Lane found that these men reacted negatively to the hypothetical prospect of more equality: it would be difficult to adjust one's behavior, there would no longer be an elite to look after things, and people would lose their incentive to work and get ahead.

> Painfully these men have elaborated an explanation for their situation in life; it helps explain things to their wives, who take their status from them; it permits their growing children to account for relative social status in school; it offers to each man the satisfaction of social identity and a measure of social worth. Their rationales are endowed with moral qualities; the distribution of values in society is seen as just and natural. While it gives satisfactions of an obvious kind to those who contemplate those beneath them, it also, oddly enough, gives order and a kind of reassurance to those who glance upward toward "society" or the "four-hundred." This reassurance is not unlike the reassurance provided by the belief in a just God while injustices rain upon one's head. The feudal serf, the Polish peasant, the Mexican peon believed that theirs was a moral and a "natural" order — so also the American workingman.[12]

12. Robert E. Lane, "The Fear of Equality," in *The White Majority: Between*

Lane's analysis is heavily psychological, and he sees the professional classes as the only true defenders of democracy. Our own interpretation of his materials is that these working class attitudes correspond to the nation's dominant ethos: Americans live in a free and equal society, and where they wind up is where nature intended them to be; thus the inherent rationality or functionality of society. In other words, the personalities of men and women in symbolic utterances reflect the operation of the class system. Out of the rich materials of their symbolic culture and the capacity of the human psyche for compartmentalization and rationalization, Americans (no more or less than other people) construct an explanation and a justification for social inequality, and, of course, for their own success or failure. To the extent that this is so, they not only sustain themselves but stabilize and maintain the overall class system.

Let us recall some of our findings in the field of values and attitudes. Mann's contention that industrial societies are not characterized by consensus on fundamental issues is a case in point. Mann argued that there is also a lack of consensus among the lower classes, and that their absorption in pragmatic role systems is the main reason for their subordination.[13] He also emphasized the role of education in keeping the lower classes off balance psychologically, and thus unable to understand their experiences or formulate their grievances.[14] Never is this failure more poignantly apparent than when education promotes (and reflects) unrealistic optimisim about the chances for personal success. A study of third- to twelfth-grade students in Baltimore reveals that even young children are aware of occupational differences. Interestingly enough, while a majority of the children denied the existence of equality of opportunity in general, a majority of the children at every combination of age, race, and socioeconomic level were fairly optimistic about *their own personal* prospects.[15] In addition, high aspirations for social mobility (even into solid middle class occupations) were expressed by working class children.

Poverty and Affluence, ed. Louise Kapp Howe (New York: Random House, 1970), p. 136f; reprinted from Robert E. Lane, *Political Ideology: Why the American Common Man Believes What He Does* (New York: Free Press, 1962), pp. 57–81.

13. For a previous discussion of this general area, see "Political Attitudes," in Chapter 12.

14. The middle class fare that permeates the mass media also undoubtedly helps to prevent the formation of a full working class subculture in which workers can find relevant and satisfying identities.

15. Charles C. Moskos' analysis of the attitudes of soldiers in Vietnam revealed little ideological support for, or understanding of, the war but rather a characteristic American tendency to blame not society or national policy but their own bad luck for being there. See his article, "Why Men Fight," *Transaction* 7 (November 1969): 13–23; reprinted in Irving Louis Horowitz and Mary Symons Strong, eds., *Sociological Realities* (New York: Harper and Row, 1971), pp. 391–401. This belief in luck runs deep in American culture, and is undoubtedly related to the essentially "irrational" notion of the individual. Whatever its source, it is a theme that has arisen consistently in our study and that deserves more systematic attention from students of society.

Asked to locate themselves in the class system, the children tended to exhibit false consciousness. Despite their awareness of occupational differences, they tended to consider their own class level higher than was warranted. The study also indicates that children become more class-conscious as they grow older, but that the greatest increase is among the *advantaged*. The implications of the foregoing for the stability of the American class system are obvious. Disadvantaged chidren have false impressions of both their realistic prospects and their true class level. While they are knowledgeable about some important aspects of the class system, they tend to accept the pervasive American assumption that the individual is distinct from society. By contrast, the advantaged — those with an objective stake in the existing system — are the ones who become most class-conscious.[16]

The school itself is an important part of the socialization process, and its effects make it an important auxiliary of the overall class system. Considered as a structure of authority, the school is a powerful transmitter of American values and beliefs. By discussing and evaluating things in universal terms, it tends to blur class differences except insofar as they support the middle class outlook. The authority of the teacher (made even more effective if accompanied by affective interaction) reinforces the ideology of middle class homes and either co-opts children from the lower classes or keeps them psychologically off-balance. The schools seem to sponsor very little discussion of the specific problems faced by specific groups or classes of Americans. They tend not to be critical of the American social system and fail to stress that groups have differing and often incompatible interests. On the whole, the schools are complacent and optimistic, and stress acceptance of authority and of established ways of doing things. Education, in other words, transmits the normative culture relatively intact and attempts to inculcate in each student generation the role needs of an industrial society and a common set of values and beliefs. That these values are often inaccurate, irrelevant, and personally disorienting renders them no less effective in promoting stability.

The various mechanisms that broadcast universalistic American beliefs and values to a population diversified by class no doubt help to keep the lower classes psychologically off-balance. But there are also specialized mechanisms that translate the abstract core culture into the specificities of class. There is not much systematic data on these mechanisms, but the impact of educational diversity, specialized television and radio programming, class-related magazines and newspapers, and so on is undoubetdly related to class stability. In any case, the role of ideology in our class system needs far more research. It may even be that those who argue that we have seen the end of ideology exaggerate the amount of ideology in the past and underestimate it in the present. It is probably truer to say that the United States has never had much ideology (that

16. Roberta G. Simmons and Morris Rosenberg, "Functions of Children's Perceptions of the Stratification System," *American Sociological Review* 36 (April 1971): 235–249.

is, rival world views), or, more accurately, that it has had only one ideology, liberalism. Actually, the thesis that ideology has ended is best understood as an aspect of liberal ideology itself.

Power processes and class stability
The expansion of political-legal rights

The right of the general population to participate in political decisions is of paramount importance to the functioning and stability of the American class system. If we remember the vital role played by government in mediating and adjusting class-prestige interests, the role of the equal vote is apparent — it legitimates the far-reaching powers of legislators and political officials and their staffs. The extension of suffrage during the pre–Civil War period, for example, went a long way toward stabilizing class (commodity, credit, labor) relations. It is of no little importance that American workers did not have to fight for the right to vote. By ending the formal identification of class with power (for example, by dropping the property qualification for voting), the extension of suffrage placed economic relations and conflicts in a wider moral, legal, and political context. As a result, class relations were disguised, and their potential for explosive confrontation was ultimately defused. Indeed, there is no better way of demonstrating the essential absence of change in the United States than to note how exactly our political and social history corresponds to Madison's argument in Federalist paper number 10. Madison, remember, argued that property differences are due to the "diversity of human faculties," that conflicts are due mostly to property, that government cannot and should not eliminate property differences (which are natural) but only cushion or regulate conflicts, and that this is best done by removing the conflict from its immediate context (representative government).

The extension of suffrage to blacks (ineffective, however, until the 1960s), to women in 1919, and to eighteen–twenty-year-olds in 1971 has also helped to defuse and diffuse class relations. The extension to blacks of political-legal rights and equality softens and disguises a heavily lopsided class relation. Similarly, the extension of the vote and the granting of a relatively full complement of legal rights to women serve to individualize American society and to disguise both the problem of the family (ascription and class advantage) and the subordinate social and economic position of women.

The lowering of the voting age to eighteen in 1971 was a response to a number of factors, the most obvious of which was the fact that an unpopular war was being fought by nonvoting conscripts. But the rise of educational standards and the variation in age requirements for performing various adult functions (voting, leaving school, working, driving a car, drinking, getting married, legal responsibility) also helped to persuade Americans to lower the voting age. A less consciously acknowledged factor is industrial society's failure to provide the young a coherent pattern of transition from high school to work. Giving eighteen-year-olds the vote will no doubt help to defuse the potential for conflict inherent in high rates of unemployment among young males (particularly blacks).

The political-legal rights of Americans are embedded in a normative system enjoying wide support,[17] and this too has a bearing on class stability. Public holidays (celebrating the birthdays of great national figures and commemorating great national achievements), public buildings and monuments, historical sites, state occasions, the mass media, religion, and, of course, education, all serve to promote this overriding normative tradition and to make it difficult for antisocial movements or ideologies to arise. Of considerable interest is Robert N. Bellah's depiction of these legitimating traditions as a civil religion.[18]

Power and the economy

Though the state — at all levels — is a prime factor in the operation of the American economy, our awareness of its functioning is less full and sophisticated than it ought to be. One of the most interesting, and largely unnoticed, ways in which government interpenetrates with the class dimension is our money and credit system. Since the origin of the republic, the issuance of currency has been a public responsibility, and the nature of the credit-banking system figured prominently in the early political struggles of the American nation. The outcome of these struggles was that the credit system of the nation was gradually placed under *fiduciary* structures, the trusteeship of government supplementing and supporting private banking. While this process was not completed until the 1930s, it now appears so normal that we fail to recognize that public money and credit, and public regulations and safeguards, have structured a specific kind of private class-based credit system.[19] By disguising a class relation in fiduciary terms, our political-legal system has helped to make this aspect of a capitalist economy seem normal. And by so doing, it has stabilized a class relationship (creditor-debtor) that has caused a great deal of trouble in our own history and in the histories of other societies.

Another notable political-legal adaptation relevant to the stability of the American class system has been the loosening of the definition of property rights. The gradual acceptance of the right of the power dimension to interfere with property rights through taxation, regulation, licensing, and the development of collective bargaining represents a significant development in the history of the American class system. Its full import is only partially understood, however, if one thinks of public economic intervention as a struggle between the principle of class and the principle of equality. Basically, the growth of public authority over the economy and the legalization of collective bargaining

17. The broad American consensus on the Lockean liberal political tradition is amply documented by Donald J. Devine, *The Political Culture of the United States: The Influence of Member Values on Regime Maintenance* (Boston: Little, Brown, 1972).

18. "Civil Religion in America," *Daedalus* 96 (Winter 1967): 1–21.

19. Basically, those who have collateral pay less to borrow money than those who do not have collateral (when and if the latter can get credit).

were adaptive responses that supported the principle of class stratification. The vast growth of public fiduciary structures and functions is also largely understandable as a way of making the overall class system work. In sum the growing array of regulatory commissions, licensing and certifying procedures, collective bargaining and mediation services, banking insurance, and presidential and congressional commissions as well as governmental purchasing and subsidization policies, tax and credit policy, moral exhortation, and wage-price controls, represent efforts to take the heat off class relations in one market after another.

The government also promotes economic well-being directly. The general (and always proportional) tax cuts during the 1950s and 1960s were implemented by a public authority deeply responsive to the class system. The government also acts as an employer, often deliberately providing jobs for specifically depressed segments of society. (For example, the federal government employs a disproportionate number of black Americans.) And, of course, the government in its roles as the military, as a research and development agency, and as a dispenser of funds for research provides for the economic stability and advancement of different portions of our economy and labor force.

Ethnic politics

The relatively successful accommodation of forty million immigrants is one of the United States' more notable achievements. The means by which it was accomplished varied: economic expansion was certainly a major factor in the successful absorption of diverse kinds of foreigners. But high on the list of factors that prevented the development of castelike foreign bodies within American society was the "politics of accommodation" that characterized the United States' urban centers during the nineteenth century and the first third or so of the twentieth (and that persists to this day in some places).[20] The United States' egalitarian political-legal tradition and urban political machines provided immigrants with ready access to political processes, and thus with a certain measure of political power. The consequences for the functioning of the class system should be apparent. Immigration provided the nation's burgeoning industrial economy with a large supply of cheap labor, and because the newcomers entered the class system at the bottom, they automatically elevated the general class positions of those above them. At the same time, this lower working class found the power dimension accessible in the process of furthering its own economic-prestige position. All in all, the American structure of liberal democracy was vital enough to guarantee that the politics of accommodation would prevail over the politics of separation and/or radicalism.

The system of ethnic politics served the United States quite well through the 1930s. Changes since 1945, however, have modified it considerably, and

20. The only full-length treatment of this important aspect of our political history can be found in Edgar Litt's excellent *Beyond Pluralism: Ethnic Politics in America* (Glenview, Ill.: Scott, Foresman, 1970).

its relative importance has declined. The growth of public welfare programs administered by public bureaucracies, and the consequent decline of patronage, has made local politics less useful in the scramble for economic advantage. Also, more and more decisions affecting our political and economic life are made in Washington; the state capitals; suburbia; the boardrooms of corporations, business and professional associations, and trade unions; and foundations and other voluntary organizations unaffiliated with the political machine. And, of course, significant portions of our various ethnic groups, especially those from Europe and Canada, have moved up the class ladder and no longer need the special help of ethnic politics. But while the ethnic politics of accommodation prevailed, it effectively served to reconcile the lower classes to hardship and the American order of things during the early stages of industrialization and urbanization.

Crime as a stabilizing process

Deviant behavior often has consequences that are functional to society. Certainly, the opportunity to better oneself through crime can be interpreted as providing social mobility, and thus satisfaction with society, for certain categories of Americans. In simplest terms, a considerable amount of American criminal behavior is an affirmation of the legitimacy of gain and success.

Thus crime can be interpreted, at least in part, as a stabilizing force. Since the arrival of Europeans in the New World, rich opportunities for illegal gain have helped to establish the primacy of acquisitive institutions and the acquisitive personality. It would be interesting to trace the social consequences of crime in American history: stealing land, claim-jumping, smuggling, tax evasion, bootlegging, illegal slave-trading, political corruption, and so on. Also of interest is the ethnic and class specialization apparent in the history of American crime. White Anglo-Saxon Protestants who committed crimes specialized, for example, in smuggling, claim-jumping, and stock swindling; many of the most successful probably invested their ill-gotten gains in respectable enterprises, eventually becoming pillars of society. Immigrant groups such as the Irish, Jews, and Italians had to respond to a different set of opportunities for crime, and our contemporary lower classes confront still other opportunities.

Of some importance in understanding how and why the class system works is the intertwining of ethnic politics, crime, and the special category of crime we call *political corruption*. It appears that significant portions of our successive immigrant groups (probably since the arrival of Europeans in the New World) entered the American class structure by amalgamating political power, crime, and political corruption.[21] Perhaps nothing illustrates the odds against black Americans more succinctly than the fact that opportunities to climb this

21. For a valuable analysis along these lines, see Daniel Bell, "Crime as an American Way of Life: A Queer Ladder of Social Mobility," *Antioch Review* 13 (June 1953): 131–154; reprinted in his *The End of Ideology: On the Exhaustion of Political Ideas in the Fifties,* rev. ed. (New York: Collier, 1962), pp. 127–150, available in paperback.

"queer ladder of social mobility" declined drastically just as they emerged on the political scene.

Regulating the poor

Though misfits by nature undoubtedly account for some members of the lower class, the vast majority are the flotsam and jetsam of society. We have no exact records on the lower class in previous generations and only an imprecise profile of today's lower class. One thing is certain, though: the American lower class is too diversified and weak ever to organize or pose a collective threat to the existing order of things. Even when programs are enacted to help the poor help themselves through organized effort — thereby incurring the risk that militants will mobilize the masses — the results have been negligible, and often outright failures. The lower class simply lacks the middle class skills and psychology necessary either to utilize existing power structures or to organize new ones.[22]

During the 1960s considerable internal unrest flared up in American cities. Hundreds of riots by black Americans combined with other strains to make the middle of this decade a turbulent period. Further unrest was prevented, in large part, by the War on Poverty and the expansion of the welfare system. The War on Poverty succeeded in disguising the new problem posed by poverty — why does chronic poverty exist in a booming economy? — as the traditional problem of determining what kind of formal opportunities the poor should be offered. At the same time, the United States managed to use the War on Poverty to blunt the edge of the more intractable problem posed by the rise of black militancy. By defining blacks as poor people, white Americans could avoid the racial issue and fall back on a familiar repertoire of programs and ideas. The political integration of American society also benefited from the recognition of poverty in that it gave the Democratic party an incentive and a means to rebuild the New Deal coalition that had faltered during the postwar period.

The lower class in industrial societies has not been a revolutionary force, and for good reason — it has been too demoralized by poverty to undertake more than sporadic outbursts of rebellion. The upper classes' basic policy toward the poor has been to adopt one form or another of the Poor Law, a policy that originated in medieval England during the first stirrings of capitalism. The history of public welfare is distinctly at odds with the popular conception of it as an act of singular morality bespeaking the growing humaneness of modern society. As Piven and Cloward have argued, relief for the poor has two central functions, to forestall civil disorder and to enforce work norms among the marginal labor force. The inauguration of relief during the Great Depression of the 1930s was a method of maintaining civil order. During the stable 1940s and 1950s, the system changed its emphasis to focus on the reinforce-

22. For a case study in the area of housing, see Harry Brill, *Why Organizers Fail* (Berkeley: University of California Press, 1971).

ment of work norms. And in the 1960s, when rural laborers congregated in our great urban centers, the relief system again expanded dramatically to forestall civil disorder. A return to the reinforcement of work norms is clearly discernible beginning in 1970–1971. As Piven and Cloward argue, the relief system does not merely enforce work norms:

> It also goes far toward defining and enforcing the terms on which different classes of men are made to do different kinds of work; relief arrangements, in other words, have a great deal to do with maintaining social and economic inequities. The indignities and cruelties of the dole are no deterrent to indolence among the rich; but for the poor man, the specter of ending up on "the welfare" or in "the poorhouse" makes any job at any wage a preferable alternative. And so the issue is not the relative merit of work itself; it is rather how some men are made to do the harshest work for the least reward.[23]

All complex societies have definite lower (and upper) boundaries. Even in traditional Indian society, whose thousands of subcastes were only ambiguously distinguishable, there was no doubt about the boundaries of the outcaste. Thus the lower class may be necessary to the continued existence of a class system of society, serving the latent function of helping to keep the marginal working masses in line. In short, without a lower class the bottom might fall out of class society.

Class and anomie: the uses of deviance
The normal and the abnormal

The major theme in the sociological investigation of social problems is recognition that the normal institutions of society are the major cause of problem behavior. Let us assume that behavior has no intrinsic meaning until it is defined by society (that is, by its power groups). As we have seen, American society has criminalized a great deal of behavior that need not be considered legal deviation at all. Once a particular form of behavior (such as homosexuality or gambling) is declared illegal, an underground subculture develops to provide such deviants with the satisfaction of their various needs. Such a subculture not only socializes new deviants, but often also bands together with other deviant subcultures for mutual support and protection. The relevance of such subcultures to social stability is obvious.

The general connection between deviance and social stability, is, however, not obvious, due to the mistaken notion that social problems are uniformly injurious to society. A long tradition of sociological analysis has attributed many positive social functions to alleged error and evil. Perhaps the most succinct statement of this tradition is provided by Kai T. Erikson,[24] who argues

23. Frances Fox Piven and Richard H. Cloward, *Regulating the Poor: The Functions of Public Welfare* (New York: Random House, 1971), p. xvii, also in paperback.
24. "Notes on the Sociology of Deviance," in *The Other Side,* ed. Howard S. Becker (New York: Free Press, 1964); reprinted in slightly revised form from *Social Problems* 9 (Spring 1962): 307–314.

that "deviance cannot be dismissed simply as behavior which disrupts social stability, but may itself be, in controlled quantities, an important condition for preserving stability." Building on Durkheim's suggestion that crime is useful to society in that its existence and its punishment helps to reaffirm what society believes in, Erikson asks whether society is actually organized to promote deviance, which may well be a necessary resource providing the indispensable boundaries needed for social integrity and stability. Institutions of control, such as prisons, actually perpetuate deviance; our stigmatization of deviance is dramatic and often permanent, since we do not allow the deviant to re-enter society easily. Our control agencies assume a high rate of recidivism among offenders. Instead of focusing on harmony and equilibrium, according to Erikson, we should perhaps think in terms of two different currents, "forces which promote a high overall degree of conformity among its members, and those forces which encourage some degree of diversity so that actors can be deployed throughout social space to patrol the system's boundaries." Erikson concludes by remarking that the stabilization in deviant roles of a defined portion of the population, largely drawn from among young adults and the lower economic classes, and the expectation that they will remain deviant indefinitely, is reminiscent of "earlier Puritan theories about predestination, reprobation, and the nature of sin." The stabilization of deviant roles among the young and the poor and the general usefulness of deviance suggested by Erikson have an obvious bearing on class stability and continuity. In order to clarify the social utility of deviance more fully, however, we must undertake a different approach.

Class and anomie

The tradition of "nonegalitarian classlessness" contains a contradiction that creates a many-sided identity problem for the American population. The tradition of universalism (twofold judgments, rational analysis, egalitarianism, assertions about what is good or bad for people in general, abstract references to the average citizen) defines cultural goals in such a way as to create enormous pressures toward deviance. In other words, the uniform application to a deeply graded class structure of a monopolistic universalistic goal (economic or class success) and a monopolistic universalistic set of means (the Protestant-bourgeois virtues) is anomic.[25] Forced to judge themselves and to fashion their aspirations in terms identical to those of the established classes,[26]

25. This is, of course, a reference to Robert K. Merton's classic article "Social Structure and *Anomie*," *American Sociological Review* 3 (October 1938): 672–682; widely reprinted and also available as Bobbs-Merrill reprint no. S-194. For an earlier discussion, see "Middle Class Values and Deviance" in Chapter 14.
26. We are speaking here in the abstract; actually, the various strata have different aspirations and definitions of success, as we have pointed out. Merton himself has recognized these and other mitigating factors, but insists that only significant numbers of the lower classes need to internalize the success theme to support his theory; see his "Continuities in the Theory of Social Structure and *Anomie*," in *Social*

AN INTERPRETATION AND SUMMARY 442

the disadvantaged could presumably charge class injustice. But so tenacious is the individualistic explanation of success and failure ("nonegalitarian classlessness") that it is rare for the disadvantaged to think in terms of class or of institutional inadequacy. Instead, the general population subdivides into five categories, only the last of which seriously questions the legitimacy of the social system:

1. Conformity — acceptance of the dynamic world view and discipline of liberalism
2. Innovation — crime, including political corruption and violation of fiduciary ethics
3. Ritualism — bureaucratic personality, the stable worker, the family man
4. Retreatism — mental illness, skidding, suicide
5. Rebellion — socialism, communism, fascism, some forms of black militancy, milleniarian movements, utopian movements

There is no exact parallel between class membership and type of deviance. Crime, for example, is not monopolized by the lower classes: members of the upper classes commit criminal acts at significant rates (with far greater monetary and moral cost to society than lower class crime). And all classes contribute to ritualist, retreatist, and rebellionist behavior. In other words, there is no easy way to relate class position to a particular deviant response, though it is possible to talk generally about class and deviance. Two points in particular are worth noting. First, it appears that by far the highest rates of deviance occur among the working and lower classes; and, second, judging by the relative smallness of the rebellion category, the United States has succeeded in inducing the victims of social anomie to blame themselves. In sum, it is difficult not to conclude that the United States relies for much of its stability on high rates of crime, divorce, mental illness, apathy, ignorance, protection of the inept, political corruption, school and social dropping-out, and the like. To state the matter as a question, to what extent has the United States rendered its social system opaque and protected itself from rebellion (peaceful or violent), class conflict, and even meaningful reform by its success in institionalizing the flow of deviance into the areas of innovation, ritualism, and retreatism?

Class and international relations

Modern social science developed simultaneous with the nation state, and it is not surprising that the single social system was seen as a valid autonomous unit of study. Despite some comparative and historical references, this text too has focused on a single society, and an effort must now be made to correct this artificial delineation of subject matter. Unfortunately, the analysis of the

---

Theory and Social Structure by Robert K. Merton (New York: Free Press, 1968), chap. 11.

relation between class and international relations is badly handicapped by the lack of research, and we can do no more than raise questions and present some of the ideas that theorists have had in this area. In keeping with the theme of this chapter, our analysis will focus on how stratification processes contribute to the functioning of the American and other systems of stratification when they operate beyond national boundaries.

Theorists are less likely than they once were to separate internal and external affairs, and are no longer content either to interpret national rivalry and war as vestiges of a predemocratic era or to see a natural trend toward prosperity and peace through free trade, international law, and education. Contemporary analysts are more likely than their predecessors to see a relation between domestic conflicts and needs and the expression of conflicts and needs on the international level. The relation between the class structure of a society and its foreign policy is only beginning to be understood, and much work remains to be done. There are many unanswered questions in this area. From the vantage-point of this study the most important questions are: to what extent do the United States' external actions and reactions provide support for its domestic class system? What level and what type of profits does the United States bring home from its economic dealings abroad? Does this process work to the relative detriment of others? Exactly what role does the export of American capital play in insuring prosperity and expansion at home, or, conversely, in hurting the domestic labor force? How dependent is the American economy, and thus the rising American standard of living, on the import of cheap raw materials from abroad? What role do specific groups — manufacturing firms, banks, law firms, trade unions, farm blocs, and professional and learned associations — play in formulating foreign policy, and how is this process related to the American class system? How important is the internationalization of domestic groups — for example, what role does the multinational corporation play in foreign affairs? What roles do international trade unions and learned, professional, charitable, and aesthetic associations play? What role do international agencies play in domestic systems of stratification? What role does military power play in preserving peace? And what role does peace play in furthering America's economic pre-eminence?

In a provocative thesis, William Appleman Williams has argued that American leaders have always seen a vital link between domestic prosperity and peace, on the one hand, and external expansion (either geographically or in terms of trade and investment) on the other. Furthermore, says Williams, these leaders consciously promoted an expansionist foreign policy (the Monroe Doctrine, manifest destiny, the Open Door policy) in order to make liberal democracy and its class system work. That these policies have steered clear of traditional forms of colonialism, argues Williams, should not obscure the imperialistic nature of the United States' foreign policy or its failure to live up to its ideals.[27]

The relevance of foreign relations to domestic structures and processes of

27. William Appleman Williams, *The Tragedy of American Diplomacy,* rev. ed. (Cleveland: World, 1962).

stratification is a staple feature of Marxist-Leninist thought. The identification of imperialism as a necessary stage of capitalism was Lenin's distinctive contribution to Marxian theory[28] (along with his vanguard of elitist theory of socialist revolution). Lenin's theory of imperialism is a logical extension of Marx's analysis of internal capitalist relations. For Marx the only source of profit is *surplus value,* the value created by a worker over and above what he is paid to live on. As an industrial economy matures, it uses more capital in relation to labor; therefore, it becomes more and more difficult to create profit, especially in the face of trade union activity and the development of welfare services. Given the inherent limitations of the profit-based domestic economy, the dominant stratum is forced to search for profit elsewhere. Hence the export of capital to take advantage of cheap labor and raw materials in less developed countries. To protect these investments, the dominant stratum uses political and military measures to insure compliant governments in its colonies or spheres of influence. Thus the exploitation of workers at home is matched by exploitation of foreign workers. National rivalries and wars, the argument concludes, are attributable to the struggle between capitalist countries for markets and dominance, a necessary outcome of advanced capitalist development.

Finally, there are questions even more abstract. Is there a stratification order and hierarchy among nations? Are there three worlds of development — a world of American-led capitalist nations, a world of Soviet-led communist nations, and a Third World of unaligned underdeveloped nations?[29] How does one classify the authoritarian Western nations, such as Portugal, Spain, and the Latin American military dictatorships? Is "Third World" a meaningful category when it includes such varied countries as India, China, Yugoslavia, Egypt, Libya, Saudi Arabia, Brazil, Indonesia, and Nigeria? What is the relevance for world stratification of the increased understanding and trade between the United States, on the one hand, and the Soviet Union and the People's Republic of China on the other? Will such relations enhance the present advantage of the industrial over the nonindustrial countries? Will the future see class alliances across nations, or will ideological, ethnic, religious, and racial barriers prove too strong to be transcended in this way? These and all the other questions we have just raised, though undoubtedly germane to any full understanding of the American class system, lie outside the scope of this work. They point to the vast unfinished business confronting stratification researchers and theorists. In any event, it is clear that international relations not only express class relations but also help to explain why and how the American class system works.

28. V. I. Lenin, *Imperialism, The Highest Stage of Capitalism* (New York: International Publishers, 1939).

29. For a pioneering study, see Irving Louis Horowitz, *Three Worlds of Development: The Theory and Practice of International Stratification* (New York: Oxford University Press, 1966).

16

The American class system: a formal summary

THE MOST IMPORTANT scientific question that can be asked in stratification analysis is: does the concept of *social class* organize diverse empirical phenomena so that the causes of behavior can be predicted at higher levels of abstraction? Based on our findings, our answer is emphatically yes.

The reality of class and class analysis

Our analysis of the three major dimensions and numerous subdimensions of stratification indicates that the distribution of American social and cultural values (material comfort and convenience, psychic development and satisfaction, political-legal power and every conceivable subcategory of behavior and benefit) can be subsumed by the concept of *social class* or *social stratum,* now understood to mean the location of families and individuals across the three major dimensions of inequality. To refer to a high school or college graduate, a blue-collar worker, a professional, and so on is not to refer to a human being with unique characteristics and entirely idiosyncratic behavior patterns — it is to suggest a fairly detailed picture of an individual and his or her family of origin, personality, spouse, life expectancy, life style, political behavior, and so on.[1]

1. It is understood that such a picture portrays statistical rates of behavior of aggregates, and not the behavior of each and every individual.

The grip of the United States' particular kind of economy on American behavior is thorough and pervasive. The economic system generates most of the needs of Americans by making products and services available (and known about through advertising) and by influencing the personality at work and in other institutional areas. (Many people mistakenly assume that "needs" precede and generate economic behavior.) The dynamics of class (both ascriptive and achievement processes) determine who will succeed in school, who will forego sex and marriage until preparation for work is completed or guaranteed, who will move from their neighborhoods of birth and upbringing, who will dress in what ways, who will participate in voluntary organizations, who will be politically active, and who will receive how much and what kind of governmental attention.

The analysis of class stratification rests on a number of key assumptions. For one thing, the concept of *class* seeks to unify phenomena and predict behavior in a specific society (discovering, of course, whatever similarities it can find with other social systems). It is a mistake to use either abstract discourse, such as Marxian theory, or a composite of stratification phenomena from various societies in various historical periods as the central definition of *social class*. As we have seen, there is no reason to assume that because the American population does not exhibit class consciousness — a unitary feeling of being different from other classes across the dimensions of class, prestige, and power — and does not engage in class struggle — overt hostility of one stratum toward another manifested as an all-or-nothing confrontation — the United States does not have classes or a class system.

All that the absence of class consciousness and class conflict means is that Marx was wrong: class consciousness and class struggle are not inherent features of industrial society. In this regard, Durkheim had the surer insight, that the complex division of labor in modern society is an integrative force. Rather than leading to massive confrontation, the division of labor assigns modern populations to specialized occupation orbits structured to limit conflicts to specific issues. While class consciousness and class struggle are associated strongly with most societies undergoing "modernization," they do not seem to be strongly associated with developed or mature industrial systems. Class consciousness and class struggle are probably manifestations of economic expansion and industrialization in a feudal context (although it is possible to industrialize a feudal society without class struggle, as in the case of Japan). But even in countries that manifested the classic Marxian hallmarks of class (Germany, France, and England), class antagonisms have been greatly muted and modified during the course of the twentieth century.

The relative absence of class consciousness and class struggle in the United States is attributable to the specific manner in which American society emerged and developed. The dimension of class — the American economy — has been marked by complex inconsistencies and multiple hierarchies (labor, credit, commodity markets), all of which have made it difficult for Americans to identify themselves as class members — that is, difficult for members of various economic groups in either the upper or lower classes to recognize that they have economic interests in common.

The problem of class identification is further complicated by historical developments affecting the American prestige dimension, especially racial slavery (an offshoot of a plantation economy) and immigration (an offshoot of an industrializing economy). The prestige realm is thus diversified by the presence of numerous racial and ethnic-religious groups. Class identification is confused still further by beliefs and values that stress moral, religious, legal, and political equality.

Much of Americans' misunderstanding of class and related matters is due to a characteristic ahistorical, abstract mentality — the American incapacity to see phenomena in terms of historical contexts and guises. Americans tend to apply simplistic notions of utility and evolution to human behavior. Many Americans assume, for example, that racism is alien to basic American values and will eventually disappear because it lacks roots in the true and valid American scheme of things. Racist inequality cannot be dismissed so lightly, however. While it emerged under historically unique conditions, it may now have acquired a new form nourished and supported by new causes. Social systems do not slough off subsystems simply because they are morally undesirable or have outlived their original purposes. Racial slavery arose to insure a dependable supply of cheap labor for the propertied class of a plantation economy. Degraded by this experience, both whites and blacks made an historically "necessary" adjustment after emancipation: blacks continued to supply cheap labor, but in a "free" labor market rather than as slaves. Today the vested interests that maintain a depressed black labor force are deeply institutionalized in terms of legitimate American values and norms (free markets and enterprise, professional standards, qualifications and credentials, equality of opportunity, black capitalism, the "competence gap," excellence).

Nor are religious diversity and rankings wholly independent entities. For one thing, they emerged from the imperatives of immigration, which was itself related to the needs of industrialization. It is more than likely that religious values today are largely explicable in terms of the functions they serve for a diverse and conflict-prone industrial society. Americans are a routinely religious people who profess what is largely a secular faith; religion, by and large, does not interfere with economic or political values.[2] In family life, in personality development, and in our economy and politics, religion helps to lubricate relations between Americans by providing them with a common faith and a common vocabulary of motives and goals. Religious rankings also provide a measure of consistency to class ranks: well-structured upper groups want well-structured forms of piety and theology, while the lower classes find hope, solace, and discipline in the more emotional, evangelical sects and churches.

Despite the teeming variety of American life, therefore, it is still possible to group individuals and families according to certain salient class characteristics

2. Will Herberg, *Protestant, Catholic, and Jew* (Garden City, N.Y.: Doubleday, 1955).

and to predict their behavior with great accuracy. The absence of class consciousness and class struggle, it should be noted, is itself a predictable outcome of the American class system. Social stratification, in short, *does* control consciousness, just as it produces the specific types of conflicts and struggles that occur between groups: its control simply does not take the form of class consciousness or class struggle!

Thus the analysis of class should take time into account — that is, contemporary phenomena must be seen in terms of the push and pull of historical forces. One of the unique and unnoticed features of liberal society is that it provides rich soil for preserving the relics of the past. The American sociocultural system is like a bulging Victorian attic, except that Americans are trying to live in it rather than to use it for storage. Liberal clichés about the dynamism, utilitarianism, and rationalism of the free market society often blind us to the fact that the United States straddles three centuries (and has deep ties to the metaphysical symbols and social practices of feudal Europe and of ancient Greece and Israel).

Most of the confusion about class (which is compounded by the use of the word *class* in various ways) can be avoided if the foregoing insights and perspectives are pursued. The essence of social stratification is the existence of a hierarchy of valued things, traits, and behaviors, which, lodged in families, are transmitted by means of social processes to children. The existence of mobility, inconsistency, lack of class consciousness, and such universal values and norms as the Bill of Rights, equality of opportunity, and universal suffrage should not obscure this fundamental fact. Liberal society has developed these phenomena as integral parts of a legitimated class inequality. To take an example, significant rates of social mobility are necessary to a class system, which is by definition derived from an expansive economy and requires extensive support and justification: thus the emphasis on success, equality of opportunity, achievement, and the like. But high rates of upward mobility are fully compatible with a high rate of ascriptive transmission of class position from one generation to the next. That this is not compatible with American ideals should remind us that class society, like past forms of society, is also a system of illegitimate inequality.

Continuity with the past

The early theorists of sociology — Condorcet, Saint-Simon, Auguste Comte, Herbert Spencer, William Graham Sumner, Lester Ward, and many others — tended to overemphasize the uniqueness and moral superiority of the middle class society whose emergence they were experiencing. In their excitement, these theorists developed a large inventory of high-order abstractions by means of which the emerging industrial society was contrasted favorably with the past. Their ideas have passed into contemporary sociology and, if used carelessly, tend to exaggerate the differences between present and past society and to identify ideals with practices. Our analysis of American society (seen as a class system) reveals not only many similarities with the past but a wide array of deeply institutionalized processes and outcomes at odds with prevailing images. Contemporary Americans' conceptions of themselves and their society are probably based on an astonishingly simplistic and self-flattering comparison with preindustrial (especially feudal) society. This contrast must be clarified and sharpened if one is to fully understand the class system of inequality and the nature of contemporary society.

In an extremely useful analysis focused on the need to distinguish between folk and feudal societies, Sjoberg provides some valuable and surprising insights into the similarities between industrial and feudal social systems.[3] According to Sjoberg, feudal society has the following characteristics:

1. A surplus of food that becomes the basis of urban development and a leisured elite that monopolizes the most valued occupations.

2. A basic cleavage between a small elite and a large working mass.

3. A diversified elite that includes political and legal functionaries, scholar-priests, and warriors as well as landed nobility.

4. An elite that is more unified and homogeneous than the masses. (According to Sjoberg, this is due largely to the existence of writing, which allows a segment of the elite to standardize the official memory and the official perception of reality.)

5. Occupations that tend to become monopolistic guilds. Sjoberg confines his list to artisans, but one should add that all favored feudal occupations tended to become monopolistic, including scholar-priests, warriors, lawyers, political functionaries. Recruitment is carefully controlled, largely through apprenticeship and control over work norms. One should add that control over favored occupations was also exercised through the principle of heredity and through education.

6. Despised groups beyond the pale of decent life (merchants, slaves, untouchables, beggars, criminals).

The power of the elite to resist social change, Sjoberg continues, rests on its command of technical intelligence and its control of symbols (oral and, especially, written language). He concludes his analysis by citing examples of the many feudal norms that have been legislated into law by modern societies, and by pointing out that feudal elites have continued to exercise great power in many industrialized nations (England, France, Germany, Japan).

The full value of Sjoberg's analysis will be lost if we fail to note that the United States has a significant number of "feudal" characteristics. At the risk of misunderstanding, one can even say that the nation's "feudal" characteristics are not simply historical vestiges that can be counted on to disappear gradually, and may belong to the essential structure of all complex historical societies. If, for example, one compares the foregoing list of feudalism's

3. Gideon Sjoberg, "Folk and 'Feudal' Societies," *American Journal of Sociology* 58, no. 3 (November 1952): 231–239; also available as Bobbs-Merrill reprint no. 270.

structural features with characteristics of the American class system, one finds an interesting similarity, a similarity that places industrial society much closer to feudal society than we like to think:

1. An abundant supply of agricultural products was an important factor in the industrialization and urbanization of the United States and thus in the development of the American business and professional elite.

2. The United States is characterized by a basic cleavage (expressed as an unequal distribution of social benefits, not as class consciousness or conflict) between an elite and a working mass, a cleavage that extends through the dimensions of class, prestige, and power. Its elite is much larger than that of feudal society.

3. The United States has a diversified elite, on a far greater scale than feudal society.

4. The American elite is also more united and homogeneous than the masses, judged, for example, by their greater class consciousness, their greater organization (interest and voluntary groups), and their control of education (the official memory).

5. Occupations in the United States, especially among the upper classes but also among a portion of the working class, tend toward being "monopolistic guilds."

6. The United States also has its despised groups (blacks, hippies, welfare recipients, the lower class), which serve to provide it boundaries and definitions of right and wrong, decent and indecent.

One of the interesting similarities between feudal and modern societies deserves special mention. The stability of the feudal system relative to folk societies has been noted by Sjoberg and many other commentators. Feudal elites are highly conscious of themselves, and defend the order of things against change with great tenacity. It is an almost unchallengeable truism that, unlike static agrarian societies, modern society is dynamic and unstable, subject to almost chronic social change. This view, is seems to me, represents a confusion between the kind of social system change and instability that occurred from roughly 1000 A.D. through the eighteenth and nineteenth centuries and the type of change that is characteristic of established industrial societies since the nineteenth century. The unique stability and continuity of industrial social systems since the nineteenth century require special attention.

Continuity and stability within class society

Nothing is so characteristic of Americans as the belief that they are on the move as individuals and as a people. Americans welcome innovation: "new" is a term of approval, and the old invites scorn. Americans believe in progress and constantly tell themselves to look to the future. They also tend to think that dynamism causes instability, though they are sure that things will eventually work out well since change is fundamentally beneficent. However, Americans do not really mean *change*, in any fundamental sense, when they search for and celebrate the new. To paraphrase Hofstadter's famous aphorism, "America is the only society which began with perfection and aspired to progress." Actually, Americans do not look kindly on proposals for social system change, and do not ordinarily have social system change in mind when they analyze problems or propose reform. (Indeed, it is more characteristic for them to be on the lookout against threats to the American way of life.)

Seen from this perspective, among the most salient features of the American class system are its stability and adaptability. The United States began as a class society, and continues as a class society unchanged in its essential structure. It cannot be said that its unique forms of equality have grown (except that racial "caste" is giving way to class), or, in other words, that class inequality (either achieved or ascribed) has declined. The essential structure of the United States' system of inequality is still found in its economic system. Throughout American history the key to differential enjoyment of social benefits has been market power — how much one's property or person is worth on various economic markets. Prestige and power assets such as moral equality and constitutional rights have not been effectively realized unless supported by class assets. (Even political office has not been a basis for lasting stratification status unless it has been transformed into economic power.)

The great age of reform that began in the 1880s should be seen as extending the values and norms of the United States' corporate, high achievement economy into the political realm. Not only was political corruption and patronage out of keeping with the logic of achievement, rationalization, and professionalism, but the American economy had to "figure out" ways to avoid disastrous and unprofitable competition. The result was the regulatory state, which represents not a movement away from capitalism but its consolidation and adaptation to new conditions.

Unbridled operations of economic forces behind a facade of laissez-faire and Social Darwinism would undoubtedly have produced more inequality had there been no reforms from the 1880s on. But such an outcome might also have endangered capitalism and its class system by giving vent to the "anarchistic" strand in liberalism. A great deal of our political reform, in other words, is either public certification of economic change or a way of facilitating it. The United States has become more explicitly coordinated by government (and other forces), but it cannot be said that our overall hierarchy of social power has changed much. As we will argue shortly, the basic power structure in the United States is neither pluralistic nor narrowly elitist — the reality behind the political dynamics of the post–Civil War period has been the struggle between various upper and middle class elements for supremacy and advantage and the effective cooptation of the lower classes.

The uniqueness of class society

While class society exhibits many similarities with previous systems of stratification, it is also unique. For one thing, it stresses achievement by *all;* there are many more occupations today than in the past that require specialized training (though most occupations probably do not require as much training as we demand and achievement norms are adhered to far less than many people think). Furthermore, competition for positions is stressed far more today than in the past (though, again, competition is not as prevalent as many think). And, finally, our symbolic world is massively and increasingly influenced by what Max Weber referred to as *formal rationality,* better known as science. Certainly the physical and psychological flavor of class society is radically different from those of the societies of the past. On the whole, our bodies do not ache from hunger and disease, and we tend to live two and three times longer than our ancestors. We also live in a different psychological universe, one that stresses personal fulfillment and responsibility in a natural and social world subject to human control. That these values are unequally enjoyed does not diminish either their reality or their uniqueness.

The general structure of American classes

The following depiction of the United States' social classes is highly abstract. It does not purport to be a precise and literal representation of the American class system. It is intended as a broadly accurate account of the distribution of cultural, social, and personality benefits in the United States, based on a composite of empirical and interpretive studies. A special effort has been made to depict classes in terms of consistency of position within and among the dimensions of class, prestige, and power.

Speaking abstractly, the things that are most valued in American life — money, psychic satisfaction, and political-legal power — are distributed among five strata. The differences between these strata are twofold: there are quantitative and qualitative differences in the sociocultural values each stratum enjoys, and qualitative differences in the consistency with which each stratum experiences sociocultural values. Since American social strata (especially the lower-middle class and the classes below) are diversified by religious, ethnic, and "racial" components, these have been summarized separately. The available evidence points to five distinct strata; the composite estimate in Table 16-1 has been drawn from the many empirical and interpretive studies canvassed above.[4] Though our estimate applies to the twentieth century, it is within the realm of reasonable conjecture to assume that no changes have taken place

---

4. The best compendium of existing research, which I have found useful in a general way, is in Richard P. Coleman and Bernice L. Neugarten, *Social Status in the City* (San Francisco: Jossey-Bass, 1971), chap. 12.

Table 16-1 The American Class Structure During the Twentieth Century: A Composite Estimate

The hierarchy of social class	Percentage range of families and unrelated individuals
Consistency: the stable top	1–3%
Near-consistency: the upper-middle class	10–15%
Mixed consistency: the lower-middle class	30–35%
Inconsistency: the working class	40–45%
The consistently depressed: the lower class	20–25%

in the American system of social stratification since European settlers first arrived (leaving aside the issue of slavery and racial segregation). Changes have taken place, of course, in the various elements that make up a class. The occupational skill levels of the various classes have risen consistently, and the nature of the family — the means by which the class system is transmitted from one generation to the next — has been modified by various factors. Also, new forms of upward and downward mobility have emerged, though overall mobility rates seem not to have changed much. All in all, however, no reduction in the relative distance from one class to another is discernible, and there has been no significant increase in equality of opportunity, competition, or justice. Simply put, our social classes represent significant and enduring differences in the benefits Americans derive from society. By referring to these strata, in other words, one can predict outcomes in a wide range of areas, including family life; health; civic, political and cultural participation; voting; type and amount of crime; justice; and so on. Obviously, some overlap between the various strata, some differences within them, and some regional and local variations exist. Despite these qualifications, however, the United States' social classes are real because each is a network of social groups sharing unequally in the totality of social benefits.

Consistency: the stable top

It is safe to assume that the United States possesses a small collection of upper class families that enjoy a thoroughgoing consistency of class, prestige, and power statuses. More specifically, this class of families has great economic power derived from its ownership and control of economic enterprises; its wealth is secure over generations; and it enjoys high and dependable income. Furthermore, it enjoys high family stability, life expectancy, and mental health; high-quality socialization and education; high occupational prestige and satisfaction; high levels of comfort and diversion; high psychic satisfaction from material and symbolic consumption; high psychic satisfaction and high prestige from primary and secondary associations; and great access to, influence over, and protection from political and legal processes. The basic causal process that maintains such families at the top is readily explicable: each of the foregoing categories of benefits reinforces the others, producing a web of causation that enables upper class families to weather and prevail over adversity, whether in the form of economic depression, an occasional economic reversal, an indiscreet marriage, or an occasional mental illness or retarded child. No understanding of this group of families is possible if one restricts oneself to individualistic explanations. On the contrary, their social position is due to the historical accumulation and consolidation of advantage, including careful attention to the socialization structures and processes that insure continuity from one generation to the next. It can be assumed that these families are fairly self-conscious about their position in society, though they do not characteristically emphasize their superiority by demanding deference or recognition from society-at-large. The main evidence for imputing self-consciousness about social class to this group is the careful and comprehensive way in which they raise their children and manage their lives and the fact that membership in this stratum is restricted to those who qualify on both class and prestige criteria. This class also derives considerable unity and social power from common upbringing, education, intermarriage, socializing and associational membership, and overlapping economic statuses. Finally, surveys have shown that in general the upper classes are more conscious of social class than the the lower classes.

The stable top has not been subjected to exact empirical study, and we must infer most of its characteristics. It is tradition-conscious without being backward or reactionary; it is civic-minded without being much interested in politics or public service. It is a leisure class, though its males work at occupations. It supports charitable, educational, and cultural activities and organizations, though its role may be declining as hard-pressed colleges, museums, service agencies, and research institutes become increasingly dependent on tax funds and business contributions to support themselves. The particular blend of class, prestige, and power represented by the stable top varies from region to region and from community to community. Its stronghold has been the small town or small city, though changes may have taken place as a result of urbanization and suburbanization. In any case, there is evidence that the distinction between the stable top and the class below it is blurring in the metropolis (specifically, Kansas City, Missouri, studied from the mid-1950s to the late 1960s).[5]

Near-consistency: the upper-middle class

Families whose breadwinners are proprietors of substantial businesses or farms or upper-level managers or professionals, in either "private" or "public" life, enjoy a high level of sociocultural-personality benefits and a high level of consistency in their various benefits and statuses.[6] The main strength and focus

5. Coleman and Neugarten, *Social Status in the City,* chap. 13.
6. This group encompasses young breadwinners with high prospects as well as the

of these families is economic position — basically the adult male's business or career. This class of families is distinguished from the stable top by its lack of certain prestige assets, but it appears not to suffer much on this account. As we have noted, one of the characteristics of a stable class system is the existence of many different ways by which individuals and families can obtain satisfaction. In any case, to join the stable top, upper-middle class families must learn to consume and to associate according to upper prestige standards and protocols. For real and lasting success in this regard, they must place their children in the socialization structures (especially private schools and prestige colleges) that old rich families have established for their own offspring. In the meantime, upper-middle class families participate in a full range of voluntary organizations, founding their own clubs and frequenting new resorts if need be. While they may occasionally experience discomfort when they consume or when they apply for membership in exclusive clubs, they tend to enjoy high consistency in all their statuses. An upper-middle class family is by definition characterized by high income, high education, high occupation (in terms of both prestige and other satisfactions), high participation in voluntary associations, and high awareness and participation in political life.[7] Such families enjoy stable family life, privacy, pleasant surroundings, and stimulating associations. Their children of both sexes receive higher education as a matter of course, and their members enjoy the comfortable feeling that they are fully normal.[8]

Post-1945 America witnessed a significant growth in the absolute numbers of the upper-middle class, though there appears to have been only slight growth in its relative size. Basically, the upper-middle class is made up of individuals (and their families) who rode the wave of post–World War Two corporate and professional expansion. Subject to the long-range process of rationalization, there has been a steady bureaucratization of the economy (the growth of corporate concentration), the professions (hospitals, law firms, universities, and so on), voluntary organizations (professionally run charitable organizations, foundations, trade and professional organizations, labor unions, churches, and so on) and, of course, government. Thought of in terms of class (and not of the ideology of "nonegalitarian classlessness" and "strategic elites"), much of what has transpired in post-1945 America makes sense as class modernization, not as the reduction of ascription and the realization of merit and equality. As the upper and upper-middle classes have grown in absolute numbers (not in relative size), elite institutions of higher education have been enlarged and others have been upgraded. As maturing industrial society has experienced long- and short-term pressures and crises (technological displace-

---

middle-aged whose prospects have been realized. Taking age into account helps to resolve or account for many apparent inconsistencies.

7. Obviously, this definition excludes the new rich (instant business millionaires, entertainment celebrities) and the criminal rich.

8. Remember that we are speaking about relative modal tendencies. The upper-middle class obviously experiences trouble of various sorts, notably as a result of the pressure on children at this level to match or exceed the attainments of their successful fathers.

ment of labor and large-scale migration, boom and bust, labor unrest, war, racial conflict, student unrest, pollution, and the like), it has increasingly turned to political solutions, which are defined by the upper-middle class and its political allies — the rich, entrenched small-town businesspeople and professionals, and small farmers. It is not surprising, therefore, that the upper-middle class is a major beneficiary of most legislation, reform and otherwise. It goes without saying that this class is not a ruling class in any traditional sense. For one thing, it is too diverse in composition to have clear-cut common economic and political interests. Furthermore, it is too deeply committed to economic functions to be committedly political. On the whole, it is conservative on most domestic economic issues and liberal on foreign policy and civil rights.

Mixed consistency: the lower-middle class

The lower-middle class is a very diverse group, unified loosely by the fact that it is not a manual (factory) laboring class, and, more importantly, by an overall level of social existence that places it above the working class and gives its children a much greater probability of rising to the upper-middle class. The lower-middle class includes small businesspeople and small farmers; small, independent professionals[9] and semiprofessionals (teachers, clergy, local elected officials, social workers, nurses, police officers, firefighters); and sales, clerical, and middle management personnel, both private and public. On the whole, members of this class enjoy stable family lives and a certain measure of occupational prestige; they are civic-minded; and while they participate in political life less than the upper classes, they are more political than the classes below (each of the segments of this class can exhibit different shades of political behavior depending on issue and context). The various segments of this class have diverse histories, and each is potentially subject to various forms of inconsistency.[10] Small businesspeople, small farmers, and independent professionals are still committed to the laissez-faire ethic of rugged individualism, even though each of these groups has suffered a decline in relative class, prestige, and power status over the past century. Quasi-professionals, as well as sales, clerical, and midde-management personnel, enjoy a measure of prestige because of their education, because they are associated with valued social functions, and because their work is clean and allegedly cerebral, but their class position is not always congruent with their prestige. One of the persistent trends in this area is the growing unionization of teachers, firefighters, police officers, and lower-level white-collar civil servants on a "professional"

9. Independent professionals such as small-town doctors and lawyers would be members of the upper-middle class or even stable top in their local contexts but are lower-middle class when ranked nationally. The reader will also recall that professionals are stratified internally on other grounds; see "Stratification Within Classes and Occupations" in Chapter 8.
10. For a discussion of class inconsistency *within* class, see "America's Unique Class Politics" in Chapter 11.

basis — that is, without associating themselves with factory and other service workers with whom they share many basic economic problems.

Among these groups, small businesspeople and small farmers experience peculiar inconsistencies in their economic (class) positions. Small businesspeople are subject to many economic markets (credit, labor, commodity) as both buyers and sellers, and thus are unlikely to develop a coherent class ideology. The inconsistency of their position probably goes a long way toward explaining the appeal of that magical mechanism, the free market, for small businesspeople. Farmers also have an inconsistent market relation: they are often buyers of credit in a seller's market and sellers of commodities in a buyer's market.

Both small farmers and small businesspeople have made a considerable effort to shore up their difficult economic positions by stressing prestige factors. Both stress the moral value of their respective ways of life (self-sufficiency, competition) and both link their activities to the health of society. Neither group, however, is above using government to lower its costs — such as of transportation and credit — to stabilize the price of what it sells ("fair trade" laws, farm price supports), or to prevent collective bargaining by labor unions. The basic defensive posture of the semiprofessions, on the other hand, is collective action (increasingly collective bargaining) and the upgrading of their professional images, especially through increased (and unnecessary?) educational requirements promoted by professional associations.

Inconsistency: the working class

When we turn our attention from the lower-middle class to the working class, we cross a rather deep cleavage in the American class system. The evidence points overwhelmingly to a significant gap between the level of social and cultural benefits received by blue-collar workers and those received by the classes above them. (A gap of similar magnitude separates the working class and the lower class.) The term *working class* obviously refers to a broad, diverse group of families encompassing highly skilled as well as semiskilled and unskilled workers — a group, in other words, that subsumes quite varied levels of income, work satisfaction, and prestige. If by *working class* one means workers who are steadily employed in manual or blue-collar occupations, regardless of other attributes, then inconsistency of class, prestige, and power statuses seems to be the normal condition of the working class. There is, first of all, the confining routine of work and the lack of prestige or public regard for manual work. Working class marriages are significantly more unstable than marriages in the classes above. At best, marriages at this level are deeply segregated into masculine and feminine roles; there is considerable isolation and even estrangement between working class husbands and wives. In comparison with the classes above, working class families manifest a significantly lower level of participation in community affairs and in the aesthetic and thought life of the nation. All in all, the working class life is seriously inconsistent with the American emphasis on freedom and individual choice; happiness; moral, political, and legal equality; and personal fulfillment and identity through work and success.

Some elite elements in the working class receive incomes in the middle class range of income levels, and are thus somewhat difficult to classify. It is of great importance that this group accounts for the bulk of the working class with college-bound children. However, extreme caution must be exercised in interpreting high working class incomes. The hourly wages of plumbers, steam-fitters, bricklayers, and the like are quite misleading, since seasonal and other forms of underemployment make it difficult to translate hourly wages into true annual incomes. Secondly, a comparison of total work-related economic benefits (pensions, insurance, sick leave, material comforts and safety on the job, and paid holidays and vacations) and power-related economic benefits (taxation, housing policies, recreational facilities, public services in general) would undoubtedly differentiate many lower-middle and working class individuals who earn similar incomes. And, of course, it is of the utmost importance not to confuse individual with family income data: the bulk of high working class incomes belong to families with two or more earners.

By and large, members of the working class earn incomes that permit only a modest level of comfort. Many working class families live austere and even impoverished lives. Few can save — accumulation is very slow — and many live on credit. Economically, they are best characterized as living close to their incomes, which has obvious psychological implications. While members of the working class are less self-conscious about residential prestige differentials than the classes above, and do not worry much about being excluded from membership in middle class clubs, they do face serious psychological insecurities and pain. Workers are typically not protected against serious medical illness, and their pension funds are ordinarily not vested — that is, a worker loses all rights if he or she is laid off or changes a job, though vesting is occasionally provided for if certain time restrictions are met.[11] Many working class males experience drudgery or heavy exertion or both in their work, compounded by the knowledge that they have little chance of improving their economic status. The working class female typically faces a life of drudgery, revolving around too many children,[12] and isolation; she often remains closer to her relatives than to her husband.

Trade unions protect only 35–40 percent of the working class, and, misconceptions about the power of unions to the contrary, many unskilled workers are not well paid — that is, they do not enjoy even a modest level of living — even when they are represented by unions. Trade unionism has not resulted in a monolithic struggle between labor and management, as the popular image has it. Employers still find it possible to appeal to workers against trade unions, and

11. In 1974 Congress passed legislation strengthening somewhat the pension rights of lower-level private employees.
12. The decline in the birthrate at this level may modify this aspect of working class life within the near future.

employers and trade union officials often reach agreements against the wishes of workers (sometimes legally and sometimes not). Whatever else it does, therefore, trade unionism also incorporates workers into a capitalist way of life — that is, helps workers accept a definition of themselves conducive to running a private property, profit-oriented market economy and society.

Politically, the working class tends to be more apathetic than the classes above it; when it votes or otherwise participates in politics, it tends to be liberal on economic-welfare issues and conservative on foreign policy and civil rights (with the obvious exception of blacks and some other minorities). The working class gets into a great deal of trouble as a result either of criminal activities or of credit and marital-family problems, but its access to justice and public aid is deeply biased by class factors. Despite the pronounced particularities of the working class life experience, however, it cannot be said that there exists anything resembling a working class subculture. Nothing so poignantly expresses the plight of the American working class as the fact that it is subject to the full force of the middle class ethos.

The consistently depressed: the lower class

The lower class in America is made up of a diverse collection of families and individuals: the permanently unemployed; the erratically employed; the underemployed; the badly underpaid,[13] the old who are poor; abandoned mothers; and the physically, mentally, and psychologically sick, disabled, or different. This group is not united by any common consciousness, nor do its members have much to do with each other. What these individuals have in common, basically, is their worthlessness on the labor market, a class position that renders them fairly worthless in terms of prestige and power as well. The worthlessness of this stratum is an outcome of American society, though there are undoubtedly a few inherently "defective" individuals among its members. Ours is a society that calls an unemployment rate of 4 percent "full employment," that is probably characterized by considerably more underemployment and unemployment than the published rates (5 to 9 percent, 1970–1975), and that has much higher rates (up to 50 percent) among certain age and racial groups. It is the American economy that displaces middle-aged unskilled workers, making them employable one day and unemployable the next. It is the American economy that pays significant numbers of workers less than its own official minimum standard of living. It is American society that, while doubling life expectancy, has defined the old as economically and therefore socially useless. (The older person who is a discard in our society is often a highly honored elder in preindustrial societies.) American society's cultural and social definitions and

13. In 1971 the federal minimum wage of $1.60 provided a full-time worker with a family of four an annual income of $3,328, about $800 below the federal poverty (destitution) level for that year, $4,137. The rise in the minimum wage to $2.00 in 1974 still leaves such a family below the poverty level.

sanctions are responsible for most mental, physical, and psychological disabilities. The physically different, such as cripples and dwarfs; the sexually different, such as homosexuals; and those who want to live differently, such as hippies, are all culturally despised and thus made deviant by cultural (and often legal) definition. Many of these outcasts are unable to earn a living, and thus our moral evaluation of these "other minorities" also takes the form of class subordination and political-legal discrimination (often open persecution).[14] It is in these areas that one finds distinctive "lower class" subcultures, such as segments of the criminal, carnival, and homosexual worlds.

We do not know the lower class very well, since it is a composite of many different types of individuals and families. Some are multigenerational members of the lower stratum who have inherited their class position as the children of migratory workers, seasonal laborers, hospital help, and the like. Others, unlucky enough to have physical characteristics that do not conform to American definitions of normality, are destined from birth for the lower class. Still others gravitate downward as a result either of defeat in economic combat or of having or developing undesired or dysfunctional personalities; examples are alcoholics, homosexuals, and the mentally ill and retarded.

The War on Poverty has had little impact on the lower class. The elderly poor have, however, been helped by Medicare and special housing programs. Perhaps the most successful aspect of the War on Poverty has been legal aid, largely because justice for the poor has received the backing of a powerful profession and enjoyed political independence through federal funding. (For this very reason legal aid for the poor has aroused powerful, sustained opposition and appears to be on the wane.) The rest of the War on Poverty has become indistinguishable from the dependency-creating, dirt-under-the-carpet welfare system. Its programs have gradually been incorporated into local government, dismantled, or starved for funds. No significant decrease in the size of that portion of the lower class whose status is attributable to unemployment and poverty-level income — by far the bulk of the lower class — seems likely without more explicit forms of social and economic planning. As for redefining the status of the "other minorities" (especially by eliminating legal stigmas) only a tentative beginning has been made toward allowing the "unbeautiful," the dwarf, the homosexual, and the like to participate fully and freely in the benefits of social life.

The basic pattern of statuses in the lower class could also be characterized, of course, as highly inconsistent. Certainly membership in the lower class is inconsistent with American ideals, especially for those who believe America's promises or who once enjoyed better times. And the apathy of this group is the mark of defeat, not personal inadequacy, though here as elsewhere American society is not above blaming its victims for their own defeat.

14. For an interesting and valuable collection of readings in this general area, see Edward Sagarin, ed., *The Other Minorities: Non-Ethnic Collectivities Conceptualized as Minority Groups* (Waltham, Mass.: Ginn, 1971).

The class system and minority groups

The foregoing characterization of the American class system contained almost no references to racial and religious-ethnic minorities. The following depiction of the positions of such minorities in the American class system is again pitched at a high level of generalization. While broadly representative of empirical phenomena, it is not intended as an empirically based theory. Its purpose, rather, is to complete our summary of social stratification in the United States. More specifically, it is designed to identify the special behavior problems created by racial, religious, and ethnic rankings, to place research in this area in context, to identify processes that mediate the relations between majority and minority, and to identify trends in this all-important realm of American social stratification.

The criteria for establishing the positions of majority-minority groups are derived from basic American values and beliefs. We can assume, therefore, the superior worth of high class achievement (income, wealth, occupation, education), of good taste and breeding (by definition, how the upper classes consume and comport themselves), and of the Protestant religion and white skin (by definition, the attributes of the upper classes).

High class, prestige, and power: the abnormal norm

The norms and values governing majority-minority relations have been fully embodied historically only by a relatively small group of white, largely Protestant upper and upper-middle class families. At this level, remember, there is great consistency among the three hierarchies of social worth. The group that first achieved pre-eminence in America happened to be white, Anglo-Saxon, and Protestant, and its members simply assumed or asserted the superiority of all they did and believed in. Today, the upper class appears to contain significant numbers of Roman Catholics and Jews; however, because no exact studies exist, we cannot specify exact numbers or determine whether such newcomers are full or only partial members.

Normal class, prestige, and power: white Protestants

By *normal class* we mean a group of families that does not exhibit unusually high or low achievement in the spheres of occupation, education, or income. White Protestants — both Anglo-Saxons of long duration in the United States and immigrant groups from Germany and Scandinavia — exhibit normal class achievement; in other words, they are well represented above the manual labor rank. As white Protestants, they also have normal prestige despite the fact that the occupations white Protestants hold and the churches they attend vary widely in class composition and prestige worth.[15]

15. There is also a depressed white Protestant Anglo-Saxon group, largely rural but also concentrated in urban "hillbilly" enclaves.

Normal class, changing prestige and power: European Roman Catholics

This category includes Roman Catholics of European origin (French, Irish, German, Polish, Italian) and European Roman Catholics who entered the United States via Canada (French Canadians). Thanks to their location in urban centers, Roman Catholics (excluding black and Latin Roman Catholics) have now achieved parity with white Protestants in class achievement. Furthermore, Roman Catholics have been assimilated culturally, which is to say that socioeconomic status predicts more about a Roman Catholic than does religion. Even on basic issues such as birth control and parochial education, it cannot be said that there is a Roman Catholic position (among the laity) that varies much from the class views of non-Catholics. And in the field of politics it appears that the historic proclivity of (underdog, working class) Roman Catholics to support the Democratic party is coming to an end. As they diversify by class, Roman Catholics will probably vote along the same class lines that divide other Americans. While basic religious attitudes have no doubt changed, there is still a prestige ranking that affects European Roman Catholics adversely. Because of both national origin (long associated with working class status) and religion, European Roman Catholics do not mingle easily with other Americans outside the dimension of class. Associational life in the United States is pervasively segregated along religious-ethnic lines, though such segregation is not necessarily enforced or characterized by feelings of resentment. Indeed, a relatively full way of life is available to the Irish of Boston, the French Canadians of Burlington, Vermont, and their counterparts elsewhere. While complaints may be expressed about this or that grievance or injustice, resentment of the system of society is minimal. Indeed, as we saw in Chapter 15, prestige segregation plays an important role in making the American system of stratification work.

Normal-to-high class, subnormal prestige and power: Jewish and Oriental Americans

A number of minorities in the United States enjoy normal-to-high class achievement but suffer from subnormal prestige and power. This category of minorities includes Jews, Japanese Americans, and Chinese Americans. By and large, these groups have exceeded the class achievements of white Christians, but suffer from adverse prestige evaluations on religious-ethnic grounds and, in the case of Oriental Americans, on racial grounds as well. While these groups have taken on the American cultural identity, they still live and associate separately from other Americans. The position of Japanese and Chinese Americans in Hawaii is somewhat different from that of their counterparts in the continental United States: the latter has a deeper racist tradition than Hawaii, though no exact comparative studies exist.

Low class, negative prestige and power: the oppressed and depressed

It is no exaggeration to say that the United States possesses a substantial group of families and unrelated individuals who exhibit all the earmarks of a "permanent" proletariat. This category of minorities includes significant numbers of black Americans, Indian Americans, Eskimos, Mexican Americans, Puerto Ricans, and Filipinos. It also includes a diverse group of white Protestants, who are not readily identifiable and thus not easily denied prestige; "hillbilly" is the most descriptive, though hardly the most flattering, term for this group.

Though each of these minorities is itself stratified, containing middle and upper class members, in the aggregate these minority groups have not made any significant relative gains *vis-à-vis* the class standing of mainstream white Protestants and white European Roman Catholics. They also suffer from a low prestige evaluation (largely associated with their historic economic subordination), which is largely expressed in racist terms. By force of class, prestige, and power, these groups are barred from full or even adequate participation in American society. The vicious process in which low class (income, wealth, occupation, education) leads to low prestige (through racist values and beliefs, ethnic prejudice, residential segregation, interactional segregation), which in turn reinforces low class is an institutionalized pattern that will not be easy to break. In addition, the power position of this group of minorities has been compromised throughout American history. Despite the rhetoric and the promises of American society, the most that can be claimed for the strenuous reform movements of recent decades is that they have lifted these groups out of "caste" subordination into class subordination. Though these minority groups achieved significant power mobility in the 1960s through the acquisition of a more effective franchise, they remain weak politically because they are weak economically; do not have access to politically relevant voluntary pressure groups; and are gerrymandered by the economics of transportation and housing, by discrimination, by various forms of public policy, and by explicitly drawn political boundaries.

The middle (and upper) class establishment

The word *establishment* has a number of synonyms, such as *ruling class, governing class, power elite, military-industrial complex,* and the like, terms that denote a group possessing great, almost unilateral, power over the rest of society. In the technical terms of social stratification, *establishment* refers to a social class possessing class, prestige, and power assets of such an order, intensity, and magnitude that it controls the structure and direction of society. The more sophisticated formulations of this idea specify the type of social system that produces such (social) power.[16]

16. The term *power* will in this section refer to social power — the combined effects of class, prestige, and power factors — as distinguished from the power dimension alone.

The best-known theory in American sociology alleging the existence of an establishment is C. Wright Mills'. Mills' thesis is that a small power elite drawn from and coordinating the upper reaches of the corporate world, the federal executive branch of government, and the military has come into being because of processes inherent in advanced industrial society. Perched atop the stratification dimensions of class and power, this group possesses, according to Mills, significantly more power than Congress, trade unions, farmers, small business, or the general public.[17] Our study has found little evidence of the existence of a ruling class or power elite in this sense. The absence of a power elite does not mean, however, that American society is without an establishment; it does not mean, in other words, that the United States has approximated either a nonegalitarian classless society or a pluralistic self-equilibrating system of power, or that it is even making progress toward pluralism or a democratic meritocracy (the theory of convergence).

The pluralist argument is that there exists a pluralistic group or power structure in which the various contending interest groups balance each other. It alleges that because no single group or combination of groups can dominate the others, the public interest is guaranteed, or at least constantly pursued and approximated. The existence of a plurality of groups, it is argued, makes for overlapping group membership, which in turn inhibits groups from acting unilaterally. A pluralistic power structure requires groups to make alliances with one another in response to specific issues, and thus both leaders and followers must learn the arts of negotiation and compromise. The public always has alternatives to choose from and is constantly supplied with a wide variety of information to help it make up its collective mind about public issues. Perhaps the best-known variant of this perspective in American sociology is the democratic elitist theory of Seymour M. Lipset.[18]

Our study has found the pluralist argument unsatisfactory, largely because pluralist thinkers tend to overlook two basic aspects of American life: (1) the existence of significant amounts of powerlessness, exploitation, privilege, waste, and ideological rhetoric, and, (2) the fact that these phenomena seem to be deeply institutionalized and thus relatively permanent, perhaps "necessary," features of American (and industrial?) society.

If American society does not conform either to the power elite or to the

17. *The Power Elite* (New York: Oxford University Press, 1956), also in paperback. G. William Domhoff, who has set himself the task of trying to substantiate Mills' thesis more fully, has investigated the upper levels of the various hierarchies in American society and offers what he considers conclusive evidence that a small, homogeneous, stable, and interchangeable collection of very rich individuals (and their families) occupies the command positions of American society; see his *Who Rules America?* (Englewood Cliffs, N.J.: Prentice-Hall, 1967), available in paperback, and *The Higher Circles: The Governing Class in America* (New York: Random House, 1971), also available in paperback. For a straightforward, sophisticated Marxist interpretation along the same lines, see Charles H. Anderson, *The Political Economy of Social Class* (Englewood Cliffs, N.J.: Prentice-Hall, 1974).

18. See especially *Political Man* (Garden City, N.Y.: Doubleday, 1960); *The First New Nation* (New York: Basic Books, 1963); and *Revolution and Counter-revolution* (New York: Basic Books, 1968).

pluralist model, to what model does it correspond? The best answer is probably that this is still an open question. The next-best answer is that we are probably governed by a middle (and upper) class power structure with strong overtones of oligarchy.[19] The model of a middle class establishment resembles the pluralist model up to a point. There is some truth, for example, in the argument that the liberal democracies are unique because the people rule. Power *is* shared by more people than was the case in the past. But this is not the same thing as saying that the people-at-large participate actively in the business of running society, which they do not, or that they have equal shares of power, which they do not. It is also true that the many groups in contemporary society tend somewhat to check and balance each other as they jostle for advantage. But closer scrutiny reveals that the articulated groups in American society are overwhelmingly middle and upper class in leadership, composition, and social philosophy. This fact is evidence of social power rather than of a natural distribution of ability, since the processes and agencies of achievement in the United States are heavily ascriptive and arbitrary. Far from being a society based on equality of opportunity (with acknowledged gaps), the United States has no equality of opportunity — except among members of the same class — and cannot as long as children are raised in families steeply differentiated by class, and thus by prestige and power.

Stated diffeerntly, it is social power that explains individualism rather than the reverse: a minority of white males and their families from middle and upper class backgrounds has managed to monopolize important social positions in the name of nonegalitarian classlessness, or the philosophy of individualism. This has led to a hierarchy of ascriptive and arbitrary power in the United States because the dominant groups believe in achievement, excellence, and progress, and constantly raise the norms required for admittance to upper-level occupations. Since these norms are largely unrelated to functional performance, their latent function is to maintain an artificial scarcity of qualified personnel. This practice is imitated at all levels as semiprofessionals and skilled workers use the state or their unions to establish unnecessary occupational qualifications. The net result is not pluralistic competition or power but a scramble for a socially created shortage of desirable positions in which the winners are largely foreordained by the rules of the game.

The dominant power groups in American society have succeeded, by and large, in inculcating their explanation of how society works in the remainder of the population. Americans not only accept large concentrations of private power, especially corporations and the professions, but also regard this situation as normal and therefore legitimate. And the same thing is true of other basic features of American society: the primacy of economic status and occupation over other institutions; the stress on work and gain; the assumed validity of highly unequal rewards; faith in the automatic beneficence of science, technology, and education; the use of religion as a secular faith; reliance on an

19. An *oligarchy* is a propertied or occupational power group, or collection of such groups, that consciously or unconsciously does not honor the ideals of its society.

individualized and psychologized human nature as the ultimate explanation of behavior; and the assumed fiduciary benevolence of private power blocs. Of course, there is evidence that Americans are highly critical of the specific ways in which their society works and, as public opinion polls have consistently revealed, have considerably less than full confidence in their leaders and institutions. The important point, however, is that the lower classes find it difficult to articulate a philosophy that would challenge the existing system of power since their Americanism predisposes them away from the concept of power and the institutional explanation of behavior. And underlying the maintenance of the status quo is the fact the the upper and lower classes are all implicated in the existing division of labor. Daily experience, interpreted in terms of the ideology of classless inequality and progress through reliance on existing processes (or variations on them) locates the various classes in orbits that seem normal and natural.

Within the upper- and lower-middle classes (and the tiny upper class, which has a far greater affinity with the middle classes than is usually assumed) there is an intricate intermeshing of interests, which the pluralist model invariably overlooks or slights. Interests are coordinated across competing groups in the same class by intermarriage; interlocking directorships; informal agreements; common experience, such as schooling, socializing, religion, and business; and "fiduciary" organizations, such as law firms, banks, professional associations, voluntary organizations of various kinds, and governments. The intermeshing of interests can take the form of reciprocal backscratching and support, such as when the insurance industry supports the American Medical Association in its fight against a public system of medical care and in turn receives support from the AMA in its own opposition to public insurance programs. Or it can take the form of reciprocal inaction, an important feature of our professional life. Indeed, the existence of noncompeting clusters of power within specific sectors of society, the economy, the professions, education, prestige groups, and politics is a salient feature of American society. These features, together with (1) economic insecurity and competition for scarce jobs and resources at lower levels, and (2) ethnic, religious, and racial hostilities, go a long way toward explaining the nature of social power in America.

The intermeshing of interests also occurs across the various classes, as is exemplified by hierarchies within the middle classes in which managers subordinate lower white-collar workers, professionals subordinate semiprofessionals, and elite members of a profession subordinate average members. There is also a complex interplay of interests that binds various classes together: for example, a plant owner will receive the support of his upper-middle class employees, clerical staff, and blue-collar workers when he fights for a government subsidy to save his bankrupt plant. Real estate owners will receive the support of tenants and small businesspeople when highway construction threatens to demolish their homes and stores. Businesspeople, local governments, farmers, and blue-collar workers will all rally to help a declining railroad (even though the same railroad has cheated and exploited them for generations). And members of all classes will defend education in the name of equal opportunity, even though equal opportunity is a myth and the educational system it disguises benefits the middle and upper classes most.

Thus the existing division of labor, and its ideological justification, is the prime mover of American behavior. The growth of mass disenchantment with institutions signifies an inadequate exercise of power, and perhaps loss of control over society, but not a relinquishment of power. It seems fairly clear that the American class system isolates those in upper-level positions from the experiences and problems of those at lower levels. To function effectively, upper groups must at least understand the sociocultural nature of behavior and reduce the wide gap between themselves and the lower classes. Despite the many, serious, and chronic problems from which American society suffers, however, there is no evidence that any such shift is taking place. The characteristic response to any given problem is to undertake more of the behavior that caused the problem in the first place: economic growth, applied technology, professionalism, an emphasis on a psychologized leadership, education, and the like.

The observer of the American scene must be careful not to succumb to the siren song of evolutionary liberalism. Many interpret higher absolute levels of income, education, and the like as evidence of the homogenization and equalization of society. Others see the United States as a postindustrial society, or one that has somehow muted its authority structures or rendered them socially benevolent; the latter view is inherent in theories of managerial revolution, "technostructure" based on knowledge, collegiality among the professions, meritocracy, strategic elites, and the like. However, the managerial revolution is exaggerated, and, on a more fundamental level, there is no reason to see in the rise of a managerial economy a growth of reason, achievement, or benevolence. Managers may be better educated and more experienced than stockholders, and these groups may occasionally quarrel, but their fundamental class interests are quite similar, especially when contrasted with those of lower-level employees and consumers. As for the professions, there is still a wide gap between the ideals of public service, scholarship, collegiality, ethical and fiduciary codes, on the one hand, and actual practice on the other, and there is no evidence that this gap is closing.

It may well be that the concept of a middle class, as either an establishment or an oligarchy or both, is too abstract, and that it hides a more fundamental structure of power. It is possible that the upper class or, as Hamilton has argued, the upper-middle class, is the dominant power group in the United States.[20] Before this question can be resolved conclusively, however, we need more explicit research into the big business managerial elite: where it comes from, how it behaves, where it gets its information, with whom it allies itself, and so on. And we need to know more about the other segment of the upper-middle class, the professions — not as idealized transmitters of the achievement ethic but as class-bound interest groups that promote ascription as well as

20. Richard F. Hamilton, *Class and Politics in the United States* (New York: John Wiley and Sons, 1972).

achievement, and that prevent significant changes and improvements in the way in which social problems are confronted. Of special interest is the political elite: government now wields enormous power, and we need to know more about how social change is prevented, and problems perpetuated, by complacent inaction as well as by reform and dynamic leadership.

We also need to know more about the lower-middle class. It may well be that lower-middle class clerical and sales workers should be grouped with blue-collar workers, as Hamilton has argued. If so, the lower-middle class would be composed of small and medium-sized businesspeople and farmers and other white-collar workers (middle management, local professionals, and semi-professionals) who identify strongly with the upper and upper-middle classes.

And certainly the stable top needs more careful study, not merely as a potential power elite, but also as a class that has derived its superior status from the historical accumulation and consolidation of advantage and is thus out of keeping with the individualist equal-opportunity ideals of the United States. Enjoying high and secure class and prestige assets and the favor of government, especially in matters of taxation and economic policy, the stable top is a potent ally of, if not the leader of, the upper-middle class.

In any case and for the time being, the differences and disparities in social power within the middle classes (defined broadly to include all propertied and advantaged occupational groups) appear to be less extreme than the differences between the middle classes and the classes below them. In our judgment, therefore, the relation of this broad middle class establishment to the rest of society constitutes not only the essential hierarchy of social power in America, but a hierarchy with pronounced, stable, and apparently inherent oligarchic features.

Author Index

Davis, Fred, 247n
Davis, James A., 211n
Davis, James W., Jr., 194n, 373n
Davis, Kingsley, 51–53, 53n, 102, 185n, 242
Davis, Rennard, 159n, 317n, 370n
Dawson, Richard E., 343n
Dean, John P., 318n
Deasy, Lelia Calhoun, 195n
DeClercq, Eugene R., 347n
Demerath, N. J., III, 87n, 168n
Dervin, Brenda, 279n
Devine, Donald J., 368n, 437n
Dewey, John, 70
Dodyk, Paul M., 123n
Doherty, Robert E., 207n
Dolbeare, Kenneth M., 194n, 373n
Domhoff, G. William, 126n, 179n, 302, 306–307, 314n, 351n, 465n
Dominick, Joseph R., 279n
Donovan, John C., 332n
Duncan, Beverly, 92n, 273n
Duncan, Otis Dudley, 92n, 170, 273n, 303n
Durkheim, Emile, 9n, 64n, 103, 134, 364, 424, 442, 447
Dye, Thomas R., 343n, 347n

Eckland, Bruce K., 211–212
Eells, Kenneth, 298n
Ehrenreich, Barbara, 192n
Ehrenreich, John, 192n
Ehrmann, Winston, 176
Eisenhower, Dwight, 258, 348, 361
Eitzen, D. Stanley, 87n
Empey, LaMar, 95–96
Engels, Fredrich, 11n
Ennis, Philip H., 409n, 410n
Erikson, Kai T., 196n, 441–442
Erlanger, Howard S., 180n
Esposito, John C., 350n
Evans, Peter, 41n
Eysenck, H. J., 10

Falk, Jacqueline M., 379n
Fallers, Lloyd A., 288–290
Farber, Bernard, 197
Featherman, David L., 92
Fei, Hsiao-Tung, 41n
Feigelman, William, 173n
Feldman, Jacob J., 191n
Feldman, Saul D., 278n

Feldmesser, Robert A., 46n
Fellmeth, Robert, 350n
Ferman, Louis A., 147n
Festinger, Leon, 88n
Feuer, Lewis S., 11n
Fisher, Wesley A., 45n
Flacks, Richard, 368n
Flanagan, John C., 221n, 222
Floud, Jean, 214n, 215n
Fonda, Jane, 260n
Foote, Nelson N., 179n
Form, William H., 49n, 60, 282n, 349n
Frazier, E. Franklin, 158, 188–189, 311n
Free, Lloyd A., 282n, 363
Freeman, Walter E., 283n
Friedman, Laurence M., 376–377
Friend, Irwin, 128, 129, 131
Fromm, Eric, 366n

Galbraith, John K., 385, 421
Galton, Francis, 8
Gamson, William, 362
Gans, Herbert J., 184n, 278n
Garfinkel, Harold, 409
Gartner, Alan, 208n
Garza, Rudolph O. de la, 391n, 392n
Gaudet, Hazel, 366n
Gaviglio, Glen, 345n
Geiger, H. Kent, 45n
George, Charles H., 172n
George, Katherine, 172n
Gerth, H. H., 13n, 20n, 40n, 228n, 325n, 330n, 331n, 337n
Geschwender, James A., 85n, 88n
Gintis, Herbert, 208n
Glazer, Nathan, 159n, 392n
Glenn, Norval D., 167, 168, 169, 177n
Glidden, William, 345n
Glock, Charles Y., 168n, 169n
Giddings, Franklin Henry, 9n
Gillespie, W. Irwin, 121n
Glenn, Norval D., 219, 280n
Goffman, Erving, 215n
Goffman, Irwin W., 86n
Gold, Ray, 247n
Goldscheider, Calvin, 190, 316n
Goldstein, Sidney, 190, 273n, 316n
Goldthorpe, John H., 49–51, 279n, 361n
Gomberg, William, 247n, 266n, 278n, 279n, 281n, 285n, 307n
Goode, William J., 176n, 178n, 180n, 183n, 246n, 426
Gordon, Gerald, 195n

Jencks, Christopher, 207n, 208
Jensen, Arthur R., 10, 207n
John of Salisbury, 6, 102
Johnson, David R., 318n
Johnson, E. L., 45n
Johnson, Elmer H., 194n
Johnson, Sheila K., 173n
Jones, F. Lancaster, 87n, 93n

Kadushin, Charles, 191–192
Kahl, Joseph H., 65n
Kain, John F., 147n, 158n
Kallenback, W. Warren, 80n, 279n
Kalven, Harry, Jr., 405n
Kaplan, D. L., 136
Kaplan, Max, 234n
Karabel, Jerome, 210n
Katona, George, 127n
Kavaler, Lucy, 297n
Kavolis, Vytautas, 280n
Keller, Suzanne, 60n, 80n, 421n
Kelly, Arlene, 194n, 405n
Kelly, D. Dennis, 87n
Kenkel, William K., 87n
Kephart, William M., 186
Kerckhoff, Alan C., 182n, 214n
Kessler, Friedrich, 404n
Key, V. O., Jr., 349n, 350n, 361n
Killingsworth, Charles C., 147n
Kimball, Penn, 352
King, Martin Luther, 258n
Kirkpatrick, Clifford, 187
Kitagawa, Evelyn M., 195
Kitano, H. L., 146n
Kitto, H. D. F., 235
Klapp, Orrin E., 257n, 423n
Klemer, Richard H., 177n
Knight, Frank H., 13n
Knight, Julie, 37n
Knowles, James C., 133n
Kohlmeier, Louis M., 350n, 384n
Kohn, Melvin L., 181, 262
Kolko, Gabriel, 112, 113n, 126n, 335n, 383
Komarovsky, Mirra, 179n, 186, 246n
Kornhauser, William, 366, 367
Kosack, Godula, 80n
Kramer, John, 345n
Kramer, Ralph M., 355n
Krislov, S., 350
Krueger, Thomas A., 345n
Kruszewski, Z. Anthony, 391n, 392n
Kuznets, Simon, 113n

Lampman, Robert J., 127n
Lane, David, 44n
Lane, Robert E., 433–434
Lansing, John B., 127n
Lauer, Roger, 173n
Laumann, Edward O., 80n, 86n, 87n, 88n, 170, 177n, 273n, 307n
Laurenti, Luigi, 274–275
Lazarsfeld, Paul, 260n, 366n
Leavitt, Helen, 132n
Lefebvre, Georges, 63n
Leggett, John C., 87n, 148n, 265n
Lenin, V. I., 49n, 445
Lenski, Gerhard, 53–58, 83, 86n, 190, 309n
Levitt, M., 407n
Lewis, Lionel S., 250n
Lewis, Oscar, 37n
Liebow, Elliot, 311n
Light, Ivan H., 161, 311n
Lincoln, Abraham, 258
Lind, Andrew W., 146n
Linder, Staffan Burenstam, 235–236
Liniger, Charles, 129
Linton, Ralph, 17n
Lipset, Seymour M., 11n, 41n, 45n, 46n, 50n, 58n, 59n, 62n, 64n, 90n, 91n, 92n, 104n, 141n, 172n, 180n, 191n, 204n, 208n, 233n, 242n, 243n, 276n, 288n, 301n, 359n, 365, 367n, 465
Litt, Edgar, 438n
Lobel, Lyle S., 104, 276, 288
Locke, John, 7, 68
Lockwood, David, 279n, 361n
Long, Huey, 368
Long, Priscilla, 368n
Lopreato, Joseph, 250n
Lord, Walter, 193n
Lorenz, Konrad A., 10
Louis, Joe, 259
Low, J. O., 71
Lowenthal, Leo, 260n
Lowi, Theodore J., 350n, 375n
Lukacs, Georg, 280n
Lundberg, Ferdinand, 126n
Lunt, Paul S., 71
Lutterman, K. A., 194n, 373n
Lydall, Harold, 113n, 114n
Lynd, Helen M., 59n
Lynd, Robert S., 59n
Lysgaard, Sverre, 181

McCarthy, Joseph R., 361
McClellan, Grant S., 403n

Powell, Elwin H., 193n
Projector, Dorothy S., 127n, 130n

Quandt, Jean B., 335n
Quinney, Earl R., 401n
Quinney, Richard, 401n, 405n

Raab, Earl, 367n
Rabkin, Judith, 197n
Rainwater, Lee, 179n, 188n, 279n, 284–285
Rankin, Jerry, 391n
Rauh, Morton A., 208n
Raye, David E., 345n
Redlich, Fredrick C., 59n, 73, 193n, 197
Reisman, David, 208, 258n
Reiss, Albert J., 241n, 248n, 404n
Reiss, Ira L., 176
Reiss, Paul J., 183n, 184
Reissman, Frank, 208n, 266n
Reissman, Leonard, 229
Reuck, Anthony de, 37n
Reynolds, J. M., 335n
Reynolds, L. T., 335n
Richardson, William C., 191
Ridgeway, James, 209
Riley, Matilda White, 31n
Rist, Ray C., 207n
Roach, Jack L., 98n, 186n, 193n
Roberts, Bertram H., 198n
Robeson, Paul, 260n
Robinson, Jackie, 259
Robinson, James A., 343n
Robinson, John P., 74n, 282n, 362n
Rodman, Hyman, 183n
Rogoff, Natalie, 92n, 205n, 221
Rogow, Arnold, 367
Rokeach, Milton, 264
Rokkan, Stein, 359n
Roosevelt, Franklin, 258
Roosevelt, Theodore, 258
Rose, Peter I., 94n
Rose, Stephen M., 355n
Rosen, Bernard C., 181–182, 205n
Rosenberg, Morris, 435n
Ross, Aileen D., 312
Rossi, Alice S., 378n
Rossi, Peter H., 242n, 243n, 244, 253n, 378n
Rothstein, Richard, 159n, 317n, 370n
Rubel, Maximilien, 11n
Rubenstein, B., 407n
Rubin, Zick, 177n
Rush, Gary B., 86n

Russell, J. W., 194n, 373n
Rytina, Joan Huber, 49n, 60, 282n, 349n

Sabine, George H., 7n
Sagarin, Edward, 461n
St. John, Nancy Hoyt, 206n
Saint-Simon, 8, 140, 449
Scanzoni, John, 188–189, 234n
Schlekat, George A., 381
Schmidt, Fred H., 163n, 164n
Schmidt, Wolfgang, 199n
Schneider, Louis, 181
Schnore, Leo F., 273n
Schuman, Howard, 257n
Schwartz, Michael, 243n
Schwartz, Mildred, 252–253
Schwartz, Richard D., 402n
Scoble, Harry M., 370n
Scott, John Finley, 177n
Scott, William G., 243n
Scott, W. Richard, 405n
Seeley, John, 179n
Segal, David R., 86n
Selznick, Gertrude, 254–255, 360n
Sewell, William H., 92n, 180n, 205n, 220n
Sexton, Patricia Cayo, 206n, 207n
Sharkansky, Ira, 334n, 341n
Shepherd, William G., 132, 133n
Shils, Edward, 228n
Shipman, Virginia C., 182n
Shostak, Arthur B., 247n, 266n, 278n, 279n, 281n, 285n, 307n
Sichel, Werner, 132n
Sidorsky, David, 190
Siegal, Paul M., 86n, 87n, 88n, 177n, 242n, 244, 273n
Silverberg, James, 37n
Silverman, Larry J., 350n
Simmel, Georg, 9n
Simmons, Roberta G., 435n
Simon, Julian A., 291n
Simon, Rita James, 291n
Simpson, Ida Harper, 242n
Simpson, Richard L., 242n
Sjoberg, Gideon, 41n, 124n, 450–451
Skolnick, Alfred M., 122n
Skolnick, Jerome H., 402n, 407n
Smart, Reginald G., 199n
Smelser, Neil J., 91n, 92n
Smith, Adam, 6, 102
Smith, James D., 121
Smith, Richard Austin, 400n
Smith, Thomas C., 64n

Socrates, 397
Spencer, Herbert, 8, 449
Spengler, Joseph J., 124n
Sprengel, Donald P., 343n, 345n
Srinivas, M. N., 37n
Srole, Leo, 71, 198n, 309n
Stalin, Joseph, 6, 102
Stanton, Frank, 260n
Stark, Rodney, 168n, 169n
Steinberg, Stephen, 254–255, 360n
Stern, Philip M., 119n
Stewart, George R., 305
Stickle, W. E., 335n
Stinchcombe, Arthur L., 41n
Stouffer, Samuel A., 233n
Straus, Murray A., 205n
Strauss, Anselm L., 91n, 192n
Strodtbeck, Fred L., 401n, 405n
Strong, Mary Symons, 249n, 434n
Stub, Holger R., 378n
Stulman, Harriet, 159n, 317n, 370n
Suchman, Edward A., 318n
Sumner, William Graham, 8, 9n, 449
Sussman, Marvin B., 179n, 183n, 184, 401n
Suter, Larry E., 32n
Sutherland, Edwin H., 399–400
Swanson, Guy E., 181n

Tabb, William K., 147n, 159n
Taeuber, Alma F., 274, 317n
Taeuber, Karl E., 274, 317n
Tavuchis, Nicholas, 184–185
tenBroek, Jacobus, 407n
Thernstrom, Stephan, 59–60
Thielbar, Gerald W., 278n
Thomas, W. I., 70
Thompson, Ralph V., 317n
Thompson, Wayne E., 367n
Tiger, Lionel, 10
Titmuss, Richard M., 113n, 238–239
Tocqueville, Alexis de, 261, 296
Toffler, Alvin, 280n
Treiman, Donald J., 87n, 243n, 250, 251n
Trow, Martin, 141n, 142, 282n
Tuckman, Howard P., 117n, 126n, 130n
Tumin, Melvin M., 52n, 98
Turner, James S., 350n
Turner, Ralph, 96, 213–215

Udry, J. Richard, 186, 189
Uyeki, Eugene S., 273n

Vander Zanden, James W., 86n, 367n
Van Riper, Paul, 332n
Vaz, Edmund W., 87n
Veblen, Thorstein, 268–269
Verba, Sidney, 355–357
Vidich, Arthur J., 72n, 421n

Ward, David A., 401n
Ward, Lester, 449
Warner, W. Lloyd, 59–60, 71–73, 77, 80, 183, 228n, 272n, 298–299, 309, 345
Warren, Roland L., 367n
Washington, George, 258
Watts, Harold W., 122n
Wax, Murray L., 146n
Webb, Lee, 345n
Weber, Max, 9n, 15, 18, 20, 33, 40, 70, 84n, 230, 251
    bureaucracy, concept of, 21, 330
    class, definition of, 19–20, 336–337
    class consciousness, explanation of, 429
    formal rationality, concept of, 453
    inequality, sociocultural explanation of, 10–14
    and politics, 330–332
    power, concept of, 21, 325–326
    status (prestige), definition of, 228–229
Wector, Dixon, 258, 297n
Weiner, David, 177n
Weisinger, Mort, 240n
Weiss, Gertrude S., 127n
Weissberg, Norman C., 84n
Weistrod, Burton A., 381–382
White, Harrison C., 91n
White, Morton, 69
Whyte, William H., Jr., 178–179
Wilensky, Harold L., 91n, 235–236, 266n
Wiley, Norbert, 84n, 94–95, 282n, 335–336, 360, 426
Williams, Chilton, 328n
Williams, J. Allen, Jr., 318n
Williams, Robin M., Jr., 97n, 318n, 422n
Williams, William A., 336n, 444
Willmott, Peter, 184n
Wilson, Alan B., 205n
Windham, Douglas M., 382n
Wiseman, Jacqueline P., 405n
Wohl, R. Richard, 90n
Wolfe, Donald M., 178n, 187n
Wolfgang, Marvin E., 193n, 194n, 405n
Wood, Robert C., 341n

X, Malcolm, 258n

Yancey, William L., 188n
Yanovitch, Murray, 45n
Young, Michael, 184n

Zeigler, L. Harmon, 345n, 349n
Zeisel, Hans, 405n
Zeitlin, Maurice, 133n, 194n, 373n
Zinkin, Taya, 37n
Zola, Irving Kenneth, 401n

Subject Index

Associations, *see* Prestige groups

Biopsychological inequality, 4, 5–10, 15,
   18, 33, 207, 265, 297, 348
   versus sociocultural inequality, 4–14,
     364, 397
Black Americans
   and assimilation, 303–306
   black capitalism, 448
   black celebrities, 258–259
   and "caste," 36n, 298n
   class system, movement into, 30n, 427
   clubs, 310–311, 317
   and the Coleman Report, 202–207
   consciousness, 358, 420
   consistency, 83, 366, 464
   and consumption, 285–287
   and crime, 402, 439–440
   and education, 154–158
   estrangement between the sexes, 188
   and family, 187–189
   and health, 191
   and income, 148–151
   and Jews, 392
   and life expectancy, 193–195
   and mental retardation, 197
   and Mexican Americans, 369
   numerical size, 146
   occupational status, 151–154
   and political participation, 368–370
   and poverty, 156–157
   and primary groups, 310–311, 319
   relation to government and law, 386–
     389, 403, 405, 409–411, 438
   and residential segregation, 219n, 274–
     275, 285–286
   and secondary groups, 316–318, 319
   and social mobility, 147–162, 365–366,
     464
   and travel, 291
   unemployment, 148–149
   white attitudes toward, 252–253
Bloodgiving and class, 238–239
Bogardus Racial Distance Scale, 256

Canada, 209n
   class self-identification in, 251n
   occupational prestige in, 243n
Capitalism
   black, 448
   rise of, 11–14, 56–57, 62–63
Carnegie Commission on Higher Education, 216n

Caste stratification, 298n
   consistency in, 39–40
   contrasted with "caste" in American
     South, 36n
   defined, 17
   in India, 35–40
Celebrities, black, 258–259
Chapin Scale, 273n
Chinese Americans, 145–146
   academic achievement of Oriental
     Americans, 206
   consistency, 463
   mobility, 303n
   residence, 275
Civil Rights Act of 1964, 202, 285
Class consciousness
   absence in the lower class, 428, 460
   absence in the United States, 30, 69,
     185, 264–266, 295, 364, 378, 428,
     430, 447, 449, 451
   class self-identification, 81, 250–251,
     266
   defined, 264
   and economic insecurity, 265
   and false consciousness, 435
   in the lower-middle class, 265
   Marx's explanation, 429
   and residence among the working
     class, 276, 459
   in the upper classes, 435, 455
   Weber's explanation, 429
Class dimension, 18–20, 111, 336–338,
     422–427, 447–448. *See also* Ameri-
     can class system; Class system; So-
     cial class; Social stratification
Class hostility, 48, 295
Classless society, *see* Liberalism; Marx;
     Nonegalitarian classlessness
Class politics, concept of, 365–368
Class self-identification
   in Canada, 251n
   and class consciousness, 81, 250–251,
     266
Class struggle
   absence in United States, 68–69, 421,
     447
   Marx's prediction, 48–49, 447
   nature of, 447
   substitutes for in United States, 368
Class system
   American, 23–30
   blacks in, 30n, 427
   in communist countries, 44–45

Equality of opportunity (*cont.*)
  disbelief in its existence, 419, 423, 434
  as disguise for unfair contest, 432
  and education, 200–204, 209, 215–216,
    219–220, 379–382, 388, 468
  as incompatible with hereditary upper
    class, 469
  and individual responsibility, 433
  as legitimating, stabilizing illusion, 287
  as liberal reform, 288
  and minorities, 252–253, 256–257,
    448
  nature of, 200–202
  and nonegalitarian classlessness, 70,
    124, 265
  no increase of, 30, 454
  and taxation, 374–375
  violation of, 107, 449
  and War on Poverty, 125
  see also Social mobility
Eskimos, 145–146
  consistency, 464
  mobility, 464
  numerical size, 146
Estate system
  consistency in, 41–43
  defined, 17
  prerevolutionary France, 62–64
  Western feudalism, 41–44
Estrangement between the sexes, 186, 310
  among blacks, 188
Ethclass, 308, 314, 317, 319
Ethnic-religious stratification, 33
  and clubs, 304, 308
Evaluated Participation, 71
Evolutionary liberalism, *see* Liberalism

Fair employment laws, 388
False consciousness, 48, 363, 435
Family (and related) behavior, 172–199
  and anomie, 187
  black, 187–189
  Jewish Americans, 190
  Mexican Americans, 189–190
  social mobility, 177–178
  trust funds, 183, 230
  and unemployment, 186, 246
Fashion, trickle down process, 104, 276
Featherbedding, 246
Federalist paper number ten, 8, 393, 436
Feudalism, *see* Estate system
Filipinos, 145–146
  consistency, 464
  mobility, 303n, 464

numerical size, 146
French Canadians
  associational segregation in Burlington,
    Vermont, 309
  consistency, 463
  mobility, 463
  in Yankee City class structure, 298
Friendship and class, 310
  among Jews, 309
  among Mexican Americans, 310
Functional illiteracy, 220, 279–280
Functionalism
  as antithetical to stratification analysis,
    6–7, 52–53, 82
  criticism of functional stratification
    theory, 52–53
  Davis and Moore, 51–53
  defined, 102
  functional school of inequality, 5–7,
    51–53, 58–60
  functional specificity as class lubri-
    cant, 82
  and manifest and latent functions,
    102–104
  and nonegalitarian classlessness, 6–7,
    53
  in Plato, 5–6
  in sociology, 49, 52n, 59–60, 100–102
  in stratification theory, 5–7, 102
Functional school of inequality, 5–7,
    51–53, 58–60

German Americans, 462, 463
Gerrymander, 161, 306, 342–343, 369,
    377, 464

Hawaiians, 145–146
Health, 191–192
Hostility, class, 48, 295
Housing
  black Americans, 219n, 274–275, 285–
    286
  Chinese Americans, 275
  and class consciousness, 276, 459
  trickle down process, 388
Human talent, *see* Distribution of human
  talent

Ideal type, 35–36
Ideology, 63
  American, 349n
  defined, 48n
  end of, 421, 435–436
  evolutionary liberalism as, 60–61, 112

Managerial revolution (*cont.*)
Postindustrial society; Property; Separation of property and management

Market power, *see* Economic concentration

Marriage, *see* Family (and related) behavior

Melting pot theory, 303–306

Men's clubs, 301–302

Mental health
and poverty, 196, 198
and social mobility, 198

Meritocracy, 60n, 207n, 209, 421, 465, 468

Mexican Americans
academic achievement, 203, 206
attitudes toward, 256
and blacks, 369
and consistency, 464
and education, 165–166, 390–391
and family, 189–190
and friendship, 310
and income, 163–164
and intermarriage, 310
and mobility, 163–165, 303n, 427, 464
and movement into the class system, 427
numerical size, 146, 162
occupational status, 165–166
and political participation, 368–370
and poverty, 190, 310, 319
and primary groups, 309–310, 319
relation to government and law, 389–391, 410–411
and residential segregation, 275
and secondary groups, 315–316, 319

Middle class mass, 28, 234–235, 273, 278–279, 280n, 284–285, 287, 293, 333n, 361

Middletown, 59n

Military-industrial complex, 464

Minimum wage, 460n

Minorities, 145–147, 291, 461, 462–464
and equal opportunity, 252–253, 256–257, 448
ethnic-religious stratification, 33
sexism, 90, 137
sex stratification, 14–16, 30–33

Miss America and class, 238–240

Mobility trap, *see* Social mobility

Monopoly, *see* Liberal monopoly

Morris, Illinois, *see* Elmtown

Multidimensional analysis, 29, 89
and additive analysis, 87
in Milton M. Gordon, 68n
in Weber, 13–14

Multiple jobholding, *see* Work

Muncie, *see* Middletown

National Advisory Commission on Civil Disorders, 253, 257n

Newburyport, *see* Yankee City

New Haven, 59n, 73, 80, 197, 314–315

Newtonian world view, 69, 219

Nonegalitarian classlessness, 7, 34, 47, 49, 51, 104, 200, 218, 220, 257, 382, 442–443, 456, 465–467
and equal opportunity, 70, 124, 265
and functionalism, 6–7, 53
and I.Q., 9, 105, 182, 196, 205, 207–208, 220, 223

Occupations, 134–138
Anglo-Saxon Protestants, 168
black Americans, 151–154
Jewish Americans, 168–169
Mexican Americans, 165–166
and prestige, 241–250
Roman Catholics, 168

Oligarchy, 466–469

Opportunity, *see* Equality of opportunity

Oriental Americans, *see* Chinese Americans; Japanese Americans

"People's capitalism," 128

Pluralism, 58, 60n, 85, 138, 296, 303, 349n, 362, 452, 465–469

Polish Americans, 315, 463

Political participation, 340–370
blacks, 368–370
Jews, 368–370

Politics
class, 365–368
Progressive movement in, 335
stratified, 326

Postindustrial society, 138–141, 468

Poverty
black, 156–157
and black health, 191
function of lower class, 441
and health, 191–192
intergenerational, 84
and life expectancy, 195
and the lower class, 28, 460–461, 464
and mental health, 198

and mental retardation, 196
and Mexican American family, 190, 310, 319
persistence of, 123–126
poverty income, 77, 125, 460n
and private and public charity, 286
types of, 124–125
see also Minimum wage; Relative deprivation; Unemployment; Welfare system
Power elite, 302, 335, 347, 365, 464, 465, 469
Premarital sex, and class, 175–176
Prestige, occupational, 241–250
Prestige groups, 281, 282–283, 294–321, 353, 354
and Anglo-Saxon Protestants, 303, 308, 315
clubs as, 295
and Roman Catholics, 303–306, 308–310, 314–316
Primogeniture, 230, 327
Progressive movement
in education, 201
in politics, 335
and upper class, 300
Project Talent, 205n, 221–222
Proletariat, 337, 464
Property
alleged decline of, 58–60
alleged replacement by trained intelligence, 421, 468
in Marx, 12
separation from management, 133–134
see also Economic concentration; Wealth
Protestant-bourgeois ethic
and anomie, 396–397
and asceticism, 270
and deferred gratification pattern, 181
Protestants, *see* Anglo-Saxon Protestants
Psychological poverty, *see* Relative deprivation
Puerto Ricans
academic achievement, 203, 206
consistency, 464
mobility, 464
numerical size, 146

Race
and clubs, 310
Racial stratification, 33
Reference groups

and the definition of poverty, 125–126
and hero worship, 258
and relative deprivation, 125–126
Relative deprivation
and the definition of poverty, 125–126, 292, 420
and prosperity, 420
and reference groups, 125–126
Religious-ethnic stratification, 33
Republic (Plato), 5–7
Reputational method, 81
Residential segregation, 219n, 274–275, 285–286
Rise of capitalism, 56–57, 62–63
and German social science, 11
in Marx, 11–13
in Weber, 13–14
Rising expectations, 420. *See also* Relative deprivation
Riverside, California, 197
Roman Catholics
assimilation, 303–306
associational life, 303–306, 308–310, 314–316
educational distribution, 169
mobility, 167, 303, 303n, 463
occupational distribution, 168
socioeconomic characteristics, 170
and upper class, 462
voting, 359, 361
Ruling class, 12, 27, 138, 184n, 302, 457, 464, 465. *See also* Power elite; Social power

Scandinavian Americans, 315, 462
Self-directed personality, 262–263
Separation of property and mangement, 133–134. *See also* Managerial revolution; Postindustrial society
SES (Socioeconomic status), defined, 73–77
Sexism, 90
Sex stratification
related to social stratification, 14–16, 30–33
and social differentiation, 14–16
Sexual behavior, *see* Family (and related) behavior
Social class (social stratum)
analysis of, 17–22, 67–107, 326
defined, 23, 27
empirical summaries, 199, 223, 318–321, 370, 393–394, 416

Social class (*cont.*)
and ideology, 349n, 433–436
as network of groups, 454
reality of, 446–449
in the United States, 23–30, 453–464
see also American class system; Class
    dimension; Class system; Social
    stratification
Social Darwinism, 69, 348, 452
Social differentiation, 14–16, 50
and social stratification, 14–16
and stability, 294
Social mobility
blacks, 147–162, 365–366, 464
Chinese Americans, 303n
and class diversification, 251, 360
in convergence theory, 50
dysfunctions of, 98, 420, 423
and education, 205, 218
Eskimos, 464
and family values, 184–185
Filipinos, 303n, 464
French Canadians, 463
functions of, 426–428
general pattern in United States, 98–
    100
Japanese Americans, 275n, 303n
Jewish, 166–167
within the legal profession, 248
and marriage, 177–178
and mental health, 198
Mexican American, 163–165, 303n,
    427, 464
among minorities, 303n
mobility trap, 94–95, 426–427
and open elite theory, 300–302
and *Playboy* magazine, 271n
in prerevolutionary France, 63–64, 365
Puerto Ricans, 464
Roman Catholic, 167, 303, 303n, 463
sponsored versus contest, 213–215
and a static distribution of values,
    130, 449, 454
in stratification analysis, 85, 89–100
substitute for, 247
and suicide, 193
types of, 89–100, 439–440
United States, and other countries, 29,
    89
United States, rates of, 59–60, 69, 89,
    124n, 421, 454
United States and Soviet Union com-
    pared, 45
Social power, 21, 29, 104, 248, 295, 325–

326, 347, 372, 452, 464–469
Social Register, 183, 283, 297n, 301, 302
Social stratification
versus age and sex stratification, 14–
    16, 30–33
and causation, 10–14, 29, 68n, 83–89,
    212–213, 353–354
definition, 15
essence of, 449
and general theory, 35–66
and life cycle, 30
and religious-ethnic stratification, 33
and social differentiation, 14–16
types of, 16–17, 47, 54
Social stratum, *see* Social class
Sociocultural inequality, 10–14, 18, 33,
    468
versus biopsychological inequality, 4–
    14, 364, 397
Marx, 10–14
Rousseau, 10
Weber, 10–14
Socioeconomic achievement status, 84–
    85
Sociology
of knowledge, 261–262, 280n
as middle class ideology, 335n
Soviet Union
class system, 44–47, 50–51
Stable unrepresentation, 362
Standard of living, 111, 114, 123–125,
    288–289, 423–424, 444
estimated distribution of, 115–117
three budgets by Department of Labor,
    77–79, 115
Status
attainment process, 92n, 205n, 212n,
    220n
consistency, 39–43, 50, 83–89, 365–
    368, 453–464
cycle, 290–291
panic, 290
politics, 365–368
socioeconomic, 73–77
Stockownership, 126–134
Strategic elites, 60n, 80n, 138, 421, 468
Stratification, *see* Social stratification
Stratified politics, 326. *See also* Politics
Stratum, *see* Social class
Style of life, *see* Consumption
Subjective method, 81
Subjective poverty, *see* Relative depriva-
    tion
Suicide, 193

Taxation
    effective tax rates, 119–120, 373
    and equality of opportunity, 374–375
    and income, 117–123
Technocracy, 60, 140, 351, 371. *See also*
    Liberalism
Technology, 334
Thematic appreception test, 182
Trade unions, 28, 130, 133, 154, 208,
    230, 250, 311, 332, 333, 349, 377,
    425, 445, 457–458, 459–460, 465
Transfer payments, 121–123
Travel, 291
Trickle down process
    in consumption, 288–290
    in fashions, 104, 276
    in housing, 388

Unemployment
    among blacks, 148–149
    and family life, 186, 246
    and featherbedding, 246
    full, defined, 245, 384, 385
    as government policy, 388
    and lower class, 460–461
    and technology, 334
    among upper and lower classes, 24
United States Commission on Civil
    Rights, 219n, 390–391, 410
United States Equal Opportunity Com-
    mission, 154n, 164n, 171n
Upper class
    class consciousness, 435, 455
    clubs, 301–302, 307
    and Jews, 462
    and Progressive movement, 300
    and Roman Catholics, 462
    and unemployment, 24
    WASP, 299–302

Values, and social mobility, 130, 184–
    185, 449, 454

Value Survey, 264
Voluntary groups, *see* Prestige groups
Voting, 342–344, 351–362. *See also* Ger-
    rymander; Political participation

War on Poverty, 125, 386, 420, 440, 461
WASP, *see* Anglo-Saxon Protestants
Wealth
    ascriptive, 130n
    distribution of, 126–134
    stockownership, 126–134
Welfare state (services), 80, 112, 332–
    335, 445
Welfare system
    administration of, 376, 390
    basic functions of, 376, 440–441
    as dependency-creating, 84n, 461
    as percentage of GNP, 122
    in Social Security Act, 375
    as substitute for employment, 388
White-collar crime, 399–402
Women, *see* Sexism; Sex stratification
Women's liberation, 31
Work
    as central value, 134, 244–245
    multiple jobholding, 236
    and personality, 260–264
    and retirement, 246
    and satisfaction, 81, 246–247, 262,
        424, 459
    as stabilizing force, 134, 249–250, 424,
        447, 467–468
    success without, 259
    transition from school to work, 436–
        437
Working class, residences of, 276, 459

Yankee City (Newburyport), 59–60, 71,
    72n, 298n, 309

Zoning, 272, 275, 286, 334, 377, 414